5/9/87

To James Siguin,

All the best,

Robert n Parting

PARKER'S WINE BUYER'S GUIDE

ROBERT M. PARKER, JR.

A Fireside Book
Published by Simon & Schuster, Inc.
New York

Simon and Schuster/Fireside Books
Published by Simon & Schuster, Inc.
Simon & Schuster Building
Rockefeller Center
1230 Avenue of the Americas
New York, New York 10020
Portions of this book were previously published in the author's
bimonthly newsletter, *The Wine Advocate*.
SIMON AND SCHUSTER and FIRESIDE and colophons are registered
trademarks of Simon & Schuster, Inc.
Designed by Levavi & Levavi
Maps by Jeanyee Wong
Drawings by Christopher Wormell
Manufactured in the United States of America
10 9 8 7 6 5 4 3 2 1
Library of Congress Cataloging-in-Publication Data
Parker, Robert M.
     Parker's wine buyer's guide.

     "A Fireside book."
     "Portions of this book were previously published in the author's
bimonthly newsletter, the wine advocate"—T.p. verso.
     Includes index.
     1. Wine and wine making.   I. Title.   II. Title:
Wine buyer's guide.
TP548.P287   1987   641.2′22   87-4539
ISBN: 0-671-64349-5
ISBN: 0-671-63380-5 (pbk.)

ACKNOWLEDGMENTS

It is the world's finest winemakers who merit a hefty endorsement and acknowledgment. Always risking foul weather, the uncertainty of supply and demand, the headaches of fluctuating international currency rates, as well as merciless and relentless wine critics, they take all the risks and work extraordinarily hard to produce the magical beverage that gives so many people so much pleasure.

I would like to thank the following people for their support and encouragement: Victor Morgenroth, Bob Cline, Paul Evans, Joel Fleishman, Steve Gilbertson, Thomas Hoving, Alan Krasner, Jay Miller, Annette Piatek, Frank Prial, Jancis Robinson, Bob Schindler, Ila Stanger, Elliott Staren, Ed Sands, and Dan Green, whose idea this was.

To Eve Metz and Frank Metz at Simon & Schuster, my appreciation for the book's design and cover, which make it at once elegant and easy to use. And special thanks to Jeanyee Wong for her beautiful maps.

Finally, special recognition is due to my magnificent seven "sitters" who are always there to offer counsel and provide reassurance when needed. I owe a great deal of thanks to my wonderfully capable team at Simon & Schuster, Carole Lalli and Nancy Kalish, their British counterpart, Jill Norman of Dorling Kindersley, my formidable yet always compassionate literary representative, Bob Lescher, my ever smiling, meticulous secretary, Joan Passman, and lastly, the two women in my life that I love so dearly, my dear and adored mother and the woman who started my obsession with wine, my wife.

This book is dedicated to my beloved wife, Patricia, my mother and father, and to Jean Claude Vrinat, a man who embodies all the finest qualities of the true oenophile— unselfishness, enthusiasm, knowledge, and remarkable passion for the subject.

CONTENTS

9

HOW TO USE
THIS GUIDE

This book is both a wine educational and buying manual; it is not an encyclopedic listing of wine producers and growers. It is intended to make you a more formidable, more confident wine buyer by providing you sufficient insider's information to permit the most intelligent choices possible when buying wine. The finest producers and growers of the world's greatest viticultural regions are evaluated, as well as most of the current releases available in the marketplace. If you cannot find a specific vintage of a highly regarded wine, you still have at your fingertips a wealth of information and evaluations concerning the best producers for each viticultural area. You should be confident in knowing that you will rarely make a mistake (unless, of course, the vintage is absolutely dreadful) with a producer rated "outstanding" or "excellent" in this buying manual. These producers are the finest and most consistent in the world.

However, to make the most of this guide, you must know how to use it.

Organization

The general organization of each specific viticultural region covered in this manual is arranged as follows:

1. The name of the viticultural region
2. A short informational introduction to the area
3. A summary of the quality of recent vintages for the area
4. A quick reference chart to that area's best producers/growers
5. A buying strategy to follow for the next two years for the wines of that area
6. And, where deemed relevant, tasting commentaries, a specific numerical rating for the wine, and the approximate retail shop price for a 750 ml bottle of that grower/producer's wine.

Viticultural Areas Covered

This guide covers the world's major viticultural regions. In Western Europe, France receives the most detailed coverage, followed by Italy, Spain, Portugal, and Germany. In North America, California receives much more significant coverage than other viticultural areas, with the exception of America's new emerging wine star, Oregon. The wine regions of the world that dominate the marketplace are given priority and much more detailed coverage than minor areas whose wines are rarely seen or exported to the United States. Consequently, the sections dealing with Bordeaux, Burgundy, Champagne, Alsace, and the Rhône in France, Piedmont and Tuscany in Italy, Rioja, Penedès, and the Duero in Spain, the northern viticultural area of California, and the Mosel in Germany receive an inordinate amount of coverage herein simply because those regions produce the world's greatest wines.

Rating the Producers/Growers

Who's who in the world of wine becomes readily apparent after years of tasting and visiting the vineyards and wine cellars of the world's producers and growers. Great producers are, unfortunately, still quite rare, but certainly more growers and producers today are making better wine, with better technology and more knowledge than ever before. The charts that follow rate the producers on a five-star system, awarding five stars and an "outstanding" rating to those producers deemed to be the very best, four stars to those who are "excellent," three stars to "good" producers, and two stars or one star to "average" and "below average" producers. Since the aim of the book is to provide you with the names of the very best producers, the content is dominated by the top producers rather than the less successful ones.

Those few growers/producers who have received five-star ratings are indeed those who make the world's finest wines. They have been selected for this rating because of two reasons: they make the greatest wine of their particular viticultural region, and they are remarkably consistent and reliable even in mediocre and poor vintages. Ratings, whether they be specific numerical ratings of individual wines or classifications of growers, are always likely to create controversy among not only the growers but wine tasters themselves. But, if done impartially, with a global viewpoint and with firsthand, on the premises ("sur place"), knowledge of the wines, the producers, and the type and quality of the winemaking, such ratings can be reliable and powerfully informative. The important thing for readers to remember is that those growers/producers who receive either a four-star or five-star rating are producers to search out; I suspect few consumers will ever be disappointed with one of their wines. The three-star-rated growers/producers are less consistent, but can be expected to make fine wines in the very good to excellent vintages. Their weaknesses come either from the fact that their vineyards are not as strategically placed, or because for financial or other reasons they are unable to make the severe selections necessary to make only the finest quality wine.

The importance of rating the growers/producers of the world's major viticultural regions is perhaps the single most salient point to this book. Years of wine tasting have taught me many things, but the more one tastes and assimilates the knowledge of the world's regions, the more one begins to isolate the handful of truly world-class growers and producers who seem to rise above the crowd in great as well as mediocre vintages. I always admonish consumers against blind faith in one grower or producer, or one specific vintage, but the producers and growers rated "outstanding" and "excellent" are as close to a guarantee of high quality as you are likely to find.

Vintage Summaries

Everyone is exposed to wine advertisements proclaiming "a great vintage," but I have never known it to occur that more than several viticultural areas of the world have a great vintage in the same year. The chances of a uniformly great vintage are extremely remote simply because of significantly different micro-climates, soils, and so on, in every wine-producing region. It is easy to fall into the trap of thinking that because Bordeaux had a great vintage in 1982, everyplace else in Europe did too. Nothing, of course, could be further from the truth. Nevertheless, a Bordeaux vintage's reputation unfortunately seems to dictate what the world thinks about many other wine-producing areas.

This obviously creates many problems, since in poor Bordeaux vintages the Rhône or Alsace or Champagne could have excellent vintages, and in great Bordeaux vintages those same areas could have bad years because of poor climate conditions. For California, many casual observers seem to think *every* year is a top year and this image is, of course, promoted by that state's publicity-conscious Wine Institute. It may be true that California rarely has a disastrous vintage, but tasting certainly proves that 1981, 1982, and 1983 are different in style and more irregular in quality than either 1984 or 1985. In this guide, there are vintage summaries for each viticultural area because the vintages are so very different in both quantity and quality. Never make the mistake of assuming that one particular year is great everywhere or poor everywhere. I know of no year when *that* has happened.

Tasting Notes and Ratings

For many of the major viticultural areas, the growers/producers are listed alphabetically and their current wines are reviewed, scored, and commented upon. In this instance, great attention has been given to trying to provide an overview of the style and quality level of the producer/grower. Such factors as whether the producer is steadily improving the wine's quality, resting on its allegedly superior reputation, or slipping in quality because of mismanagement, replanting, or simple negligence are issues that I deem extremely important for consumers to be aware of.

Virtually all of my tastings are done in peer-group, double-blind conditions—meaning that the same type of wines are tasted against each other and the producers' names are not known. The ratings reflect an independent, critical look at the wines. Neither price nor the reputation of the producer/grower affect the rating in any manner. I spend three months of every year tasting in vineyards both here and abroad. During the other nine months of the year, six- and sometimes seven-day work weeks are devoted solely to tasting and writing. I do not participate in wine judgings or trade tastings for many reasons, but principal among these are the following: (1) I prefer to taste from an entire bottle of wine, (2) I find it essential to have properly sized and cleaned professional tasting glasses, (3) the temperatures of the wine must be correct, and (4) I alone will determine the time allocated to the number of wines to be critiqued.

The numerical rating given is a guide to what I think of the wine vis-à-vis its peer group. Certainly, wines rated above 85 are very good to excellent, and any wine rated 90 or above will be outstanding for its particular type. While some have suggested that scoring is unfair to a beverage that has been so romantically extolled for centuries, the fact of the matter is that wine is no different than any product being sold to a consumer—there are specific standards of quality that full-time wine professionals recognize, and there are benchmark wines against which all others can be judged. I know of no one with three or four different glasses of wine in front of him or her, regardless of how good or bad the wines might be, who cannot say "I prefer this one to that one." Scoring wines is simply taking a professional's opinion and applying some sort of numerical system to it on a consistent basis. Scoring permits rapid communication of information to expert and novice alike.

The rating system I employ in my wine journal, *The Wine Advocate*, is the one I have utilized in this buying guide. It is a 100-point scale, the most repugnant of all wines meriting 50, and the most glorious, perfect gustatory experience commanding 100. I prefer my system to the more widely quoted 20-point scale called the Davis Scale, of the University of California at Davis, because it permits much more flexibility in scoring. It is also easier to understand because it corresponds to the grading system most of us have experienced in school, and it avoids the compression of scores from which the Davis Scale suffers. It is not without its own problems, though, because readers will often wonder what the difference is between 86 and 87, both very good wines. The only answer I can give is a simple one, that when tasted side by side, I thought the 87-point wine slightly better than the 86-point wine.

The score given for a specific wine reflects the quality of the wine at its best. Wines from obviously badly corked or defective bottles are re-tried, since a wine from such a single bad bottle does not indicate an entirely spoiled batch. Many of the wines reviewed here have been tasted several times, and the score represents a sort of cumulative average of the wine's performance in tastings to date. However, the written commentary that accompanies the ratings is often a better source of information regarding the wine's style and personality, its relative quality level vis-à-vis its peers, and its relative value and aging potential than any score could ever possibly indicate. The easiest way for the reader to understand my scoring system is to remember the grades received in school.

Here, then, is a general guide to interpreting the numerical ratings:

90–100 is equivalent to an A and it should be given for an outstanding or excellent special effort. Wines in this category are the very best produced for their type and, like a three-star Michelin restaurant, worth a special effort to find and try. There is a big difference between a 90 and a 99, but both are top marks. As you will note throughout the text, there are few wines that actually make it into this top category simply because there just are not many truly great wines.

80—89 is equivalent to a B in school and such a wine, particularly in the 85–89 range, is very, very good; many of the wines that fall into this range often are great values as well. I would not hesitate to have any of these wines in my own personal collection.

70—79 represents a C, or average mark, but obviously 79 is a much more desirable score than 70. Wines that receive scores between 75 and 79 are generally pleasant, straightforward wines that simply lack complexity, character, or depth.

Below 70 is a D or F, depending on where you went to school; for wine, too, it is a sign of an imbalanced, flawed, or terribly dull or diluted wine that will be of little interest to the smart wine consumer.

In terms of awarding points, my scoring system gives a wine 50 points to start with. The wine's general color and appearance merit up to 5 points. Since most wines today have been well made thanks to modern technology and the increased use of professional oenologists, most tend to receive at least 4, often 5 points. The aroma and bouquet merit up to 15 points. Obviously, the intensity of the aroma and bouquet are important, and equally so is the wine's cleanliness. The flavor and finish merit up to 20 points, and again, intensity of flavor, balance, cleanliness, and depth and length on the palate are all important considerations when giving out points. Finally, the overall quality level or potential for further evolution and improvement—aging—merits up to 10 points.

Scores are important for the reader to gauge a professional critic's overall qualitative placement of a wine vis-à-vis its peers. However, don't ignore the description of the wine's style, personality, and potential, which is just as important. No scoring system is perfect, but a system that provides for flexibility in scores, if applied without prejudice and fairly, can quantify different levels of wine quality. If implemented properly, then, this guide will lead you to the finest wines as well as to the very finest wine values. But no scoring system could ever convey the hedonistic experience of wine that might arise from the ambience, gorgeous setting, excellent food, and fine company that may accompany it.

Quoted Prices

The prices quoted in this manual reflect what prevails as the normal retail price at some of the major wine shops around the country. However, for a number of reasons there is no single suggested retail price for a particular wine that is valid throughout the country. Take Bordeaux as an example. Bordeaux is first sold as "wine futures" two full years before the wine is bottled and shipped to America. This opening or base price can often be the lowest price one will encounter for a Bordeaux wine, particularly if there is a great demand because the vintage is reputed to be excellent or outstanding. Prices will always vary for Bordeaux, as well as for other imported wines, according to the quality of the vintage, the exchange rate of the dollar against foreign currencies, and the time of purchase by the retailer, wholesaler, or importer. Was the Bordeaux wine purchased at a low futures price in the spring following the vintage, or was the wine purchased when it had peaked in price and was very expensive?

Another consideration in pricing is that in some states wine retailers can directly import the wines they sell and thereby bypass the middlemen, such as wholesalers, who usually tack on a 25% markup of their own. The bottom line in all this is that in any given vintage for Bordeaux, or any imported wine, there is no standard suggested retail price. Prices can differ by at least 50% for the same wine in the same city. However, in cities where there is tremendous competition among wine shops, the retail markup for wines can be reduced to as low as 10% or even 5% versus the normal 50–55%. This can result in significantly lower overall prices for wine, whereas in cities where there is little competition the prices often charged are full retail and can be more expensive. I always recommend that consumers pay close attention to the wine shop advertisements in major newspapers. For example, every Wednesday the *New York Times*'s Living Section is filled with wine advertisements that are a wonderful barometer of the market price of a given wine. For most of the listings here I have used *The Beverage Journal*, a trade bible for wine availability and wholesale prices. Readers should remember, however, that prices differ considerably, not only within the same state, but also within the same city. The price that is used generally—and reported here—reflects the suggested retail price with a 50% markup by the retailer in most major metropolitan areas. Therefore, in many states in the Midwest and less populated areas where there is little competition among wine merchants, the price may be significantly higher. In major marketplaces where there is brisk competition, such as Washington D.C., New York, San Francisco, Boston, Los Angeles, Chicago, and Dallas, prices are often lower because of the discount wars that frequently occur. The key for you as the reader and consumer is to follow the advertisements in major newspapers and to shop around. Most major wine retailers feature sales in the fall and spring; summer is the slow season and generally is the most expensive time to buy wine.

BACK TO THE FUTURE: THE YEARS IN REVIEW

Crystal Gazing for the Future

Before I predict what will happen during the next several years in the wine world, I want first to go back a dozen years to 1975 and look at the situation in the wine market then, what the wine consumer was drinking, and the wine trends of that year. To know the past will help to understand the events of the future.

In wine terms, 1975 seems more like an eternity ago. Nothing resembling the three hottest items in the wine news today existed then. First, there was no such thing as the soda-pop-like wine coolers that have helped California wineries unload their bloated inventories. Second, there were no such things as blush wines, made from any number of red wine grapes, that are in essence rosé wines. Third, there were no such magical wine-making adulterants as diethylene glycol or methanol, which have plagued portions of the European wine industry with one scandal after another. What then was happening in 1975?

For one thing, there was a tremendous wine glut from the European wine-producing countries being dumped on the American market. Earlier in the decade, wine investors (you hear that same term applied today) had determined that wine was a great investment.

These investors, largely corporations heavily involved in the spirits and beer business, relied significantly on worldwide interest in the 1970 Bordeaux vintage and purchased large portions of that and subsequent vintages, especially 1972, 1973, and 1974. While 1970 was indeed a wonderful vintage, 1972, 1973, and 1974 were poor years. Then, when the international oil crisis arrived in 1974, the wine market collapsed. The international oil crisis had an unsettling effect on major wine-buying markets, particularly their economies; and investors from countries that were holding large wine inventories, principally England and America, became nervous and began to unload their wine stocks at English auction houses. This was led by the bureaucratic beer and whiskey corporations, which knowing not a whole lot about wine, decided to dump huge inventories of mediocre to poor Bordeaux on a market unwilling and financially unable to accept it. The result was a massive crash and subsequent reorganization of the entire wine trade, particularly that of Bordeaux, where many large companies were either crippled or put out of business.

It is hard to believe, but in 1975 California's wine star had barely begun to ascend. Although California had just finished two consecutive top-notch vintages, 1973 and 1974, these wines had not yet been released for sale. Nineteen seventy-five was one whole year before wine authority Steven Spurrier's now-famous tasting in Paris in which French Bordeaux were tasted against California's best Cabernets and white burgundies against California's best Chardonnays. As is now known by everyone who follows wine news, the California wines scored unanimous and consistent triumphs over their French counterparts. One year later, after the results of this historic tasting had been ballyhooed over and over by the press, the California wine industry was on an upward surge in growth, fame, prosperity, optimism, and vineyard expansion and development. This was to last only five short years. But before the boom was over, *Time* magazine ran a story called "The Golden Age of California Wine."

What was available for purchase in 1975? Well, in 1975 the wine consumer was largely restricted to a choice of prestigious labels from Bordeaux, Burgundy, Champagne, and innocuous, often shabbily made shippers' blends. Many of today's recognized superstars in California wine production were not even producing wine. However, there were plenty of old standbys in 1975 that are still out there today— Louis Martini, Inglenook, BV, Krug, Gallo, Paul Masson, and Almaden. Today's California superstars, Opus One, Dominus, Duckhorn, Caymus, Chateau St. Jean, Joseph Phelps, Grgich, Sonoma-Cutrer, Jordan, and William Hill, were either not yet in the business or were just beginning to make wine. At wine shops in 1975 it was largely impossible to find the better East Coast wines, wines from the Pacific Northwest, fine Italian wines, the best Rhône wines, good Alsace wines, and the very competently made but not terribly well-known smaller châteaux from Bordeaux.

In 1975 there was little consumer-oriented wine writing. The primary outlets for wine education in America were the Les Amis du Vin chapters that had proliferated successfully throughout the country. Along with Alexis Lichine and Frank Schoonmaker, the peripatetic Englishman Harry Waugh was the wine authority consumers wanted to hear speak and to meet, and I suspect that the impact his extensive travels in the early and mid-'70s had on the wine-consuming public has never fully been given the credit it deserves. It was, in fact, enormous. Today he is retired and no longer the best-known English wine authority. Two experts who were little known in 1975 are Hugh Johnson and Michael Broadbent, and today anyone with an interest in wine knows their names and sterling reputations.

If 1975 was a period of hope, enthusiasm, and zest for wine knowledge, while remaining to some extent a period of wine provincialism at the trade and consumer levels, how does the state of wine differ today? First, while there is a glut of wine in the marketplace, there is little likelihood that a wine crash is imminent. For one, unlike the early seventies, while there has been tremendous investment in top-quality wines, it has been at a consumer and worldwide level, rather than by specific corporations and financial entities that can then control large chunks of the wine market.

What has happened to California's stardom? There is no question that the remarkable period of growth and enthusiasm for California wines that started in 1976 and ended in 1981 has been the result of a number of factors: 1) There were wild swings in styles of wine. In the seventies, California winemakers went for full-extract, high-intensity, very tannic, big, rich, dramatic wines. Some of these wines met with criticism because they did not go well with food and, in turn, in the eighties there was a lemminglike rush in the other direction to what were often referred to as "food" or "sculptured" wines, which in fact were double-digit-priced wines that were often innocuous, bland, and very simple. 2) There was a proliferation of wineries and a multitude of offerings available to the wine consumer. For example, Chateau St. Jean produced as many as six different Chardonnays in a given vintage, and there are many wineries that produced three or four different Cabernets. Most consumers found that overwhelmingly confusing to deal with. 3) A sort of musical chairs for winemakers has confused the wine consumer and added to the chaotic situation. One had only to look at some of the best and most talented winemakers in the state —Chuck Ortman, Rick Forman, Jerry Luper, and Bill Bonetti to name some—to see that they were pretty much switching wineries every few years. They took their style of winemaking with them, and just when the consumer settled in to thinking that he liked one winery's wine, the winemaker left and a totally different style of wine was produced by the next person in charge. Lastly, perhaps the biggest reason California's image suffered was a very strong American dollar from 1981 to 1985 that ironically coincided with a remarkable succession of top-quality, big-quantity vintages from Europe. The competition from lower-priced, higher-quality imports did significant damage to the California wine trade. Yet, in 1987, the California wine industry has rebounded strongly and though it is still too trendy, the quality of current releases is consistently better than five years ago.

What should wine consumers be buying today? There is no question that the wine consumer today is more educated than ever before; it is increasingly difficult for the wine trade to unload poor wine or vintages. Smart consumers today will go anywhere that excellence is offered. One sees shrewd wine buyers selecting wines from the Rhône Valley, from Alsace, from the East Coast of the United States, from Oregon, from the Piedmont section of Italy, as well as from Spain and Australia. Unlike 1975, the wine consumers of 1987 are not loyal, nor are they captives of any one wine region; and they are less likely to be label snobs.

Perhaps the most important development in 1987 is the emergence of viticultural regions that for all intents and purposes were ignored twelve years ago. In this country, there has been tremendous development and interest in the fine wines of the East Coast and the Pacific Northwest. Even in states such as Texas, Pennsylvania, and New York the quality of the wines continues to increase with each passing vintage. In France, the underrated Rhône wines, Alsace wines, Loire Valley wines, and small but impeccably run properties in Bordeaux are finally getting more and more attention. In Italy, the wines of the north in the Piedmont section have at long last been given their due as world-class, outstanding, complex wines. The new breeds of light, white, crisp, and fresh wines of the Friuli region of Italy, which offer such great value and quality, are being recognized for their satisfying personalities. The best wines from Australia are much more widely available in this country than twelve years ago, as are the better wines from Chile and Argentina.

The other major development in 1987 is the proliferation of wine educational courses, schools, better, more informed wine consultants at the retail level, and a glut of wine writers dispensing advice—some very good, some arrogant, some irresponsible, and some just boring. However, there are two things clear about 1987: The buyer has access to a remarkable array of information, and it continues to be a great buyer's market. Perhaps the late eighties is less sensational than the period of the low-priced imports (1982–1985), but there are great wines from virtually every viticultural area in the world available on the retail shelves, and the prices are generally competitive. There is plenty of professional wine advice to be had and the quality of wines in all price ranges has never been better than it is today.

For the future, will things get worse or better? Here are my predictions and comments on the wine market and price trends, consumer trends, and possible external factors that could have significant impact on the wine market.

Prediction number one. The glamour French wines, meaning those from the top two dozen Bordeaux châteaux as well as the best Grands Crus and Premiers Crus, and red and white burgundies, will become increasingly more expensive and affordable only by the super-rich. The simple reason for this is that the quantities are finite. The great vineyards cannot be expanded and they are already at their maximum level of production. Given the continued worldwide demand for these wines, with an increasingly aware wine-drinking public, demand will continue to outstrip supply and will push the prices for these wines into a very expensive, elitist arena.

Prediction number two. Other French wine prices, as well as other imported wine prices from countries such as Italy, Spain, Germany, and Portugal, will remain largely stable because they are producing quantities of wine at a rate that outstrips demand. In addition, the huge crop of 1985 was succeeded by another bumper crop in 1986 and only one vintage since 1980, the 1984 vintage, could be considered below average in quantity and less than good quality. There is an ocean of fine imported wine in the pipeline.

Prediction number three. Domestic wine prices will generally remain stable as the producers rebound from a sluggish period of sales between 1981 and 1985 and hold their prices in order to gain more and more control over the market. Should any wine increase in price, it will be Chardonnay, and that only slightly.

Prediction number four. The greatest values in imported wine in 1987 will come from the white wines from Alsace, France, white and red wines from Chile and Australia, and the red wines from Spain.

Prediction number five. Oregon will emerge as a superstar, a fertile and enormously promising region for Pinot Noir as well as Pinot Gris and Chardonnay. These wines will rival not only the best made in California, but also in France. In connection with this prediction, I believe Pinot Noir, particularly those made in Oregon, will become one of the most fashionable red wines in the late '80s. For one reason, it is more flexible with food than many Cabernets. For another, it is less tannic, much more fragrant and supple, and much easier to drink and enjoy when young.

Prediction number six. California will continue its strong rebound in the marketplace, begun in 1986, largely because it has two outstanding vintages coming—1984 and 1985—that will continue to generate excitement about the wines from that region over the next several years. In addition, after a period of experimentation in the late seventies and early eighties, many of California's top wineries are finally settling into definable and consistent styles of winemaking.

Prediction number seven. The death knell for some domestic wineries will continue. Despite the healthy rebound in interest in California wines, there will be winery casualties, because production continues to outrace demand and consumption. New wineries unable to produce great wine will not survive in the very competitive wine market of the future. In addition, the huge investment in the sparkling wine business in California will largely turn sour. California cannot (without protective legislation) compete in price with the European sparkling wines coming primarily from Spain and Italy, and they have not yet shown any ability to compete with quality French champagne.

Prediction number eight. Italy, always known for its production of fine red wine, will become wider known as a major supplier of excellent-quality white wine at very reasonable prices.

Prediction number nine. The East Coast wine industry, particularly that centered in New York, Pennsylvania, Maryland, and Virginia, will get more and more respect and will continue to build support for its growers. However, most of these growers will not be able to compete financially with imports and the snob appeal that continues to exist for California wines. As optimistic as one can be about the quality prospects on the East Coast, there is little likelihood that producers can sell the wine in sufficient quantities and at sufficient price levels to make the business lucrative. Unfortunately for its pioneers, the East Coast wine business will remain for the near future very much a gentleman's hobby rather than a viable, commercial, profit-making business.

Prediction number ten. The ocean of wine is swelling at a staggering rate, and in fact one could even say there is a glut already in the marketplace. In the years to come, America will certainly be consuming more wine, but it is not now and is unlikely ever to be a wine-drinking country. For 1987, America is still ranked thirtieth in the world in wine consumption per person. In 1975 we drank 6.5 liters per person and in 1987 we are drinking just under 9 liters per person. While this is a healthy 30% growth rate, even if Americans increased their consumption by 50% by the year 1995, America will only move up to twenty-fifth place (based on today's figures), behind such wine-thirsty countries as Rumania, Bulgaria, Czechoslovakia, and, yes, the vodka kingdom, Russia. The two leading wine-drinking countries in the world, France and Italy, have seen their consumption of wine per person drop by almost 25% between 1975 and 1987. Where is the slack going to be made up, since more vineyards are being planted than ever before and modern technology allows wineries to make much better wine in mediocre vintages and to produce much more wine in great vintages? Certainly there is the possibility that Japan, which has doubled its consumption in the last ten years from 0.5 liters per person to 1 liter per person, may be developing a keen interest in wine. I see many Japanese touring the vineyards of France and they seem to be taking wine more seriously than ever. There may also be help from England, which has quadrupled its wine consumption from 2.7 liters per person in 1975 to 10+ liters per person in 1987, but I don't see the wine glut being evaporated by significantly increased wine consumption in the near future. To sum up, this all means that there will be tremendous competition and stability in prices except for the aforementioned glamour wines, which will be able to maintain their exorbitant prices only if their quality is also exceptionally high.

Prediction number eleven. While technology allows winemakers to produce better and better quality wine, the continuing obsession with technically perfect wines is unfortunately stripping wines of their identifiable and distinctive character. Whether it is the excessive filtration of wines or the excessive emulation of winemaking styles, it seems to be the tragedy of modern winemaking that it is now increasingly difficult to tell an Italian Chardonnay from one made in France or California or Australia. When the corporate winemakers of the world begin to make wines all in the same way, designing them to offend the least number of people, wine will no doubt lose its fascinating appeal and individualism to become no better than most brands of whiskey, gin, scotch, or vodka. One must not forget that the great appeal of wine is that it is a unique, distinctive, fascinating beverage and different every time one drinks it. Winemakers and the owners of wineries, particularly in America, must learn to take more risks so as to preserve the individual character of their wines, even at the risk that some consumers may find them bizarre or unusual. It is this distinctive quality of wine that will ensure its future.

Prediction number twelve. Will the average American's perception of wine change over the next several years? First, and unfortunately, wine today is still regarded as an elitist drink for snobs, and this ridiculous notion continues to be fostered not only by restaurant wine pricing but also by the absurd, elitist advertising of the wine industry. Certainly, things are better today than they were ten years ago as more and more progressive, forward-thinking restaurants are offering a greater array of wines at 50–100% markups rather than the 200–300% of the recent past. And wine advertising from some wineries has toned down. However, the great majority of restaurant wine prices and wine advertising continues to reinforce an image of wine that is not at all necessary, correct, or true.

Second, there is a continued apprehension concerning the new prohibitionist movement in the United States and a worry that if it continues to grow it will have a negative effect on wine sales and the appreciation of wine as a fascinating beverage of moderation and good, healthy living.

Third, the wine scandals of 1986 involving dangerous chemical additives have caused many consumers to wonder what really is in a bottle of wine, despite the fact that these scandals involved only a tiny percentage of the producers who make wine.

There is no question in my mind that the key to increased wine consumption and comprehension of wine as a beverage of moderation is at the restaurant level. There is an unbelievable amount of discretionary income being spent by Americans eating out, and restaurants are the cornerstone of a broader public acceptance of wine and its benefits. Will restaurants make wines more accessible and affordable to the average diner, or will they continue to treat them as a special-event beverage that must be served by pompous sommeliers adorned with jingling tastevin cups, and marked up 200% to 400% above cost so that the only people who might order them are the businessman or woman who has a generous expense account, or the person who doesn't mind getting ripped off on his birthday or anniversary? If such attitudes persist, wine will still be viewed as a mysterious beverage of the rich life. Will wine advertisers promote many of the proven health benefits of wine instead of featuring wine as a drink of snobs who have it served to them by their black-tied butler? I predict that things will get better, but only slowly.

Final thoughts. For each major viticultural area in this manual,

specific buying strategies are set forth. However, there are some overall directions and guidelines that will help you maximize your purchasing power:

• A knowledge of the international financial climate, as well as
the top vintages in demand, can always put you ahead of the pack in
developing an intelligent buying strategy for wine. With respect to
imports, the most recent story has been that of the American dollar,
which sadly has slipped from its record strength in 1985 when, for
example, it traded as high as 10 francs to the dollar—a whopping
150% higher than its value in 1979 and 35% higher than its value
today. The dollar's decline has had a dramatic impact on the prices
for imported wines since these prices have skyrocketed across-the-
board. In addition, the current trade war brewing between the United
States and the European Common Market may result in even higher
tariffs on European wines in retaliation against European tariffs on
American products. In short, the international wine market in 1987 is
in a state of rapid change. However, on the positive side, there are
bumper crop productions in the pipelines and aside from the so-called
glamour wines, prices should remain stable though higher than they
were a mere 18 months ago.

• With respect to French wine prices, which have reached dan-
gerously high levels, my advice with regard to red and white burgundies is to avoid them altogether. I see no reason to buy white
burgundies such as Meursault or Puligny-Montrachet that are selling
between $25 and $60 a bottle when better Chardonnays from California and Australia, not to mention Italy, are available at a half to a
third the price. (The situation for red burgundy is the same.) You need
the income of a movie star or superstar athlete to afford them. The
area in France that still merits considerable consumer interest is Bordeaux. It remains the leader in the world for producing large quantities of superb wines. The 1986 vintage, a gigantic and very good
crop, followed the 1985 vintage, which was also a record-setting production in terms of size and another very good, even excellent, vintage
in terms of quality. The prices being asked for these wines, which will
not be released until spring 1988 for the '85s and spring 1989 for the
'86s, are approximately double, sometimes triple the prices asked for
the 1981s, a vintage of comparable quality.

Furthermore, the fact that there is so much Bordeaux in unsold
inventory means that prices could conceivably soften for the less
glamorous châteaux of this region. However, do not forget for one
second that there are many delicious, very charming wines from other
vintages that are still available at remarkably modest prices, and that

today's best Bordeaux bargains are not the very good 1985s but the monumentally great Cru Bourgeois wines from 1982, as well as the 1979s and 1981s. The latter two vintages produced very good, stylish, elegant wines that have been ignored since all the media and consumer attention was directed toward the 1982 vintage and subsequently to the 1983 vintage. Prices for the 1979s and 1981s, wines which by and large can be drunk now and over the next decade, are approximately half those asked for the 1985 futures and a third of the asking price for the few glamorous 1982s that remain in stock. Be sure to consult the reviews herein, but the following châteaux merit a serious look by interested consumers for both 1981 and 1979: Gruaud-Larose, Talbot, Ducru-Beaucaillou, Léoville-Las Cases, Branaire-Ducru, Giscours, Chasse-Spleen, and Cos d'Estournel. These châteaux are all making some of Bordeaux's finest wines. From 1982, virtually any of the Crus Bourgeois are as good as classified growth in other vintages, and most of them can be drunk today or cellared for 5–10 more years.

Elsewhere in France, champagne prices, like those of Bordeaux, have increased significantly, but there still are bargains to be had. The non-vintage champagne prices have remained more stable than the vintage and luxury cuvées. Be sure to try some of the higher-rated producers of non-vintage champagne, decide on the style you prefer, and then stock up. Other bargains are also available from France. The 1985 wines of Beaujolais were as good as these wines can be and prices are reasonable, particularly those of the best producer of that region, Georges Duboeuf. In addition, look for the 1985s from the Loire Valley, where many producers consider it the best vintage in over 20 years. Loire Valley wines, particularly those from such regions as Muscadet, are still quite reasonable, selling for $5 to $7 a bottle. Unfortunately, the highly regarded wines of Sancerre and Pouilly Fumé have reached double-digit prices in the last year. Still among the great values in French wines are the distinctive wines produced in scenic Alsace on the German border. By and large, they also represent the greatest white wine values in all of Europe. From the spicy Gewürztraminers and smoky Tokays to the steely Rieslings and straightforward Pinot Blancs there are plenty of top-notch wines at excellent prices. Nineteen eighty-three is an outstanding vintage, but 1985 is almost as good and the marketplace is now loaded with these wines. Be sure to look for bottles from the top producers of Alsace. These wines, contrary to what many consumers think, are quite dry and taste much more full-bodied and powerful than their counterparts across the Rhine River in Germany made from the same varietal grapes.

• Italy produces and consumes more wine than any other country in the world; however, the current international furor over the criminal adulteration of cheap wine with lethal chemical additives had far-reaching effects on Italian wine sales in 1986. Of course, this is history, but a cloud still seems to hang over the Italian wine producers. This is unfortunate, for the top producers in Italy make majestic wine and for years have tried to improve the image of Italy as a producer of great, not cheap wine. My buying strategy with respect to the white wines of Italy would be to concentrate on two areas that offer spectacular values—the vibrant, zesty, light, refreshing, white wines of Fruili-Venezia Giulia at less than $7 a bottle have no peers in the world for freshness and lightness. These wines, made from such grapes as Riesling, Ribolla, Chardonnay, Pinot Grigio, and Müller-Thurgau, never see an oak barrel and are bottled and sold just months after they are made to retain their vivacity and freshness. The 1985s are excellent and these would be the wines I would look for. There is no need to look for any older vintages since these wines are meant to be drunk young, not cellared. The other white wines of Italy that offer great value are from the scenic countryside of Tuscany. Vernaccia di San Gimignano is a dry, medium-bodied wine that is refreshingly crisp and flavorful, and an ideal complement to fish and poultry. Again the 1985s are the stars, excellent across-the-board, and they can be bought for less than $6 a bottle.

Italy has made tremendous progress with its white wines, but the real glories of this country continue to be its majestic, long-lived reds. Italy's finest red wines come from Piedmont and the best of them are the massive, very tannic, rather tough, stern Barolos and the more elegant yet no less complex Barbarescos. Both are made from the Nebbiolo grape and are not inexpensive. Expect to pay anywhere from $15 and up for the greatest wines from the greatest producers, but remember, these are world-class wines that in a great vintage such as 1982 or 1985 require a full decade of cellaring to reach their summit of maturity. A less expensive and less time-consuming way to introduce yourself to the glories of the red wines of Piedmont is to try a wine called Nebbiolo d'Alba, often called the poor man's Barolo or Barbaresco, or Piedmont's answer to a French Beaujolais, the soft, fruity, dry Dolcetto. Both these wines have broad, popular appeal in Italy but have yet to be discovered by wine enthusiasts in this country. Consequently, the prices are often less than $7 a bottle.

• With respect to other imports, Australia merits more and more attention from quality-conscious, serious wine consumers. Traditionally, the big, high-alcohol reds have been the stars here. However, with modern winemaking technology, the quality of this country's white wines has increased dramatically. Australia is now turning out beautifully made Chardonnays for under $10 a bottle. Many of them compete with the best Chardonnays of California and the better-quality French white burgundies. Distribution in America is still rather uncertain in many areas, but should you see any of the Chardonnays from such producers as Tyrrell, Montrose, Rosemount, or Lindeman's, don't hesitate to give them a try. Only the powerful, opulent Rosemount sells for more than $10 a bottle.

• South American wines are normally relegated to the back shelf by wine merchants, but I have praise for the wines of Chile's best winery, Cousino Macul, which merit plenty of attention from consumers looking for value rather than prestige.

• With respect to Spain, prices, like those for wines from the other less glamorous wine-producing countries, should remain completely stable and offer the best rapport in quality and price. In Spain, the three areas that are filled with great wine buys are the Rioja, Penedès, and the Ribera del Duero. Just remember that the Spanish style is generally more noticeably oaky in taste than others; this has considerable appeal to an increasing number of Americans, but it may take some time and practice getting used to.

• Lastly, German wines. Wine consumers seem to have a difficult time taking these wines seriously, but they should be looked at, particularly the Kabinetts and Spätleses from the 1983 vintage and the 1985 vintage. Prices have remained generally stable despite the declining dollar and a rather macho German mark.

• With respect to domestic wines, as much as I would like to be able to give support to some of the viticultural regions outside of California and Oregon, it's going to be hard for other wine regions to match the success and brilliance of the wines coming from California's 1984 and 1985 vintages and Oregon's 1985 vintage. For the immediate future, California looks ready to position itself strongly in the marketplace. The two best vintages since the legendary 1974 vintage are 1984 and 1985, and prices should remain generally stable and attractive compared to the glamorous imports. What California wines would I be buying over the next several years? I would certainly be looking for the top producers of Chardonnay from both 1984 and 1985, and, unless I knew the wine well, I would ignore anything older than 1983. California's best Cabernets are again on the verge of challenging the French for supremacy in the fine red wine market. The 1982 vintage turned out fruity, immensely drinkable wines, although some irregularity tends to plague many wineries in this vintage. However, the excellent and opulent 1984s and classic 1985s will become available over the next several years. The 1984s, deep, ripe, with a creamy richness, are well-balanced wines loaded with fruit. They should prove to be the best overall Cabernet vintage for California since 1974. In assessing the wines from the barrel samples I tasted, the following 1984s look potentially outstanding: the three different Cabernets of Diamond Creek, Ridge's Monte Bello, Ravenswood's Merlot, Santa Cruz's Mountain Vineyards, Dunn, William Hill, Caymus, Joseph Phelps, Monticello, Buehler, Carmenet, Dominus, Forman, Girard, Groth, Laurel Glen, Lyeth, Chateau Montelena, Rubicon, the three wines from Silver Oak Vineyards, and the Matanzas Creek Merlot. Certainly, 1984 will offer a great opportunity for California Cabernet and Merlot fanatics to stock their cellars as this vintage should mature well over a ten-year period.

With respect to Oregon, run, don't walk to your local wine merchant and secure a few bottles of the 1985 Pinot Noirs released by such wineries as Eyrie, Ponzi, Adelsheim, Peter Adams, Rex Hill, and Oak Knoll. In addition, the 1985 Pinot Gris white wines offer remarkable quality and value at less than $7 a bottle. They will no doubt sell out fast once word gets out as to just how good they are. They seem perfectly matched to the wonderful salmon of the Pacific Northwest.

Yes, the world's wine market is changing considerably, but armed with the right facts about the top vintages and the best producers and growers, a consumer can maximize his purchasing power and become a formidable authority when buying wine.

Ten Propositions to Consider for 1987–1988

I would like every reader to seriously consider the following propositions for satisfying the palate without punishing the purse.

1. For dry white wines under $7, try some of the best 1983 and 1985 Pinot Blancs from Alsace, which will convince that in a quality sense, they are worth at least twice the price.
2. For serious white wines, there are numerous alternatives to over-priced French white burgundy. Try a 1983 or 1985 Pinot Gris (also called Tokay) from either Alsace or Oregon.
3. Until prices come down, avoid red burgundy; there are far better wines made at significantly lower prices in France's Rhône Valley. As an alternative to burgundy, any of the half-dozen Oregon Pinot Noirs from the 1983 or 1985 vintages.
4. As for great, rich, complex, red wines, make a special effort

to try a Côte-Rôtie, Hermitage, Crozes-Hermitage, Cornas, St.-Joseph, Gigondas, or Châteauneuf-du-Pape from one of the excellent or outstanding growers enumerated herein. Look for wines from the 1982, 1983, and 1985 vintages.

5. For a wonderfully fresh, crisp, delicious apéritif wine, try a 1983 or 1985 German Kabinett or Spätlese, or 1985 Italian white wine from Friuli-Venezia Giulia, or from Tuscany's famed medieval town of San Gimignano.

6. Buy, taste, and finally accept the fact that Spanish red wines offer the greatest quality/price rapport in the world. I would try a bottle each of the 1981 or 1982 Torres Gran Coronas, 1978 or 1981 Torres Black Label Gran Coronas, the 1983 Cabernet Sauvignon-based wine from Remelluri, and Pesquera 1983 Tinto from Ribera del Duero. These are among the world's greatest wines, regardless of their modest prices.

7. Try all three wines made by the Chilean winery of Cousino Macul —the 1985 Chardonnay for $6, the 1982 Cabernet Sauvignon priced at $5.99, and the 1980 Cabernet Sauvignon Antiguas Reserva for $7.99. They are, qualitywise, as good as wines twice their price.

8. Until Bordeaux prices moderate, search out the following 12 red wine-producing overachievers, châteaux that make great wine at modest prices: Potensac (Médoc), Haut-Marbuzet (St.-Estèphe), Les-Ormes-de-Pez (St. Estèphe), Meyney (St.-Estèphe), Bon Pasteur, (Pomerol), L'Enclos (Pomerol), La Dominique (St.-Emilion), L'Arrosée (St.-Emilion), La Louvière (Graves), Sociando-Mallet (Médoc), Chasse-Spleen (Moulis), Belles Graves (Lalande-de-Pomerol), and Balestard-La-Tonnelle (St.-Emilion). Look for the 1981s, 1982s, 1983s, and 1985s.

9. Buy all of the best producers' California white wines you can get your hands on from vintages such as 1984 and 1985, and approach with caution anything made earlier. For California red wines, be extremely selective with choices from the two irregular years of 1982 and 1983, and concentrate on the excellent 1984s coming on the market.

10. If you immensely enjoy drinking a particular red wine *now*, do not hide it away in a cool closet for four to five years in the belief that it will be significantly more enjoyable to you even if its reputation indicates it will continue to improve with aging. If you like the wine now, drink it; you will be happier for it. I may disagree with your drinking strategy, but the most important thing is that you enjoy the wine.

THE WINES OF WESTERN EUROPE

France

Alsace
Bordeaux
Burgundy
Champagne
The Loire Valley
Languedoc
Provence
The Rhône Valley
The Southwest

Italy

Piedmont
Tuscany
Other Significant Red Wines of Italy
Other Significant White Wines of Italy

Germany

Portugal

Spain

1. FRANCE

ALSACE

France's Least-Known Great
White Wines

For years I thought that my unabashed fondness for the distinctive, spicy, unique wines of Alsace was because my first exposure to wine and France was in this highly picturesque region as a visiting student in 1967. As I have learned more about the great wines of France as well as the world, I have come to realize that these wines are among the greatest white wines of France. Furthermore, they are curiously and terribly undervalued, and, to a large part, misunderstood by the wine-consuming public.

Alsace, in the northeastern section of France, sits strategically between the Vosges Mountains and the Rhine River. Although it remains fervently French in its free spirit, Alsace looks as if it belongs in Bavaria. The plethora of cute little villages overflowing with quaint, timbered houses with windows bursting with boxes of vividly colored flowers makes Alsace France's loveliest wine region. The 70-mile stretch of Alsace's "Route du Vin" goes through one fairy-tale village after another. The most picturesque towns, Riquewihr, Ribeauvillé, Colmar, Kayserberg, Eguisheim, and of course, the major city of the area, gorgeous Strasbourg, with its magnificent rose-colored cathedral that still dominates the skyline, are alone reason enough to devote significant attention to this largely undiscovered area of France.

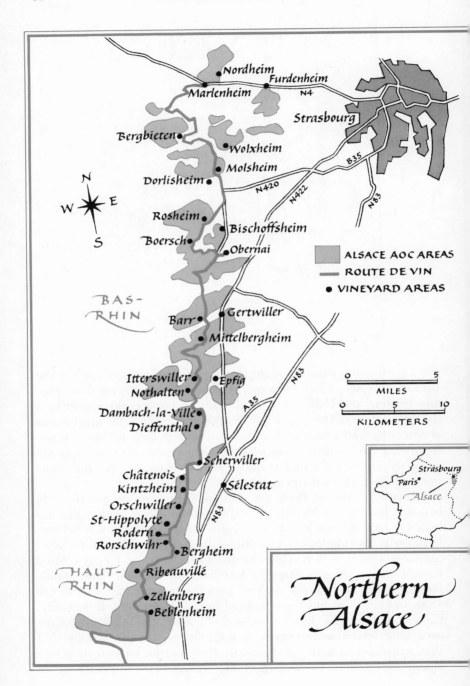

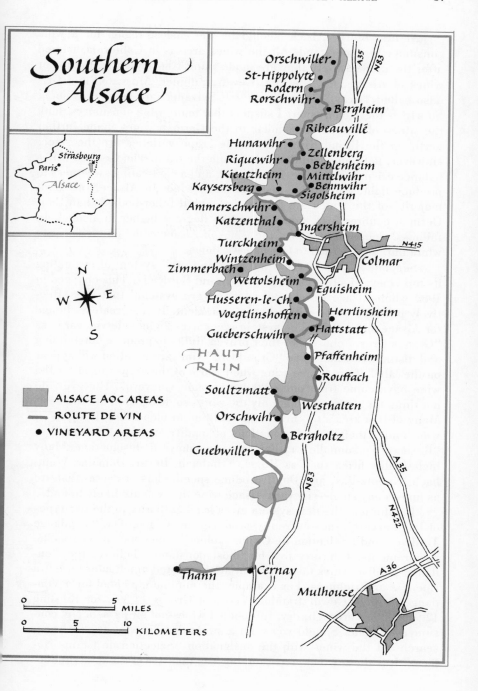

Southern Alsace

Strasbourg
Paris
Alsace

Orschwiller
St-Hippolyte
Rodern
Rorschwihr
Bergheim
Ribeauvillé
Hunawihr
Riquewihr
Zellenberg
Kientzheim
Beblenheim
Kaysersberg
Mittelwihr
Bennwihr
Sigolsheim
Ammerschwihr
Katzenthal
Ingersheim
Turckheim
Wintzenheim
Zimmerbach
Colmar
Wettolsheim
Eguisheim
Husseren-le-Ch.
Herrlinsheim
Voegtlinshoffen
Hattstatt
Gueberschwihr
HAUT
RHIN
Pfaffenheim
Rouffach
Soultzmatt
Westhalten
Orschwihr
Bergholtz
Guebwiller
Thann
Cernay
Mulhouse

N   N83   N415   N83   N422   A35   A36

ALSACE AOC AREAS
ROUTE DE VIN
VINEYARD AREAS

N
W   E
S

0   5   MILES
0   5   10   KILOMETERS

At first blush, Alsace should be the easiest region for a wine consumer to understand. All the wines are, as in California, named after the grape variety they are made from. Consequently, the major wines of Alsace, the Riesling, Gewürztraminer, Muscat, Pinot Gris (also called Tokay), Pinot Blanc, and Sylvaner, are labeled as such. So why is there confusion? I suspect that many wine consumers think the wines of Alsace are similar to the German wines made further north up the Rhine River. True, the grape varieties are the same. However, nothing could be further from the truth. The German wines balance crisp, tart acidity, low alcohol, and a captivating sweetness to produce light, elegant, refreshing, clean wine. In Alsace, the great majority of the wines are totally dry, much fuller-bodied than their German counterparts, and a good 2–4 degrees higher in alcohol. In fullness, richness, and size, the wines of Alsace come much closer to white burgundies than to German Rieslings.

Second, Alsace has not had a "grand cru" system of evaluating its top vineyard sites, as do Burgundy and Bordeaux. This changed in 1983 when Alsace developed a "grand cru system" that was effectively put into action with what is coincidentally the greatest vintage for Alsace since 1971. The system recognizes 25 hillside vineyards as "Grands Crus," chosen for their proven ability to produce outstanding and distinctive wines. The "Grand Cru" vineyard notation will appear on the label of an Alsace wine when 100% of the grapes used for the wine have come from one of these specific vineyards. However, do not think for a moment that only the wines so designated are the best. Many of this area's top firms will continue to blend their best lots of wine under their own designations of quality such as "Réserve" or "Réserve Personnelle" rather than by vineyard designation. Many high-quality firms such as Hugel, Trimbach, Beyer, Domaine Weinbach, Kuentz-Bas, and Dopff produce specific lots or *cuvées* that are as fine as any single-vineyard Alsace wine that you are likely to find.

In addition, the new system gives legal authority to the two types of late-harvest wines currently produced in Alsace. The "Vendange Tardive" and "Sélection de Grains Nobles" wines now meet specific requirements. Contrary to what most consumers believe, the Vendange Tardive wines taste dry, but are harvested much later for extra ripeness and richness. For example, the minimum alcohol for a Vendange Tardive Gewürztraminer or Pinot Gris is 14.3%, for Riesling 12.9%. These are rich, dry, full-bodied wines not sweet as many consumers assume. Should you want a sweet dessert wine from Alsace, search out the wines with the designation "Sélection de Grains Nobles." It is these wines, representing less than 1% of the total production of Alsace, that are unctuous dessert wines and though they have the sweetness of German Beerenauslese, they are considerably higher in alcohol. Legally, the minimum requirements for these wines are 16.4 degrees alcohol for Gewürztraminer and Pinot Gris, and 15.1 degrees alcohol for Riesling and Muscat. They are indeed powerful wines.

These changes in the wine laws of Alsace could not have come at a better time as the 1983 vintage was a monumental year. The wines are opulently fruity, powerful, rich, and deep. Furthermore, they are still available in abundant quantities at the retail level. Looking ahead, 1985 is another excellent vintage, so there is a plentiful supply of fine Alsace. You will be in for some unbelievable gustatory experiences with these wonderful 1983s and 1985s from Alsace.

What does one eat with a wine from Alsace? The most spicy and distinctive of the Alsatian wines are the fragrant, rich Gewürztraminers. These full-flavored and full-bodied wines require full-flavored foods. Perfect matches include oriental or Indian cuisine, rich pâtés, and duck or quail. The Riesling of Alsace is a drier, fuller-bodied wine than its German counterpart, less aromatic, spicy, and unique than Gewürztraminer, and much more flexible when paired with food. All fish and chicken dishes are excellent. The Pinot Gris or Tokay d'Alsace can be Alsace's biggest, richest, fullest wine. I have often mistaken a top-notch Pinot Gris for a great white burgundy. Yes, I did say that. Pinot Gris is smoky, buttery, nutty, and very flavorful. It goes marvelously well with richly sauced fish and fowl dishes, and is superb with fresh foie gras. Lastly, but for different reasons, Pinot Blanc and Muscat are perfect apéritif wines. Pinot Blanc is light, fresh, medium-bodied, and fruity. The Muscat is softer, more perfumed, often rounder and slightly sweeter.

Most of the rich, dry, intense, full-bodied Vendange Tardive (or late-harvest) wines and the sweet dessert Sélection de Grains Nobles wines are very rare and much more expensive. Keep in mind that the top Gewürztraminers will evolve and improve in the bottle for 5–10 years and the top Rieslings for 5–15 years in vintages such as 1983 and 1985. The Vendange Tardive and Sélection de Grains Nobles wines will last 20 or more years.

ALSACE
QUICK VINTAGE GUIDE

1986—Because of significant rainfall as well as rot, it is expected that Alsace's 1986 crop will range in quality from average to above average. The size of the crop is much smaller than in 1985 or in 1983 because of the rot and hailstorms that plagued this area. Most growers hope that the wines will turn out as good as the light yet charming 1979s.

1985—An excellent vintage, 1985 appears to be a close match for the exceptional 1983s. There was less intense, full-bodied Vendange Tardive wine made and the wines are less opulent, rich, and alcoholic than the 1983s, but otherwise this is a lovely vintage of top wines that should drink well for 5–7 years, if not longer. Cask samples of 1985s from Domaine Weinbach, Hugel, Zind-Humbrecht, Sparr, and Gustave Lorentz looked like more elegant, finesse-styled competitors to their great 1983s. Interestingly, the Rieslings of 1985 looked overall to be the weakest group of wines; the Gewürztraminers and Tokays, the strongest.

1984—As in all of France a difficult but not disastrous year, as press reports had indicated. Most wines are quite light, a trifle too acidic, and less intensely fruity than their 1983 and 1985 counterparts. If priced reasonably, the best of these wines offer decent drinking for the next few years.

1983—A great vintage, the best since 1976 and 1971, the 1983s from scenic Alsace have everything—intense, pungent, aromatic bouquets, long, rich, ripe flavors, plenty of body, and great balance and length. At the top levels, the wines will last until the mid to late '90s. It was also a splendid year for the titans of Alsace, the rich, alcoholic, but generally dry Vendange Tardive wines.

1982—A huge crop of rather sound, commercial wines that are soft, fruity, and pleasant. They are aging fast and should, by and large, be drunk up before the end of this decade.

1981—Forgotten in all the (justifiable) hype surrounding 1983 and 1985, this is a good, sometimes very good, vintage of medium-bodied, fruity, well-defined wines. They have good acidity and structure, and though now at their peak, can be drunk with a good deal of pleasure over the next 4–5 years.

1980—A mediocre to below-average-quality vintage. Interestingly, the wines, which were tart and green when first released in 1982/1983, have mellowed substantially with aging. Nothing exciting is to be found here, but as elsewhere in France the wines are better than their initial reputation.

1979—A huge crop of sound, fruity, medium-bodied wines were produced in 1979. The wines have aged nicely, surprising most observers who felt they would not last. All of the wines should be drunk up over the next 4–5 years. This vintage can render a number of surprises, particularly in Gewürztraminer, Tokay, and Riesling.

Older Vintages

The 1976s are luscious wines—intense, full-blown, rather powerful wines of great dimension. The sweet, nectarlike Sélection de Grains Nobles wines are just now coming of age. Two other great vintages for Alsace were 1971 and 1967. Except for the well-cellared examples of Gewürztraminer, Tokay, and Riesling, particularly the richer, fuller-bodied Vendange Tardive wines, the glory days of these wines have passed.

A GUIDE TO ALSACE'S BEST PRODUCERS

* * * * * (OUTSTANDING PRODUCERS)

Dopff "Au Moulin" (Riquewihr)
Hugel (Riquewihr)
Josmeyer (Wintzenheim)

Kuentz-Bas (Husseren-les-
  Châteaux)
Weinbach (Kientzheim)
Zind-Humbrecht (Wintzenheim)

* * * * (EXCELLENT PRODUCERS)

Léon Beyer (Eguisheim)
Marc Kreydenweiss (Barr)
Landmann-Astholt (Soultzmatt)
Gustave Lorentz (Bergheim)
Jerome Lorentz (Bergheim)
René Schaefle (Rouffach)

Charles Schleret (Turckheim)
Schlumberger (Guebwiller)
Pierre Sparr (Sigolsheim)
Trimbach (Ribeauvillé)
A. Willm (Barr)
A. Zimmerman (Orschwiller)

* * * (GOOD PRODUCERS)

Aussay (Eguisheim)
E. Boekel (Mittelbergheim)
Bott Frères (Ribeauvillé)
Joseph Cattin (Voegtlinshoffen)
Dopff & Irion (Riquewihr)
Sick-Dreyer (Ammerschwihr)
W. Gisselbrecht (Dambach-La-
Ville)
Klipfel (Barr)

Klug (Eguisheim)
Muré (Rouffach)
Ostertag (Epfig)
Preiss Henny (Mittelwihr)
Martin Schaetzel
(Ammerschwihr)
René Schmidt (Riquewihr)
Louis Sipp (Ribeauvillé)

* * (AVERAGE PRODUCERS)

Baumann (Mittelwihr)
F. Brucker (Wettolsheim)
La Cigogne (Seva)

Klack (Riquewihr)
H. Krick (Wintzenheim)

IN SEARCH OF THE BEST WINES OF ALSACE
(A List of Some of the Very Best Producers and Their Best Wines)

Gewürztraminer

Léon Beyer: Comtes
D'Eguisheim
Dopff & Irion: Les Sorcières
Dopff "Au Moulin": Eichberg
Hugel: Réserve Personnelle
Josmeyer: Hengst Vyd.
Marc Kreydenweiss: Kritt Vyd.
Kuentz-Bas: Réserve
Personnelle
Gustave Lorentz: Altenberg
Vyd.
Muré: Clos St.-Landelin
Ostertag: Moenchberg Vyd.
Schleret Cuvée Speciale

Schlumberger Kessler Vyd.
Schlumberger Christine
Schlumberger
Sick-Dreyer: Kaefferkopf Vyd.
Pierre Sparr Mambourg Vyd.
Trimbach Ribeaupierre
Weinbach Cuvée Theo
Weinbach Réserve Personnelle
Willm Clos Gaensbroennel
Zind-Humbrecht Hengst
Wintzenheim Vyd.
Zind-Humbrecht Gueberschwihr
Vyd.

Riesling

Léon Beyer Ecaillers
Dopff "Au Moulin"
Schoenenberg
Hugel Réserve Personnelle
Josmeyer Hengst
Kuentz-Bas Réserve Personnelle

Gustave Lorentz Altenberg Vyd.
Ostertag Moenchberg Vyd.
Schaetzel Kaefferkopf
Schlumberger Saering Vyd.
Schmidt Schoenenberg
L. Sipp Kirchberg

Pierre Sparr Altenbourg
Trimbach Frédéric Emile
Trimbach Clos Ste.-Hune
Weinbach Schlossberg
Weinbach Sainte Catherine
Willm Kirchberg

Zind-Humbrecht Rangen
Zind-Humbrecht Herrenweg
  Turkheim
Zind-Humbrecht Brand
Zind-Humbrecht Clos Hauserer

Tokay d'Alsace (Pinot Gris)

L. Beyer Réserve
Hugel Réserve Personnelle
Kuentz-Bas Réserve Personnelle
Landmann-Astholt "Bollenberg"
Gustave Lorentz Altenberg

Schaetzel
Weinbach
Zind-Humbrecht St. Urbain
  Rangen
Zind-Humbrecht Rangen

Alsace's Very Best Wine Values—Pinot Blanc and Crémant

Virtually all of Alsace's white wines offer good values in the world-wide wine market, but two stand out as particularly fine values: Pinot Blanc and the sparkling wine of Alsace called Crémant d'Alsace. Pinot Blanc is the poor man's Chardonnay, fresh, lively, crisp, and pleasantly fruity. It is not a wine to buy in lean, tart vintages such as 1984 and 1980 because it is then too acidic. However, it flourishes in vintages such as 1983 and 1985, rivaling in quality Chardonnays that sell for two or three times the price. Pinot Blanc, a dry spicy wine, but not one to age well, is best drunk up within 3–4 years of the vintage. Alsace's other bargain, Crémant d'Alsace, is hardly known outside of the area where it is produced. This inexpensive, sparkling alternative to champagne can be a delicious, fairly priced, dry wine. It rarely sells for more than $10 a bottle.

Alsace's Best Pinot Blancs

Josmeyer Hengst
Josmeyer Les Lutins
Hugel Cuvée les Amours
Marc Kreydenweiss

M. Schaetzel
Schlumberger Princess Abbes
Weinbach Réserve
Willm Cordon d'Alsace

Alsace's Best Crémants

Aussay
Dopff
Laugel

Muré
Willm

Two Alsace Wines That Rarely Merit Attention

Not everything in Alsace is a great bargain. One of Alsace's biggest selling wines is Sylvaner. It can be good—Domaine Weinbach's is in fact always pleasant—but, in general, it is a rather dull, flat wine with little charm. It is best avoided. Alsace also makes red wines from the Pinot Noir grape. They are fashionable and rather expensive, and the local cognoscenti have a great deal of pride in the wine. However, it usually looks like a blush or rosé wine in color and often tastes insipid and diluted, although the 1983 Muré could have been confused for a minor red burgundy. Yes, one can find an exception or two, but Pinot Noirs from Alsace are by and large extremely mediocre.

Alsace—Today's Buying Strategy

The primary thrust in buying Alsace wines should be to search out the better 1983s that are still around on the shelves. Most of these wines will offer splendid drinking for the rest of this decade, with the Vendange Tardive wines lasting well into the next decade. The 1984s are light and somewhat acidic. They are not bad wines. The 1983s are generally outstanding, and the newly released 1985s excellent. Buy 1983s and 1985s—you are not likely to be disappointed.

AUSSAY (EGUISHEIM)* * *

This new line of products is made by the Caves Vinicole d'Eguisheim. This cooperative has one of the best reputations in France and now also makes the wines of the famous firm of Willm. The Aussay wines showed especially well in comparative blind tastings and, as the prices indicate, they offer excellent value. The style of the wines emphasizes crisp, dry fruitiness and medium body. They are not opulent, but all are faithful to their grape varieties.

1983 Crémant d'Alsace   ($8.99)   83

This sparkling wine from Alsace no doubt has a proportion of Pinot Gris in its composition, as the buttery, spicy bouquet suggests. The bubbles are persistent and a little large, but this sparkling wine is quite dry and has surprising flavor and character.

1983 Gewürztraminer   ($6.49)   84

A flowery, almond-scented, fruity bouquet, it is less spicy than normal for Gewürztraminer, but this medium-bodied, stylish wine has good concentration and very fine length, is dry, crisp, and quite well made.

1983 Pinot Blanc d'Alsace   ($3.99)   81

Light- to medium-bodied, fresh, fruity, dry yet very refreshing and
quite cleanly made, this is a very charming wine for drinking now.

1983 Pinot Gris d'Alsace   ($5.49)   85

A lovely wine, as are so many 1983s from Alsace, this wine has a
subtle, smoky, buttery, creamy bouquet that is reminiscent of a good
white burgundy. Medium to full body with very good length, adequate
acidity, and good dryness make this wine an excellent value.

1983 Riesling   ($4.99)   84

Quite an attractive Riesling, this medium-bodied wine is aromatic,
spicy, and fresh, with solid fruit flavors.

BAUMANN (MITTELWIHR)* *

1983 Riesling Schoenenbourg   ($9.99)   86

Quite an excellent Riesling, this rather large-framed, big, rich wine is
quite full-bodied, with an exotic, smoky, spicy bouquet, long, deep
flavors, and at least 3–5 years of evolution ahead of it.

LÉON BEYER (EGUISHEIM)* * * *

1978 Gewürztraminer Cuvée Comtes Eguisheim   ($11.99)   87

The 1978 is still quite youthful but showing excellent ripeness, full
body, and the rich, exotic bouquet that typifies Gewürztraminer. Quite
a successful wine for the 1978 vintage in Alsace, this wine will last for
at least another decade.

1981 Gewürztraminer Cuvée Comtes Eguisheim   ($8.59)   85

No doubt 1981 for Alsace has been forgotten with all the justified
hoopla over 1983. However, 1981 was a good vintage. This wine is still
quite young and unevolved, but has oodles of the rich, exotic Gewürztraminer fruit, a powerful, heady punch, and long finish. Its bouquet
has yet to open and develop, but that will come.

1983 Gewürztraminer Cuvée Comtes Eguisheim   ($9.49)   88

A powerful, authoritative, spicy, exotic Gewürztraminer for sure, but
at present this wine, despite considerable promise, is quite closed.
The bouquet hints at rich, ripe fruit but remains tight and generally
restrained. On the palate, the wine is full-bodied, very concentrated,

but like a spring flower in bud, it has yet to blossom. Quite dry, quite concentrated, and impeccably vinified, this wine will merit a higher score in 2–3 years when it is showing all its considerable charm.

1983 Riesling	($4.99)	80

1983 Riesling Cuvée des Écaillers	($8.99)	82

Here is a case where the regular Riesling is almost as good as the special cuvée and is $4 a bottle less expensive. Both wines are medium-bodied, with light-intensity, floral, spicy bouquets, dry, nicely textured flavors and good crisp finish. Both should last for 4–6 years.

1983 Tokay (Pinot Gris) Réserve	($8.99)	86

1983 Tokay (Pinot Gris) Sélection de Grains Nobles	($40.00)	92

The Réserve is another very fine Pinot Gris in what looks to be an outstanding vintage for this grape variety. In Alsace, the Pinot Gris in this great vintage has a buttery, creamy richness that is not unlike a fine Chardonnay. This example from Beyer is big like most 1983 Alsatian Pinot Gris wines, yet more restrained and elegant than others. A flowery yet buttery, creamy bouquet is just beginning to emerge. On the palate, the wine is full-bodied, relatively rich, quite long, and should improve for 3–5 years. As for the nectarlike 1983 Tokay Sélection de Grains Nobles, it is like tasting a blend of a great Montrachet and Yquem. Powerful, unctuous, rich, dense, and incredibly long on the palate, this wine will age for 15 or more years.

E. BOEKEL (MITTELBERGHEIM)* * *

Boekel is a good, even very good, producer that offers solid, well-flavored wines at very reasonable prices.

1983 Gewürztraminer Réserve	($7.99)	86

This is not an overly aggressive, intense Gewürztraminer, but it is well-balanced and spicy, with rich fruit and a fine, dry finish.

1983 Pinot Blanc	($4.99)	84

Boekel's Pinot Blanc is one of the vintage's best. It is rather fresh, ripe, rich, and full-bodied, and all in all quite impressive.

1983 Riesling	($5.99)	84

The 1983 Riesling from Boekel is a good, solid Riesling with flowery, spicy flavors and excellent balance.

1983 Riesling Zotzenberg	($7.99) 86

An excellent Riesling with a fragrant, intense bouquet, it is very long on the palate, and has fine balance. An impressive wine.

BOTT FRÈRES (RIBEAUVILLÉ)* * *

This tiny firm in the lovely town of Ribeauvillé produces a small amount of wine from its own vineyards. The only wines I have experienced are the 1983s, which are excellent and very reasonably priced.

1983 Gewürztraminer Cuvée Exceptionnelle	($6.99) 86

1983 Gewürztraminer Réserve Personnelle	($7.99) 87

Both of these wines are textbook Gewürztraminers at prices that are simply superb. The only difference between them I could perceive was that the Réserve Personnelle had a slightly more exaggerated bouquet and perhaps a little more depth. They are both rather big, intense wines with excellent concentration, but also possess a measure of elegance and avoid the heaviness that can sometimes be found in Gewürztraminer. Both wines will drink well for 3–5 years.

1983 Riesling Réserve Personnelle	($7.49) 86

An excellent Riesling, rather full and flavorful, but wonderfully balanced with dry, rich, spicy, medium-bodied flavors, plenty of concentration, and a long finish. A textbook example of a dry, rather full-flavored Alsace Riesling from an outstanding vintage. Drink over the next 4–5 years.

1983 Tokay d'Alsace Cuvée Exceptionelle	($6.95) 80

Light golden with a rich, smoky, spicy, almost buttery and bacon-scented bouquet, this nicely proportioned wine is not so rich and opulent on the palate as some Alsatian Tokays, but has good flavor authority, balancing acidity, and a good finish.

F. BRUCKER (WETTOLSHEIM)* *

This is another label of the firm of A. Gaschy. The wines are quite inexpensive and offer sound, rather one-dimensional, simple drinking at very fair prices. On occasion, this winery can turn out something special, as it did in 1983 with its Vendange Tardive Riesling and Gewürztraminer.

1983 Gewürztraminer Cuvée Tradition   ($3.99)   75

1983 Gewürztraminer Pfersigberg Vendange Tardive   ($9.99)   85

1983 Gewürztraminer Réserve Personnelle   ($4.99)   75

The star here is the dry, rich, full-bodied Pfersigberg, which has an exotic, smoky, spicy bouquet, and soft, round, clean flavors. It is quite spicy and should be served with pâté or game. The Réserve Personnelle is clean, pleasant, but of standard quality, and the Cuvée Tradition is quite palatable, but very simple and short in the finish.

1983 Pinot Gris Réserve Personnelle   ($4.99)   70

Faint, spicy, creamy aromas suggest a rather watery Pinot Gris. On the palate, the wine is light, but clean and fresh.

1983 Riesling Cuvée Tradition   ($3.59)   72

1983 Riesling Réserve Personnelle   ($4.99)   75

1983 Riesling Steingrubler Vendange Tardive   ($9.49–$9.99)   84

The Riesling Steingrubler is a finely made wine, concentrated, full and spicy, with good acidity and length. It should age well for 1–3 years. The Réserve Personnelle is lean and tart, the Cuvée Tradition even more so. Nevertheless, for the money, it is hard to criticize the quality.

LA CIGOGNE (SEVA)* *

These wines are also produced by a cooperative, and while no one is likely to confuse them with the wines of Hugel, Weinbach, Zind-Humbrecht, or Trimbach, these inexpensive wines offer considerable appeal and value, particularly the Riesling and Gewürztraminer.

1983 Gewürztraminer   ($5.49)   83

I suspect this is the least expensive Gewürztraminer on the market. It is neither powerful nor opulently fruity, but spicy, perfumed, fresh, lively, medium-bodied, with good varietal fruit and a good finish. An understated yet very nice style of dry Gewürztraminer.

1983 Riesling   ($4.89)   80

A straightforward, slightly spicy, rather fruity, dry, medium-bodied wine that is very cleanly made and stylish.

1983 Sylvaner   ($4.49)   70

As Sylvaners go, this wine is decent and palatable. Lean, austere fruit
offers aromas of herbs and minerals.

DOPFF & IRION (RIQUEWIHR)* * *

One of the most important firms of Alsace, Dopff & Irion produce
significant quantities of wines that are usually good but rarely spectacular. The firm has excellent vineyards, but the wines have been criticized for having a commercial dullness rather than any individualistic
or unique style. I would tend to agree with such observations for the
1983s from Dopff & Irion, with the exception of the firm's sensational
top-of-the-line Gewürztraminer, Les Sorcières. Certainly the prices
for Dopff & Irion wines remain quite reasonable.

1982 Gewürztraminer   ($5.99)   70

1983 Gewürztraminer   ($6.49–$7.49)   83

The 1983 Gewürztraminer shows good ripeness, a typically big, rich,
smoky, lychee-nut-scented aroma, a touch of coarseness in the finish,
and medium body. The 1982 is quite light, rather soft and flabby, and
should be drunk soon. The 1983 will keep well for the balance of this
decade.

1981 Gewürztraminer Les Sorcières   ($12.99)   83

1982 Gewürztraminer Les Sorcières   ($9.99)   70

1983 Gewürztraminer Les Sorcières   ($12.99)   89

These three wines illustrate the greatness of the 1983 vintage. The
1981 is good, delicate, spicy, rather restrained for a Gewürztraminer,
but stylish and well made. The 1982 is a trifle diffuse and borders on
being watery and bland. However, the 1983 is the finest wine made by
Dopff & Irion in at least a decade. An intense, powerful bouquet of
ripe, spicy fruit is followed by a wine that has layers of flavor, full
body, an intense, lingering finish and great balance. The 1983 is quite
a big wine that begs for a rich pâté or a duck or quail dish. It should
improve for at least 4–5 more years and last well unto the '90s before
fading.

1982 Riesling   ($5.99–$6.29)   72

1983 Riesling   ($6.49–$6.79)   82

The 1983 regular Riesling shows good, crisp acidity, medium body
and an attractive perfume of spicy, floral fruit. It is stylish and well
made rather than dramatic and concentrated. The 1982 is quite light,
lacks flavor authority, and finishes short and pale.

1983 Sylvaner   ($4.49)   72

I have never been a great admirer of Sylvaner, a wine that I find to be
acidic, with little charm and often some bitterness. I suspect these
wines have turned out better than usual in 1983 because of the exceptional ripeness attained in this vintage, but I have yet to find many
1983 Sylvaners that I can enthusiastically recommend. This is a clean
yet rather thin, bland wine that is neutral and, one might say, honest,
but even at its low price is no bargain.

DOPFF "AU MOULIN" (RIQUEWIHR)* * * * *

A top house of Alsace, Dopff "Au Moulin" has an impressive list of
vineyards and also produces the best sparkling wine of Alsace. The
wines drink young but age well. They are definitely wines to seek out.

N.V. Crémant d'Alsace   ($9.99)   84

A fresh, lively wine with good concentration of fruit and medium body.
Very stylish.

1983 Gewürztraminer Eichberg   ($15.95)   90

The 1983 Gewürztraminer Eichberg is simply extraordinary. A spectacular bouquet of lychee nuts and exotic fruit, great concentration
and length, plus super balance all combine to make this an outstanding wine.

1983 Gewürztraminer Réserve   ($9.97)   87

The 1983 Réserve has an exceptional nose, ripe, spicy, deep, long,
massive fruit on the palate, and is very rich and deep.

1983 Riesling Réserve   ($8.99)   86

A fragrant, rich, flowery, spicy nose, and deep, long, rich flavors
combine to produce a very well-made wine.

1983 Riesling Schoenenberg Vendange Tardive   ($15.45)   90

This wine is a superb Riesling. It has a long, rich, fabulous bouquet,
long finish, and is quite dry on the palate. Should last 10 years.

WILLY GISSELBRECHT (DAMBACH-LA-VILLE)* * *

A reliable rather than exciting producer of wine; Gisselbrecht's wines often represent very good values.

| 1983 Gewürztraminer Cuvée Réserve | ($8.99) | 84 |

The Cuvée Réserve has rather deep color, is ripe and round, juicy and concentrated. It tends to be one-dimensional, but is still quite satisfying.

| 1983 Pinot Blanc | ($4.99) | 83 |

A ripe, flavorful, rather plump and succulent wine.

| 1983 Riesling | ($5.99) | 83 |

Gisselbrecht's 1983 Riesling has a ripe peachlike nose with a good, supple palate.

HUGEL (RIQUEWIHR)* * * * *

Alsace's most famous wine firm, this family-run operation began in the lovely town of Riquewihr in 1637 and is now run by the ebullient Jean (or "Johnnie") Hugel. For many Alsace enthusiasts, the name Hugel is synonymous with these special and distinctive wines. The quality here is very high and, fortunately, the wines easy to find in major markets. The style of wine made here is quite rich, concentrated, opulent, and full-bodied. The Gewürztraminers and late-harvest Sélection de Grains Nobles wines, whether they be Gewürztraminer, Riesling, Muscat, or Tokay, are truly brilliant. In addition, Hugel wines keep exceptionally well, though one suspects that most of them are drunk when they are still in a prepubescent state for the simple reason that they show so well. The 1983s of Hugel are truly superb, easily the equals of the great wines this firm produced in 1976 and 1971.

1976 Gewürztraminer Grains Nobles Fut 20	($49.50)	95
1976 Gewürztraminer Grains Nobles Fut 28	($49.50)	95
1976 Gewürztraminer Réserve Personnelle	($24.95)	88
1976 Gewürztraminer Vendange Tardive	($22.95)	87

All four of these wines can still be found at both the retail and, in some areas, the wholesale level. The prices have remained unchanged since the wines were released in the late '70s. Consumers are unaware that these wines, particularly the two nectarlike Sélections de Grains Nobles, are as spectacular in their own distinctive style as a great vintage of Yquem, and therefore have let them sit. The 1976 Beerenauslese-styled Gewürztraminers are still adolescents in terms of their evolution, but are truly stunning wines. Claimed by the Hugel firm as the greatest Sélection de Grains Nobles wine they have ever produced, these wines have layers of exotic tropical fruit, finishes that last a full 60 seconds (which is extremely long), intense, magnificently aromatic bouquets, and unbelievable balance. It is worth latching onto a bottle to celebrate the year 2000. The Vendange Tardive is very, very good, but lacks the depth, dimension, and balance of the Sélection de Grains Nobles wines. As for the totally dry, intense 1976 Réserve Personnelle, it smells of ripe pineapples, almonds, candied lychee nuts, has a powerful, heady punch to its full-bodied, rich texture, and is ready to drink now.

1979 Gewürztraminer Réserve Personnelle	($14.99)	85

Hugel produced an excellent Gewürztraminer in 1979. It may not rival the 1983 or 1976 Réserve Personnelle, but it is still quite full-bodied, powerful, nicely balanced, and dry, with ample length and acidity. Drink over the next 2–3 years.

1981 Gewürztraminer Réserve Personnelle	($14.00)	86
1981 Gewürztraminer Vendange Tardive	($17.49)	85

These two 1981 Gewürztraminers are very fine, but when compared to the great efforts of Hugel in 1983 and 1976, lack the breadth and depth of the wines of the two latter vintages. Both are typically "Hugelian"—concentrated, ripe, plump, deep, but not complex. The Vendange Tardive is a trifle soft and leans toward being flabby. However, it and the Réserve Personnelle are authoritative examples of Gewürztraminer from one of France's great wine families.

1983 Gewürztraminer	($8.69)	86
1983 Gewürztraminer Réserve Personnelle	($13.99)	90
1983 Gewürztraminer Vendange Tardive	($22.95)	92

Three outstanding examples of the Hugel style of Gewürztraminer, these wines all share this firm's rich, powerful, deep, full-bodied style. The late-harvest Vendange Tardive is not sweet, but rather incredibly ripe and rich, powerfully built, with a full-blown bouquet of almonds and flowers. It is quite long and sensationally concentrated. It should drink well for 10–20 years. Slightly less exuberant, but still an authoritatively rich, dense, full-bodied wine, the Hugel Réserve Personnelle is probably the finest in a long line of superb Gewürztraminers since Hugel's great 1971. Even the regular Gewürztraminer shows surprising richness and strength, with a big, rich, spicy bouquet, lush, full-bodied flavors, and good balance.

1983 Pinot Blanc Cuvée les Amours   ($5.49)   84

1985 Pinot Blanc Cuvée les Amours   ($6.49)   84

Hugel's Pinot Blanc has rarely been one of the firm's better wines, but in the 1983 they are justifiably proud of the quality. This dry wine is spicy, quite fruity, round and generous, with good, crisp balance and acidity. The 1985 is slightly less opulent and lush, but stylish, quite well made, and ready to drink.

1983 Riesling   ($6.99)   84

1983 Riesling Réserve Personnelle   ($14.49) 85

Hugel's regular Riesling has a wonderfully fresh, perfumed character, medium to full body, is quite dry, but round, fruity, and surprisingly long. The Réserve Personnelle is riper, longer on the finish, slightly deeper and fuller, with oodles of ripe Riesling fruit. These are big wines with alcohol contents of 12.5%, an interesting contrast to their German counterparts with 8% alcohol.

1983 Tokay Réserve Personnelle   ($14.49) 86

The poor man's Meursault? Many of the 1983 Tokays from Alsace are so buttery, smoky, full-bodied, and rich that one could easily assume he was drinking a great Meursault. Full-bodied and powerful, this strongly scented, big, rich wine will age well for 4–7 years.

JOSMEYER (WINTZENHEIM)* * * * *

One of the least known of the great wine firms of Alsace, the family-run winery of Joseph Meyer, which appears on the label as Josmeyer, produces outstanding wines, particularly Gewürztraminer, Pinot Blanc, and Riesling. His Pinot Blanc is unquestionably one of the best in Alsace, and is remarkably cheap. Josmeyer's wines are very rich and concentrated, yet slow to mature, and older examples such as the

1966 Riesling and 1964 Gewürztraminer Vendange Tardive can be incredible wines and are among the least-known great dry white wines of the world.

1983 Gewürztraminer Cuvée des Centenaire-Hengst	($13.99)	91

1983 Gewürztraminer Les Archenets	($9.99)	87

Josmeyer's successes extend throughout his line of wines, but certainly his 1983 Gewürztraminers are quite special. His blended Gewürztraminer from different vineyard sites, the Les Archenets, is splendid enough, rich, powerful, deep, quite dry, rather alcoholic, exotically fruity and big. However, the special Gewürztraminer Cuvée des Centenaire, from the chalky soil of the Hengst vineyard, is magical in 1983. It is one of the greatest dry Gewürztraminers I have ever tasted. Decadently rich and opulent, this full-bodied, intensely perfumed wine has stupendous length and layers of ripe, rich fruit. It is drinking well now and will last for well over a decade.

1985 Pinot d'Alsace Les Lutins	($5.99)	82

1983 Pinot Auxerrois Hengst-Vieilles Vignes	($5.99)	85

1983 Pinot Blanc Réserve Fourways	($5.99)	84

The 1983 Vieilles Vignes from the chalky soil of the Hengst vineyard, made from a Pinot clone called Pinot Auxerrois, is a remarkably stylish, spicy, clean, medium-bodied, dry, flavorful wine with real elegance and breeding. It is ideal for drinking over the next 3–4 years. The 1983 Pinot Blanc Fourways has ripe flavors and surprising richness and length. The Les Lutins is Josmeyer's blend of Pinot Blanc grapes. It is quite good and certainly one of the best Pinot Blancs from the 1985 vintage, but is upstaged by the firm's other two wines.

1983 Riesling Les Pierrets	($8.99)	84

1983 Riesling Vendange Tardive Hengst	($15.99)	87

The Les Pierrets, the firm's blend of Riesling from different sites, is opulent, lovely, spicy, very flowery, quite dry, with well-defined flavors, good depth, and a solid finish. It should be drunk soon. The Hengst Vendange Tardive is as expected, quite rich, medium- to full-bodied, spicy, ripe, and concentrated, with a long, round, luscious finish. It is very impressive and will last more than a decade.

1983 Sylvaner d'Alsace   ($5.69)   77

Not a bad Sylvaner, this effort from Josmeyer shows good ripeness, a touch of acidity in the finish, but is generally pleasing, albeit simple.

KLACK (RIQUEWIHR)* *

Apparently, Klack is a very small producer or secondary label, and the only wines I have seen from this firm are the 1983s, which are quite good.

1983 Gewürztraminer   ($8.49)   84

Rather soft, ripe, and lush, this aromatic wine has the Gewürztraminer spicy character, medium to full body, and good length. Drink over the next 1–2 years.

1983 Riesling   ($8.25)   85

A distinctive Riesling, smoky, quite spicy, with rather dramatic, intense flavors, this is an impressive Riesling for drinking over the next 3–4 years.

KLIPFEL (BARR)* * *

This estate is in the very northern section of Alsace's viticultural region. The 1983s were good rather than spectacular.

1983 Gewürztraminer Clos Zisser   ($7.99)   85

A rich, authoritative, spicy, intense wine.

1983 Pinot Gris Freiberg   ($6.49)   80

A satisfactory rather than excellent Pinot Gris, this offering from Klipfel is round, slightly sweet, quite spicy and fruity, but it lacks acidity and finishes a little short.

1983 Riesling   ($5.99)   84

1983 Riesling Kirchberg   ($6.99)   86

The standard cuvée of Riesling is quite good, fresh, aromatic, dry, with a bouquet suggestive of walnuts and flowers; it is a nicely textured wine, but the Kirchberg has a big, complex, fragrant bouquet, spicy, fresh, concentrated flavors, and an impressive finish. The Kirchberg should drink well for 4–5 years.

KLUG (EGUISHEIM)* * *

Klug is one of the labels produced at the top-notch cooperative in Eguisheim. The wines represent very good values and on occasion can be excellent (e.g., the 1983 Gewürztraminer is amazing for the price).

| 1983 Gewürztraminer | ($5.49) | 86 |

A great value in Gewürztraminer, this rich, spicy, surprisingly intense wine has excellent depth and richness, full body, some round, ripe sweetness in the long finish, and a powerful, heady bouquet. Quite impressive.

| 1983 Riesling | ($4.99–$5.49) | 75 |

Rather tart and lean, with some herbal overtones, this dry, austere Riesling may develop more flesh and character with several more months of bottle age.

KUENTZ-BAS (HUSSEREN-LES-CHÂTEAUX)* * * * *

This tiny firm does indeed have an excellent reputation in Alsace, but as yet is little known in America. The quality of its wines, in particular the 1983s, should do much to establish this tiny family firm's place among the most successful of Alsace's producers. My favorite wines from Kuentz-Bas have been the splendidly rich Gewürztraminers and Tokays. The Pinot Blancs and Rieslings do not seem to be of the same caliber. The firm believes its Muscat is the best. The style of wines produced by Kuentz-Bas is neither the most full-bodied and opulent à la Weinbach, Schlumberger, or Hugel, nor the most restrained and elegant à la Trimbach or Beyer. It lies somewhere between these two general approaches to Alsace wines.

| 1983 Gewürztraminer Cuvée Tradition | ($5.99) | 88 |

| 1983 Gewürztraminer Réserve Personnelle | ($7.99) | 89 |

| 1983 Gewürztraminer Vendange Tardive Cuvée Caroline | ($16.99) | 91 |

Here are three very fine Gewürztraminers, two of which are sold at sensational prices. The regular or standard cuvée, called Cuvée Tradition, is a powerful wine with a huge, smoky, bacon fat and exotic fruit bouquet, rich, concentrated flavors, a good measure of alcohol, and long finish. It should be drunk over the next 3–4 years. One of my favorites here is the Réserve Personnelle (which is also a great buy) because it is a powerful, authoritative, deeply concentrated Gewürztraminer with a big, aromatic, smoky, almondlike bouquet, long, gorgeously fruity flavors, full body, and I would guess at least 13.5% alcohol. The Vendange Tardive is immense in stature, and a remarkably alcoholic and powerful wine that has more in common with a great Montrachet than a typical Alsace wine.

1983 Muscat Réserve Personnelle ($8.99) 82

Very aromatic, as one would expect, this is one of the Kuentz-Bas wines that is certainly good but a trifle heavy and lacking in acidity. Drink over the next year. Curiously, Kuentz-Bas regards Muscat as one of the firm's specialties.

1983 Pinot Blanc Cuvée Tradition ($3.99) 78

For the price, this wine may merit a look, but it is not one of the top Pinot Blancs of the vintage. It has a good, clean, spicy, fruity nose, but has a touch of harshness in the finish.

1983 Riesling Réserve Personnelle ($6.99) 84

1983 Riesling Sélection de Grains Nobles ($35.00) 90

The Réserve Personnelle is a good, clean, stylish, dry, medium-bodied Riesling with a concentration of fruit and good acidity. The Sélection de Grains Nobles has 15.2% alcohol, a gorgeous, perfumed, fragrant bouquet, intense and powerful flavors, and an amazing finish. It should age for 20–25 years.

1983 Tokay d'Alsace Pinot Gris Réserve Personnelle ($8.99) 87

1983 Tokay d'Alsace Pinot Gris Vendange Tardive ($16.99) 85

The 1983 Tokay Réserve Personnelle is splendidly concentrated, rich, buttery, smoky, and better than 85% of the burgundies on the market. It is a dry, full-bodied, very rich wine with stunning length. The Vendange Tardive would have scored higher, but some slight sulphur in the nose kept the score lower.

GUSTAVE AND JEROME LORENTZ (BERGHEIM)* * * *

Two separate firms, Gustave Lorentz and Jerome Lorentz, are managed by the same staff, and although the wines come from different vineyards, both the winemaking philosophy and care of the wines are under the control of Charles Lorentz, Jr. The Gustave Lorentz operation is twice the size of Jerome's, but both are moderate in size—a production of 160,000 cases for Gustave and 80,000 for Jerome. Both firms are highly respected for their Gewürztraminers, which usually come from the two Grand Cru vineyards of Altenberg and Kanzlerberg. I would enthusiastically agree with such observations, since these wines are clearly both firms' best. However, I would not disregard the Riesling of Jerome Lorentz from the Altenberg vineyard or the Muscat and Tokay (from Altenberg) from Gustave Lorentz. The basic cuvées, or regular bottlings, from both Jerome and Gustave Lorentz are generally sound, but usually not on the same level of quality as the regular cuvées of Hugel, Trimbach, or Zind-Humbrecht. The style of wine produced at Lorentz is one that emphasizes ripeness, power, and opulent flavors.The specific vineyard wines are the wines to search out from these two firms.

GUSTAVE LORENTZ

1983 Gewürztraminer	($6.79)	78
1983 Gewürztraminer Altenberg	($16.99)	90
1983 Gewürztraminer Réserve	($6.99)	84
1983 Gewürztraminer Sélection de Grains Nobles	($50.00)	98
1983 Gewürztraminer Vendange Tardive	($22.00)	88

The standard cuvée of Gewürztraminer I found to be a little lacking in character and a disappointment. The Réserve is a big step up in quality as it is a rather fat, ripe, full-bodied, well-made wine. The other three wines are all huge, ripe, intense, monumental Gewürztraminers. The Altenberg has an immense structure, a chewy texture, great ripeness and length, and staggering concentration. It will drink well and improve for over a decade. the Vendange Tardive is similarly styled, even more powerful, with a head-spinning alcohol content of 14.5–15%, a dry finish, and enough body and flesh to make one think it is an old-style Chalone Chardonnay. Finally, the Sélection de Grains Nobles, which is 90% from the Grand Cru vineyard Altenberg, is a legendary wine, virtually perfect, with an incredible perfume, incredible richness and concentration, and simply outlandish length (over 90 seconds) and 15–30 years of evolution. It held up without oxidation for 8 days in an open bottle. An astonishing wine!

1983 Muscat   ($7.49)   85

One of the best Alsatian Muscats I have tasted, this full-bodied wine
has plenty of fruit, a long, lingering finish, and adequate acidity.

1983 Riesling Altenberg   ($13.95)   88

1983 Riesling Réserve   ($6.99)   83

The Riesling Altenberg ranks as one of the outstanding Rieslings from
this great vintage. A lovely bouquet of spices and ripe pineapple gives
way to a complex, rich, dry, medium- to full-bodied Riesling with
excellent presence in the mouth. It should improve for 6–8 years. The
Réserve Riesling is more austere, with a steely, mineral-scented bouquet and tight, austere flavors.

1983 Sylvaner Réserve   ($5.29)   74

Not very interesting, but clean, spicy, with a rather herbal, weedy
character and some acidity in the finish, this wine is rather typical of
the common Sylvaner grape.

1983 Tokay d'Alsace Altenberg   ($11.95)   87

This wine is a dead ringer for a fat, buttery, smoky Meursault. The
intense bouquet is followed by a wine that is spicy, unctuous, rich,
and full-bodied, with a super finish. Quite powerful, creamy, and rich,
one should think of this wine as one would a great white burgundy—
serve it with fowl or fish.

JEROME LORENTZ

1983 Gewürztraminer   ($7.49)   85

1983 Gewürztraminer Vendange Tardive   ($19.95)   87

The regular Gewürztraminer is quite fat and forward, with the superb
ripeness and richness of this special vintage very capably displayed.
It is intensely spicy, light golden in color, lush, ripe, and very opulent.
Because of its forward character, I would opt for drinking this wine
over the next several years. As for the Vendange Tardive, it is very
long and rich on the palate, with considerable alcohol, a deep, full-
bodied, concentrated texture, and intensely aromatic bouquet. It
should be drunk over the next 4–6 years.

1983 Pinot Blanc   ($3.99)   82

Another lovely Pinot Blanc, the 1983 has a light golden color, medium body, and a crisp finish; it is spicy, very attractive, and fruity. Drink now.

1983 Riesling   ($6.49)   78

Very crisp, a little lean and ungenerous for an Alsace Riesling, this is an acceptable but undramatic wine. Drink over the next 3–4 years.

1983 Sylvaner   ($13.49)   76

Pleasant, simple, light, cleanly made and medium-bodied, this Sylvaner is free of the annoying acidity and blandness this grape variety usually possesses.

MURÉ-CLOS SAINT-LANDELIN (ROUFFACH)* * *

The firm of Muré, which owns 44 acres of the excellent vineyard Clos St.-Landelin, produces full-flavored, rather strongly scented wines that usually have been put through a malolactic fermentation for additional complexity and lower acidity. I have generally found the wines of Muré good, but I am less enthusiastic about them than other well-regarded growers in Alsace. Not infrequently, the wines seem to have a rather flabby character and a slightly bizarre bouquet. The Gewürztraminers tend to be the best wines.

1983 Gewürztraminer Clos St.-Landelin   ($7.49)   85

1983 Gewürztraminer Clos St.-Landelin
Sélection de Grains Nobles   ($15.95,375 ml)   90

The regular Gewürztraminer has a relatively deep color, a typical ripe, exotic bouquet, and soft, fat flavors that taste a little low in acidity but do have plenty of length and concentration. It should be drunk over the next 2–3 years. The Sélection de Grains Nobles has a full-blown bouquet of ripe peaches and apricots, very concentrated, sweet, fruity flavors, full body, a huge finish, and at least 8 years of evolution.

1983 Muscat Clos St.-Landelin   ($4.49)   85

One of the best 1983 Muscats I tasted from Alsace, this dry, very aromatic, spicy, fruity wine has delicious flavors, medium body, and a crisp, clean, long finish. Drink it as a distinctive apéritif.

1983 Pinot Blanc Clos St.-Landelin ($5.99) 76

Quite different from the other Alsatian Pinot Blancs, the Muré has a fennel-dominated bouquet, is rather austere and tart, with some harshness in the finish.

1983 Pinot Noir ($9.99) 80

This wine has surprisingly good color, but resembles a good Beaujolais rather than a Pinot Noir.

1983 Riesling Clos St.-Landelin ($7.49) 83

For a 1983 Riesling, this offering is lean, with an earthy yet pleasant bouquet, good, solid, varietal, Riesling flavors, and a moderate finish.

1983 Sylvaner Clos St.-Landelin ($4.99) 72

Not much of interest can be found in this Sylvaner, which is straight-forward and has a touch of acidity.

1983 Tokay Clos St.-Landelin ($7.49) 80

Somewhat unusual in that this wine has a slight rosé blush to it, Muré Tokay is very ripe, a trifle too soft and flabby, but full-bodied and unctuous. Drink over the next several years because of low acidity.

OSTERTAG (EPFIG)* * *

1983 Gewürztraminer Moenchberg ($10.99) 87

This is a firmly structured, young, potentially outstanding Gewürztra-miner. The bouquet is just beginning to open and emerge. The flavors show wonderful richness, ripeness, and concentration. Quite deep and full-bodied, this wine should continue to develop for 3–6 years.

1983 Pinot Gris (Tokay) ($6.99) 84

A plump, substantial wine with plenty of round, creamy, buttery Tokay fruit, a heady alcoholic punch, and rather long finish. Not so complex as many of the Tokays, but this is still a big, hefty, husky wine.

1983 Riesling ($6.79) 68

1983 Riesling Moenchberg ($9.95) 85

The regular Riesling is so tart and green that is is hard to believe it could have come from the 1983 vintage. This is certainly not the case with the Moenchberg, which has very good ripeness, deep, medium-to full bodied flavors, a mineral-scented bouquet, and good acidity.

PREISS HENNY (MITTELWIHR)* * *

A little-known but generally well-regarded producer, the several 1983s of this firm I tasted were well-made, attractive wines, with the Gewürztraminer being particularly good.

1983 Gewürztraminer Château de Mittelwihr   ($8.99)   87

Close to being a superb Gewürztraminer, this is a very powerful, rich, deep, spicy, almond-scented wine with excellent palate presence, full body, a strong, alcoholic punch, and very firm length. It is an extroverted, big, luscious, dry Gewürztraminer for drinking over the next 2–3 years.

1983 Riesling Château de Mittelwihr   ($7.99)   83

Rather reserved and restrained to smell, this youthful Riesling is lean and tight, but shows good fruit, medium body, and a crisp, fruity finish. Drink over the next 2–3 years.

MARTIN SCHAETZEL (AMMERSCHWIHR)* * *

Schaetzel has very high quality wines that retail at excellent prices. His 1983s are rich, rather full-bodied, with oodles of ripe fruit present. They may well be the sleepers of the 1983 vintage in Alsace.

1982 Gewürztraminer Réserve   ($6.99)   78

1983 Gewürztraminer   ($6.99)   86

The 1982 is rather thin and high in acidity, whereas the 1983 is rich, full-bodied, deeply fruity, long on the palate and so, so lush. It should be drunk over the next 1–2 years.

1983 Pinot Blanc   ($5.49)   84

One of the finest Pinot Blancs on the market, the 1983 Schaetzel is quite concentrated and rather full for a Pinot Blanc, with plenty of spice and length. Drink now.

1983 Riesling Kaefferkopf Cuvée Réservé   ($5.49)   85

Quite a complex wine, the Riesling has a bouquet suggestive of flowers, mint, and pineapple. Quite youthful on the palate, with good acidity and a long finish, this wine will improve for 4 years or more.

1983 Sylvaner   ($5.49)   77

Certainly a good Sylvaner, but typically herbaceous, spicy, dry, and aromatic, this light- to medium-bodied wine should be drunk over the next year.

1983 Tokay d'Alsace   ($6.99)   87

A Meursault look-alike, this dry, big, full-bodied wine is quite rich and powerful, with a smoky, butterscotch aroma, long, deep flavors, and good balancing acidity. Drink over the next 2–3 years.

CHARLES SCHLERET (TURCKHEIM)* * * *

Schleret's wines are quite popular among connoisseurs; fortunately, they are now available in several markets in America. My only exposure with Schleret's wines are the 1983s, which are all quite good and among the finest regular cuvée wines I have tasted from any grower in Alsace. The prices are quite modest given the quality.

1983 Gewürztraminer Cuvée Speciale   ($7.95)   87

One of the most smoky, exotically rich bouquets I have ever encountered was from this gorgeously perfumed, complex wine. Medium- to full bodied, with excellent concentration and balance, this spicy, totally dry Gewürztraminer is a delight to drink now.

1983 Riesling   ($6.49)   84

This is not a flamboyant Riesling, but rather a well-knit, clean, fresh, dry, fruity, medium-bodied wine that has impressive structure. Drink over the next 4–5 years.

SCHLUMBERGER (GUEBWILLER)* * * *

In the drab town of Guebwiller, one of the few in Alsace that has little tourist value, the Schlumberger firm produces a bevy of good Alsatian wines that are well-colored, fat, ripe, sometimes heavy and too alcoholic, but always interesting. This firm's best wines are its intense, rich, almost unctuous Gewürztraminers, which run the gamut from dry regular cuvées like the Fleur de Guebwiller and Kessler to the late-harvest, Vendange Tardive wines called Cuvée Christine Schlumberger and Cuvée Anne Schlumberger. As for the other wines, I have often been left unexcited and have even found a few rather tiresome to drink. The Riesling Kitterlé has the best reputation, though it rarely inspired me. This is a firm where lovers of the lusty, rich Gewürztraminers will find a great deal of pleasure, but the other wines can be flabby and heavy.

1983 Gewürztraminer Cuvée Christine Schlumberger ($20.00)   90

The Cuvée Christine Schlumberger is a dessert wine with a nectar-like, honeyed sweetness, and sensational length and concentration. It will improve for 10 or more years.

1983 Gewürztraminer Kessler   ($11.99)   88

I was struck by the sheer power, richness, and balance of this huge, rather massive Gewürztraminer. Power and ripeness are the two principal assets of this wine.

1983 Gewürztraminer Kitterlé   ($11.99)   88

The Kitterlé is ripe and exotic, with plump, luscious, big flavors. A very big, assertive wine.

1983 Pinot Blanc Cuvée Princess Abbes   ($5.99)   85

This dry cuvée is one of the market's great values in white wine. It is full-bodied, ripe, spicy, long, and deep on the palate.

1983 Riesling Saering   ($7.49)   86

A classic, deeply flavorful, well-textured, fruity Riesling with style and complexity.

RENÉ SCHMIDT (RIQUEWIHR)* * *

This small firm, in the quaint, touristy town of Riquewihr, produces sound, good quality wines that I have always found to be a little high in acidity and austere in personality. The 1983s, no doubt because of the superb vintage, taste considerably rounder and richer, with a creamier texture than I normally associate with this grower. Schmidt's wines tend to be quite fairly priced.

1983 Gewürztraminer Cuvée Particulière   ($6.99)   85

Surprisingly round, fruity and ripe, with a floral, peachlike bouquet, this lush Gewürztraminer has good spice and length, medium to full body, and a soft finish. It should be drunk over the next 1–2 years.

1983 Muscat Schoenenberg Cuvée Particulière   ($6.49)   75

One rarely sees Muscat from the Schoenenberg vineyard, and I could hardly get excited about this one, which is rather lean, bland, and characterless.

1983 Riesling Réserve   ($6.99) 83

1983 Riesling Schoenenberg   ($7.99) 86

The Réserve Riesling is quite attractive, nicely concentrated, dry, a little tart, medium-bodied, and crisp. The Schoenenberg has a complex bouquet of ripe fruit and cinnamon, is rather rich and deeply concentrated, with a ripe, long finish. It is an excellent, medium-bodied Riesling.

1983 Tokay d'Alsace Cuvée Particulière   ($6.99) 82

A rather light Tokay for Alsace in 1983, but nevertheless charming and ready for drinking now, this medium-bodied, pleasant wine has round, creamy flavors.

LOUIS SIPP (RIBEAUVILLÉ)* * *

This firm in Ribeauvillé specializes in Riesling and Gewürztraminer. The firm's reputation is one for good rather than spectacular wines. The 1983s look to be quite good.

1983 Gewürztraminer Medaille d'Or   ($7.99) 88

1983 Gewürztraminer Sigille Qualité   ($8.99) 83

Both of these wines are quite powerful Gewürztraminers. However, the Medaille d'Or has the ultimate class and distinction because it has the balance to go along with its huge power, ripeness, and length. It should be drunk young, preferably over the next 3–4 years. The Sigille Qualité has the same power and richness, but an otherwise much higher score is brought down by some coarseness and bitterness in the finish.

1983 Riesling Kirchberg de Ribeauvillé   ($7.99) 85

1983 Riesling Sigille Qualité   ($8.99) 78

The Sigille Qualité Riesling is pleasant, a little tart and green, but varietal and correct. The Grand Cru Kirchberg is very flavorful, with quite well-defined, long, rich flavors and a medium-bodied texture and finish. It needs 1–2 years to exhibit all its charm.

PIERRE SPARR (SIGOLSHEIM)* * * *

I was unable to track down many wines from Sparr, a producer with a good reputation and some good vineyards, particularly Brand in Turckheim.

1981 Gewürztraminer Réserve	($7.99)	86
1983 Gewürztraminer Cuvée Particulière	($8.99)	83
1983 Gewürztraminer Mambourg Cuvée Centenaire	($13.99)	90

These are all robust, rather rich, spicy Gewürztraminers that offer power rather than finesse. The 1981 Réserve is showing very well, with excellent ripeness, length, and full body. The 1983 Cuvée Particulière is a less rich and less weighty Gewürztraminer, but it finishes well. However, the 1983 Mambourg is a real head-turner. A very powerful, opulent, full-bodied, dry, rich wine with a perfumed, exotic aroma of lychee nuts and tropical fruits. This wine has sensational ripeness, excellent structure, and a finish that lasts over 40 seconds.

1983 Riesling Altenbourg Centenaire	($11.99)	84
1983 Riesling Carte d'Or	($6.49)	75

The Carte d'Or is a nice yet simple Riesling with some tartness and austere qualities, but lacking a bit in the middle as well as the finish. However, the Altenbourg, though quite light in color, exhibits very good ripeness, medium to full body, a spicy, perfumed bouquet, and good finish.

TRIMBACH (RIBEAUVILLÉ)* * * *

Along with the firm of Hugel, Trimbach is one of the very best-known and largest Alsace firms that is capable of producing high-quality wines. The style of wine aimed at here is for wines less powerful and opulently fruity, but more delicate, crisp, refined, and austere. As with many producers, their 1983s are particularly successful. This is a firm that can often be a bit spotty in performance, particularly in years where the crop is enormous and the wines a little light. It seems that in such years the Trimbach wines lack concentration and stuffing. However, in the superb vintages for Alsace, 1971, 1976, 1983, and 1985, this firm produces very refined, beautiful wines. The top wines are always the special bottlings of Riesling called Frédéric Emile and Clos Sainte-Hune (the latter an uncompromisingly brilliant wine), and the special Gewürztraminer called Cuvée des Seigneurs de Ribeau-pierre. The firm also produces Vendange Tardive wines with these cuvée designations. Trimbach's wines have the virtue of being widely available, and the 1983s, particularly the regular cuvées, are very fairly priced.

1983 Gewürztraminer	($8.49)	83

1983 Gewürztraminer Ribeaupierre	($15.00)	92

1983 Gewürztraminer Ribeaupierre Vendange Tardive	($25.00)	96

Trimbach's 1983s, like so many growers' in Alsace in this marvelous vintage, are very, very successful. The standard cuvée of Gewürztra-miner is less flamboyant and extroverted than many of the vintage, but exhibits lovely balance, a seductive, spicy fruitiness, medium body, and surprising elegance. It will drink well for 1–2 years. The Cuvée Ribeaupierre is simply sensational. Extraordinarily deep, rich, and full-bodied, yet impeccably balanced and elegant, it is a wine-making tour de force. Even better is the Ribeaupierre Vendange Tardive. This is a "must have" wine for connoisseurs, for it is as rich, opulent, and complex as the greatest Yquem or German Eiswein. Words hardly do it justice—just let me say that it is pure nectar, honeyed, and so, so powerful and rich, but brilliantly balanced by crisp acidity.

1983 Pinot Blanc	($4.49)	83

Quite a good wine as well as value, this lovely Pinot Blanc offers uncomplicated charm and fruity flavors in a dry, medium-bodied for-mat.

1982 Pinot Gris Réserve	($4.49)	82

1983 Pinot Gris Réserve	($5.99)	84

These are two very stylish Pinot Gris wines. The 1983 has more con-centration and character, a buttery, almost toasty character, excel-lent, round, ripe fruit flavors, and a crisp finish. The 1982 is softer, more diffuse, but still very enjoyable and quite a bargain.

1983 Riesling	($5.99)	82

1983 Riesling Frédéric Emile	($12.99)	88

1983 Riesling Frédéric Emile Vendange Tardive   ($25.00)   96

Again, one sees the progression in quality in Trimbach's wines since the special cuvées are notably superior to the standard cuvées. The standard Riesling is rather light for a 1983, but fragrant, crisp, clean and lively and very much in the Trimbach style of lighter, leaner wines. The Cuvée Frédéric Emile is a textbook Riesling: spicy, clean, crisp, rich in flavor, medium-bodied, concentrated, but so well knit that it will not be until 1992–1995 that it is fully mature. The Vendange Tardive Frédéric Emile is an almost perfect wine. With layers and layers of Riesling fruit, impeccable balance, great length and richness, this powerful wine is worth knowing about now because of its greatness.

1983 Sylvaner   ($4.49)   79

Given my hostility to Sylvaners, I was surprised by the fact that Trimbach's Sylvaner has good fruit, some character, and a touch of finesse. Drink it now for its freshness.

DOMAINE WEINBACH (KIENTZHEIM NEAR KAYSERBERG)* * * * *

It would be unfair to state that the Domaine Weinbach is producing Alsace's greatst wines; however, there is no question that some of the finest, most concentrated, powerful, and opulent wines from this beautiful region are being made at this estate. Madame Faller runs this property with a fanatical dedication to quality. The entire line of wines is excellent, but the Rieslings made here are definitely the best in Alsace and the specific vineyard wines from the Clos des Capucins vineyard are nothing short of spectacular. The top wines are designated by the words "Cuvée Théo" across the top of the label, a tribute to the founder of the estate, Théo Faller, who died in 1979. To reiterate, the Domaine Weinbach provides intense, very rich, strikingly powerful wines. The 1983s of this small firm are particularly outstanding; however, should you run across any of the 1981s or 1985s of Weinbach, they too were quite good. They are expensive, but the high quality justifies the price.

1983 Gewürztraminer   ($8.99)   84

1983 Gewürztraminer Cuvée Théo   ($13.49)   92

1985 Gewürztraminer Cuvée Théo   ($19.95)   87

1983 Gewürztraminer Réserve Personnelle   ($9.49)   91

1985 Gewürztraminer Réserve Personnelle   ($17.95)   88

Weinbach consistently produces superb Gewürztraminer, but it is hard to top the splendidly concentrated, exotically perfumed 1983 Cuvée Théo and 1983 Réserve Personnelle. The bouquets explode with aromas of rosebuds, lychee nuts, and grapefruit. They are both very rich and full-bodied, and to my palate there is little difference between them. They both should provide sensational drinking over the next 4–5 years. The regular Gewürztraminer is just a down-sized version of the other two wines. It is quite full-bodied, spicy, slightly sweet, and deep. The 1985s are significantly more expensive, less intense than the 1983s, but both wines are admirably concentrated, rich, and excellent examples of their types. The Réserve seems to have slightly more elegance.

1983 Pinot Réserve   ($5.99–$6.49)   85

What makes 1983 such a special vintage for Alsace is that the rank-and-file wines, notably Pinot Blanc, are so good—and inexpensive. This is a full-throttle Pinot Blanc, rich, spicy, full-bodied, dry and just oozing with fruit. Drink over the next year.

1983 Riesling Cuvée de la Sainte-Catherine   ($13.95)   91

1985 Riesling Cuvée de la Sainte-Catherine   ($19.95)   90

1983 Riesling Schlossberg   ($11.95)   88

1985 Riesling Schlossberg   ($18.95)   88

I can't recall ever tasting a dry, young Riesling from Alsace with as much promise and potential as these wines. The Sainte-Catherines in both vintages in particular are breathtakingly beautiful wines that are oh, so fragrant, so pure and concentrated, so well balanced, and so long and deep that they are a true gustatory tour de force. Both overwhelm the lovingly proportioned but less expressive Schlossbergs, two wines which would be considered classic Rieslings from Alsace. Both are dry wines and will improve for 3–5 years.

1983 Sylvaner   ($5.99)   83

I do not like Sylvaner, but this is the best of this normally dull, bland variety that I have found. It is surprisingly good and interesting, spicy, fruity, dry, and flavorful. Drink over the next year for its freshness.

1983 Tokay d'Alsace Vendange Tardive   ($16.99)   91

A luxuriously rich, velvety wine with adequate acidity, full body, stupendous length and concentration, this young, great wine will drink
well (and continue to develop) for at least a decade.

A. WILLM (BARR)* * * *

The firm of Alsace Willm is generally well known, but the production
of 42,000 cases per year is not very large. The firm specializes in
Gewürztraminer and Riesling, although there is an entire range of
wines, including a sparkling Crémant d'Alsace. The pride of the firm
is the intense, rich Gewürztraminer from the 17-acre Clos Gaensbroennel. It starts off life slowly but ages magnificently. The Cuvée
Emile Willm in both Riesling and Gewürztraminer is quite good, as is
the bottom-of-the-line Cordon d'Alsace, made from Pinot Blanc.

1983 Gewürztraminer   ($4.99–$6.49)   85

1983 Gewürztraminer Clos Gaensbroennel   ($8.99–$10.99)   89

1983 Gewürztraminer Clos Gaensbroennel
Vendange Tardive   ($13.45)   90

1983 Gewürztraminer Cuvée Emile Willm   ($6.99–$8.99)   87

1983 Gewürztraminer Cuvée Emile Willm
Vendange Tardive   ($11.95)   89

Given the prices for these wines, the Willm lineup of Gewürztraminers
offers a bacchanal paradise. The regular Gewürztraminer is richly
varietal, with lovely aromas of almonds, roses, and grapefruit. Rich
and full-bodied, with surprising power and length, it is a wine that
Gewürztraminer fanatics should buy by the carload. The Cuvée Emile
Willm is even richer, fuller-bodied and dry, with the Emile Willm
Vendange Tardive exceptionally powerful (14.6% alcohol) and heady.
At the pinnacle, however, are the two Gewürztraminers from the famous Clos Gaensbroennel. The regular Clos Gaensbroennel is still
almost totally unevolved, but behind the bouquet of spice and flowers
is an enormously rich, well-structured, powerful, full-bodied wine.
The Clos Gaensbroennel Vendange Tardive is slightly richer and
fuller, if you can believe that. It is almost too overpowering and rich,
but remember, it is dry and capable of a decade of improvement.

1985 Pinot Blanc Cordon d'Alsace   ($3.99–$4.49)   83

Another surprisingly good Pinot Blanc from Alsace, this crisp, fresh, vibrantly fruity, medium-bodied wine has solid fruit and a crisp finish.

1983 Riesling   ($4.99)   76

1983 Riesling Cuvée Emile Willm   ($5.99)   78

1983 Riesling Cuvée Emile Willm Vendange Tardive   ($9.95)   86

1983 Riesling Réserve Kirchberg   ($6.99)   83

Willm's Rieslings are no match for the firm's Gewürztraminers in 1983. They are sound, cleanly made, but generally uninteresting wines, except for the Emile Willm Vendange Tardive, which is quite good, round, dry, medium- to full-bodied, long, intense, and very flavorful.

ZIND-HUMBRECHT (WINTZENHEIM)* * * * *

Léonard Humbrecht of the Domaine Humbrecht produces wines from some of Alsace's best vineyards, Herrenweg, Hengst, Brand, Clos Hauserer, Rangen, three of which are Grand Cru under the new law. The wines of Zind-Humbrecht, many of which are vineyard-designated, are among the most palatable and intellectually satisfying and distinctive wines of Alsace. The wines, particularly the top-of-the-line specific vineyard wines, can be absolutely brilliant as well as rare and quite expensive. Léonard Humbrecht is a fanatical perfectionist and his wines reflect the great care he obviously gives them.

1983 Gewürztraminer   ($4.95–$6.95)   85

1983 Gewürztraminer Gueberschwihr
Vendange Tardive   ($36.00)   92

1983 Gewürztraminer Hengst Wintzenheim   ($15.99)   90

1983 Gewürztraminer Rangen Vendange Tardive   ($36.00)   90

Four excellent Gewürztraminers, of which three are close to being called monumental. That is quite an achievement. The 1983 regular is a great buy and has an exotic, spicy, full-bodied character. However, it cannot compare to the other three Gewürztraminers, which are truly sublime. The Hengst Wintzenheim is a marvelous wine with a big, rich, spicy bouquet of honey and almonds, full body, long, classic flavors, and a superb finish. Between the two "très cher" Vendange Tardive Gewürztraminers, there is hardly any difference. I rank the Gueberschwihr the finer, a truly great wine of sensational intensity and power, dry to taste, yet with a framework akin to the greatest white burgundies. It will age for 15–20 years. The Rangen is less open but equally spectacular in its perfect balance of power, opulence, finesse, and richness.

1983 Muscat d'Alsace	($7.99)	75

Pleasant, slightly aromatic, clean, and fresh, this is a decent wine, but given all the outstanding wines and values from Alsace in 1983, this wine hardly merits much attention.

1983 Riesling	($5.95)	84

1983 Riesling Brand Vendange Tardive	($36.00)	86

1983 Riesling Clos Hauserer	($19.99)	82

1983 Riesling Clos Saint-Urbain Rangen	($14.99)	85

1983 Riesling Herrenweg Turkheim	($11.96)	87

Zind-Humbrecht's Rieslings are made in a rather high-acid, lean style; however, each has a very distinctive personality that justifies his vineyard-designating these wines. For high quality, the Herrenweg, with its highly aromatic bouquet, and the Rangen are very good, albeit expensive, examples of top-notch Rieslings. The Brand Vendange Tardive is dry, rather long, but has nowhere near the same richness that Zind-Humbrecht's Tokays and Gewürztraminers do. The Clos Hauserer has a great reputation, but I find it lean, rather tart, with a bouquet of stones and herbs, and needing a decade to develop.

1983 Tokay d'Alsace Rangen Vendange Tardive	($30.00)	91

1982 Tokay d'Alsace Saint-Urbain Rangen	($14.95)	82

1983 Tokay d' Alsace Saint-Urbain Rangen	($14.95)	92

1982 Tokay d'Alsace Vieilles Vignes   ($15.95)   84

Here are four Tokays, two from the outstanding 1983 vintage and two
from the rather average 1982 vintage. The two 1983 Tokays are as
good a dry Tokay or Pinot Gris as one is likely to find anywhere. The
straight Rangen is intense and concentrated, with an incredible bouquet of smoky bacon, butter, and rich, ripe fruit. The palate impression is similar to that of a great white burgundy: creamy, powerful,
very concentrated, and long. The Rangen Vendange Tardive is less
evolved but very rich, dry, full-bodied and powerful, and very much
like the normal Rangen, only less evolved. The 1982 Rangen is good,
but lacks the overall dimension and complexity of the 1983. The
Vieilles Vignes is also good, but finishes a little hot and seems short
in acidity.

BORDEAUX

*The World's Largest Supplier of
High-Quality Wine*

Bordeaux's "Golden Age" continues unabated. The
succession of good to extraordinary vintages that began in 1975 has,
except for 1977, continued uninterrupted. Never in the history of this
great wine region in southwest France has there been so much fine
wine produced in so many back-to-back vintages. Of course, the consumer has been the beneficiary of Bordeaux's good fortune, with an
array of high-quality wine available in all price ranges. On the negative
side, insatiable worldwide demand for Bordeaux's best wines and best
vintages has caused prices to skyrocket. For American consumers,
the weakening of the American dollar by 35% in 1986 has served as a
double whammy. However, one remarkable thing about Bordeaux is
that the quality level of wine is very high, even at the lower price

The Bordeaux Appellations

Bordeaux

1 St-Estèphe
2 Pauillac
3 St-Julien
4 Listrac
5 Moulis
6 Margaux
7 Cérons
8 Barsac
9 Sauternes

10 Ste-Croix-du-Mont
11 Loupiac
12 Premières Côtes de Bordeaux
13 Côtes de Bordeaux St-Macaire
14 Ste-Foy-Bordeaux
15 Graves de Vayres
16 St-Emilion
17 Lussac St-Emilion
Montagne-St-Emilion
St-Georges-St-Emilion
Parsac-St-Emilion
Puisseguin-St-Emilion
18 Côtes de Castillon
19 Côtes de Francs
20 Lalande de Pomerol
21 Pomerol
22 Fronsac
23 Côtes de Bourg
24 Cadillac
25 Blayais

GIRONDE

MÉDOC

Soulac

Lesparre-Médoc

BLAYAIS

ÉTANG

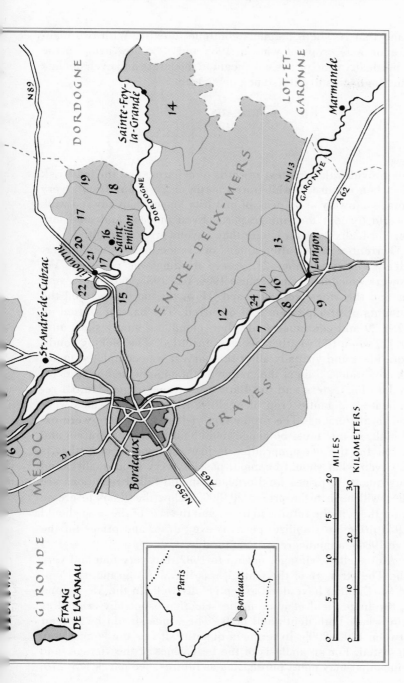

levels, and that is where bargains continue to exist. With two high-quality, enormous crops of wine in 1985 and 1986 now aging in the cellars, Bordeaux wine prices may begin to moderate and even decline as production begins to outdistance demand.

BORDEAUX
QUICK VINTAGE GUIDE

Bordeaux provides the greatest rewards of cellaring and the least risk because, when mature, a well-stored bottle of Bordeaux from a very good vintage can stay at its peak of maturity longer than any red wine in the world (except for vintage port). Even in poor and mediocre vintages, Bordeaux lives for longer than anyone gives it credit.

1986—Torrential rains buffeted most of France in early September. In Bordeaux, on September 24, severe flooding was reported. Yet most growers welcomed rain because 1986, like 1985, had been a very dry year and the vines were stressed. However, no one wanted the huge amounts of precipitation that occurred. The harvest started on September 29 and continued under hot, cloudless, sunny skies until October 12, when the weather became unsettled. The picking conditions were ideal and virtually all of the harvest was completed under textbook conditions. Rain at the end no doubt complicated matters for the very late harvesters and the Barsac-Sauternes region. Initial reports indicate a gigantic crop of healthy, fruity, sound wines were produced in all regions. The production yields per hectare were extremely high, so one must be concerned about the concentration and acidity, but for the consumer, this is just the type of crop that is needed. Given what should be good, possibly very good quality, and enormous quantity, prices for Bordeaux should fall. Predictions are that 1986s will have to be priced 20–30% below the 1985s to create interest for them in the futures market, and the size of the crop should cause 1985 prices to stabilize, perhaps even drop, and prices for the expensive 1984s (a mediocre year) to tumble.

1985—An excellent vintage, not up to 1982, but very fine and very desirable. The strength of the vintage was the Merlot grape, so Pomerol and St.-Emilion have done exceptionally well. In the Médoc and Graves, the huge yield of juice made selection especially critical as some wines lack both depth and body. The wines should be at their best between 1990–2005. In terms of quantity, it was the largest crop ever harvested. For an analysis of the best wines of the vintage, and those wines that may merit purchasing as futures, see pages 175–176, which contain a chart of the best wines of 1985 based on cask evaluations done in March and October 1986.

1984—The wine press wrote it off before the harvest, but the quality of the Médoc and Graves wines is at least good, in many cases very good. Due to a bad crop of Merlot grapes, St.-Emilion and Pomerol produced mediocre wines at best, with some of the top châteaux declassifying their entire crop. This will be a vintage to consume within its first 10 years of life.

1983—A difficult year because of rot in the vineyards, the wines, initially believed to be harder, tougher, more typical or classical wines than the more massive, intense 1982s, have turned out soft, very fruity, delicious, but destined in most cases to mature well before the fuller-bodied, richer 1982s. The sweet wines are outstanding in 1983, as are the red wines from the Margaux appellation.

1982—The greatest vintage since 1961, the 1982s have begun to close up and their considerable tannin content is now becoming very apparent. The masses of fruit are still present, but as the wines have recovered from their transatlantic voyage, the huge structure and potential for extended longevity is obvious. The petits châteaux are marvelous in this vintage and can be drunk now or aged for 5–7 years. As for the big shots of the vintage, 1995–2010 would be the likely period when these wines will enter their plateau of maturity.

1981—Almost all of the 1981s are developing quickly. Most will be ready to drink by 1990, but not Pétrus, Margaux, or Lafite-Rothschild.

1980—The top wines from this vintage are delicious now and quite appealing (e.g., Pichon Lalande, Domaine de Chevalier, Gruaud-Larose). Except for Château or CH. Margaux, these are wines to drink over the next 2–4 years. The sweet wines of Sauternes and Barsac are especially good in 1980 and represent very good values.

1979—A vintage that continues to show more and more class every time I go back to it. The petits châteaux are quite mixed, but the classified growths are developing a harmonious charm, show a lovely fruitiness, and may, in the best cases, turn out like the terribly underrated 1962s. For the top wines, 1987–1997 looks to be the decade of enjoyment for the 1979s.

1978—This is a wonderful vintage for the classified growths of the Médoc and Graves. The wines are just beginning to open up and develop. The petits châteaux are surprisingly not up to the quality one might expect and must be picked carefully. The Pomerols are generally ready to drink, the St.-Emilions need another 1–2 years, and the Médocs and Graves need 5 years. Peak drinkability for the Médocs and Graves should be 1990–2000.

1977—All the 1977s require drinking now.

1976—A very irregular vintage that could have been great had the harvest rains not bloated the grapes. The best 1976s are almost always from the Médoc. They offer deliciously supple, charming drinking now. In restaurants, this is the Bordeaux vintage I look for. Drink over the next 2–4 years, except for Ausone and the great Lafite-Rothschild, both of which need until 1992 to be fully ready. The sweet wines of Barsac and Sauternes are remarkably rich and unctuous and will continue to drink well for 1–2 more decades.

1975—More irregular in quality than initially believed, 1975 still produced a bevy of very great, rich, big, tannic wines that will turn out to be some of the longest-lived Bordeaux of the last several decades. For the top wines, their bouquets are just now emerging from behind a wall of tannin. Peak drinkability for the best wines will be 1990–2010. The petits châteaux can be excellent and are now ready to drink.

1974—The sleepers of this vintage are the Graves, which turned out quite well. However, these are wines to drink over the next 3–4 years, save for La Mission-Haut-Brion, which will last for 10 more years.

1973—Unless you have Pétrus cellared, run, don't walk, to your cellar, because these wines have been fully mature for the last 7–8 years and are now almost comatose. Beware!

1972—Drink now if ever.

1971—Virtually every 1971 is fully mature and is not likely to get better. One must pick carefully in this vintage, but the rewards are there. The Pomerols and Graves are particularly seductive at present.

1970—A great vintage that several writers naïvely criticized when released. They were said to be the product of Bordeaux's new vinification. The critics thought that because the wines had so much supple fruit, they would not last until 1980. In 1987, the top wines are still not ready—this vintage is unquestionably the most totally satisfying vintage after 1961 and before 1982. The petits châteaux are fully mature. The Graves, St.-Emilions, and Pomerols have reached their plateau of maturity, but will hold for at least another decade. The Médocs need 2–5 more years, but are drinking well now. This is a marvelous vintage at all levels.

1969—I have never tasted a 1969 claret that I did not dislike. Avoid.

1968—Avoid.

1967—All of the wines have been mature for a decade. However, the top wines are still holding together and can be revelations to drink, provided they have been well stored.

1966—Initially was believed to be a classic, potentially excellent vintage. The wines have developed so slowly, and in some cases even lost fruit, that the opinion of this vintage has been revised downward. There are some very fine wines, but they are generally somewhat lean and austere. Most 1966s should be drunk over the next 10 years.

1965—Avoid,

1964—For Graves, St.-Emilion, and Pomerol, a beautiful vintage of wines that are in full bloom. For the Médoc, caution is the watchword since persistent harvest rains plagued growers in this area. Drink over the next 5–8 years.

1963—Avoid.

1962—Apparently this vintage never went through an awkward stage of development. Delicious young, delicious old, well-stored bottles of 1962 claret are beautifully harmonious wines that have been mature for a decade but have been able to stay at their plateau of maturity without fading. However, all of the 1962s require consumption now. If you are buying them, they must be from good, cool cellars or you may end up with expensive vinegar.

1961—Nineteen sixty-one is, of course, a great vintage, not so consistently great as 1982, but the top 1961s, have incredible concentration and richness that is unmatched in any Bordeaux vintage this century. Most can be drunk now, but the top wines will go on improving for decades.

Older Vintages

The 1959s are powerful and where well stored, excellent. The 1955s are more spotty than initially predicted, but overall very good. The 1953s are beginning to tire, but well-cellared examples of this vintage can be incredibly satisfying, rich, luxurious wines with great intensity of flavor and finesse. The 1952s are hard, the 1950s underrated, and the trio of vintages in the forties, 1945, 1947, 1949, if well-cellared examples can be found, can be pure perfection, particularly the 1949s.

A GUIDE TO BORDEAUX'S BEST PRODUCERS
DRY RED WINES AND SAUTERNES/BARSAC

***** *(OUTSTANDING PRODUCERS)*

L'Arrosée (St.-Emilion)

Ausone (St.-Emilion)

Canon (St.-Emilion)

Certan de May (Pomerol)

Cheval Blanc (St.-Emilion)

Domaine de Chevalier (Graves)

Cos d'Estournel (St. Estèphe)

Ducru-Beaucaillou (St.-Julien)

L'Evangile (Pomerol)
De Fargues (Sauternes)
Giscours (Margaux)
Gruaud-Larose (St.-Julien)
Haut-Brion (Graves)
Lafite-Rothschild (Pauillac)
Lafleur (Pomerol)
La Lagune (Ludon)
Latour (Pauillac)
Latour à Pomerol (Pomerol)
Léoville-Barton (St.-Julien)
Léoville-Las Cases (St.-Julien)

Lynch-Bages (Pauillac)
Château Margaux (Margaux)
La Mission-Haut-Brion (Graves)
Mouton-Rothschild (Pauillac)
Palmer (Margaux)
Pétrus (Pomerol)
Pichon-Longueville, Comtesse
   de Lalande (Pauillac)
Raymond-Lafon (Sauternes)
Rieussec (Sauternes)
Trotanoy (Pomerol)
Yquem (Sauternes)

* * * * (EXCELLENT PRODUCERS)

Beychevelle (St.-Julien)
Bon Pasteur (Pomerol)
Boyd-Cantenac (Margaux)
Branaire-Ducru (St.-Julien)
Cadet-Piola (St.-Emilion)
Calon-Ségur (St. Estèphe)
Cantemerle (Macau)
Chasse-Spleen (Moulis)
Climens (Barsac)
La Conseillante (Pomerol)
Coutet (Barsac)
La Dominique (St.-Emilion)
L'Eglise-Clinet (Pomerol)
Figeac (St.-Emilion)
La Fleur Pétrus (Pomerol)
Forts de Latour (Pauillac)
Le Gay (Pomerol)
Gilette (Sauternes)
Grand-Puy-Lacoste (Pauillac)
La Grave Figeac (St.-Emilion)
Haut-Bailly (Graves)
Haut-Marbuzet (St. Estèphe)

D'Issan (Margaux)
Lafaurie-Peyraguey (Sauternes)
Langoa-Barton (St.-Julien)
Larmande (St.-Emilion)
Lascombes (Margaux)
Léoville-Poyferré (St.-Julien)
Magdelaine (St.-Emilion)
Montrose (St. Estèphe)
Pavillon Rouge de Margaux
   (Margaux)
De Pez (St.-Estèphe)
Le Pin (Pomerol)
Prieuré-Lichine (Margaux)
Sociando-Mallet (Haut-Médoc)
St.-Pierre-Sevaistre (St.-Julien)
Suduiraut (Sauternes)
Talbot (St.-Julien)
Tertre-Rotebouef (St.-Emilion)
La Tour-Haut-Brion (Graves)
Vieux-Château-Certan
   (Pomerol)

* * * (GOOD PRODUCERS)

L'Angélus (St.-Emilion)
d'Angludet (Margaux)
Balestard-La-Tonnelle (St.-
   Emilion)

Bastor-Lamontagne (Sauternes)
Batailley (Pauillac)
Beauséjour (Duffau-Lagarrosse)
   (St.-Emilion)

Bel Air (Lalande-de-Pomerol)
Belair (St.-Emilion)
Belles Graves (Lalande-de-
Pomerol)
Le Boscq (Médoc)
Brane-Cantenac (Margaux)
Brillette (Moulis)
Camensac (Haut-Médoc)
Canon (Canon-Fronsac)
Canon de Brem (Canon-
Fronsac)
Cantenac-Brown (Margaux)
Cap de Merle (Lussac-St.-
Emilion)
Cap de Mourlin (St.-Emilion)
Les Carmes Haut-Brion
(Graves)
Certan-Giraud (Pomerol)
Cissac (Haut-Médoc)
Clarke (Listrac)
Clerc-Milon (Pauillac)
Clos du Clocher (Pomerol)
Clos des Jacobins (St.-
Emilion)
Clos René (Pomerol)
Corbin (St.-Emilion)
Corbin-Michotte (St.-Emilion)
Coufran (Haut-Médoc)
Couvent des Jacobins (St.-
Emilion)
La Croix (Pomerol)
La Croix de Gay (Pomerol)
Croque-Michotte (St.-Emilion)
La Dauphine (Fronsac)
Destieux (St.-Emilion)
Doisy-Daëne (Barsac)
Doisy-Védrines (Barsac)
Duhart-Milon-Rothschild
(Pauillac)
Durand-Laplagne (Puisseguin-
St.-Emilion)
Durfort-Vivens (Margaux)

L'Enclos (Pomerol)
Faurie-de-Souchard (St.-
Emilion)
Ferrand (St.-Emilion)
de Fieuzal (Graves)
Fonbadet (Pauillac)
Fonplégade (St.-Emilion)
Fonroque (St.-Emilion)
Fourcas-Hosten (Listrac)
La Gaffelière (St.-Emilion)
Gazin (Pomerol)
Gloria (St.-Julien)
Grand-Ormeau (Lalande-de-
Pomerol)
Grand-Puy-Ducasse (Pauillac)
La Grave Trigant de Boisset
(Pomerol)
Greysac (Médoc)
Guiraud (Sauternes)
La Gurgue (Margaux)
Haut-Bages-Libéral (Pauillac)
Haut-Batailley (Pauillac)
Haut-Brisson (St.-Emilion)
Haut-Sarpe (St.-Emilion)
Hortevie (St.-Julien)
Kirwan (Margaux)
Labégorce-Zédé (Margaux)
Lafon-Rochet (St. Estèphe)
Lagrange (St.-Julien)
Lalande Borie (St.-Julien)
Lanessan (Haut-Médoc)
Larose Trintaudon (Haut-
Médoc)
Liversan (Médoc)
La Louvière (Graves)
Maison Blanche (Montagne-St.-
Emilion)
Malescot St.-Exupéry (Margaux)
Marquis-de-Terme (Margaux)
Maucaillou (Moulis)
Mazeris (Canon-Fronsac)
Meyney (St. Estèphe)

Mouton-Baronne-Philippe
(Pauillac)
Nairac (Barsac)
Les-Ormes-de-Pez (St.-Estèphe)
Pape-Clément (Graves)
Patache d'Aux (Médoc)
Pavie (St.-Emilion)
Pavie-Decesse (St.-Emilion)
Petit-Village (Pomerol)
Phélan-Ségur (St. Estèphe)
Pichon (Haut-Médoc)
Pichon Longueville, Baron de
Pichon Longueville (Pauillac)
Pitray (Côtes de Castillon)
Plagnac (Médoc)
Pontet-Canet (Pauillac)
Potensac (Médoc)
Pouget (Margaux)
Pougeaux (Moulis)
Rahoul (Graves)
Rausan-Ségla (Margaux)
Rauzan-Gassies (Margaux)
Roudier (Montagne-St.-Emilion)
Rouet (Fronsac)

Rouget (Pomerol)
de Sales (Pomerol)
Sigalas Rabaud (Sauternes)
Siran (Margaux)
Soudars (Haut-Médoc)
Soutard (St.-Emilion)
Tayac Prestige (Côtes de Bourg)
Terrey-Gros-Cailloux
(St.-Julien)
du Tertre (Margaux)
Tertre-Daugay (St.-Emilion)
La Tonnelle (Côtes de Blaye)
La Tour Figeac (St.-Emilion)
La Tour-de-Mons (Margaux)
La Tour-du-Pin-Figeac
(St.-Emilion)
La Tour St.-Bonnet (Médoc)
Tronquoy-Lalande (St.-Estèphe)
Troplong-Mondot (St.-Emilion)
Vieux-Château Guibeau
(Puisseguin-St.-Emilion)
Villars (Fronsac)
Villemaurine (St.-Emilion)
La Violette (Pomerol)

* * (AVERAGE PRODUCERS)

d'Agassac (Haut-Médoc)
d'Arche (Sauternes)
L'Arrivet-Haut-Brion (Graves)
Beau Séjour-Bécot (St.-Emilion)
Beaumont (Haut-Médoc)
Bel-Orme-Tronquoy-de-Lalande
(Haut-Médoc)
de Belcier (Côtes de Castillon)
Belgrave (Haut-Médoc)
Bonalgue (Pomerol)
Bouscaut (Graves)
Broustet (Barsac)
Caillou (Barsac)
Canon-La-Gaffelière (St.-
Emilion)
Carbonnieux (Graves)

La Cardonne (Médoc)
Caronne-Ste.-Gemme (Haut-
Médoc)
Clinet (Pomerol)
Clos L'Eglise (Pomerol)
Clos Fourtet (St.-Emilion)
Clos des Tempiers (Lalande-de-
Pomerol)
La Clotte (St.-Emilion)
La Commanderie (St.-Emilion)
Cos Labory (St.-Estèphe)
Croizet-Bages (Pauillac)
Curé-Bon-La-Madeleine
(St.-Emilion)
Dauzac (Margaux)
Desmirail (Margaux)

Domaine de L'Eglise (Pomerol)
Ferrière (Margaux)
Filhot (Sauternes)
La Fleur Gazin (Pomerol)
Fombrauge (St.-Emilion)
Fourcas-Dupré (Listrac)
Garraud (Lalande-de-Pomerol)
du Glana (St.-Julien)
Gombaude-Guillot (Pomerol)
Grand-Corbin-Despagne
  (St.-Emilion)
Gressier Grand-Poujeaux
  (Moulis)
Hanteillan (Médoc)
Haut Chatain (Lalande-de-
  Pomerol)
Haut Plantey (St.-Emilion)
Haut Sociando (Cotes de Blaye)
Labégorce (Margaux)
Lagrange (Pomerol)
Lamarque (Haut-Médoc)
Larcis-Ducasse (St.-Emilion)
Lestage (Listrac)
Loudenne (Médoc)
Malartic-Lagravière (Graves)
Marquis d'Alesme-Becker
  (Margaux)

Monbousquet (St.-Emilion)
Moulin des Carruades (Pauillac)
Nenin (Pomerol)
Les Ormes-Sorbet (Médoc)
Peyrabon (Haut-Médoc)
Plince (Pomerol)
La Pointe (Pomerol)
Rabaud-Promis (Sauternes)
Ramage La Batisse (Haut-
  Médoc)
Rayne-Vigneau (Sauternes)
Ripeau (St.-Emilion)
La Rivière (Fronsac)
Romer du Hayot (Sauternes)
Smith-Haut-Lafitte (Graves)
St.-Bonnet (Médoc)
Tailhas (Pomerol)
Taillefer (Pomerol)
La Terrasse (Côtes de Castillon)
La Tour Blanche (Sauternes)
La Tour de By (Médoc)
La Tour-Carnet (Haut-Médoc)
Trottevieille (St.-Emilion)
Verdignan (Médoc)
Vraye-Croix-de-Gay (Pomerol)

* *(OTHER PRODUCERS)*

Beauregard (Pomerol)
Bel-Air-Marquis d'Aligre
  (Margaux)
Bourgneuf-Vayron (Pomerol)
La Bridane (St.-Julien)
Citran (Haut-Médoc)
Ferrande (Graves)

La Garde (Graves)
Moulinet (Pomerol)
Olivier (Graves)
Tayac (Margaux)
La Tour-Martillac (Graves)
Villegeorge (Haut-Médoc)

A GUIDE TO BORDEAUX'S BEST PRODUCERS
DRY WHITE WINES

** * * * * (OUTSTANDING PRODUCERS)*

Domaine de Chevalier (Graves)   Haut-Brion (Graves)
Fieuzal (Graves) (starting in   Laville-Haut-Brion (Graves)
  1985)

** * * * (EXCELLENT PRODUCERS)*

La Louvière (Graves)   Pavillon Blanc de Château
Malartic-Lagravière (Graves)   Margaux (Margaux)
     La Tour-Martillac (Graves)

** * * (GOOD PRODUCERS)*

L'Arrivet-Haut-Brion (Graves)   Olivier (Graves)
Bouscaut (Graves)   Pirou (Graves)
Caillou Blanc de Talbot   Pontac-Monplaisir (Graves)
  (Bordeaux)   Rahoul (Graves)
Carbonnieux (Graves)   Respide (Graves)
Loudenne (Bordeaux)   Smith-Haut-Lafitte (Graves)

THE BEST WINE VALUES IN BORDEAUX

St.-Estèphe

Haut-Marbuzet   Marbuzet
Meyney   Les-Ormes-de-Pez
de Pez

Pauillac

Haut-Batailley   Haut-Bages-Libéral
Fonbadet   Haut-Bages-Averous

St.-Julien

Branaire-Ducru   Hortevie
Gruaud-Larose   St.-Pierre
Talbot   Clos du Marquis
Léoville-Barton

Margaux

du Tertre	La Gurgue
d'Angludet	Siran
d'Issan	

Médoc & Haut-Médoc

Chasse-Spleen	Liversan
Cissac	LaRose-Trintaudon
Sociando-Mallet	La Tour St.-Bonnet
Potensac	Greysac
Lanessan	Plagnac

Sauternes/Barsac

Bastor-Lamontagne	Les Justices
Doisy-Daëne	

Pomerol

La Croix de Gay	Rouget
de Sales	Clos René
L'Enclos	

St.-Emilion

La Dominique	Cadet-Piola
L'Arrosée	La Grave-Figeac
Clos des Jacobins	Destieux
Balestard-La-Tonnelle	Cap de Mourlin

Côtes de Bourg

La Grolet	Tayac

Côtes de Blaye

La Tonnelle	Haut-Sociando

Fronsac & Canon-Fronsac

Canon	Rouet
La Dauphine	Dalem
La Grave	Mazeris
Villars	Canon de Brem
Haut Laroque	

Lalande-de-Pomerol

Belle Graves   Clos des Templiers
Grand-Ormeau   Bertineau St.-Vincent

Graves

Haut-Bailly   Cheret-Pitres
La Louvière   Rahoul
Picque-Caillou

Montagne St.-Emilion

Roudier   Tour Musset

Côtes de Castillon

Pitray

Lussac St.-Emilion

Cap de Merle   Villadière
Tour de Grenat   Bel Air
Carteyron

Bordeaux—Today's Buying Strategy

Because of the recent succession of high-quality Bordeaux crops and also because Bordeaux has traditionally been offered for sale on a pre-arrival "futures" basis, the Bordeaux wine market has been quite active each year. Buying Bordeaux futures makes a lot of sense if you are sure you are buying top wines from a top vintage that are likely to be in great demand and cost considerably more when they arrive on the market. However, due to worldwide supply and demand, and the wide fluctuation in the value of the dollar, buying futures only makes sense with specific wines in specific vintages. Regardless of all the wine trade hype insisting that you buy Bordeaux futures, there are only three reasons to invest your money in unbottled Bordeaux wines two years prior to taking delivery. They are:

1. To buy great wine from an excellent or great vintage.
2. To save money based on the assumption that the wines will be at least 25–50% more expensive when they arrive on the market.
3. To guarantee getting glamour wines of high quality from estates that have small productions, for example, Pomerols and St.-Emilions.

If any of these three criteria can be satisfied, then buying futures may make sense. If none of these conditions exist, then save your money until the wines arrive on the market. Nineteen eighty-two was the best recent case demonstrating the wisdom of buying as much as one could afford at the earliest possible time. Since the futures were offered, the prices doubled and tripled because the demand for the '82s was unparalleled. The 1978, 1979, and 1981 vintages, and to a lesser extent, 1985, are the best recent examples for not buying futures since the wines came on the market at the same price (or lower in some cases) than the prices consumers had paid for them as futures two years in advance of their arrival.

Today, the best values in Bordeaux vintages are the 1979s, which are drinking deliciously, the 1981's, similarly styled to the 1979s, and the 1983s, a rather overlooked, very good vintage that just got lost in the huge shadow cast by the great 1982s. As for the 1982s, they are great, but the famous as well as glamorous wines are very rare and very expensive. However, the top 1982 Crus Bourgeois still represent great value given their splendid quality in this vintage. The highly regarded 1985s also appear rather costly, but that has a lot to do with the fact that the dollar is much weaker.

All things considered, there is a tremendous glut of high-quality Bordeaux in the marketplace. Yes, the glamour châteaux, those top two dozen or so estates that represent the summit of quality, have become extremely expensive in the last several years, but there are hundreds of lesser-known châteaux, the Crus Bourgeois, and top wines from less renowned but up and coming regions such as Lalande-de-Pomerol, Fronsac, and Canon-Fronsac that represent remarkable rapports in quality/price.

When buying Bordeaux, remember one cardinal fact—in the last five years, the quality difference between the top Crus Bourgeois and petits châteaux and glamour classified growths has gotten narrower and narrower. Yet the difference in price has only widened between these two groups of Bordeaux wines. The message to the shrewd, value-conscious consumer is obvious—search out the top Crus Bourgeois. Wouldn't you rather have four or five cases of the luscious Lalande-de-Pomerol Grand-Ormeau than one case of La Conseillante?

D'AGASSAC (HAUT-MÉDOC)* *

1982	($10.00)	82
1983	($10.00)	80

This property has been off form for sometime, but the first several vintages of the '80s have offered encouraging new evidence that the

wine is improving in quality. The 1983 is spicy, rather tannic and
backward, and the 1982 more supple and richly fruity.

L'ANGÉLUS (ST.-EMILION)* * *

1981	($15.95)	84
1982	($15.95)	85
1983	($15.95)	87

L'Angélus, like many wines, has recently made a strong effort to
improve its quality. The wine still tastes better out of barrel than out
of bottle, but the last couple of vintages have looked promising. The
1983 is an exuberantly fruity, ripe, lush wine; the 1982, no ugly duck-
ling, is precocious, supple, and sumptuous. The 1981 is light, herbaceous and ready to drink.

D'ANGLUDET (MARGAUX) * * *

1981	($12.95)	83
1982	($15.95)	84
1983	($15.95)	88
1984	($9.99)	80

The highly respected Bordeaux winebroker Peter A. Sichel lives at
d'Angludet and has taken this modest property from obscurity to international prominence. It tends to be a spicy, elegant, supple wine
with a decade of aging potential in the top vintages. The best recent
vintage is the superb 1983, a rich, intense, remarkable wine that will
make people take more notice of d'Angludet. The 1984 is light and
ready to drink, the 1982 supple and easy to understand.

D'ARCHE (SAUTERNES) * *

1982	($9.99)	80
1983	($9.99)	86

A property in Sauternes that can make solid, reliable wines that represent good value. Nineteen eighty-three is their best wine in several
decades.

L'ARRIVET-HAUT-BRION (GRAVES) * *

1982	($14.95)	83

L'Arrivet-Haut-Brion produces a rather fruity, soft, but interesting red wine of which 1982 is a good example.

L'ARROSÉE (ST.-EMILION) * * * * *

1981	($15.00)	86
1982	($25.00)	90
1983	($15.00)	90
1984	($15.00)	86

L'Arrosée is one of the least-known great wines of Bordeaux and is to be sought out for its expansive, broad flavors of almost burgundian-like richness. The 1984 may be St.-Emilion's best wine in a very, very difficult vintage, fragrant, rich, and showing surprising ripeness. The 1983 has a big bouquet of black cherries, is wonderfully spicy and lush. The 1982 is equally deep but more tannic, a lovely, multidimensional wine and the 1981 elegant, lighter, but still very, very attractive.

AUSONE (ST.-EMILION) * * * * *

1981	($75.00)	80
1982	($100.00)	90
1983	($50.00)	89

One of the most impressive châteaux and remarkable locations of all the châteaux in Bordeaux, Ausone has emerged from a period of long mediocrity and since 1976 has made classic, long-lived wines that should last well given their firm tannic structures. There is no 1984 as it was declassified. The 1983 is rich and jammy, with very soft flavors but a good deal of power. The 1982 was extraordinary, virtually perfect from cask, but has closed up and seems rather unyielding and backward despite an impressive color and an enormous richness and power. The 1981 is rather light and a little lean and angular, the least attractive of the vintages in the 1980s.

BALESTARD-LA-TONNELLE (ST.-EMILION) * * *

1981	($12.95)	84
1982	($12.95)	85
1983	($12.95)	85

Balestard is an immensely enjoyable wine. The style produced here is dense, big, deep and rich, with a chewy texture. Both the 1983 and 1982 are beefy, full-tilt St.-Emilions with little finesse but plenty of power and hedonistic flavors. The 1981 is lighter but also fruity and uncomplicated.

BASTOR-LAMONTAGNE (SAUTERNES) * * *

1982	($6.99)	85
1983	($9.99)	87

This is a wonderful property making very fine Sauternes at a very good price. The 1983 is voluptuous and luscious. The 1982 is a distinct success.

BATAILLEY (PAUILLAC) * * *

1982	($17.95)	87
1983	($14.95)	83

Batailley produces wines that are never in the top class of Pauillac but are solid, well colored, and somewhat one-dimensional in quality. The 1983 is straightforward, chunky, pleasant, but not complex. The 1982 is similarly styled, only more concentrated and longer on the palate.

BEAU-SÉJOUR BÉCOT (ST.-EMILION) * *

1981	($14.95)	70
1982	($14.95)	78
1983	($14.95)	86

A property involved in a boiling controversy since it was demoted in the new St.-Emilion classification, after which the owner appealed to the French government and lost his case. The demotion was probably justified, based on the vintages in the 1960s and 1970s, but Bécot is now making much better wines, as its 1983 and 1985 dramatically attest. The 1983 is the best recent effort, with a ripe, raspberry, oaky bouquet and lush flavors.

BEAUMONT (HAUT-MÉDOC) * *

1982	($7.50)	83
1983	($7.50)	81

Beaumont can make very good wine at very reasonable prices. The 1983 is slightly herbaceous, but the 1982 shows more depth of fruit and character. Both are made in a very quick-maturing, soft, commercial style.

BEAUREGARD (POMEROL) *

1982	($16.00)	81
1983	($16.00)	80

Beauregard generally makes light-style Pomerols that lack a little in body and richness, with sometimes pronounced herbaceous bouquets. Both the 1982 and 1983 are ready to drink, fruity, soft, easy wines.

BEAUSÉJOUR (DUFFAU-LAGARROSSE) (ST.-EMILION) * * *

1981	($15.95)	82
1982	($25.00)	87
1983	($25.00)	88

One of the two Beauséjours in St.-Emilion, this estate produced numerous mediocre wines in the 1960s and 1970s, but has come on strongly in the 1980s. The 1983 is a wonderfully rich, complex wine, with a bouquet of roasted fruit and subtle herbs. The 1982 is also intense, expansive, rich, and quite delicious now. The 1981 is much lighter than the latter two wines and a little more angular and harsh on the palate. A property to watch.

BEL-AIR (LALANDE-DE-POMEROL) * * *

1982	($8.99)	83

1983   ($7.99)   82

Bel-Air produces ripe, fruity wines that are among the best in Lalande-de-Pomerol.

BEL-AIR-MARQUIS D'ALIGRE (MARGAUX) *

1983   ($12.99) 78

This wine can be well colored but generally lacks harmony and finesse.

BEL-ORME-TRONQUOY-DE-LALANDE (HAUT-MÉDOC) * *

1981   ($10.00) 75

1982   ($10.00) 83

This property can make outstanding wine, but recent vintages have
not looked as strong so one might have hoped, compared with older
vintages that sometimes appear to have been made in a higher-quality,
longer lasting style. The 1982 is supple, chunky, but uncomplex. The
1981 is an austere, mean, tannic wine.

BELAIR (ST.-EMILION) * * *

1981   ($15.95) 74

1982   ($19.95) 85

1983   ($19.95) 90

The sister château of Ausone, Belair shares the same winemaking and
recent efforts have shown remarkable improvements in quality, particularly since 1976. There was no 1984 from Belair, but the 1983 is
the best in over 20 years, a rich, surprisingly powerful, deep wine that
is better than the more famous 1982. The 1981 is light, fruity, soft,
and lacking concentration.

DE BELCIER (CÔTES DE CASTILLON) * *

1982   ($5.99)   82

1983   ($5.99)   78

De Belcier is a largely unknown yet fine Côtes de Castillon representing excellent value for money. The 1982 is the best recent vintage.

BELGRAVE (HAUT-MÉDOC) * *

1982	($12.95)	84
1983	($10.00)	65

Although a classified growth, Belgrave had fallen into great disrepair and only considerable amounts of money invested by its owners have brought it up in quality. The 1982 is a fruity, supple, early-maturing wine. The 1983 is disappointingly thin and light.

BELLES GRAVES (LALANDE-DE-POMEROL) * * *

1982	($6.99)	86
1983	($8.99)	84

One of the leading estates in Lalande-de-Pomerol, Belles Graves produces very rich, blackberry-scented wines with considerable character. The 1983 is delicious, the 1982 rich, plummy, and has 5–6 more years of aging potential.

BEYCHEVELLE (ST.-JULIEN) * * * *

1981	($18.95)	84
1982	($25.00)	92
1983	($19.95)	85
1984	($12.95)	80

Beychevelle is one of the most scenic châteaux on Bordeaux's Route du Vin. The wines tend to be smooth, supple, and very fruity, forcing them to be drunk at a very young age. Recent vintages have shown a bit more backbone and tannin than the quick-maturing wine that was made here in most vintages of the '60s and '70s. The 1984 is a good, straightforward wine that should be drunk over the next 3–4 years. The 1983 is more aggressive, with more tannin in the finish and a good concentration of fruit. The 1982 has a wonderful, sweet, ripe nose and deep, rich, long flavors. It is very impressive. The 1981 is light and ready to drink now.

BON PASTEUR (POMEROL) * * * *

1982	($25.00)	90
1983	($15.95)	86
1984	($12.95)	80

Bon Pasteur is owned and managed by one of the gifted oenologists of Bordeaux, Michel Rolland. His commitment to quality is no better evidenced than in his own property, which makes wonderfully fruity, rich wines that can age for up to 10 years. The 1984 is a modest success given the difficulties of the vintage; the 1983 ripe, rich, quite supple and destined for early maturity; and the 1982 an atypically powerful wine with a wonderful aroma and flavors of ripe black cherries and toffee.

BONALGUE (POMEROL) * *

1981	($12.00)	83
1982	($12.00)	85
1983	($14.00)	82

The wines of Bonalgue exhibit surprising strength and richness. While not complex, they are well made, with deep, black cherry fruitiness and medium to full body. The 1982 is the best of the vintages in the '80s so far.

LE BOSCQ (MÉDOC) * * *

1982	($6.99)	84
1983	($5.99)	83

Le Boscq has rewarded me on more than one occasion with its rather impressive richness and straightforward, robust, fleshy character. It is always quite reasonably priced.

BOURGNEUF-VAYRON (POMEROL) *

1981	($15.00)	75

| 1982 | ($12.00) | 78 |

Bourgneuf is a relatively unknown wine, well situated, and generally makes satisfying wines with richness, power, and aging potential of 5–8 years.

BOUSCAUT (RED) (GRAVES) * *

| 1982 | ($18.95) | 85 |
| 1983 | ($12.99) | 84 |

This property has potential but has yet to live up to it. The wine is always a little lean and lacking in character, although the 1982 and 1983 are two of the best wines in the last 15–20 years.

BOUSCAUT (WHITE) (GRAVES) * * *

1983	($12.00)	84
1984	($14.00)	82
1985	($15.00)	85

I have always enjoyed the white wine of Bouscaut more than the red. It is usually a lean, rather austere wine that is best drunk within 5–8 years of the vintage. The 1985 is the best of the recent vintages.

BOYD-CANTENAC (MARGAUX) * * * *

1981	($15.95)	70
1982	($19.95)	86
1983	($15.95)	88
1984	($9.99)	80

Boyd-Cantenac, for whatever reason, remains largely unknown, yet offers a full-bodied, rich, plump, quite long-lived style of Margaux that remains somewhat undervalued given its quality. The 1984 is one-dimensional but cleanly made and ready to drink. The 1983 is one of this property's top wines, very dark in color, full-blown, spicy, with a ripe plummy aroma, and plenty of tannin for longevity. The 1982 is not unlike the 1983, only softer, with unctuous, fat, fleshy flavors. The 1981 has proved to be soft and diluted, with a distinct vegetal character.

BRANAIRE-DUCRU (ST.-JULIEN) * * * *

1981	($15.95)	86
1982	($28.00)	93
1983	($14.95)	85
1984	($9.99)	83

Branaire-Ducru is one of those curiously underrated, undervalued properties that somehow gets forgotten when wine enthusiasts discuss their favorite wines. Nevertheless, it can make splendid wines, as it has in 1975, 1976, and 1982, that rival the best Bordeaux could produce. The 1984 is supple, and richly fruity, with a cedary, berry-scented bouquet. The 1983 is rather soft and lacking concentration for Branaire, but nevertheless charming. The 1982 is a superlative wine and one of the great successes for this château. Its smoky, opulent, exotic qualities give it tremendous appeal. The 1981 is more understated in personality, but very supple, fruity, and drinking very well now.

BRANE-CANTENAC (MARGAUX) * * *

1981	($14.95)	83
1982	($19.95)	87
1983	($17.95)	88
1984	($14.95)	73

Brane-Cantenac produces a tremendous amount of wine and although it has enjoyed a large measure of commercial success throughout the world because of its official classification as a second-growth, the wine in the period between 1967 and 1977 was quite mediocre, if not poor. However, the vintages in the 1980s have gone from one strength to another. The 1981 is a charming, fruity wine that is ready to drink. The 1982 is a rich, deep, fat, intensely perfumed wine with lovely fruity flavors. The 1983 is the best wine this property has made since 1961. The 1984 is straightforward and rather diluted.

LA BRIDANE (ST.-JULIEN) *

1982	($8.99)	82

La Bridane produces solid, reliable, unexciting wines. The 1982 is its most recent good vintage and it is ready to drink. It is fruity, quite ripe, and soft.

BRILLETTE (MOULIS) * * *

1981	($10.00)	84
1982	($12.00)	86
1983	($12.00)	82

The wines of Brillette are not yet well known, but the quality of wine-making here is very high. The wine produced is in the spicy, oaky, richly fruity style that appeals to many tasters. The 1983 is not up to the quality of either the 1981 or 1982, but is still an attractive, soft, plummy wine dominated by the smell of new oak. The 1982 is a rich, concentrated, rather exotic wine with plenty of character. The 1981 is a more elegant and lighter version of the 1982.

BROUSTET (BARSAC) * *

1978	($12.95)	80
1980	($12.95)	82

This is a property to watch since great improvements are being made to the vineyard and *chai* and improved quality is expected.

CADET-PIOLA (ST.-EMILION) * * * *

1982	($19.95)	87
1983	($17.95)	86

The Jabiol family, who make this wine, are conservative winemakers and the wine produced has a wonderful black/ruby color and, usually, an intense, full-bodied, rich fruitiness. It is generally a good value. The 1983 is quite good, the 1982 rich, full-bodied, and quite concentrated, and the unreleased 1985 quite impressive. A very underrated estate worth more attention.

CAILLOU (BARSAC)* *

1982	($7.99)	78
1983	($10.99)	85

Caillou produces straightforward, fruity, easygoing wine that can age well and should be drunk young. The 1983 vintage, an outstanding one for Sauternes and Barsac, produced a very rich wine.

CALON-SÉGUR (ST.-ESTÈPHE) * * * *

1981	($14.95)	83
1982	($25.95)	95
1983	($18.95)	82
1984	($14.95)	75

The white château of Calon-Ségur has a magical name, but the wines continue to be very spotty in their performance. The 1981, 1983, and 1984 are not notable successes, though decent wines in their respective vintages. However, Calon-Ségur did everything right in 1982 and this is probably the best vintage for this property since 1947. It is a voluptuous, tannic, and very backward wine with great potential.

CAMENSAC (HAUT-MÉDOC) * * *

1981	($12.00)	81
1982	($12.00)	85
1983	($12.00)	84

Camensac is one of the least known of the 1855 classified growths. The wine is made in a very supple, soft style that is meant to be drunk young, although it is capable of aging in top vintages like 1982 and 1985 for at least 10 years. The 1981 is elegant and spicy with a taste of blackcurrants. The 1982 is quite richly concentrated, with plenty of fruit and obvious vanillin character. The 1983 is almost as good as the 1982.

CANON (CANON-FRONSAC) * * *

1982	($7.99)	84
1983	($7.99)	84

Canon makes a more supple style of wine than many Canon-Fronsacs and both the 1982 and 1983 are superlative, richly fruity, interesting, elegant wines.

CANON (ST.-EMILION) * * * * *

1981	($15.95)	75
1982	($40.00)	93
1983	($25.00)	90

The wines of Canon have increased in quality greatly, and although this has always been one of St.-Emilion's best wines, it is also, curiously, one of its best kept secrets. The wines are splendidly rich, deep, and concentrated, and this can be seen in both the excellent tobacco-scented, rich, classic 1983 and sublime, extraordinarily rich 1982. The 1981 comes up short when compared to these two vintages since it lacks the fruit to handle the tannin and leanness.

CANON DE BREM (CANON-FRONSAC)* * *

1982	($8.99)	86
1983	($8.99)	86

The top estate of Canon-Fronsac, this property makes very forceful, aggressive, rich, big, robust, intense wines that can last for 10–15 years. Both the 1982 and 1983 are quite good.

CANON-LA-GAFFELIÈRE (ST.-EMILION) * *

1981	($8.99)	70
1982	($12.95)	83

| 1983 | ($9.99) | 82 |

Rather light, bland, mediocre wines are produced by this property; both the 1982 and 1983 showed adequate, supple fruit and a fresh, berry character.

CANTEMERLE (MACAU) * * * *

1981	($16.95)	85
1982	($19.95)	85
1983	($19.95)	92
1984	($15.95)	86

Cantemerle, a "Sleeping Beauty" château in a park just north of Bordeaux, after a period of mediocrity and inconsistency in the '70s is in full form in the '80s. The 1984 has wonderful intensity and richness for a wine of this vintage and the 1983 is one of the very top wines of the vintage, with a remarkable bouquet of ripe plums, flowers, and oak. The 1982 is elegant, soft, and loaded with berry fruit, and the 1981 a lighter version of the 1982.

CANTENAC-BROWN (MARGAUX)* * *

1981	($12.95)	85
1982	($18.95)	85
1983	($17.95)	84
1984	($16.95)	82

Cantenac-Brown, after a long period of mediocrity and a history of producing rather charmless, coarse, hard wines, has made a number of changes in its winemaking with a new team of people and the results have been increasingly impressive in the 1980s. The 1984 is supple, with an attractive bouquet and easy drinkability. The 1983 is a full-bodied wine that needs 5 full years of cellaring. The 1982 is quite rich, with long, ripe flavors and excellent concentration, and the 1981, a big, tannic, chocolatey, rich wine, will age for a long time.

CAP DE MERLE (LUSSAC-ST.-EMILION)* * *

1982	($5.99)	84
1983	($5.99)	84

The leading estate of Lussac-St.-Emilion, Cap de Merle's 1982 and 1983 are both deliciously fruity, spicy, ripe wines with plenty of character.

CAP DE MOURLIN (ST.-EMILION)* * *

1982	($12.95)	85
1983	($12.95)	85

There have always been two Cap de Mourlin estates, but starting with 1983 there is only one, under the name Jacques Capdemourlin. The wine here is powerful, dense, huge, and massive, with little complexity but tremendous richness and power. Both the 1982 and 1983 are this style.

CARBONNIEUX (RED) (GRAVES)* *

1982	($15.95)	82
1983	($10.99)	80

Another property better known for its white wine than red, Carbonnieux tends to make very fruity, easy to like, easy to drink, soft red wine. Both 1982 and 1983 are typical of its style.

CARBONNIEUX (WHITE) (GRAVES)* * *

1983	($14.99)	85
1984	($13.99)	80
1985	($14.59)	85

Carbonnieux produces a large quantity of very reliable, crisp, fruity, elegant white Graves. The 1983 is a textbook white Graves that should keep for 5–10 years. The 1985 is slightly fruitier and less ageworthy, but very attractive.

LA CARDONNE (MÉDOC)* *

1982   ($8.99)   80

This is an interesting Cru Bourgeois owned by the Rothschild family
(of Lafite-Rothschild). There has been a tremendous amount of money
invested, but to date the wines have been rather light and lacking in
character.

LES CARMES HAUT-BRION (GRAVES)* * *

1982   ($10.99)   82

Rarely seen, Les Carmes Haut-Brion's vineyard is well placed and in
1982 made a rich, lush, easy to drink wine that will mature quickly.

CARONNE-STE.-GEMME (HAUT-MÉDOC)* *

1982   ($10.00)   84

This is a big, powerful, richly fruity, tannic wine that needs another
3–5 years of cellaring to reach its peak.

CERTAN DE MAY (POMEROL)* * * * *

1981   ($50.00)   90

1982   ($75.00)   97

1983   ($30.00)   87

The tiny property of Certan de May has in the last 10 years emerged
from a period of mediocrity into the top echelon of Pomerols. It is a
connoisseur's wine, slow to evolve, but powerful, rich, and multidimensional in personality. The 1983, which will need a long cellar stay,
is perhaps too tannic and oaky for its own good. The 1982, a fantastic
wine with unbelievable concentration, is one of the truly colossal efforts from this vintage. The 1981, broodingly dark and backward, is a
powerful, rich, fruity wine destined for 10–15 years of life.

CERTAN-GIRAUD (POMEROL)* * *

1982   ($22.00)   89

1983   ($20.00)   88

1984   ($12.00)   81

Certan-Giraud is a Pomerol on the move upward in quality. The 1984, given the difficulties of the vintage, is a success. The 1983 is filled with the scent of garden herbs and ripe fruit, and is an unctuous, rich wine for drinking over the near future. The 1982 is a big, dense, full-bodied Pomerol loaded with flavor.

CHASSE-SPLEEN (MOULIS)* * * *

1981   ($8.99)   84

1982   ($14.99)   87

1983   ($14.99)   87

Chasse-Spleen is an outstanding property that produces one of Bordeaux's best wines as well as best wine values. The wine is always characterized by a very pronounced deep ruby color, a bouquet of plummy ripeness, and rich, round, substantial flavors. The 1983 and 1982 are two very fine vintages for Chasse-Spleen, producing big, full-flavored, rich, large-scaled wines with enormous potential. The 1981 is ready to drink and is a bit lighter and more precocious in style.

CHEVAL BLANC (ST.-EMILION)* * * * *

1981   ($50.00)   90

1982   ($100.00)   98

1983   ($65.00)   93

1984   ($35.00)   75

Cheval Blanc, one of Bordeaux's greatest wines, is also unique, being made from more than two-thirds Cabernet Franc, the only major wine in Bordeaux to have that distinction. The wine is exotic, rich, very easy to drink young but cunningly made to last. The 1984, from a disastrous vintage for St.-Emilion, is light, herbaceous, and should be drunk soon. The 1983 is a rich, exotic, full-bodied, lush wine with a sweet, long finish. Nineteen eighty-two is Cheval Blanc's greatest wine since some of its legendary vintages in the late 1940s. It is voluptuous and extremely intense, with a cascade of exotic, rich aromas. There is plenty of tannin, but the immense concentration of fruit will cause many to drink the wine before it is fully mature. The 1981 is a lighter wine, but very elegant, spicy, plummy, with soft, silky, lovely flavors.

DOMAINE DE CHEVALIER (RED) (GRAVES)* * * * *

1981	($19.95)	85
1982	($25.95)	90
1983	($19.95)	87
1984	($19.95)	86

For sheer elegance and consistency the tiny Domaine de Chevalier has always been a connoisseur's favorite. Recent vintages have all been very successful and this is also a property to look for in off vintages such as 1980 and 1984. The 1984 is, in fact, a top success of the vintage, the 1983 rather hard, tough, and tannic, and just needing 7–8 years of patience. The 1982 is rich, long, fat, and quite concentrated, and the 1981 elegant, with a pronounced vanillin oakiness.

DOMAINE DE CHEVALIER (WHITE) (GRAVES)* * * * *

1982	($35.00)	88
1983	($35.00)	93
1984	($25.00)	88

On average, only 500–600 cases of this exceptional white wine are produced each year. It is remarkably long-lived and though usually overpoweringly oaky when young, becomes increasingly more complex with age. The 1983 is a monumental effort, the 1982 and 1984, very fine.

CISSAC (HAUT-MÉDOC)* * *

1981	($6.99)	78
1982	($7.99)	84

| 1983 | ($6.99) | 80 |

Cissac is one of the best of the Cru Bourgeois properties in the Médoc. The wine is generally made in a very long-lived, tannic style. The 1982 shows more supple richness and is quite full-bodied and powerful. The 1981 is rather austere and a little too lean, and the 1983 plump and showing an uncomplicated fruitiness and character.

CITRAN (HAUT-MÉDOC)*

1981	($6.99)	65
1982	($7.99)	73
1983	($5.99)	70

This winery produces a significant amount of wine that is often highly promoted. However, it is also often quite diluted and emaciated in taste and texture. The latter comment would characterize the 1981, 1982, and 1983.

CLARKE (LISTRAC)* * *

| 1982 | ($12.00) | 81 |
| 1983 | ($12.00) | 80 |

The Baron Edmond de Rothschild has totally restored and rejuvenated this property, and when the 1985 is released people will see how far in quality it has come. Both the 1982 and 1983 reflect the youth of the vineyard and while they are adequate wines, they lack the richness and depth we will see in the upcoming 1985.

CLERC-MILON (PAUILLAC)* * *

1982	($20.00)	84
1983	($18.00)	83
1984	($18.00)	85

A great effort has been made by the Baron Philippe de Rothschild to improve the quality of Clerc-Milon in the '80s. Ironically, the 1984 (the vintage of the least pedigree) is the best vintage of Clerc-Milon, even better than the 1983 and 1982. The 1984 is richer, with a lush, fruity quality and should be drunk in the near future. The 1983 seems rather lightweight for the vintage. The 1982 is again charming and very forward, an open-knit wine with a very pleasing bouquet.

CLIMENS (BARSAC)* * * *

1980	($19.95)	90
1982	($19.95)	80
1983	($19.95)	90

Climens is the best sweet wine for sheer racy and stylish elegance. It is never overpowering, but oh so delicious and crisp, with great balance. The 1983 is superb, the 1982 a disappointment, and the 1980 a fabulous vintage for this château, with an exotic bouquet of tropical fruit, pineapples, and melons.

CLINET (POMEROL)* *

1982	($15.00)	75
1983	($12.00)	80

I have usually found the wines of Clinet to be rather light and lacking the exuberant, fleshy, rich fruit for which Pomerols are so renowned. The 1982 and 1983 are typical.

CLOS DU CLOCHER (POMEROL)* * *

1982	($18.00)	85
1983	($12.00)	83

This is a terribly underpublicized property that generally makes very good wine. The 1982 is surprisingly dense, concentrated, and deeply fruity, and the 1983 elegant, spicy, well-colored, and ready to drink.

CLOS L'EGLISE (POMEROL)* *

1982	($16.00)	82
1983	($16.00)	80

Clos L'Eglise produces one of the more Médoc-like and austere wines of Pomerol, with a heavy reliance on the Cabernet Franc and Cabernet

Sauvignon grapes. The 1983 is slightly herbaceous and a little shallow. The 1982 is light for the vintage but attractive in a simple, fruity way.

CLOS FOURTET (ST.-EMILION)* *

1981	($12.95)	80
1982	($18.95)	86
1983	($14.95)	78

Clos Fourtet's main claim to fame is its remarkable wine cellars, but the wine has been off form for some time, though recent vintages look more promising. The 1983 is soft, fruity, and rather commercial. The 1982 is the best recent vintage, with a full-blown bouquet of toasty oak and berry fruit, and the 1981 is pleasant but rather one-dimensional.

CLOS DES JACOBINS (ST.-EMILION)* * *

1981	($15.95)	86
1982	($19.95)	89
1983	($15.95)	87
1984	($9.99)	80

The well-known *négociant* Cordier owns this little château and produces deeply colored, rich, creamy, plummy wines that have a cedary fragrance when mature. Recent vintages have all been successful, including the 1984, which is ready to drink. The 1983, is lush, ripe, fat, and alcoholic, the 1982 sweet with layers of voluptuous fruit, and the 1981 herbaceous but intensely fruity and elegant.

CLOS RENÉ (POMEROL)* * *

1982	($20.00)	87
1983	($15.00)	86

After a period of rather uninspired activity, Clos René has come on strong in the '80s with a succession of good vintages. Both the 1983 and 1982 are ready to drink, rich, lush, fat wines with considerable flavor and power, but lacking a little in finesse.

CLOS DES TEMPLIERS (LALANDE-DE-POMEROL)* *

1982	($6.99)	83
1983	($6.99)	80

A very good, reliable estate in Lalande-de-Pomerol making supple, silky wines for drinking within the first 5–6 years.

LA CLOTTE (ST.-EMILION)* *

1982	($12.99)	84
1983	($8.99)	75

The owners of the lovely little bistro in St.-Emilion, Logis de la Cad-ène, also own this vineyard. The wine, made to be drunk young, is supple, fat, fruity, as well as delicious, as in 1982.

LA COMMANDERIE (ST.-EMILION)* *

1982	($12.00)	81
1983	($9.00)	84

This is a tiny property next to Cheval Blanc that in 1983 made a delicious, densely colored, chunky wine.

LA CONSEILLANTE (POMEROL)* * * *

1981	($35.00)	90
1982	($50.00)	90
1983	($30.00)	87

La Conseillante makes one of Pomerol's most elegant and burgundy-like wines. It always seems to have a smell of toasty oak and raspberry fruit not unlike a fine Chambolle-Musigny. The 1983 is creamy, velvety with lovely fruit, the 1982 voluptuous, decadently ripe, a rather big wine from La Conseillante, but with a smell of raspberry and other fruits. The 1981, lighter than both the 1982 and 1983, is a remarkably elegant, balanced wine with layers of gorgeous, plummy, sweet fruit.

CORBIN (ST.-EMILION)* * *

1982	($19.95)	87
1983	($19.95)	86

Corbin, which borders Pomerol, tends to make wine in a very lush, fruity style. It seems to excel in the hot, sunny years. Both the 1983 and 1982 are supple, fat, jammy, ripe wines that offer wonderful drinking for the next 5–6 years.

CORBIN-MICHOTTE (ST.-EMILION)* * *

1982	($14.99)	85
1983	($12.99)	84

A sound, reliable, fat, plummy, deeply colored, Graves-like St.-Emilion that is excellent in both 1982 and 1983.

COS D'ESTOURNEL (ST.-ESTÈPHE)* * * * *

1981	($15.95)	86
1982	($45.00)	97
1983	($25.95)	87
1984	($16.95)	87

Cos d'Estournel has risen not only to the top of its class in St.-Estèphe, but is now among the great wines in all of Bordeaux. Since 1976 the wines have improved, going from one strength to another. The 1984 is one of the top successes of the vintage; the 1983 is certainly the best St.-Estèphe, though not a great wine. The 1982 is a monumental wine of explosive richness and length on the palate, and the 1981 elegant, a much lighter-weight wine than the 1982 or 1983. The unreleased 1985 from the cask looked to have enough potential to be the wine of the vintage—no small accomplishment.

COS LABORY (ST.-ESTÈPHE)* *

1982	($15.95)	78
1983	($10.99)	73

1984   ($10.99)   78

Cos Labory, although a classified growth, is one of the most disappointing. Improvements continue to be made, but the wine is generally
fruity, bland, and light, often feebly colored as well. The 1984 is light
and pleasant, the 1983 again very light, and the 1982 a decent wine,
but in the context of the vintage, a disappointment.

COUFRAN (HAUT MÉDOC)* * *

1982   ($10.00)   83

1983   ($10.00)   82

Coufran is one of the most unique wines in the Médoc since it is made
of a very high percentage of Merlot (85%). Consequently, the wine
tends to be richly fruity and very precocious in style. The 1983 is a
succulent, juicy, grapy wine, ready to drink, and the 1982 a little more
serious effort with greater richness and length.

COUTET (BARSAC)* * * *

1981   ($14.95)   78

1983   ($17.00)   87

A lighter-styled wine from Barsac, Coutet makes very fresh, easy to
drink wines with a lemony, melon fruitiness. The 1983 is their best
wine from the most recent vintages.

COUVENT-DES-JACOBINS (ST.-EMILION)* * *

1981   ($9.95)   78

1982   ($12.95)   85

1983   ($14.95)   85

The gorgeous Château Couvent-des-Jacobins is one of the most interesting in all of Bordeaux and its underground cellars are among the
most impressive. The wine is increasingly well made by the owners,
the Joinaud-Borde family. The 1983 is a soft, supple, fruity, deliciously styled, elegant wine. The 1982 has an impressive color and a
complex bouquet of cedar and rich, fruity scents. The 1981 is a bit

herbaceous and lacking the concentration of the latter two vintages. The 1984 was declassified totally by this meticulously run property.

LA CROIX (POMEROL)* * *

1981	($12.00)	84
1982	($12.00)	86
1983	($12.00)	86

La Croix produces a very plump, fat, deliciously fruity, uncomplex style of Pomerol that has wide appeal. The 1982 and 1983 are both big wines with a lot of alcohol and flavor but not much finesse. The 1981 is lighter in style.

LA CROIX DE GAY (POMEROL)* * *

1982	($15.00)	75
1983	($15.00)	84

La Croix de Gay had a great reputation in the '40s and '50s, but by the 1970s the wine became rather light in style. Now in the 1980s, the '82 is somewhat of a disappointment given the vintage, but the 1983 shows effusively fruity, round, supple texture and good fruit, and the unreleased 1985 is perhaps the best La Croix de Gay in more than two decades. A property to watch since greater efforts are being made to upgrade the quality.

CROIZET-BAGES (PAUILLAC)* *

1982	($14.95)	75
1983	($9.99)	68
1984	($9.99)	70

Croizet-Bages is among the lightest and quickest maturing of all the Pauillacs. The wine is often lacking in class as well as concentration. The 1984 is surprisingly fruitier and more interesting than the disappointing 1983. The 1982 has simple cherry flavors and a rather flabby structure.

CROQUE-MICHOTTE (ST.-EMILION)* * *

1982	($11.95)	86
1983	($9.99)	80

This is a rather uncomplicated style of wine, fruity, fleshy and alcoholic in style. The 1983 is a bit too alcoholic and lacking acidity, the 1982 ripe, savory, very flavorful, and quite full-bodied.

CURÉ-BON-LA-MADELEINE (ST.-EMILION)* *

1982	($19.95)	87
1983	($19.95)	84

Despite a remarkable reputation, this wine is rarely seen due to the tiny production of 1,500 cases. The 1983 is herbaceous but soft and very fruity, the 1982 is richer, denser, riper, and ready to drink.

LA DAUPHINE (FRONSAC)* * *

1982	($8.99)	85
1983	($8.99)	85

The star of Fronsac, La Dauphine produces fragrant, rich, medium- to full-bodied wines that can age up to 10 years. Both the 1982 and 1983 are very successful here.

DAUZAC (MARGAUX)* *

1981	($9.99)	80
1982	($12.95)	82
1983	($9.95)	80

Despite a new ownership in 1978 that has invested considerable sums of money, Dauzac remains one of the least impressive wines in Margaux. The wine is simple, with decent cherryish flavors and medium body. The best recent vintage is the 1982, which is plump, fruity, with good color and an attractive ripeness on the palate.

DESMIRAIL (MARGAUX)* *

| 1981 | ($9.95) | 75 |

| 1982 | ($9.95) | 82 |

| 1983 | ($9.95) | 80 |

This property has been resurrected by the owner of the famous Brane-Cantenac, Lucien Lurton. The wine to date has been uncomplicated, fruity, with attractive suppleness and richness, and is meant to be drunk young.

DESTIEUX (ST.-EMILION)* * *

| 1982 | ($9.99) | 84 |

| 1983 | ($9.99) | 85 |

Destieux makes an attractive, plummy, fleshy, open-knit wine with plenty of alcohol. The 1983 is the best of the recent vintages since it has a bit more concentration and flesh to it. These wines are to be drunk young.

DOISY-DAËNE (BARSAC)* * *

| 1982 | ($9.95) | 82 |

| 1983 | ($12.95) | 90 |

One of the most ambitiously and innovatively run estates in Bordeaux, Doisy-Daëne is capable of making very fine sweet wines from the Barsac region. The 1983 is one of their best vintages in recent history, with a big, ripe bouquet of pineapples, peaches, and spring flowers and a very concentrated, full-bodied, unctuous feel on the palate.

DOISY-VEDRINES (BARSAC)* * *

| 1982 | ($9.99) | 84 |

| 1983 | ($9.99) | 87 |

This well-placed estate in Barsac can make very good wines that tend to be fatter, richer, more intense than many of the Barsacs. The 1983 is excellent and the 1982 is a success for the vintage; both are viscous, ripe, coconut-scented wines with sweet, rich flavors.

LA DOMINIQUE (ST.-EMILION)* * * *

1981	($10.95)	84
1982	($25.00)	92
1983	($18.95)	87

A remarkably underrated wine from St.-Emilion, La Dominique is recently making wines on a level of any St.-Emilion save for Cheval Blanc. The property has produced a number of great wines in recent vintages, including an incredibly opulent, rich, sublime 1982, a well-structured, flavorful, full-bodied 1983, and a lighter, but complex, fully mature 1981. There was no 1984 made.

DUCRU-BEAUCAILLOU (ST.-JULIEN)* * * * *

1981	($19.95)	90
1982	($55.00)	96
1983	($27.95)	88
1984	($19.95)	83

Ducru-Beaucaillou is one of Bordeaux's most famous properties and has been elevated to greatness by its modest owner, Jean-Eugène Borie. The top vintages for Ducru-Beaucaillou in recent decades have all been excellent. This wine seems to combine the most cedary, majestic richness of a Pauillac with the ripe, intense fruitiness of a classic St.-Julien. The 1984 is one of the more tannic wines of the vintage and needs several more years to fully develop. The 1983 is a very good rather than great vintage for Ducru. It is tannic and needs a good decade of aging. The 1982, along with the 1953 and 1961, is one of the three greatest Ducrus I have ever tasted. It is closed at present, but with another 10 years of aging should reveal its voluptuous, extremely concentrated, stunning density of extract and power. The 1981 is a more elegant, lighter version of the intense 1982. It is a beautifully crafted wine made to last and last.

DUHART-MILON-ROTHSCHILD (PAUILLAC)* * *

1981	($15.95)	84
1982	($19.95)	88
1983	($17.95)	86
1984	($14.95)	80

Duhart-Milon is one of the Pauillac châteaux owned by the Roth-schilds. The vineyard is still quite young and while there were many disappointing wines produced in the 1970s, the '80s have shown greater consistency and quality. The 1984 is light but pleasant, the 1983 has good color, a firm structure, and some pleasant cassis flavors. The 1982 is the best Duhart-Milon I have tasted in the last several decades, rich, full-bodied, with loads of tannin and fruit. The 1981 is light but extremely elegant, with a cedary, rich bouquet.

DURAND LAPLAGNE (PUISSEGUIN-ST.-EMILION)* * *

1982	($7.99)	82
1983	($7.99)	84

This is the top estate of Puisseguin-St.-Emilion; both 1982 and 1983 produced surprisingly rich and fruity wines with generous textures.

DURFORT-VIVENS (MARGAUX)* * *

1981	($14.95)	74
1982	($19.95)	85
1983	($18.95)	86
1984	($11.95)	73

Durfort-Vivens, one of the principal properties of the Lurton family, has a record of 20 years of mediocrity. However, vintages since 1978 have shown improvement, particularly in 1982 and 1983, both years having produced rather rich, ripe, lovely wines with good concentration and aging ability. The 1981 is angular and weedy and 1984 rather light and thin.

L'EGLISE-CLINET (POMEROL)* * * *

1982	($19.95)	86
1983	($19.95)	86
1984	($15.00)	84

L'Eglise-Clinet is one of the properties to watch in Pomerol since it is making great strides in quality. The 1984 is one of Pomerol's top wines in what was a disappointing vintage. The 1983 and 1982 are fat and powerful, with rich, black cherry bouquets and chewy, dense textures. The unreleased 1985 (which rivals Pétrus) will make L'Eglise-Clinet justifiably famous.

DOMAINE DE L'EGLISE (POMEROL)* *

1982	($14.00)	80
1983	($14.00)	82

Domaine de L'Eglise has not distinguished itself in recent vintages and remains a dull, chunky Pomerol with little character. However, the unreleased 1985 may prove to be a move toward making a better-quality wine than before.

L'ENCLOS (POMEROL)* * *

1982	($15.00)	87
1983	($10.99)	86

L'Enclos is always a supple, fruity wine with an opulent, blackberry fruitiness. Both the 1982 and 1983 are very smooth and velvety, and delicious for drinking over the next 5–6 years. As Pomerols go, this wine represents good value.

L'EVANGILE (POMEROL)* * * * *

1981	($18.00)	72
1982	($50.00)	96
1983	($30.00)	91

1984	($20.00)	78

L'Evangile is one of the most complex and interesting Pomerols, and in the last several vintages has been a worthy rival to the great Pétrus itself. The 1984 is light, flavorful, but rather simple. The 1983 is the top wine of Pomerol, dark, with a full-blown, blackberry bouquet and plenty of tannin. The 1982 is extraordinary, with explosive, jammy, blackcurrant fruit and a full-bodied, unctuous texture. The 1981 is diffuse and a disappointment for this property. Lastly, keep an eye out for the great 1985, which is likely to turn out to be among the top four or five wines of the vintage.

DE FARGUES (SAUTERNES)* * * * *

1980	($35.00)	91

1981	($45.00)	90

The ancestral home of the Lur Saluces family (who own Yquem), Fargues is under the Yquem management and given exactly the same winemaking and cellar treatment. In fact, it resembles Yquem much more closely in character, style, and texture than the Lur Saluces family would like to admit. The 1981 may even be better than Yquem, a rich, sweet, exotic, concentrated wine; the 1980 is a great vintage, with an opulence and power that is exceptional. In short, the Yquem junior of Sauternes wines.

FAURIE-DE-SOUCHARD (ST.-EMILION)* * *

1982	($13.95)	85

1983	($12.99)	85

This little-known but excellent property makes firm, rich, muscular wines that can take up to 10 years of aging.

FERRAND (ST.-EMILION)* * *

1982	($11.99)	86

1983	($11.99)	84

The famous ballpoint pen king, Baron Bich, owns this up and coming property and is sparing no expense to produce one of St.-Emilion's top wines. The unreleased 1985 is superb, but the 1982 is a good introduction to the rich, full-bodied yet balanced style of this wine. The 1983 is a little lean and hard. Prices can only go up once the quality of this wine is no longer a secret.

FERRANDE (GRAVES)*

1981	($7.99)	82
1982	($9.99)	82

Ferrande produces supple, round, warm, soft red wines for drinking within the first 5–6 years.

FERRIÈRE (MARGAUX)* *

1981	($15.95)	79
1982	($19.95)	84
1983	($19.95)	82

The obscure and tiny property of Ferrière produces wine that is largely sold in France. The wine is made at Lascombes and shows a similarity in style to it. The 1983 is supple and earthy, with a nice plummy fruitiness. The 1982 shows more depth than the 1983 and better color than the 1981, with very forward elegance that makes it drinkable over the next couple of years.

DE FIEUZAL (RED) (GRAVES)* * *

1982	($19.95)	84
1983	($15.95)	83

Fieuzal is a relatively unknown property in the southern Graves area making both red and white wine. The soon to be released 1985 shows the great potential of this well-placed property; although the 1982 and 1983 are good, they are not exciting given their vintages. However, this is a property on the move upward.

DE FIEUZAL (WHITE) (GRAVES)* * * * *

1983	($15.00)	86
1984	($18.00)	86

1985   ($25.00) 92

Starting in 1985, due to a huge effort on the part of the owners to put Fieuzal in the top class of white Graves wines, Fieuzal can now challenge Laville-Haut-Brion, Haut-Brion, and Domaine de Chevalier. The 1985 is fabulous; both the 1984 and 1983 quite good. Prices, unfortunately, are skyrocketing.

FIGEAC (ST.-EMILION)* * *

1981   ($19.95) 82

1982   ($45.00) 92

1983   ($19.95) 87

1984   ($15.95) 70

Figeac makes the wine that is most commonly compared to Cheval Blanc. It seems to be less consistent than Cheval Blanc in recent vintages and in some years has a distinctive, if not annoying, vegetal, overtly herbaceous character. The 1984 is disappointing; the 1983 soft, rich, fruity, and a lovely wine for drinking over the next decade; the 1982 a sensational Figeac and the best since the property's outstanding 1964. The 1981 is dull, herbaceous, but soft and fruity.

FILHOT (SAUTERNES)* *

1982   ($11.99) 78

1983   ($14.99) 85

This property makes fruity, aromatic, delicate wines that lack a little in power and richness but are attractively elegant. The 1983 is the best in recent vintages.

LA FLEUR GAZIN (POMEROL)* *

1982   ($15.00) 83

The tiny vineyard of La Fleur Gazin produces a rather supple, fruity, uncomplicated style of wine that should be drunk before its sixth or seventh birthday.

LA FLEUR PÉTRUS (POMEROL)* * * *

1981	($25.00)	84
1982	($30.00)	90
1983	($20.00)	86

Although this property has a famous name, it is a much lighter wine than Pétrus; it often shows very elegant, forward flavors and can be drunk quite young. Whether it has the requisite power to last with the great Pomerols is questionable. The 1983 is fruity, very charming, plummy and ready. The 1982 is a bigger, denser wine with a good future ahead of it, and the 1981 soft, a trifle jammy, but very supple and charming.

FOMBRAUGE (ST.-EMILION)* *

1982	($9.99)	82
1983	($9.99)	82

Fombrauge is a very commercial wine that is made to be drunk within its first 4–5 years. It is sold at reasonable prices and has appeal for its forward and fruity flavors.

FONBADET (PAUILLAC)* * *

1982	($19.95)	87
1983	($15.95)	86
1984	($12.95)	72

This rather unknown property in Pauillac makes very intense, chewy, rich wines that have very good style and character. The 1984 is somewhat of a disappointment for Fonbadet—light, rather diluted, and vegetal. The 1983 is quite concentrated, rich, full-bodied, with moderate tannins. The 1982 is a gorgeous wine, with intense blackberry aromas and viscous, rich flavors.

FONPLÉGADE (ST.-EMILION)* * *

1981	($9.95)	82

1982	($15.95)	84

Fonplégade makes uncomplicated, fruity, soft wines that drink well for the first 5–8 years of life. The 1982 is soft and fruity, the 1981 plummy, slightly lighter, but enjoyable.

FONROQUE (ST.-EMILION)* * *

1981	($12.00)	84

1982	($14.00)	84

1983	($15.00)	87

Fonroque has a splendid location in St.-Emilion and is a property to watch carefully since huge efforts have been made to upgrade its quality. The 1983 may be the best Fonroque in over two decades, ripe, rich, full-bodied, lush with plenty of toasty, new oak aromas. The 1982 does not have the same concentration, nor does the more open-knit, lighter 1981. This is a property on the way up.

LES FORTS DE LATOUR (PAUILLAC)* * * *

1975	($30.00)	84

1976	($30.00)	82

1978	($25.00)	90

The second wine of Latour is often as good as some classified growths of Bordeaux. The 1978 is the best Forts de Latour I have ever tasted —rich, complex, with great bouquet and long, rich flavors. The 1976 is beginning to dry out. The 1975 is hard, unyielding, but still showing promise if it ever softens.

FOURCAS-DUPRÉ (LISTRAC)* *

1982	($8.00)	84

1983	($8.00)	80

Fourcas-Dupré is generally reliable and consistent, if usually unexciting, though certain vintages, the 1982 and 1978, have been excellent.

The 1982 shows a great deal of richness and a plump, fat texture. The 1983 is a rather light, short, uninteresting wine.

FOURCAS-HOSTEN (LISTRAC)* * *

1981	($9.00)	84
1982	($9.00)	84
1983	($10.00)	85

Fourcas-Hosten is perhaps the leading vineyard of Listrac. The wine is made in a very intelligent style that combines supple richness and adequate tannin for longevity of 8–10 years. The best recent vintage, the 1983, is a classic, elegantly styled wine with a complex, spicy, richly fruity bouquet and good length. The 1982 is soft and drinkable already, as is the 1981.

LA GAFFELIÈRE (ST.-EMILION)* * *

1981	($15.95)	78
1982	($19.95)	87
1983	($19.95)	86

No one doubts the fabulous location of La Gaffelière, but its track record until 1982 had been one of mediocrity. Since 1982, La Gaffelière seems to be getting serious about turning out high-quality wines. The 1983 and 1982 are a big step in the right direction, fruity, ripe, elegant, not deep or powerful, but well-balanced, graceful wines for drinking at a young age.

LA GARDE (GRAVES)*

1982	($8.99)	75

A soft, fruity, medium-bodied, rather one-dimensional wine that should be drunk young.

GARRAUD (LALANDE-DE-POMEROL)* *

1982	($6.99)	82

1983   ($5.99)   75

This can be a well-made, chunky, robust, often tannic Lalande-de-Pomerol that takes some time to age.

LE GAY (POMEROL)* * * *

1981   ($15.00)   72

1982   ($25.00)   89

1983   ($20.00)   85

Le Gay is a tiny property that makes deep-colored, robust, tannic, backward wines that need cellaring. The 1983 is alcoholic, tannic, but a powerful and ripe wine. It seems a good bet for cellaring. The 1982 is even more powerful, very rich, with a blackberry, earthy, peppery bouquet. The 1981 is disappointing and flawed because of dirty barrels.

GAZIN (POMEROL)* * *

1981   ($20.00)   81

1982   ($20.00)   84

1983   ($19.00)   83

There is no question that the vineyard of Gazin has one of the better locations in Pomerol, but the wine produced has been rather light and uninspiring. Both the 1982 and 1983 are light, supple, and fruity, but not up to the quality one expects given the location of this vineyard and the price charged for the wine.

GILETTE (SAUTERNES)* * * *

1953   ($65.00)   86

1955   ($60.00)   88

1959   ($65.00)   94

Gilette's proprietor does not release his wines until they have had 20–25 years of aging; consequently the vintages that are now available are all from the 1950s. The 1955 is deep golden with a honey bouquet, the 1953 less rich and fat, with a bouquet suggesting melted caramel. The 1959 is extraordinary, a hedonistic symphony of earthly and heavenly delights. These are wines that are unique and remarkably well made.

GISCOURS (MARGAUX)* * * * *

1981	($17.95)	87
1982	($19.95)	87
1983	($19.95)	88
1984	($14.95)	85

The vast estate of Giscours is impeccably managed by the Tari family and the wines are consistently rich and supple, with robust body and fleshiness. They can be especially good in off vintages such as 1984 and 1980. The 1984 is very perfumed, very supple, a notable success. The 1983 is delicious to drink now, will evolve quickly, but offers a silky texture and oodles of fruit. The 1982 is similarly styled but slightly fatter, perhaps not so well balanced overall. The 1981 is a totally charming wine with a supple, graceful fruitiness, and rich, spicy, berry fruit bouquet.

DU GLANA (ST.-JULIEN)* *

1982	($5.99)	83
1983	($5.99)	82
1984	($6.99)	75

Du Glana is a sizable vineyard that had a very spotty record of achievement until 1978. Since then reliable wines have been made. The 1982 is fat, concentrated, full-bodied and supple. The 1983 has been irregular in tasting, but is fruity, soft, and ready to drink.

GLORIA (ST.-JULIEN)* * *

1981	($12.95)	80
1982	($15.95)	85

| 1983 | ($9.99) | 82 |

| 1984 | ($9.99) | 82 |

Gloria has lightened its style of winemaking, but the wine still remains a very stylish, delicious, richly fragrant and fruity wine meant to be drunk young and capable of aging for up to a decade. The 1984 is simple and fruity, the 1983 very spicy and somewhat herbaceous. The 1982 is gloriously fruity, grapy, velvety, and ready to drink. The 1981 is light, supple, and a trifle disappointing for this property.

GOMBAUDE-GUILLOT (POMEROL)* *

| 1982 | ($20.00) | 82 |

This is a middle-of-the road Pomerol that is generally sold to private customers in France. The wine can be good but is rarely exciting.

GRAND-CORBIN-DESPAGNE (ST.-EMILION)* *

| 1982 | ($9.99) | 82 |

| 1983 | ($10.99) | 83 |

A well-situated property that makes a great deal of wine that tends to be rather stern, darkly colored, chunky, and robust in flavor. The 1983 looks quite good.

GRAND-ORMEAU (LALANDE-DE-POMEROL)* * *

| 1982 | ($7.99) | 86 |

| 1983 | ($7.99) | 78 |

Another of the up and coming stars of Lalande-de-Pomerol, this estate made an excellent 1982 that is rich, fruity, and loaded with extract. The unreleased 1985 also looks to be a knockout. These are wines to drink within 5–8 years of the vintage.

GRAND-PUY-DUCASSE (PAUILLAC)* * *

| 1981 | ($9.99) | 82 |

| 1982 | ($14.95) | 86 |

1983   ($12.95)   84

Grand-Puy-Ducasse is one of the most ignored wines in Pauillac, which is rather unfortunate. The wine is made in a style that is supple and easy to drink young. Yet the wines have a way of holding their own for 8–10 years. The 1983 is herbaceous, cedary, silky, attractively fruity and ready. The 1982 is richer, fuller-bodied, but also ripe, round, and will drink well for 5–10 more years. The 1981 is quite light and ready to drink now. For a classified-growth Pauillac, these wines are always fairly priced.

GRAND-PUY-LACOSTE (PAUILLAC)* * * *

1981   ($15.95)   78

1982   ($25.00)   91

1983   ($17.95)   85

1984   ($14.95)   75

Grand-Puy-Lacoste is still not as well known as its quality merits. It has always been a somewhat inconsistent property, but under the current ownership, which has run the property since 1978, the wine has been a textbook Pauillac. Nineteen eighty-four is good but rather simple. The 1983, a tannic, somewhat angular wine, has yet to show its full pleasures. The 1982 is a stupendous vintage for Grand-Puy-Lacoste, with a great intensity of fruit, very dark color, and a huge aroma, even though it will not be ready to drink for 10 years. The 1981 is very light, rather elegant, but soft and ready to drink.

LA GRAVE FIGEAC (ST.-EMILION)* * * *

1982   ($9.95)   87

1983   ($9.95)   89

This is a tiny gem of a property located right next to Cheval Blanc that produces only 1500 cases per year. The wines are rich, fragrant, and very, very concentrated. The 1983 is absolutely sensational, with lots of ripe blackberry fruit, and the 1982 nearly as good with a lusher, more opulent texture.

LA GRAVE TRIGANT DE BOISSET (POMEROL)* * *

1981	($17.00)	83
1982	($20.00)	88
1983	($20.00)	86

The personal property of Christian Moueix, the brilliant winemaker of Pétrus and other major Pomerols, La Grave Trigant sits on lighter soil and produces a very fruity, more elegant wine than some of the larger-scaled Pomerols from better-situated vineyards. It is a wine that has gotten better and better as the vineyard has gotten older. The 1983 is a big, richly fruity wine, the 1982 is gorgeously ripe, richly scented with significant power for La Grave Trigant. The 1981 is elegant and a wine more of finesse than power. This is certainly a Pomerol to drink young, before its tenth birthday, but also one to watch as the vineyard gets older.

GRESSIER GRAND-POUJEAUX (MOULIS)* *

1981	($10.00)	81
1982	($10.00)	83

This tiny estate in Moulis makes good but not exciting wines. The 1982 shows good body and depth and potential for improvement of 4–5 years.

GREYSAC (MÉDOC)* * *

1981	($5.99)	80
1982	($6.99)	82
1983	($6.99)	83

One of America's most popular Cru Bourgeois wines, Greysac combines suppleness and elegant complexity and consistency even in weaker vintages. The 1983 needs a few years to soften, the 1982 is plump, quite soft and ripe, and the 1981 a little light for Greysac. This wine is capable of aging in good vintages for 5–8 years.

GRUAUD-LAROSE (ST.-JULIEN)* * * * *

1981	($19.95)	88
1982	($35.00)	96
1983	($24.95)	90
1984	($13.95)	84

Gruaud-Larose produces a tremendous amount of wine and is probably St.-Julien's most popular wine. Its style is big, richly fruity, and full-bodied. The 1984 is a chunky wine with very good flavor, not much complexity, but satisfying palate impressions. The 1983, one of the top wines of the vintage, is a deep, plummy wine with an excellent extract of fruit, and very dark color for the vintage. The 1982 is a massive, incredibly rich and concentrated wine that is extremely tannic and should live for 30 or more years. It's one of the greatest wines Gruaud-Larose has ever made. The 1981, another top success for the vintage, is dark in color, with a full-intensity bouquet of ripe blackcurrants, spicy oak, plums, and tarry scents.

GUIRAUD (SAUTERNES)* * *

1981	($17.95)	85
1982	($17.95)	78
1983	($17.95)	88

One of the larger estates of Sauternes, now run by an ambitious Canadian, the wines of Guiraud bear watching as the quality seems to get better with each vintage. The best current release is the marvelous 1983, which has excellent balance and a full-bodied, lush, rich fruitiness.

LA GURGUE (MARGAUX)* * *

1982	($9.99)	85
1983	($9.99)	87

This superb little property in the village of Margaux is making itself noticed because of its rich, ripe, intense style of wine. The 1982 is very good, but the 1983 is a superior wine, with an intense, blackcurrant, chocolatey fruitiness and plenty of quality and tannin. This is an up and coming star.

HANTEILLAN (MÉDOC)* *

1982	($8.99)	75
1983	($8.99)	77

There is a great deal of effort being made at Hanteillan, but to date the wines have continued to be rather lean and cleanly made, and lack intensity and charm. However, I am convinced this is a property to keep an eye out for.

HAUT-BAGES-LIBÉRAL (PAUILLAC)* * *

1982	($14.99)	87
1983	($12.99)	87
1984	($9.99)	80

Haut-Bages-Libéral is one of Pauillac's best kept secrets and great values. The wine is easy to understand, rich, and, since the mid-'70s, increasingly well made. The 1984 is above average in quality and ready to drink, the 1983 is a big, brash, aggressive wine with intense color and excellent ripeness. The 1982 is very similarly styled, a voluptuous, silky wine that will drink well for the next 5–6 years.

HAUT-BAILLY (GRAVES)* * * *

1981	($14.95)	84
1982	($19.95)	87
1983	($15.99)	85
1984	($10.99)	78

Haut-Bailly produces one of the lightest Graves wines that may at first seem to lack power and richness but has an uncommon elegance and finesse. Many of the vintages in the '70s turned out very poorly due to the declining health of the former owner. Since 1979 the property has been in full form, making wines that are voluptuous, ripe, and easy to drink young. The 1982, 1983, and 1985 are the best recent vintages.

HAUT-BATAILLEY (PAUILLAC)* * *

1981	($15.95)	83
1982	($25.00)	86
1983	($14.95)	84
1984	($12.95)	77

This Pauillac sits on the border of St.-Julien and perhaps because of this is a lighter, more elegant, yet very fragrant, silky style of wine. The 1984 is light and not very substantial, but clean and pleasant if drunk young. The 1983 is good, rather soft, with decent concentration. The 1982 started life promisingly but is now in a rather awkward, closed stage and one will have to wait another 4–5 years to see its real potential. The 1981 is quite silky, velvety, and ready to drink.

HAUT-BRION (RED) (GRAVES)* * * * *

1981	($45.00)	84
1982	($130.00)	96
1983	($55.00)	88
1984	($45.00)	87

The only official first-growth of Graves (and American-owned as well), Haut-Brion makes magnificently elegant, early to mature wines that have a way of lasting in the bottle longer than most people think. They develop very characteristic tobacco smells with age. The 1984 is one of the top successes of this vintage, with an open-knit fruitiness and lush flavors. The 1983 is rather light and elegant but very forward and should be fully mature in 3–4 years. The 1982 is Haut-Brion's best since the great 1959: densely colored, with a gorgeous bouquet and long, lush, intense flavors. The 1981 is a bit light, angular, and lean for a first-growth.

HAUT-BRION (WHITE) (GRAVES)* * * * *

1983	($65.00)	84
1984	($60.00)	87

| 1985 | ($65.00) | 90 |

The tiny production of Haut-Brion's white wine (around 1,500 cases in a good vintage) guarantees a high price for the wine. In vintages such as 1985 it is well worth its price since the wine is rich, distinctive and capable of 15–20 years' longevity. In other years, 1983 for example, it is not worth its high price.

HAUT BRISSON (ST.-EMILION)* * *

| 1982 | ($9.99) | 84 |
| 1983 | ($9.99) | 84 |

This vineyard, planted on very gravelly soil and using a high percentage of Merlot, produces ripe, stylish, fruity, moderately concentrated, cleanly made wines. Both the 1982 and 1983 will provide delicious drinking over the next 4–5 years.

HAUT-CHATAIN (LALANDE-DE-POMEROL)* *

| 1982 | ($8.49) | 84 |
| 1983 | ($8.49) | 65 |

Haut-Chatain made a wonderful, fruity, delicious, complex 1982, but a disappointing 1983. The as yet unreleased 1985 is also poor.

HAUT-MARBUZET (ST.-ESTÈPHE)* * * *

1981	($11.95)	85
1982	($25.00)	92
1983	($14.95)	88
1984	($9.99)	78

Haut-Marbuzet is an immensely popular wine because it is a unique tasting experience. Aged in 100% new oak barrels, it has an opulent, almost overwhelming intensity that appeals to those who love powerful, rich, extroverted wines. The 1984 is a somewhat disappointing wine for Haut-Marbuzet; however, the 1983 is ripe, plummy, fat— simply a hedonistic drinking experience. The 1982 is a ravishing, decadently rich wine with extraordinary concentration and the potential to live for another 7–8 years. The 1981 is another intriguing Haut-Marbuzet, deeply colored, ripe, spicy, very oaky, but loaded with fruit.

HAUT PLANTEY (ST.-EMILION)* *

1982	($9.99)	84
1983	($9.99)	84

A typical, uncomplicated style of St.-Emilion, with a fat, plummy, chewy texture and good concentration in the top vintages.

HAUT-SARPE (ST.-EMILION)* * *

1981	($12.95)	83
1982	($12.95)	85

This is another rustic, rather generously flavored, firm St.-Emilion that needs 3–4 years to show its best. The 1982 has aromas and flavors of ripe blackberry fruit with good tannin, while the 1981 is rather lean and medium-bodied.

HAUT SOCIANDO (CÔTES DE BLAYE)* *

1982	($5.99)	82
1983	($5.99)	78

A very good Côtes de Blaye property that can excel in the really good vintages such as 1982 and 1985.

HORTEVIE (ST.-JULIEN)* * *

1982	($10.99)	86
1983	($9.99)	85

Hortevie is a selection of the oldest part of the vineyard of Terrey-Gros-Cailloux and shares with it much the same character—a silky, lush, rich, jammy quality, although Hortevie, since it is made from older vines, has more depth and richness.

D'ISSAN (MARGAUX)* * * *

1981	($12.99)	86
1982	($15.99)	86
1983	($19.95)	88
1984	($12.95)	78

One of the prettier châteaux in Bordeaux, d'Issan produces a very elegant, plummy, supple wine that has plenty of appeal and, of all wines, tends to remind me of Palmer. The 1984 is light, but clean and destined to be drunk very young. The 1983 is one of d'Issan's most impressive recent efforts, with rich, cherry, fruity flavors and a lush texture. The 1982 is spicy and earthy, and displays good black cherry fruit. The 1981 is ready to drink with an oaky, plummy bouquet, and soft, light tannins in the finish.

KIRWAN (MARGAUX)* * *

1981	($14.95)	78
1982	($18.95)	84
1983	($14.95)	85
1984	($9.95)	84

An underachiever in Margaux for most of the '60s and '70s, Kirwan's wines of the '80s have taken on a higher quality as a result of an extensive rehabilitation program begun in the early 1970s. The 1984 is a success, with supple, spicy fruit. The 1983 is one of the best Kirwans: rich, tannic, with very good length. The 1982 is charming, with a very precocious personality, and the 1981 is sound but uninspiring.

LABÉGORCE (MARGAUX)* *

1982	($12.95)	82
1983	($9.99)	75

Labégorce produces rather light but fragrant, typical Margaux wines that offer good value. The 1982 is particularly supple, fruity, and distinctive. The 1983 is rather unexciting for a Margaux.

LABÉGORCE-ZÉDÉ (MARGAUX)* * *

1981	($9.95)	82
1982	($9.95)	86
1983	($14.95)	87

Labégorce-Zédé produces solid, plump, chunky, flavorful wines. The 1983 is excellent, rich, full-bodied, and long on the palate. The 1982 is very similarly styled. The 1981 is a little light, but elegant.

LAFAURIE-PEYRAGUEY (SAUTERNES)* * * *

1981	($25.00)	89
1982	($25.00)	87
1983	($25.00)	92

Owned by the Cordier family, this is the least known of the great wines of Sauternes, but due to a concentrated effort to improve the quality, the vintages of the '80s have been nothing short of spectacular, topped by the fabulous and fantastic apricot-flavored, unctuous 1983, a delicious, fresh, lively, stunningly balanced 1982, and an exceptionally rich, intense 1981.

LAFITE-ROTHSCHILD (PAUILLAC)* * * * *

1981	($60.00)	92
1982	($160.00)	96
1983	($65.00)	88
1984	($60.00)	84

Bordeaux's most famous wine, Lafite-Rothschild, is among the most elegant and lightest of all the famous wines of Bordeaux. Its reputation rests on its fabulous bouquet rather than on the power and intensity of its flavors. For that reason, it can often be disappointing and too light in poor years. The 1984, though good, is hardly worth the price. The 1983 is still a very tannic, closed wine, and has not aged so well as I would like. The 1982, along with the 1975, is the best Lafite since '59, a powerful, rich, fabulous wine with a great bouquet and decades of evolution ahead. The 1981 is another classic Lafite with a fabulous bouquet and rich, complex, elegant flavors.

LAFLEUR (POMEROL)* * * * *

1981	($30.00)	78
1982	($100.00)	95
1983	($50.00)	90

Lafleur is the only wine in Pomerol capable of matching the power and majesty of Pétrus in certain vintages. The 1983 is an even more powerful and rich wine than Pétrus. The 1982 is an enormous wine with great potential and depth, and the 1981 a somewhat flawed, very inconsistent wine that has turned out disappointingly.

LAFON-ROCHET (ST.-ESTÈPHE)* * *

1982	($15.99)	85
1983	($11.99)	86
1984	($8.99)	82

Lafon-Rochet gets little publicity these days, but the wine can be very good and often a good value. The 1984 is attractively fruity and well-colored for the vintage. The 1983 is quite backward, very tannic, and in need of long-term cellaring. The 1982 is not as impressive as it should be given the vintage, but has plenty of ripe, lush, fat flavors and a good measure of tannin.

LAGRANGE (POMEROL)* *

1982	($20.00)	84
1983	($18.00)	78

Lagrange is a rarely seen Pomerol that produces rather hard, burly wines with plenty of body and tannin but little charm. Both the 1982 and 1983 are typical.

LAGRANGE (ST.-JULIEN)* * *

| 1981 | ($9.99) | 78 |

| 1982 | ($25.00) | 84 |

| 1983 | ($20.00) | 86 |

| 1984 | ($15.00) | 85 |

Lagrange has suffered numerous blows to its reputation because of its poor track record in the '60s and '70s. However, the property looks to have a brilliant future since it is now owned by a Japanese firm that has pumped tremendous amounts of money and expertise into the property. The 1984 is a good wine for the vintage: chunky, tannic, well colored. The 1983 is surprisingly rich and long, and is certainly one of the top values of that vintage. The 1982, less successful than 1983 at Lagrange, is a big wine, but a little awkward.

LA LAGUNE (LUDON)* * * * *

| 1981 | ($17.95) | 83 |

| 1982 | ($30.00) | 92 |

| 1983 | ($19.95) | 87 |

| 1984 | ($17.95) | 87 |

La Lagune is one of Bordeaux's shining success stories. From virtual obscurity in the late 1950s and early 1960s, La Lagune has become in 25 years one of the most conscientiously run properties, making top-quality wine consistently in all vintages. The style of wine is rich and fleshy, with a sometimes overpowering bouquet of oak and plummy fruit. Nineteen eighty-four is an outstanding success in this vintage, with ripe, rich, plummy fruit. The 1983 suffers only in comparison with the incredible 1982, which the château believes is the greatest wine it has ever made. The 1981 is a plummy, cherry-flavored wine that is medium-bodied and ready to drink now.

LALANDE BORIE (ST.-JULIEN)* * *

1982	($12.99)	85
1983	($9.99)	84

The highly respected Jean-Eugène Borie produces this wine from a young vineyard planted in 1971–72. The 1982 is dense and gorgeously colored with deep flavors. The 1983 is tannic and more angular.

LAMARQUE (HAUT-MÉDOC)* *

1982	($6.99)	82
1983	($6.99)	78

Lamarque is one of the prettier and more interesting châteaux in the Médoc. The wines are made in an elegant, light style, to be drunk within the first 6–7 years. The 1983 is light, somewhat herbaceous, and the 1982 is supple, fruity, and ready to drink.

LANESSAN (HAUT-MÉDOC)* * *

1981	($9.99)	78
1982	($12.00)	86
1983	($10.00)	83

Lanessan produces wine of a big, rich, gutsy style that often lacks finesse but more than compensates for that deficiency with plenty of power and flavor authority. The 1982 is the best recent vintage, a powerful, unique wine of great color and depth on the palate. The 1983 is a little disjointed and needs several years of aging. The 1981 is light for a Lanessan and fully mature.

LANGOA-BARTON (ST.-JULIEN)* * * *

1981	($15.95)	84
1982	($19.95)	88
1983	($17.95)	85

| 1984 | ($14.95) | 78 |

Langoa-Barton is an impressive château sitting directly on the heavily traveled Route du Vin in the Médoc. It shares its cellar with Léoville-Barton, which has no château or winemaking facilities. The wine is very traditionally made, easily taking years to show its true character. The 1984 is an uninspiring wine, but flavorful and drinkable over the next several years. The 1983 is tannic and rather angular; good, but not special. The 1982 looks to be one of the best in the last several decades, with its rich, intense bouquet and big, tough, full-bodied framework. The 1981 is spicy and ready to drink, but will not be long-lived.

LARCIS-DUCASSE (ST.-EMILION)* *

1981	($12.95)	75
1982	($12.95)	80
1983	($12.95)	72

A well-respected property, well situated on the Côtes of St.-Emilion. The wines have yet to make an impression, though a 1945 drunk several years ago was remarkable. The wines are light and simple.

LARMANDE (ST.-EMILION)* * * *

1981	($9.95)	83
1982	($14.95)	86
1983	($15.95)	87

This is a relatively unknown yet up and coming estate in St.-Emilion that should be sought out for its high-quality wines. The 1983 is rich, full-bodied, deep and lush, the 1982 very, very similar in style, and the 1981 the lightest and most elegant of these three vintages, with a slightly more herbaceous bouquet. Also keep an eye out for the 1985, which showed enormous potential from the cask.

LAROSE-TRINTAUDON (HAUT-MÉDOC)* * *

1982	($8.99)	84
1983	($8.99)	84

This huge vineyard in the Médoc produces over 65,000 cases of wine in a very silky, supple, intelligent style that shows well young but can also age for 5–8 years. The wine is always clean and fruity, with a certain spiciness to it. Both the 1982 and 1983 are very good values and attractive wines for drinking over the next 4–5 years.

LASCOMBES (MARGAUX)* * * *

1981	($12.95)	74
1982	($19.95)	87
1983	($17.95)	87
1984	($12.95)	83

One of the largest estates in the Médoc, Lascombes has produced many great vintages in the 1950s and 1960s, but then in the '70s fell from grace with a succession of mediocre wines. However, since 1982 the property has been back on track. The 1984 is a lovely, plummy, spicy, supple wine for drinking soon. The 1983 is quite an impressive wine, with deep intensity of flavors and a rich, spicy, berrylike aroma. The 1982 is similarly styled, perhaps slightly deeper and fatter on the palate. Nineteen eighty-one is the last of a poor line of Lascombes wines that began with the 1976.

LATOUR (PAUILLAC)* * * * *

1981	($60.00)	90
1982	($125.00)	98
1983	($65.00)	90
1984	($40.00)	88

Latour is one of France's and the world's greatest wines, known for its remarkable longevity and majestic richness. The 1984 is a successful wine that will develop fast. The 1983 is much more evolved and ready to drink than one usually expects of a Latour, but it is excellent. The 1982, the best Latour since the 1961, is incredibly deep and rich, and is very, very tannic. The 1981, an elegant, complex, silky Latour, will also mature quite quickly.

LATOUR À POMEROL (POMEROL)* * * * *

1981	($35.00)	87
1982	($40.00)	93
1983	($20.00)	90

Another of the outstanding Pomerols that is hard to find and expensive as well. The 1983 is a muscular, brawny, big, ripe wine with plenty of tannin to carry it into the next century. The 1982 is even more powerful, decadently rich and multidimensional with explosive fruit, and the 1981 supple, rich, elegant, and drinking beautifully now.

LAVILLE-HAUT-BRION (WHITE) (GRAVES)* * * * *

1983	($55.00)	92
1984	($65.00)	86
1985	($65.00)	90

Arguably the greatest dry white wine produced in Bordeaux, Laville-Haut-Brion can easily age and improve for 15–20 years in the bottle. The last three vintages have been superb: a great, rich, deep 1985, a fragrant, early to mature 1984, and a splendidly rich, long, honeyed, dense 1983.

LÉOVILLE-BARTON (ST.-JULIEN)* * * * *

1981	($15.95)	78
1982	($19.95)	93
1983	($15.95)	86
1984	($10.99)	84

The late Ronald Barton was one of Bordeaux's great personalities and since he passed away the winemaking and management of the very traditionally made Léoville-Barton has been run by his nephew, Anthony Barton. This is a wine that has as much of the character of a Pauillac as it does a St.-Julien. The 1984 is good, with a cedary, spicy, blackcurrant bouquet. The 1983 seems hard and in need of at least 5–6 years of cellaring to develop. The 1982 is a great wine and one of the best that Léoville-Barton has made in the last three decades. It is a big wine and will take 10 years to develop further. The 1981 is good, but not special in this vintage. The unreleased 1985 should propel this estate into the same league as such stars of St.-Julien as Ducru-Beaucaillou, Léoville-Las Cases, and Gruaud-Larose.

LÉOVILLE-LAS CASES (ST.-JULIEN)* * * * *

1981	($19.95)	88
1982	($55.00)	99
1983	($29.95)	90
1984	($20.95)	86

One of the great wines of Bordeaux, the wines of Léoville-Las Cases are in demand the world over. They are very slow to develop and in the great vintages behave like the best first-growths—possessing majestic depth of flavor and remarkable tannins for longevity. The 1984 is quite a successful wine for the vintage and can be drunk over the next 5–6 years for its round fruitiness. The 1983 is also a top success in an irregular vintage. It is quite tannic and backward, shows a very classic cedary bouquet and very ripe flavors. In 1982 this property made a monumental wine that its owner, Michel Delon, feels is the greatest wine he could ever possibly make. It is extraordinary in its flavors and richness, but will not be ready to drink before the turn of the century. The 1981 is a very elegant rendition of Las Cases. It has a spicy, oaky, berryish bouquet and long, ripe flavors.

LÉOVILLE-POYFERRÉ (ST.-JULIEN)* * * *

1981	($15.95)	81
1982	($25.00)	92
1983	($19.95)	87

1984   ($15.95)   75

Léoville-Poyferré has long been considered to have one of the greatest
vineyards in all of the Médoc. The problem has been one of unrealized
potential. However, things in the '80s have improved considerably,
with the 1982 being a really great wine and the best that this property
has made in over three decades. The 1983, which was so promising
from the cask, seems extremely hard and tannic and needs at least 7–
10 years to prove its quality. The 1984 has turned out to be rather
shallow, but adequate. The 1981 is soft, jammy, and lacking in complexity.

LESTAGE (LISTRAC)* *

1982   ($5.99)   82

1983   ($5.99)   80

Both vintages produced very fruity, supple, straightforward wines that
are meant to be drunk within their first 4–5 years of life.

LIVERSAN (MÉDOC)* * *

1982   ($9.99)   84

1983   ($9.99)   82

Liversan is one of the up and coming Crus Bourgeois of the Médoc
and its owners are giving it a great deal of attention, both financially
and personally. The 1983 is rather soft, yet elegant, fruity, and easy
to drink. The 1982 is a bit richer and more multidimensional.

LOUDENNE (RED) (MÉDOC)* *

1982   ($9.99)   83

1983   ($9.99)   80

The showpiece château of the northern Médoc produces very light,
picnic-styled claret for drinking young. The 1982 is the best of recent
vintages since it shows a bit more richness and flesh than one normally
finds in this wine.

LA LOUVIÈRE (RED) (GRAVES)* * *

1982	($10.99)	86
1983	($9.99)	87
1984	($9.99)	79

La Louvière is making great progress in the southern part of the Graves area, producing very supple, rich, gloriously fruity and fleshy wines of considerable character. Nineteen eighty-four is satisfactory; however, the 1983 and 1982 are both rich, with wonderful ripeness, balance, concentration, and aging potential of 5–10 years.

LA LOUVIÈRE (WHITE) (GRAVES)* * * *

1983	($11.99)	87
1984	($9.99)	84
1985	($11.99)	86

La Louvière shows equal ability with its fleshy, ripe, fruity white wines that are made in a style perfect for drinking young. The 1985 and 1983 are both top successes.

LYNCH-BAGES (PAUILLAC)* * * * *

1981	($17.95)	85
1982	($25.00)	93
1983	($20.00)	90
1984	($19.95)	87

Lynch-Bages is one of the Médoc's most popular wines. Impressively colored, hefty, full-bodied, and savory, it is always a satisfying wine. The last several vintages have been extremely strong for Lynch-Bages, including a very fragrant, supple, rich 1984, a ripe, big, full-blown, substantial 1983, a super-concentrated, extroverted, intense 1982, and a great (not yet released) 1985. The 1981 is the lightest of the above quartet of wines, but is rich in blackcurrant fruit and is ready to drink.

MAGDELAINE (ST.-EMILION)* * * *

1981	($18.95)	80
1982	($45.00)	90
1983	($29.99)	85

Althought Magdelaine does not produce a lot of wine, there is a great deal of demand for it among knowledgeable connoisseurs. It tends to be a very slow to evolve wine despite the fact that it is made from over 80% Merlot. It is also rather expensive. The 1983 has been an incredibly inconsistent though certainly very good wine. It is quite tannic and closed. The 1982 is powerful, rich, deep, and opulent and the 1981 lean, overly oaky, and lacking in fruit.

MAISON BLANCHE (MONTAGNE-ST.-EMILION)* * *

1981	($8.99)	82
1982	($8.99)	85

A top estate in Montagne-St.-Emilion, this property made a delicious 1982 with excellent power and ripeness.

MALARTIC-LAGRAVIÈRE (RED) (GRAVES)* *

1982	($15.95)	84
1983	($15.95)	80

This property tends to make better white wine than red, but the red has a likable ripe cherry fruitiness, moderately intense flavors, and rather light to medium body. The 1982 is the best recent vintage.

MALARTIC-LAGRAVIÈRE (WHITE) (GRAVES)* * * *

1983	($17.95)	85
1984	($15.95)	84
1985	($15.95)	84

This property produces very fresh, lively, crisp, lighter-styled white wines with a distinctively pungent, herbaceous bouquet. The 1983 looks to be the best in the last three vintages.

MALESCOT ST.-EXUPÉRY (MARGAUX)* * *

1981	($15.95)	78
1982	($19.95)	85
1983	($17.95)	83
1984	($12.95)	80

Malescot St.-Exupéry has always had an excellent reputation for making very long-lived, traditional, firm, hard wines. However, they have never fared particularly well in my tastings. The 1984 and 1981 are rather light and lack charm and flesh. The 1983, though good, is not one of the leaders in a vintage that was extremely successful in the Margaux region. The 1982 is round, lusciously fruity, but not so deep as other top wines from this vintage.

CHÂTEAU MARGAUX (MARGAUX)* * * * *

1981	($45.00)	92
1982	($100.00)	98
1983	($85.00)	98
1984	($40.00)	90

After a period of mediocrity in the '60s and '70s, the wines of Château Margaux, since 1978, have been as grand as any in Bordeaux. One wonders how such greatness at this high level can continue to be maintained. The 1984 is one of the top two wines of the vintage, rich, intense, and surprisingly dark-colored given the year. The 1983 is the wine of the vintage, with a remarkable aroma of violets, ripe cassis fruit, and vanillin oakiness; it will develop for at least another 15–20 years. The 1982, another celestial wine, is creamier and fuller-bodied than normal for Margaux, and extremely rich and intense. The 1981 is lighter, but only in comparison to recent vintages from Margaux. It is a fabulous wine with an exceptional bouquet and great class and finesse.

MARQUIS D'ALESME-BECKER (MARGAUX)* *

1982	($15.95)	83

1983	($9.95)	85

This wine is rarely seen in America and although it is well colored it often tastes rather simple and one-dimensional. The 1983 is the most recent top success, with a rich and solid texture and very good length. The 1982 is solid and reliable, but not complex.

MARQUIS-DE-TERME (MARGAUX)* * *

1982	($15.95)	84

1983	($15.95)	82

This is another wine that is rarely seen in American commercial channels but is widely available in Europe, particularly in the Benelux countries. The 1983 is chunky and fruity, but lacks finesse. The 1982 shows a bit more depth and a fragrant, precocious, soft texture.

MAUCAILLOU (MOULIS)* * *

1981	($9.99)	83

1982	($15.99)	86

1983	($12.99)	83

Maucaillou in Moulis is a wine made in an early-maturing style, but it offers a savory, supple character and relatively complex, fragrant bouquet. The 1981 and 1983 are good wines, but the 1982 is very rich, quite deeply flavored, and undoubtedly a great buy in a vintage that has become very expensive because of worldwide demand.

MAZERIS (CANON-FRONSAC)* * *

1982	($5.99)	83

1983	($5.99)	80

This is a forceful, aggressive, dense, chunky, tannic wine that can excel. The unreleased 1985 is excellent.

MEYNEY (ST.-ESTÈPHE)* * *

1981	($10.99)	85
1982	($14.99)	87
1983	($9.99)	85
1984	($8.99)	82

Meyney is an extremely large property and one of the most reliable wines in Bordeaux. Shrewd consumers have been beating a path to Meyney for years, knowing of the fine value of the wines and their potential for 15–20 years of longevity. The 1984 is a surprisingly elegant, deeply colored wine for the vintage. The 1983 is extremely successful, with rich, ripe, deep flavors. The 1982 is jammy, very intense, very full-bodied, and will take at least 10 years to mature. The 1981 is delicate, elegant, and attractive for early drinking.

LA MISSION-HAUT-BRION (GRAVES)* * * * *

1981	($55.00)	90
1982	($65.00)	96
1983	($45.00)	89
1984	($35.00)	86

One of the greatest wines of Bordeaux, La Mission-Haut-Brion is first-growth in quality, if not in name. It is always a big, rich, powerful wine that has had remarkable consistency in even the worst Bordeaux vintages over the last four decades. The 1984 is quite attractive and rich, with a big, tobacco-scented bouquet. The 1983 is full-bodied, rather tannic, and more austere than usual, the 1982 a monumental bottle of rich, intense, fruity flavors, and a very long evolution ahead of it. The 1981 is rather elegant, but quite well balanced, fairly rich and powerful for a 1981, and impressively long on the palate.

MONBOUSQUET (ST.-EMILION)* *

1982	($7.99)	78
1983	($7.99)	80

This large estate is owned by the amiable Querre family that makes very commercial yet fruity, supple, delicious wines. Both the 1982 and 1983 were mediocre and not up to some of the previous vintages.

MONTROSE (ST.-ESTÈPHE)* * * *

1981	($16.95)	84
1982	($24.95)	87
1983	($19.95)	83
1984	($14.95)	83

Montrose is one of the best kept and best situated vineyards in all of the Médoc. However, the style since 1978 has changed from a huge, massive, tannic wine to a rather elegant, lighter style that is still quite attractive but a disappointment to the old Montrose fans. The 1984 is a success for the vintage and is ready to drink. The 1983 is rather medium-bodied and light for Montrose, but attractive and elegant. The 1982, probably the best Montrose since the 1970, is a rich, full-bodied wine with an unctuous texture. The 1981 is ready to drink, light, fruity, and very pleasant.

MOULIN DES CARRUADES (PAUILLAC)* *

1981	($19.95)	82
1982	($19.95)	83

The second wine of Lafite-Rothschild is not nearly so attractive as its name might suggest. The wine tends to be rather light and not so impressive as the second wines of some other notable first-growths, Latour's Forts de Latour or Château Margaux's Pavillon Rouge de Margaux, to name two.

MOULINET (POMEROL)*

1982	($12.00)	75
1983	($10.00)	72

Moulinet produces a very light, rather unsubstantial Pomerol that is faintly perfumed and very commercial in style. At its best it is round, fruity, and elegant, but it is generally rather bland.

MOUTON-BARONNE-PHILIPPE (PAUILLAC)* * *

1982	($14.95)	86
1983	($14.95)	85
1984	($14.95)	75

Mouton-Baronne-Philippe's 1984 is light and lacking in concentration. The 1983 is more amply proportioned and noticeably richer and fruitier on the palate. The 1982 is the best effort recently, with a rich, cedary, blackcurrant bouquet, and long, rich, full-bodied flavors.

MOUTON-ROTHSCHILD (PAUILLAC)* * * * *

1981	($45.00)	88
1982	($150.00)	100
1983	($60.00)	92
1984	($40.00)	89

Mouton-Rothschild is the brilliant wine that has been produced for over six decades by the Baron Philippe de Rothschild. Like its owner, it is a flamboyant, extroverted wine that, in great vintages, has no equal. The 1984 is an outstanding success for the vintage. Ripe, exotic, and rich, it is delicious already. The 1983 is also an exotic wine that should mature rather rapidly and is very fine. The 1982 is perhaps the single greatest young wine this writer has ever tasted, and certainly a wine of legendary proportions. Don't touch it until 1995 or later. The 1981 is light for Mouton, but elegant, stylish, and ready to drink now.

NAIRAC (BARSAC)* * *

1981	($9.99)	83
1982	($11.99)	84
1983	($15.95)	87

This is a meticulously and passionately operated Barsac estate making better and better wines as time goes on. The 1983 is powerful and rich, the 1982 has a spicy, pineapple and vanillin bouquet and flavors, and the 1981 is plump, fat, but perhaps a little dull.

NENIN (POMEROL)* *

1982	($20.00)	70
1983	($15.95)	72
1984	($15.00)	75

Nenin has always produced a rustic-style Pomerol, but the early vintages of the '80s have looked increasingly poor, except for the unreleased 1985, which exhibits the kind of richness and style one expects from this property.

OLIVIER (RED) (GRAVES)*

1982	($12.99)	78
1983	($9.99)	72

The wines here are no better than a mediocre shipper's blend—light, innocuous, and lacking richness and character.

LES-ORMES-DE-PEZ (ST.-ESTÈPHE)* * *

1981	($8.99)	82
1982	($14.99)	87
1983	($8.99)	84
1984	($8.99)	84

Le Ormes-de-Pez is one of Bordeaux's most popular wines; it is made by the owner of Lynch-Bages. It is a supple, very fruity, fragrant, delicious wine to drink young, yet it has the uncanny ability to age well. The 1984 is a top success in this vintage. The 1983 is fat, ripe, round, and very fruity; the 1982 is deep, seductive, very soft in the finish, but will last well; the 1981 is the least successful of the last four vintages. It is always a good value.

LES ORMES-SORBET (MÉDOC)* *

1982	($8.99)	82

This is always a rather one-dimensional but solid, well-colored wine lacking finesse but possessing good richness and a chunky, satisfying feel on the palate.

PALMER (MARGAUX)* * * * *

1981	($20.00)	82
1982	($30.00)	86
1983	($35.00)	94
1984	($19.95)	82

Until the resurgence of Château Margaux, Palmer was usually the finest wine made in the Margaux appellation. Although it now takes a back seat to the greatness of Margaux, Palmer can be an exceptional wine. The vintages in the '80s have not been among the great Palmer successes except for the fabulous 1983. The 1984 is light, straightforward, supple, and fruity. The 1983 is a powerful, deep, concentrated, chewy wine with a fabulous bouquet. The 1982, from a legendary vintage, is not as good as it should be, but it does offer precocious, fat, oaky flavors and early maturity. The 1981 is also good, but given Palmer's level of quality, somewhat of a disappointment.

PAPE-CLÉMENT (GRAVES)* * *

1981	($14.95)	68
1982	($19.95)	68
1983	($19.95)	75

1984   ($16.95)   80

One of the best placed vineyards in all of Graves, Pape-Clément made fabulous wines in the '50s and '60s and then fell on hard times due to neglect in the '70s, particularly after the 1975 vintage. The above vintages are all rather poor and not representative of what this property can produce. Look for the unreleased excellent 1985 that will resurrect the reputation of Pape-Clément and begin to put this property back in the forefront of Graves.

PATACHE D'AUX (MÉDOC)* * *

1981   ($6.99)   73

1982   ($6.99)   84

1983   ($6.99)   84

Patache d'Aux makes a solid, firm wine that in 1982 and 1983 resembles a California Cabernet with its olive-scented, rich, blackcurrant bouquet. The 1981 is rather meagerly endowed, but both the 1982 and 1983 are rich, medium- to full-bodied wines with lots of character.

PAVIE (ST.-EMILION)* * *

1981   ($16.95)   83

1982   ($25.00)   89

1983   ($16.95)   86

1984   ($15.95)   80

Pavie produces elegant, fruity, attractive wines with a great deal of style. While the 1984 is ready to drink and rather light, 1983 is backward and tannic, and the 1982 uncommonly rich and full for Pavie. The most recent typical vintage for Pavie may be the 1981, which is classy and complex and has a bouquet of ripe cherries.

PAVIE-DECESSE (ST.-EMILION)* * *

1982   ($15.95)   86

1983   ($11.99)   86

| 1984 | ($9.99) | 77 |

This tiny vineyard behind and further up the hill from Pavie is making better and better wines with each vintage. The 1984, from a terrible vintage, is light and slightly herbaceous. The 1983 is tannic, rich, tough and brawny, the 1982 lush and full-bodied, with an excellent extract of fruit.

PAVILLON ROUGE DE MARGAUX (MARGAUX)* * * *

1978	($19.99)	85
1979	($19.99)	86
1981	($19.99)	87
1982	($19.99)	87

The second wine of Margaux, Pavillon Rouge is a supple, fragrant, ripe, very seductive wine that is released only by the château when they deem it ready to drink. The first four vintages released have all shown well, with much of the character of the "grand vin." Expect these wines to drink well for 5–8 years.

PETIT-VILLAGE (POMEROL)* * *

1981	($15.95)	84
1982	($19.99)	89
1983	($16.99)	85

The highly respected Bruno Prats owns this château and has improved the quality dramatically in the '80s. The 1981 is fully mature, elegant, and very supple and fruity. The 1982 has an explosive bouquet of blackberry fruit and spicy oak. It should be fully mature by 1989–90. The 1983 is chunky, not complex, but very satisfying, round, and ready to drink.

PÉTRUS (POMEROL)* * * * *

| 1981 | ($130.00) | 95 |
| 1982 | ($250.00) | 100 |

1983	($125.00)	89

1984	($100.00)	84

Pétrus, in the short 35 years since it was first introduced to the United States, has become the most expensive and sought after red wine, not only in France but in the world. Its character is one of great, concentrated intensity of flavor that comes from being made primarily from Merlot. It ages incredibly well despite its accessibility as a young wine. The 1984, a disastrous vintage for Pomerol, is good, though rather light, but does show some of the Pétrus character. The 1983 is a bit clumsy, but a big, full-bodied, chewy, powerful wine that has yet to show much finesse. The 1982 is believed by the owners to be the greatest Pétrus ever made, a powerful, rich, yet so perfectly balanced wine it should last for 30–40 years. The 1981 is not far behind and is incredibly rich, full-bodied, and still quite backward.

PEYRABON (HAUT-MÉDOC)* *

1982	($8.50)	78

This is a one-dimensional, soft, supple, fruity wine with little character.

DE PEZ (ST.-ESTÈPHE)* * * *

1981	($8.99)	79

1982	($14.95)	86

1983	($10.99)	85

1984	($8.99)	82

De Pez is one of the most carefully maintained, well-run Cru Bourgeois properties and always represents one of the better wines and better wine values for long-term cellaring. The 1984 is ready to drink, clean, and fruity. The 1983 is ripe, has a good amount of tannin, and needs plenty of cellaring. The 1982 is rounder and richer than the 1983 and will be drinkable at an earlier age. The 1981 is not a great success for Pez, but is a pleasant, elegant, if somewhat austere wine.

PHÉLAN-SÉGUR (ST.-ESTÈPHE)* * *

1981	($8.99)	74
1982	($10.99)	84
1983	($7.99)	82
1984	($8.99)	75

Phélan-Ségur is one of the lesser known wines of St.-Estèphe, but it can be very good, although its problem has been its inconsistency. The 1984 is rather light, but pleasant; the 1983, which tasted poor from cask samples, has turned out to be a pleasant, fruity, elegant wine with decent body. The 1982, which also showed poorly early on, has turned out to be a very fruity, very soft, grapy, but quite enjoyable wine for drinking over the next several years. The 1981 is herbaceous and beginning to brown in color, which is a bad sign.

PICHON (HAUT-MÉDOC)* * *

1982	($9.99)	85
1983	($9.99)	85

Pichon is an up and coming star from the southernmost portion of the Médoc. The vineyard is still extremely young, but the first several vintages of the '80s have been surprisingly good. Each vintage is stronger as the vines get older. Both the 1982 and 1983 are deeply colored, rich in fruit, very supple, and delicious to drink now and over the next several years.

PICHON LONGUEVILLE BARON DE PICHON LONGUEVILLE (PAUILLAC)* * *

1981	($15.95)	83
1982	($19.95)	86
1983	($15.95)	84

Pichon Baron is the noble-looking château sitting across from the more famous Pichon Lalande. It can make great wines, as it did in the '40s, '50s, and early '60s, but it has been casually run since and many of the wines have turned out to be extremely disappointing. The three vintages in the 1980s are all successes, but one wishes, and one suspects, that they could have been a lot better. The 1983 Pichon Baron looked to be one of the best Pichon Barons since 1961, but as it has turned out the wine lacks a little bit of richness on the palate and should have been more concentrated than it is. Nevertheless, it is a good wine. The 1982 is fat, very low in acidity, and should be drunk over the next 4–8 years. The 1981 is rather oaky, fairly light for a Pauillac in that vintage, and is fully mature now.

PICHON LONGUEVILLE, COMTESSE DE LALANDE (PAUILLAC)* * * * *

1981	($28.00)	91
1982	($40.00)	96
1983	($40.00)	95
1984	($30.00)	90

At present, Pichon Lalande is unquestionably the most popular and consistently successful wine in the Médoc. The vintages since the late '70s have been brilliant expressions of winemaking at its best. The 1984 is a revelation given the mediocre vintage overall. Rich, intense, exotic, and so, so delicious, it is a candidate for the wine of the vintage. The 1983 is also one of the greatest wines of the vintage, even better than the first-growths that year. The 1982 is superb, creamy, intense, with layers of ripe, rich, cedary fruit. The 1981 is a more elegant example and slightly lighter, but again, a lovely, medium- to full-bodied wine that is drinking beautifully now.

LE PIN (POMEROL)* * * *

1982	($30.00)	91
1983	($30.00)	87
1984	($20.00)	81

This is a brand new vineyard owned by the famous Thienpont family of Pomerol, and the wine is given the attention of a spoiled child, à la Pétrus. It is a rich, unctuous wine dominated by Merlot. The 1984 is supple and ready to drink, the 1983 rich, oaky, lush, and fruity, and the 1982 extraordinarily voluptuous, filled with the smell of ripe black-currants and spicy oak. The unreleased 1985 is sensational.

DE PITRAY (CÔTES DE CASTILLON)* * *

1982	($5.99)	84

1983	($5.99)	82

Pitray is the classic Côtes de Castillon wine, very supple, fruity, and early maturing. The 1985 and the 1982 can rival some classified growths.

PLAGNAC (MÉDOC)* * *

1982	($6.99)	84

1983	($6.99)	83

This Cru Bourgeois of the large broker Cordier seems to get little attention, but like all the Cordier wines is quite well made and very reasonably priced. The 1983 is supple, quite fruity, elegant, and ready to drink. The 1982 is similarly styled, with a touch more richness.

PLINCE (POMEROL)* *

1982	($15.00)	84

1983	($14.00)	82

Plince produces a rather peppery, chunky, fruity wine with good body but not much complexity. The 1983 is good but a trifle dull and the 1982 rich and unctuous.

LA POINTE (POMEROL)* *

1982	($15.00)	75

1983	($15.95)	80

La Pointe tends to make mediocre Pomerols, but this may be changing because the gifted oenologist Michel Rolland has been making the wines since 1983; the 1985 is the best La Pointe I have seen in some time.

PONTET-CANET (PAUILLAC)* * *

1982	($19.95)	85
1983	($14.95)	86
1984	($12.99)	82

Pontet-Canet has one of the largest productions of any Médoc classified growth. The property is quite capable of making top-quality wine, but in the period between 1961 and 1981 slipped considerably. Recently there has been much improvement. The 1984 is undoubtedly a success and should be drunk over the next 3–4 years for its medium-bodied, savory fruitiness. The 1983 is quite tannic and needs 4–5 years to soften. The 1982 is the deepest in color and is a big, corpulent wine that is just a little overweight.

POTENSAC (MÉDOC)* * *

1981	($7.99)	82
1982	($9.99)	87
1983	($8.99)	84

Potensac is one of the very finest wine values produced in the Médoc. Recent vintages, particularly the 1982 and 1983, have been excellent. The property is managed by Michel Delon, who has remarkable winemaking talents; the wine made here is dark in color, rich, medium- to full-bodied, and capable of aging for up to 10 years. It remains a stunning bargain. The 1982 is superb, 1981 elegant and ready to drink, the 1983 also very good, deep, and capable of living 10 years in the bottle.

POUGET (MARGAUX)* * *

| 1982 | ($18.95) | 83 |
| 1983 | ($14.95) | 82 |

Pouget's wines tend to be sturdy and robust, rather well colored, but lacking in charm or finesse. Both the 1983 and 1982 are compact, sturdy wines that have decent color but taste severe and hard; it is quite difficult to know what direction they will take.

POUJEAUX (MOULIS)* * *

1981	($8.99)	82
1982	($12.95)	87
1983	($12.95)	86

Poujeaux, another excellent wine value from Bordeaux, is known for producing full-bodied, deeply colored wines that last and last. Both the 1983 and 1982 are quite excellent, with the 1983 more austere and the 1982 very rich and full-bodied. The 1981 is the most elegant and lightest of this trio, and can be drunk now.

PRIEURÉ-LICHINE (MARGAUX)* * * *

1981	($15.95)	78
1982	($19.95)	87
1983	($17.95)	87
1984	($9.99)	75

The home of one of the world's most famous wine writers, Alexis Lichine, Prieuré makes light but complex, elegant wines that are supple and fast-maturing, yet have enough tannin to last 8–12 years. Nineteen eighty-four and 1981 are perhaps too light for further aging, but the 1983 is a top success that should age well for at least 10–12 years. The 1982 should do the same with its rich, blackcurrant aroma and sumptuous, fragrant bouquet and long flavors.

RABAUD-PROMIS (SAUTERNES)* *

1981	($10.99)	80
1983	($15.95)	85

This estate, which has been run down for years, is beginning to experience a renaissance in quality; recent vintages have shown well, particularly the 1983, which is rich and has a good deal of flavor and intensity.

RAHOUL (GRAVES)* * *

1981	($10.99)	81
1982	($12.99)	84
1983	($9.99)	80

Rahoul is an up and coming property in the Graves area making rather oaky red wines with character. The 1982 is the best recent vintage.

RAMAGE LA BATISSE (HAUT-MÉDOC)* *

1982	($12.00)	75
1983	($12.00)	74

After producing a trio of good wines during the period 1978–1980, this property has fallen on hard times. Recent vintages have lacked charm and fruit, and have tasted severe and tannic. Both the 1982 and 1983 are disappointments given the vintages.

RAUSAN-SÉGLA (MARGAUX)* * *

1981	($15.95)	74
1982	($18.95)	87
1983	($17.95)	87
1984	($12.95)	75

Rausan-Ségla has always been considered to have one of Bordeaux's great vineyards, but over the recent decades the wine has rarely lived up to its outstanding reputation. However, while the 1984 is a bit vegetal, soft, and undistinguished, the 1983 is rich, spicy, intense, and very long on the palate. The 1982 is similarly styled, perhaps slightly softer, but rich and very fragrant, and showing a great deal of complexity. The 1981 is light and one-dimensional, though palatable.

RAUZAN-GASSIES (MARGAUX)* * *

1981	($9.95)	74
1982	($19.95)	85

| 1983 | ($15.95) | 84 |

Rauzan-Gassies tends to produce rather hard wines that lack a great deal of the famous Margaux fragrance and finesse. The 1983 is very tannic and chunky, and lacks charm. The 1982 is fat, plummy, and very precocious, with quite low acidity. The 1981 lacks depth and richness, and is rather disappointing.

RAYMOND-LAFON (SAUTERNES)* * * * *

1980	($25.00)	90
1982	($20.00)	86
1983	($35.00)	93

The up and coming superstar of the Sauternes region, this wine is made by the winemaker at Yquem; it is a decadently rich, full-bodied, viscous wine with layers of sweet fruit. The 1983 is astonishing, the 1982 a total success from a difficult vintage, and the 1980 a truly great wine that is just now coming into its plateau of maturity.

RAYNE-VIGNEAU (SAUTERNES)* *

| 1982 | ($9.99) | 75 |
| 1983 | ($10.95) | 82 |

These are straightforward, fruity wines that lack much character.

RIEUSSEC (SAUTERNES) * * * * *

1981	($19.95)	86
1982	($19.95)	82
1983	($29.95)	94

Rieussec produces powerful wines with the smell of crème brûlée and deep, rich flavors that are neither heavy nor cloying. The 1983 is an extraordinary vintage for Rieussec. The 1982 is a good wine in a difficult vintage, and 1981 one of the best wines of a so-so vintage for the region.

RIPEAU (ST.-EMILION)* *

1982	($10.99)	82
1983	($10.99)	78

This property has always had good potential, but has been an inconsistent performer. The 1983 is a little light and herbaceous, the 1982 medium weight but richer and of more interest.

LA RIVIÈRE (FRONSAC)* *

1982	($7.99)	84
1983	($7.99)	80

La Rivière is one of the most splendid châteaux, with some of the most remarkable underground cellars in all of Bordeaux. The wines tend to be a bit inconsistent, but at their best, as in 1982, rich, fruity, soft, and delicious to drink within the first 7–8 years of life.

ROMER DU HAYOT (SAUTERNES)* *

1982	($9.99)	80
1983	($9.99)	84

Romer du Hayot makes fruity, fresh, medium-bodied wines of no great character but with a satisfying flavor.

ROUDIER (MONTAGNE-ST.-EMILION)* * *

1982	($8.99)	85
1983	($9.99)	84

The top estate in Montagne-St.-Emilion, Roudier makes very fleshy, rich, ripe wines with a lot of character and intensity. The 1982 is drinking deliciously now and the 1983 is also very good.

ROUET (FRONSAC)* * *

1982	($4.99)	82
1983	($5.99)	83

Rouet makes very fragrant, supple, fruity wines in Fronsac that represent very good values.

ROUGET (POMEROL)* * *

1982	($20.00)	88

1983	($15.95)	83

Rouget is potentially one of the best wines of Pomerol, but it is made in a very traditional manner, is often very tannic when released, and so needs a minimum of 8–10 years, rather atypical in order for a Pomerol to show its best. The 1983 is a big, full-bodied, moderately tannic wine, and the 1982 quite concentrated, very tannic, with layers of fleshy fruit, but very backward.

DE SALES (POMEROL)* * *

1982	($15.00)	87

1983	($12.00)	85

1984	($10.00)	78

De Sales makes a very commercial, very easy to enjoy and easy to understand wine of suppleness and early maturity. It satisfies virtually everyone who tastes it. The 1984 is light but pleasant, the 1983 a touch overripe but soft, low in acidity, and delicious now. The 1982 is an exceptionally elegant, richly fruity, round, and generous wine. It is a good value for a Pomerol.

SIGALAS RABAUD (SAUTERNES)* * *

1982	($9.95)	75

1983	($15.95)	86

This is a lighter-style Sauternes that must be drunk young, generally before 7–8 years of age. The 1983 is the best recent vintage, with a wonderfully fruity bouquet suggestive of pineapples.

SIRAN (MARGAUX)* * *

1981	($12.95)	84

1982	($18.95)	85

1983   ($14.95)   86

This is an up and coming property in Margaux that has been making consistently delicious, fragrant, and deeply colored wines in the 1980s. Nineteen eighty-three looks to be the best; it is the most powerful and densely colored. The lush, supple 1982 makes for lovely drinking now, and the stylish, lighter 1981 is quite pleasant. A property to watch.

SMITH-HAUT-LAFITTE (RED) (GRAVES)* *

1982   ($15.95)   82

1983   ($10.99)   82

Another property in Graves better known for its white wines than its reds, Smith-Haut-Lafitte tends to produce very light, very easy to drink, pleasant wines of no particular character. Both the 1982 and 1983 represent this style.

SMITH-HAUT-LAFITTE (WHITE) (GRAVES)* * *

1983   ($14.99)   85

1985   ($11.99)   85

A better producer of white wine than red, both the 1985 and 1983 are crisp, lively, fresh, medium-bodied wines of character.

SOCIANDO-MALLET (HAUT-MÉDOC)* * * *

1981   ($8.99)   81

1982   ($17.95)   90

1983   ($15.00)   87

1984   ($10.00)   82

Sociando-Mallet has in the last 4 or 5 years become one of the most sought after wines of France's wine connoisseurs. Its reputation for excellence and longevity has surged to the forefront because of the fanatical and meticulous winemaking style of its owner, Jean Gautreau. This is an inky black/ruby wine with great concentration and plenty of tannin. The 1981 can be approached now, but ideally needs several more years. The 1982 is a fabulous wine, but it won't be ready to drink until the late '90s. The 1983 is almost as good as the 1982, and the 1984 is light but well made and will be drinkable relatively soon.

SOUDARS (HAUT-MÉDOC)* * *

1982	($7.50)	82
1983	($8.49)	84

This relatively new estate is making very good wine from a high percentage of Merlot. The 1983 is fat, ripe, round, and very playful. The 1982 is also lovely to drink in a supple, smooth, velvety style. This is a wine to search out because, as the vineyard gets older, one suspects the wine will get even better.

SOUTARD (ST.-EMILION) * * *

1981	($18.95)	84
1982	($18.95)	88
1983	($18.95)	86

Soutard is another one of St.-Emilion's best-kept secrets. However, the wine is made in such a backward, rich, tannic style that one must usually wait 8–10 years for its tannic ferocity to subside. The 1983 is very dark, full-bodied, quite rich; the 1982 opulent and huge, but also tannic and broodingly backward. The 1981 is not so impressive, but has plenty of ripe, spicy, plummy fruit.

ST.-BONNET (MÉDOC)* *

1982	($5.99)	84
1983	($5.99)	78

This can be an excellent, very modestly priced wine to look for in the very good Bordeaux vintages. The 1982 is an example of a full-flavored, very well-made, rich Cru Bourgeois that should last at least 7–8 years.

ST.-PIERRE-SEVAISTRE (ST.-JULIEN)* * * *

1981	($15.95)	89
1982	($22.95)	87
1983	($16.95)	88
1984	($12.95)	84

A terribly underrated property in St.-Julien, St.-Pierre tends to produce a big, hefty, beefy style of wine with great color and wonderful richness, if somewhat lacking in finesse and charm. The 1984 is quite a success for the vintage, as is the 1983, which is very seductive in its lushness and full-bodied appeal. The 1982 is similarly styled, even softer. The 1981, one of the great successes of the vintage, is impressively colored, with a great depth of fruit and richness that is surprising for a 1981.

SUDUIRAUT (SAUTERNES)* * * *

1981	($20.00)	84
1982	($35.00)	90
1983	($25.00)	87

An outstanding yet often inconsistent property that can make great wines in certain vintages. The 1982 Suduiraut is fabulously honeyed, luscious, deep, with great concentration in a difficult vintage. The 1983 is very, very good, rather elegant, and the 1981 attractive, rich, with less power than normal but drinking well now.

TAILHAS (POMEROL)* *

1981	($15.00)	72
1982	($15.00)	84
1983	($15.00)	82

Tailhas is a fairly well-respected vineyard that makes a full-bodied, robustly styled Pomerol with good richness and weight. The 1983 is loaded with good berry fruit, has medium body, and is very soft. The 1982 is a deeper and richer wine, the 1981 disappointingly thin and dirty to smell.

TAILLEFER (POMEROL)* *

1982	($12.95)	77
1983	($9.99)	75

Taillefer produces one of Pomerol's lightest-styled wines. It never has a great deal of depth, but is soundly made, round, fruity, and capable of evolving for 5–7 years before losing its fruit. The 1982 is the best of the recent vintages, but is hardly an inspiring wine.

TALBOT (ST.-JULIEN)* * * *

1981	($14.95)	85
1982	($25.00)	89
1983	($18.95)	89
1984	($11.95)	84

Talbot is owned by the famous Cordier family and tends to produce a robust yet fruity, full-bodied wine that offers excellent value. Recent vintages since 1978 have been particularly successful. The 1984 is ripe, medium-bodied, and quite fruity. The 1983 is a big, full-bodied, tannic, rich wine that will last a long time. The 1982 is massive, dense, earthy, with a very powerful, round, ripe, rich taste and long finish. The 1981 is more elegant and ready to drink.

TAYAC (MARGAUX)*

1981	($8.99)	75
1982	($9.99)	78

Tayac produces easy to drink, decent wines that lack complexity, but are generally soundly made.

TAYAC PRESTIGE (CÔTES DE BOURG)* * *

1982	($12.95)	87
1983	($11.95)	84

The leading property of the Côtes de Bourg, Tayac produces a number of different wines, but their top label is their special cuvée called

Prestige. The 1982 could be mistaken for a first-rate Pomerol: a rich, intense, very full-bodied wine with excellent character.

LA TERRASSE (CÔTES DE CASTILLON)* *

1982	($5.99)	82
1983	($5.99)	80

A deliciously fruity, fragrant, easy to drink wine that should be drunk before its fifth birthday. Both the 1982 and 1983 are quite delicious.

TERREY-GROS-CAILLOUX (ST.-JULIEN)* * *

1982	($11.99)	84
1983	($9.99)	83

Both wines are jammy, meaty, fleshy mouthfuls of wine without a great deal of finesse, but they show good concentration and potential for evolution of 5–7 years.

DU TERTRE (MARGAUX)* * *

1981	($12.95)	84
1982	($15.95)	87
1983	($15.95)	87
1984	($9.99)	75

Du Tertre has yet to become well known, but great efforts are being made to elevate the quality of wine produced here. The vintages since 1978 have been quite successful. The 1984 is light, but cleanly made and ready to drink. The 1983 is a full-bodied, tannic, tough wine that needs time to round out. The 1982 promised well young, but has now closed up and needs at least another 5 years of aging. The 1981 is light and lean.

TERTRE-DAUGAY (ST.-EMILION)* * *

1982	($12.95)	82
1983	($12.95)	84

One of St.-Emilion's oldest estates, this property completely lost credibility for its poor wines in older vintages, but the new owners are making a strong effort to bring it back to form. The 1982 and 1983 are both more impressive efforts.

LA TONNELLE (CÔTES DE BLAYE)* * *

1982	($5.99)	84
1983	($5.99)	84

La Tonnelle is one of the leading estates of the Côtes de Blaye, making delicious wine for drinking upon release. Both the 1982 and 1983 represent excellent bargains for drinking over the next 3–4 years.

LA TOUR BLANCHE (SAUTERNES)* *

1982	($8.99)	79
1983	($9.99)	84

La Tour Blanche, run by the French Ministry of Agriculture, tends to make a very light, fruity wine that lacks character. The 1983 seems to be a step in the right direction, but this probably has more to do with the vintage, which was superb in this area.

LA TOUR DE BY (MÉDOC)* *

1982	($5.99)	84
1983	($7.99)	81

La Tour de By is another of the very reliable, well-made, good values from the upper Médoc. The wine can last very well and both the 1983 and the 1982 (which is richer and fleshier than the 1983) are good candidates for lasting 5–7 years.

LA TOUR-CARNET (HAUT-MÉDOC)* *

1982	($12.00)	80
1983	($12.00)	83

La Tour-Carnet has been extensively replanted and the disappointing wines from the 1970s seem to be giving way in the 1980s to wines with a bit more character and richness. The 1983 wines are riper and richer than those of any recent vintage. The 1982 is also good. A property to watch.

LA TOUR-FIGEAC (ST.-EMILION)* * *

1982	($9.99)	85
1983	($9.99)	84

La Tour-Figeac consistently produces fat, supple and fruity wines rarely worth keeping beyond 5–6 years, but they offer delicious fruit and an uncomplicated style. The 1982 is the best recent vintage; the 1983 also has plenty of appeal.

LA TOUR-HAUT-BRION (GRAVES)* * * *

1981	($25.00)	85
1982	($35.00)	95
1983	($19.95)	85
1984	($19.95)	82

A separate vineyard in principle, La Tour-Haut-Brion has traditionally been the second wine of La Mission-Haut-Brion, with a bit more tannic press wine added in to give it its character; in some vintages, it has been identical but for that addition. The 1984 is very soft, fruity, and straightforward, the 1983 good, but a lot more supple than past vintages. The 1982 is a blockbuster—rich, massive, very tannic, and almost as good as La Mission-Haut-Brion, at half the price. The 1981 lacks some finesse and is rather robust and aggressive.

LA TOUR-MARTILLAC (GRAVES)*

1982	($11.99)	83

1983	($11.99)	82

La Tour-Martillac makes relatively light, sometimes hard, tannic wines that consistently taste mediocre. The quality of the 1982 and 1983 is more encouraging than other efforts have been.

LA TOUR-DE-MONS (MARGAUX)* * *

1981	($9.95)	72

1982	($11.95)	82

This property made wonderful wines in the '60s and '70s, but has been inconsistent since the late 1970s. The 1981 is light, herbaceous, and rather high in acidity, and the 1982 supple, fruity, but not terribly complicated.

LA TOUR-DU-PIN-FIGEAC (ST.-EMILION)* * *

1982	($14.95)	85

1983	($9.99)	81

One of the many châteaux in St.-Emilion with name Figeac, this moderately sized vineyard produces straightforward, fleshy, fruity wines with good body. The 1982 is the best recent effort, with an attractive ripe berryish, spicy bouquet and silky, lengthy flavors.

LA TOUR ST-BONNET (MÉDOC)* * *

1982	($8.99)	85

1983	($6.99)	84

La Tour St.-Bonnet makes a full-bodied, fleshy, deeply colored wine that is supple enough to drink young but can keep 6–8 years. Both the 1982 and 1983 are serious wines with a lot of character and intensity.

TRONQUOY-LALANDE (ST.-ESTÈPHE)* * *

1981	($9.99)	81
1982	($9.99)	83
1983	($8.99)	80

Tronquoy-Lalande is one of the more attractive châteaux in St.-Es-
tèphe. The wine is a rather clumsy one, very earthy, very rich in color,
often lacking finesse but compensating for that with plenty of power.
The 1983 is extremely tannic and perhaps too austere and hard for its
own good. The 1982 is corpulent, very high in concentration as well
as tannin, and very exaggerated in style. The 1981 is immense as well,
but very tough and hard.

TROPLONG-MONDOT (ST.-EMILION)* * *

1982	($15.95)	84
1983	($12.95)	84

The wines of Troplong-Mondot have generally been very light in style,
but the last several vintages have shown a bit more concentration and
stuffing. The 1983 is elegant, fruity, and medium-bodied, the 1982
soft, supple, with a lovely berry fruitiness.

TROTANOY (POMEROL)* * * * *

1981	($30.00)	87
1982	($100.00)	96
1983	($40.00)	86
1984	($30.00)	83

If there is one wine that often resembles Pétrus in tastings, it is
Trotanoy. The 1984 is light, but charming and tasty; the 1983 a little
disappointing for Trotanoy, but a very good wine. The 1982 is a powerful, exotic, chocolatey, rich, massive wine, and the 1981 elegant,
yet authoritatively flavored, with good concentration.

TROTTEVIEILLE (ST.-EMILION)* *

1981	($18.95)	70
1982	($18.95)	85
1983	($18.95)	72

One of the more celebrated Premiers Grands Crus of St.-Emilion, this property has produced an embarrassing array of wines that have lacked concentration and character, and were often disturbingly light and dull. However, the vintages of the '80s have shown improvement, with the unreleased 1985 perhaps the best yet. The vintages of the '80s are light but fruity and soft, with 1982 being your best bet.

VIEUX CHÂTEAU CERTAN (POMEROL)* * * *

1982	($35.00)	88
1983	($19.95)	87

Vieux Château Certan for decades was considered the second-best wine of Pomerol. It has lost some of its appeal as other Pomerols have surpassed it. However, for elegance and a more Médoc style of wine, it is hard to beat. The 1983 is slightly minty, with attractive berry flavors and good body; the 1982, a rich deep, perfumed wine with layers of lush fruit, can be drunk now.

VIEUX CHÂTEAU GUIBEAU (PUISSEGUIN-ST.-EMILION)* * *

1982	($5.99)	82
1983	($5.99)	82

This is the leading estate in Puisseguin-St.-Emilion. Both the 1983 and 1982 are soft, fruity, and quite delicious.

VILLARS (FRONSAC)* * *

1982	($5.99)	84
1983	($5.99)	82

Villars tends to produce supple, fruity wines of good concentration. Recent vintages have been quite successful and the unreleased 1985 may be the best yet.

VILLEGEORGE (HAUT-MÉDOC)*

1981	($7.99)	72
1982	($8.99)	80
1983	($8.99)	83

This property has a good reputation in Europe. The best recent vintage has been 1983—the wine is generously fruity, supple, spicy, with good concentration and smooth texture.

VILLEMAURINE (ST.-EMILION)* * *

1982	($11.99)	84
1983	($11.99)	82

Named after an ancient Moorish encampment, the enormous underground cellars here have considerable tourist interest. The wine, after a period of mediocrity, is better made in the '80s than in previous decades. Both the 1982 and 1983 are fruity, supple, and soft.

LA VIOLETTE (POMEROL)* * *

1981	($15.00)	78
1982	($15.00)	87
1983	($13.00)	83

This rather obscure Pomerol produces only 1,800 cases, but the wine is made primarily from the Merlot grape and can be stunningly rich, as in 1982. The 1983 has a ripe berry fruit bouquet and flavors and soft tannins, but is a simple wine. The 1981 is light and watery.

VRAYE-CROIX-DE-GAY (POMEROL)* *

1982	($12.00)	84
1983	($15.00)	80

One sees very little of the wines of this tiny property in Pomerol, which usually makes darkly colored, dense, powerful, very flavorful, tannic wine. It suffers from inconsistency, though both the 1982 and 1983 are smoky, exotic, chocolatey flavored wines.

YQUEM (SAUTERNES)* * * * *

1979	($55.00)	88
1980	($60.00)	93
1981	($65.00)	90
1982	($120.00)	93

The world's most unique and expensive wine to produce, Yquem costs a fortune, but the owners claim they have never made a profit trying to produce it. Its nectarlike richness and legendary aging potential are indeed all for real. The 1981 is an outstanding rather than great Yquem; both the 1980 and 1982 are perfect examples of fabulous Yquems from two vintages that were not considered textbook years for the Sauternes region. The 1979 is very, very good, but lacks the honeyed richness and incredible power and intensity that this wine seems to possess in most vintages. It will keep for 30–60 years.

THE 1985 RED BORDEAUX
A PREVIEW GUIDE

EXCEPTIONAL POTENTIAL (94–96 POINTS)

Cos d'Estournel (St.-Estèphe)
L'Evangile (Pomerol)
Pétrus (Pomerol)
Trotanoy (Pomerol)

OUTSTANDING POTENTIAL (90–93 POINTS)

Canon (St.-Emilion)
Cheval Blanc (St.-Emilion)
Ducru-Beaucaillou (St.-Julien)
L'Eglise-Clinet (Pomerol)
Haut-Brion (Graves)
Lafite-Rothschild (Pauillac)
Lafleur (Pomerol)
Léoville-Barton (St.-Julien)
Léoville-Las Cases (St.-Julien)
Lynch-Bages (Pauillac)
Magdelaine (St.-Emilion)
Margaux (Margaux)
La Mission-Haut-Brion (Graves)
Mouton-Rothschild (Pauillac)
Pichon Lalande (Pauillac)
Le Pin (Pomerol)

VERY GOOD POTENTIAL (86–89 POINTS)

L'Angélus (St.-Emilion)
L'Arrosée (St.-Emilion)
Ausone (St.-Emilion)
Beauséjour-Duffau (St.-Emilion)
Belair (St.-Emilion)
Beychevelle (St.-Julien)
Bon Pasteur (Pomerol)
Boyd-Cantenac (Margaux)

Cadet-Piola (St.-Emilion)
Clerc-Milon (Pauillac)
La Conseillante (Pomerol)
Destieux (St.-Emilion)
Ferrand (St.-Emilion)
Fieuzal (Graves)
Figeac (St.-Emilion)
Le Gay (Pomerol)
Grand-Puy-Lacoste (Pauillac)
La Grave Trigant de Boisset
  (Pomerol)
Gruaud-Larose (St.-Julien)
Haut-Bages-Libéral (Pauillac)
d'Issan (Margaux)
La Fleur Pétrus (Pomerol)
La Lagune (Médoc)
Lagrange (St.-Julien)

Langoa-Barton (St.-Julien)
Larmande (St.-Emilion)
Lascombes (Margaux)
Latour à Pomerol (Pomerol)
Meyney (St.-Estèphe)
Palmer (Margaux)
Pape-Clément (Graves)
Pavie (St.-Emilion)
Pontet-Canet (Pauillac)
St.-Pierre (St.-Julien)
Sociando-Mallet (Médoc)
Soutard (St.-Emilion)
Talbot (St.-Julien)
Le Tertre-Roteboeuf
  (St.-Emilion)
Vieux Château Certan (Pomerol)

SLEEPERS OF THE VINTAGE
(The underpublicized high-quality wines that represent great values)

L'Arrosée (St.-Emilion)
Belles Graves (Lalande-de-
  Pomerol)
Bertineau St.-Vincent (Lalande-
  de-Pomerol)
Bon Pasteur (Pomerol)
Cadet-Piola (St.-Emilion)
Canon-de-Brem (Canon-
  Fronsac)
Destieux (St.-Emilion)
L'Eglise-Clinet (Pomerol)
Ferrand (St.-Emilion)

Fieuzal (Graves)
Gran Ormeau (Lalande de
  Pomerol)
Lagrange (St.-Julien)
Larmande (St.-Emilion)
La Louvière (Graves)
Mazeris (Canon-Fronsac)
Le Pin (Pomerol)
Sociando-Mallet (Médoc)
Le Tertre-Roteboeuf
  (St.-Emilion)

BURGUNDY

Including Beaujolais and Chablis

The Côte de Nuits and Côte de Beaune

Burgundy is by far the most challenging wine region one could encounter. The notorious range in the quality of wine here is greater than anywhere else. The top wines are often produced in such minute quantities that the exhilaration of finding and tasting a great burgundy is dashed when the grower tells you that only 50 cases will be sent to America. Combine this with the fact that truly excellent vintages here are far less frequent than elsewhere in France. Furthermore, the demand for burgundy, whether it be poor, mediocre, or superb, is far greater than the supply, and prices are therefore excruciatingly high. Unfortunately, for far too many growers there is simply no incentive to produce smaller yields and greater quality wines. In short, small quantities, high prices, a plethora of mediocre vintages, and greedy as well as incompetent growers are an integral part of Burgundy's story—whether it be past, present, or future.

Even where high-quality wines are produced from recognized excellent vineyards and carefully vinified by good growers, there is no guarantee that what is in the barrel will make it into the bottle. The commercial madness of today's modern wine world has caused many good growers to overfilter their wines so that no sediment will form in the bottle. The result of sterile filtrations—through German-made micropore filters—is that most of the character, flavor intensity, and aging potential is left behind in the filter pads. Even if a wine somehow miraculously survives the trauma of filtration, many growers and *négociants* are making sure that no "living wine" is sent abroad since the wines are also put through a flash pasteurization prior to bottling. Even the great burgundies that are famous for their expansive fragrance and broad, rich, velvety flavors resemble jug wines with cooked, compact aromas and cardboard flavors after they are subjected to this abusive treatment. Yet there are advantages for those importers who insist on this treatment for their wines. They will never

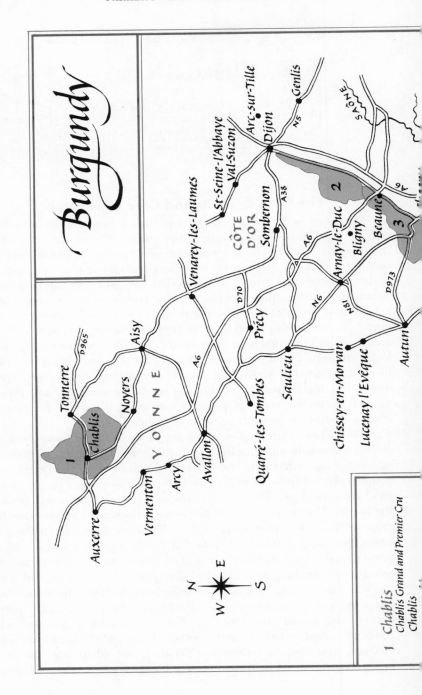

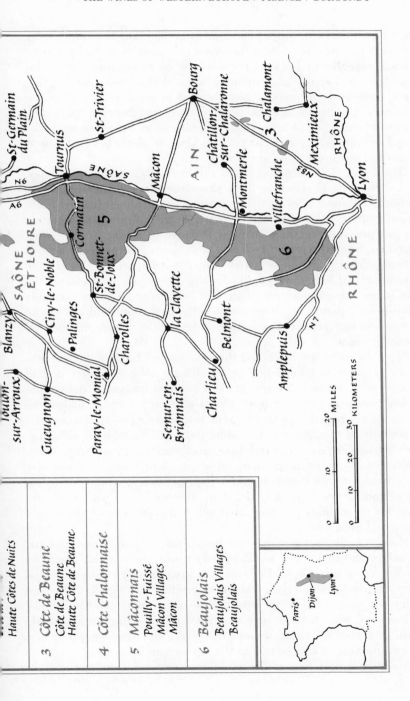

Haute Côtes de Nuits

3 Côte de Beaune
   Côte de Beaune
   Haute Côte de Beaune

4 Côte Chalonnaise

5 Mâconnais
   Pouilly-Fuissé
   Mâcon Villages
   Mâcon

6 Beaujolais
   Beaujolais Villages
   Beaujolais

have to contend with stupid consumers or ignorant restaurants that send back the wine because it has some sediment in it. And of course they will save money because these wines, now castrated and sterile, are generally incapable of developing in the bottle. Consequently, they do not have to be protected and shipped in temperature-controlled containers. Unfiltered, natural wines can spoil or become unstable if exposed to extremes of heat. However, filtered and pasteurized wines are not so vulnerable; they can take all kinds of abuse because, for all intents and purposes, they are already dead.

The Pinot Noir grape produces rather fragile, very subtle wines. The overzealous filtration or flash pasteurization will literally kill off its character. Most conscientious growers are dead set against filtration or pasteurization; they argue that it is their American importers who put pressure on them to filter because of a fear that a living, natural, unfiltered wine will go bad if subjected to extreme heat in shipment. This is definitely a risk, but not if importers who sell 20-dollar bottles of burgundy would only ship the wines in "reefers," the trade name for temperature-controlled containers. They are readily available and, though more expensive—the cost is only a dollar or two per case—a tiny price to pay for guaranteeing the proper shipment of expensive wines.

Why the difficulty in finding the best wines? Finding the top producers of great red burgundy is as difficult as hunting for one of France's other remarkable sensory and culinary treasures, the truffle. It takes patience, plenty of time, plenty of money, and the realization that there are just not so many great Burgundy wine producers who are committed to making outstanding red wine. Combined with Burgundy's troublesome and unpredictable climate for Pinot Noir, which usually results in no more than three excellent vintages a decade, wine enthusiasts the world over have the right to lament the herculean task of finding fine burgundy. In short, burgundy is a wine perfectly suited for masochists . . . you must suffer a great deal of abuse and pain to find pleasure!

However, the fact remains that both good and bad burgundies are expensive, and that really top Burgundy wines are incredibly hard to find. Why, you might ask? Unlike Bordeaux, where on the average, a moderate-sized estate or vineyard may produce 15,000–20,000 cases of wine per year, a top-notch grower in Burgundy may make only 300–500 cases of wine from a specific Premier or Grand Cru vineyard. Divide that production up around the world and you can easily see how exasperating it can be to find the top burgundies.

Scarcity is only part of the problem, however. Take one of Burgundy's most famous and expensive wines, Clos de Vougeot. There are 125 acres of vineyard at Clos de Vougeot, which makes it about the size of one moderate château in Bordeaux. However, in 1985 there were in excess of 80 different growers who owned a part of these 125 acres, whereas in Bordeaux, the château's vineyard is under one management and ownership. Not all of these 80 + growers bottle their own wine, of course—some sell to the large brokers in Burgundy. However, there are at least 30 or more different Clos de Vougeot wines on the market in any given vintage. Some are totally insipid wines made by incompetent growers who overcrop and carelessly vinify their wines, whereas a few are splendid wines, rich, majestically scented, and truly representative of what a great burgundy should be. Yet whether that wine is poor, mediocre, or superb, there is one constant —the wine will always be expensive, and when it is from one of the top growers, very hard to find as well, because knowledgeable burgundy connoisseurs rush to snap up the limited supplies of the real thing. In short, the problem facing top-quality burgundy is a classic example of supply and demand. The region's top vineyards are entirely too small to produce enough wine to satisfy the world demand. Take a look at Burgundy's most famous estate, the Domaine de la Romanée-Conti (DRC). This estate is the sole owner of such fabulously expensive and famous vineyards as Romanée-Conti and La Tâche. The Romanée-Conti vineyard comprises a full 4.75 acres, whereas the La Tâche comprises 15 acres. These two wines fetch prices of $120 and $70 a bottle respectively, regardless of how good the vintages are. There are simply too many people wanting to buy these wines in spite of their price or quality. However, if you are going to buy burgundy, you must rely not just on the prestige of the vineyard, but also on the quality and competence of the grower. In Burgundy, the French have an expression that sums it all up, "C'est l'homme qui fait la différence" (it is the man who makes the difference). Those words alone sum up the realities of buying burgundy yesterday, today, and tomorrow. In summary, the good growers in Burgundy make much better wine in mediocre and poor years than the careless and sloppy growers make in the great years.

BURGUNDY
QUICK VINTAGE GUIDE

1986—Due to heavy rains before the harvest and rains at the end of the harvest, Burgundy will be a very difficult area to generalize about. Production was much higher than in 1985 and early reports suggest that the white wines should be very good and the red wines very irregular, with quality depending in large part on when the grower picked. The size of the crop should help stabilize prices, which at the time of writing are absurdly high.

1985—Overall, 1985 looks to be the most promising vintage since 1978. The drought during the late summer and fall caused the grapes to ripen well. The red wines are deeply colored, very fruity and ripe, with clean, rich, very fruity aromas. They have much less tannin and more charm than the irregular, rather massive 1983s. Despite early reports that the quantity was small, the vintage has turned out a good-sized yield of wine. Most of the wines have excellent balance, and though they will be approachable in their youth, should age well for a decade. Prices are already absurdly high, so the wines will continue to be extremely expensive. The white wines, even more expensive, are fat, supple and lush, and will have to be drunk early. In style, they resemble the 1982 white burgundies. Cask tastings showed a remarkably high level of quality from such red wine producers as Faiveley, Domaine de la Romanée-Conti, Bruno Clair, Dujac, Jean Gros, Hubert Lignier, Maume, Mongeard-Mugneret, Georges Mugneret, Ponsot, Pothier Rieusset, Pousse d'Or, Joseph Roty, A. Rousseau, and Mérode.

1984—All of us remember 1984. This year, like 1980, was declared by several wine writers to be a major catastrophe long before they ever tasted the wines. In 1980 the source of information was the *négociant* Louis Latour, who had all sorts of problems with the vintage, and indeed made poor wine that year. As all burgundy-lovers know, 1980 has turned out some of the most delicious and best-balanced wines of the last 7–8 years, and some of the wines from the Côte de Nuits (e.g., Domaine de la Romanée-Conti and Robert Arnoux) are superb. Well, 1984 is not likely to be so good as 1980, but many of the good growers have made wines that I predict will be better-balanced, richer wines than the 1982s. The vintage was late, and everyone had to chaptalize because the natural alcohol contents were only 9% to 10%. However, the resulting red wines are often quite elegant, very cleanly made, fruity, soft, and agreeable. The yields were low because of poor flowering. There is the normal irregularity, but the wines of the Côte de Nuits are better colored and richer than those of the Côte de Beaune. I would guess that the good 1984s will reach full maturity between 1988–1990. They will certainly not be long-lived, but when well chosen, will be very pleasant wines.

1983—A knowledgeable oenologist once asked me, "Is 1983 really a great vintage or the Burgundy sham of the century?" It is hard to judge any vintage in black and white terms because of the innumerable variables that affect quality, but I have always felt that only 15% of the wines I tasted had the potential, concentration, and overall balance to be considered great. The severe hailstorms that hit the Côte de Nuits in July and the rampant rot in the vineyards from the tropical heat and rain in August and early September created significant problems. Many wine journalists, who do not look very closely at all the facts or laboriously taste across the field of play, obviously read that the hot dry weather in late September and October caused sugar readings to soar in the grapes and the harvest to occur under textbook conditions.

So they concluded that it must surely be a great vintage, and like the prophets of doom who also talk and write before tasting, the reports went out that this *was* truly a great vintage. One single thing was forgotten—it is difficult to make wine from unhealthy grapes, and in 1983 there were plenty of rot-infested and scarred grapes from both rot and hail damage. The key to making great burgundy in 1983 was to separate the rotten grapes from the healthy ones. This had to be done at the time of picking. It was extremely time-consuming, but absolutely essential if one was to produce a clean, well-balanced wine. There were, of course, other factors that would have a significant effect on the outcome. Because the grape skins were extremely thick and ripe, one had to be careful with the vinification so as not to extract an excess of tannin. Some growers pulled the fermenting grape juice off the skins too fast for fear of obtaining a taste of rot and getting too much tannin. Their wines tend to be lighter in color and much more precocious in style. Other growers went for maximum extract and produced wines so tannic that 1976 burgundies (known for their tannic ferocity) almost look supple in comparison. Other growers used too much new wood, some obviously in an attempt to hide or mask the smell of rot. Some did not use enough new wood. Some growers fined their wines excessively, hoping the egg white fining would help soften the bite from the harsh tannins. This worked in some cases, but often both color and flavor were also removed by the fining. And of course, some growers have overzealously filtered and/or pasteurized their

wines, a sort of double whammy to the wine that destroys any taste or
smell that would identify its place of origin.

And so for the red burgundies of 1983, you will find many abrasive, harsh, tannic, dry wines with a *"goût de sec"* and *"goût de
moisi."* (This is the smell and taste of rot closely resembling damp,
moldy cardboard in aroma; a sharp, bitter, very dry impression is
produced by the flavor.) There are also wines that have lost significant
color because of the rot. Unlike the terribly underrated 1980 Burgundy
vintage, in which the wines seemed to deepen in color and flavor
concentration as they aged in the cask, the 1983s have lightened up
considerably in color, with some taking on orange, brownish edges, a
particularly dangerous sign. If you do not like the 1976 red burgundies
because of their hard tannins and firmness, don't imagine for a moment that the 1983s will be more pleasant.

As for the white burgundies, they are simply the most enormous
white wines from Burgundy I have ever tasted. Ranging to 14–16%
alcohol, they are extremely alcoholic, heavy, clumsy wines that will
leave your head spinning. Some can be magnificent if the balancing
acidity is present (e.g., Leflaive, Sauzet, Coche Dury, Jadot, Jobard),
but many are oafish wines that will please when young but fall apart
within 3–4 years as the fruit fades and the ugly level of alcohol becomes dominant.

Does all of this sound very pessimistic? You bet it does, but there
are small quantities of very good to superb wines produced in 1983
that will permit connoisseurs of burgundy to replenish their cellar
stocks. Of course, it will not be cheap, because many of the very best
burgundies were made in exceptionally small quantities since the
growers ruthlessly discarded any tainted grapes. For a few growers,
1983 is truly a great vintage. For the rest, the vintage is a mixed bag
of high alcohol, harsh, rather imbalanced wines that taste a little
bizarre. For those lucky enough to get a hold of any of the greatest
wines, they will undoubtedly be real treasures. However, everyone
should remember that these wines are quite tannic and most of them
will not be ready to drink before 1995. If you don't want to wait that
long—and that is minimum—then take a look at the dozen or so top
1982s, which by and large are delicious now. But whatever you decide
to do, remember that 1983 is an extremely irregular and overrated
vintage. Only the very best wines are worth the high price.

1982—A huge crop of grapes was harvested in 1982. Had it not been
for the extremely wet month of August, this year could have been
quite special. However, the enormous yield produced very fragile
wines, somewhat watery, but generally charming, soft, and fruity.

Where the conscientious growers were able to pick before the harvest rains and control the vinification temperature, some good, round, adequately concentrated wines have been produced. As for the white wines, they have turned out to be extremely successful—fat, lush, ripe wines for drinking over the next 2–3 years while waiting for the 1981s to open. Most top growers compare their white burgundies with the 1973 vintage.

In general, the wines of the Côte de Beaune are more consistent than those of the Côte de Nuits. However, the Domaine de la Romanée-Conti and Georges Mugneret, both in Vosne-Romanée, Armand Rousseau, Maume, both Philippe and René Leclerc, all of Gevrey-Chambertin, Domaine Dujac and Pierre Amiot in Morey St.-Denis, as well as the *négociant* Faiveley did quite well in the Côte de Nuits.

1981—A difficult vintage for certain, the great majority of 1981 red burgundies lack flesh and charm, and are too hard, shallow, and austere. Several optimistic reports have indicated they will turn out like the 1972s, but the 1972s had significantly more concentration. For white burgundies it is a very good year, but for reds one must pick very carefully. Notable successes among the small growers include the wines of Philippe Leclerc in Gevrey-Chambertin, Pierre Amiot and Domaine Dujac in Morey St.-Denis, Robert Chevillon in Nuits St.-Georges, and Domaine de la Pousse d'Or and Michel Lafarge in Volnay. Among the *négociants*, the wines of Faiveley are excellent and perhaps the finest 1981s produced.

1980—A disappointing to mediocre year for the white wines, and an average year for the reds of the Côte de Beaune. As for the Côte de Nuits, a vastly underrated vintage in which there are considerable numbers of rich, medium-bodied, very elegant, cleanly made, technically sound red burgundies that can be drunk now or cellared for another 3–5 years. The reds of the Côte de Nuits are probably the best bargains of Burgundy today.

1979—A good to very good year for white burgundy. The wines are fully mature and should be consumed. For the red burgundies, the wines are generally showing their age, are soft, rather frail and best drunk up.

1978—The most consistently pleasing and successful vintage for Burgundy over the period 1972–1984. The whites, which are just now reaching full maturity, are classic wines with power, richness, depth, and balance. The reds from the Côte de Beaune are quite good and ready to drink; from the Côte de Nuits, the red wines can be drunk, but the best of them need a few more years. Interestingly, the greatest red wines of the 1983 vintage are better than the greatest red wines of the 1978 vintage. However, in 1978 there is a general level of consistent good quality, whereas in 1983 there are numerous failures.

1977— For red burgundies, a terrible year, in which even the most conscientious growers could not overcome Mother Nature's cruel blows. For the white burgundies a surprisingly good year of wines that seemed acidic at first, but which have matured well. Nineteen seventy-seven white burgundies are in beautiful condition today and are real sleepers.

1976— Along with the 1983, 1976 must surely be the most controversial Burgundy vintage of recent years. A hot drought year resulted in tiny berries with thick skins. The major difference from 1983 is that there was no hail or rot damage. The reds, very deeply colored, very tannic, and very concentrated, continue to lack charm and character, but they have all the characteristics necessary to age well. Since they have richer, more concentrated fruit than the 1983s, I suspect that all they need is more time—4–7 more years. As for the whites, they were low in acidity, powerful, rich, alcoholic wines that in size resembled the 1983s, but without the taint of rot. They should be drunk immediately since they are not likely to get any better.

1975— An undisputably terrible vintage for virtually everyone. Several very good wines were made in Chablis; otherwise this is a vintage to avoid.

1974— When it rains, it pours, and 1974 was another very bad year for the growers and *négociants* of Burgundy. The palatable wines I have had have all been white burgundies from Meursault and Chassagne-Montrachet.

1973— A very good, sometimes excellent vintage for the white wines. Like the 1982s, the white wines tasted good from the beginning, and while lacking some firmness and acidity, were full of fruit and charm. They should have been consumed by now, because they are no longer fresh. The reds were watery, pale, light, and generally in full retreat into oblivion by 1978. They are now comatose.

1972— Like 1980, at first a maligned, poorly regarded vintage that has developed so well that lovely vinous surprises are everywhere and the vintage's reputation clearly on the rise. The reds, deeply colored but high in acidity and dumb when first assessed in 1973–1974, have developed slowly but surely. The top wines have rich, complex bouquets, deep flavors, and a touch of firmness. A keeping vintage of wine that should be drunk over the next 5–8 years. The whites were less successful, but certainly good. They are now cracking up and must be drunk.

1971— A splendid vintage of ripe, rich, voluptuous, deeply scented red and white wines. The only disappointment has been how fast these wines have matured. Virtually all the wines have been mature for several years and the telltale orange/amber colors have become apparent. The whites are somewhat risky unless stored in a cold cellar. The reds are just beginning to lose some fruit, but the well-preserved red burgundies of this vintage are delectably opulent and fragrant.

1970—A good vintage of round, fruity, soft wines was produced everywhere in Burgundy. If both the whites and reds lacked greatness, there were plenty of satisfying wines produced. They matured quickly and should be drunk without delay.

1969—An excellent vintage for the red wines, a very good one for the white wines. The wines were slow to mature because they were powerful but backward and quite firm. The reds are all mature and should be drunk up. The only recent white burgundies I have tasted from this vintage seemed to be losing their fruit and becoming oxidized. Nevertheless, this is a vintage to look for on the auction markets.

Rating the Red Burgundy Growers, Producers, and *Négociants*

No one will ever have a great deal of success selecting a burgundy without a thorough knowledge of the finest growers and *négociants*. The most meticulous producers often make better wine in mediocre vintages than many less dedicated growers and producers make in great vintages. Knowing the finest producers in Burgundy is unquestionably the most important factor in your success in finding the best wines.

The following is a guide to the best red burgundy producers. Consistency from year to year among the producers' total range of wines was the most important consideration. One should be cognizant of the fact that many lower-rated producers may make specific wines that are qualitatively above their placement here.

A GUIDE TO RED BURGUNDY'S BEST PRODUCERS

* * * * * *(OUTSTANDING PRODUCERS)*

Faiveley (Nuits St.-Georges)	Domaine de la Romanée-Conti
Henri Jayer (Vosne-Romanée)	(Vosne-Romanée)
Leroy (Meursault)	

* * * * (EXCELLENT PRODUCERS)

Robert Arnoux (Vosne-
Romanée)
Pierre Bourée (Gevrey-
Chambertin)
Castagnier (Vosne-Romanée)
Cathiard Molinier (Vosne-
Romanée)
Robert Chevillon (Nuits St.-
Georges)
Bruno Clair (Marsannay)
Clair-Daü (Marsannay)
Courcel (Pommard)
Joseph Drouhin (Beaune)
Drouhin Larose (Gevrey-
Chambertin)
Dujac (Morey St.-Denis)
Michel Gaunoux (Pommard)
Pierre Gelin (Fixin)
Machard de Gramont (Nuits
St.-Georges)
Jean Grivot (Vosne-Romanée)
Jean Gros (Vosne-Romanée)
Gros Soeur et Frère (Vosne-
Romanée)
Hospices de Beaune
Hudelot Noëllat (Vosne-
Romanée)
Louis Jadot (Beaune)
Lucien Jayer (Vosne-
Romanée)
Michel Lafarge (Volnay)
Clos des Lambrays (Morey
St.-Denis)

Philippe Leclerc (Gevrey-
Chambertin)
René Leclerc (Gevrey-
Chambertin)
Hubert Lignier (Morey
St.-Denis)
Maume (Gevrey-Chambertin)
Prince Florent de Mérode
(Ladoix-Serrigny)
Moine Hudelot (Chambolle-
Musigny)
Hubert de Montille (Volnay)
Mongeard Mugneret (Vosne-
Romanée)
Albert Morot (Beaune)
Georges Mugneret (Vosne-
Romanée)
Mussy (Pommard)
Pernot Fourrier (Gevrey-
Chambertin)
Ponsot (Morey St.-Denis)
Pothier Rieusset (Pommard)
Pousse d'Or (Volnay)
Joseph Roty (Gevrey-
Chambertin)
Roumier (Chambolle-Musigny)
Armand Rousseau (Gevrey-
Chambertin)
Bernard Serveau (Morey
St.-Denis)
Tollot-Beaut (Chorey-les-
Beaune)
Tollot-Voarick (Aloxe-Corton)

* * * (GOOD PRODUCERS)

Pierre Amiot (Morey St.-Denis)
Marquis d'Angerville (Volnay)
Comte Armand (Pommard)
Barthod Noëllat (Chambolle-
Musigny)
Adrian Belland (Santenay)

Guy Berthaut (Fixin)
Berthaut (Chambolle-Musigny)
Besancenot-Mathouillet
(Beaune)
Bichot-Clos Frantin (Beaune)
Billard Gonnet (Pommard)

Simon Bize (Savigny-Les-Beaune)
Bouchard Aîné (Beaune)
Bouchard Père (Beaune)
Henri Boillot (Volnay)
Lucien Boillot (Gevrey-Chambertin)
L. J. Bruck (Nuits St.-Georges)
Georges Bryczek (Morey St.-Denis)
Alain Burguet (Gevrey-Chambertin)
Champy Père (Beaune)
Domaine Chandon de Briailles (Savigny-Les-Beaune)
Domaine de la Charrière (Santenay)
Jean Chauvenet (Nuits St.-Georges)
George Clerget (Vougeot)
Edmond Cornu (Ladoix)
Deroubaix-Indelli (Clos Vougeot)
Armand Douhairet (Monthelie)
Dubreuil-Fontaine (Pernand-Vergelesses)
Duchet (Beaune)
M. Ecard (Savigny-Les-Beaune)
René Engel (Vosne-Romanée)
Robert Groffier (Morey St.-Denis)
Jaffelin (Beaune)
Jacqueline Jayer (Vosne-Romanée)
Domaine Jacqueson (Chagny)
Jayer Gilles (Nuits St.-Georges)
Philippe Joliet (Fixin)
Lamy Pillot (Chassagne-Montrachet)
Domaine Comte Lafon (Meursault)

Henri Lamarche (Vosne-Romanée)
Lejeune (Pommard)
Lequin-Roussot (Santenay)
Georges Lignier (Morey St.-Denis)
Château de la Maltroye (Chassagne-Montrachet)
Manière-Noirot (Vosne-Romanée)
Matrot (Meursault)
Jean Meo (Vosne-Romanée)
Mestre (Santenay)
Alain Michelot (Nuits St.-Georges)
Moillard (Nuits St.-Georges)
Charles Moncault (Beaune)
Gerard Mugneret (Vosne-Romanée)
Charles Noëllat (Vosne-Romanée)
Andre Nudant (Nuits St.-Georges)
Jacques Parent (Pommard)
Pierre Ponnelle (Beaune)
M. Prunier (Auxey Duresses)
Rapet (Savigny-Les-Beaune)
Henri Rebourseau (Gevrey-Chambertin)
Remoissenet (Beaune)
Daniel Rion (Nuits St.-Georges)
Philippe Rossignol (Gevrey-Chambertin)
Daniel Senard (Aloxe-Corton)
Servelle Tachot (Clos Vougeot)
Robert Siruge (Vosne-Romanée)
Robert Suremaine (Monthelie)
Gabriel Tortochot (Gevrey-Chambertin)
Louis Trapet (Gevrey-Chambertin)

Vachet Rousseau (Gevrey-   Domaine des Varoilles (Gevrey-
   Chambertin)   Chambertin)

* * *(AVERAGE PRODUCERS)*

Arlaud (Nuits St.-Georges)   Lupé Cholet (Nuits St.-Georges)
Bernard Bachelet (Chassagne-   J. P. Magien (Gevrey-
   Montrachet)   Chambertin)
Bertagna (Vougeot)   Mommessin (Macon)
Chanson (Beaune)   Naigeon-Chauveau (Gevrey-
F. Chauvenet (Nuits   Chambertin)
   St.-Georges)   Patriarche (Beaune)
Chevalier (Aloxe-Corton)   Jacques Prieur (Meursault)
Coron (Beaune)   Prosper Maufoux (Santenay)
Damoy (Gevrey-Chambertin)   Charles Quillardet (Marsannay)
Albert Derey (Marsannay)   A. Rodet (Beaune)
Henri Gouges (Nuits   Charles Viénot (Nuits
   St.-Georges)   St.-Georges)
Jaboulet-Vercherre (Beaune)   Henri de Villamont (Beaune)
Labouré Roi (Beaune)   Comte de Vogüé (Chambolle-
Louis Latour (Beaune)   Musigny)

* *(OTHER PRODUCERS)*

Thomas Bassot (Gevrey-   Geisweiler (Nuits St.-Georges)
   Chambertin)   Pascal (Meursault)
Robert DuBois (Nuits   La Reine Pedanque (Beaune)
   St.-Georges)

The Best Wine Values in Red Burgundy

The glamour appellations of the Côte de Nuits and Côte de
Beaune offer exorbitant prices as well as irregular quality. Consequently, more and more wine-lovers are simply looking elsewhere for
Pinot Noir wines or are considering some of the less glamorous appellations of Burgundy where values can still be found. The following
chart lists the best red wine appellations when quality/price rapport is
important to you. In addition, the best producers of these appellations
are noted.

Fixin (Côte de Nuits) The only reasonable value left among the extravagantly expensive wines of the Côte de Nuits. Located next to
Gevrey-Chambertin, the wines of Fixin tend to be rustic, big, rather
full red burgundies. The top four producers to look for are Pierre
Gelin, Philippe Joliet, Guy Bertheau, and Bruno Clair.

Savigny-Les-Beaune (Côte de Beaune) A terribly underrated appellation, the Savigny wines often have a good, ripe, rich, strawberry and cherry fruitiness. Simon Bize, Ecard, Tollot-Beaut, Bruno Clair, and Tollot Voarick have very high standards.

Pernand-Vergelesses (Côte de Beaune) Perhaps the varying assessments of this appellation have kept its wines from an expensive notoriety. They are light, fragrant, and aromatic and resemble good Beaunes or Aloxe-Cortons, at a much lower price. Three producers stand out here—Robert Rapet, Dubreuil-Fontaine, and Domaine Chandon des Briailles.

Monthelie (Côte de Beaune) The neighbor of the much sought after, elegant, suave, lush wines of Volnay, Monthelie is terribly overlooked for robust, quality, fragrant Pinot Noir. Robert Suremain and Armand Douhairet are two growers to take note of.

Auxey-Duresses (Côte de Beaune) An up and coming appellation for both red and white burgundy, Auxey-Duresses does not have a charming, lyrical name, but Leroy and Michel Prunier make very fine wine here.

Chassagne-Montrachet (Côte de Beaune) Internationally famous for its splendidly perfumed, rich, white wines, Chassagne-Montrachet does not get enough respect for the fragrant, supple, red wines made here by such top growers as Château de la Maltroye and Lequin-Roussot.

Santenay (Côte de Beaune) Perhaps the most underrated appellation in the entire Cote d'Or, the quality level of wine made in Santenay is particularly high. The wines are sturdy and ageworthy, particularly for the Côte de Beaune, with rather deep, rich, long flavors when made by the likes of Lequin-Roussot, Adrian Belland, Domaine de la Charrière, Domaine de Pousse d'Or, Phillipe Mestre, and the *négociants* Joseph Drouhin and Remoissenet. All make delicious Santenays in the good vintages.

Values from Burgundy's Underbelly— The Côte Chalonnaise

Smart Europeans who enjoy red burgundy but cannot afford the luxurious prices of the famous wines have been seeking relief in the wine of the Côte Chalonnaise for decades. There is much good, not great, red burgundy made here that normally sells for under $15 a bottle, often for less than $10 a bottle. The following are the wines to look for and their best producers. The 1982s and 1985s from these appellations are more consistently successful than the 1983s and 1984s.

Rully Rully is best known as the closest wine village to the drab town of Chagny, which contains one of France's greatest restaurants, the hotel/restaurant Lameloise. There are five top red wine producers making very good Rully. The best are the Domaine de la Folie and Henri Jacqueson, then Jean-François Delorme, Chanzy, and the *négociant* Faiveley.

Mercurey Mercurey, though hardly world famous, is the best known of the appellations of the Côte Chalonnaise. The best wines are made by the excellent *négociants* Faiveley, Michel Juillot, Yves de Launay, and Chanzy Frères.

Givry My favorite wines of this area come from Givry. They have more richness and color than the other appellations. The Givry from Baron Thénard is first-class, followed by those of Gardin, who owns a vineyard called Clos Saloman.

Montagny Of the red wines of the Côte Chalonnaise, the wines of Montagny offer the least appeal. On the bright side, they are not expensive, but I know of no grower here making red wine as good as the aforementioned producers.

Burgundy—Today's Buying Strategy

More than any other wine of France, purchasing burgundy is fraught with the risk of paying top dollar for a mediocre or poor wine —it is a classic example of buying the proverbial pig in a poke. However, you have the names of the best producers. Mediocre vintages like 1984 and 1982 are very risky, but then so is a generally accepted top vintage like 1983. Thankfully, 1985 looks much more consistent in quality, with supple, fruity wines that are easy to taste and to understand. What does one do? In lieu of avoiding the region altogether, concentrate on buying only the very finest wines from the finest growers. They will be hard to find and very expensive, but if you want to taste what some experts think is the world's greatest wine, then this is the only way, as painfully expensive as it is. Look out also for any remaining 1980s that may turn up on the shelves, and if you can afford them, have a go at the excellent 1985s, Burgundy's most consistent vintage for red wines since 1978. Some 1983s will be fabulous, but proceed with great caution since the great majority of wines from this vintage are harsh and astringent. And remember . . . even the great 1983s need 8–10 years of cellaring. Worldwide demand for burgundy is simply too great for the tiny quantities of wines made; it will never be cheap, or even reasonably priced. To buy intelligently, you must learn—memorize is a better word—who the greatest producers are and then buy only their wines. They will make better wines in vintages such as 1984 and 1982 than less conscientious growers will in high-quality years such as 1985.

PIERRE AMIOT (MOREY ST.-DENIS)* * *

In my experience, Amiot is one of Burgundy's most hospitable vignerons. More importantly, he is an excellent winemaker. In contrast to many of his peers who produced poor and insipid wines in 1981 and 1982, Amiot did quite well in both vintages. His 1983s are also quite good, though not spectacular. Amiot's style of burgundy emphasizes velvety, soft, ripe, rich flavors. His wines are round and fruity with considerable charm and flavor. My instinct tells me that they are not candidates for long-term cellaring, but then how many burgundies are? Amiot was also very successful in 1984 and his wines will be worth looking for in that terribly maligned vintage.

1983 Clos de la Roche	($40.00)	85
1983 Gevrey-Chambertin Aux Combottes	($27.00)	84
1983 Morey St.-Denis Aux Charmes	($25.00)	84
1983 Morey St.-Denis Les Baudes	($25.00)	84
1983 Morey St.-Denis Millandes	($25.00)	82
1983 Morey St.-Denis Villages	($18.00)	80

As the scores indicate, the wines are quite consistently successful, if not at the very highest level of quality. In general, Amiot's 1983s typify the Michael Broadbent expression "an iron fist in a velvet glove." They have a good measure of tannin but also more supple, lush, voluptuous fruit than one usually finds in the 1983s.

Most of Amiot's 1983s need a good 5–6 years of cellaring, but are clearly much more accessible, fragrant, and precocious than other 1983s. Comparing them, the Clos de la Roche has the most class, slightly more concentration and complexity, but both the Morey St.-Denis Les Baudes and Morey St.-Denis Aux Charmes are delicious, rich, and fruity wines with broad, authentic Pinot Noir flavors. The Les Baudes is slightly more tannic and darker in color and will evolve less quickly. The Gevrey-Chambertin Aux Combottes is perhaps the biggest wine Amiot made in 1983, rather substantial and alcoholic, with ripe, earthy flavors. It clearly begs for 5–6 years. The Morey St.-

Denis Villages has lovely, open-knit, broad, round, fruity flavors and at present is the most easily drunk wine of Amiot. In contrast, the Morey St.-Denis Millandes is Amiot's darkest colored as well as his most backwardly tannic wine. It needs 8 years of cellaring.

1982 Clos de la Roche	($28.95)	86

1982 Gevrey-Chambertin Aux Combottes	($19.00)	83

1982 Morey St.-Denis Aux Charmes	($18.00)	83

There are not many 1982s, particularly from the Côte de Nuits, that are this good. Unlike the 1983s, which require some patience, these wines are best drunk over the next 1–3 years. Amiot's 1982s are more concentrated than many of his peers, quite perfumed, fruity, and lush, with low acidity, soft tannins, and good, round yet long finishes. The Clos de la Roche is very, very good and has quite a complex bouquet of raspberries, flowers, and spicy oak. It should be drunk over the next 3 years. Both the Morey St.-Denis Aux Charmes and Gevrey-Chambertin Aux Combottes are lighter in weight and less rich. The Gevrey-Chambertin is also more spicy and earthy.

DOMAINE ARLAUD (NUITS ST.-GEORGES)* *

Located on the back streets of Nuits St.-Georges, the Domaine Arlaud has 12 hectares spread throughout the Côte de Nuits. The wines produced here in 1982 and 1983 are rather fat, highly chaptalized, well-colored wines that purists might criticize as being too sweet, but they are inexpensive and actually quite delicious to taste. Surprisingly, the 1982s had more color and richness than the 1983s.

1983 Chambolle-Musigny	($12.95)	85

1983 Charmes-Chambertin	($18.00)	84

These two 1983s from Arlaud have the tannic toughness of the vintage but also show the apparent house style in that they are rather fat, alcoholic, jammy, and richly fruity. There is quite a lot of Pinot Noir flavor and a pleasing lushness. No doubt both should be drunk over the next 2–4 years. The Chambolle-Musigny is much the better value.

1982 Clos de la Roche	($17.95)	86

1982 Morey St.-Denis	($16.95)	85

Two legitimate "sleepers," these two succulent 1982s are surprisingly deep colored, have rather sweet tastes with some powerful alcohol present, but do indeed exhibit masses of fruit, a rich, perfumed, spicy, ripe, plummy bouquet, and round, velvety finishes. They should be drunk over the next few years because of low acidity, but now offer quite a mouthful of burgundy.

ROBERT ARNOUX (VOSNE-ROMANÉE)* * * *

The towering, somewhat formidable looking Robert Arnoux has received excellent reviews for his fragrant, rich, spicy, deeply flavored burgundies. Both his 1978s and 1980s were among the very best wines of those respective vintages. I find the style of wine of Arnoux to be somewhat like that of the famous Domaine de la Romanée-Conti: perhaps not as broad and deep, but similarly rich, expansive, pure Pinot Noir wines. The 1982s are somewhat weak by Arnoux's standards, and I doubt that his 1983s are better than either his best 1980s or 1978s. Interestingly, he bottled his 1983s very early, in late winter of 1985. Arnoux employed 30% new oak barrels for the 1983 vintage, and does not filter his wines. His 1984s looked mediocre from the cask; his 1985s are great successes.

1983 Clos Vougeot	($35.00)	87
1983 Nuits St.-Georges Les Corvées-Paget	($26.95)	79
1983 Nuits St.-Georges Les Poisets	($23.95)	82
1983 Vosne-Romanée	($15.95)	78
1983 Vosne-Romanée Les Chaumes	($26.95)	85
1983 Vosne-Romanée Les Suchots	($26.95)	86
1983 Vosne-Romanée Premier Cru	($21.95)	78

As the above scores indicate, Arnoux made good 1983s, but given a choice, I would opt for his lineup of 1980s and 1978s over these wines, if they can still be found. My main criticism of the Arnoux 1983s is that, with the possible exception of the Clos Vougeot and Vosne-Romanée Les Suchots and Les Chaumes, they are extremely tannic, perhaps to excess. From cask and from bottle, the Clos Vougeot looks to be the best. It has the deepest color of all Arnoux's wines, with an exotic bouquet of toasty oak, licorice, and blackcurrants. Full-bodied, tannic, but balanced, it needs 8–10 years of cellaring. Next best, and usually the top wine from Arnoux, the Vosne-Romanée Les Suchots shows less complexity than the 1980 and 1978 did at a similar stage, but has a deep color, hard tannin, plenty of power and fruit, and a dry finish. It needs 7–8 years to develop fully. Les Chaumes is also very good, but lacks the dimension in flavor and depth compared to the Clos Vougeot and Les Suchots. Arnoux's two selections from Nuits St.-Georges are good, but given the reputation of Arnoux and the vintage, are not terribly exciting wines. Les Poisets is deeper and more attractive, with a spicy blackcurrant fruitiness. The Les Corvées-Paget has less color, is rather light, with an excess of tannin in the finish. Both the Vosne-Romanée and Vosne-Romanée Premier Cru share adequate color, body, and depth, but are extremely harsh and astringent. I doubt that the fruit can outlast the tannin.

1984 Bourgogne	($10.00)	76
1982 Clos Vougeot	($30.00)	84
1982 Nuits St.-Georges Les Corvées-Paget	($20.00)	80
1982 Nuits St.-Georges Les Poisets	($18.00)	75
1982 Romanée St.-Vivant	($35.00)	84
1982 Vosne-Romanée Les Chaumes	($20.00)	80
1982 Vosne-Romanée Les Suchots	($20.00)	82

All of these wines are sound, generally above-average examples of the 1982 vintage. Fruity, medium ruby wines with soft textures, decent concentration, the Nuits St.-Georges Les Poisets is the most tannic, angular, and charmless. The two best wines are the Clos Vougeot and Romanée St.-Vivant. The latter has broad, soft, raspberry fruit flavors with a nice touch of vanillin oakiness. It will make a fine bottle for drinking over the next 1–2 years, but at a very high price. The former wine, the Clos Vougeot, is elegant, rather light, medium-bodied, and soft, but effusively fruity, clean, and charming. Les Suchots is marked more by new oak, but is an agreeable, fruity wine.

BERNARD BACHELET (CHASSAGNE-MONTRACHET)* *

This small estate in Chassagne-Montrachet makes both red and white burgundy of good quality. Most consumers probably ignore the red wines for more prestigious appellations, but red wines from Chassagne-Montrachet do indeed represent good values.

1983 Chassagne-Montrachet	($15.99)	80
1983 Côte de Beaune-Villages	($14.99)	78
1983 Santenay	($12.99)	84

These three wines exhibit the irregularity one finds in the 1983 vintage. The Côte de Beaune-Villages is quite alcoholic and big, with an aggressive finish. Rather awkward at the moment, it should be better in 1–2 years. The Chassagne-Montrachet has very fine color, but suffers from an excessively high level of hard tannins, though the underdeveloped bouquet of leather and berry fruits hints at finer things. My favorite is the Santenay, a dark, rather tannic but full-bodied, rich, deep wine that provides the concentration of fruit to outlast the tannins. It needs 4 years.

BARTHOD NOËLLAT (CHAMBOLLE-MUSIGNY)* * *

The elderly Monsieur Barthod is one of the tiny growers in Burgundy who make awfully good, natural, pure Pinot Noir wine that is unfiltered. He is rather aloof, perhaps even shy, but seems to warm up when sufficient interest is taken in his wines. His 1983s are full of charm and elegance, without the excess of tannin one so often finds in the wines of this vintage. He is also another viticulteur who succeeded admirably in overcoming the problems of both the 1982 and 1984 vintages and managed to make good wine. Barthod's winemaking style produces rather lightly colored wines that are much more flavorful and rich than their color suggests. His 1983s are likely to be drunk young because of their soft textures, although there is good tannin in the finish.

1983 Chambolle-Musigny	($16.95)	84
1983 Chambolle-Musigny Les Charmes	($19.95)	86

Both of these wines were rather light in color, particularly for 1983s, but one whiff of the rich, complex, fruity, smoky, spicy bouquet leaves no doubt that some serious wine is in the glass. They are ripe, fat, fleshy wines with surprisingly soft tannins. The Les Charmes has more to it in both aroma and flavor. Somewhat hard to resist even at this early stage, but 4–6 years will reveal more pleasures.

ADRIAN BELLAND (SANTENAY)* * *

I only wish more and more consumers wanting to enjoy reasonably priced red burgundy would seek out the wines of Santenay. This sleepy little town is in the southern part of the Côte de Beaune and its treasures are a bevy of underpublicized wines and producers. When I visited Belland, I was struck by the quality of his wines and the reasonable prices. He makes a range of wines (even a Chambertin), but in 1983 most of his best came from the surrounding vineyards. His wines are deeply colored, tannic, quite concentrated and full-bodied, and if they have a flaw at all, it is a lack of finesse. Nevertheless, these are burgundies with flavor.

1983 Chambertin	($35.00)	84
1983 Corton Clos de la Vigne Cent	($18.99)	87
1983 Corton Grèves	($18.95)	75
1983 Santenay	($10.99)	83
1983 Santenay Les Gravières	($14.99)	85

The near-classic in this group is the lovely Corton Clos de la Vigne Cent, which is a very rich, beautifully concentrated, full-bodied wine with an impressive, leathery, rich, plummy bouquet, and very long finish. The Santenay Les Gravières is also very good and quite a fine value given its quality. It has a big, toasty, spicy, rather full-blown bouquet, ripe, rich flavors, deep color, and a clean, moderately tannic finish. Neither of the aforementioned wines will be at their peaks before 1990. The Santenay is big and alcoholic, but very tannic, and though I have scored it high, I am concerned about the fruit/tannin balance. The Corton Grèves is the lightest, and while there is plenty to like—a leathery, spicy aroma, rich, alcoholic flavor—I believe there is an excess of tannin and a touch of rot in the taste that has also caused the color to lighten. Belland makes some Chambertin, and the 1983 is quite good, smoky, rather light in color, but rich and powerful, with plenty of alcohol. It is, however, too expensive.

DOMAINE GUY BERTHAUT (FIXIN)* * *

Fixin is, of course, the little town that sits several kilometers north of Gevrey-Chambertin. The wines have always represented good values. Berthaut's wines are quite robustly styled, big, and rather forceful. He is quite an honest winemaker and willing to discuss problems he has had in a particular year. Interestingly, his 1983s tasted severe and dry, with traces of the ominous *"goût de sec."* Berthaut's wines are rather modestly priced, but quite limited in availability. No filtering occurs at this estate.

1983 Fixin Les Arvelets	($16.00)	80
1983 Fixin Les Clos	($16.00)	78
1983 Fixin Les Crais	($15.00)	75
1983 Gevrey-Chambertin	($22.00)	78

All of these wines are terribly tannic in a rather severe way. With the exception of Les Arvelets, I just could not detect enough fruit to balance out the tannins. Perhaps 10 years of cellaring will prove me wrong, but I think Berthaut's 1983s are real gambles.

1982 Fixin Clos d'Entre Deux Velles	($14.95)	85
1982 Fixin Les Arvelets	($14.95)	85
1982 Fixin Les Clos	($10.99)	84
1982 Fixin Les Crais	($10.99)	82
1982 Gevrey-Chambertin	($13.95)	75

Berthaut's production per acre was significantly less than most growers in 1982, and the results are wines that are deeply colored, rich in ripe fruit, and quite well balanced. They are much better than his 1983s and are perfect examples of why vintage charts are not to be blindly relied upon. All of these wines, save for the mediocre, light, diluted Gevrey-Chambertin, are rich, fruity, and delicious. They will all last 4–6 years minimum. The Les Arvelets is simply lovely, sweet, ripe, rich, and full-bodied, and will be a fine bottle of wine in 4–5 years. The Les Clos is nearly its equal, deeply colored, a little bigger and more tannic, but shockingly deep for a 1982. The Clos d'Entre

Deux Velles is the most precociously styled, with ripe, rich fruit, a fleshy fatness, and a lively, robust, leathery, peppery bouquet.

DOMAINE BÉSANCENOT-MATHOUILLET (BEAUNE)* * *

This small, well-run domaine right outside the walls of Beaune makes very elegant, fragrant, supple, silky, easy to enjoy wines from vineyards in the Côte de Beaune. In previous years (1979 and 1980) the wines tasted fully mature when released, but the 1983 Besancenot's wines will need 4–5 years to reach their peak. The two top wines tasted were very, very fine, exhibiting no signs of rot and showing excellent balance. He made very fine 1985s.

1983 Beaune Cent Vignes	($15.95)	86
1983 Beaune Clos du Roi	($15.95)	85

Both of these wines were quite impressive from the cask, showing rich, concentrated cherry fruit, spicy, fragrant bouquets, long, lush textures, and moderate, ripe, round tannins. They had a good measure of alcohol (13–13.5%), as do most 1983s, but were impeccably clean and well-made wines for drinking over the near future.

BICHOT-CLOS FRANTIN (BEAUNE)* * *

This firm makes a lot of mediocre burgundy, but at the top level its estate-bottled wines from the Domaine du Clos Frantin and Chablis from their estate called Long-Depaquit can be excellent. The 1983 reds from Clos Frantin are irregular. They will need time in the bottle to shed their tannins.

1983 Clos Vougeot	($27.00)	87
1983 Corton	($22.00)	82
1983 Echézeaux	($25.00)	80
1983 Gevrey-Chambertin	($14.00)	75
1983 Vosne-Romanée Malconsorts	($23.00)	85

The star here is the Clos Vougeot, which is ripe, rich, very tannic and well colored. The Vosne-Romanée Malconsorts is more advanced but still in need of 5–7 years of aging. As for the other wines, the Gevrey-

Chambertin is tough and severe, the Echézeaux very tannic but light on the palate, and the Corton very closed, dry, and rather astringent.

DOMAINE BILLARD-GONNET (POMMARD)* * *

My experience with Billard-Gonnet's wines has been very young vintages, all of which have tasted rather tough, closed, and quite backward. Not surprisingly, his 1983s were reserved and restrained wines obviously made for long-term cellaring. His Pommards looked to be the best, but if you are not willing to wait a minimum of 10 years, then you had best seek out a more supple style of burgundy from these pages.

1983 Beaune La Lune Montrevenots	($22.00)	72
1983 Pommard	($22.00)	80
1983 Pommard Les Chaponnières	($28.00)	85
1983 Pommard Les Rugiens	($32.00)	86

The Beaune is very light in color, has a pleasant bouquet, but tastes weak and simple on the palate. The Pommard is certainly a good run-of-the-mill wine, but lacks excitement and personality. The Pommard Les Chaponnières has considerably more personality, a dark ruby color, a chocolate and spice box aroma, long, ripe, sufficiently deep flavors, but hard, rather dry tannins. It has the balance, but one must wait until 1995. The Pommard Les Rugiens is an even bigger, richer, more alcoholic wine, with considerable depth, flavor, and mouth-searing tannins. It may be ready by 1995.

LUCIEN BOILLOT (GEVREY-CHAMBERTIN)* * *

There are a number of Boillots making wine in Burgundy. Lucien usually does a respectable job (his 1982s were lovely); however, the 1983s tasted were terribly tannic and astringent and may be totally tainted by the rot and mildew that was such a problem for many winemakers in 1983. They have good color, but are totally out of balance. The Nuits St.-George Les Pruliers is the best of an otherwise dreary lot of wines.

1983 Côte de Nuits-Villages	($12.50)	62
1983 Gevrey-Chambertin	($24.95)	55

1983 Gevrey-Chambertin Les Cherbandes	($32.50)	75
1983 Nuits St.-Georges Les Pruliers	($32.00)	82
1983 Pommard	($24.00)	60
1983 Volnay Les Angles	($32.00)	70

DOMAINE PIERRE BOURÉE (GEVREY-CHAMBERTIN)* * * *

This has always been an intriguing *négociant* to follow. There is no Pierre Bourée, but instead a shy yet very professional Monsieur Valait who runs the operation. The wines of the Bourée firm have, justifiably, a loyal following. Generally well colored, chunky and slow to develop, I have always found them to be of a good level of quality but stubbornly backward. This is a very traditionally run operation. The 1983s were bottled directly from the barrel (no assemblage to avoid barrel-to-barrel differences) and, thankfully, there was no flavor-stripping filtration. The firm is excited about the 1983s, which they claim are better than the 1978s. There are quite a few wines produced here, and though I tasted no great wines, I tasted quite a few good to very good ones.

Bourée (Côte de Beaune)

1983 Beaune Premier Cru	($19.95)	84
1983 Bourgogne Passetout Grains	($8.50)	80
1983 Chassagne-Montrachet	($11.95)	80
1983 Corton	($25.00)	87
1983 Pernand-Vergelesses	($14.95)	80
1983 Santenay Gravières	($15.95)	87
1983 Volnay	($15.95)	79

As the above scores reflect, there is a greater range in quality in Bourée Côte de Beaune wines than those from the Côte de Nuits, where, of course, the firm is based. The two stars from the Côte de Beaune are the wonderful Santenay Gravières and the powerful Corton. The Santenay Gravières may ultimately merit a higher score. It was among the very finest Santenays I tasted and could clearly hold its own against many Grand Cru red burgundies. Fleshy, deeply colored with rich, ripe, concentrated fruit, it should prove to be a real eye-opener between 1995–2000. The Corton is equally impressive, perhaps a trifle more rustic, alcoholic, and powerful, but very, very fine, and again has enough fruit to outlast the tannins. Like the Santenay, 1990–2000 should be this wine's glory years.

Bourée (Côte de Nuits)

1983 Bonnes Mares	($40.00)	86
1983 Chambertin	($50.00)	85
1983 Chambolle-Musigny	($19.95)	74
1983 Charmes-Chambertin	($32.95)	84
1983 Clos Vougeot	($35.00)	87
1983 Côte de Nuits-Villages	($9.95)	83
1983 Echézeaux	($40.00)	87
1983 Gevrey-Chambertin Clos de la Justice	($19.95)	88
1983 Gevrey-Chambertin Premier Cru	($18.95)	86
1983 Latricières-Chambertin	($35.00)	84
1983 Morey St.-Denis	($17.95)	84
1983 Nuits St.-Georges	($18.95)	78
1983 Vosne-Romanée	($19.95)	78

The Bourée firm produces an extensive range of red burgundies from the Côte de Nuits, as the above list reflects. In 1983 the quality here was quite consistently good. The "villages" or commune wines, Morey St.-Denis, Vosne-Romanée, Nuits St.-Georges, Chambolle-Musigny, and so on, are what one expects. The Morey is much better than the others, the Chambolle-Musigny too dry and severe and perhaps affected by the hail that hit this commune. Certainly, the Gevrey-Chambertin Clos de la Justice, always one of Bourée's best wines, is especially rich, tannic, full-bodied, and concentrated in 1983. Its smoky, plummy, earthy bouquet and big, rich flavors beg for 5–7 years of cellaring. The Gevrey-Chambertin Premier Cru is almost as good, more supple, but rich, savory, fat, and quite forward-tasting. It should be at its best in 4–5 years. Curiously, the Grand Cru Latricières-Chambertin is less rich than the Clos de la Justice or Premier Cru. Nevertheless, it is quite flavorful, robust, and in need of 3–6 years of cellaring. The Clos Vougeot is excellent, with a rich bouquet of berry fruit, some toasty, vanillin oakiness, long, deep, rich flavors, immense body, and very good length. It will be excellent in 1995. Both the Echézeaux and Bonnes Mares are rather atypical 1983s in that they are surprisingly light in color, very lush and accessible, and should be ready to drink soon, say in 3–4 years. Both are lovely wines with the bouquet of the Echézeaux particularly fine. The Charmes-Chambertin looked and felt promising, but was quite closed, and the Chambertin was alcoholic, fat, spicy, long in the finish, but rather forward. I suspect it will be ready by 1992. Lastly, don't overlook Bourée's Côte de Nuits-Villages, which in 1983 is like previous renditions of this wine, always a good value and one of the better wines of its type. It should be drunk over the next 2–3 years.

L. J. BRUCK (NUITS ST.-GEORGES)* * *

A medium-sized *négociant* in Nuits St.-Georges, this firm produces wines that are generally well colored, tannic, and firm, but perhaps a little dry and dull. The wines from vineyards in Nuits St.-Georges and Gevrey-Chambertin have been, in my opinion, the best.

1983 Chambolle-Musigny	($20.00)	68
1983 Côte de Nuits-Villages	($12.00)	80
1983 Echézeaux	($35.00)	84
1983 Gevrey-Chambertin	($18.00)	81
1983 Gevrey-Chambertin Lavaux St.-Jacques	($25.00)	85
1983 Hautes Côte de Nuits	($8.00)	78

1983 Nuits St.-Georges Corvées-Pagets	($25.00)	86

One sees the house style in all of these burgundies, from the lower-priced Hautes Côtes de Nuits to the Echézeaux. The wines have good color, full body, some tough tannin, but a trace of dullness. The Nuits St.-Georges Corvées Pagets, aged in 100% new oak barrels, is a big, forceful, rich, ripe wine with plenty of concentration and a big, alcoholic finish. It certainly was the best of the red wines I tasted from Bruck. The Gevrey-Chambertin Lavaux St.-Jacques also stood out for having the requisite richness of fruit to balance out the hard tannins of the 1983 vintage. The expensive Echézeaux is well made, perhaps a little too alcoholic, but tasty and rather precociously styled.

ALAIN BURGUET (GEVREY-CHAMBERTIN)* * *

This small grower makes only a Gevrey-Chambertin, but it is usually quite concentrated and powerful, and for a straight *village* appellation wine, perhaps the best one can find.

1983 Gevrey-Chambertin	($15.95)	72
1982 Gevrey-Chambertin	($15.95)	83
1981 Gevrey-Chambertin	($15.95)	80

The highly touted 1983 vintage has produced a wine that is quite darkly colored but abrasively tannic. Ten years of cellaring is the bare minimum, but will the fruit hold? In contrast, the forward, rich, ripe, fruity 1982 has oodles of berry fruit, good spice and color, and can be drunk over the next 4 years. The 1981 is tannic and has power, but lacks elegance and charm.

CHAMPY PÈRE (BEAUNE)* * *

This is the oldest *négociant* in all of Burgundy, dating from 1720. The 1983s I tasted were not that impressive, but acceptable, save for the Clos Vougeot. They seemed to be made in a rather old, heavy style.

1983 Beaune Avaux	($18.95)	83
1983 Clos Vougeot	($27.95)	75
1983 Savigny Dominode	($12.95)	78

Considering how very successful the wines of Clos Vougeot were in 1983, I was surprised by the lack of quality apparent in this bottle, which was good but not special. The Savigny Dominode is robust and beefy, a solid, rather heavy, rustic sort of wine that should be at its best in 1990. The Beaune Avaux was the best of these Champy wines. It had a vivid bouquet of cherry fruit and oak, a full-bodied texture, and 12 years of evolution ahead of it.

DOMAINE DE LA CHARRIÈRE (SANTENAY)* * *

The wines from this estate are another example of why consumers should take more notice of the good values that emanate from Santenay. Monsieur Girardin makes solid wines at this estate that are chunky, robust, deeply fruity, and ageworthy. The 1985s are delicious here.

1983 Santenay La Combe	($9.99)	85

1983 Santenay Maladière	($9.99)	85

Both of these wines are quite robust, well colored, fleshy, and ripe and should age well for up to a decade. The Maladière has more interest to its aroma and flavor. It is hard to find burgundies of this quality for this price.

1982 Santenay	($8.99)	78

1982 Santenay Clos Roussot	($9.99)	81

The *village* Santenay is round, gentle, light, and pleasant. The Clos Roussot has more flavor and character. Both should be drunk soon.

JEAN CHAUVENET (NUITS ST.-GEORGES)* * *

This moderate sized grower located just north of Nuits St.-Georges makes very elegant, medium-bodied wines that are well balanced and clean. Based on the vintages I have tasted in the 1980s, his wines are best drunk within the first 5–6 years, but the more tannic 1983s are likely to require longer. Chauvenet also made above-average-quality wines in both 1984 and 1982. His best wine looks to be consistently Les Vaucrains, the Premier Cru Nuits St.-Georges. Chauvenet does not filter his wines.

1983 Mazis-Chambertin	($40.00)	87

1983 Nuits St.-Georges	($15.00)	83

| 1983 Nuits St.-Georges La Perrière | ($18.00) | 83 |

| 1983 Nuits St.-Georges Les Vaucrains | ($22.00) | 85 |

| 1983 Vosne-Romanée | ($18.00) | 81 |

Chauvenet's Vosne-Romanée and Nuits St.-Georges are rather understated but graceful wines, yet typical of his winemaking style. They should drink well within the first 4 years of life, but will not be for the long term. The Nuits St.-Georges La Perrière has more weight and richness but in effect is still on the charming lighter side for a 1983. The Mazis-Chambertin and Nuits St.-Georges Les Vaucrains have the broadest and most expansive flavors, and show very good winemaking, some subtle, smoky notes, and firm tannins. Both should be at their best by 1990 and hold for 5–7 years thereafter.

| 1982 Nuits St.-Georges | ($12.95) | 78 |

| 1982 Nuits St.-Georges Les Vaucrains | ($16.95) | 85 |

Chauvenet's 1982 Les Vaucrains is every bit as good as his 1983. Softer and quite ready to drink, it is a very classy, supple wine with a smooth, broad, gentle berry fruitiness, some subtle, spicy oak, and a good finish. The Nuits St.-Georges is pleasant, cleanly made, but a little too simple and bland.

ROBERT CHEVILLON (NUITS ST.-GEORGES)* * * *

Robert Chevillon has, since 1978, clearly established his domaine as one of the finest in the Cote d'Or. If one were to judge the 1983 vintage by his wines, then all the hoopla and hype would be totally justified. His 1983s are marvelous and among the very finest and best-balanced wines of this notoriously overrated vintage. His 1982s are especially good, and he has turned out super 1985s.

| 1983 Nuits St.-Georges | ($20.00) | 81 |

| 1983 Nuits St.-Georges La Perrière | ($30.00) | 87 |

| 1983 Nuits St.-Georges Les Cailles | ($30.00) | 86 |

| 1983 Nuits St.-Georges Les Saint Georges | ($34.95) | 90 |

1983 Nuits St.-Georges Les Vaucrains   ($34.95)   88

One wishes that all producers of red burgundy had been as successful as Chevillon in 1983. The wines from La Perrière, Les Vaucrains, and Les Saint Georges are rich and intense, pure and clean, and show no evidence of rot or hail damage. The colors are dark, the bouquets explosive, and the length and balance truly superb. They are bigger and much more full-bodied than usual, with a powerful alcoholic clout. Expect these three wines to be at their best between 1992–2000. As the scores note, the Les Saint Georges is one of the great wines of this vintage. As for the other 1983s, Les Cailles is slightly tougher and more tannic and I have less confidence that it will hit the heights of Chevillon's other wines. The *village* wine is good, a little stern and unyielding, but well made.

1982 Nuits St.-Georges   ($11.95)   78

1982 Nuits St.-Georges La Perrière   ($16.95)   80

1982 Nuits St.-Georges Les Roncières   ($15.95)   81

1982 Nuits St.-Georges Les Saint-Georges   ($19.95)   83

1982 Nuits St.-Georges Les Vaucrains   ($19.95)   88

All of these wines are above-average 1982s, except for Les Vaucrains, which is very good. Les Vaucrains has an open-knit, smoky, spicy, marvelous bouquet, a ripe raspberry fruitiness, good body, and a round, gentle finish. It should be drunk over the next 2–3 years. Chevillon's other 1982s are lighter in weight but generally ready for consumption since they are only moderately concentrated and have light, soft tannins.

BRUNO CLAIR (MARSANNAY)* * * *

I doubt that many burgundy-lovers spend much time in Marsannay, the tiny village between Dijon and Fixin that is known for producing Burgundy's best rosé wine. This new domaine was started in 1979 by Bruno Clair after he left the famous domaine Clair-Daü because of a family squabble. The young Bruno Clair is a very serious winemaker. His 1984s are quite good and the few 1983s he made even more noteworthy. There is also a little bit of a white Fixin made here from Pinot Blanc that is outstanding for its quality and low price. The 1985s are marvelous.

1982 Bourgogne	($10.00)	82
1983 Fixin La Colle Blanche	($15.00)	84
1983 Morey St-Denis	($15.00)	81
1983 Savigny-Les-Beaune Dominode	($20.00)	88

One look at the scores might cause some to think there is a typo for the Savigny "Dominode." Yes, the darkly colored wine does merit the score. It is extremely powerful, dense, rich, full-bodied wine with plenty of tannin and a great finish. Clair told me it was made from 80-year-old vines. It will need 8–10 years of cellaring. The Fixin La Colle Blanche may suffer in comparison, but it is a rich, beefy, ripe, very well-made wine that should be ready in 4–5 years. The Morey St.-Denis is above average, but a little tough and perhaps excessively tannic. The generic Bourgogne is one of the best of its type, fruity, fat, clean and very attractive, for drinking over the next several years.

DOMAINE CLAIR-DAÜ (MARSANNAY)* * * *

Between 1971 and 1980 this estate produced quite mediocre wines that in no way merited the price demanded for them nor reflected the excellent reputation this very important domaine had in the '60s. Several 1970s tasted recently very extremely rich, fine wines. Well, the 1983s were among the finest red burgundies I sampled. Rich in color and extract, there was none of the *"goût de sec"* or *"goût de moisi"* (dryness or musty flavors) that taints many 1983 red burgundies. The prices for the Clair-Daü 1983s seem reasonable, given the quality, and I urge readers to try these wines as examples of some of the best 1983s I saw. In 1985, the Clair-Daü firm was purchased by the large, important Beaune *négociant*, Louis Jadot. The wines will appear under Jadot's label in the future.

1983 Bonnes Mares	($36.00)	90
1983 Bourgogne	($5.99)	83
1983 Chambertin Clos de Bèze	($40.00)	89
1983 Chambolle-Musigny Les Amoureuses	($35.00)	88
1983 Chapelle-Chambertin	($25.00)	86

1983 Clos Vougeot	($30.00)	87

1983 Gevrey-Chambertin Clos de Fonteny	($17.50)	86

1983 Gevrey-Chambertin Clos St.-Jacques	($25.00)	85

1983 Gevrey-Chambertin Les Cazetiers	($18.00)	89

1983 Vosne-Romanée Champs Perdrix	($17.50)	85

It is easy to start with superlatives concerning the 1983 Clair-Daü wines, certainly this domaine's best vintage since 1970. All of the wines have excellent color and clean, ripe Pinot Noir aromas. They all possess various degrees of rich, fat character, good, ripe tannins, and very good to great depth. Most of the 1983 Clair-Daü wines should reach maturity between 1990 and 1995. For value, the Bourgogne is very good at $6. At the top level, the Bonnes Mares was dense, ripe, rich, and close to being spectacular. It already had a hauntingly great perfume. The Chambertin Clos de Bèze and Gevrey-Chambertin les Cazetiers are both strong, robust, alcoholic, rich wines; they have powerful bouquets, deep colors, layers of Pinot Noir fruit, and a total absence of any taste or smell of rot. The Chambolle-Musigny Les Amoureuses is notable for its sheer elegance and lush seductiveness; it is named appropriately in 1983. The Clos Vougeot is a very big wine, perhaps a little rustic and overblown in size and weight, but if it reveals some finesse with bottle aging, it could well prove to be outstanding. Of all these wines, the Chapelle-Chambertin and Clos St.-Jacques have the lightest color and appear to be the two wines (along with the Bourgogne) that should mature fully before 1990. Both are still packed with fruit and are simply more precocious than the others. The Clair-Daü 1983s were extremely exciting wines to taste and marked the return of this domaine to one of the leaders in Burgundy.

DOMAINE GEORGE CLERGET (VOUGEOT)* * *

There are several Clergets in Burgundy, but to my knowledge this is the only one from the Côte de Nuits. My only experience with this estate's wines were the five different 1983s. The wines were good, with surprisingly rich, deep colors and enough fruit to stand up to the tannins.

1983 Bourgogne	($10.00)	82
1983 Chambolle-Musigny	($18.00)	82
1983 Chambolle-Musigny Les Charmes	($25.00)	86
1983 Echézeaux	($45.00)	88
1983 Vosne-Romanée La Violette	($20.00)	84

All of these wines have surprisingly deep colors and show none of the bitter, harsh, dry, dusty tannins that frequently show up elsewhere. The simple Bourgogne is inexpensive and offers robust, ripe, plummy fruit. It should be drunk over the next 1–2 years. I liked it as much as the Chambolle-Musigny, which is a solid, chunky, fruity wine but, for its appellation, lacks a little complexity. The Vosne-Romanée La Violette is a rather rich, fat, moderately tannic wine with good concentration, clean, pure Pinot Noir flavors, and 5–6 years of development ahead of it. The two best wines are the Chambolle-Musigny Les Charmes, which is quite concentrated, chewy and rich, with full body and a deep, dark color, and the Echézeaux, a dark ruby-colored wine that has rich cassis and plumlike fruit, medium to full body, and a lingering finish. It should be at its best between 1988–1995.

DOMAINE EDMOND CORNU (LADOIX)* * *

The tall, lean Edmond Cornu is not yet one of Burgundy's best-known producers. I have followed his wines since 1981; they are very good quality and are reasonably priced. His wines are generally from Burgundy's least-known appellations of Chorey-Les-Beaune, Ladoix, and Savigny, but as any connoisseur knows, this is where the values are. He did not produce great 1983s—few producers did—but he did make very attractive wines.

1983 Aloxe-Corton	($14.00)	85
1983 Aloxe-Corton Les Moutottes	($16.00)	83
1983 Chorey-Les-Beaune	($12.00)	83
1983 Corton Bressandes	($24.00)	87
1983 Ladoix	($12.00)	84

1983 Savigny-Les-Beaune   ($14.00)   82

The obvious star from Cornu's 1983 wines is the Corton Bressandes. It is a powerful wine, rich in color and extract, with layers of ripe fruit, and good, firm, but not astringent tannins. However, it will need 8–10 years of cellaring. Those who cannot defer their gratification would be better advised to try the less expensive Chorey-Les-Beaune, with its bouquet of leather and cherries, medium body, and good, clean fruit, or the spicy, cherry-scented, medium-bodied Ladoix. Two tough, tannic customers are the Savigny-Les-Beaune, which may turn out to be too tannic for its own good, although it seems to have ample fruit, and the Aloxe-Corton Les Moutottes, a leathery, spicy yet hard, *"très dur"* wine, as the French say. The Aloxe-Corton is a contrast to these two wines, almost jammy with rather deep, alcoholic, rich flavors. It needs 5–8 years.

ALBERT DEREY (MARSANNAY)* *

A little-known, yet from what I have seen, competent, producer of red burgundy, this man's wines are generally quite reasonably priced.

1983 Bourgogne Coteaux de Couchey   ($7.99)   83

1983 Bourgogne Les Vignes Marie   ($7.49)   81

1983 Fixin   ($8.99)   60

The two generic wines represent good values for burgundy. The Les Vignes Marie is a good, medium-bodied, somewhat robust, earthy wine for drinking over the next 1–2 years. It has plenty of appeal. The Coteaux de Couchey is somewhat of a sleeper in this vintage of mixed results. Supple, ripe, rather broad Pinot Noir flavors show good depth, an alcoholic punch, and some complexity. It is best drunk over the next 1–2 years. The Fixin had an orange rim and a smell of rot. It is a real risk.

JOSEPH DROUHIN (BEAUNE)* * * *

This popular firm in Beaune has a large international following. After slumping a bit in the early '70s, the wines have recently been back to top form. As a general rule, I prefer the Drouhin white wines to the red, but the red wines are well made, very clean, generally elegant, medium-bodied, well balanced, and are ready to drink within 5–7 years. The 1983s were given an intense filtration, no doubt because many of them are sold to American restaurants, where one is unlikely to find many who understand the virtues of sediment.

1983 Beaune Clos des Mouches	($36.95)	86
1983 Chambolle-Musigny	($29.95)	80
1983 Chambolle-Musigny Les Amoureuses	($52.95)	84
1983 Clos Vougeot	($45.00)	87
1983 Griottes-Chambertin	($45.00)	82
1983 Santenay	($16.95)	81
1983 Vosne-Romanée Les Suchots	($35.95)	82

The Santenay is a spicy, fruity, medium-weight wine that has a good finish but little excitement. It should be at its best in 2–3 years. The red Beaune Clos des Mouches, always one of this firm's best wines, has a moderately deep color, a lovely ripe cherry and spicy oak bouquet, good flavor concentration, and moderate tannins. It should be at its best between 1988–1995. The Chambolle-Musigny has some very dusty, astringent tannins and a very dry finish. It has plenty of fruit, but I sensed a touch of rot. The Clos Vougeot, absurdly costly, was clearly the star, although not a great wine—only priced that way. It had a dark ruby color, excellent sweet fruit, full body and a rich, long finish. It should peak between 1990–2000. The Vosne-Romanée Les Suchots lacked balance, seemed awkward, its color seemed light, and the tannins were very hard and severe. The Chambolle-Musigny les Amoureuses was somewhat perplexing to evaluate. It had very good color, ripe, rich fruitiness and good body, but once again, very astringent, almost bitter tannins. I liked it, but one will have to wait 7–8 years for it to mature. The Griottes-Chambertin seems to have the *goût de sec*, and is very astringent in the finish without sufficient underlying fruit.

DROUHIN-LAROSE (GEVREY-CHAMBERTIN)* * * *

This is a very wealthy estate—its cellars well hidden by large iron gates monitored 24 hours by cameras—in the town of Gevrey-Chambertin. Bernard Drouhin, the cocky, self-assured owner, feels no one makes better wine than he does, and for that reason prices his wines accordingly. The style of wine here is hardly classic, but one that produces rich, alcoholic, fat wines with plenty of fragrance, body, sweetness, and color. They are hedonistic rather than classic wines. Unfortunately, Bernard Drouhin recently began to filter the wines that are sent to America because it is "the safe thing to do." By his own admission, the 1983 vintage is "great because the journalists said it was." Outspoken Drouhin prefers his 1985s, 1980s and 1978s. For the record, his 1983s are quite good, with the Clos de Bèze outstanding.

1983 Bonnes Mares	($45.00)	78
1983 Chambertin Clos de Bèze	($45.00)	89
1983 Chapelle-Chambertin	($35.00)	85
1983 Clos Vougeot	($40.00)	87
1983 Gevrey-Chambertin	($25.00)	82

With the exception of the Clos Vougeot and Chambertin Clos de Bèze, the 1983s from Drouhin-Larose were light in color but, surprisingly, had broad flavors. The Gevrey-Chambertin is a good, ripe, round wine that will be ready in 1–2 years. The Chapelle-Chambertin has plenty of clean, supple, ripe berry fruitiness, an attractive, oaky note in the bouquet, and a long, sweet finish. It should be ready in 4–5 years. The Clos Vougeot is much darker in color, with an intense perfume of vanillin oak and raspberries. Long, rich, deep and moderately tannic, it should be ready by 1990–1992. The Bonnes Mares had a slight taste of rot and dry bitterness in the finish. Light in color with dusty tannins, it shows all the warning signs of having been afflicted by both rot and hail. The Chambertin Clos de Bèze ("la fleur de la cave") of Drouhin-Larose is a wonderful wine, long, ripe, succulent, rich and fruity, with excellent depth and a great finish. It should be ready by 1990–1992.

DOMAINE DUJAC (MOREY ST.-DENIS)* * *

This is one of my favorite estates in Burgundy. The wines are filled with ripe, rich Pinot Noir fruit and aromas but are never heavy or overly chaptalized. The color of the Dujac wines is never very dark, even in years such as 1978, and the wines have never been filtered, so they must be shipped and stored properly because they are very much alive. It is no secret that this estate did not have the success in 1983 that one might have expected. Jacques Seysses was apprehensive about the rampant rot in the vineyards and pulled the skins off the macerating grape juice very quickly in order to avoid the taste of rot in his wines. Consequently the vines are less colored than other 1983s. They are, however, certainly very, very good. With respect to the 1982s, Dujac was extremely successful, and along with the Domaine de la Romanée-Conti, produced what must be the best wines. His 1985s will prove to be his best wines since 1978.

1983 Bonnes Mares	($45.00)	86
1983 Clos de la Roche	($38.00)	86
1983 Clos St.-Denis	($37.00)	85
1983 Gevrey-Chambertin Les Combottes	($28.00)	85
1983 Morey St.-Denis	($28.00)	82

No doubt the Bonnes Mares, the best of Dujac's 1983s, will be impossible to obtain for only two barrels (50 cases) were produced. It is a very fragrant, richly perfumed wine with a medium ruby color and long, spicy flavors suggestive of berry fruit and cinnamon. Some firm tannins are present, so expect the Bonnes Mares to be at its peak in 1992–1995. The same can be said for the very fine Clos St.-Denis and Gevrey-Chambertin Les Combottes. The Clos St.-Denis is Dujac's darkest-colored 1983, has a rich, ripe, deep, fruity texture, medium to full body, and long finish. The Gevrey-Chambertin Les Combottes is extremely spicy on the nose, with big, rich, alcoholic flavors and a powerful finish. The Morey St.-Denis tasted much less complex and serious than the other wines, but appears to be quite precocious and may be ready to drink by 1987. The Clos de la Roche is undoubtedly very good, but rather closed, quite tannic, and unyielding. It should be given at least 5–7 years of cellaring. For the moment, I prefer the 1982 Clos de la Roche.

1982 Clos de la Roche	($32.00)	89
1982 Clos St.-Denis	($28.00)	85
1982 Gevrey-Chambertin Les Combottes	($26.00)	84

Jacques Seysses was one of only a handful of growers to make a rosé wine by running off some of the juice from the bloated Pinot Noir grapes. The result was that he got more concentration in his red wines, which are among the very best 1982s. The Clos de la Roche is quite excellent. Ready to drink now but capable of improving for 2–5 years, it is loaded with spicy, earthy, rich berry fruit and has a succulent sweetness and long finish. The Gevrey-Chambertin Les Combottes is not so concentrated, but is very spicy, fragrant, and fruity, and should be drunk over the next 1–2 years. The Clos St.-Denis is richly fruity, medium-bodied, sweet, fat, and altogether charming and elegant.

DOMAINE RENÉ ENGEL (VOSNE-ROMANÉE)* * *

This estate has been highly regarded for some time. The 1983s are good rather than exciting or great. The wines here are filtered.

1983 Clos Vougeot	($24.99)	84
1983 Echézeaux	($32.00)	85
1983 Grands-Echézeaux	($35.00)	84
1983 Vosne-Romanée	($14.99)	78
1983 Vosne-Romanée Les Brûlées	($22.95)	75

Given the vineyards that this Domaine owns, one would have expected a greater level of quality. However, the Clos Vougeot is certainly fine with a rich, sweet texture, very good depth, a spicy, leathery, jammy bouquet, and 5–8 years of aging potential. Both the Grands-Echézeaux and Echézeaux have a lovely, rich, sweet fruitiness, medium body, and lush texture, but also a trace of hard, dry astringent tannins due to the rot. They have plenty of appeal and character, but they are not sure bets. The Vosne-Romanée Les Brûlées has even more noticeable rot in its flavors. As for the straight Vosne-Romanée, it is supple and fruity, with a very attractive color. It should be drunk over the next 2–3 years.

FAIVELEY (NUITS ST.-GEORGES)* * * * *

This moderate-sized firm in Nuits St.-Georges is unquestionably the most underrated producer of great red burgundy. Most consumers probably don't realize that while Faiveley is a *négociant,* 85% of the wines they produce come from their own vineyards, which are some of the best in the Côte d'Or. The business is now run by François Faiveley, a young man in his mid-thirties who is meticulous and conservative. His father, the jovial Guy, still provides assistance. Faiveley refuses to filter his wines, refuses to shorten the long barrel-aging period, and refuses to make a commercial burgundy that is fully mature by age 3 or 4 and comatose by age 6. These are lusty, rich, powerful, full-bodied wines that, quite truthfully, are among the very finest made. They age magnificently. Importers who do not ship these unfiltered, natural wines in temperature-controlled containers and store them properly are doing both Faiveley and their clients a great injustice. The 1981s of this firm are excellent, by far the best wines I tasted from this vintage in Burgundy. In richness and strength, they are superior to many producers' 1983s. They make a joke of any vintage chart. The 1982s are typically soft but generally much better than most producers'. The 1983s look to be outstanding. Burgundy-lovers, take note; Faiveley may be your best bet.

1983 Chambertin Clos de Bèze	($65.00)	90
1983 Clos Vougeot	($50.00)	89
1983 Corton Clos des Cortons	($35.00)	87
1983 Gevrey-Chambertin Combe aux Moines	($35.00)	88
1983 Gevrey-Chambertin Les Cazetiers	($35.00)	87
1983 Mazis-Chambertin	($45.00)	89
1983 Nuits St.-Georges Clos de la Maréchale	($25.00)	85

None of the Faiveley 1983s show signs of the astringent, dry tannins and moldy flavors caused by rot. They are very powerful, rich, deep, tannic wines that ideally need 8–10 years of cellaring. The firm regards them very highly. The Gevrey-Chambertin Les Cazetiers and Combe aux Moines are very brawny, fleshy, rich and tannic, full-bodied wines, and have excellent underlying sweetness and length. The colors are dark, but the Combe aux Moines is the darker. These two wines may deserve a higher score in 1995 when they reach maturity. The Nuits St.-Georges Clos de la Maréchale has plenty of rich, meaty fruitiness, a heady alcoholic content, wonderful texture, and firm tannins. One must wait until 1992. The Corton was very closed on the nose, but dark in color, with a very big framework; it will need plenty of time. The Clos Vougeot is one of the richest and biggest wines of Faiveley's 1983s. With great depth of flavor and length, it has plenty of alcohol, rich, round tannins, and an exceptional finish. It needs a decade of cellaring. The Mazis-Chambertin has a bouquet of leather and berry fruit, great density, an explosive fruitiness, and superb length. The Chambertin Clos de Bèze has even more. Huge, powerful, dense, and rich, it is truly a great red burgundy from the 1983 vintage. These wines are among the very finest produced in 1983. Bravo!

1982 Chambertin Clos de Bèze	($42.00)	87
1982 Corton Clos des Corton (Tastevinage)	($30.00)	86
1982 Fixin (Tastevinage)	($12.95)	84
1982 Gevrey-Chambertin Combe aux Moines	($25.00)	86
1982 Gevrey-Chambertin Les Cazetiers	($25.00)	85
1982 Mercurey	($9.99)	84
1982 Nuits St.-Georges Clos de la Maréchale	($25.00)	85
1982 Nuits St.-Georges Les Saint-Georges	($30.00)	86

I am not a great admirer of the 1982 vintage for red burgundy. The wines are generally quite watery, but there are some notable exceptions. The DRC, Dujac, the Leclerc brothers, Georges Mugneret, and Faiveley have done better jobs than just about everyone else. These eight wines will please anybody. They are ready to drink, but will last for at least 2–4 more years. They have some real depth. The Fixin and Mercurey are very good values, the two wines from Nuits St.-Georges surprisingly big and rich. The Clos de la Maréchale has a smoky, ripe Pinot nose, and lovely, round flavors. The Les Saint-Georges is dominated more by the smell of new oak barrels, has some tannin to lose, but is quite good. Both Les Cazetiers and Combe aux Moines are shockingly deep, with the latter wine showing a significant concentration of ripe fruit and full body. The Clos des Cortons actually needs 3–4 years to reveal its big fleshy character. Lastly, the firm's top wine is the Chambertin Clos de Bèze. It is a deeply scented, rich, full-bodied, particularly concentrated wine in 1982. It will drink well for at least 4–5 years. I am shocked by how good these 1982s are.

1981 Chambertin Clos de Bèze	($45.00)	90
1981 Chambolle-Musigny	($25.00)	85
1981 Charmes-Chambertin	($40.00)	88
1981 Clos Vougeot	($40.00)	87
1981 Côte de Nuits-Villages (Tastevinage)	($10.00–$12.00)	84
1981 Echézeaux	($40.00)	85
1981 Gevrey-Chambertin	($20.00)	85
1981 Gevrey-Chambertin Les Cazetiers	($25.00)	87
1981 Latricières-Chambertin	($37.00)	88
1981 Morey St.-Denis	($25.00)	85

The quality Faiveley obtained in 1981 is hard to believe. Some of the wines are better than many producers' 1983s. Nineteen eighty-one is not a good vintage for red burgundy, but Faiveley made exceptional wines that, quite frankly, overwhelm anything else I have tasted from this vintage. I urge retailers and consumers to try these wines and compare them against the likes of the DRC, Leclerc, Maume, whomever you want. They have no qualitative peers in 1981. Start with the smoky, spicy Côtes de Nuits-Villages, that tastes like it came from Gevrey-Chambertin. This is a rich, fruity wine that will drink well for 3–4 years. The Gevrey-Chambertin is similarly styled, only bigger and more concentrated. Less virile but more elegant and charming is the Chambolle-Musigny, which has broad, pure, sweet Pinot Noir flavors. It is supple and will drink well over the next 3–4 years. The Morey St.-Denis is softer, quite deep, rich and fruity, and a real crowd-pleaser. The surprises continue with the Gevrey-Chambertin Les Cazetiers, which is big, rich, deep, smoky, full-bodied, and so flavorful that one would never guess it was a 1981. If I sound enthusiastic, I was stunned by the quality of Faiveley's 1981s. The Latricières-Chambertin is a powerful wine, full-bodied, spicy, rich, with extremely long, pure flavors, and lovely balance. It will drink well for 5–8 years. The story is the same for the Clos Vougeot. Not smoky or spicy like the wines from Gevrey-Chambertin, it possesses full-blown, ripe, rich, fleshy, berry fruitiness, full body, super length, and 5–10 years of aging potential. As good as the Echézeaux is, it suffered in comparison with the other Faiveley Grand Cru wines. The Charmes-Chambertin also is a full-bodied, ripe, rich, very flavorful wine with considerable character. It will be at its best between 1988–1995. Lastly, the Chambertin Clos de Bèze is a powerhouse of a wine. Aromas of fresh leather, berry fruit, and exotic spices are top-notch. Quite big, full-bodied and deep, this superb wine should be drunk between 1990–2000. This unbelievably fine line of 1981 red burgundies must be tasted to be believed.

DOMAINE HENRI GOUGES (NUITS ST.-GEORGES)* *

This famous and important estate historically produced some of the finest red burgundies in the Côte d'Or. However, the wines of the '70s slipped considerably in quality, and in good vintages like 1971, 1976, and 1978, the wines have looked strikingly pale and tasted meagerly endowed when compared against their peers. I know Michel Gouges and his son, Christian, well, having visited them on three different occasions; therefore, it is all the more difficult to say that I do not believe their wines are nearly as concentrated and as rich as they should be. Nevertheless, I write for the wine consumer, not the wine trade, and that is my opinion. The 1983s are quite frankly very light in color and seem also lacking in concentration except for the Les Saint-Georges. The 1984s also were rather weak. Gouges does filter his wines, perhaps too aggressively. This famous old firm, whose wines of the '60s still remain superb, has sadly dropped significantly in quality since 1970.

1983 Nuits St.-Georges	($15.00)	72
1983 Nuits St.-Georges Les Chaignots	($25.00)	75
1983 Nuits St.-Georges Les Porets	($25.00)	75
1983 Nuits St.-Georges Les Pruliers	($25.00)	80
1983 Nuits St.-Georges Les Saint-Georges	($32.00)	86
1983 Nuits St.-Georges Les Vaucrains	($27.00)	80

The only wine of interest here is the Les Saint-Georges. The other five wines have the color of most 1982s, and lack richness and concentration. The Les Vaucrains is quite good, has medium ruby color, and should be at its peak by 1992. The Les Saint-Georges is deep ruby in color, has a concentrated richness, and is clearly the best wine Gouges made in 1983. Expect it to be fully mature by 1992.

MACHARD DE GRAMONT (NUITS ST.-GEORGES)* * * *

This estate has been going through a family dispute, the vineyards being divided among family members. The 1983s are the first Machard de Gramont wines I have seen since the excellent 1978s and 1979s. These are very good, deeply colored, richly fruity wines that are quite well made.

1983 Nuits St.-Georges Les Damodes	($22.00)	85
1983 Nuits St.-Georges Les Hauts-Pruliers	($25.00)	84
1983 Nuits St.-Georges La Perrière Noblot	($20.00)	84
1983 Pommard Clos Blanc	($30.00)	86

If none of these wines can be called outstanding, they can certainly be considered very good. Dark in color with no trace of rot or hail damage, these plummy, rather chunky wines have good tannins and fleshy textures. The Pommard Clos Blanc is the richest and deepest and suggests that it needs 5–6 years to reach its prime. The Nuits St.-Georges Les Damodes is similarly styled, a little more lush and less tannic. Both the Nuits St.-Georges Perrière and Hauts Pruliers have the same house style, but are slightly less elegant and complex.

DOMAINE JEAN GROS (VOSNE-ROMANÉE)* * * *

Madame Gros is the mayor of Vosne-Romanée in addition to looking after this highly respected domaine. The 1983s here have very fine color, a silky, lush richness wrapped in a velvet, but firm, glove. As the notes below indicate, two of the Gros wines are very special.

1983 Hautes Côtes de Nuits	($8.49)	81
1983 Richebourg	($40.00)	90
1983 Vosne-Romanée	($15.99)	84

1983 Vosne-Romanée Clos des Réas   ($35.00)   90

The Hautes Côtes de Nuits is a pleasant, soft, very agreeable wine
with good fruit and some complexity. The Vosne-Romanée has supple,
sweet, plummy fruitiness, medium body, good length and 5–6 years
of potential evolution. The Vosne-Romanée Clos des Réas is outstanding. It is dark ruby with an explosive blackberry bouquet complemented by vanillin oak and scents of licorice. Rich and full-bodied,
with very fine extract, this is a wine to lay away for 5–6 years. It will
last until 2000. It is as good as the Richebourg, which has a remarkably complex bouquet, layers of fruit, medium to full body, and firm
tannins. It needs all of 6–7 years to develop. Her 1985s may prove to
be even better.

DOMAINE GROS SOEUR ET FRÈRE (VOSNE-ROMANÉE)* * * *

This estate was somewhat of a discovery. Gustave Gros is the son of
Madame Gros and has his own small cellar. He owns what is generally
considered the best part of the Clos Vougeot vineyard, a tiny section
next to Musigny. His 1983 Clos Vougeot is fabulous, one of the single
greatest red burgundies I tasted from this vintage. His other wines are
inconsistent. However, only 25 cases of the Clos Vougeot were sold to
America.

1983 Clos Vougeot   ($30.00)   92

1983 Richebourg   ($45.00)   83

1983 Vosne-Romanée   ($18.00)   83

Inexplicably, neither the Richebourg, which was extremely tannic and
dry, nor the Vosne-Romanée, which was spicy but simple, approach
the Clos Vougeot made here. The 1983 Clos Vougeot has exceptional
color, a huge bouquet of intense berry fruit, coconut, ripe oranges,
and spices. Enormous on the palate, with layers of ripe, very concentrated fruit, this moderately tannic wine will be a real treasure for
those lucky to find a bottle or two.

1982 Richebourg   ($40.00)   87

1982 Vosne-Romanée   ($15.00)   84

Two very good 1982s, both surprisingly deep in color, have obviously
been chaptalized, but offer ripe, sweet, supple fruit in a medium-

bodied, high-alcohol style. The Richebourg has significantly more fragrance and greater length and class.

HOSPICES DE BEAUNE* * * *

I did not taste the entire selection of Hospices wines, but did have the opportunity to sample several of the more famous names. These wines are imported by different firms throughout the country.

1983 Corton Cuvée Charlotte Dumay	($35.00)	87
1983 Corton Cuvée Dr. Peste	($35.00)	85
1983 Mazis-Chambertin Madeleine Collignon	($45.00)	88
1983 Savigny-Les-Beaune Arthur Girard	($20.00)	87

All of these wines are very well made. I must admit to being a little disappointed with the Cuvée Dr. Peste, perhaps because I expected much more. It is extremely tannic and severe, with good underlying sweet fruit and medium to full body. It needs a full 10–12 years. Just as tannic, but showing considerably better, is the Cuvée Charlotte Dumay which appears to have a greater concentration of sweet Pinot fruit, full body, some strong scents of new oak barrels, and very good length. It needs 10 years. Curiously, the Savigny-Les-Beaune Cuvée Arthur Girard was darker in color and every bit as concentrated as the two Hospices de Beaune Cortons. It is a powerful, full-bodied, rich and tannic Savigny that needs 7–9 years of cellaring. It is a sleeper! Lastly, the Mazis-Chambertin Madeleine Collignon is very rich, smoky, earthy, and rather ponderous, but excellent depth of fruit and structure are present. It may well merit an outstanding score when mature in 1995–1998.

One final comment about the Hospices wines. They are extremely expensive and have been widely criticized for not always being as good as they should be. However, since 1977 a totally new team has been responsible for the management of the vineyards and the making of the wines. They are aged in 100% new oak and have since 1978 generally been models of excellence. Of course, the competence of the buyer of these wines and the manner in which they are cellared can make a difference. In my experience, the best wines from Hospices are:

Red Wines	*White Wines*
Nicolas Rolin (Beaune-les-Avaux)	Francois de Salins
Maurice Drouhin (Beaune)	(Corton-Charlemagne)
Charlotte Dumay (Corton)	Cuvée Goureau
Cuvée Dr. Peste (Corton)	(Meursault)
Madeleine Collignon (Mazis Chambertin)	Cuvée Loppin (Meursault)
Arthur Girard (Savigny Les Beaune)	Albert Grivault
Jehan de Massol	(Meursault-Charmes)

DOMAINE JACQUESON (CHAGNY)* * *

The wines from this domaine offer good value, are cleanly made, with rather vivid and rich, chewy flavors. This is definitely a domaine to seek out when it comes to good values.

1983 Mercurey Les Naugues	($9.99)	82
1983 Rully Les Chaponnières	($9.99)	85
1983 Rully Les Clouds	($11.99)	85

These wines are all similar. They have deep, bright ruby colors, moderately intense bouquets of black cherries, a lovely, silky, ripe concentration of fruit, and light tannin. The Les Clouds is a very seductive, medium-weight, lush wine. The Les Chaponnières has a very attractive Pinot fragrance, and the Mercurey Les Naugues soft, spicy, chewy flavors. Jacqueson's 1985s were even better than his 1983s, rich, supple and loaded with flavor.

LOUIS JADOT (BEAUNE)* * * *

This excellent firm in Beaune has now been purchased by its American importer, Kobrand, Inc. I hope the quality of the wine will remain at its current level, which is very high. For white wines, Jadot's wines are as good as anybody's, both the elegant, rich 1982s and powerful 1983s belong in everyone's collection, provided you have the funds of a rock star. The red wines here don't receive the publicity of the white wines, but no wine cellar has any better management than André Gagey and his enthusiastic cellarmaster, Jacques Lardière. Gagey and Lardière succeeded in 1983, but admitted that it was a tough year and there are frequent failures elsewhere in the Côte d'Or. Their red wines are not filtered (the only other major *négociant* not to filter is Faiveley). The red wines here are of very high quality in 1983.

1983 Beaune Boucherottes	($25.00)	85

1983 Beaune Clos des Ursules	($25.00)	85

1983 Bourgogne	($10.00)	82

1983 Chambertin Clos de Bèze	($50.00)	88

1983 Clos Vougeot	($40.00)	90

1983 Corton Pougets	($30.00)	88

1983 Côte de Beaune-Villages	($15.00)	83

1983 Côte de Nuits-Villages	($18.00)	84

1983 Nuits St.-Georges Clos de Corvées	($25.00)	86

1983 Pernand-Vergelesses Clos de Vergelesses	($20.00)	85

There is a lot to like in these wines from Jadot. The lower-priced wines, the Bourgogne, Côte de Beaune-Villages, and Côte de Nuits-Villages, offer good value and are ready to drink, with solid Pinot Noir flavors. The Côte de Nuits-Villages is particularly fine for its class. The Pernand-Vergelesses tastes like many people's Corton, ripe, rich, rustic, big and full, and in need of 7–8 years of cellaring. Jadot's Beaune Boucherottes and Clos des Ursules already exhibit big, complex bouquets of black cherries and vanillin oak. The Boucherottes has richer and riper fruit; the Clos de Ursules has more body and is more marked by oak. Both should be *en pleine forme* in 5–6 years. The Nuits St.-Georges Clos des Corvées is smoky, robust, quite aromatic, full-bodied, and tannic. It needs 5–7 years of cellaring. The Corton Pougets should make a delicious bottle of savory, ripe, broadly flavored wine. It is already extremely impressive, with excellent concentration, super ripeness, a long finish, and moderate tannins. Drink it in 1990–1995. The Clos Vougeot is outstanding. Great color, great fragrance, great richness—this wine has the texture and intensity of a top 1982 Bordeaux. It will need 8–10 years to fully develop. Lastly, the Chambertin Clos de Bèze is surprisingly forward and accessible, with a voluptuous, seductive richness, long, deep flavors and ripe tannins. The secret to Jadot's success in 1983 was to avoid the hail and rot damage. After severe selections were made, the wines were fermented at very hot temperatures for a short period. It obviously worked.

JAFFELIN (BEAUNE)* * *

This firm is run by Robert Drouhin, the owner of the Drouhin firm. Both firms share the same facility for bottling, but the wines are different. The Jaffelin wines are certainly above average in quality but rarely exciting.

1983 Aloxe-Corton	($17.95)	78
1983 Chambertin	($55.00)	87
1983 Chambolle-Musigny	($21.95)	80
1983 Clos Vougeot	($39.95)	86
1983 Corton	($31.95)	83
1983 Côte de Nuits-Villages	($10.95)	75
1983 Echézeaux	($35.95)	83
1983 Gevrey-Chambertin	($21.95)	80
1983 Volnay	($19.95)	82

There are hardly any exciting wines here, though technically the wines are pleasant, fruity, medium-bodied, with some tough tannin in the fruit. The best of the lot are the Clos Vougeot, an appellation that did extremely well in 1983, and the rich, perfumed, ripe, and sensual Chambertin. It has an extra measure of depth and length on the palate, and needs 6 years of cellaring.

DOMAINE HENRI JAYER (VOSNE-ROMANÉE)* * * * *

This small domaine is consistently one of the greatest producers of red burgundy. Everything is aged in new oak, never filtered, and Jayer is the only Burgundian I know to have a fully temperature-controlled wine cellar. He is a passionate winemaker. Several brokers in Burgundy suggested that his 1983s were not so good as they should have been. Perhaps this is true, because Jayer lost a significant portion of his crop due to hail and rot. I found his 1983s to be sumptuous wines, as super as his 1985s.

1983 Echézeaux	($80.00)	88
1983 Nuits St.-Georges Meurgers	($35.00)	86
1983 Richebourg	($85.00)	92
1983 Vosne-Romanée	($25.00)	84
1983 Vosne-Romanée Clos Parantoux	($35.00)	89
1983 Vosne-Romanée Les Beaumonts	($30.00)	87
1983 Vosne-Romanée Les Brûlées	($35.00)	85

There is no question that Jayer's Richebourg is his finest wine in 1983, but he only made 25 cases of it, so the chances of getting any are nil. There are 175 cases of Vosne-Romanée Clos Parantoux, which is extremely elegant, with broad, deep flavors tinged with spicy oak. It has the best length of all Jayer's Vosne-Romanées and should be ready to drink by 1990. The Vosne-Romanée Les Brûlées is a more spicy, more expressive wine with harder tannins, very good color, full body, but less concentration. The Vosne-Romanée Les Beaumonts is a fat yet tannic wine with dark ruby color, clean flavors of ripe, sweet Pinot Noir, and a long finish. It has more concentration than the Les Brûlées. The Nuits St.-Georges Meurgers is quite good, with fat, fleshy flavors, supple for a 1983, and will probably be mature by 1990. The Echézeaux is excellent, elegant, complex, highly aromatic, with seductive, round, rich flavors wrapped in a glove of tannin. Jayer's straight Vosne-Romanée is good. All of these wines are very hard to obtain, unless you live in California, the only state to which Jayer sells his wines.

DOMAINE JACQUELINE JAYER (VOSNE-ROMANÉE)* * *

Another Jayer, this woman is a relative of both Henri and Lucien. Her 1983s did not show very well at all. However, the 1982s produced by this estate are very, very good and will make excellent drinking over the next 2–3 years.

1983 Echézeaux	($35.00)	?
1983 Nuits St.-Georges Les Lavieres	($25.00)	?
1983 Vosne-Romanée	($20.00)	?
1983 Vosne-Romanée Les Rouges	($25.00)	?

These wines were so abrasively tannic and astringent, and seemed so devoid of fruit, that I must raise serious reservations about their balance. I will be shocked if there is enough fruit here to outlive the excessive tannin levels.

1982 Echézeaux	($25.00)	86
1982 Nuits St.-Georges Les Lavieres	($20.00)	85
1982 Vosne-Romanée	($18.00)	79

J. Jayer produced very good 1982s. They have healthy dosages of vanillin oakiness; lovely, seductive, and very lush Pinot Noir fruit; and fleshy textures. They are extremely enjoyable to drink now, but should last 1–3 years. The Echézeaux is a very fine 1982 with a top-rank bouquet of ripe berry fruit, spicy oak, coconuts, and plums. The Nuits St.-Georges Les Lavieres is almost as good. It has a healthy deep ruby color, a big, plummy, oaky bouquet, and soft, lush flavors. It should be drunk over the next few years. The Vosne-Romanée is quite pleasant, but finishes short.

DOMAINE MICHEL LAFARGE (VOLNAY)* * * *

This very serious Domaine makes an excellent red burgundy with richness, complexity, elegance, and power. The top wine is always the Volnay Clos des Chenes, and in both 1981 and 1983 it is excellent.

1983 Beaune Grèves	($25.00)	86
1983 Volnay	($18.00)	86
1983 Volnay Clos des Chenes	($30.00)	90
1983 Volnay Premier Cru	($25.00)	87

All of these wines have a rich ruby color; a deep, seductive, velvety black-cherry fruitiness interlaced with smells of vanillin oakiness, and medium to full body. The tannins are obvious but not astringent or harsh. The Beaune Grèves is more open-knit and has a lighter color with a strong alcoholic finish. It should be ready by 1990. The Volnay has very harmonious flavors; a smoky, ripe-berry fruit bouquet; and long finish. The Volnay Premier Cru is slightly deeper with layers of rich fruit and 5–8 years of further evolution. The Volnay Clos des Chenes is excellent. It is the richest, deepest, and most aromatic and complete of all these wines. It should be at its peak by 1990–1995.

DOMAINE COMTE LAFON (MEURSAULT)* * *

This estate has a deservedly high reputation for its white Meursaults (the 1982s were fabulous, the 1983s less so), but moderate quantities of red Volnay are produced here as well that can be very, very good. The 1983s were not filtered.

1983 Volnay Champans	($25.00)	83

1983 Volnay Santenots	($25.00)	86

These two 1983s show no signs of rot or astringent bitterness. The Champans is a velvety yet big, fruity wine, which will mature by 1990. The Santenots is bigger framed, quite ripe, rich, fat, and alcoholic with a good, firm edge and tannins for support. It should be mature between 1990–1995.

1982 Volnay Champans	($17.95)	80

1982 Volnay Santenots	($17.95)	84

Neither of these wines has the concentration or power of the 1983s, but they offer immediate drinkability. The Champans is soft, well made, but a trifle simple and straightforward. The Santenots has more richness, a lush, supple texture, and good finish. It should be drunk over the next 1–2 years.

DOMAINE CLOS DES LAMBRAYS (MOREY ST.-DENIS)* * *

This famous estate, now under the new ownership of Louis and Fabien Saier, is making numerous changes in an effort to modernize the style of wine produced at the Clos des Lambrays. The wine is now aged in one-third new oak barrels and bottled after 18–22 months. Based on the 1982, 1983, and 1984 I tasted, the wine is lighter and fruitier than the old style, which had a tendency toward heaviness and inconsistency, although some vintages—the 1945, 1947, and 1949—could be sublime. The 1983s were filtered prior to bottling.

1983 Clos des Lambrays	($35.00)	82

1983 Mercurey Les Chevelots	($18.00)	81

1983 Morey St.-Denis	($25.00)	83

The Clos des Lambrays exhibits fine winemaking. It needs 8–10 years to fully develop, but shows an elegant, complex, cherry fruit, and spicy bouquet. It has adequate concentration but hard tannins in the finish. The Morey St.-Denis is a medium-weight, very stylish wine with charm and sufficient tannins to age nicely for 8–10 years. The Mercurey has a complex bouquet of ripe cherries and leather, but finishes hard and tannic. If the fruit holds, it will be better than the above score.

DOMAINE LAMY-PILLOT (CHASSAGNE-MONTRACHET)* * *

René Lamy's 1983s, the only wines from this Domaine I have tasted, did not fare well in comparative tastings. The prices are reasonable, but with the exception of the Blagny, the wines had very vegetal, rather bizarre aromas.

1983 Blagny La Piece Sous Le Bois	($12.00)	80

1983 Chassagne Montrachet Clos Saint Jean	($12.00)	73

1983 St.-Aubin Les Castets	($12.00)	72

1983 Santenay Les Charrons	($12.00)	65

Unless you get excited over vegetal aromas interlaced with the scent of manure, there is nothing much to like about these wines except the Blagny, which has some tobacco, vegetal aromas but also more clean berry ripeness and richness. The Blagny should be at its best by 1988.

PHILIPPE LECLERC (GEVREY-CHAMBERTIN)* * * *

This wild and crazy man who seems to be the most unlikely sort to make wine has become one of the Côte d'Or's finest growers or vignerons. His wines have been consistently brilliant almost regardless of the vintage. His 1980s, 1981s, 1982s, and 1983s are among the very finest of those vintages. His 1984s are exceptionally good. The secret is severe pruning in the vineyard, a very slow, hot, highly extractive vinification, 2½ years in new oak barrels, and absolutely no filtration. The intensity and majesty of flavor he succeeds in obtaining make his wines worth a special search of the marketplace. Don't pass up his 1985s which will be excellent when he releases them in 1988.

1983 Gevrey-Chambertin	($20.00)	84
1983 Gevrey-Chambertin Combe Aux Moines	($25.00)	89
1983 Gevrey-Chambertin Les Cazetiers	($25.00)	87
1983 Gevrey-Chambertin Les Champeaux	($25.00)	84

Not surprisingly, all of these wines are powerful, deeply scented wines which will show no trace of rot or bitter tannins. The Gevrey-Chambertin is alcoholic, well-colored, rich, and in need of 1–3 years cellaring. The Les Champeaux is also rather soft and surprisingly accessible but has broad, spicy, ripe flavors. The two stars here are Les Cazetiers, a powerful, rich, substantial wine with layers of sweet Pinot Noir fruit. It is a full-bodied, big, alcoholic wine which will be close to full maturity by 1990–1992. The top wine is Combes Aux Moines, which has an intense old vine flavor; a rich, chewy, and lush texture; moderate rather than excessive tannins; and a huge finish. It should be superb between 1990–1995.

1982 Gevrey-Chambertin	($13.95)	83
1982 Gevrey-Chambertin Combe aux Moines	($19.95)	86
1982 Gevrey-Chambertin Les Cazetiers	($18.95)	85
1982 Gevrey-Chambertin Les Champeaux	($18.95)	84

Leclerc did very well in 1982. All of these wines are ready to drink, but both the Les Cazetiers and Combe aux Moines will easily last 4–5 years. Soft, fat, chewy, plummy flavors complemented by vanillin oak and long, clean finishes are the rule here. If the Les Cazetiers is very good, the Combe aux Moines is slightly denser, richer, and longer on the palate.

RENÉ LECLERC (GEVREY-CHAMBERTIN)* * * *

Another long-haired Leclerc, René is the brother of Philippe. Like his brother, he produces very rich, intense, broodingly dark-colored Pinot

Noir. His vinification and approach to long-term barrel aging and his policy against filtration are exactly the same as Philippe's. However, there is one big difference. René uses no new oak barrels; his brother uses 100% new oak. Consequently, René's wines have less tannin and a richer, more accessible fruitiness. Obviously this is another small grower worth a special effort to seek out.

1983 Gevrey-Chambertin Clos Prieur	($27.00)	85
1983 Gevrey-Chambertin Combe aux Moines	($30.00)	90
1983 Gevrey-Chambertin Lavaux St.-Jacques	($30.00)	89

All three of these wines are rich, robust, darkly colored, full-bodied wines with excellent extract and potential. The Clos Prieur is rich, long, typically alcoholic, but also very hard. It will need 10 years. The Lavaux St.-Jacques is a dense, very fat, rich, immense wine with 10–12 years of positive evolution ahead of it. The layers of flavor are very impressive. The Combe aux Moines is clearly one of the great wines of this vintage. It is very concentrated, dense, and powerful, and has a huge finish. It is much better than most growers' Chambertins.

1982 Gevrey-Chambertin Combe aux Moines	($22.00)	86
1982 Gevrey-Chambertin Lavaux St.-Jacques	($22.00)	84

Like his brother Philippe, René also made very fine 1982s that have a surprising intensity of color and richness, though they are ready to drink now. If you have a choice to make, go for the Combe aux Moines, which resembles the Lavaux St.-Jacques but is larger in the mouth, with more concentration and character.

DOMAINE LEQUIN-ROUSSOT (SANTENAY)* * *

This moderate-sized estate in Santenay is extremely well run. They make excellent white wines and quite good red wines. The honesty of the two brothers is refreshing, and they, like many growers, are concerned about the ferocity of tannin in the red burgundies of 1983. The 1983s were aged in 50% new wood. The red wines have plenty of character but are quite hard and tannic. The 1982s, both red and white, were successful here as are their 1985s.

1983 Chassagne-Montrachet Morgeot	($18.00)	78
1983 Corton	($18.00)	85

1983 Pommard	($16.00)	68

1983 Santenay	($12.00)	83

1983 Santenay Clos de Haut Villages	($12.00)	78

1983 Santenay La Combe	($18.00)	85

The Pommard was so hard, tough, and tannic that I am quite concerned that it will never be balanced. Otherwise, Lequin-Roussot produced a very good, spicy, full-bodied Santenay for drinking in 1990, a very hard, tannic Chassagne-Montrachet Morgeot, and Santenay Clos de Haut Villages. The Santenay La Combe exhibits much riper, plummier fruit, a big, spicy bouquet, deep color, and long finish. Equally good is the Corton, which has a healthy, deep color, full body, very good depth, but is also very tannic. It will need 10 years of cellaring.

LEROY (MEURSAULT)* * * * *

M. Lalou Bize-Leroy is certainly one of Burgundy's, if not France's, most dynamic and respected wine producers. She calls herself the "Gardienne des Grands Millésimes," and with a stock in excess of 2.2 million bottles, no one argues. Her wines are extremely expensive, but also consistently among the greatest, perhaps are *the* greatest, made in Burgundy. She has the habit of releasing vintages when they are just beginning to show some maturity. The prices are astronomically high, but the quality is superb. Leroy's burgundies are capable of 15–30 years of life in the bottle and are natural, unfiltered wines of profound character and complexity. I cannot recommend them enthusiastically enough, but be prepared to pay a premium for such glories. The great vintages (for Leroy) are the 1964s, 1969s, and 1971s. While all of Leroy's wines are special, she seems to be at her impeccable best with respect to the wines from such appellations as Gevrey-Chambertin, Chambolle-Musigny, Nuits St.-Georges, and Pommard. Yet, as the following scores evidence, this woman produces an unparalleled line of great wines, even from lesser appellations. Burgundy's single greatest producer?

1955 Mazis-Chambertin	($169.95)	90

1961 Gevrey-Chambertin Les Cazetiers	($129.95)	95

1964 Chambolle-Musigny Les Amoureuses	($150.00)	92

1964 Chambolle-Musigny Les Charmes	($150.00)	88
1964 Chapelle-Chambertin	($175.00)	95
1964 Gevrey-Chambertin Les Combottes	($155.00)	92
1964 Gevrey-Chambertin Les Cazetiers	($160.00)	95
1964 Mazis-Chambertin	($180.00)	97
1964 Pommard Grands Epenots	($165.00)	90
1964 Pommard Rugiens	($125.00)	90
1966 Gevrey-Chambertin Les Cazetiers	($90.00)	92
1966 Musigny	($110.00)	87
1966 Pommard Grands Epenots	($70.00)	87
1969 Clos Vougeot	($110.00)	80
1969 Gevrey-Chambertin Lavaux St.-Jacques	($110.00)	89
1969 Gevrey-Chambertin Les Cazetiers	($110.00)	90
1969 Mazis-Chambertin	($140.00)	90
1972 Chambolle-Musigny	($28.00)	85
1976 d'Auveney Bourgogne	($8.95)	84
1976 Monthélie	($14.00)	82
1978 d'Auveney Bourgogne	($8.95)	84
1978 Auxey-Duresses	($15.00)	85
1978 Beaune	($22.00)	85
1978 Chassagne-Montrachet	($22.00)	85

1978 Côte de Beaune-Villages	($18.00)	85

1979 Gevrey-Chambertin	($25.00)	86

1979 Pommard	($24.00)	85

1979 Santenay	($18.00)	86

1979 Vosne-Romanée	($19.00)	86

DOMAINE HUBERT LIGNIER (MOREY ST.-DENIS)* * * *

There are two separate Ligniers, Georges and Hubert, making wines in Morey St.-Denis. Both are highly respected. Hubert produces velvety, rich, and graceful wines and has been on a good streak of late, producing very fine wine in 1978, 1979, 1980, 1981, 1982, and 1983. His 1984s are good, his 1985s superb, so Lignier is clearly a grower who knows what he is doing. His wines are bottled unfiltered. He gets tremendous color in his wines and they are magnificently scented red burgundies.

1983 Clos de la Roche	($40.00)	90

1983 Morey St.-Denis	($22.00)	85

Lignier's Morey St.-Denis is quite attractive, rich, supple, yet powerful and firm. It has dark color, a lovely bouquet, and still needs 4–6 years to develop fully. His Clos de la Roche is truly superb, deep, ripe, with the scent of ripe plums and violets; it is remarkably fruity and complex, but needs 6–8 years to shed the moderate tannins that are present.

1982 Clos de la Roche	($25.00)	83

1982 Morey St.-Denis	($17.00)	82

Lignier made good 1982s. Both wines are much more open-knit than usual, with some spicy vanillin oakiness, soft, supple, ripe fruit, good concentration, but not much tannin. They should be drunk over the next year.

LUPÉ-CHOLET (NUITS ST.-GEORGES)* *

This firm produces rather standard quality wine, their best being the Château Gris. The wines are commercially made and unexciting.

| 1983 Beaune Clos du Roi | ($22.00) | 78 |

| 1983 Château Gris Nuits St.-Georges | ($30.00) | 85 |

| 1983 Pommard | ($20.00) | 70 |

The Pommard is stemmy and harsh. The Beaune has a pleasant, light, strawberry fruitiness, and the Château Gris a ripe, rich yet aggressively tannic texture. It needs 8–9 years of age, but it may not have the fruit to last that long.

CHÂTEAU DE LA MALTROYE (CHASSAGNE-MONTRACHET)* * *

One thinks of this estate usually as a very fine white wine producer. However, they also produce several red wines. The 1983s were all quite good.

| 1983 Chassagne-Montrachet Clos de la Maltroye | ($17.95) | 85 |

| 1983 Chassagne-Montrachet Clos Saint-Jean | ($17.95) | 85 |

| 1983 Santenay La Comme | ($16.95) | 84 |

All three wines have moderately intense bouquets of leather, spice, and ripe cherry fruit. Rather elegant for 1983s, but still rather powerful and fuller-bodied than one might normally expect, these wines need a minimum of 5 years to mature. The Clos Saint-Jean is slightly more forward than the others, the Clos de la Maltroye more tannic and tough, the La Comme the lightest.

DOMAINE MAUME (GEVREY-CHAMBERTIN)* * * *

This traditionally run estate makes very powerful, almost inky-colored wines. When I first visited Maume in 1981, I could not believe the color he obtained from Pinot Noir grapes. His 1980s are impenetrably deeply colored wines that will not be fully mature until 1990. His 1982s are among the best made in this vintage, his 1983s extremely dense and robust with no trace of astringence or rot, and his 1985s rich, intense, and the best I have tasted yet from this estate. Maume's wines are not filtered.

| 1983 Gevrey-Chambertin | ($20.00) | 83 |

| 1983 Gevrey-Chambertin Lavaux St.-Jacques | ($35.00) | 87 |

1983 Mazis-Chambertin   ($40.00)   89

The *village* Gevrey-Chambertin has plenty of good, ripe fruit, but its
score is kept low by some hard tannins in the finish. Both the Lavaux
St.-Jacques and Mazis-Chambertin are powerfully built wines meant
to mature slowly. Both should not be mature until 1993–1995. The
Mazis-Chambertin has a huge aroma of violets, leather, and ripe
plums. It is dense and huge on the palate, with full body and outstanding length. The Lavaux St.-Jacques is almost identically styled, perhaps more tannic, but equally rich and full-proportioned.

DOMAINE JEAN MÉO (VOSNE-ROMANÉE)* * *

The Domaine Méo is one of the small but important estates in the Côte
de Nuits. I have never seen the wines in America, but was told they
are rarely exported. I tasted through the 1983s, but was extremely
impressed. This appears to be a domaine that succeeded admirably in
the difficult 1983 vintage.

1983 Corton Clos Rognet   ($20.00)   87

1983 Nuits St.-Georges Boudots   ($25.00)   87

1983 Nuits St.-Georges Meugers   ($20.00)   68

1983 Richebourg   ($45.00)   86

1983 Vosne-Romanée Les Brûlées   ($25.00)   84

The 1983s are not tainted by rot, although the Nuits St.-Georges Meu-
gers was clearly bizarre and unusual when I last tasted it. The Nuits
St.-Georges Boudots is quite excellent, potentially outstanding. Deep
ruby in color, with a full-intensity bouquet of spicy new oak, plums,
truffles and licorice, this rich, concentrated wine will make a fine
bottle in 1990–1995. The Corton Clos Rognet and Richebourg had
similarly dark colors, excellent extract, clean, well-delineated Pinot
Noir flavors with a pure, ripe character. The Richebourg tasted
slightly less tannic. Give both wines a full 5–6 years of cellaring. The
Vosne-Romanée Les Brûlées was in the same style, only by comparison showed less depth and fragrance.

PRINCE FLORENT DE MÉRODE (LADOIX-SERRIGNY)* * * *

This well-known estate has long held a very fine reputation for graceful and elegant wines produced from vineyards at Aloxe-Corton and

Pommard. The wines are made by Pierre Bitouzet, an engaging man who knows his business and is responsive to queries. The 1983s were aged in oak barrels (50% of which were new) and bottled surprisingly early. The wines here are filtered. They are surprisingly light and less powerful than most 1983s, yet totally free of any traces of rot. Mérode also made good 1984s and excellent 1985s that will mature much faster than his 1983s.

1983 Aloxe-Corton	($18.00)	82
1983 Corton Bressandes	($30.00)	86
1983 Corton Clos du Roi	($35.00)	85
1983 Corton Maréchaudes	($22.50)	83
1983 Corton Renardes	($25.00)	84
1983 Pommard Clos de la Platière	($22.50)	84

The Aloxe-Corton and Corton Maréchaudes have good fruit, a light to medium ruby color, spicy vanillin aromas intermixed with cherry fruit, and rather short finishes. They are clean, elegant, rather understated wines. The Pommard Clos de la Platière is a more serious wine with ripe, round, forward, cherry fruit, better color, some depth and weight. It can be drunk now or aged for 4–5 years. The Corton Renardes bouquet is all cherry and vanillin. On the palate, it is a medium-bodied, pleasant, elegant wine that will be ready to drink soon. The star of the Mérode 1983s is the Corton Bressandes. It is by far the richest and deepest of these wines, fragrant, loaded with ripe, cherry fruit complemented by spicy new oak. Fuller, richer, and more complex than the others, the Bressandes should be fully mature by 1990–1992. The Corton Clos du Roi is almost as good, only its toughness and dryness kept it from scoring higher. It does seem to have the concentration of fruit to outlast the tannins. It will need 6–8 years.

DOMAINE MOILLARD (NUITS ST.-GEORGES)* * *

Moillard is a large *négociant* with some very important vineyard holdings. The wines are always quite dark in color, beefy, robust, and concentrated. In fact, they are very pleasing wines, but my experience with older vintages is that they do not develop much bouquet. Perhaps this is because the wines are pasteurized; while such a practice (also employed by the *négociant* Louis Latour) has its proponents, the result is wines that often taste very much alike and have slightly cooked bouquets and flavors. Moillard's best wines are those from the firm's own vineyard holdings. These tend to be big, rich, chocolatey wines that have little complexity, but deliver chunky, mouth-satisfying flavors. The 1983s are more alcoholic than usual but continue this style.

1983 Auxey-Duresses	($8.29)	75
1983 Beaune	($10.79)	73
1983 Beaune Grèves	($16.99)	80
1983 Bonnes Mares	($45.00)	85
1983 Bourgogne Hautes Côtes de Nuits	($6.99)	80
1983 Chambertin Clos de Bèze	($37.00)	87
1983 Clos Vougeot	($32.00)	83
1983 Corton Clos du Roi	($19.99)	83
1983 Corton Clos des Vergennes	($16.99)	85
1983 Côte de Nuits-Villages Domaine Chevillon	($8.99)	82
1983 Fixin	($8.99)	78
1983 Fixin Clos de la Perrière	($14.00)	80
1983 Nuits St.-Georges Clos des Thorey	($19.99)	86
1983 Nuits St.-Georges Les Richemondes	($26.00)	86
1983 Romanée St.-Vivant	($45.00)	86
1983 Volnay Clos des Chênes	($25.00)	85
1983 Vosne-Romanée Les Beaux Monts	($25.00)	83

1983 Vosne-Romanée Les Malconsorts   ($25.00)   83

These wines I tasted from Moillard show several things. One, this firm produces consistently above-average wines; there were no bad wines tasted. Second, while the wines are not great, there are some very fine, fleshy, rich, dense, chunky selections that offer plenty of palate pleasure. The two best values are the Côte de Nuits-Villages and Bourgogne Hautes Côtes de Nuits. To briefly summarize the highlights here, the Romanée St.-Vivant and Bonnes Mares have the most complexity and reflected their appellation the best. The Chambertin Clos de Bèze was the biggest and most concentrated with an easy 10-year lifespan ahead of it. The two wines from Nuits St.-Georges, Moillard's home base, the Richemondes and Clos des Thorey, are both big, thick, jammy, almost opaque wines. Both were rather atypical Pinot Noirs, but offered dense, smoky, very rich fruit, and full body. The Volnay Clos de Chênes has aromas and flavors of black cherries, is alcoholic and rich, the Corton Clos des Vergennes quite good, spicy, deep, fat, rich, and long. Both wines should be cellared for 5 years. As for the other wines, it was difficult to tell them apart (except that some were more intense than others).

DOMAINE MOINE-HUDELOT (CHAMBOLLE-MUSIGNY)* * * *

This tiny estate is run by Daniel Moine-Hudelot, the mayor of Chambolle-Musigny. He is a philosophical chap who explains quite succinctly why burgundy is so expensive and irregular in quality—too much demand, not enough quantity, and too much illegal stretching, by means of blending in the wine from weak, overcropped, inferior vineyards with that of better vineyards. Moine-Hudelot is a serious winemaker, but he makes so little wine that only tiny quantities are exported.

1983 Chambolle-Musigny   ($20.00)   80

1983 Chambolle-Musigny Les Amoureuses   ($40.00)   85

Both wines have deep ruby color and a pronounced raspberrylike bouquet. The Chambolle-Musigny is a little dry and astringent in the finish. The Les Amoureuses ripe, full-bodied, alcoholic, and rich. Give both 4–5 years.

DOMAINE MONGEARD-MUGNERET (VOSNE-ROMANÉE)* * * *

Jean Mongeard is the master architect behind this estate, which can make truly superb burgundies. To my taste, they have everything I really want in a wine—the scent of ripe fruit and violets, lush, deep, berry flavors, a touch of oak and a super finish. Mongeard is a believer in very hot vinifications, long aging in small oak (of which 50% is new), and absolutely no filtration. His 1983s are great successes, as are his 1985s, particularly Richebourg and Grands-Echézeaux. He also made very good 1984s, especially his Grands-Echézeaux. However, his wines are not always the model of consistency. The 1979s were disappointing.

1983 Clos Vougeot	($45.00)	90

1983 Echézeaux	($35.00)	88

1983 Fixin	($20.00)	82

1983 Grands-Echézeaux	($50.00)	92

1983 Vosne-Romanée	($20.00)	85

All of Jean Mongeard's wines have great color and clean, ripe, deeply scented bouquets. His Fixin offers a lighter-weight version of his more serious wines. Broad, ripe, alcoholic flavors are complex and soft in this medium-bodied wine; it will be mature by 1990. The Vosne-Romanée has excellent color and depth and the richness of most growers' Premiers Crus. Deep flavored, full-bodied, high in alcohol with moderate tannins present, this delicious wine will also be ready to drink by 1990. The Echézeaux, Clos Vougeot, and great Grands-Echézeaux are wines to lay away for 10 years. The Echézeaux is wonderfully fruity, chewy, fleshy and very concentrated. Its bouquet is one of vanillin, violets, and ripe berry fruit. It is potentially outstanding, but next to the spectacular Clos Vougeot and Grands-Echézeaux, it is overwhelmed. Mongeard's Clos Vougeot has remarkable intensity, great depth of flavor, super richness, and is altogether a great young wine. Give it 8 years. The Grands-Echézeaux is, along with several of Roumier's wines, the DRC 1983s, and Ponsot's Clos de la Roche Vieilles Vignes, among the greatest red burgundies of the vintage. The bouquet is filled with complex scents of flowers, plums, oak, and exotic spices. Incredibly rich and concentrated with layers of fruit, this is a great wine that should be at its best between 1995–2000. Mongeard thinks it is his best wine since the 1949.

DOMAINE ALBERT MOROT (BEAUNE)* * * *

This old estate is surely going to get a strong following as the quality of its wines becomes better known. Madame Chapin runs the business from the old, rather run-down Château de la Creusotte in Beaune. The wines are all from her own vineyards. Having tasted through the 1979s, 1972s, and 1964s, these are full-throttle, natural burgundies that age well, have excellent flavor, and are not filtered. The prices are very reasonable.

1983 Beaune Bressandes	($15.95)	86
1983 Beaune Cent Vignes	($16.95)	87
1983 Beaune Grèves	($16.95)	86
1983 Beaune Marconnets	($15.95)	86
1983 Beaune Theurons	($15.95)	85
1983 Beaune Toussaints	($15.95)	84
1983 Savigny-Vergelesses	($12.99)	85

This is an impressive array of Beaune wines. For elegance and drinking in 4–5 years, the Savigny-Vergelesses and Beaune Toussaints would be my choices. The most tannic wine, and most backward at the moment, is the Beaune Theurons, which is dark ruby, medium- to full-bodied, but very tannic. Don't touch it before 1993. The Beaune Marconnets needs 5–8 years, but has excellent color, a big, tarry, berry-scented bouquet, long, ripe flavors, and firm tannins. The Beaune Bressandes is very similar, perhaps slightly more fruity, but deep and broad, particularly for a Beaune. The Beaune Cent Vignes tastes the richest and most concentrated, with just something extra in the bouquet and flavor. Again, it would be a shame to drink it before 1993. The Beaune Grèves is excellent, has deep color, no trace of rot or hail damage, firm tannin, and rich, jammy fruit with medium to full body. Looking for some unadulterated Pinot Noir to lay away for 10–15 years at a reasonable price? Then consider these very fine offerings from Albert Morot.

DOMAINE GEORGES MUGNERET (VOSNE-ROMANÉE)* * * *

This is a very serious domaine run by Dr. Georges Mugneret, who has retired from the medical profession to make wine. Only new oak barrels are used to age the wine, and this estate refuses to filter its wines. The two best wines are almost always the Ruchottes-Chambertin and Clos Vougeot. Several of the 1982s of Georges Mugneret are excellent and his 1983s very good. His wines are beginning to obtain a cult following, so make reservations now for his splendid 1985s, which he feels are the best he has made.

1983 Clos Vougeot	($27.00)	90
1983 Echézeaux	($25.00)	86
1983 Nuits St.-Georges Les Chaignots	($22.00)	85
1983 Nuits St.-Georges Les Vignes Rondes	($22.00)	80
1983 Ruchottes-Chambertin	($30.00)	86
1983 Vosne-Romanée	($20.00)	81

When I visited Mugneret in 1984, I feared that his use of 100% new oak barrels for the 1983s was a mistake. The wines were already very tannic and they hardly needed any additional wood tannins. Well, the wines have turned out to be very good, with the Clos Vougeot potentially outstanding. The Vosne-Romanée has a roasted, ripe, spicy bouquet, very good concentration, a trace of astringence, but should age well for 5–8 years. The Nuits St.-Georges Les Vignes Rondes tasted less concentrated, a little too hard and dry. It has good, ripe fruit, but I worry about it drying out before it matures. On the other hand, the Nuits St.-Georges Les Chaignots, despite the presence of very aggressive tannins, has a ripe, roasted character, deep color, and a long finish. It must have 10 years of cellaring. The Echézeaux, another wine that requires a 10-year wait before drinking, is dark ruby, very spicy, quite robust and concentrated, but very, very tannic. The Ruchottes-Chambertin has less charm than the lovely, seductive 1982, but is a very big wine, dark in color, and potentially better than scored, but it is extremely tannic. The Clos Vougeot gets my nod as Mugneret's best. It is very intense and powerful with mouth-searing tannins, but also oodles of ripe, plummy fruit. It should be sublime between 1995–2005.

1982 Echézeaux	($28.00)	85

1982 Ruchottes-Chambertin	($19.95)	88

With respect to the best 1982s, one might say they are composed of "sugar and spice and everything nice." No doubt that 1982s have been chaptalized to give them a fat, fruity, alcoholic character, and if a grower was meticulous with his/her selection process, the diluted, watery lots of wine were discarded. Well, both these 1982s are extremely alluring. Round, sweet, and spicy, with captivating aromas, lush, gentle flavors, and surprising concentration, this is the type of red burgundy that is easy to drink and easy to understand. The 1982 Ruchottes-Chambertin should drink well for 3–4 years and then fade quickly. However, it is a top 1982. The Echézeaux is a trifle tannic and may last 4–6 years, but it should be viewed as a hedonistic red burgundy for drinking soon.

NAIGEON-CHAUVEAU (GEVREY-CHAMBERTIN)* *

DOMAINE DES VAROILLES* * *

The Domaine des Varoilles has a loyal following for its long-lived wines, particularly those from Gevrey-Chambertin. The owners are the Naigeon-Chauveau family, who also sell wines as a *négociant* under their own labels. The 1984s here are not very promising, but the 1983s are quite good, very tannic, deeply colored, true *vins de garde*. The quality of the wines under the Domaine des Varoilles label is vastly superior to those under the *négociant* label, Naigeon-Chauveau. Burgundy enthusiasts should make a special search for the Clos des Varoilles Cuvée Vieilles Vignes and Clos des Meix Ouches Cuvée Vieilles Vignes.

Naigeon-Chauveau

1983 Chassagne-Montrachet	($14.00)	78

1983 Côte de Beaune-Villages	($10.00)	73

1983 Côte de Nuits-Villages	($12.00)	69

1983 Nuits St.-Georges	($18.00)	79

1983 Nuits St.-Georges Les Damodes	($25.00)	80

1983 Nuits St.-Georges Les Pruliers	($25.00)	83

1983 Santenay Le Passe Temps	($12.00)	78

None of these wines is bad, but none of them is particularly interesting. The Nuits St.-Georges Les Pruliers had the most color and concentration, but was somewhat dull and overly tannic. The others are quite aggressively tannic, raising serious questions about whether they would dry out before the tannins subside.

Domaine des Varoilles

1983 Bonnes Mares	($40.00)	87

1983 Charmes-Chambertin	($30.00)	85

1983 Clos Vougeot	($38.00)	87

1983 Gevrey-Chambertin	($15.00)	78

1983 Gevrey-Chambertin Champonets	($22.00)	87

1983 Gevrey-Chambertin Clos de Couvent	($18.00)	85

1983 Gevrey-Chambertin Clos de Meix Ouches Vieilles Vignes	($25.00)	88

1983 Gevrey-Chambertin Clos de Prieur	($20.00)	79

1983 Gevrey-Chambertin Varoilles	($25.00)	86

1983 Gevrey-Chambertin Clos des Varoilles Vieilles Vignes	($25.00)	89

1983 Vosne-Romanée La Romanée	($30.00)	80

Given the fact that the wines of the Domaine des Varoilles are made in a tight, lean, hard style that takes most of a decade to open and develop, the 1983s provided the precise natural products this estate needed. These are very tannic, backward wines. I would guess that 1995 or beyond will be a good time to take another look at these wines to see if they are mature. Even the lower level wines, such as the Gevrey-Chambertin, are 8–10 years away from maturity. The Gevrey-Chambertin Clos de Prieur seemed to lack richness and color, and the Vosne-Romanée La Romanée is good, but somewhat light, particularly for a 1983. Otherwise, the Gevrey-Chambertin Clos de Couvent, made from 40-year-old vines, is dark in color, with good body and rich fruit to balance out its considerable tannic clout. The excellent Gevrey-Chambertin Champonets may need 10 years, but it has the requisite concentration to outlast the tannins, and is nearly as good as the Clos des Meix Ouches Vieilles Vignes, which has oodles of ripe, sweet Pinot Noir fruit, a spicy, rich but restrained bouquet, and tough tannins. The Clos des Varoilles Vieilles Vignes is probably better than the 1978 version of this wine; at least it is more powerful and tannic. It will need 10–15 years, but it has excellent concentration and makes a forceful impression on the palate. The regular cuvée of the Clos des Varoilles is not so rich nor as tannic; it may be ready by 1995. As for the Grands Crus, the Charmes-Chambertin is a typical, very good 1983, big and rich, but so tough and tannic. The Bonnes Mares had tons of tannin but deeper fruit and better color than the Charmes-Chambertin. The Clos Vougeot is the most precocious of this latter trio, has excellent ripeness, full body, and a long finish, provided you are willing to cellar it for 10 years.

DOMAINE PERNOT-FOURRIER (GEVREY-CHAMBERTIN)* * * *

Over the years I have tasted some marvelous wines from this estate, particularly the 1964s, 1969s, and 1971s. They have broad, lush Pinot flavors and smoky, quite fragrant bouquets. Normally the wines need 5–8 years to develop fully, though I suspect the 1983s from Pernot-Fourrier will need 10–15 years. This estate made several good 1982s and their 1984s are certainly successful. The wines of Pernot-Fourrier are filtered prior to bottling, but, interestingly, they are never fined while aging in the cask. His 1983s are extremely tannic and several of them are problematic.

1983 Gevrey-Chambertin	($20.00)	70
1983 Gevrey-Chambertin Clos St.-Jacques	($30.00)	87
1983 Gevrey-Chambertin Combe aux Moines	($30.00)	86
1983 Gevrey-Chambertin Premier Cru	($25.00)	72

1983 Griottes-Chambertin	($35.00)	78

1983 Vougeot Premier Cru	($28.00)	85

These are real macho wines. In fact, several may be far too tannic to ever develop properly. The Gevrey-Chambertin tastes severe and astringent. The Gevrey-Chambertin Premier Cru is even more abrasively tannic and its future is suspect. The Griottes-Chambertin has plenty of ripe, rich, sweet fruit, but the musty taste of rot is present. That is a shame, because the wine has a lot of power and richness. Some growers claim that with extended aeration this smell blows off. Perhaps you are willling to take that chance; I am not. As for the others, the Vougeot is very tannic and full-bodied, but also has a lot of rich, ripe, deep fruit. It should peak in 8–10 years. The Combe aux Moines is another tannic titan, but has very fine concentration, some lush, sweet fruit in the midrange, and 8–10 years of evolution ahead. The Clos St.-Jacques is the best of these wines, a big, alcoholic, rich, deep, tannic wine that has balance and depth. However, it begs for 8–10 years.

DOMAINE PONSOT (MOREY ST.-DENIS)* * * *

Jean-Marie Ponsot and his son make some of Burgundy's richest and most concentrated wines. However, the estate is far from consistent; the 1984s are weak and feeble here, the 1985s excellent. They still hold to the opinion that 1983 is "an extraordinary year" and the best since 1947 and 1949. For several of their wines, they may be right. Some of their 1983s are, quite frankly, unbelievably concentrated and powerful. Consequently, they did not bottle their 1983s until late 1986. Some of the 1982s produced here are good, but, by Ponsot's own admission, they were not happy with the quality of their 1984s. Ponsot's wines can be truly great. The 1980 Clos de la Roche Vieilles Vignes is one of the greatest young burgundies I have ever tasted. In addition to their superb Clos de la Roche, the Latricières-Chambertin and Clos St.-Denis are the top wines from this estate. Ponsot never filters its wines.

1983 Chambertin	($55.00)	85

1983 Clos de la Roche	($55.00)	88

1983 Clos de la Roche Vieilles Vignes	($75.00)	96

1983 Clos Saint-Denis	($60.00)	91

1983 Griottes-Chambertin	($45.00)	87

1983 Latricières-Chambertin	($55.00)	88

These wines are all very good, even spectacular, in quality, but they differ considerably in style and will be ready to drink at different times. The Griottes-Chambertin is fairly precocious, with oodles of supple, yet soft, ripe fruit. It is so rich it is almost jammy. Drink it between 1990–1995. The Chambertin, a greater name but not greater wine, is rather light in color, especially for a Ponsot wine, has soft, classy, complex flavors, but is ready to drink. It is extremely long in the mouth but too light for a Chambertin. The regular Clos de la Roche (250 cases produced) is very dark in color, with a huge aroma of black cherries, apricots, and spicy oak. Quite full-bodied, deep and concentrated, this excellent wine should be at its best by 1998. The Latricières-Chambertin is similar: dense, dark, almost jammy, with full body, a long, rich, deep texture, and excellent concentration. It is more exotic and fragrant than the Clos de la Roche and should peak between 1992–2000. As for the two sensational wines of Ponsot, the Clos Saint-Denis (75 cases produced) combines power with finesse, has a voluptuous, deeply concentrated, long taste, is highly aromatic, and superbly flavored. It can be drunk now, but promises to be extraordinary in 5–7 years. Lastly is the monument of the 1983 red burgundies, the Clos de la Roche Vieilles Vignes (200 cases produced). It is in the same class as the staggering 1980, only the wine is more powerful (the alcohol is 14.5%) and denser. It simply must be tasted to be believed. This is an old heavyweight style of red burgundy that no one but Ponsot produces anymore. It should be mature by 1998 and last at least several decades. The concentration of flavor and length have more in common with a Guigal La Mouline or Pétrus than any red burgundy I have ever tasted.

DOMAINE POTHIER-RIEUSSET (POMMARD)* * * *

Virgile Pothier is one of those charming, red-cheeked vignerons who makes a visit to his cellars a memorable stop. Pothier made several great wines in 1983 and appears to have triumphed again in 1985. His 1984s are quite light, but clean and fruity; his 1982s are relatively disappointing given the standards here. Pothier's wines are not filtered.

1983 Beaune Boucherottes	($18.00)	84
1983 Bourgogne	($10.00)	82
1983 Bourgogne Grand Ordinaire	($9.00)	78
1983 Pommard	($18.00)	86
1983 Pommard Clos des Vergers	($20.00)	89
1983 Pommard Epenots	($25.00)	88
1983 Pommard Rugiens	($25.00)	90

The basic Bourgogne Grand Ordinaire, which is made from Gamay, not Pinot Noir, is a pleasant, rather simple but fruity wine. The Bourgogne is a step up in quality and interest. Pothier's Bourgognes generally have been excellent values (his 1979 and 1980 are very nice) and the 1983 actually needs 2–3 years to fully develop. It is spicy and fruity, with good body and length. The Beaune Boucherottes is, of course, a more serious wine. It will be ready to drink soon for a 1983, probably by 1990. It has a lovely Pinot fragrance, good, ripe, round, spicy fruit, medium body, and soft, moderate tannins. The real specialties of this house are the Pommards, and all of them are stunning in 1983. The Pommard has plenty of ripe, sweet fruit, a long, unctuous finish, round tannins, a very forward, precocious personality. It should be at its best between 1989–1996. The Pommard Epenots has a ripe, exotic aroma, deep, rich, long, broad flavors of raspberries tinged with vanillin oakiness, and moderate tannin. It should be delicious by 1989 and hold for a decade. As good as the Epenots is, the two stars are the Pommard Clos des Vergers and Pommard Rugiens. In both 1979 and 1983 these two wines stood out as greats of the vintage. The Clos des Vergers is perhaps the more classically structured. It has 13.5% alcohol without chaptalization, a staggering perfume of cedarwood, truffles, flowers, and ripe berry fruit. Full-bodied, rich and lush, with good supporting tannins, the Clos des Vergers can be drunk in 5 years or cellared for 10–20. The Rugiens is, by comparison, a more extroverted, exotic, fleshy wine. Sweet, oaky aromas intermingled with ripe plums fill the olfactory senses. On the palate, it has stupendous richness and none of the harsh, astringent tannins frequently found elsewhere. Pothier thinks it is the best Rugiens since his 1949 (which is a legendary wine). I am not quite sure when to drink it; by 1995 it will be outstanding, but it already has oodles of ripe fruit showing.

1982 Beaune Boucherottes	($14.95)	78
1982 Bourgogne	($8.99)	77
1982 Pommard	($14.95)	80
1982 Pommard Clos de Vergers	($18.95)	82
1982 Pommard Rugiens	($18.95)	82

These are all rather light, fruity, pleasant wines, but except for a good Clos de Vergers and Rugiens, they are simple. Even the latter two are rather shallow and watery for Pothier.

GÉRARD POTEL–DOMAINE DE LA POUSSE D'OR (VOLNAY)* * * *

I have a great deal of admiration for Gérard Potel and his lovely estate perched in Volnay with a full view of the vineyards. His wines have been textbook examples of elegant, refined, complex burgundies that show very well young but age beautifully. At a vertical tasting at the Domaine covering the vintages 1964–1983, I was struck by the splendid velvety richness these wines attain in vintages such as 1980, 1978, 1976, 1971, 1969, 1966, and 1964. The two greatest vintages for this property were 1964 and 1976. As for the 1983s, they are not among my favorites. While certainly good, they are perhaps too dry and tannic. I prefer his 1980s to his 1983s. Potel has begun to filter his wines.

1983 Pommard Les Jarollières	($22.00)	?
1983 Santenay Clos d'Audignac	($18.00)	77
1983 Santenay Clos Tavannes	($18.00)	80
1983 Volnay Bousse d'Or	($25.00)	84
1983 Volnay Les Caillerets	($25.00)	83
1983 Volnay Les Caillerets 60 Ouvrées	($25.00)	85

In general, these wines are medium ruby in color, quite hard and tannic, and one, the Pommard Les Jarollières, just too severe and unpleasant to judge at the moment. Neither Santenay greatly impressed me since they both had light color and a dry *(sec)* finish. The Volnay Caillerets has more obvious depth and fruit, but needs 8–10 years of cellaring. Certainly the Volnay Bousse d'Or and Volnay Les Caillerets 60 Ouvrées show richer and greater fruit, more depth and richness, and long finishes. Don't drink either until 1993.

DOMAINE CHARLES QUILLARDET (MARSANNAY)* *

This estate makes wines that I find clumsy, dull, and very Rhône-like. They are dark in color, chewy, sometimes too barnyardlike in aroma, but rarely do I find accurate Pinot Noir flavors. Nevertheless, the wines have a certain following and are fairly priced, save for the Chambertin, which can be overpriced. The 1983s are pretty mediocre wines. I do have a very good note on the 1982 Chambertin, but the price is too high.

1983 Bourgogne Les Grands Vignes	($7.49)	72
1983 Bourgogne Montre Cul	($7.99–$8.99)	60
1983 Chambertin	($40.00)	83
1983 Fixin	($8.49)	75
1983 Gevrey-Chambertin	($15.00)	82
1983 Gevrey-Chambertin Le Bel Air	($18.00)	82
1983 Gevrey-Chambertin Champeaux	($18.00)	83

The problem is that all the wines from Gevrey-Chambertin taste alike. The prices are different, but I see little or no difference between the *village* Gevrey-Chambertin and Chambertin. I would also like to know how Quillardet gets Pinot Noir to produce wines with this color and such a chunky, dense, heavy character. The Montre Cul is a wine that is truly in poor taste, from its adolescent label (featuring a woman's derriére in full view) to its heavy, coarse flavors.

1982 Chambertin	($40.00)	85

This is quite a lovely wine. Ready to drink, with rich, spicy, fat, deep flavors, medium to full body, and an earthy, trufflelike aroma, I find this quite an attractive offering from Quillardet.

DOMAINE HENRI REBOURSEAU (GEVREY-CHAMBERTIN)* * *

This is a historic old property that the now-ancient General Rebourseau made famous. The late Frank Schoonmaker claimed that the
1929s from Rebourseau were among the greatest burgundies he had
drunk. Now the younger Rebourseau runs the show, and the wines
are less rich and full-bodied than they were in the past. The 1983s are
very difficult wines to judge. They are suspiciously light in color, but
do make a powerful, heady, alcoholic impact on the palate. However,
after 20–30 minutes in the glass, moldy smells of rot emerge, and after
an hour these smells have overtaken everything in the glass. I went to
the trouble and expense to taste these wines three separate times to
be sure I was right. My conclusion is that they are badly affected by
rot and are flawed. The 1984s also seem poor, but for different reasons
(dilution and poor winemaking).

1983 Chambertin	($35.00)	60
1983 Charmes-Chambertin	($25.95)	55
1983 Clos Vougeot	($30.00)	65
1983 Gevrey-Chambertin	($13.99)	70
1983 Mazis-Chambertin	($28.95)	73

These wines, though quite alcoholic and powerful on the palate, are
very light in color, browning at the edges, and after 20–30 minutes in
the glass take on the unmistakable moldy smell of rot. The Mazis and
Clos Vougeot are less afflicted, the Charmes totally flawed. Some
tasters may not object to this character. It resembles the smell and
taste of a "corked" bottle.

REMOISSENET (BEAUNE)* * *

This is unquestionably one of the wealthiest domaines in Burgundy.
Roland Remoissenet is the gregarious genius behind this empire. The
quality of wines here has always been quite good, perhaps not as
exciting as the prices charged for the wines suggest, but nevertheless
ripe, round Pinot Noir-flavored wines. While tasting through the line
of Remoissenet wines, I got the impression that Roland Remoissenet
thinks 1983 is a good vintage, but no more. The quality level in 1983
at Remoissenet is good, but I found no great red burgundies, adding
evidence to my feeling that 1983 is by no means a super vintage.

Remoissenet did not bottle his wines until December 1985, in order to soften the tannins as much as possible. His wines are quite expensive.

Côte de Beaune (Remoissenet)

1983 Beaune Grèves	($28.00)	85
1983 Beaune Marconnets	($25.00)	87
1983 Beaune Toussaints	($25.00)	84
1983 Bourgogne Passe-Tout-Grains	($8.00)	74
1983 Corton Clos du Roi	($40.00)	86
1983 Givry Baron Thénard	($15.00)	83
1983 Mercurey Clos Fourtoul	($15.00)	75
1983 Pommard	($18.00)	76
1983 Le Renommée	($8.00)	72
1983 Santenay Gravières	($15.00)	75
1983 Volnay	($20.00)	80

The range of Remoissenet wines from the Côte de Beaune was surprisingly mediocre. Only five wines stood out. The 1983 Givry from Baron Thénard, always a good value from Remoissenet, is robust, fruity, substantial on the palate and interesting. Look for it to be fully mature between 1988–1994. Several of the Beaune wines are quite good. The Beaune Toussaints has a lovely black cherry bouquet, spicy, rather hard, tannic flavors, and medium body, and at least 5–8 years of positive evolution ahead. The Beaune Marconnets was my favorite Côte de Beaune wine from Remoissenet. Rich, ripe cherry and spicy oak aromas inundate the nose. On the palate, the wine is dense and concentrated, moderately tannic, and simply longer and deeper in flavor than the other wines. Give it 6–8 years of cellaring. The Beaune Grèves has broad flavors, but not the length or complexity of the Beaune Marconnets. The Corton Clos du Roi is the biggest and most alcoholic of these wines. Deep, fat, but also hard and tough in the finish, it should make a fine bottle in 8 years or so.

Côte de Nuits (Remoissenet)

1983 Charmes-Chambertin	($35.00)	78
1983 Clos Vougeot	($50.00)	86
1983 Gevrey-Chambertin	($20.00)	70
1983 Gevrey-Chambertin Aux Combottes	($35.00)	87
1983 Gevrey-Chambertin Clos St.-Jacques	($35.00)	87
1983 Grands-Echézeaux	($50.00)	84
1983 Mazis-Chambertin	($45.00)	83
1983 Nuits St.-Georges	($18.00)	84
1983 Nuits St.-Georges Les Perdrix	($25.00)	86
1983 Richebourg	($55.00)	72
1983 Vosne-Romanée Les Beaumonts	($30.00)	80

Remoissenet's wines from the Côte de Nuits show somewhat better quality than the wines from the Côte de Beaune. That is not to say there are not any disappointments. The Gevrey-Chambertin is thin and hard, the Charmes-Chambertin totally one-dimensional and musty in flavor. The Vosne-Romanée Les Beaumonts smelled herbaceous and stemmy. Lastly, the Richebourg tasted uncommonly harsh and astringent. As for the good news, the Nuits St.-Georges exhibits a smoky, earthy richness, deep color, good body and 6–8 years of life ahead. The Nuits St.-Georges Les Perdrix is even better, rich, smoky, dark in color, full-bodied, tannic, and powerful. Give it 8–10 years. The Gevrey-Chambertin Clos St.-Jacques is a definite winner, deep in color, full-bodied, ripe, intense, rich, and loaded with fruit. I liked the Gevrey-Chambertin Aux Combottes equally for its spicy, rich, very complex bouquet, ripe, dense, alcoholic, powerful flavors, and excellent finish. It is quite a big-impact wine that needs 7–10 years of cellaring. The Grands-Echézeaux is delicious, but rather light and not as concentrated as one might expect. The Clos Vougeot, while very tannic and in need of 10 years of cellaring, is rich in extract, spicy, full-bodied, with a long, deep finish.

DOMAINE DANIEL RION (NUITS ST.-GEORGES)* * *

I have tasted most of Rion's wines over the last four vintages; the wines have shown considerable consistency and now avoid the lapses in quality that plagued them in the late '70s. The Rion wines tend to be round, ripe, and fruity, with moderate levels of tannins. For the last several years, the Nuits St.-Georges Les Hauts Pruliers, Clos Vougeot, and Vosne-Romanée Les Beaumonts have tended to be the best wines from this domaine.

1983 Clos Vougeot	($30.00)	87
1983 Côte de Nuits-Villages	($12.00)	81
1983 Nuits St.-Georges Les Hauts Pruliers	($25.00)	86
1983 Vosne-Romanée	($20.00)	84
1983 Vosne-Romanée Les Beaumonts	($25.00)	84

These 1983s are more forward and accessible than many wines from this vintage. I would expect them to peak around 1990 and last a half-dozen more years; Rion's wines generally are not long-lived. A tasting in the summer of 1985 showed the 1978s to be drying out. The 1983 Côte de Nuits-Villages is a solid, chunky, straightforward wine with moderate tannins and some elegant Pinot Noir character. It should last for 5 years. The Vosne-Romanée is a lively, medium-bodied wine with a suppleness and pleasing lushness that give it appeal now. It should be drunk over the next 3–4 years. Curiously, the Vosne-Romanée Les Beaumonts has a similar character and, while more tannic, seems too close in style and quality to the Vosne-Romanée to merit the additional price. I liked both the Nuits St.-Georges Les Hauts Pruliers and Clos Vougeot considerably more than the other Rion wines. The Les Hauts Pruliers has a lot of spicy oak in its bouquet as well as some ripe plums. On the palate, it is deep and relatively rich, with very good length and depth. The Clos Vougeot is even better, with a dense-looking, dark ruby color, a very fragrant plum and oak bouquet, fat, rich fruit, full body, and moderate, rounded tannins. Both the Les Hauts Pruliers and Clos Vougeot should be at their best between 1990–1995.

DOMAINE DE LA ROMANÉE-CONTI (VOSNE-ROMANÉE)* * * * *

After a number of years of futile efforts, I was finally permitted to visit the Domaine in 1985. I can appreciate the Domaine's feelings that certain writers have maliciously criticized this estate, which produces Burgundy's most expensive and sometimes its most remarkable wines. However, the Domaine should be able to accept constructive criticism. I was the very first writer to highly praise their excellent 1980s, but when I criticized several of the 1981s, I was persona non grata. In any event, since 1978 this estate has produced many of the greatest wines in Burgundy, the 1978s superb, the 1979s excellent, 1980s exceptional, the 1981s somewhat mixed, and the 1982s very, very good. The 1983s here are outstanding, but begin to save your money for them now since they are extremely expensive.

1983 Echézeaux	($50.00)	87
1983 Grands-Echézeaux	($75.00)	90
1983 Richebourg	($100.00)	90
1983 Romanée-Conti	($150.00)	92
1983 Romanée-St.-Vivant	($85.00)	87
1983 La Tâche	($135.00)	92

The 1983 vintage for DRC was a very tough year. First there was hail, then the advent of rot in August because of tropical heat and humidity. When the harvest occurred, the DRC instructed its pickers to pick only the grapes, not the whole bunches, by hand and to discard all the rotten grapes. The results are splendidly concentrated and rich wines, but wines that also are extremely expensive and need at least a decade of cellaring, as they are not showing well at present because they are so tannic. At the summit of quality is the Romanée-Conti and La Tâche, two sensational wines with rich yet youthful fragrances, long, deep flavors, and plenty of body. The Richebourg is closed, the Grands-Echézeaux the most velvety and forward, and, given its quality, also the best value for a DRC wine. The Romanée-St.-Vivant is very spicy, a little rustic, but tannic and big. The Echézeaux is the lightest, but quite good. Yet, despite the obvious success, these wines all need at least 7–10 more years of cellaring, except for the Echézeaux.

1982 Echézeaux	($25.00)	83

1982 Grands-Echézeaux	($35.00)	87

1982 Richebourg	($55.00)	87

1982 Romanée-Conti	($95.00)	88

1982 Romanée-St.-Vivant	($37.50)	86

1982 La Tâche	($75.00)	88

The fact that the Domaine, or the DRC as it is often called, is on top in Burgundy is well evidenced by these 1982s. Considering the vintage, they are remarkably rich, deep, broadly flavored wines. They are expensive, but extremely high in quality. The Echézeaux is light and slightly herbaceous, aromatic, very spicy, and ready to drink. It will keep for 5–7 years. The Grands-Echézeaux is normally the "best buy" (for a DRC wine) and in 1982 it seems to offer the most for your dollar. It has surprisingly deep color, a big, rich, open-knit bouquet of exotic spices, plums, and wood. On the palate it is rich, medium-bodied and fairly heady, with moderate tannins. It should be at its best between 1988–1994. The Romanée-St.-Vivant is intensely spicy, round, and fruity, with plenty of complexity, moderate tannins, and 5–7 years of evolution. The Richebourg actually needs 5 years to mature fully. It is deep in color (in fact, one of the darkest 1982s), quite long and rich on the palate, with a lush, rich finish, and some firm tannins clearly noticeable. Give it 4–5 years. The La Tâche and Romanée-Conti are both very, very fragrant. Exotic spices, new oak, and ripe berry fruit all intermingle to create an orgy of wonderful scents. Both wines need 3–5 years to lose some of their tannic bite, but they are surprisingly deep, rich, and well-colored wines for this vintage. The DRC clearly looks to have made some of the finest wines of the 1982 vintage.

DOMAINE ARMAND ROUSSEAU (GEVREY-CHAMBERTIN)* * * *

This is a very serious domaine where Charles Rousseau makes altogether classic long-lived wines. They are expensive and hard to find, but very much deserve their acclaim and price. Rousseau compares 1983 to 1976, only he admits that the grapes were much more difficult to deal with. Some of the 1983s here are exceptional, but very tannic;

some have noticeable rot problems. Rousseau says they need a minimum of 15 years of cellaring.

1983 Chambertin	($55.00)	67
1983 Chambertin Clos de Bèze	($49.00)	90
1983 Charmes-Chambertin	($45.00)	70
1983 Clos de la Roche	($50.00)	70
1983 Gevrey-Chambertin	($20.00)	82
1983 Gevrey-Chambertin Clos St.-Jacques	($30.00)	90
1983 Gevrey-Chambertin Les Cazetiers	($30.00)	85
1983 Mazis-Chambertin	($48.00)	72
1983 Ruchottes-Chambertin	($45.00)	88

With the exception of the Gevrey-Chambertin, which may be mature by 1990, all of these wines require a minimum of 10 years of cellaring. However, the tannins are ripe and hard, though not the dry and astringent tannins caused by rot. All the wines are very deep in color, with the Clos de Bèze, Clos St.-Jacques, and Ruchottes the deepest. The most forward wine is the Clos de la Roche, but it still needs 10 years. The most backward wine is the Chambertin. If I had just one of these wines to buy, it would be the Clos St. Jacques, which has layers of sweet fruit and is significantly less expensive than the Clos de Bèze or Chambertin. If you have a good cellar and plenty of discretionary income, the Clos de Bèze will be superb in 10–15 years. The others may or may not turn out well, because rot definitely appears to be a problem with the Chambertin, Charmes Chambertin, and Clos de la Roche.

DOMAINE ROUMIER (CHAMBOLLE-MUSIGNY)* * * *

When I first looked at the 1983s at Roumier, I thought they were among the very best of the vintage. There is no reason to change my opinion now, though I wish Roumier had not bowed to pressure from his American importer and filtered his 1983s. His wines were pre-sold by a number of retailers, so I doubt that his greatest wines are still available; he did not make much wine in 1983 due to hail and rot. Several of Roumier's 1982s are also attractive for drinking now. The 1985s look very good rather than great.

1983 Bonnes Mares	($58.00)	92
1983 Chambolle-Musigny	($22.00)	84
1983 Chambolle-Musigny Les Amoureuses	($52.00)	88
1983 Clos Vougeot	($46.00)	90
1983 Morey St.-Denis Clos de la Bussière	($25.00)	87
1983 Musigny	($55.00)	90
1983 Ruchottes-Chambertin	($45.00)	93

Roumier always makes top-quality burgundy, but the 1983s are the best I have ever tasted from him, including the sensational wines he produced in 1976 and 1969. His 1983s have an opulence and richness to go along with their power and firm tannins. They are not likely to be fully mature until 1995–2000. These are truly great red burgundies —worth a search of the marketplace to find. The Morey St.-Denis Clos de la Bussière is an excellent red burgundy by any standard, but when tasting it alongside the other top wines here it gets lost. It has dark ruby color, an intense, sweet fruitiness, medium to full body, and firm tannins. It should be ready by 1992. The Chambolle-Musigny is a bit more tough and tannic, and while the color and concentration are excellent, the wine has some dry, astringent tannins in the finish that suggest hail or rot problems; it is the only Roumier wine I noticed this in. The Chambolle-Musigny Les Amoureuses (only 200 cases made) is rather powerful and alcoholic, but extremely deep and concentrated. Give it 10 years. The four great wines produced by Roumier include a staggeringly rich Clos Vougeot, so packed with ripe Pinot Noir fruit and so complex and aromatic that this powerful, massive red burgundy will not be fully mature for 10 years. Roumier's Musigny is also a great wine, more sensual and elegant, but extremely ripe and rich, dark in color, with an intense, supple lushness to its fruit. It has great balance and should drink beautifully between 1995–2000. Two of the very greatest wines are the Bonnes Mares and Ruchottes-Chambertin. I truly don't think one can taste better burgundy. The Bonnes Mares tastes denser and richer than the Musigny. The Ruchottes-

Chambertin is a monument, a prodigious and magnificent wine of incredible power, richness, and depth.

1982 Bonnes Mares	($35.00)	82
1982 Chambolle-Musigny	($18.00)	78
1982 Clos Vougeot	($30.00)	82
1982 Musigny	($40.00)	84

These are good wines, light, fruity, clean, and supple, but the prices for burgundy are so high that, unless the wine is truly superb, your money is better spent elsewhere. The Musigny is clearly the best; it has a vivid, oaky, and cherry-scented bouquet, but compared to the 1983, is rather light and watery.

DANIEL SENARD (ALOXE-CORTON)* * *

In America one hears little about this fine estate in Aloxe-Corton. Senard's specialty is Corton, but for connoisseurs of trivia, he makes a tiny amount of white wine from the Pinot Gris grape called Corton Blanc. It is an exotic, rich wine. Senard's red 1983s are typical for the vintage, big, backward, dry, tannic, and undeveloped. Hopefully, 10–12 years of cellaring will see the fruit emerge from behind the wall of tannin.

1983 Corton	($28.00)	70
1983 Corton Bressandes	($25.00)	86
1983 Corton Clos du Meix	($25.00)	85
1983 Corton Clos du Roi	($28.00)	87

Patience is required here . . . a lot of it. With the exception of the Corton, which I found awkward to judge because of the mouth-searing tannins and apparent absence of ripe fruit, the other three Cortons, though tannic and hard, do seem to have the concentration of fruit for balance. The Corton Clos du Roi is the most impressive since it has the finest deep color and density of fruit, with a promising bouquet of vanillin oak and ripe cherries. Give it 10 years of storage. The Corton Bressandes is a trifle more supple, medium weight, yet a fragrant, ripe, medium- to full-bodied wine that also needs 10 years of cellaring. The Corton Clos du Meix is similarly styled, yet very tannic and in need of 12–15 years of aging. It does have plenty of ripe fruit and a rustic, alcholic punch.

BERNARD SERVEAU (MOREY ST.-DENIS)* * * *

I have begun to visit Serveau regularly since I regard his wines as benchmark examples of the elegant, graceful, supple style of burgundy winemaking. His wines are made to be drunk young, as they are never tannic, alcoholic, or full-bodied enough to age past 7–8 years. The 1985s are excellent, the 1984s also well above average, and the 1983s generally less impressive than his 1985s. However, the 1983 Chambolle-Musigny Les Amoureuses should prove to be a winner.

1983 Chambolle-Musigny Les Amoureuses	($30.00)	88

1983 Chambolle-Musigny Les Sabiots	($18.00)	84

1983 Morey St.-Denis Les Sorbets	($18.00)	83

The Morey St.-Denis Les Sorbets has lost color, but still retains a pleasing ripeness and sweetness of Pinot Noir fruit. It is a delicate rather than powerful 1983, and should be drunk over the next 4–5 years. The Chambolle-Musigny Les Sabiots has a trifle more concentration, surprising suppleness for a 1983, and very good ripeness. It should be ready to drink by 1987. The Chambolle-Musigny Les Amoureuses is quite fine, dark in color, with an expansive, fragrant, ripe bouquet of flowers and plums. This silky, medium-bodied wine has very good concentration and moderate, rather gentle tannins. It should be at its peak between 1990–1995.

ROBERT SIRUGE (VOSNE-ROMANÉE)* * *

This small grower in Vosne-Romanée produces elegant, supple wines that generally mature quite quickly. His 1983s are above average to good wines, with the exception of the Grands-Echézeaux, which is outstanding.

1983 Grands-Echézeaux	($52.00)	90

1983 Vosne-Romanée	($16.00)	80

1983 Vosne-Romanée Les Petits Monts   ($25.95)   84

The *village* Vosne-Romanée is light to medium ruby in color, has a pleasing oaky, spicy bouquet, a strong lashing of tannin, and a powerful alcoholic punch. It needs 5–6 years of cellaring. The Vosne-Romanée Les Petits Monts is darker in color, ripe, and alcoholic, but finishes hard and dry with a touch of the *goût de moisi* (a taste of moldy, damp cardboard from rot-damaged grapes). It is certainly a good wine, but its development must be watched. The Grands-Echézeaux is quite outstanding, dark ruby in color with a really superb, intense bouquet of very ripe fruit and spicy oak. It is quite concentrated, very deep and rich, with good tannins that add firmness rather than astringence. It should be at its best between 1992–2000.

DOMAINE GABRIEL TORTOCHOT (GEVREY-CHAMBERTIN)* * *

Tortochot is a serious winemaker. His wines are not filtered and therefore, if not cared for properly, can become unstable. His 1983s are very big, full-bodied with an almost roasted ripeness. Like most of the big 1983s, the wines will require significant cellaring.

1983 Chambertin   ($45.00)   89

1983 Clos Vougeot   ($35.00)   84

1983 Gevrey-Chambertin Lavaux St.-Jacques   ($30.00)   83

1983 Mazis-Chambertin   ($35.00)   88

Both the Gevrey-Chambertin Lavaux St. Jacques and Clos Vougeot tasted closed and tough, and had good concentration, some underlying suppleness, but a tannic toughness in the finish. They showed no signs of rot damage. They definitely need 6–8 years of cellaring. The Mazis-Chambertin and Chambertin are very old-style wines, thick, rich, full-throttle burgundies with roasted, spicy, intense bouquets, rich, sweet, almost creamy flavors, full body, and ripe, round tannins. They are approachable now, but please cellar them 6–8 years for their potential to be realized.

DOMAINE LOUIS TRAPET (GEVREY-CHAMBERTIN)* * *

I have not always been pleased with the Trapet wines. They certainly have an excellent reputation, but in some vintages they have turned out too light and have had a tendency to turn brown in color at an early age. Jean Trapet, the current Trapet in charge, is a short, affable man. His wines are aged 15–18 months in oak barrels, of which one-third are new. His 1983s were bottled in May 1985, after a slight filtration. Trapet used the new "Bouteille Bourgogne" for his 1983s, an ugly, cheap-looking bottle that resembles the bottle used for generic Côtes du Rhône wines and does no justice to the product. The style of wine produced here is generally lighter than that made at such domaines as Leclerc, Rousseau, Clair-Daü, and Varoilles. The 1983s from Trapet are very, very good, probably the best wines I have yet tasted from this estate.

1983 Chambertin	($40.00)	86
1983 Chambertin Cuvée Vieilles Vignes	($55.00)	90
1983 Chapelle-Chambertin	($27.00)	86
1983 Latricières-Chambertin	($27.00)	86

All of these wines have light to medium ruby color. They also exhibited very broad, ripe, smoky, sweet Pinot flavors. Firm tannins are present, but these wines are much more accessible and forward than most 1983s. I expect all of them to be drinking well by 1990 and to last 5–10 years. The Chapelle-Chambertin is quite rich, round, and fruity, with a complex, smoky, deep bouquet. The flavors are lush and intense. It should be ready in 3–4 years. The Latricières-Chambertin is less evolved and more obviously tannic, yet develops beautifully in the glass, revealing scents of toffee, caramel, and hickory. It has a velvety texture and very long finish. It should be drunk by 1990; no later than 1996. The Chambertin is the most closed and tannic of these four wines. It is spicy and rich, but for the moment does not reveal the same depth and complexity of flavor as the other wines. The Chambertin Cuvée Vieilles Vignes, produced from 80-year-old vines on an average of only once every decade (there were 100 cases in 1983), is a decadently rich and opulent Pinot Noir. It has the deepest color (though not very dark) and concentration, with a huge-scented bouquet of smoky fruit and crème brûlée. Sweet, ripe, long, and very expansive on the palate, this medium- to-full-bodied wine is already tasting exceptionally fine. However, 5–6 years of bottle age should reveal even more character.

COMTE DE VOGÜÉ (CHAMBOLLE-MUSIGNY)* *

This estate in Chambolle-Musigny is certainly one of the most famous in all of Burgundy. Burgundy collectors continue to rush to buy these wines, even though the quality has slipped considerably. I have not tasted a great Vogüé wine since the 1972s. Yet the price is as high as ever, and the wine is more often than not extremely light, sometimes insipid, overly filtered and, in truth, a total embarrassment. The 1983s are better than many of the wines made in the dismal 1973–1982 period, but are not anywhere close to being considered among the best in this variable vintage.

1983 Bonnes Mares	($50.00)	84
1983 Chambolle-Musigny	($30.00)	75
1983 Chambolle-Musigny Les Amoureuses	($40.00)	83
1983 Musigny	($65.00)	85

For fear of tainting the macerating grape juice with the *goût de moisi* from rot- and hail-scarred grapes, the decision was made to pull the skins off after only a week. Several other producers made similar decisions and the results were rather lightly colored, elegant, fruity wines that lacked depth and concentration. The *village* Chambolle-Musigny is very light, but clean and pleasant. The Chambolle-Musigny Les Amoureuses has considerably more fruit and flavor, decent body, some attractive vanillin oakiness, and a good, lush finish. It should be at its best by 1990. The Bonnes Mares is very precocious-tasting, has medium body, good concentration, an underlying, pleasing suppleness, and 4–6 years of evolution ahead of it. The Musigny is darker in color, with more tannin and slightly more concentration. Its tannins are soft, the bouquet dominated by the smell of new oak and cherries. The Musigny should reach full maturity between 1990–1994.

1982 Bonnes Mares	($40.00)	73
1982 Chambolle-Musigny Les Amoureuses	($35.00)	72
1982 Musigny	($45.00)	74

There is not much flavor or color to these wines, so all I will say is that they look and taste like simple, pleasant rosés with some faint

Pinot Noir character in the distant background. How any respectable producer, particularly the Comte de Vogüé, could release such over-priced mediocrities under a famous label is quite clearly beyond my comprehension. Caveat emptor!

Beaujolais

The summer heat and humidity, which affects most areas of the United States in May, June, July, August, and September, are not conducive to enjoyable drinking of many types of rich, full-bodied red wines, particularly fine French Bordeaux, Rhônes, and bigger-style burgundies, as well as Italian Barolos, Barbarescos, and California Cabernet Sauvignons and Zinfandels. I, like most wine enthusiasts, will not totally abstain from drinking one of these wines, even on the most torrid of days, but they are best served in fall, winter, and spring. There is, however, a perfect summer red wine, and it is Beaujolais, the refreshingly forthright, effusively fruity wine from France. In fact, it can be the right wine for any season.

Beaujolais, produced from the Gamay grape, will never be a great or profound wine, but it has the potential to be one of the most flexible, enjoyable, and seductive. At its best, served slightly chilled (50° F is a perfect temperature), it is a heady, perfumed, intensely fruity, soft, lush wine that can be rapaciously gulped down without feeling any guilt for not commenting on its bouquet, complexity, or finesse. Simple, lush and delicious, Beaujolais can be a hedonistic summer pleasure for wine drinkers.

The Beaujolais hierarchy is simple. At the lowest echelon is "straight" Beaujolais, followed by Beaujolais-Villages, which is usually better. At the top level of quality are the nine "crus," each offering the inimitable soft, lush fruitiness that has made Beaujolais so popular, but each slightly different in style.

Today the difference between a Moulin-à-Vent, historically the fullest, most ageworthy and richest Beaujolais "cru," and Brouilly, the lightest "cru," is not always as apparent as the textbooks say. The other seven crus include Chiroubles, always one of my favorites for decadently fruity wines; Julienas, fleshy and rich; St.-Amour, very fruity and supple, Morgon, among the most ageworthy, Fleurie, lush, silky, and fruity, Côtes de Brouilly, light, delicate, though rarely seen in this country, and Chénas, full, darkly colored, and potentially excellent, but also rarely seen.

Most Beaujolais will be at their best in 1–3 years after the vintage. Some will last longer. Despite this possibility of longevity, the wines do lose fruit and change in character as the freshness and zesty, exuberant fruitiness of the wines dissipate. They may taste good in three years, but clearly their effusively fruity character begs for them to be drunk up over the first few years.

Recent Vintages

As for recent vintages, 1985 is the best bet since the wines are ripe, fragrant, rich, and supple. They should be drunk up by the end of 1988. Avoid the 1984s, which are hollow and lack charm. The rather large-proportioned 1983s were atypical Beaujolais—tannic, full-bodied, rich, but "too big." Surprisingly, the best Morgons, Fleuries, and Moulin-à-Vents from 1983 can still be drunk with great pleasure. However, given a choice, I would opt for the 1985s.

A GUIDE TO THE BEST PRODUCERS OF BEAUJOLAIS

* * * * * (OUTSTANDING PRODUCERS)

René Berrod	Georges Duboeuf
J.P. Bloud	Jacky Janodet
Michel Chignard	Petit Perou
B. Diochon	Bernard Sauté

* * * * (EXCELLENT PRODUCERS)

Serge Aujas	Domaine Matray
Jean Bédin	Jean-Paul Ruet
Louis Champagnon	Domaine Savoy
Jacques Depagneux	Thevenet
Pierre Ferraud	Château Thivin
Château des Jacques	Trenel
Mathelin	Georges Trichard

* * * (GOOD PRODUCERS)

Paul Beaudet	Chanut Frères
Georges Boulon	Jaffelin
Domaine Dalicieux	André Large
Joseph Drouhin	Moillard
Henry Fessy	Piat
Sylvain Fessy	Roger Rocassel

* * (AVERAGE PRODUCERS)

Loron	Pasquier-Desvignes
Mommessin	Paul Sapin
Robert Pain	Louis Tête

The King of Beaujolais

No other person dominates a wine region of France as Georges Duboeuf, *le grand roi de Beaujolais*, does there. The reasons for his remarkable success are simple—fair prices, consistently high quality, and a huge production. His famous flower-labeled bottle has inspired a new colorful era of wine labels and his single domaine-designated Beaujolais wines are the best that money can buy. In recent vintages, Duboeuf's wines have been priced at $5.50 to $8 a bottle; his 1985s are the finest he has made to date. Duboeuf's wines are always in demand.

RATING DUBOEUF'S BEST SINGLE-VINEYARD BEAUJOLAIS

Outstanding

Chiroubles Desmeures

Fleurie Les Deduits

Morgon Jean Descombes

Moulin-à-Vent Heritiers Tagent

Excellent

Beaujolais Regnie (du Potet)

Beaujolais-Villages (Grand Grange)

Brouilly (du Prieuré)

Brouilly (de Nervers)

Chiroubles (de Raousset)

Chiroubles (de Javernand)

Chénas (La Combe Remont)

Chénas (Manoir des Journets)

Fleurie (Quatre Vents)

Julienas (des Mouilles)

Julienas (des Vignes)

Morgon (des Versauds)

Morgon (Princesse Lieven)

Moulin-à-Vent (La Tour du Brief)

Moulin-à-Vent (des Caves)

Saint-Amour (du Paradis)

White Burgundy
(The Price of Glory)

Puligny-Montrachet, Chassagne-Montrachet, Meursault, Corton-Charlemagne

There can be no doubt that the tiny region of southern Burgundy, centered around the small towns of Puligny-Montrachet, Chassagne-Montrachet, and Meursault, produces the world's greatest dry white wine from the Chardonnay grape. However, the production is strictly limited by law, and insatiable worldwide demand has caused prices for white burgundy in 1987 to reach such absurd levels that one is

hard pressed to recommend any of these wines. However, I have
provided a rating of the growers for someone willing to spend the small
fortune necessary for a bottle of white burgundy.

Chablis

Located at Burgundy's northernmost end, Chablis has never been
fully understood by Americans. Chablis wines, less opulent, fat, buttery and rich than white burgundy made further south, are crisp,
sometimes flinty, often austere and tart, but in great years are classic
examples of tightly knit Chardonnay ripeness and crisp acidity. In
most years, a huge quantity of wine is made here, all of it white and
all of it from Chardonnay vines spread out around the town of Chablis.
But this is a risky area since the vineyards lie quite far north and it is
cool in Chablis. Consequently the frequent spring frosts can occur
very late, putting a tragic halt to vine growth and significantly curtail-
ing production. Yet, when the climate is hospitable from March
through October, Chablis at its best has a remarkable richness of
fruit, a firm, fresh acidity that gives it a zesty taste and a penetrating
bouquet. The best Chablis comes from several Grand Cru vineyards
(which represent less than 5% of the total produced), but some Chablis
Premiers Crus from vineyards such as Montée de Tonnerre, Four-
chaume, and Vaillons can, in the hands of the best growers, be as
good. Chablis, which has had its name bastardized by both the California and Australian wine industry, is not a wine to seek out in cold,
rainy years, since the wines then tend to be too acidic, lean, and hard.
But in the great vintages, 1985, 1983, 1978, and 1975, Chablis can last
and improve in the bottle for 5, 10, even 15 years in some cases. Prices
here too have skyrocketed in the last 24 months and Chablis at the
top levels (Premier or Grand Cru) is now very, very expensive.

When choosing a top Chablis, I recommend staying away from
straight Chablis except in the ripe, sunny vintages. It is often a green,
very neutral wine with an acidic character. Also, decide whether
you like a toasty oaky character to your Chablis or want pure, unin-
fluenced, crisp Chardonnay fruit to taste. If you like the barrel-
fermented, aged in cask, "traditional," buttery, toasty, ripe style
of Chablis, no one does it better than Dauvissat, Raveneau, and
Long-Depaquit, but expect to pay upwards of $25 a bottle for
Grands Crus from these producers. For pure Chardonnay fruit that
never sees a trace of oak aging, Louis Michel's wines are brilliant
expressions.

QUICK VINTAGE GUIDE

1985— An outstanding year for Chablis, a very good year for Puligny, Chassagne, and Meursault. Forward, lush, soft wines were made that have good, not excessive alcohol content, relatively low acidity, and no trace of any annoying rot or hail damage. Unfortunately, prices are at absurd levels and show no signs of dropping. The crop size was normal in Chablis. A vintage to buy if you can afford it.

1984— The small crop of wine was maligned for no reason prior to the harvest, but for both Chablis and Puligny, Chassagne, and Meursault, medium-bodied, clean, fresh, lively wines were produced that will drink nicely for 3–4 years. They are not great wines, but neither are they poor. The wines have begun to lose some of their annoyingly high acidity and greenness, but they lack fruit and flesh.

1983— The best year for Chablis since the great vintage of 1978. For Puligny, Chassagne, and Meursault, a very irregular year of massive, high-alcohol wines. Where balancing acidity is present, the wines are spectacular. When it is not, they are heavy, clumsy, and grotesque. The top wines from Chablis are explosively rich, powerful, and alcoholic, but they are slightly out of balance and though immensely enjoyable, should be drunk before the end of this decade.

1982— A prolific crop of lush, rich, very fruity, low-acid wines was produced in both Chablis and Puligny, Chassagne, and Meursault. Some wines, particularly from the growers/producers who overcropped or made no selections, are watery and light. The best, however, are voluptuous, lush, elegant, and ideal for drinking over the next 2–4 years. A very good, sometimes outstanding vintage, but frequently the wines will not keep long.

1981— Initially considered a classic year of slow to mature, high-acid, lean, angular wines that just needed time to develop. Some wines lack flesh and charm and will never develop. Those that have the requisite intensity and richness will be long-lived and classic. The wines from Chablis are good, but a trifle austere and in some cases very lean. This is a vintage in which one should pay particular attention to the producer.

1980— A dull summer led to adverse pre-harvest publicity that doomed the reputation of the vintage. The wines are solid, reliable, but uninspiring. They should be drunk up.

1979— A huge crop everywhere, but the wines show a lack of depth as well as low acidity. They all should be drunk up; only a few of the big wines from the best growers are worth holding onto.

1978—In the last ten years, the only uncontested and consistently great vintage for both Chablis and Puligny, Chassagne, and Meursault. The wines are both powerful and graceful, with splendid balance, rich, ripe flavors, and further evolution of at least 5 years ahead of them.

Older Vintages

I suspect few consumers give the best white burgundies and top Chablis much of a chance to prove their remarkable longevity. Older vintages of the best producers can be eye-opening in their freshness. The best 1978s are presently in full bloom, revealing all of their majestic ripeness and richness, since this was unquestionably a great year. The 1979s should have been consumed by now. (Examples from cool cellars can be wonderful.) The 1976s were ripe, alcoholic, and similar to the 1983s, but all 1976s should be drunk up. The 1975s from Chablis are still classics, and were certainly France's best-kept secret in this vintage.

A GUIDE TO THE BEST PRODUCERS OF PULIGNY-MONTRACHET, CHASSAGNE-MONTRACHET, MEURSAULT, AND CORTON-CHARLEMAGNE

* * * * * (OUTSTANDING PRODUCERS)

Coche-Dury	Leroy
Louis Jadot	André Ramonet
Comtes Lafon	Etienne Sauzet
Vincent Leflaive	

* * * * (EXCELLENT PRODUCERS)

Bitouzet-Prieur	Château de Maltroye
Bonneau de Martray	Château de Meursault
Louis Chapuis	Michelot-Buisson
Chartron and Trébuchet	Albert Morey
Delagrange-Bachelet	Niellon
Joseph Drouhin	Prieur-Brunet
Gagnard	Ramonet-Prudhon
Jaffelin	Remoissenet
François Jobard	Ropiteau
Louis Latour	Guy Roulot
Lequin-Roussot	

* * * *(GOOD PRODUCERS)*

Robert Ampeau   Duc de Magenta
Henri Boillot   Joseph Matrot
Bouchard Père   Moillard
Bouzereau-Gruère   Charles Moncaut
Caillot   Jean Monnier
Coche-Debord

A GUIDE TO THE BEST PRODUCERS OF CHABLIS

* * * * *(OUTSTANDING PRODUCERS)*

René Dauvissat   Raveneau
Long-Depaquit

* * * *(EXCELLENT PRODUCERS)*

Domaine Auffray   Louis Pinson
Paul Droin   Guy Robin
William Fèvre   Robert Vocoret
Louis Michel

* * * *(GOOD PRODUCERS)*

La Chablisienne   Lamblin
Jean Colin   Domaine Laroche
Domaine Defaix   Moillard
Joseph Drouhin   J. Moreau
Marcel Duplessis   Albert Pic
Domaine de L'Eglantière   A. Regnaud
Alain Geoffrey

Where are Burgundy's White Wine Values?

If one is willing to be a bit adventurous and avoid the glamour appellations of white burgundy, values can be found. The little-known Saint-Romain, Auxey-Duresses, Saint-Aubin, and Santeney provide four appellations where it is still difficult to find a white burgundy for more than $15 a bottle. Further south, in the area called the Chalonnais, the white wines of Rully and Montagny are where the values are produced. Further south of Chalonnais, just to the north of Lyon, is the Mâconnais, the consumer's best chance for enjoying fruity, crisp Chardonnay wines for under $8. The Mâcon-Villages wines and neighboring wines of St.-Veran are increasingly well made, and represent very fine values. The following is a list of the best producers of these wines. Vintages should be regarded as approximately the same as in Puligny, Chassagne, Meursault, and Corton-Charlemagne.

Burgundy's Best White Wine Values

Delorme (Rully)   J. Lamy (St.-Aubin)
Duboeuf (St.-Veran)   Lequin-Roussot (Santenay)
Duboeuf (Mâcon-Villages)   Leroy (Auxey-Duresses)
Domaine de la Folie (Rully)   Leroy (St.-Romain)
Guffens-Heynen (Mâcon-   Prunier (Auxey-Duresses)
    Pierreclos)   Vachet (Montagny)

Chablis, Puligny-Montrachet, Chassagne-Montrachet, Meursault, Corton-Charlemagne
A Buying Strategy

Unless you have the riches of a successful rock star or movie star, the glories of the outstanding 1985 Chablis will seem, justifiably, too expensive an indulgence. The currently weak dollar and worldwide demand have caused prices to skyrocket. If that is discouraging news, I can hardly recommend the lean, acidic 1984s, not only unattractive wines, but also expensive—a double whammy for consumers. The 1983s are drinking beautifully, but I will bet the top wines have long disappeared from the marketplace. Wine from the bountiful crop of 1982 can still be found, but unless you can find those from the top producers, these wines are beginning to show a little fatigue. In short, this is not a good time to buy white burgundy unless you want to pay the outrageously high prices asked for the 1985s, and that seems senseless to me, given the numerous high-quality, less expensive alternatives.

CHAMPAGNE

A vast amount of champagne, the festive wine par excellence, is purchased and drunk by consumers. For the last several years, champagne buyers have never had it so good. The strong dollar, bumper crops of solid quality wine in Champagne, and intense price competition by importers, wholesalers and retailers all combined to drive prices down, and for a time, it was a wonderful buyer's market. However, this has all changed. A small, mediocre crop in 1984, a top-quality but tiny crop in 1985, and a sagging American dollar have caused an upward surge in champagne prices. The shift was first noticed in 1986, as prices soared higher—a good 20–40% in many cases. Price instability appears to be the rule now, but those who stocked up in 1985 can consider themselves fortunate, since prices now are considerably higher.

In buying champagne, I recommend paying close attention to the following guidelines.

1. The luxury or prestige cuvées of the Champagne houses are almost always overpriced (all sell for $35–$80 a bottle). The pricing plays on the consumer's belief that higher price signifies a higher level of quality. In many cases it does not.
2. Purchase your champagne from a merchant who has a quick turnover in inventory. More than any other wine, champagne is vulnerable to poor storage and bright shop lighting. Buying bottles that have been languishing on the shelves of retailers for 2–3 months can indeed be risky business.
3. Don't hesitate to try some of the best non-vintage champagnes recommended herein. The best of them are largely comparable to the best luxury cuvées, but sell for a quarter to a fifth the price.
4. There has been a tremendous influx of high-quality champagnes from small firms in Champagne. Although most of these wines may be difficult to find outside of major metropolitan markets, some of these small houses produce splendid wine worthy of a search of the marketplace.

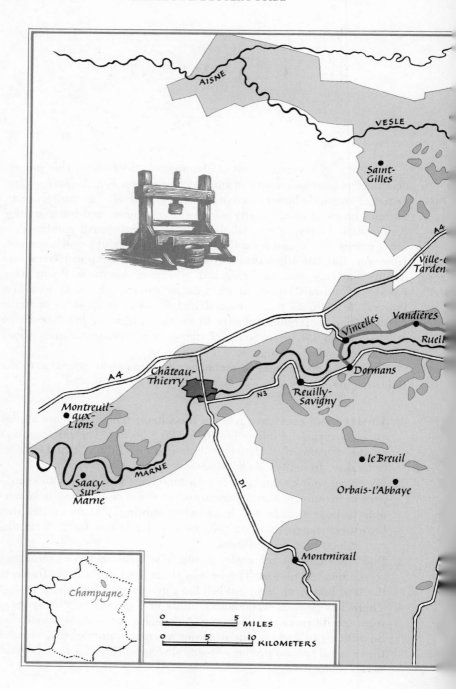

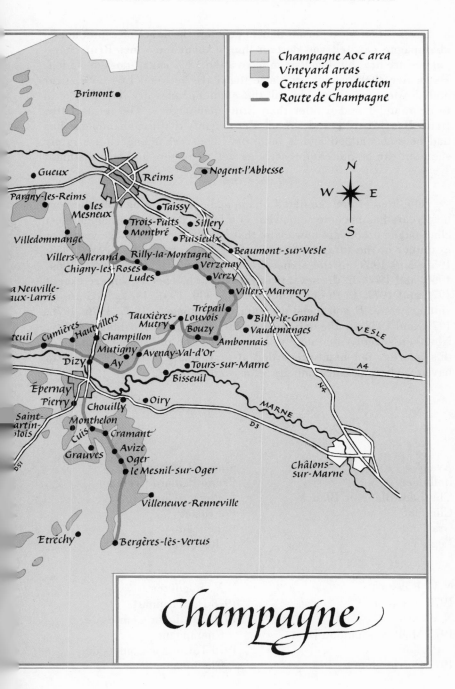

Champagne

5. Several technical terms that appear on the label of a producer's champagne can tell you certain things about the wine. **Brut** champagnes are dry, but legally can have up to 1.5% sugar (dosage) added. **Extra dry** champagnes are those that have between 1.5–3.5% sugar added. Most tasters would call these champagnes dry, but they tend to be rounder and fruitier than Brut champagnes. The terms **Ultra Brut, Brut Absolu,** and **Dosage Zéro** signify that the champagne has had no sugar added and is bone dry. These champagnes are rarely seen but can be quite impressive as well as austere and lean-tasting.

Recent Vintages

The idea of vintage-dated champagne representing only the very best years has become somewhat of a farce. It seems as though most champagne producers now claim that every year is a vintage year. For example, in the fifties there were four "vintage" years, 1952, 1953, 1955, and 1959, in the sixties five vintage years, 1961, 1962, 1964, 1966, and 1969. In the seventies, every year has been a vintage except 1972 and 1977. In the current decade, 1980, 1981, 1982, 1983 are all vintage years. If you insist on vintage champagne, 1975, 1976, 1978, 1979, and 1982 are the only recent years that are truly vintage quality. Nineteen seventy-nine may well turn out to be the sleeper vintage of this quartet; not highly regarded at first, many of the '79s seem to have excellent balance and grace, as well as flavor.

CHAMPAGNE—FINDING THE BEST WINES

Non-vintage Brut

Ayala	Mumm Crémant
Bollinger	Bruno Paillard Crémant
Charbaut Blanc de Blancs	J. Perrier Cuvée Royale
Clicquot	Pol Roger
Gratien	Rapeneau
Legras	L. Roederer Premier

Rosé

N.V. Billecart	N.V. Roederer
1979 Clicquot	1978 Dom Ruinart
N.V. Krug	1976 Taittinger Comtes de
1975 Moët & Chandon Dom	Champagne
Pérignon	1979 Taittinger Comtes de
1979 Perrier-Jouët	Champagne

Vintage Brut

1982 & 1979 Billecart Blanc de
Blancs
1982 Bonnaire Blanc de Blancs
1979 Charbaut Blanc de Blancs
1978 Clicquot

1979 H. Germain Blanc de
Blancs
1979 Gratien
1976 Bruno Paillard
1979 Pol Roger
1976 Pol Roger

Luxury cuvées

1979 Billecart Cuvée Billecart
1975 Bollinger "R.D."
N.V. Cattier Clos du Moulin
1976 Charbaut Certificate
1979 Clicquot La Grande Dame
1979 Deutz Wm. Deutz
N.V. Gosset Réserve
1979 Henriot Rothschild
1979 Heidsieck Monopole
Diamant Bleu
1969 Jacquesson Late Disgorged
N.V. and 1979 Krug
N.V. Laurent-Perrier Ultra Brut
1979 and 1978 Laurent-Perrier
Grand Siècle

N.V. Lechere Orient Express
N.V. Lechere Blanc de Blancs
1980 and 1978 Moët & Chandon
Dom Pérignon
1975 Pol Roger Blanc de
Chardonnay
1979 Pol Roger Winston
Churchill
1981 and 1979 L. Roederer
Cristal
1976 Taittinger Comtes de
Champagne
1979 Taittinger Comtes de
Champagne
1981 Taittinger Collection

A GUIDE TO CHAMPAGNE'S BEST PRODUCERS

* * * * * (OUTSTANDING PRODUCERS)

Bollinger (full-bodied)
Veuve Clicquot (full-bodied)
Krug (full-bodied)

Pol Roger (medium-bodied)
Louis Roederer (full-bodied)
Taittinger (light-bodied)

* * * * (EXCELLENT PRODUCERS)

Billecart-Salmon (light-bodied)
Bonnaire (light-bodied)
Charbaut (light-bodied)
Gosset (full-bodied)
Alfred Gratien (full-bodied)
Henriot (full-bodied)
J. Lassalle (light-bodied)

Laurent-Perrier (medium-
bodied)
Lechere (light-bodied)
Moet & Chandon (medium-
bodied)
Dom Ruinart (light-bodied)

* * * (GOOD PRODUCERS)

Ayala (medium-bodied)
Paul Bara (full-bodied)
Barancourt (full-bodied)
Cattier Brut (light-bodied)
Deutz (medium-bodied)
H. Germain (light-bodied)
Heidsieck Monopole (medium-
  bodied)
Charles Heidsieck (medium-
  bodied)
Jacquesson (light-bodied)

Lanson (light-bodied)
Launois Père (light-bodied)
R. & L. Legras (light-bodied)
Bruno Paillard (light-bodied)
Perrier-Jouët (light-bodied)
Joseph Perrier (medium-bodied)
Philipponnat (medium-bodied)
Piper Heidsieck (light-bodied)
Pommery and Greno (light-
  bodied)

* * (AVERAGE PRODUCERS)

Beaumet (light-bodied)
Besserat de Bellefon (light-
  bodied)
Boizel (light-bodied)
Nicholas Feuillatte (light-
  bodied)
Goldschmidt-Rothschild (light-
  bodied)
Michel Gonet (medium-bodied)

Jacquart (medium-bodied)
Jestin (light-bodied)
Guy Larmandier (medium-
  bodied)
Mumm (medium-bodied)
Oudinot (medium-bodied)
Rapeneau (medium-bodied)
Alfred Rothschild (light-bodied)
Marie Stuart (light-bodied)

Champagne—A Buying Strategy

One should have stocked up in 1985 and early 1986, before prices began to skyrocket. However, what do you do now? For vintage champagnes, unless you are dealing with those producers who make long-lived, full-bodied champagnes (e.g., Bollinger, Pol Roger, Krug, Veuve Clicquot), you are advised to avoid vintages before 1978. Concentrate on the 1979s, which are very good and the best vintage for drinking until the 1982s appear on the market. Also concentrate on the top non-vintage champagnes listed. Most experienced tasters cannot begin to tell the difference between a vintage and a non-vintage champagne when tasted blind, yet the price differential is considerable. Lastly, if you think champagne prices are too high, don't ignore the fine sparkling wines made in Alsace or the Loire Valley. The best of them offer attractive and inexpensive alternatives.

AYALA (MEDIUM-BODIED)* * *

Brut Non-Vintage   ($9.95–$12.95)   86

This is a very good champagne that I have seen discounted to $9.95 a bottle, making it an exceptional bargain. Quite dry, medium-bodied, and frothy, with crisp acidity, this is an aromatic, spicy, toasty champagne with a dramatic bouquet and well-balanced, dry taste.

PAUL BARA (FULL-BODIED)* * *

1979 Brut   ($18.95)   85

Bara's style makes his among the most forceful, aggressive, and full-bodied champagnes. His 1979 is relatively rich, toasty, spicy, and full, and for that reason should be served with food rather than as an apéritif.

BARANCOURT (FULL-BODIED)* * *

1979 Cuvée des Fondateurs   ($39.95)   84

This is a well-made, tightly knit, austere yet large-framed champagne at a ridiculous price. It needs several years of aging to shed its tartness and austere qualities.

BEAUMET (LIGHT-BODIED)* *

Brut Blanc de Blancs Non-Vintage   ($12.99)   85

Brut Non-Vintage   ($11.99)   78

1979 Brut Rosé   ($11.99)   75

This is a very reasonably priced line of light-bodied, clean, fresh, straightforward champagnes. The Non-Vintage Brut is acceptable, but rather bland, the 1979 Brut Rosé has little character other than freshness and pretty packaging. The Non-Vintage Blanc de Blancs is fresh, has a moderately intense, toasty, buttery bouquet, lovely, fresh, light flavors, and a good lingering finish.

BESSERAT DE BELLEFON (LIGHT-BODIED)* *

Brut Non-Vintage   ($12.95–$14.95)   78

Quite light, rather tart and lean, with some annoyingly high acidity in the finish, this wine has good freshness, but suffers in comparison with the other non-vintage champagnes on the market.

BILLECART-SALMON (LIGHT-BODIED)* * *

1979 Blanc de Blancs	($30.00)	90
1982 Blanc de Blancs	($30.00)	88
1979 Cuvée Billecart	($25.00)	89
Non-Vintage Brut	($18.00)	83
Non-Vintage Rosé	($25.00)	92
1982 Cuvée Billecart	($25.00)	?

One cannot say too many good things about this small house that produces wonderfully light, elegant yet flavorful champagnes. In every one of my champagne tastings, Billecart has shown exceptionally well. This year the remarkable Rosé edged out the wonderful but superexpensive Taittinger Comtes de Champagne Rosé and Perrier-Jouët Flower Bottle Rosé and Perrier-Jouët Blason Rosé wines. As for the Non-Vintage Rosé, it is a gorgeously balanced, light salmon-colored wine with pinpoint bubbles, faint yet noticeable aromas of framboises and strawberries, lovely, light yet flavorful and frothy character. The Blanc de Blancs is an equal match for the Rosé in terms of finesse and gracefulness. It is dry and steely, but has very crisp, light flavors, a zesty, refreshing acidity, and dry finish. In contrast, the 1979 Cuvée Billecart is rounder and has a creamy, toasty richness that one does not find in the Blanc de Blancs. It is fuller and fruitier than the Blanc de Blancs, but has less finesse. The Non-Vintage Brut is light and serviceable, but is less interesting than previous releases. On a negative note, two out of three bottles of 1982 Cuvée Billecart tasted flabby and out of balance.

BOIZEL (LIGHT-BODIED)* *

1978 Joyau de France	($19.95)	84
Non-Vintage Brut Réserve	($12.95)	74

The non-vintage is neutral, quite bland, cleanly made, but has no focal point of interest. The 1978 Joyau de France is richer, medium-bodied, with a hint of buttery fruit, is fully mature, and rather attractive.

BOLLINGER (FULL-BODIED)* * * * *

1973 Année Rare	($49.95)	85
1979 Grande Année Brut	($29.95)	85
1979 Grande Année Rosé	($39.95)	86
Non-Vintage Special Cuvée	($22.95)	87
1975 R.D.	($55.95)	92
1979 Vieilles Vignes Françaises	($89.95)	90

Bollinger is clearly one of Champagne's most respected and cele-brated houses. The wines are very high in quality and made in a full-bodied, dry style with considerable character. The non-vintage is fer-mented in stainless steel, but the other champagnes are still fer-mented in oak. On the negative side, the prices for Bollinger champagnes are high and the availability tight. As for these new offer-ings from Bollinger, the 1979 Vieilles Vignes is listed for academic purposes only. Less than 150 cases were produced and less than a third of these were sent to America. The 1979 is lighter than other vintages I have had the pleasure of tasting, but still full, with authori-tative flavors and good body for a champagne. The bubbles are ex-tremely small and well defined, which is always a sign of high quality. However, the price is ludicrous. The 1975 R.D., despite spending 9 years on its lees, tastes remarkably young and undeveloped. It is full-bodied for a champagne, deeper in color than the other Bollinger champagnes, quite dry, austere, complex and outstanding. The 1973 Année Rare spent 11 years on its lees and though refined and ob-viously well made, it tastes lean, a trifle too tart and acidic. My notes show it has a pH of 2.95, which is extremely low. As for the two Grande Année releases from Bollinger, the 1979 Grande Année Rosé is very dry, quite austere, medium- to full-bodied, with tiny pinpoint bubbles. The 1979 Grande Année Brut is medium-bodied, a trifle tart and reserved, but very stylish. Lastly, the non-vintage Bollinger Spe-cial Cuvée surprisingly showed more of the famed Bollinger full-bod-ied, creamy, toasty style than the more expensive bottlings. I found it quite tasty and complex.

BONNAIRE (LIGHT-BODIED)* * * *

1982 Blanc de Blancs   ($17.95)   89

1981 Blanc de Blancs Cuvée Anniversaire   ($12.95)   87

Non-Vintage Cramant   ($14.95)   83

This is quite a good producer of champagne from the village of Cramant. The 1982 is toasty, with a spicy, yeasty-scented aroma, good, clean crisp flavor, medium body, and good, lingering effervescence. The Cuvée Anniversaire is a special bottling to honor the famous New York wine merchant Sam Aaron of Sherry Lehmann. It is identical to the 1981 Bonnaire Blanc de Blancs (which was almost as good as the 1982), only less expensive. The non-vintage Cramant is a good, dry, yeasty brut champagne.

CATTIER BRUT (LIGHT-BODIED)* * *

1979 Brut   ($16.95)   80

Non-Vintage Brut   ($14.99)   81

Non-Vintage Clos du Moulin   ($24.95)   86

This house produces quite light, flowery champagnes. The non-vintage is straightforward, frothy, light, and gentle on the palate. The 1979 Brut is also light, a trifle dull and unexciting, but pleasant. The non-vintage Clos du Moulin exhibits considerably more style and interest. Delicate and subtle, with a flowery, clean bouquet, light yet flavorful palate impression, the Clos du Moulin is an ideal champagne to serve as an apéritif.

CHARBAUT (LIGHT-BODIED)* * * *

1979 Blanc de Blancs Brut   ($25.00)   87

Brut Non-Vintage   ($19.95)   84

Brut Non-Vintage Blanc de Blancs   ($19.95)   87

Brut Non-Vintage Rosé   ($20.95)   86

1976 Certificate Blanc de Blancs Tête de Cuvée   ($59.95)   90

These releases from Charbaut were among the surprises in my series of blind tastings of champagne. This is a house that I have always regarded as producing reliable, middle-of-the-road, fruity, soft champagnes that lacked excitement and drama. However, these wines may well suggest a move to a higher plateau of quality; all turned in very good performances. At the top level, the 1976 Certificate, made from 100% Chardonnay, tastes like a buttery, flavorful yet effervescent white burgundy, spicy with soft, impeccably balanced, rich, delineated flavors. It will not age well, so enjoy it now while it is showing its best. Very similarly styled is the 1979 Blanc de Blancs Brut, which showed much of the same subtle, spicy, buttery character as the 1976 Certificate. However, it is less than half the price. It has a frothy effervescence, a graceful Chardonnay fruitiness, and crisp, clean finish. Remarkably, even the Brut Non-Vintage Blanc de Blancs has plenty of Chardonnay character and a creamy, buttery, medium-bodied feel on the palate. The Brut Non-Vintage does not have the finesse or broad richness of the other wines, but it is a good, soft, fruity, nonvintage champagne that is very cleanly made. The Brut Non-Vintage Rosé is one of the best rosé champagnes on the market and undoubtedly one of the better values in the generally exorbitantly priced rosé champagne marketplace. It has a lovely pink salmon color, a subtle, complex, berry fruit aroma, and crisp, light- to medium-bodied texture.

VEUVE CLICQUOT (FULL-BODIED)* * * *

1978 Brut	($28.00)	88
Brut Extra Dry	($17.00)	67
1979 Brut Rosé	($32.00)	89
1976 La Grande Dame	($50.00)	70
1979 La Grande Dame	($50.00)	90
Ponsardin Brut Non-Vintage	($20.00)	88

1980 Texas Sesquicentennial Cuvée	($30.00)	85

This excellent firm is generally regarded as a producer of full-bodied, creamy, large-scaled champagnes that can age well. This is a house I like quite a bit, and the recent champagnes are very well made in a medium- to full-bodied style. The wines are more richly flavored than most other champagne houses. As for the two disappointments, the Brut Extra Dry tasted like ginger ale, soft, slightly sweet, and oddly perfumed. The 1976 La Grande Dame is tired and, in this vintage, better named the Senile Dame. Otherwise, the current offerings are delectably full, fruity, yeasty, rich, and interesting. The Ponsardin Brut Non-Vintage is light golden, spicy and full, with excellent flavor concentration. Among the bigger, boldly flavored champagnes on the market, it is one of the very best. The 1979 Brut Rosé is delicious and quite full-bodied and full-flavored for a rosé. The 1979 La Grande Dame is in top form, rich, round, toasty, and creamy, with fine length and tiny bubbles that linger and linger. The 1978 Brut is the most robust champagne in this group, with plenty of flavor, a mouth-filling, toasty, spicy richness, and crisp finish. Lastly, the special cuvée of champagne to honor the 150th birthday of Texas is good, very attractively packaged, but obviously a marketing gimmick. Because of their fullness, these champagnes are better drunk with food than as apéritifs.

DEUTZ (MEDIUM-BODIED)* * *

1978 Blanc de Blancs	($40.00)	82
1976 Brut	($25.00)	78
Brut Non-Vintage	($18.00)	78
1981 Brut Rosé	($25.00)	80
1979 Cuvée G. Mathieu	($45.00)	84
1979 Cuvée William Deutz	($45.00)	90

Somewhat to my surprise, the Deutz champagnes did not fare as well in my tastings as I had expected. While the 1979 Cuvée William Deutz is excellent, frothy, elegant, medium-bodied, and delicious, the others tasted one-dimensional, almost too mild and bland. They are dry, light in body and, though clean and crisp, seemed to offer little excitement or flavor interest. Oddly enough, the 1981 Brut Rosé had almost no bouquet whatsoever.

NICHOLAS FEUILLATTE (LIGHT-BODIED)* *

Non-Vintage Brut	($19.95)	75
Non-Vintage Rosé	($19.95)	85

The labels are pretty, but with the exception of the very charming and captivating Non-Vintage Rosé, I have been unimpressed by the other champagnes. The Rosé is light, frothy, and dry, with a bouquet vaguely reminiscent of strawberries.

H. GERMAIN (LIGHT-BODIED)* * *

1979 Blanc de Blancs	($25.00)	87
Brut Non-Vintage	($16.00)	85

This small house is highly reputed in France and it is easy to see why. Both the above champagnes showed well in my tastings. The Brut Non-Vintage has a full-blown, spicy, yeasty, intense bouquet, good, elegant, dry flavors, medium body, and a crisp finish. The 100% Chardonnay 1979 Blanc de Blancs was even more impressive, with a complex, fruity, spicy, moderately intense bouquet, clean, well-defined, crisp flavors, tiny uniform bubbles, and good effervescence.

MICHEL GONET (MEDIUM-BODIED)* *

1981 Blanc de Blancs Brut	($13.99)	85

With champagne prices going up, one suspects that buys like this will not be available much longer. This is a Blanc de Blancs, and a light one at that, but it does have considerable finesse, clean, light-intensity, toasty Chardonnay scents, light to medium body, and an overall refreshing character. It is perfect as an apéritif champagne.

GOSSET (FULL-BODIED)* * * *

Réserve Brut Non-Vintage	($19.95)	84
Special Réserve Brut Non-Vintage	($29.95)	89

The Special Réserve Brut is a classic champagne, rich, creamy, deep, complex, full-bodied, yet impeccably balanced and graceful. One is hard pressed to find a better non-vintage champagne. As for the regular Réserve Brut Non-Vintage, it has plenty of flavor, but seems slightly tired and oxidized. Those with an English palate for mellow, well-aged champagne will like it better than I did.

ALFRED GRATIEN (FULL-BODIED)* * * *

1979 Brut	($30.00)	88
Brut Non-Vintage	($25.00)	87
Brut Non-Vintage Rosé	($25.00)	85

One of the few champagne firms to still ferment their wines in small barrels, the wines of Gratien are traditional and full-flavored. The Brut Non-Vintage Rosé has plenty of depth, well-defined bubbles, a crisp, dry, but not tart or acidic finish. The Brut Non-Vintage has toasty, creamy, yeasty flavors, good body, an assertive personality and real style. The 1979 Brut is richer, perhaps softer on the palate, but complex, flavorful, and quite effervescent.

HEIDSIECK MONOPOLE (MEDIUM-BODIED)* * *

Brut Non-Vintage	($20.00)	84
1976 Diamant Bleu	($30.00)	78
1979 Diamant Bleu	($35.00)	88
Extra Dry Non-Vintage	($17.00)	75

The luxury cuvée from Heidsieck Monopole, the Diamant Bleu, has generally been one of the most fairly priced Tête de Cuvée champagnes. The 1975 was a long-time favorite of mine, while the 1976 is rather light, dull, and a trifle too tart and acidic. However, the 1979 Diamant Bleu is quite a stylish, delicate wine with tiny bubbles, a creamy, graceful, well-balanced texture, and a good, crisp finish. The Brut Non-Vintage is fuller-bodied, somewhat toasty and spicy, and a seemingly bigger, more aggressive style of champagne. The Extra Dry Non-Vintage has a straightforward, fruity bouquet, and somewhat dull flavors.

CHARLES HEIDSIECK (MEDIUM-BODIED)* * *

Brut Non-Vintage   ($19.95)   85

1979 Cuvée Charlie   ($50.00)   85

Here is an example of a luxury cuvée, Cuvée Charlie, that for three times the price is no better than the good Brut Non-Vintage. Charlie, affectionately named (presumably) after the founder of this firm, Charles-Henri Heidsieck, is a light, delicate, very restrained, medium-bodied champagne that is obviously well made, but in quality is more like a $20 bottle than a $50 bottle. The Brut Non-Vintage is more dramatic, if only because it is more fruity, spicy, and possesses a soft, creamy texture.

HENRIOT (FULL-BODIED)* * * *

Brut Non-Vintage   ($18.00)   85

1976 Réserve Baron Philippe de Rothschild   ($35.00)   90

1979 Réserve Baron Philippe de Rothschild   ($40.00)   90

It is hard to beat the quality of these two luxury champagnes from Henriot. But be warned, those who prefer light, flowery champagnes will no doubt find these two wines too rich, dramatic, and creamy for their tastes. The 1976 Réserve Baron Philippe de Rothschild is fully mature and has a full-blown, spicy, toasty bouquet, round nutty flavors and very fine length. The 1979 is very similar, only slightly lighter and more elegant. The Brut Non-Vintage is very similarly structured and styled—creamy, toasty, ripe, and quite dramatic. It, too, is fully mature, and should be drunk rather than aged.

JACQUART (MEDIUM-BODIED)* *

Brut Non-Vintage   ($14.99)   82

Extra Dry Non-Vintage   ($14.29)   75

The Brut Non-Vintage is fruity, soft, cleanly made and very straightforward in style. It lacks personality, but is satisfying. The Extra Dry Non-Vintage is quite soft, slightly sweet, a little tiring to taste, but serviceable.

JACQUESSON (LIGHT-BODIED)* * *

Blanc de Blancs Brut Non-Vintage	($19.99)	84
1979 Brut	($25.00)	85
1969 Brut Late-Disgorged	($40.00)	90
Brut Non-Vintage	($18.99)	70
Brut Rosé Non-Vintage	($19.99)	80
1976 Brut Signature	($27.00)	86

The Jacquesson champagnes are very reasonably priced and made in a very light, delicate style not unlike that of Taittinger. The Brut Non-Vintage is musty in the nose, has fairly insipid flavors, and no finish. The 1979 Brut is quite light, but also complex and flavorful, with subtle toasty, yeasty aromas, soft, very refined flavors, and a good lingering effervescence. The Blanc de Blancs Brut Non-Vintage is one of the lightest champagnes I have ever tasted. In fact, its lightness is an attribute and a curse. Delicate, almost ethereal, and unbelievably light, it seems to disappear on the palate once in the mouth. It is probably a controversial champagne, but very cleanly made and ideal as an apéritif. The 1976 Brut Signature is also made in the very light, delicate style, but has more flavor, some hint of toasty, aged fruit, and is still very fresh and crisp. It is a good value for a luxury cuvée. The Brut Rosé Non-Vintage is standard quality, but the rare 1969 Brut Late-Disgorged is a super, very complex, interesting, provocative champagne with considerable interest in both flavor and bouquet.

JESTIN (LIGHT-BODIED)* *

Brut Non-Vintage	($15.00)	78
Brut Rosé Non-Vintage	($18.00)	78

There is little to comment on here. These are dry, cleanly made, crisp, tart, straightforward champagnes at very reasonable prices. In fact, their prices are all that should draw interest to these champagnes.

KRUG (FULL-BODIED)* * * * *

1976 Brut	($65.00)	91
1979 Brut	($60.00)	90
Grand Cuvée Non-Vintage	($35.00–50.00)	88
Rosé Non-Vintage	($85.00)	88

In the first year (1978) that Krug launched the Grand Cuvée Non-Vintage, the batch released in this country was sublime. Since then, this champagne has vacillated from tart, green, and austere to light, elegant, and graceful. It is impossible to know when a new blend is released, but the Krug Grand Cuvée I purchased in November 1986 from a shop with a huge turnover of stock is back to top form. Lighter and more elegant than one would assume from the reputation Krug's wines have, the new batch of Grand Cuvée is very flavorful, very elegant, with scents of vanillin and toast, medium body, and long, crisp, yet gentle flavors. The new Rosé Non-Vintage from Krug sets a new benchmark in price absurdity, but otherwise is full-bodied, quite well made, deeply flavored, with crisp acidity and tiny bubbles. Both vintage champagnes (1976 and 1979) get top marks because they have even more character, exquisite noses of fruit and toast, and loads of refined flavors. These latter two wines will keep for a decade.

LANSON (LIGHT-BODIED)* * *

Brut Black Label	($19.99)	84
1979 Brut Red Label	($25.00)	86

Lanson's Brut Black Label Non-Vintage continues to represent a good value. It is very consistent in style, with a soft, light, lively fruitiness, light to medium body, crisp acidity, and adequate finish. It is a good party champagne, not too austere, not too flabby and soft. The 1979 Brut Red Label is a classier champagne. It tastes as if it has plenty of Chardonnay since it is delicate yet flavorful, cleanly crisp, medium-bodied, and well made.

GUY LARMANDIER (MEDIUM-BODIED)* *

Blanc de Blancs Non-Vintage   ($22.95)   86

Not for those who prefer soft, round champagnes, this austere, 100% Chardonnay-based wine exhibits plenty of character, a chalky, clean refined bouquet, average effervescence, medium body, a dry, firm, interesting texture, and very crisp finish. It tastes quite dry, like an ultra or *zéro* brut.

J. LASSALLE (LIGHT-BODIED)* * * *

1979 Blanc de Blancs   ($18.95)   86

This small producer produces a lovely, delicate, flavorful, and graceful wine. The 1979 Blanc de Blancs is crisp, aromatic with scents of fresh wheat and dough. On the palate, it is medium-bodied, zesty, and fresh, with well-delineated flavors and a lovely finish.

LAUNOIS PÈRE (LIGHT-BODIED)* * *

1980 Blanc de Blancs   ($16.95)   71

Blanc de Blancs Non-Vintage   ($13.95)   65

Both of these champagnes showed poorly in my tastings. The 1980 Blanc de Blancs is watery and thin. The Blanc de Blancs Non-Vintage has a bizarre, almost artificial perfumed character and little character on the palate.

LAURENT-PERRIER (MEDIUM-BODIED)* * * *

Cuvée Speciale Non-Vintage Brut   ($15.99)   85

Cuvée Ultra Brut Non-Vintage   ($25.00)   91

1978 Grand Siècle   ($55.00)   88

1979 Grand Siècle   ($55.00)   92

For the last several years the non-vintage Laurent-Perrier has represented one of the great bargains in high-quality champagne. The Cuvée Speciale Non-Vintage Brut is less bold and toasty than previous renditions, as well as a little lighter and noticeably more flowery. It is still a very good champagne and can often be found discounted to $10–$12 a bottle. The Cuvée Ultra Brut Non-Vintage is a gloriously refined, flavorful champagne that is better than the very good Grand Siècle (and at half the price). Light golden with a rich, toasty, fragrant bouquet, it has tiny bubbles, good effervescence, a crisp yet medium- to full-bodied feel on the palate, and a very impressive finish. It is hard to find a better champagne at any price. The 1978 Grand Siècle is also quite an elegant, graceful, refined champagne. Crisp and fruity, yet so delicate, with aromas of vanillin and bread dough, it lingers on the palate and has a good measure of flavor. The 1979 is even richer.

LECHERE (LIGHT-BODIED)* * *

Blanc de Blancs Non-Vintage	($22.00)	88
Orient Express Non-Vintage	($25.00)	90
Rosé Brut	($25.00)	84

The special cuvée called the Orient Express (because it is served on that famous European train) is an ethereal, sublime champagne. It is outstanding, light golden with a toasted wheat, spicy, vanillin bouquet, crisp, well-focused flavors, and a lovely, lingering effervescence. For the sheer delicacy of its flavors, it is stunning. The Blanc de Blancs Non-Vintage is very similar, only slightly lighter and perhaps a trifle more tart on the palate. The Rosé Brut is good, dry, crisp, but a trifle too understated; it is not in the same league as the others.

R. & L. LEGRAS (LIGHT-BODIED)* * *

1979 Blanc de Blancs	($28.95)	86
Blanc de Blancs Non-Vintage	($21.95)	86

These are both very polished, refined, lighter-styled champagnes that are produced from 100% Chardonnay grapes. Given the choice, why not save several dollars and opt for the non-vintage? Both are similar: elegant, flowery, and subtle, but crisp, flavorful, fresh, and light- to medium-bodied. The 1979 has some toasty, spicy notes in its bouquet that I could not find in the non-vintage.

MOËT & CHANDON (MEDIUM-BODIED)* * *

1980 Brut Imperial	($30.00)	78
Brut Imperial Non-Vintage	($18.00–$22.00)	82

1980 Brut Imperial Rosé	($30.00)	85
1978 Dom Pérignon	($55.00)	90
1980 Dom Pérignon	($65.00)	88
1975 Dom Pérignon Rosé	($60.00)	90
White Star Extra Dry Non-Vintage	($18.00)	73

The largest producer of champagne, Moët & Chandon's products are visible in virtually every hotel, wine shop, and restaurant in the world. Dom Pérignon is, of course, Champagne's most famous wine, and in America the ultimate for those who collect labels. It can be superb, as it was in 1964 and 1971. The 1978 Dom Pérignon is back to top-notch form, the 1980 slightly lighter, but elegant and very tasty. The 1978 has authoritative, impeccably balanced flavors, a very classy, refined, yeasty, spicy bouquet, and lovely, moderately rich flavors. The 1975 Dom Pérignon Rosé is quite outstanding as well, but good luck finding a bottle. Only 400–500 cases are produced, and its rich, strawberry fruitiness, captivating color, and crisp flavors as well as its super snob appeal make it the hardest champagne in the world to find. As for the other champagnes, they offer the prestige of the Moët & Chandon name, but little else. The rather sweet-tasting White Star Extra Dry Non-Vintage is heavy and cloying. I liked the Brut Imperial Non-Vintage, yet it is hardly a classic champagne in the sense that it relies too much on softness and a puffy, frothy character for its appeal. The 1980 Brut Imperial is hardly the stuff of vintage champagne. It is lean, light, a little green, and does not have much of a finish. As for the 1980 Brut Imperial Rosé, it has surprisingly deep color for a rosé, a tomato, herb-scented bouquet, fat, round, slightly soft flavors, and some character.

MUMM (MEDIUM-BODIED)* *

1979 Cordon Rouge	($35.00)	80
Cordon Rouge Non-Vintage Brut	($20.00)	83
Crémant de Cramant Blanc de Blancs	($35.00)	90

1979 René Lalou	($40.00–$45.00) 83

I have never been a great admirer of the Mumm champagnes, which I find rather average in quality and rarely exciting. The luxury cuvée René Lalou can often be terribly mediocre; the 1979 René Lalou is above average to good, but given the outrageous price, hardly a bargain. Austere, a trifle tart and too lean, one is hard pressed to find enough to like to merit the price. The 1979 Cordon Rouge is even more bland and simple, with straightforward, fruity flavors. The Cordon Rouge Non-Vintage Brut shows as much character as the luxury cuvée. It has a more interesting, spicy, vanillin, fruity nose and is less austere. My favorite Mumm champagne is the gorgeously well-balanced, light, delicate, but rare and expensive, 100% Chardonnay Crémant de Cramant. This is a frothy, very refined wine of considerable finesse. It is a shame the other Mumm wines don't show this style and class.

OUDINOT (MEDIUM BODIED)* *

Blanc de Blancs Brut Non-Vintage	($19.99) 78

1976 Brut	($20.00) 75

1976 Gold Label Brut	($22.00) 80

The Oudinot champagnes seem to be quite standard in quality, not objectionable, but simple, straightforward, light- to medium-bodied. The 1976 Gold Label Brut has some pleasant, spicy, fruity, yeasty scents in its aroma, and clean, decent flavors. These are rather light, innocuous champagnes.

BRUNO PAILLARD (LIGHT-BODIED)* * *

1976 Brut	($17.95) 87

1979 Brut	($18.95) 85

1975 Brut Blanc de Blancs	($19.95) 79

Non-Vintage Brut	($13.95) 83

Non-Vintage Brut Rosé	($16.95) 74

Non-Vintage Brut Zéro	($15.95)	85

Non-Vintage Crémant Blanc de Blancs	($16.95)	87

This is a new house in Champagne that has quickly moved upward in the ranks of champagne producers because of the reasonable prices charged for its well-made champagnes. First, the mediocrities. The Non-Vintage Brut Rosé is clean, soft, but lacks style and has absolutely no character. The 1975 Brut Blanc de Blancs is beginning to tire a bit, and has an annoying greenness to it. The Non-Vintage Brut is well above average in quality, sensibly priced, but at $10 one can do better with Lanson or Laurent-Perrier. The stars of Bruno Paillard are the austere, totally dry, classy Non-Vintage Brut Zéro, which (for those who like really dry champagne) is very nice in an elegant, leaner style. The 1976 Brut should be mandatory drinking for anyone on a high-fiber diet. It smells like toasty bran flakes, has a marvelous, frothy appeal, medium body, and lovely balance. It is a real bargain among the lighter yet flavorful champagnes on the market. The Non-Vintage Crémant Blanc de Blancs is a real winner. It tastes like a very good Puligny-Montrachet with bubbles. Creamy, very obviously Chardonnay in taste, with small pinpoint bubbles, it is a delicious champagne that, because of its lightness and creamy texture, is just perfect as an apéritif. Lastly, the 1979 Brut is light, frothy, and quite flavorful. It tastes like it has a good measure of Chardonnay in it. Medium-bodied, dry and yeasty, its price should cause considerable interest.

PERRIER-JOUËT (LIGHT-BODIED)* * *

Blason de France Rosé Non-Vintage	($30.00)	90

1979 Flower Bottle Brut	($54.00)	?

1979 Flower Bottle Rosé	($60.00)	90

Grand Brut Non-Vintage	($18.00)	81

I have enjoyed many a bottle of Perrier-Jouët champagne. This house is owned by Mumm and controlled by Seagram's. The champagnes are made in a light, delicate style. The famous Flower Bottle luxury cuvée was an ingenious marketing invention to publicize their best champagnes. Their 1979 Flower Bottle Rosé is outstanding, delicate, very subtle in flavor, with hints of berry fruit, spice and yeast. The 1979 Flower Bottle Brut can merit 87–88 points: delicate, charming, light, frothy champagne. It can also taste tart, green, and acidic. At its extravagant price, I expect consistency. Apparently, the Blason de France Rosé Non-Vintage suffers from the same malady. It too can be sublime; however, one bottle I tasted was tired and oxidized, while a second was stunningly crisp, flavorful, and quite excellent. Since it can be 90–92 point champagne, it may be worth the risk. The Grand Brut Non-Vintage is soft, round, quite fruity and obvious in style.

JOSEPH PERRIER (MEDIUM-BODIED)* * *

1979 Brut	($25.00)	86
Cuvée Royale Non-Vintage Brut	($20.00)	87

The 1979 Brut is well made, straightforward, pleasant, with faint, toasty vanillin aromas, some good, crisp acidity in the finish, good effervescence, and medium body. Difficult as it may be to comprehend, the Cuvée Royale Non-Vintage Brut is richer, more flavorful, and has more to it. Slightly fuller, quite tasty, with subtle, yeasty, buttery, toasty flavors, medium body, and good, well-defined bubbles that last, it is a very fine non-vintage champagne.

PHILIPPONNAT (MEDIUM-BODIED)* * *

1980 Blanc de Blancs	($21.00)	84
Brut Rosé Non-Vintage	($19.99)	78
1978 Clos de Goisses	($48.00)	82

This house has a considerable reputation, but I was left unmoved by these champagnes. The Brut Rosé Non-Vintage was standard in quality, dry, pleasant, a touch high in acidity. The single-vineyard Clos de Goisses tasted very tart, lean, and surprisingly reserved. Perhaps time will see it emerge from its rather dormant, closed personality. The 1980 Blanc de Blancs has more character. Spicy, yeasty, Chardonnay aromas exhibited style and subtlety. It is dry, medium-bodied, and pleasant rather than sublime.

PIPER HEIDSIECK (LIGHT-BODIED)* * *

1976 Année Rare	($60.00)	83
1979 Brut Sauvage	($30.00)	77

Cuvée des Ambassadeurs Non-Vintage	($21.00)	83

1976 Pink	($27.00)	74

This house rarely makes exciting champagne. There was a tremendous amount of hoopla about the release of the 1976 Année Rare, which is quite light, crisp and tart, but all things considered, should sell for $20, not a ridiculous $60. The rosé champagne called Pink (I appreciate the firm's candor in naming this champagne) is already tired and taking on the color of an old Tavel from the Rhône. It still has flavor, but is a little flat and not very interesting. The Cuvée des Ambassadeurs Non-Vintage is pleasant, dry, light- to medium-bodied, with a decent, frothy, yeasty character. It is a better champagne than the expensive wines from Piper Heidsieck. The ultra-dry Brut Sauvage is steely, very austere, lean, and a trifle green and tart. This house does a considerable amount of business in America, but their champagnes are hardly inspiring and, for the most part, notably overpriced.

POL ROGER (MEDIUM-BODIED)* * * * *

1979 Blanc de Chardonnay	($27.00)	90

1976 Brut	($22.00)	88

1979 Brut	($22.00)	88

Brut Non-Vintage	($16.00)	86

1979 Cuvée Winston Churchill	($50.00)	88

Pol Roger is one of the best producers of classic, rich, flavorful champagnes; it can also be particularly long-lived. In my tastings there were no disappointments. The Brut Non-Vintage is medium-bodied, creamy, and rich, has plenty of flavor, a lot of bubbles, and considerable style. As for the other champagnes, both the exquisite 1979 Blanc de Chardonnay and 1979 Cuvée Winston Churchill need 2–3 years of cellaring. They are impeccably made, dry, toasty, medium-bodied, loaded with fruit and tiny, symmetrical bubbles, but are extremely unevolved and young. If I were Pol Roger, I would have waited and released them in 1989. The 1976 Brut is fully mature, creamy, rich, toasty, and has a wonderfully complex bouquet. The 1979 Brut is more or less a younger version of the 1976. It is rich and creamy, medium-bodied, but could benefit handsomely from several years of cellaring. Pol Roger's champagnes are among the most consistent in quality on the market.

POMMERY & GRENO (LIGHT-BODIED)* * *

1981 Brut	($19.95)	77
Brut Rosé Non-Vintage	($19.95)	80
Brut Royal Non-Vintage Brut	($12.95)	85
1979 Cuvée Speciale-Louise Pommery	($60.00)	87

The 1981 Brut is very frothy, very light, and lacks flavor. The Brut Rosé Non-Vintage is straightforward, dry, very light, with a nice pale salmon color, crisp finish, and lively acidity. The Brut Royal Non-Vintage Brut is usually one of Pommery's best champagnes and best values. It has medium body, a crisp, refreshing dry fruitiness, yeasty, clean bouquet, and adequate finish. It is frequently discounted to $10–$12 a bottle, making it a fine value. The newly released luxury cuvée is toasty, rather unevolved and backward in taste and aroma, but has quite long, lingering flavors. Give it 2–3 years of cellaring.

RAPENEAU (MEDIUM-BODIED)* *

1979 Brut	($14.99)	86
Brut Blanc de Blancs Non-Vintage	($13.99)	85
Brut Cuvée L'Escalape Non-Vintage	($16.49)	86

This new entry into the ranks of champagne producers represented in this country offers both notable quality and value. Rapeneau's champagne seems to fall in style between the light-bodied, fluffy champagne of Taittinger and the fuller-bodied, robustly flavored champagne of Veuve Clicquot. The 1979 Brut has a buttery, almond-scented nose, crisp, medium-bodied flavors, and impressively small, symmetrical bubbles. The Brut Blanc de Blancs Non-Vintage is crisp and flavorful, and the Brut Cuvée L'Escalape Non-Vintage is spicy, clean, with good-intensity flavors in a medium-bodied format.

LOUIS ROEDERER (FULL-BODIED)* * * * *

Brut Premier Non-Vintage	($20.00)	87
Brut Non-Vintage	($20.00)	84
1979 Cristal	($60.00)	88
1981 Cristal	($65.00)	90
Extra Dry Non-Vintage	($16.00)	75
Rosé Brut Non-Vintage	($25.00)	87

Roederer's champagnes are usually among the best made, full-flavored and assertive, with aromas of nuts, toasted wheat and spices. Both the 1979 and 1981 Cristal are obviously overpriced but excellent champagnes. The 1979 is lighter than previous vintages, but has the telltale personality of Roederer—the toasty, hazelnut-scented aroma, ripe flavors, and great balance and finesse. I was also quite surprised by how good the dry Rosé Brut Non-Vintage is. It is very pale-colored yet has a lovely, complex, faint berry fruitiness, soft yet lively flavors, and good length. The Brut Non-Vintage is surprisingly soft, with a sweet yeasty nose. I found it atypical of Roederer's style. I preferred the new non-vintage Brut Premier, which is quite elegant and full-flavored and one of the best of its type on the market. The Extra Dry Non-Vintage was sweet and rather diffuse in character.

ALFRED ROTHSCHILD (LIGHT-BODIED)* *

1979 Brut	($18.00)	72
Brut Réserve Non-Vintage	($15.00)	80

The 1979 Brut is acidic and sharp on the palate and, though cleanly made, has little redeeming social value. The Brut Réserve Non-Vintage is soft, round, fruity, quite frothy, and easy to like, albeit very simple.

DOM RUINART (LIGHT-BODIED)* * * *

1976 Blanc de Blancs	($35.00)	75
1978 Blanc de Blancs	($35.00)	87

1976 Rosé	($45.00)	90

1978 Rosé	($60.00)	90

The 1976 Blanc de Blancs is lean, tart, lacking fruit and interest, and quite tired. On the other hand, the 1978 Blanc de Blancs has plenty of elegantly rendered fruit, a crisp, dry, yeasty, toasted-wheat scent, and good dry finish. It is the best Dom Ruinart since the lovely 1971. The 1976 Rosé is a gorgeous champagne, medium-bodied, quite aromatic with scents of strawberries, and is round, crisp, and quite flavorful, with good, zesty acidity. The 1978 Rosé is just as good, perhaps lighter, but also fresher and still remarkably elegant and flavorful.

TAITTINGER (LIGHT-BODIED)* * * * *

1980 Brut Millésime	($30.00)	77

1976 Comtes de Champagne Brut	($45.00)	90

1979 Comtes de Champagne Brut	($45.00)	91

1976 Comtes de Champagne Rosé	($65.00)	91

1979 Comtes de Champagne Rosé	($65.00)	90

1981 Arman Collection Series Brut	($70.00)	92

La Française Brut Non-Vintage	($24.00)	80

Taittinger's top-of-the-line *tête de cuvée*, the Comtes de Champagne, is one example of a luxury champagne that rarely disappoints. In fact, it is consistently ethereal, light, and delicate as well as being impeccably made. Both the 1976 and 1979 Comtes de Champagne Blanc de Blancs (made from 100% Chardonnay) are remarkably light, frothy, delicate, and complex champagnes that exemplify the words breed and finesse. I believe I detect even more character in the 1979. The Comtes de Champagne Rosé is quite rare and of course expensive, but is among the most delicate and delicious of the luxury cuvée champagnes on the market. It is rounder in texture than the Blanc de Blancs, but stunningly crisp, subtle, and sublime. The 1979 is slightly lighter than the 1976, but both are truly superb. The 1981 Arman Collection Series Brut is, in essence, the Comtes de Champagne Blanc de Blancs. It is quite light, with soft, gorgeous flavors, some complex, toasty wheat notes in its bouquet, and a sensational finish. As for the other selections from Taittinger, the 1980 Brut Millésime is quite light, rather thin and tart, and for Taittinger, a disappointment. The Brut Français Non-Vintage is soft, creamy, very light, and rather sweet for a brut champagne.

THE LOIRE VALLEY

Most wine drinkers can name more historic Loire Valley châteaux than Loire Valley wines. It's a pity, really, because the Loire Valley regions offer France's most remarkable array of wines. The wine-producing region stretches along one-third of the meandering 600-mile Loire River, and the astonishing diversity of grapes planted in this valley is far greater than that in the better known wine-growing regions of Burgundy or Bordeaux.

One of the most highly regarded grape varieties of the Loire is the Sauvignon Blanc, which makes such distinctive and delicious wines in the most eastern part of the valley, around the towns of Gien, Briare, Sancerre, and Pouilly-sur-Loire. At the western end, surrounding the city of Nantes, the Muscadet reigns supreme. Midway between these two areas is the historic cathedral city of Tours, where the Chenin Blanc is king. Certainly, these three white grape varieties are the most frequently encountered when sampling Loire wines, but there are other varieties that are also widely planted in this vast wine region. The Chardonnay, Pinot Gris, Arbois, and Gros Plant are the other white grape varieties found in abundance. And for red and rosé wines, there is the Gamay, Cabernet Franc, Cabernet Sauvignon, Malbec, Pinot Noir, and Pinot Meunier.

Muscadet

Muscadet is made from the grape of the same name in an area just southeast of the city of Nantes in the western Loire Valley. The best Muscadet is called Muscadet de Sèvre-et-Maine, after the two local rivers. Muscadet is really the perfect white wine for shellfish, particularly briny clams and oysters. Muscadet must be drunk young, always within two to three years of the vintage, when its best attributes can be fully appreciated. Textbook Muscadet is exuberantly fruity, extremely fresh, totally crisp, dry, and light- to medium-bodied. Consumers in search of top Muscadet should bypass any of the stale 1982s (with the exception of the long-lived Château de Chasseloir) or older vintages that remain on retailers' shelves. Look instead for the highly successful 1985s, which, because of their excellent freshness and crisp fruitiness, are rounder and fuller than usual, and for the recently released 1986s, which are more typical of the Muscadets normally turned out in a good vintage. Finally, don't buy more Muscadet than you will drink over the next 12 months; these wines don't improve in the bottle.

MUSCADET
QUICK VINTAGE GUIDE

1986—A good vintage of fresh, tart, well-balanced, typical wines.
1985—A very good vintage, very similar in style to the 1982s, but perhaps superior. Soft, fruity, and delicious, the wines must be drunk before the end of 1987.
1984—Lean, tart, high-acid wines that will last 2–3 years, but in general are lacking in charm and flavor.
1983—Ripe, fruity, soft, very flavorful wines that are now beginning to tire a bit.

A GUIDE TO MUSCADET'S BEST PRODUCERS

* * * * *(EXCELLENT PRODUCERS)*

André-Michel Bregeon
Château de Chasseloir
Marquis de Goulaine

Château La Noë
Sauvion Cardinal Richelieu
Sauvion Château du Cléray

The Loire Valley and Central France

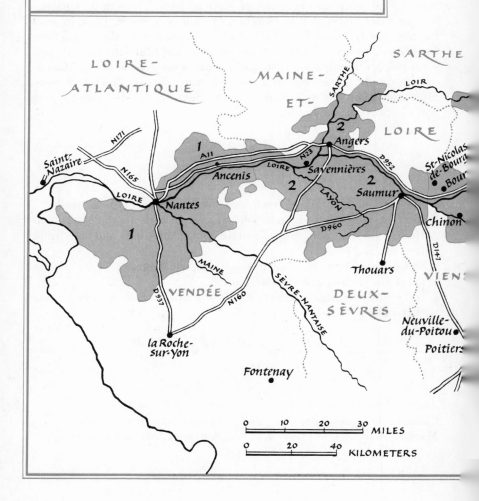

LOIRE-ATLANTIQUE

MAINE-ET-LOIRE

SARTHE

LOIR

SARTHE

N171

N165

Saint-Nazaire

LOIRE

1
A11

Ancenis

LOIRE

N23

Angers *2*

Savennières

St-Nicolas de-Bourg

Bour

Nantes

2

LAYON

Saumur *2*

Chinon

1

MAINE

D960

D937

VENDÉE

N160

SÈVRE-NANTAISE

Thouars

DEUX-SÈVRES

D141

VIEN

la Roche-sur-Yon

Neuville-du-Poitou

Poitiers

Fontenay

| 0 | 10 | 20 | 30 | MILES |

| 0 | 20 | 40 | KILOMETERS |

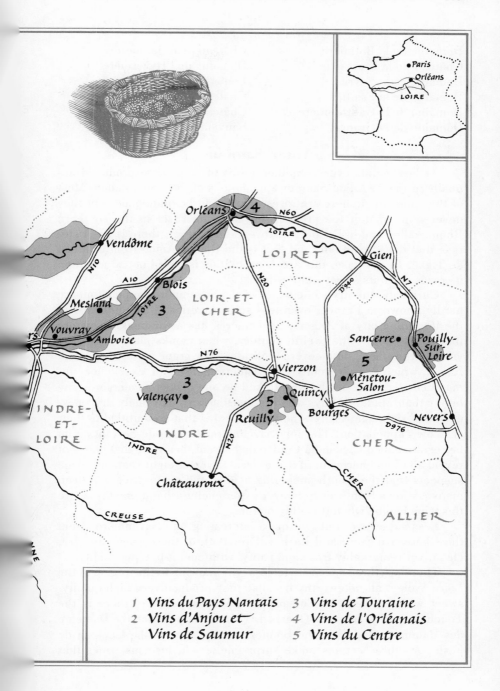

Paris
Orléans
LOIRE

Orléans **4** N60
LOIRE
Vendôme
LOIRET
A10
N10
Gien
Blois
Mesland
LOIR-ET-
CHER
N20
D940
N7
LOIRE
Vouvray
rs
Amboise
3
Sancerre
Pouilly-
sur-
Loire
N76
Vierzon
5
Ménetou-
Salon
Valençay
3
Quincy
INDRE-
ET-
LOIRE
Reuilly
5
Bourges
Nevers
INDRE
D976
INDRE
N20
CHER
Châteauroux
CHER
CREUSE
ALLIER

1 Vins du Pays Nantais	3 Vins de Touraine
2 Vins d'Anjou et Vins de Saumur	4 Vins de l'Orléanais
	5 Vins du Centre

*** (GOOD PRODUCERS)

Domaine de la Botinière	Château de la Jannière
Château de la Bretesche	Domaine de l'Hyvernière
Domaine de la Fevrie	Louis Metaireau
Domaine de la Fruitière	Chateau l'Oiselinière
Domaine de la Gautronnière	Château de la Ragotière
Domaine de la Grange	Sauvion (other cuvées)

Anjou-Saumur

At last count, over 11 million cases of wine were produced an-
nually in the 25 Anjou-Saumur appellations of the Loire Valley. Most
of the wines made here are rosés, which can be quite good, but they
never quite match the great rosés made in Tavel in the southern
Rhône valley and in Bandol in Provence. However, there is one Loire
rosé that does stand out, and that is the Rosé d'Anjou from Château
de Tigné. In any case, this area's reputation is based not so much on
its rosés as on its sweet white wines.

Curiously, the dry white wines of the Savennières appellation are
hardly known in France, even less so in America. Just southwest of
the intriguing city of Angers, Savennières has a winemaking history
that dates back to the twelfth century, when monks planted the first
vines in the steep, slate-covered hillsides. The grape variety is Chenin
Blanc, which here reaches an aristocratic level of excellence unmatched elsewhere in the world. And no one makes Savennières any
better than Madame Joly, who produces a rare, extremely dry, powerful and rich, ageworthy wine from 17 acres that are entitled to their
very own appellation. The Joly Savennières-Coulée-de-Serrant, from
her estate called Clos de la Coulée de Serrant, is a wine that does not
reveal all of its charms until it is at least seven or eight years old. One
suspects that the mouth-puckering acidity and steep price will keep
many a wine adventurer from ever experiencing what a great treasure
this wine can be when it is fully mature.

Less expensive, but still quite interesting, are Savennières from
the Château d'Epiré and La Bizolière. Both of these wines are dry,
clean, yet remarkably fresh and fruity, with mouth-bracing acidity.

There are three special estates worth knowing in this region of the
Loire Valley, all noteworthy because they produce very high-quality,
sweet wines. From the Coteaux du Layon appellation there is the
Touchais family, from the Quarts de Chaume appellation the Domaine
des Baumard, and from the Bonnezeaux appellation the Château de
Fesle. All three estates make surprisingly rich, luscious wines that

can often rival the better-known wines from the Sauternes/Barsac region of Bordeaux.

The most remarkable thing about these sweet wines, in addition to their quality, is that few people know they even exist, still fewer realize that they will last for thirty or more years without losing their freshness, delicacy, sweetness and vigor, and hardly anyone realizes that they are made from the Chenin Blanc grape, a grape that in America is considered synonymous with bland, cheap, jug wines. These French wines are splendid with foie gras, poached chicken, mildly sweet desserts, or where served as an apéritif.

Like the famous Sauternes/Barsac of Bordeaux, the sweet wines from these Loire appellations can be produced only in years when the climatic conditions are right for the Chenin Blanc grape to be attacked by the famed fungus, Botrytis Cinerea. Consumers can still find older vintages of the Touchais Coteaux du Layon wines back to 1959, which are all in marvelous condition. Other excellent vintages for the Coteaux du Layon, the Quarts de Chaume, and the Bonnezeaux are 1985, 1978, 1976, 1971, 1969, and 1964. These limited-production wines are not cheap, but most of the recent vintages sell for $8 to $12 a bottle, which is far less than their qualitative equivalent from Bordeaux.

Before leaving the Anjou-Saumur area, it is necessary to mention the booming, sparkling wine industry of Saumur. A number of firms specialize in producing surprisingly good, low-priced, sparkling wines from the Chenin Blanc grape, but no one does it better than Bouvet-Ladubay in St.-Hilaire-St.-Florent. Their sparkling Saumur, highly promoted in this country under the name Bouvet Brut and selling for under $10, is a high-quality alternative to champagne—dry, lively, medium-bodied, and fruity.

ANJOU-SAUMUR
QUICK VINTAGE GUIDE

1985—The best vintage since 1978—rich, long-lived, sweet wines from the Coteaux du Layon, Quarts de Chaume, and Bonnezeaux, and remarkably long-lived dry white wine from Savennières.

1984—The balance between fruit and acidity is missing in 1984; the wines lack fruit and are too high in acidity.

1983—Wonderfully mature, ripe grapes produced fat, rich, big wines that lack a little finesse, but have plenty of flavor and intensity. For the sweet wines, this could turn out to be a great vintage.

Older Vintages

The sweet wines of the Coteaux du Layon, Bonnezeaux, and Quarts de Chaume do indeed survive and even flourish and improve in the bottle for 15, 20, 25, or more years. Given their modest prices, these wines are undoubtedly the greatest bargains in sweet white wines on the market. The dry Savennières can be drunk young, but is at its best when 5 to 10 years old. Older vintages to look for are 1978, 1976, 1971, 1969, 1964, 1962, and 1959. The rosés and light, fruity red wines should be drunk up within three years of the vintage.

A GUIDE TO ANJOU-SAUMUR'S BEST PRODUCERS

* * * * * (OUTSTANDING PRODUCERS)
Coulée de Serrant (Savennières)

* * * * (EXCELLENT PRODUCERS)

Domaine des Baumard (Quarts de Chaume)
Château de Chamboureau (Savennières)
Philippe Delesvau (Coteaux du Layon)

Château de Fesles (Bonnezeaux)
Château de Plaisance (Coteaux du Layon)
Château de la Roulerie (Coteaux du Layon)
Touchais (Anjou)

* * * (GOOD PRODUCERS)

Jacques Beaujeau (Coteaux du Layon)
Château de Bellerive (Quarts de Chaume)
Château de la Bizolière (Savennières)
Château Bonin (Coteaux du Layon)
Domaine du Closel (Savennières)
Domaine de la Croix de Mission (Bonnezeaux)

Diot-Autier (Coteaux du Layon)
Château d'Epiré (Savennières)
Vincent Goizel (Coteaux du Layon)
Château de la Guimonière (Coteaux du Layon)
Logis du Prieuré (Coteaux du Layon)
Château des Rochettes (Coteaux du Layon)
Château de Tigné (d'Anjou)

Touraine

Chinon is the first appellation that one encounters in this part of the Loire Valley after leaving Anjou-Saumur to head upriver. Chinon's historic château is reason enough to visit this beautiful area, but Chinon makes the Loire Valley's best red wine, as well as some distinctly fresh, fruity rosés. The region also makes white wines, but they do not compare favorably with the white wines from other parts of the Loire.

The best-known producer of Chinon is the firm Couly-Dutheil. Although I have found some of Jacques and Pierre Couly's white wines not impressive enough to warrant their high reputation, their red wines from Chinon and Bourgueil, produced from the Cabernet Franc grape, can be surprisingly complex and interesting. Look for the following trio of fruity, spicy, slightly herbaceous, complex wines, with scents of wild strawberries and vanillin oak: the Chinon Domaine de Versailles ($7) and Clos de l'Echo ($7) and the Bourgueil Réserve des Closiers ($10)—all quite well-made wines that represent excellent value.

My favorite Chinon producer is Charles Joguet. He makes a marvelous rosé; try his stunningly refreshing, lively, fruity Chinon Rosé ($5), and you will see what I mean. His loyal following, however, is based on his red wines—all rich, full, complex and savory—that require five to six years of aging to show their real character. This is especially true of his best wine, the Chinon Cuvée Clos de la Dioterie Vieilles Vignes (about $9). The 1978 version of this wine could have been confused with an excellent St.-Emilion. Other selections from Joguet to look for are his Chinon Cuvée Clos du Chêne Vert ($6), Chinon Cuvée des Varennes du Grand Clos, and Chinon Cuvée du Clos du Curé.

The other major Loire Valley appellation in Touraine is Vouvray, which is famous for its white wines. They are produced from the Chenin Blanc grape, and range in style from dry to sweet, as well as bubbly. I have enjoyed immensely the Vouvrays from the largest producer of this appellation, Chateau Moncontour; the Vouvray Sec is a brilliantly made wine, with its vivid, ripe fruitiness counterbalanced against crisp, taut acidity. The small growers of Vouvray, such as Gaston Huet at the Domaine de Haut-Lieu, produce excellent Vouvrays, as does A. Foreau at his property called Clos Naudin. Interestingly, Foreau's Brut Reserve ($10) is one of the best sparkling Vouvrays I have tasted, resembling, believe it or not, rich, old vintages of champagne. Foreau also does a nice job with his dry (or *sec*) style of wine. The regular Vouvray ($6) is clean, stylish, fruity, with good acidity and at least five to six years of positive evolution.

TOURAINE
QUICK VINTAGE GUIDE

1985—A potentially great year for the sweet wines of Vouvray, and at the very least a very good year for the dry white wines and an excellent year for the red wines.

1984—A poor vintage, with the wines lean, acidic, and thin.

1983—An excellent vintage for Vouvray, both dry and sweet wines, and a very good vintage for the red wine producers since everything ripened well.

1982—The dry white wines are fading quickly. The red wines are perfect for drinking now, the sweet whites are above average but overshadowed by the two recent vintages of 1983 and 1985.

Older Vintages

Gaston Huet's sweet Vouvrays from 1959 and 1962 were tasted last year and are in superb condition. Why don't more people realize just how fine these wines are? Charles Joguet's best cuvées of red wine from his Chinon vineyards, unfiltered and rich, can easily last 10 years. His 1978s are excellent now. The same can be said for Olga Raffault's Chinons. Otherwise, the wines from Touraine should generally be drunk within their first 5–6 years of life for their freshness.

A GUIDE TO TOURAINE'S BEST PRODUCERS

* * * * * *(OUTSTANDING PRODUCERS)*

Gaston Huet (Vouvray)   Charles Joguet (Chinon)

* * * * *(EXCELLENT PRODUCERS)*

Couly-Dutheil (Chinon)   Château Moncontour (Vouvray)
A. Foreau (Vouvray)

*** *(GOOD PRODUCERS)*

Audebert (Bourgueil)

Marc Brédif (Vouvray)

Caves Coopèratives de Haut
  Poitou (Touraine)

Domaine de la Charmoise
  (Touraine)

Le Clos Neuf des Archambaults
  (Cobeaux)

La Croix de Mosny (Touraine)

Jean-Pierre Freslier (Vouvray)

Sylvain Gaudron (Vouvray)

Lamé-Delille-Boucard
  (Bourgueil)

Jean Louet (Touraine)

J. M. Monmousseau (Vouvray)

D. Moyer (Vouvray)

Prince Poniatowski (Vouvray)

Olga Raffault (Chinon)

Upper Loire

The upper Loire Valley is synonymous with Sauvignon Blanc. There are other grape varieties planted here, the bland Chasselas and some Pinot Noir, but the real glories are the Sauvignon Blanc-based wines from such appellations as Sancerre and Pouilly-Fumé and from the two little-known appellations of Quincy and Ménétou-Salon. Sauvignon Blanc, when grown in these appellations, produces dry white wines that are very aromatic, sometimes too aggressively pungent for some tastes, but always smoky, herbal, earthy and distinctive. They are usually medium- to full-bodied wines, with crisp, high acidity, plenty of fruit, and a dry finish. They are marvelous with fish, poultry and, not surprisingly, the freshly made earthy goat cheeses of the area.

Happily, 1985 was an especially kind vintage to these appellations, which often produce wines too high in acidity and too abrasively sharp and angular in texture. The hot summer and fall rendered wines slightly lower in acidity than normal but rich and lush with Sauvignon Blanc fruit. From Sancerre and Pouilly-Fumé, the following producers' 1985s are excellent choices. Nobody produces a greater Sancerre than Paul Cotat, and his wines are also capable of evolving for 5–6 years. In addition, J. C. Chatelain's Pouilly-Fumé Cuvée Prestige ($12) is loaded with intense, ripe Sauvignon fruit, very aromatic, and quite long in the finish. Another excellent Pouilly-Fumé is Ladoucette ($15) from Château du Nozet, but this wine tends to be more expensive than other Pouilly-Fumés.

From Sancerre, the pickings are even better. Five producers have consistently made excellent, estate-bottled Sancerres that stand far above their peers. All were extremely successful in both 1984 and 1985. Jean Reverdy's Domaine de Villots, Vincent Delaporte's Sancerre from Chavignol, Lucien Crochet's two Sancerres, Clos du

Chêne Marchand and Clos du Roy Blanc, Jean-Max Roger's Clos
Derveau, and Lucien Thomas's Clos de la Crele—all have the pungent, herbaceous bouquet and dry, lively, fruity flavors that one expects from a fine Sancerre. They retail for between $7 and $9 a bottle,
making them attractive wines for the price. All of these 1985s will
keep and drink well through the end of 1988. Keep in mind, however,
that the 1985s, being lower in acidity, are fuller, fleshier wines
than the 1984s, which are more typical, but more austere, leaner
wines.

Last, the two tiny wine hamlets of Quincy and Ménétou-Salon also
make Sauvignon Blanc-based wines, which can be almost impossible
to distinguish from a fine Sancerre. (They also have the advantage of
probably being unknown to your wine-smart guests.) The only wine
from Quincy imported into the United States that I know of is from
the highly acclaimed producer Raymond Pipet (his '85 is $8). From
Ménétou-Salon, I know of one producer whose wines are imported
into the United States—Henri Pellé, whose wines are excellent. His
1985 and 1984 Ménétou-Salons (both $8) are quite spicy, pungently
herbaceous, dry, medium-bodied, fruity wines, with crisp acidity.
They would do justice to any fish or fowl dish. One thing is certain in
this area—the overall quality of winemaking is by far the best of any
in the Loire Valley area.

UPPER LOIRE
QUICK VINTAGE GUIDE

1985—This is a very fine vintage in the same style as the 1982s—
fat, ripe, juicy wines that are a little low in acidity. They have more
finesse and freshness than the heavy-handed 1983s, more charm and
fruit than the 1984s. Drink them over the next 12–36 months.

1984—High-acid wines were made that will keep several years in
the bottle, but may lack fruit. However, the best wines of this vintage
will turn out to be surprisingly good, but they need time to drop some
of their sharp acidity.

1983—Ripe, alcoholic, rather ponderous wines were produced in
1983. When first released, they tasted quite good, if more powerful
than normal. However, they are now just beginning to turn the corner
and should be consumed soon.

1982—Somewhat similar to the 1985s in style, these wines should be
drunk up.

Older Vintages

Nineteen seventy-eight and 1976 were excellent vintages, but the wines of Sancerre, Pouilly-Fumé, Ménétou-Salon, and Quincy are made intentionally to be drunk within the first 3–4 years and can be appreciated for their zesty, tart, lively fruitiness. They will keep longer, but they won't get any better.

The Loire Valley—A Buying Strategy

The wines of the Loire Valley, as popular as they are in France, particularly Paris, have never been considered glamor wines elsewhere in the world. Consequently their prices have remained stable. There are numerous fine values, particularly among the sweet wines of Coteaux du Layon, Bonnezeaux, Quarts de Chaume, and Vouvray, where wines that are five, ten, even fifteen years old, and in impeccable condition, can be purchased for under $15, the starting price for a young Barsac or Sauternes of similar quality. Among the dry white wines, the exuberant, fresh Muscadets from the 1985 vintage should cost about $6, the top Sauvignon Blancs from Sancerre, Pouilly-Fumé, and Ménétou-Salon in 1985, under $10. The red wines, except for those of Charles Joguet and Olga Raffault, have never struck me as terribly interesting, but if you can find the Chinons from these two producers, the $7–$10 per bottle price is well worth it. As for vintages, if you like to indulge your palate with a nectarlike sweet wine, you can go back to 1959 with no problem, but for the dry white wines make it 1985. For the red wines you can also consider 1983, but avoid 1984.

A GUIDE TO THE UPPER LOIRE'S BEST PRODUCERS

* * * * * (OUTSTANDING PRODUCERS)

J. C. Chatelain (Pouilly-Fumé)   Château du Nozet (Pouilly-
Paul Cotat (Sancerre)   Fumé)

* * * * (EXCELLENT PRODUCERS)

Lucien Crochet (Sancerre)   H. Reverdy (Sancerre)
Vincent Delaporte (Sancerre)   Jean-Max Roger (Sancerre)
Gitton (Sancerre)   Lucien Thomas (Sancerre)
Jean Reverdy (Sancerre)

* * * (GOOD PRODUCERS)

Roger Neveu (Sancerre)   Château de Tracy (Sancerre)
Henri Pellé (Ménétou)   Clos de la Poussie (Sancerre)
Raymond Pipet (Quincy)

LANGUEDOC

For years, this vast, sun-drenched area running parallel to the Mediterranean between Perpignan near the Spanish border and Arles in Provence was considered the major supplier of inexpensive, high-alcohol, red wines for the French supermarket trade. Much of the wine from this area still finds its way into these grapy, thick blends, but a few producers are trying to rise above the tide of mediocrity and produce something with more class and distinction. There are many viticultural regions and appellations in this enormous area, but five seem to have the most potential—Costières du Gard, Faugères, Minervois, Corbières, and Fitou. None produce particularly refined, graceful, long-lived wines, but the best producers make immensely satisfying, round, generous, fruity wines that are very inexpensive and meant to be drunk within their first 4–5 years of life. Don't hesitate to slightly chill any of these red wines, since many seem to taste better when served at a cool temperature. Lastly, there is one red wine producer that is not in an approved French appellation but is widely recognized for making not only the greatest wines of the Languedoc region but one of the great wines of all France. The red wine of Mas de Daumas Gassac in L'Hérault (which is legally only a *vin de pays*) is an extraordinary wine with great potential for a longevity of 15–20 years. It is primarily a Cabernet Sauvignon-based wine made in a distinctly Bordeaux style. The first vintage was 1978, the most recent 1985, and all have been stunningly rich, powerful, potentially very long-lived wines. To date they have sold for under $10 a bottle, but given the quality and demand, one wonders how much longer this price can hold.

Recent Vintages

Heat and sun are constants in this region. Vintages are incredibly consistent and the quality of most wines has more to do with the availability of modern technology to keep the grapes and grape juice from overheating in the intensely hot temperatures. Nevertheless, recent vintages that stand out are 1985, 1983, and 1982, with 1984 the closest thing this area has had to a mediocre year.

A GUIDE TO LANGUEDOC'S BEST PRODUCERS

***** *(OUTSTANDING PRODUCERS)*

Mas de Daumas Gassac
(L'Hérault)

**** *(EXCELLENT PRODUCERS)*

St. Jean de Bebian (L'Hérault)

*** *(GOOD PRODUCERS)*

Gilbert Alquier (Faugères)
Domaine des Bories (Corbières)
Domaine du Bosccaute
  (L'Hérault)
Domaine de Fontsainte
  (Corbières)
Château de Gourgazaud
  (Minervois)
Château de Grezan (Faugères)
Haut Fabrèges (Faugères)
Domaine de la Lecugne
  (Minervois)

Domaine de Mayranne
  (Minervois)
Caves de Mont Tauch (Fitou)
Château de Nouvelle (Fitou)
Château de Paraza (Minervois)
Cuvée Claude Parmentier
  (Fitou)
Château de Queribus
  (Corbières)
St. André (L'Hérault)
Château de Villerambert-Julien
  (Minervois)

Languedoc—Today's Buying Strategy

For serious collectors, the Mas de Daumas Gassac is a revelation and a highly desirable addition to any wine cellar. For the other wines, stick to younger vintages, thereby avoiding anything older than 1982. Expect to pay under $8 a bottle for a wine from any of the recommended producers.

PROVENCE

For most Americans, Provence is known as France's vacation land and not as a source of high-quality wine. Such an impression would have been largely true a decade ago, but of all the viticultural areas of France, none has made greater progress. Long regarded for its excellent, crisp, fresh, dry rosé wines, Provence is beginning to win many converts for its up and coming red and white wines. Many producers in this region produce three wines—rosé, white, and red. For the most part, the high quality of the best estates of Provence has yet to be recognized in America; consequently this is a splendid area for bargain hunters.

Recent Vintages

Given the area's constant sunshine and heat, one can expect every year to be at least good. Although this is generally true, certain years can be too hot and dry, which in Provence creates more of a problem than cooler, wetter years. For the white and rosé wines, I know of none that should not be consumed within 2–3 years of the vintage. They are best when fresh, lively, and vibrant. In short, don't drink anything before 1984; and concentrate on 1985s and 1986s. As for the red wines, those from the top estates itemized here can last in the top vintages for 10 years or more, but most are in their full prime by the time they are 5–6 years old. Of recent vintages, 1985 and 1982 are superb, 1983 very good, and 1984 mediocre. For the white and rosé wines, 1985 gets first place, followed by 1986 and 1984.

A GUIDE TO PROVENCE'S BEST PRODUCERS

***** *(OUTSTANDING PRODUCERS)*

Domaine Richeaume (Coteaux d'Aix)

Domaine Tempier (Bandol)

Domaine de Trevallon (Coteaux de Baux)

Château Vignelaure (Coteaux d'Aix)

* * * * *(EXCELLENT PRODUCERS)*

Château de Crémat (Bellet)
Château de Fonscolombe (Aix-en-Provence)
Mas de la Rouvière (Bandol)
Domaines Ott (Côtes de Provence)
Commanderie de Peyrassol (Côtes de Provence)
Château Pradeaux (Bandol)
Domaine de Rimauresq (Côtes de Provence)

Saint-André de Figuière (Côtes de Provence)
Domaine de St.-Jean de Villecroze (Coteaux Varois)
Château Simone (Palette)
Château Val-Joanis (Côtes du Luberon)
Château Vannières (Bandol)
La Vieille Ferme (Côtes du Luberon)

Provence—Today's Buying Strategy

For the white and rosé wines, 1985 is the year. For the red wines, 1982, 1983, and 1985 are all first-rate. Prices are extremely reasonable for the wines of Provence. Domaine Tempier's splendid long-lived reds go for $8–$15, and Domaine de Trevallon's voluptuous red wines are under $10. Most Provencal wines retail for $6–$10, with many as low as $4–$5.

CHÂTEAU DE CRÉMAT (BELLET)* * * *

1984 Blanc	($9.90)	84
1985 Blanc	($9.90)	84
1985 Rosé	($7.99)	84
1982 Rouge	($9.90)	84
1983 Rouge	($9.99)	82

Anyone who has enjoyed a bottle of wine in a good restaurant in Nice has probably noticed the wines of Château de Crémat on the wine list. This property sits in the hills above Nice and has been run by the Bagnis family since 1957. They produce the best wines of Bellet. The red wine tends to be a little high in alcohol, jammy and heavy, but the white wine is fresh, with scents of nuts, apple blossoms, and fresh fruit. The rosé is a rather full-bodied wine, but fresh, deliciously fruity, and long on the palate.

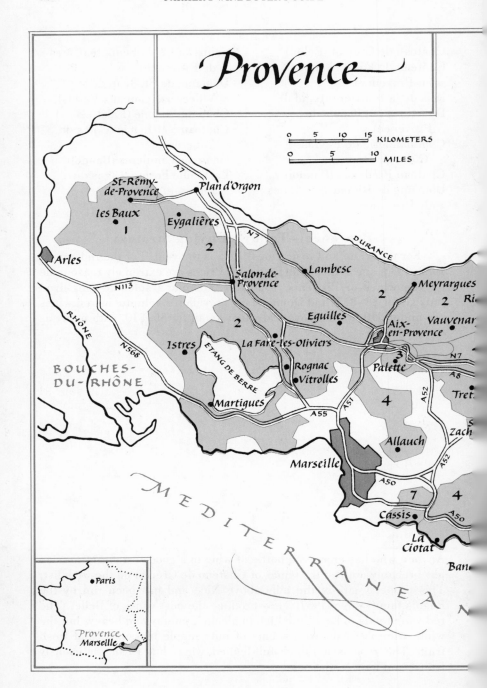

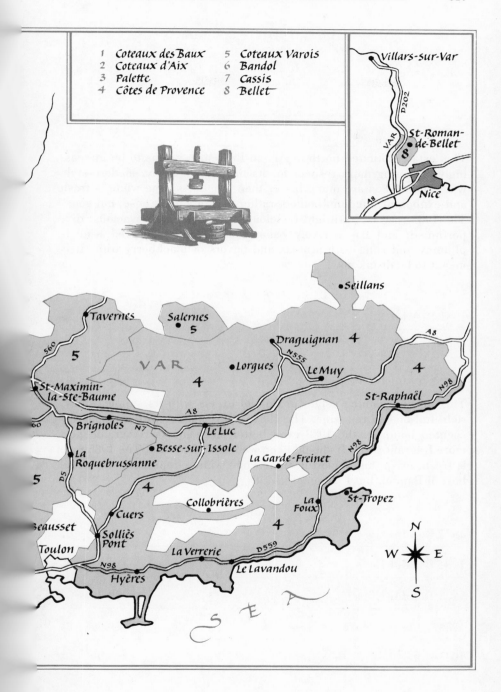

1 Coteaux des Baux   5 Coteaux Varois
2 Coteaux d'Aix   6 Bandol
3 Palette   7 Cassis
4 Côtes de Provence   8 Bellet

Villars-sur-Var

D202

VAR

St-Roman-
de-Bellet

8

Nice

A8

Seillans

Tavernes   Salernes
                 5

VAR

Draguignan 4

560   5   Lorgues   N555
                              4   Le Muy

St-Maximin-   St-Raphaël
la-Ste-Baume   A8

60   Brignoles   N7   Le Luc
                  Besse-sur-Issole
     La   La Garde-Freinet
Roquebrussanne

5   D5   La   St-Tropez
                   4   Collobrières   Foux

Beausset   Cuers   4
                Solliès
Toulon   Pont
                    La Verrerie   D559
          N98   Le Lavandou   N
                Hyères   W   E

                                                     S

S E A

CHÂTEAU DE FONSCOLOMBE
(COTEAUX D'AIX-EN-PROVENCE)* * * *

1985 Blanc	($5.99)	83
1985 Red	($6.49)	84
1985 Rosé	($5.99)	84

This estate, situated north of Aix-en-Provence, seems to be increasingly garnering more respect for its fine, fresh, lively, modern-style wine. The 1985s are much better than the 1984s. The white is fresh and exuberant, medium-bodied, rather neutral on the nose, but good. The 1985 rosé is downright delicious, very fresh and vivacious, dry, perfumed, and has a lovely balance and length. The red wine is plummy and ripe, with aromas and flavors of blackberry fruit. It is meant to be drunk now.

MAS DE LA ROUVIÈRE (BANDOL)* * * *

1981 Bandol Rouge	($8.99)	84
1982 Bandol Rouge	($8.99)	86
1985 Bandol Rosé	($7.49)	85

This up and coming estate in Bandol excels with its supple, spicy, rich, full-bodied red wine. The 1981 is fully mature with a raspberry-scented bouquet, the 1982 even better since it is a richer, deeper, more fragrant wine. It should keep well for 5–10 years. The 1985 rosé is fresh, crisp, and flavorful; their white wine is reputedly one of the best of Bandol, but I have not had it.

DOMAINE OTT (CÔTES DE PROVENCE)* * * *

1985 Bandol Rosé	($8.99)	85
1984 Bandol Rosé	($8.99)	85
1983 Bandol Rouge	($8.99)	85
1984 Côtes de Provence Rosé	($8.99)	83
1985 Côtes de Provence Rosé	($6.99)	84

1985 Cuvée Comtes de Provence Blanc de Blancs	($6.99)	85

1983 Cuvée Comtes de Provence Rouge	($7.99)	85

1984 Château de Selle Blanc	($6.99)	84

Provence's most famous and successful winery, Domaine Ott's wines are on virtually every important wine list in France. Their success is well earned. The rosé wines are crisp, fragrant, fresh and lively, the white wines rich, full-bodied and made to stand up to a big, spicy, local garlic-scented soupe de poissons or bouillabaisse. In the last 5 years, Ott's red wines have improved dramatically in quality and have intense aromas of Provençal herbs, black cherries, and cassis. Ott's white and rosé wines should be drunk up before they are 4 years old. The reds will keep well for 5–7 years.

CHÂTEAU PRADEAUX (BANDOL)* * * *

1978 Bandol Rouge	($8.99)	84

1983 Bandol Rouge	($8.99)	81

This particular Bandol usually is aged 3–4 years in oak casks prior to bottling and represents a rather big, rustic style of wine. The 1983 is a trifle coarse, but a big, fleshy mouthful. The 1978 has a cedary, rich, intense personality, full body, and long, alcoholic finish.

DOMAINE DE RIMAURESQ (CÔTES DE PROVENCE)* * * *

1982 Rouge	($4.95)	84

1983 Rouge	($4.95)	84

This estate makes round, generously flavored, very fruity, supple wines that should be drunk within their first 5–6 years of life. They are notable values and resemble in style a very good Côtes du Rhône. The estate began producing wine in 1981.

SAINT-ANDRÉ DE FIGUIÈRE (CÔTES DE PROVENCE)* * * *

1983 Blanc de Blancs	($5.99)	83

1984 Blanc de Blancs	($5.99)	83

| 1982 Cuvée du Marquis Rouge | ($6.49) | 86 |

| 1982 Cuvée Speciale Rouge | ($6.49) | 84 |

One of France's few wineries dedicated totally to organically produced wine, Saint-André uses no insecticides or chemical fertilizers in the vineyards. The wines, particularly the reds, tend to be rich and robust, with powerful, exotic aromas and fleshy flavors. The vintages I have tasted have been at their best in 3–4 years. Certainly, both 1982s are fully mature but will last for 4–5 more years. The white wines have flowery, peach-scented aromas, soft, voluptuous flavors, and a lush finish; they should be drunk up as they will not get any better.

DOMAINE DE SAINT-JEAN DE VILLECROZE (COTEAUX VAROIS)* * * *

| 1982 Cabernet Sauvignon | ($6.99) | 85 |

| 1982 Cuvée de l'Heritier | ($4.99) | 78 |

| 1984 Rosé | ($5.99) | 84 |

| 1983 Syrah | ($6.49) | 86 |

This is a serious estate that was established in the early '70s by an American and his French wife. The wines are organically made; no insecticides or chemical fertilizers are used. Like many Provence rosés, this wine is fresh, lively, and loaded with fruit, as well as dry. The Syrah, aged in oak barrels, is quite impressive, rich, deep, and full-bodied, with 4–6 years' aging potential. The Cabernet is round, generously flavored, and shows the potential for this grape in the south of France. The Cuvée l'Heritier is straightforward, fruity, soft, and pleasant, but lacks complexity.

CHÂTEAU SIMONE (PALETTE)* * * *

| 1981 Blanc | ($8.99) | 81 |

| 1982 Blanc | ($8.99) | 83 |

| 1982 Rosé | ($7.99) | 78 |

| 1981 Rouge | ($8.99) | 83 |

| 1982 Rouge | ($8.99) | 85 |

Palette, located just south of Aix-en-Provence, is one of France's smallest appellations. The Rougier family runs Simone with great care and makes three very distinctive wines. The rosé is, to my taste, a trifle oaky and heavy. The white wine is spicy, rich in fruit and body, with a long, fleshy finish. Much of Simone's fame is based on its red wine, an herb-scented, spicy, red wine that has medium to full body and is generally quite tannic and long-lived. For both the white and red, 1982 and 1985 are the two best recent vintages.

DOMAINE TEMPIER (BANDOL)* * * * *

1982 Bandol La Migoua	($14.99)	90
1982 Bandol La Tourtine	($14.99)	90
1984 Bandol Rosé	($8.99)	85
1985 Bandol Rosé	($10.99)	86
1982 Bandol Rouge	($9.99)	86
1983 Bandol Rouge	($9.99)	85

Domaine Tempier is considered by many knowledgeable authorities to be the finest estate not only in Bandol, but in all of Provence. Certainly their splendidly complex, refreshing rosé is one of the best of its type I have ever tasted. Tempier makes no white wine, but their red Bandol is a very complex, very long-lived wine that in vintages such as 1961, 1970, 1975, and 1982 can last 15–20 years. Their regular Bandol is a ripe, rich, powerful wine with excellent concentration. The two single-vineyard wines, La Migoua and La Tourtine, are wonderfully complex, rich wines that are fragrant, deep, and velvety on the palate. The 1982s will be particularly long-lived as will their 1985s.

DOMAINE DE TREVALLON (COTEAUX DE BAUX)* * * * *

1981 Rouge	($6.95)	85
1982 Rouge	($6.95)	90
1983 Rouge	($6.95)	91

1984 Rouge   ($6.95)   86

These marvelous wines, made from a blend of 60% Cabernet Sauvignon and 40% Syrah, are among the shining new stars of Provence.
The wines, dense in color, are very richly perfumed with fascinating
aromas of cassis, apricots, and thyme. They are full-bodied, rich, very
concentrated wines that exhibit great complexity and potential. The
proprietor, Eloi Durrbach, planted the vineyards 15 years ago and is
now realizing the full fruits of his labor, for this winery is surely an up
and coming superstar of France, and its wines, a revelation to those
who think Provence cannot produce great wine.

CHÂTEAU VAL-JOANIS (CÔTES DU LUBERON)* * * *

1985 Blanc   ($5.99)   82

1985 Rosé   ($5.99)   82

1985 Rouge   ($5.99)   84

This estate has received a remarkable amount of favorable publicity
in recent years. The vineyards, planted only in 1978, are still very
young, but the ambitious efforts and fresh, lively wines made here are
sure to please. The 1985s are better than the 1984s. The Rouge is
light, fruity, with a vibrant raspberry-scented bouquet and soft, round
flavors. The rosé is clean, fresh, and best drunk within its first 1–2
years of life, and the Blanc is round, crisp, and quite fruity. This is a
property to keep an eye on.

CHÂTEAU VIGNELAURE (COTEAUX D'AIX-EN-PROVENCE)* * * * *

1979 Rouge   ($8.99)   85

1981 Rouge   ($8.99)   84

1982 Rouge   ($8.99)   85

1983 Rouge   ($8.99)   88

This Provençal estate is one of the most famous properties in Provence. The proprietor, Georges Brunier, gained fame by resurrecting
a renowned Bordeaux château, La Lagune, to prominence. He now
runs this property with equal care and, not surprisingly, his wines
have an affinity with those of Bordeaux. The 1979 is velvety and fully

mature; the 1981 is round, generous, and elegant, with 5 more years of evolution ahead of it; and the 1982, a more muscular, richer, fuller-bodied effort. Brunier thinks the 1983 is the finest wine yet made at Vignelaure. Vignelaure is usually at its best within 6–9 years of the vintage.

THE RHÔNE VALLEY

France's Least-Known Great Wines

T he Rhône's top wines continue to represent France's least-known and most undervalued great wines.

The Rhône Valley offers something vinous for everyone—from soft, round, plump, fruity generic Côtes du Rhône selling for under $6, which provide the wine consumer with immediate thirst gratification and value, to the stunning and profound hand-crafted estate-bottled wines that collectors must cellar for 8–10 years before seeing their full majestic richness.

QUICK VINTAGE GUIDE

1986—About 20% of the grapes in the Rhône Valley had not been harvested when the area was inundated with heavy rains on October 12 and the weather that followed over the next two weeks was equally miserable. However, the early pickers should have done well, and in both the northern and southern Rhône, quality should at least be good. Production was less than in the bountiful year of 1985, but because of the late-harvest deluge, selection will be critical and one can expect a great deal of irregularity in the range of quality.

1985—My tastings indicate that this vintage has produced excellent wines in the northern Rhône and very good wines in the south. For

Côte Rôtie, it is a great vintage. The wines are very deep in color, quite rich, but not particularly tannic. The overall impression is one of wines fully ripe, rich in fruit, very opulent in style, and quite forward. Overall, the vintage is very close in quality to 1978. In Côte Rôtie and Châteauneuf-du-Pape it is better than 1983. Everywhere it is certainly better than 1982, 1981, and 1980. The white wines are very powerful and rich.

1984—A mediocre vintage of light- to medium-bodied wines that will offer straightforward, one-dimensional drinking for the near future. There are many surprisingly good wines from Châteauneuf-du-Pape and Gigondas, and the white wines of the entire region are quite good.

1983—An outstanding vintage in the north, a very good yet irregular vintage in the south. A hot, dry summer resulted in fully mature grapes loaded with sugar, flavor extract, and hard tannins. For Hermitage, Crozes-Hermitage, and St.-Joseph, the wines are clearly the best since 1978 and 1961, neither so massive and rich as the 1978s nor as opulent as the 1985s, but more elegant and potentially very long-lived. The southern Rhônes should be moderately long-lived since they are ripe yet full of tannin. In Châteauneuf and Gigondas, 1983 is just behind 1978, 1981, and 1985 in quality.

1982—Initially believed to be outstanding in the north, but mediocre in the south, only the latter half of the early prognosis has held true. The great heat during the harvest created significant problems and those growers not equipped to keep the fermenting grapes cool had problems with volatile acidity. The northern Rhônes are very flavorful but quite forward and will mature quickly. Most will keep until the early '90s, not much longer. At present, they are showing better than the more tannic, more sought after 1983s. The southern Rhône had many more problems with both the heat and the huge crop. The wines are rather frail and somewhat unstable. However, there are some pleasant surprises, yet one must tread very carefully here.

1981—A much better vintage in the southern than northern Rhône, where many vineyards lacked fully mature grapes. Most of the big red wines from Hermitage, Côte Rôtie, and Cornas are lean and lack charm; however, exceptions do exist. In the south it is a very good, even excellent vintage for both Gigondas and Châteauneuf-du-Pape, the best between 1978 and 1985. The wines here are quite powerful, deep in color, and offer excellent value.

1980—A large crop of easy to drink, medium-weight wines was produced in 1980. They are all relatively mature today and if stored well will continue to provide delicious drinking for the rest of this decade. Both the north and south were equally successful in this attractive, commercial vintage of fruity, soft, medium-bodied wines. Clearly, in 1980, the Rhône was France's most successful viticultural district.

1979—A very underrated yet consistently excellent year in both the northern and southern Rhône. Nineteen seventy-nine had the misfortune to follow 1978, the Rhône's greatest vintage since 1961. The wines are just now entering their mature period (where the best of them should remain for another 7–10 years). They are rich, full-bodied, deep in color, and quite flavorful and scented. The 1979s can still be found at very low prices.

1978—An undeniably great vintage in both sectors of the Rhône Valley. Most of the top wines, even though they are just short of their tenth birthday, are still not mature, yet can be drunk with pleasure because of their explosive fruit and remarkable depth. The 1978s are collectors' items and the well-cellared examples of Côte Rôtie, Hermitage, Cornas, and Châteauneuf-du-Pape will easily make it into the next century.

1977—Between 1976 and 1986, this is the Rhône's worst vintage. The wines are light, a little green, and lack character and charm. Some of the white wines from the northern Rhône, particularly those of Hermitage, which were very acidic when young, have opened up, but this is by and large a vintage to ignore.

1976—Some reports called this a great vintage, but time has taken its toll on these wines that in reality lacked depth from the beginning. Côte Rôtie was by far the most successful appellation, but many other northern Rhônes were problematic and the southern Rhônes in most cases lacked balance and were excessively tannic. Whereas 1979 is the Rhône's most recent underrated vintage, 1976 is its most overrated.

A GUIDE TO NORTHERN RHÔNE'S BEST PRODUCERS

***** *(OUTSTANDING PRODUCERS)*

J. L. Chave (Hermitage)
A. Clape (Cornas)
A. Dervieux Thaize (Côte Rôtie)
Gentaz Dervieux (Côte Rôtie)
E. Guigal (Côte Rôtie)

Paul Jaboulet Aîné (Hermitage)
R. Jasmin (Côte Rôtie)
R. Rostaing (Côte Rôtie)
N. Verset (Cornas)

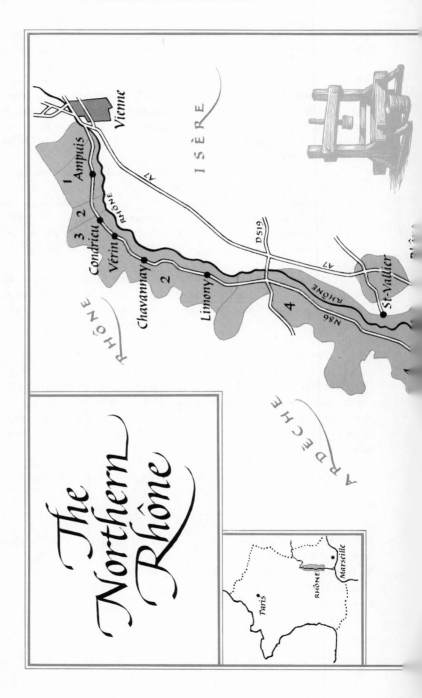

The Northern Rhône

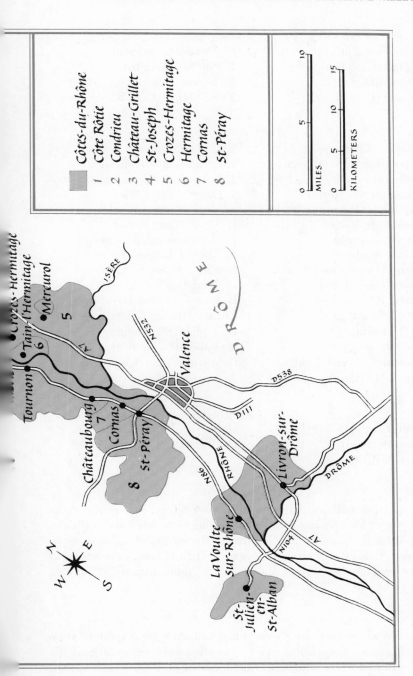

Côtes-du-Rhône

1 Côte Rôtie
2 Condrieu
3 Château-Grillet
4 St-Joseph
5 Crozes-Hermitage
6 Hermitage
7 Cornas
8 St-Péray

MILES
KILOMETERS

DRÔME

Crozes-Hermitage
Tain-l'Hermitage
Mercurol
5
6
Tournon
ISÈRE
N532
A7
Valence
N532
D538
Châteaubourg
Cornas
7
St-Péray
8
D111
Livron-sur-Drôme
RHÔNE
N86
DRÔME
A7
La Voulte-sur-Rhône
FOIN
St-Julien-en-St-Alban

N
W E
S

* * * * *(EXCELLENT PRODUCERS)*

G. Barge (Côte Rôtie)   P. Multier (Condrieu)
R. Burgaud (Côte Rôtie)   J. Pinchon (Condrieu)
Delas (Hermitage)   H. Sorrel (Hermitage)
P. Dumazet (Condrieu)   Vidal-Fleury (Côte Rôtie)

* * * *(GOOD PRODUCERS)*

G. de Barjac (Cornas)   Gray (Hermitage)
Caves des Clairmonts (Crozes-   Château Grillet (Condrieu)
  Hermitage)   J. L. Grippat (Hermitage)
E. Champet (Côte Rôtie)   J. Jamet (Côte Rôtie)
M. Chapoutier (Hermitage)   M. Juge (Cornas)
R. Clusel (Côte Rôtie)   B. Levet (Côte Rôtie)
Courbis (St.-Joseph)   J. Marsanne (St.-Joseph)
Coursodon (St.-Joseph)   R. Michel (Cornas)
Desmeures (Hermitage)   Domaine Pradelle (Crozes-
A. Drevon (Côte Rôtie)   Hermitage)
E. Duclaux (Côte Rôtie)   R. Roure (Crozes-Hermitage)
B. Faurie (Hermitage)   C.Tardy (Crozes-Hermitage)
Fayolle (Hermitage)   R. Trollat (St.-Joseph)
Ferraton (Hermitage)   de Vallouit (Côte Rôtie)
E. Florentin (Crozes-Hermitage)   Georges Vernay (Condrieu)
A. Gerin (Côte Rôtie)   A. Voge (Cornas)

* * *(AVERAGE PRODUCERS)*

A. Fumat (Cornas)   Union des Propriétaires
J. Lionnet (Cornas)   (Hermitage)
J. Teysseire (Cornas)

Northern Rhône

The northern Rhône viticultural district begins just south of the historic city of Vienne and winds south along both sides of the Rhône, running through Côte Rôtie, Condrieu, Château Grillet, St.-Joseph, Hermitage, Crozes-Hermitage, Cornas, and St.-Peray, concluding at the large commercial city of Valence. The total distance is only 42 miles.

Côte Rôtie

Côte Rôtie can be France's most magnificent wine. Produced from the Syrah grape, Côte Rôtie can by law also have up to 20% of the highly perfumed white Viognier grape blended in. Producers use considerably less than the maximum Viognier permitted, but do use some for its aromatic personality.

The top Côte Rôties will handsomely repay 8–10 years of cellaring, yet for most consumers, the greatest difficulty is finding the top wines from the small, excellent producers such as Jasmin, Gentaz-Dervieux, Rostaing, and Jamet. Fortunately, the wines from the four major *négociants*, E. Guigal, P. Jaboulet, M. Chapoutier, and Vidal-Fleury, can be found in most metropolitan markets.

What does a mature Côte Rôtie taste like? Imagine the scent of rich, ripe raspberry fruit, combined with exotic spices, floral aromas, the scent of vanillin from oak wood, and smoky hickory wood. In texture and palate impression, imagine rich, opulent, silky fruit that coats the mouth and just lingers and lingers.

GILLES AND PIERRE BARGE* * * *

1981 Côte Rôtie	($12.99)	78
1982 Côte Rôtie	($14.99)	84
1983 Côte Rôtie	($17.99)	88
1984 Côte Rôtie	($16.99)	82

Little of Barge's rustic, deeply colored Côte Rôtie makes it to these shores, but this traditional winemaker, who works his craft off a back street of Ampuis, consistently makes fine, tannic, robust Côte Rôtie. His wines lack the finesse and grace of a Jasmin, Rostaing, or Guigal, but they do offer chunky, spicy fruit, full body, and a tough, tannic overlay. I was somewhat surprised that the 1982 did not show more concentration. The 1981 needs 1–2 years to reach full maturity, but for now, its attractive and spicy nose is more interesting than the overly tannic, compact palate impression. The 1982 needs 4–6 years. The star, however, is the 1983, a powerful, rich, dark ruby wine with a scent of bacon fat, full body, and 5–10 years of further aging potential. The 1984 has a complex bouquet, but is high in acidity and lean. The 1985 will be a sensation when released in late 1987.

ROGER BURGAUD* * *

1983 Côte Rôtie	($15.95)	88
1984 Côte Rôtie	($15.95)	88

One of the youngest growers in Côte Rôtie, Burgaud is making people take notice of his talents. The 1983 is very tannic and rich, the 1984 one of the top successes of the vintage in Côte Rôtie. Both wines could use 3–4 more years, particularly the 1983.

E. CHAMPET* * *

1982 Côte Rôtie	($15.95)	87
1983 Côte Rôtie	($17.95)	88
1984 Côte Rôtie	($16.95)	85

I have had experience with only a few vintages of Champet's wines; they are very good, rustic, rich, earthy examples of Côte Rôtie. The wines share a dark ruby color with pleasant, berryish, leathery, fruity bouquets, moderately tannic, straightforward, medium- to full-bodied flavors, and tannic finishes. The 1982 is very ripe, tannic, a little low in acidity, but clearly a Côte Rôtie to drink after at least 5–6 years of bottle age. The unreleased 1985 is a little more concentrated and tannic; it will need 5–6 years. Champet's 1984 is quite good for the vintage, and the 1983 is full-bodied, sumptuous, and concentrated.

CHAPOUTIER* * *

1981 Côte Rôtie	($10.99)	82
1982 Côte Rôtie	($11.99)	84
1983 Côte Rôtie	($11.99)	84

The ebullient Max Chapoutier seems to have succeeded in the last couple of years in upgrading the quality of his family's wines, which had slipped noticeably. Nevertheless, the best cuvées of Châteauneuf-du-Pape, Côte Rôtie, and Hermitage are still blended together and sold under the firm's top-of-the-line label, the non-vintage Gran Cuvée. The vintage offerings from Chapoutier show good fruit, an attractive, woodsy, raspberry-scented bouquet, medium to full body, and soft, easygoing textures. Both the 1983 and 1982 are rounder, riper, richer, and overall just have more to them. They should drink well for 5–6 years.

R. CLUSEL* * *

1983 Côte Rôtie	($16.50)	86
1984 Côte Rôtie	($16.00)	78

The 1983 is ripe, rich in fruit, and powerfully scented with the smell of raspberries. This seductive wine can be drunk now or held for 5–6 years. The 1984 is light yet pleasant.

ALBERT DERVIEUX-THAIZE* * * * *

1983 Côte Rôtie Fongent	($18.00)	87
1984 Côte Rôtie La Garde	($18.00)	80
1983 Côte Rôtie La Viaillère	($20.00)	90
1984 Côte Rôtie La Viaillère	($18.00)	86

The affable Albert Dervieux has been president of the Côte Rôtie growers and for years his well-placed vineyards have made a very traditional, rich, deep, tannic wine. His 1983s are top successes, but his 1985s look to be even greater. His 1984s are good, a trifle lean, but are interesting, complex wines. His best wine is his La Viaillère, a tiny vineyard on the Côte Brune with vines that average 55 years old. Dervieux's wines are best drunk between 6–15 years after the vintage.

GENTAZ-DERVIEUX* * * * *

1982 Côte Rôtie Côte Brune	($14.95)	90
1983 Côte Rôtie Côte Brune	($24.95)	91
1984 Côte Rôtie Côte Brune	($24.95)	87

Here are spectacular 1982 and 1983 Côte Rôties, and a great success in 1984 as well. In 1982, Gentaz-Dervieux harvested his tiny vineyard (1.25 hectares on Côte Rôtie's precipitous Côte Brune) in the morning to avoid the intense heat and probability of overheated grapes, which could cause vinification problems. His 1982 is extremely dark in color, has a powerful, jammy, framboise-scented aroma, with exotic aromas of smoky hickory wood and black pepper. Quite rich and full-bodied, with firm, plentiful tannins, this wine will need 7–10 years of cellaring. Don't despair if you miss the wonderful 1982, because the 1983 is even better. It is even more concentrated, dense, very aromatic, but again in need of 5–7 years of cellaring. Even the 1984, with its profound aromas of raspberries and dense fruit, is excellent. This is another grower who made a truly great 1985.

GERIN* * *

1978 Côte Rôtie	($11.99)	72
1980 Côte Rôtie	($11.99)	75
1982 Côte Rôtie	($12.95)	86

The Domaine Gerin has a badly situated vineyard, on the level ground above the Côte Rôtie hill, and the vines are still young, particularly by the standards of most ancient Côte Rôtie vineyards. Perhaps this explains why these wines, except for the 1982, are lacking in richness and character. Both the 1978 and 1980 exhibit annoyingly high acid levels and sinewy, compact personalities. The 1978 is especially distressing in view of the greatness of the vintage. As the vines get older, the wine here may get better.

GUIGAL* * * * *

1979 Côte Rôtie	($14.95)	85
1980 Côte Rôtie	($12.95–$14.49)	85
1981 Côte Rôtie	($15.95)	83
1982 Côte Rôtie	($15.95)	89
1983 Côte Rôtie	($20.00)	90
1980 Côte Rôtie La Landonne Côte Brune	($29.95–$35.00)	95
1981 Côte Rôtie La Landonne Côte Brune	($29.95)	90
1982 Côte Rôtie La Landonne Côte Brune	($37.50)	95

1983 Côte Rôtie La Landonne Côte Brune	($55.00)	100

1980 Côte Rôtie La Mouline Côte Blonde	($29.95–$35.00)	96

1981 Côte Rôtie La Mouline Côte Blonde	($29.95)	90

1982 Côte Rôtie La Mouline Côte Blonde	($47.50)	98

1983 Côte Rôtie La Mouline Côte Blonde	($55.00)	100

It is obvious that I admire Guigal's wines, but I admire even more his philosophy of making wine naturally, and not overmanipulating it. My only fear is that his recently found superstar status will, as with so many who have become stars before him, cause him to forget the reasons for his success. Guigal owns vineyards only in Côte Rôtie. He purchases wine from growers for his other products and does a superb job of blending. His Côte Rôties are his best. His 1982s were the most successful northern Rhônes I tasted. The two rare, single-vineyard wines, La Mouline and La Landonne, are among the world's half-dozen greatest wines. La Mouline is more voluptuous and lush, La Landonne more brawny and tannic. Both should benefit nicely from 3–6 years of cellaring, but both have otherworldly concentration and aroma. The regular 1982 Côte Rôtie is spicy, quite aromatic, richly fruity, very concentrated and opulent in texture, soft, and long. It can be drunk now or aged 4–8 years. The 1981s, though not the greatest La Mouline and La Landonne ever made, are excellent wines, particularly in view of the difficult vintage conditions. The 1981 La Mouline is more precocious in style than the 1980, 1979, and 1978. The fragrant, open-knit, gorgeous bouquet of ripe blackberry fruit, oak, and violets lingers and lingers. It is firm on the palate, with very good fruit and a hint of the great, lush, silky quality this wine is famous for; expect it to mature in 7–8 years. In contrast, the 1981 La Landonne is closed in, tannic, dark in color, with a tarry, blackberry fruitiness, and impressive weight, but it is currently austere. It will need a full decade to show its best. The 1980 regular Côte Rôtie is quite successful, more supple and accessible than the tannic 1979, and of course not so profound and tannic as the 1978. Quite spicy, richly fruity, lush, the 1980 Côte Rôtie is quite concentrated, smooth and round, and can be drunk now or cellared for 6–7 years. The 1981 regular Côte Rôtie does not have quite the concentration and lush, rich fruitiness of the 1980 or structure, body, and potential of either the great 1978 or very fine 1979 Côte Rôties. However, it is round, very attractive, with soft, ripe fruit, light tannins, and immediate appeal. The 1983s are monumental wines here and the 1983 La Mouline and 1983 La Landonne, two of the greatest wines one could ever hope to encounter, should last and evolve for 20–30 years.

PAUL JABOULET AINÉ* * * * *

1981 Côte Rôtie Les Jumelles	($11.99–$12.49)	74
1982 Côte Rôtie Les Jumelles	($11.99–$12.49)	85
1983 Côte Rôtie Les Jumelles	($11.95)	86
1984 Côte Rôtie Les Jumelles	($12.95)	78

Louis and Gérard Jaboulet do a lovely job with Côte Rôtie, and while it rarely matches the sheer majesty of their famed Hermitage La Chapelle, it can be quite good. Vintages such as 1970, 1976, and 1978 were successful for the Jaboulet Côte Rôtie Les Jumelles, as anyone who has cellared these gorgeously succulent wines knows. The 1981 is a satisfying bottle of wine, but it lacks the richness and breadth that one normally expects. It is now ready to drink. The 1982 is my sensual favorite of these four. It bursts forth from the glass, revealing scents of raspberry fruit, flowers, and spices. Supple, round, medium-bodied, quite elegant and seductive, this precociously styled wine should be drunk over the next 5 years. Not so the 1983, which has a big, tannic clout, full body, surprising strength and power, and good length. It is the best Côte Rôtie Les Jumelles since the wonderful 1976. It will need 5–6 years before it can be drunk. The 1984 is light, ready to drink, but simple.

R. JASMIN* * * * *

1981 Côte Rôtie	($13.95)	81
1982 Côte Rôtie	($15.95)	87
1983 Côte Rôtie	($18.95)	90
1984 Côte Rôtie	($17.95)	85

The affable Robert Jasmin makes Côte Rôtie's most elegant and fruity wine. It is delicious from the barrel or the bottle, but is best drunk up within 6–8 years of the vintage, since it rarely has the stamina to last much beyond a decade. Jasmin has the habit of keeping a barrel or two of his best Côte Rôtie, from his oldest vines, for his personal consumption, and those who have had the pleasure of visiting his private wine cellar under the kitchen floor will be amazed how concentrated and rich this wine can be, and lament that it is not blended into his Côte Rôtie for "l'exportation." The 1981 Jasmin Côte Rôtie is pleasant, too straightforward and light to merit high marks, but certainly a charming, fully mature wine. His 1982 is from a much better vintage, but again lacks a bit of grip, richness, and depth, yet is quite fruity, spicy, generous, warm, and round, and apt to please virtually any taster. It should be drunk over the next 5 years. The 1983, which Jasmin said was the "best in quality and quantity since 1947," was clearly his finest wine since 1978, until the 1985. Dark ruby with an expansive bouquet of ripe, rich fruit, and vanillin oak, the 1983 is quite perfumed, fat, and concentrated, and long and silky in the finish. Moderate tannins are present, but they are simply overwhelmed by the fruit. It should be drunk over the next 10 years. The 1984 is ready to drink, quite charming, and seductive. His 1985, to be released in the fall of 1987, is exceptional.

B. LEVET* * *

1983 Côte Rôtie	($22.95)	88

This is an extremely impressive wine in need of 5–6 years of cellaring. Rich, dense in color, it has aromas and flavors of ripe raspberries, pepper, and chocolate.

R. OGIER

1980 Côte Rôtie	($7.99–$8.99)	60

Côte Rôtie? This large *négociant* has made an unsavory wine with hot, southern Rhône flavors, plenty of alcohol, and not one trace of the character of Côte Rôtie. Need I say more?

R. ROSTAING* * * * *

1981 Côte Rôtie Côte Blonde	($13.95)	87
1983 Côte Rôtie Côte Blonde	($24.95)	87
1984 Côte Rôtie Côte Blonde	($24.95)	90

| 1981 Côte Rôtie Côte Brune et Blonde | ($13.95) | 83 |

| 1983 Côte Rôtie La Landonne Côte Brune | ($24.95) | 87 |

| 1984 Côte Rôtie La Landonne Côte Brune | ($24.95) | 86 |

One of the new up and coming producers in Côte Rôtie, Rostaing's first releases have been quite impressive. They have their own unique style and are not copycat versions of Guigal or Jasmin, but something quite individual. They seem exotic and especially spicy for Côte Rôtie, with full-blown, peppery, raspberry aromas. Both 1983s need 5–7 years of bottle age, but both are impressive wines of grace, richness, and excellent flavor. The 1983 Côte Blonde is more open and more obvious at this time; the 1983 La Landonne deeper, more tannic, and more peppery and spicy. The 1981 Côte Blonde is really quite excellent—velvety, long, rich, and ideal for drinking over the next 5 years. The other 1981 is tight, austere yet promising, but not possessed of the fruit of the 1981 Côte Blonde. His 1984 Côte Blonde is among three top Côte Rôtie of the vintage, a decadently rich, gorgeously scented wine. The 1984 La Landonne is more tannic and hard. His 1985s are simply incredible—make your reservations now.

VIDAL-FLEURY* * * *

| 1979 Côte Rôtie La Chatillonne | ($13.99) | 83 |

| 1980 Côte Rôtie La Chatillonne | ($13.49) | 81 |

| 1983 Côte Rôtie | ($14.99) | 84 |

In the late '70s and early '80s, the venerable firm of Vidal-Fleury was in one of those awkward periods where effective leadership and management were missing, and the lack of direction was reflected in the wines, which were still solid and reliable, but lacked the majesty of previous efforts. Côte Rôtie enthusiasts who have cellared Vidal-Fleury's Côte Rôties of 1966, 1969, 1971, and 1978 realize how stunning these wines can be. The 1978, which, for the lucky few who have some, still needs a good 6–8 years of cellaring, was the last great Côte Rôtie from Vidal-Fleury. Change is certain since the firm of Guigal purchased Vidal-Fleury and is now making great efforts to rebuild its reputation. The 1985s made here confirm this. Both of the above wines are from Vidal-Fleury's best vineyard on the Côte Blonde sector of the famous terraced hillside of Côte Rôtie. The 1979 La Chatillonne is medium ruby with a spicy, woody, ripe berryish bouquet, medium to full body, and good concentration. It should be fully mature in 2–3 years. The 1980 La Chatillonne is straightforward, plummy, enjoyable, but lacking character and complexity, as is the 1983. One will have to wait for this release of this firm's 1985s to see the obvious potential this old house has.

Château Grillet and Condrieu

Just several minutes' drive south from Ampuis is the sleepy town of Condrieu; several miles further still is the famed Château Grillet. The wines produced in both appellations are intensely perfumed, viscous, individualistic wines made from one of the rarest white wine grapes in the world, the Viognier. Condrieu is an opulent wine, intense, rich, and full-bodied, with a viscous texture, astonishing density of fruit, and a bouquet that suggests pears, peaches, tropical fruit, roses, and lychee nuts. With such a glowing and enticing description of the wine, why isn't Condrieu better known? Scarcity and price are two reasons: There are only 57 acres to the Condrieu appellation, and a scant 7.5 acres to the Château Grillet appellation. The result, very tiny quantities of Condrieu available for worldwide distribution, has kept the price for Condrieu between a low of $16 a bottle to a high of $25. For Château Grillet, the price is usually in the neighborhood of $35 and higher. The difficulty with Condrieu is that it can overwhelm most foods. In Condrieu, the preferred dish is quenelles of river fish with a Nantua sauce. Condrieu also goes well with foods grilled over mesquite, particularly salmon and bass.

P. DUMAZET* * * *

1984 Condrieu	($24.95)	82
1985 Condrieu	($28.95)	90

The 1984 here is light and a little short, but the 1985 is explosively rich, lush, with a deep, ripe, intense fragrance of spring flowers and lychee nuts.

CHÂTEAU GRILLET* * *

1982	($45.00)	86
1983	($45.00)	82

| 1984 | ($45.00) | 80 |

For the last several years, the wines of the fabled Grillet vineyard have not been all that their precious reputation would seem to suggest. The wine is obviously overpriced simply because the property makes so little wine. The 1982 is the best wine since 1978. Full-bodied, rich, honeyed, viscous, ripe, and fruity, it is very similar to a fine Condrieu (made just a few kilometers away). Drink over the next 4–5 years. The 1983 is more austere and lacks the richness of the 1982. The 1984 is lean and a bit acidic.

E. GUIGAL* * * * *

| 1983 Condrieu | ($24.95) | 89 |

| 1984 Condrieu | ($24.95) | 84 |

| 1985 Condrieu | ($24.95) | 90 |

The progress Guigal has made with white wines is amazing. His Condrieu is now one of the best of this appellation. Guigal toned down the oaky character of the 1983 (his 1982 was delicious, but too oaky), and to my palate, the results are excellent. All of these wines, particularly the 1985 and 1983, are highly perfumed with aromas suggesting honey, flowers, and apricots. Silky, loaded with fruit, opulent and exciting, these luscious wines will make excellent drinking over the next 2 years. The 1984 is pleasant, but lacks the richness of the 1983 and 1985.

PAUL MULTIER* * * *

| 1982 Condrieu Château du Rozay | ($18.00–$24.00) | 90 |

| 1983 Condrieu Château du Rozay | ($18.00–$24.00) | 88 |

| 1984 Condrieu Château du Rozay | ($24.00) | 82 |

| 1985 Condrieu Château du Rozay | ($30.00) | 87 |

The late Paul Multier was one of Condrieu's finest winemakers, and if there is just one Condrieu to purchase, it is Château du Rozay. The 1982 and 1983 are absolutely superb, with bouquets suggesting lychee nuts, apricots, and lilacs; the wines have great density, richness, viscosity, and lushness on the palate. Both are best drunk now for their glorious, exuberant character. The 1984 is reticent and shy in comparison. It has plenty of punch, the heady, perfumed quality that makes Condrieu wonderful, as well as the lush, rich texture on the palate, and is much thinner than the 1982. The newest vintage, 1985, is very rich and opulent, with decadent flavors and a tremendous depth of fruit.

J. PINCHON* * * *

1982 Condrieu	($25.00)	90
1983 Condrieu	($25.00)	86
1984 Condrieu	($25.00)	85
1985 Condrieu	($25.00)	90

Pinchon's Condrieu can rival Multier's Château du Rozay, but unfortunately, Pinchon makes such a tiny quantity that little escapes France. The 1982 is one of the best knit Condrieu wines, and if I were going to cellar one of these wines for 4 or 5 years, it would be the Pinchon. A bouquet of ripe pears and tropical fruits is enticing enough. On the palate, the wine has surprisingly good acidity, a very rich, intense, honeyed texture, and long, long finish. The 1985 is very similar in style. The 1983 is a smaller-scale model of the 1982 and 1985, yet still wonderfully fruity and exotic. Pinchon's 1984 was the best Condrieu that I tasted from that difficult vintage.

G. VERNAY* * *

1982 Condrieu	($18.95)	85
1983 Condrieu	($18.95)	87
1983 Condrieu Coteaux de Vernon	($19.95)	88
1984 Condrieu Coteaux de Vernon	($19.95)	83
1985 Condrieu Coteaux de Vernon	($28.95)	92

Condrieu's best-known name, as well as its largest producer, Vernay is quite good, but in most vintages not quite at the same level of brilliance as Pinchon or Multier. However, if you can latch on to his top cuvée of Condrieu (Coteaux de Vernon) from old hillside vines, it is extremely unctuous, rich, lush, and opulently fruity, except for the 1984 which lacked length and tasted a trifle too acidic. The 1983 Vernay is very fresh, with a wonderful perfume of roses and spices. Fresh, intensely fruity, medium- to full-bodied, with layers of fruit, it is a round, sumptuous wine for drinking over the next 1–3 years. The 1982 is at its peak, lush and fruity, full-bodied, and a trifle alcoholic, but the heady perfumed bouquet of peaches, pears, and flowers is extremely seductive.

Hermitage (Red)

The most panoramic view of the famed Hermitage "hill" is from across the bridge over the Rhône on the Tournon side, and it is simply spectacular. Steep, huge, and jutting up from the ground behind the small, commercial town of Tain L'Hermitage is a massive outcropping of granite covered with vines and the huge painted white walls advertising the names of two of Hermitage's famed producers, Paul Jaboulet Ainé and M. Chapoutier.

The wine of Hermitage used to be, in great years, closest in texture and richness to a vintage port. Despite the fact that many growers have lightened up in style and routinely filter their wines, Hermitage is still a very big, rich, full-bodied, full-tilt, winter-weight wine. Even the minuscule quantities of white wine produced here are expensive, big, ripe, and viscous. Red Hermitage mandates game or beef on the table, but it can go splendidly well with strong cheese. White Hermitage seems like the perfect wine for the mesquite- and fruitwood-fired cooking that has swept this country; it is big and distinctive enough to stand up to the pungent aromas of grilled foods.

M. CHAPOUTIER* * *

N.V. Hermitage Le Pavillon	($45.00)	88
1981 Hermitage La Sizeranne	($10.99–$11.99)	82
1982 Hermitage La Sizeranne	($10.99)	84
1983 Hermitage La Sizeranne	($12.99)	86

The 1981 Chapoutier Hermitage is quite fat, supple, with good color and fruit, a chunky, ripe cherry aroma, and a full-bodied, solid finish. It lacks complexity and style, but is quite satisfying. The 1982 is fuller, deeper, and more concentrated, richly fruity, with a blackberry taste and soft tannins. It should mature rapidly. The 1983 is very similarly styled, perhaps slightly firmer. Nineteen eighty-three may be Chapoutier's best vintage of Hermitage since the early '60s. The non-vintage luxury cuvée, Le Pavillon, is very rich, long, deep and has an aged complexity to its flavor.

J. L. CHAVE* * * * *

1981 Hermitage	($14.49)	84
1982 Hermitage	($14.49)	90
1983 Hermitage	($19.95)	93
1984 Hermitage	($19.95)	87

Unquestionably one of the most respected growers in the Rhône, Chave is also one of the great wine drinkers and gourmets of the entire region. His propensity to talk enthusiastically about his most recent culinary innovation often leaves questions concerning the latest vintage or Rhône Valley gossip unanswered. Despite their remarkable reputation, his wines are not always the model of consistent excellence that might be suggested. The 1976 and 1969 are two vintages that I find to be lacking in fruit and entirely too austere. However, his 1978 is a monumental wine, and his 1982 and 1983 wines are top-flight. The 1981 Chave is certainly good for the vintage, precocious, medium weight, charming, and fruity, with a pleasant spicy character. It needs 2–3 years to be fully mature. The 1982 has altogether more to it. It is quite dark ruby, rich and full-bodied, with a powerful, ripe berry, blackcurrant aroma, deep, viscous, fat, fruity flavors and firm tannins. Acidity is average; the wine should mature fully in 10 years. Consumers should make a note to look for the 1983, Chave's best Hermitage since 1978. The 1984 is a top success for the vintage and very similar to Chave's excellent 1979.

DELAS* * * *

1979 Hermitage Cuvée de la Tourette	($25.00)	87
1983 Hermitage Cuvée de la Tourette	($25.00)	91

This firm tends to assume a very low profile and consequently its wines are not nearly as well known as they should be. Their Hermitage is top-drawer in quality. The 1979 is just beginning to open, displaying rich aromas of cassis and smoky, tarry fruit. It has excellent concentration. The 1983 is sweet, smoky, with gobs of fruit, a cedary, ripe, rich, very complex bouquet, and 5–10 years of further evolution ahead.

B. FAURIE* * *

| 1982 Hermitage | ($13.99) | 85 |

| 1983 Hermitage | ($16.95) | 87 |

I have found Faurie's wines to be good. Both the 1982 and 1983 are quite full-bodied, supple, spicy, with a rich blackberry fruitiness, full body, plenty of power and alcohol, and excellent color. They should be mature by 1990.

J. FAYOLLE* * *

| 1982 Hermitage Les Dionnières | ($12.99) | 89 |

| 1983 Hermitage Les Dionnières | ($15.95) | 87 |

Except for 1983, 1982 is considered the best vintage for Hermitage after 1978, provided the grower could properly handle the vinification, which took place in torrid heat. Fayolle, a tiny grower, has produced a blockbuster wine, inky ruby/purple with huge, chewy, viscous fruit, a very intense blackberry bouquet, moderate tannins, and an amazing finish. A winter wine for serving with game, stews, and ripe cheeses, this excellent Hermitage, produced by the only winemaking twins I know of in the Rhône Valley, will be mature by 1987–1990. The 1983 has shown considerable bottle variation, so judgment is somewhat reserved; the good bottles have been rich and portlike, but the bad suffer from off aromas.

FERRATON* * *

| 1981 Hermitage La Cuvée des Miaux | ($9.99) | 86 |

| 1982 Hermitage La Cuvée des Miaux | ($12.99) | ? |

| 1983 Hermitage La Cuvée des Miaux | ($15.99) | 89 |

A small grower, Ferraton produces tiny amounts of Hermitage and Crozes-Hermitage. His 1981 is an excellent wine in a vintage that was mediocre for the area. Still very young, this deep ruby/purple wine has an intense, spicy, oaky, plummy aroma with the gamey scent of

Syrah very evident. Full-bodied, and quite tannic, this big, rich, complex wine will handsomely repay those who have the foresight to buy it and the patience to cellar it for 5–8 years. The 1982, which should easily surpass the 1981, was quite poor on the two occasions I tasted it. Intolerable levels of volatile acidity make me wonder if all of Ferraton's 1982 Hermitage is flawed. The 1983, however, is smoky, rich, very concentrated, full-bodied, with great depth. Ferraton's 1985 looks to be even better.

E. GUIGAL* * * * *

1979 Hermitage	($14.49–$14.99)	87
1980 Hermitage	($14.99)	82–86
1981 Hermitage	($14.99)	86
1982 Hermitage	($16.50)	87
1983 Hermitage	($20.00)	90

I am impressed with the consistency in style and quality of Guigal's wines of Hermitage. He purchases the grape juice for these wines and then "brings it up" ("*élévage*") in his wine cellars in Ampuis. The 1982 is rich and supple, with a big blackberry, licorice-scented bouquet, and long, lush flavors. It should drink nicely for 5–8 years. The 1983 is Guigal's finest red Hermitage to date—a profound wine of great depth and stature. The 1979 is still on the market, and is the best of the remaining three wines. Richer, fuller-bodied, and more concentrated than either the 1980 or 1981, it still has plenty of tannin to shed, but is loaded with ripe cassis fruit, and it lingers on the palate. The 1980 is actually two different wines because there are two separate lots. Unfortunately, there is no way to tell which lot you may be getting. One lot of 1980 is good, but harshly tannic and austere, with a short, compact finish. Another lot has a much greater concentration of fruit, is still very tannic, but is rich and well balanced. Guigal's 1981 is a great success in this mixed vintage. A wonderful cassis aroma is followed by a big, deep, rich, full-bodied wine that has more in common with the 1979 than one would expect for the vintage.

PAUL JABOULET AINÉ* * * * *

1981 Hermitage La Chapelle	($12.49)	80
1982 Hermitage La Chapelle	($14.49)	90
1983 Hermitage La Chapelle	($30.00)	96
1984 Hermitage La Chapelle	($15.00)	85
1985 Hermitage La Chapelle	($20.00)	89

I was surprised that Gérard Jaboulet decided to declare a La Chapelle in 1981, because the first time I tasted his 1981 Hermitage he said the quality wasn't high enough to be called La Chapelle. However, his initial reaction to the wine has obviously changed, because it does indeed exist. It is a light, charming wine with soft, blackcurrant fruit, and light tannins. It should be drunk over the next 2–4 years. The 1984 is similarly styled, but noticeably richer and deeper in color. As for the 1983, Gérard Jaboulet thinks this wine is one of the very best he has ever made. I doubt whether it is better than the extraordinary 1978 or 1961 La Chapelles, but it looks to be a real winner. Opaque and ruby/purple in color, this full-bodied wine has an intense aroma of black cherry fruit, hickory wood, freshly ground black pepper and cassis. Voluptuous and full-bodied on the palate, with layers of silky, lush, viscous, chewy fruit, high tannins, and average acidity, this big, potentially great wine will mature in 10–15 years, well before Jaboulet's stunning 1978. Both the 1982 and 1985 are similarly styled—quite deep, rich, full-bodied, but very precocious, fruity, and lush. Both should drink well young and last 8–12 years. People who buy and cellar great Hermitage will be shocked at how sensational they will be at maturity. It can be a great value.

H. SORREL* * * *

1982 Hermitage Le Gréal	($15.95)	60
1983 Hermitage Le Gréal	($25.95)	90
1984 Hermitage Le Gréal	($18.00)	85

The ancient Monsieur Sorrel has passed away, and with him the talent to produce great Hermitage from his splendid parcel of vines on the Le Méal sector of the Hermitage hill. His son at first let things get out of hand, but one suspects that he found the right winemaker to assist him in 1983 and quality has returned. His 1983 is vastly superior in quality, exhibiting rich, deep fruit, and a long, tannic finish. It needs 5–6 years. The 1982 is spoiled by excessive volatile acidity, not to mention faulty winemaking.

UNION DES PROPRIÉTAIRES* *

1982 Hermitage	($9.99)	78
1983 Hermitage	($9.99)	80

The 1982 bottling from this cooperative is soft, gamy, grapy, fruity and pleasant. Drink up. The 1983 is very tannic but rich and full-bodied.

VIDAL-FLEURY* * * *

1979 Hermitage	($13.95)	83

This offering from Vidal-Fleury is a robust, spicy, chunky wine, with good color, a ripe, black cherry bouquet, full body, and a brawny, hefty texture. The tannins are beginning to mellow, so this plump wine should be ready to drink in 2–3 years.

Hermitage (White)

White Hermitage can be remarkable, long-lived, rich, intense wine. Last year I drank the 1955 and 1929 white Hermitage from the firm of Chapoutier that Max Chapoutier poured in a tasting of his old vintages. I was also lucky enough to drink the 1929, 1952, and 1969 of Gérard Chave. These wines smell of grilled almonds; their intense, lively fruit, incredible length and richness reinforce the fact that they are almost always drunk too young. I use these examples not to suggest that you cellar white Hermitage for 20 or more years before consuming it, but to consider latching onto a few bottles, because they can be truly great wines.

White Hermitage is produced from two grapes, the Marsanne and Roussanne. Most growers primarily use the Marsanne, since it is easier to cultivate and more prolific. Traditionally, the top producers of white Hermitage have been Chave, Chapoutier, and Grippat. Paul Jaboulet Aîné, for all their splendid success with reds, has lagged behind in quality with the firm's white wines, although the white 1983s and 1985s are very good. Guigal also makes white Hermitage, and it can be quite good.

M. CHAPOUTIER* * *

1982 Hermitage Chante Alouette	($12.49)	84
1983 Hermitage Chante Alouette	($12.49)	87
1984 Hermitage Chante Alouette	($12.49)	87
N. V. Hermitage Cuvée l'Orvée	($30.00)	92

Chapoutier's vintage white Hermitage, called Chante Alouette, is one of this firm's very best wines. The 1982 is soft, flavorful, ripe, and generous. It should be drunk now and over the next 5 years for its full-bodied, fleshy texture. Both the 1983 and 1984 are very powerful wines, very deep, very full, and Max Chapoutier thinks they are among his finest in the last two decades. They linger on the palate, and seem to have the potential to last for at least a decade. His luxury blend of white Hermitage, the Cuvée l'Orvée, is an extraordinary wine of great depth and dimension, and must be tasted to be believed.

J. L. CHAVE* * * * *

1981 Hermitage	($13.49)	86
1982 Hermitage	($13.49)	87
1983 Hermitage	($14.49)	90
1984 Hermitage	($19.49)	87
1985 Hermitage	($19.99)	92

Chave's white Hermitage is made to last and last, and with few exceptions, will keep and improve for 15 years or more. The 1981 is the lightest of these, and lacks the power and richness of the subsequent two years. It shows charming mineral-scented fruit, a medium-weight texture, and crisp acidity; it is rather light for Chave, but stylish and flavorful. The 1982 is very accessible, unusually opulent for a young wine from Chave, with very ripe, intense, soft, fat flavors. It is a trifle deficient in acidity, so consumers should drink it up over the next 7–10 years. It is extremely flavorful, full, and rich. The 1983 is even bigger than the large-scaled 1982, but has better acidity and superb balance. It is very concentrated, quite full-bodied, very firm, and is a stunning example of white Hermitage. The 1984 is stylistically similar to the 1981, the 1985 absolutely stunning in its power and graceful harmony.

B. FAURIE* * *

1982 Hermitage	($14.49–$14.99)	83

This 1982, like many of the white Hermitage wines of this vintage, is a trifle low in acidity, but has a full-intensity aroma of hazelnuts and ripe fruit. On the palate, the wine is full-bodied, ripe, viscous, a bit heavy, and has a long finish. Drink over the next 2–4 years.

FERRATON* * *

1982 Hermitage La Reverdy	($14.99)	50
1983 Hermitage La Reverdy	($14.99)	70
1985 Hermitage La Reverdy	($15.99)	85

Two bottles of the 1982 revealed the same inexcusable problem— excessive volatile acidity. Dark golden and quite flawed, this wine should never have been released by Ferraton. The 1983 is also a trifle odd and bizarre, but clearly more palatable. However, the 1985 is crisp, well balanced, and has no technical problems.

GRAY* * *

1978 Domaine de l'Hermite	($13.50)	88
1980 Domaine de l'Hermite	($14.50)	75

The elderly Gray made a great, viscous, ripe, heavyweight old-style Hermitage in 1978 that may still be available in certain retail areas. It's a marvelous example of a big, rich, decadently powerful and full Hermitage. The 1980 suffers not only by comparison, but tastes flat and too low in acidity, although it has solid, fruity flavors and full body.

GRIPPAT* * *

1982 Hermitage	($13.99)	87
1983 Hermitage	($13.99)	90

| 1984 Hermitage | ($13.99) | 85 |

| 1985 Hermitage | ($15.99) | 90 |

Grippat makes excellent white Hermitage and the 1982, 1983, and 1985 are among his best. Quite full-bodied with a big, luscious, ripe pear and almond-scented aroma, deep, fat alcoholic, rich flavors that coat the palate with oodles of fruit, Grippat's white Hermitage usually needs 5 years to show its best. However, there is no reason not to enjoy this big, rich wine now.

E. GUIGAL* * * * *

| 1981 Hermitage | ($13.99) | 72 |

| 1982 Hermitage | ($13.99) | 84 |

| 1983 Hermitage | ($15.99) | 86 |

| 1984 Hermitage | ($15.99) | 79 |

Guigal's style of Hermitage leans toward an austere, tightly knit, well-structured wine that should improve with age. Unfortunately, the oldest white Hermitage of his I have tasted is the 1978, which is just now beginning to unfold. The 1981 and 1984 are lean, closed, medium-bodied and tight. Two to three years of cellaring should prove beneficial, but they are not big, highly concentrated Hermitages. The 1982 is also tightly knit, closed up, but has more weight, length, and concentration. The 1983 looks to be the best of the four.

PAUL JABOULET AINÉ* * * * *

| 1982 Hermitage Le Chevalier de Sterimbourg | ($10.99–$13.99) | 82 |

| 1983 Hermitage Le Chevalier de Sterimbourg | ($10.99–$13.49) | 85 |

| 1984 Hermitage Le Chevalier de Sterimbourg | ($10.99–$13.49) | 78 |

| 1985 Hermitage Le Chevalier de Sterimbourg | ($15.99) | 86 |

For over a decade and a half, the weakest link in the Jaboulet family's strong Rhône wine lineup has been the white wines. However, over the last 3 years there has been a strengthening in character and richness in these wines, and the 1983 and 1985 are Jaboulet's best in memory. The 1982 is a good white Hermitage, but makes no pretensions of challenging the quality of a Chave, Chapoutier, or Grippat. It is a clean, fresh, fruity, straightforward wine that should be drunk over the next 5 years. The 1983 is much more concentrated, powerful, very deep and fruity, with a nose suggesting straw, almonds, and mineral scents. Quite full-bodied, it should last at least a decade. The 1984 is tart, rather light, but fragrant and fruity. The 1985 is the firm's best white Hermitage in years.

Crozes-Hermitage and St.-Joseph

Both Crozes-Hermitage and St.-Joseph are the stepchildren of the northern Rhône. If the wines of Hermitage and Côte Rôtie are notoriously underrated and undervalued, then you can imagine how little credibility the wines from these two appellations receive. However, they are the great values of the northern Rhône, since they rarely will cost the consumer more than $8 a bottle. Consequently the top red wines from these communes are almost always drunk too young by consumers who think that 8-dollar wine will not keep. In fact, a good Crozes-Hermitage or St.-Joseph is usually best at 4–6 years after the vintage, and in great vintages like 1978 and 1983 can last 10 or more years. As for white wines, they too are little known except by real Rhône wine enthusiasts who know what great, undervalued finds they can be.

Red Wines—Crozes-Hermitage and St.-Joseph

CAVES DES CLAIRMONTS* * *

1983 Crozes-Hermitage	($6.50)	84

A ripe, round, supple, very lovely wine with very good richness for drinking over the next 4–5 years.

COURBIS* * *

1981 St.-Joseph	($7.99–$8.49)	82
1983 St.-Joseph	($7.99–$8.49)	84

Both the 1981 and 1983 are chunky, big, spicy, fruity wines with plenty of cherryish fruit, full body, and a long finish. They are not complex, but substantial and satisfyingly full. Drink them over the next 2 years.

DESMEURES* * *

| 1983 Crozes-Hermitage | ($5.99) | 81 |

Dark in color, rich, rather deep, but still savage and raw, this is a very traditional backward wine for drinking in 2–3 years.

FAYOLLE* * *

| 1982 Crozes-Hermitage Pontaix | ($5.99) | 84 |

| 1983 Crozes-Hermitage Pontaix | ($6.99) | ? |

The 1982 wine could easily be mistaken for most producers' Hermitage. The ripe, tarry, gamelike aroma is full and interesting. On the palate, the wine has excellent concentration, big, thick flavors, and a soft, long finish. Drink over the next 3–4 years. The 1983 has proved itself to be both very good and very bad.

E. FLORENTIN* * *

| 1981 St.-Joseph Clos de l'Arbalestrier | ($6.95) | 78 |

| 1982 St.-Joseph Clos de l'Arbalestrier | ($7.95) | 82 |

| 1983 St.-Joseph Clos de l'Arbalestrier | ($8.95) | 84 |

The 1981 is a trifle tight, hard and lean, but seems to have the depth of fruit to outlast its tannins. Hold for 2–3 years before drinking. It is above average in quality, but too angular. The 1982 has more to it, greater ripeness and length, but top among this trio is the 1983, a rustic, rich, authoritative wine with plenty of body and length.

J. L. GRIPPAT* * *

| 1983 St.-Joseph | ($9.99) | 84 |

A velvety wine with rich cherry and strawberry fruit flavors, medium to full body, this soft, round, plump wine has a lush texture, lingering finish, and is ideal for drinking over the next 4 years.

PAUL JABOULET AINÉ* * * * *

| 1982 Crozes-Hermitage Thalabert | ($5.99–$6.99) | 83 |

| 1983 Crozes-Hermitage Thalabert | ($9.99) | 86 |

| 1984 Crozes-Hermitage Thalabert | ($9.99) | 83 |

| 1985 Crozes-Hermitage Thalabert | ($9.99) | 86 |

| 1982 St.-Joseph Le Grand Pompée | ($5.49–$6.49) | 83 |

| 1983 St.-Joseph Le Grand Pompée | ($8.99) | 83 |

| 1984 St.-Joseph Le Grand Pompée | ($6.99) | 72 |

| 1985 St.-Joseph Le Grand Pompée | ($8.99) | 84 |

The 1982, 1983, and 1985 vintages were extremely successful for the firm of Paul Jaboulet. The 1982s are lower in acidity and much more forward, the 1983s are dark, broodingly tannic, and loaded with potential. As for the Grand Pompée, the 1982 is a perfect wine for casual drinking. Decadently fruity and lush, with lots of round, silky raspberry fruit and an intensely perfumed bouquet, it is a real crowd-pleaser. The 1983 is atypically big, dense, full, and rich. It will need 2–4 years of cellaring. The 1982 Crozes-Hermitage Thalabert, usually the best wine of this appellation, was the best wine from the Thalabert vineyard since 1978. Dark ruby, with a wild, spicy, plummy gamelike aroma, soft, richly fruity flavors and medium body, it should be drunk over the next 3–4 years. However, the 1983 and 1985 Thalaberts are the best Thalaberts I have ever tasted, including the much heralded 1978. Tasting like a really big Hermitage, they are quite black ruby in color, very ripe, rich, full-bodied and tannic, and have everything going for them. Both should last 10–12 years. The 1984s are light and ready to drink now. The 1985s are much more opulent and loaded with ripe fruit.

R. ROSTAING * * * * *

| 1982 St.-Joseph | ($6.99) | 75 |

I am fond of Rostaing's Côte Rôtie, but his St.-Joseph is only average in quality, with a straightforward, simple, fruity bouquet and average-intensity flavors. Drink over the next 1–2 years.

C. TARDY* * *

1981 Crozes-Hermitage Domaine des Pierrelles	($4.99)	82

1983 Crozes-Hermitage Domaine des Pierrelles	($5.99)	82

Both the 1981 and 1983 are very solid and substantial wines with good body and concentration, plenty of spicy Syrah fruit, and excellent color. They lack a little complexity, but offer gutsy, mouth-filling flavors.

R. TROLLAT* * *

1982 St.-Joseph	($7.99–$8.99)	84

1983 St.-Joseph	($7.99–$8.99)	85

These offerings from the very fine 1982 and 1983 vintages in the northern Rhône, from the highly respected grower Trollat, have more in common with a good burgundy than with a wine made from the Syrah grape. Medium to dark ruby in color, with lovely, moderately intense bouquets of crushed raspberries and strawberries, on the palate the wines are lush, very concentrated, medium- to full-bodied, clean, dry, with lingering finishes, and that ability to make one come back time and time again for another glass. Isn't that what's called complexity?

White Wines—Crozes-Hermitage and St.-Joseph

COURBIS* * *

1982 St.-Joseph	($8.99)	84

This fine offering exhibits big, robust, deep flavors of buttered nuts, ripe, spicy fruit, and a powerful finish. A chunky, fat wine with a lush, weighty feel on the palate, this is an excellent, robust wine for drinking with full-flavored dishes.

FAYOLLE* * *

1982 Crozes-Hermitage Pontaix	($6.99)	83

1983 Crozes-Hermitage Pontaix	($6.99)	82

Full-bodied, quite aromatic, very fruity, dry, and surprisingly powerful (14% alcohol), the 1982 Fayolle white Crozes-Hermitage is a big, juicy, well-balanced white wine for having with grilled fish or poultry.

The 1983 is almost as good, but a little more angular. Drink over the next 1–2 years.

GRIPPAT* * *

1982 St.-Joseph	($6.99–$7.49)	85
1983 St.-Joseph	($8.99)	86
1984 St.-Joseph	($8.99)	84
1985 St.-Joseph	($8.99)	86

These wines are beautiful white St.-Josephs with more of a resemblance to fine, expensive Condrieus than lesser-known white Rhônes. In particular, the 1985, 1983, and 1982 have a perfumed bouquet of ripe apricots, pears, and floral scents. On the palate, these wines are round and very lush, with a heady, high alcohol content, long finish, and layers of fruit. The 1984 is the lightest and is slightly less concentrated. Drink over the next 2 years.

PAUL JABOULET AINÉ* * * * *

1982 Crozes-Hermitage La Mule Blanche	($6.99)	83
1983 Crozes-Hermitage La Mule Blanche	($6.99)	84
1984 Crozes-Hermitage La Mule Blanche	($6.99)	78
1985 Crozes-Hermitage La Mule Blanche	($7.99)	86

These are the best examples of white Crozes-Hermitage that Jaboulet has made in recent memory. The 1982 and 1983 are similar in style, with rich, aromatic, spicy bouquets, luxurious, fruity flavors, and lovely balance. The 1982 is a trifle softer. The 1983 is fuller, bigger in size, and more concentrated; the 1985 even richer and more powerful than the 1983. The 1984 is tart, pleasant, but austere. I yearn for a grilled salmon or bass when I taste these wines.

RAYMOND TROLLAT* * *

| 1984 St.-Joseph | ($8.99) | 83 |

| 1983 St.-Joseph | ($8.49) | 84 |

Always reliable and fairly priced, Trollat's wines tend to be elegant
for the northern Rhône, with lovely peachlike bouquets. A moderately
intense, fruity, slightly spicy, perfumed aroma is followed by a wine
that has good acidity, a fleshy, interesting texture, and supple, generous flavors. Both are fine choices for fowl or fish. The 1983 is a trifle
longer on the palate.

Cornas

I doubt there is any writer alive today who has argued the case for
Cornas as fervently as I have. Of course, I have no interest other than
gustatory pleasure in seeing that the savage and wild wines of Cornas
find a place in your cellar. I believe passionately in these wines,
because they are anachronisms in the new world of wine—Cornas
producers have yet to realize the technology of the twentieth century.
A visit to the caves of Cornas growers such as Clape, Michel, Juge,
Barjac, and Voge is like stepping into a time machine and getting off
around the end of the American Civil War. The wines produced make
no compromises to consumers who want supple, forward, easy to
drink wine. Cornas is broodingly dark, rustic, sometimes coarse, mas-
sively proportioned in great vintages such as 1978 and 1983, brutally
tannic and nasty to taste, but after 8–12 years, the wine has a majestic
perfumed nose, rich, long, savory flavors, and just enough tannic kick
to remind you of its origins. Properly mature Cornas is one of the great
gustatory treasures. John Livingstone Learmonth, in his excellent
book *The Wines of the Rhône* (Faber and Faber, 1983), comments,
"the sight of a mature Cornas tumbling into a broad-based wine glass
is unforgettable. What richness, vigour and virility are portrayed in
that startling dash of colour – and the heady scent of blackcurrant and
raspberry that accompanies it is sufficient to surprise the most cos-
mopolitan of wine tasters." Indeed it is!

With respect to vintages, 1981 was not an especially good vintage
for Cornas, although Juge, Clape, and Barjac did well. Nineteen
eighty-two had the potential to be good, but the tremendous heat
during the harvest and vinification caused problems. Verset's 1982
Cornas looks to be the one outstanding success of this vintage. In 1983
the conditions were perfect, and virtually everyone made a wine that
they claimed to be the best since 1978, perhaps better. Nineteen

eighty-four was a more sobering type of vintage, but 1985 is again excellent. This recent vintage provides an excellent opportunity to become acquainted with the wines of Cornas.

G. DE BARJAC* * *

1981 Cornas	($12.49)	86
1982 Cornas	($12.49)	83
1983 Cornas	($12.99)	87
1984 Cornas	($10.99)	82

Barjac makes one of the most robust and coarse wines of Cornas. There is neither fining nor filtration here, and consequently he makes wines that are opaque in color, throw a heavy sediment, and age endlessly. The 1981 is a fiercely tannic, full-bodied, savage wine loaded with Syrah fruit, peppery, blackcurrant flavors, and abrasive tannins. Give it 6–10 years. The 1982 is much softer, will mature much earlier, and does not have the depth of the 1981. The 1983 is black in color, thick, deeply concentrated, and brutally tannic. It will live for decades. The 1984 is good, given the vintage, and can last 3–4 years.

A. CLAPE* * * * *

1981 Cornas	($11.99)	86
1982 Cornas	($11.99)	83
1983 Cornas	($14.00)	90
1984 Cornas	($12.00)	87
1985 Cornas	($15.00)	90

Unquestionably the finest producer of Cornas, Clape's wines tend to have the best balance and to lack the ferocious tannins found in the wines from his peers. His 1981 is a very good wine for the vintage, dark ruby, with a spicy, peppery bouquet and good, solid, deep flavors as well as full body. The 1984 is similar, but lighter. Neither is as good as the 1978, 1979, and 1980, but both should be very attractive by 1990. The 1982 is a little light in color, of medium weight, surprisingly soft, and a trifle diffuse. Surprisingly, it is not so good as the 1981. On the other hand, the 1983 is a blockbuster of a wine, with a gorgeous perfumed aroma of peppery, blackberry fruit and spicy oak. Massive in size, with tremendous power and extract, and a tannic, long, rich finish, it is a Rhône wine collector's item. It will need 6–10 years of cellaring. The 1985 is just as concentrated and deep, but not nearly so tannic as the 1983.

A. FUMAT* *

| 1981 Cornas | ($7.99) | 75 |

Peppery, slightly herbaceous, and medium ruby in color, this is a satisfactory wine, but it lacks interest and character. Surprisingly for a Cornas, it is ready to drink.

PAUL JABOULET AINÉ* * * * *

1981 Cornas	($9.99)	80
1982 Cornas	($9.99)	84
1983 Cornas	($10.99)	88
1984 Cornas	($9.99)	78
1985 Cornas	($10.99)	86

Jaboulet's Cornas tends to get overlooked in his fine lineup of Rhône Valley wines, but it can be fabulous. The 1962, 1972, and 1978 are vivid examples of Cornas at its best. The 1983 is one of the greatest Cornas wines from Jaboulet that I have ever tasted. Impenetrably black, with a colossal aroma of cassis, truffles and pepper, it is both voluptuous and firm on the palate, and has great weight and richness. It is worth waiting for as it will need 10 years of cellaring. The 1982 is a very good, typical Cornas, virile, tough, brawny, a trifle coarse, but rich, very full-bodied, and has the standard mouth-shattering tannin. It needs 10 years of cellaring. The 1981 is lighter, pleasant, in need of 3–4 years of cellaring, but is not nearly on the level of quality of the 1982s and 1983s. The 1984 is light, simple, and ready to drink. The 1985 is fat, ripe, loaded with fruit, and much more accessible than normal.

MARCEL JUGE* * *

| 1981 Cornas | ($11.99) | 86 |

| 1982 Cornas | ($9.49) | 84 |

| 1983 Cornas | ($10.99) | 88 |

| 1984 Cornas | ($10.99) | 86 |

Juge's cellar is well worth a visit, not only because of the good wine he makes, but also because he has the only alcoholic dog I have ever seen. This dog has a voracious appetite for young Cornas wine, and actually drinks from Juge's pipette or "wine thief." As he is another who believes neither in fining nor filtration, Juge's Cornas has more finesse than the wines of other producers. The 1981 won't be mature until 1988 or later, but it is a very flavorful, stylish wine with excellent texture and fruit. The 1982 is more successful than others, but the 1983 is absolutely superb. Its huge structure and density of both fruit and tannin will require quite a wait. The 1984 is lighter, but an unqualified success. Juge made a special hillside cuvée in 1985 that looks to be one of the greatest wines of Cornas I have tasted—keep an eye out for it.

N. VERSET* * * * *

| 1982 Cornas | ($8.99) | 86 |

| 1983 Cornas | ($9.99) | 90 |

| 1984 Cornas | ($9.99) | 86 |

The 1983 Verset Cornas is the best wine I have tasted from this small grower. The 1983 is a beauty and appears to be among the best wines made in Cornas in 1983. The wine has a dark black/ruby color, a ripe, gamy aroma intermingled with ripe cassis flavors, moderate tannins, and a clean, long, savory finish. It should be fully mature by 1990. The 1982 is similarly styled, rich, lush, long, and very seductive. The 1984 is somewhat of a sleeper, a broadly flavored, rich, supple, deeply fruity wine. Verset's 1985 is stupendous—join me in line for it.

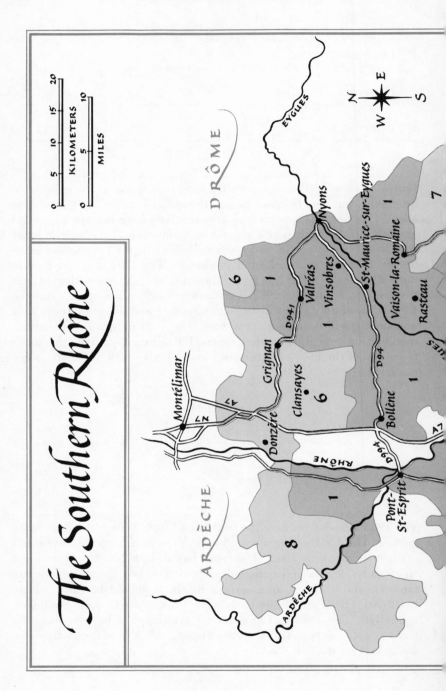

The Southern Rhône

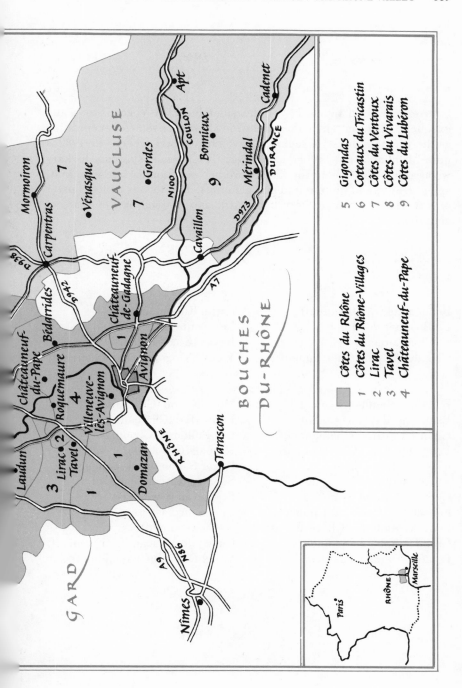

A. VOGE* * *

1982 Cornas	($8.99)	84

1983 Cornas	($9.99)	87

I have very fond memories of the splendid 1978 Voge Cornas and excellent 1979, but since then the wines have lost some concentration as the winemaking style seems to have changed. However, the 1982 is quite drinkable now. Very attractive, the bouquet suggests hickory wood and frying bacon; the flavors are not very tannic, but open knit, spicy, fruity, and quite round and generous. The 1983 is a blockbuster of a wine, very tannic, very backward, and in need of 7–8 years of cellaring.

A GUIDE TO SOUTHERN RHÔNE'S BEST PRODUCERS

* * * * * (OUTSTANDING PRODUCERS)

Beaucastel (Châteauneuf)
Le Bosquet des Papes
  (Châteauneuf)
Clos des Papes (Châteauneuf)

Fortia (Châteauneuf)
Les Gouberts (Gigondas)
Rayas (Châteauneuf)
Vieux Télégraphe (Châteauneuf)

* * * * (EXCELLENT PRODUCERS)

Beaumet Bonfils (Gigondas)
Beaurenard (Châteauneuf)
Chante Perdrix (Châteauneuf)
Les Clefs d'Or (Châteauneuf)
Clos du Mont-Olivet
  (Châteauneuf)
Georges Faraud (Gigondas)
Fonsalette (Côtes du Rhône)
Font de Michelle (Châteauneuf)
Grand Tinel (Châteauneuf)
Longue Toque (Gigondas)

Mont-Redon (Châteauneuf)
La Nerthe (Châteauneuf)
Les Pallières (Gigondas)
Raspail (Gigondas)
Roger Sabon (Châteauneuf)
Sénéchaux (Châteauneuf)
St.-Gayan (Gigondas)
Cuvée du Tastevin
  (Châteauneuf)
Cuvée du Vatican (Châteauneuf)
Vieux Donjon (Châteauneuf)

* * * *(GOOD PRODUCERS)*

d'Aqueria (Tavel)
P. Archimbaud (Gigondas)
P. Berard (Châteauneuf)
Busset (Côtes du Rhône)
Cabasse (Côtes du Rhône)
Cabrières (Châteauneuf)
Chante Cigale (Châteauneuf)
Chapoutier (Châteauneuf)
Clos de L'Oratoire
  (Châteauneuf)
Clos St.-Jean (Châteauneuf)
Combe (Gigondas)
Coudelet (Côtes du Rhône)
Devoy (Lirac)
Durieu (Châteauneuf)
Fines Roches (Châteauneuf)
Font du Loup (Châteauneuf)
Forcadière (Tavel)
La Fourmone (Côtes du Rhône)
La Gardine (Châteauneuf)
Genestière (Tavel)
Guigal (Châteauneuf)
Haut des Terres Blanches
  (Châteauneuf)

Paul Jaboulet Ainé
  (Châteauneuf)
Marcoux (Châteauneuf)
Montmirail (Gigondas)
Nalys (Châteauneuf)
Père Caboche (Châteauneuf)
J. Quiot (Châteauneuf)
Relagnes (Châteauneuf)
de Ségriès (Lirac)
La Solitude (Châteauneuf)
St.-Anne (Côtes du Rhône)
St. Roch (Lirac)
Trignon (Côtes du Rhône)
Trinquevedel (Tavel)
Trintignant (Châteauneuf)
Vaudieu (Châteauneuf)
La Vieille Ferme (Côtes du
  Rhône)
Vieux Chêne (Côtes du Rhône)
Vieux Julienne (Châteauneuf-
  du-Pape)
Vieux Lazaret (Châteauneuf)

* * *(AVERAGE PRODUCERS)*

Anselme (Châteauneuf)

Buying Strategy 1987–1988

For the wines of the northern Rhône, those who have the patience to cellar them should be looking for the remaining yet very tannic 1983s and newly arriving 1985s. For the Côte Rôties in 1985, a special effort is needed to secure some of these exceptional wines. Avoid the 1984 northern Rhônes as a general rule. For drinking now, the 1982s, powerful, rich, tannic 1983s, supple 1980s, and 1979s are the vintages in which to concentrate your efforts. The 1978s, should you be lucky enough to find any, are rare and extraordinary.

For the southern Rhône, all the generic Côtes du Rhônes are made to be drunk within 4–5 years of the vintage. So look for the 1982s, 1983s, and delicious 1985s. Anything older is definitely a risk unless it is a great Côtes du Rhône such as Fonsalette or Coudelet. For

Gigondas and Châteauneuf-du-Pape, the vintages to buy are 1981, 1983, and 1985. Also, there are a number of surprisingly good wines from 1984. Some 1982s can offer charming drinking, but the best two vintages for mature drinking over the next several years are 1979 and 1980. If you are lucky enough to see any 1978s or 1981s languishing on retailers' shelves, you may want to acquire them, for they can represent the pinnacle of winemaking in Châteauneuf. Some 1985s will have the potential to be as good as the greatest 1978s, 1979s, 1981s, or 1983s. The 1985 white wines from Châteauneuf as well as other appellations are excellent, but should be drunk up over the next year.

Southern Rhône

Châteauneuf-du-Pape

With an average production of one million cases, Châteauneuf-du-Pape easily has the largest production of the serious wines of the Rhône Valley. It is also the unofficial capital of this vast wine region. The wonderful city of Avignon, a major tourist attraction, is only 14 kilometers to the south, so many a traveler has tasted the roundness and heady power of a Châteauneuf-du-Pape.

Up until four or five years ago, the highest quality Châteauneuf-du-Pape wines, those produced from single vineyards and estate bottled, were difficult to find in America. What were usually encountered on the retailers' shelves were *négociant* wines, many of which were simple, grapy trash, hideously thick and heavy, and excessively high in alcohol. Many of these wines still remain, but the new wave of quality-conscious importers and growing numbers of smarter wine consumers have resulted in easier access to a plethora of top-quality Châteauneuf-du-Papes that offer outstanding value and quality. The truth is that there are at least three dozen estates here making serious, delicious, excellent wine.

The wine consumer, in order to understand the wines of Châteauneuf-du-Pape, must first realize that, like all wine-producing regions, the range in quality is vast, but just as important, the styles of wines in Châteauneuf-du-Pape can be dramatically different. If you seek a round, generous, soft wine that is ready to drink when released, there are numerous estates—Clos de l'Oratoire, Maucoil, Vieux Lazaret, Domaine de Nalys, Marcoux, Domaine de Beaurenard, Domaine du Père Caboche, and Vieux Télégraphe—all of which produce wines that are ideal for immediate gratification. If you prefer a rich, full-bodied, complex, intense wine that must be cellared for 5–10 years after the vintage in order to develop fully, look to Beaucastel, Les Cailloux, Clefs d'Or, Bosquet des Papes, Clos des Papes, Fortia, La Nerte, Rayas, Chante Cigale, and Chante Perdrix, a few of the properties that produce very full, tannic, deep wines that can be drunk young but improve with aging.

Châteauneuf-du-Pape's appellation laws permit 13 different grape varieties to be grown, but in practical terms, most estates use no more than three or four major grapes for their red wines. Topping the list in grape popularity is the ubiquitous Grenache, followed by Mourvèdre, Syrah, and Cinsault. The red grape varieties that some growers proclaim will be planted in more abundance in the future are Vaccarèse and Counoise. The Grenache grape provides color, alcohol, and fleshiness, yet its shortcoming is its vulnerability to oxidation. Mourvèdre provides great color, great firmness, tannic richness, and the ability to age, but in its youth it is nasty to taste and often eccentric to smell. The Syrah provides rich fruit, firmness, and complexity, and Cinsault gives a certain dimension to a wine's bouquet, but lacks color and richness. A small amount of white wine is made in Châteauneuf-du-Pape, and where the vinification is done properly, the wine can be extremely full, flavorful, and quite interesting. Vieux Télégraphe, Nalys, Père Caboche, Mont-Redon, and Font de Michelle make some of the best modern-style white Châteauneuf-du-Pape available. However, white Châteauneufs rarely age past 4–5 years, and the general rule of thumb, unless you are drinking a Beaucastel or Clefs d'Or, is to drink them within 3–4 years of the vintage.

Red Châteauneuf is a fall and winter wine; its full-bodied strength (13.5% alcohol and up is normal) makes it a perfect match for game, beef, lamb, stews, and grilled meats. White Châteauneuf would overpower a delicate fish course, and it is too full for using as an apéritif, but when matched with fowl or with grilled foods, particularly mesquite or wood-grilled fish or chicken, it is a marriage that is likely to provide a lasting memory.

Red Wines—Châteauneuf-du-Pape

L. BARROT (CUVÉE DU TASTEVIN) * * * *

1979	($9.99)	88
1980	($8.99)	84

1981	($9.99) 87

1983	($9.99) 88

There are two growers' associations in Châteauneuf-du-Pape in which the producers share bottling and storage premises. One is Les Reflets and the other is Prestige et Tradition. Barrot belongs to the latter and is one of the top growers of this group. His wines have good aging potential as well as the typical Châteauneuf-du-Pape fullness and peppery, spicy bouquet. The 1979, 1981, and 1983 are all quite full-bodied, with big, peppery, blackberry bouquets, ripe yet tannic flavors, a large frame, and aging potential of 5–7 years. The 1980 is even more tannic, quite full-bodied, surprisingly backward for a 1980, yet it has potential. The 1981 is the best of these: black/ruby, rich, full-bodied, deep, with 10–12 years of further aging potential.

BEAUCASTEL (PERRIN)* * * * *

1981	($11.99) 93

1982	($8.49) 84

1983	($16.99) 92

1984	($14.49) 87

Beaucastel makes Châteauneuf-du-Pape's longest-lived and most profound and complex wine. It is also one of the greatest of France. Perhaps the most memorable tasting I have ever attended was a vertical tasting of Beaucastel from 1942 to 1978, which for those in attendance proved beyond a reasonable doubt that at around age 8 or 9 a red Beaucastel begins to unfold its richness and complexity, at age 12–15 it is simply magnificent, and at 20–25 years is one of the truly great gustatory pleasures. It is, however, a wine for collectors since it needs considerable time, unless of course, the vintage produced light-bodied, soft wines. That's just the case in 1982 and 1984. I had expected Beaucastel to declassify its entire crop in 1982, but after an extremely strict selection (50% was sold to *négociants*), a small amount of 1982 was produced; it has turned out much better than I anticipated. Resembling the 1973, only lighter, the 1982 is fruity, soft, charming and, unlike most Beaucastels, can be drunk immediately. It is an ideal wine for restaurants. The 1984 is similarly styled, only a trifle deeper. The 1981 is the best Châteauneuf-du-Pape of the vintage and has enormous potential. Dark ruby/purple with a bouquet of blackberries, pepper, flowers, and tarry scents, this full-bodied, deeply concentrated wine should be at its best in 1991 and last for another 15–20 years. The 1983 is superb, rich, intense, full-bodied, and will be quite long-lived. The 1984 is slightly higher in acidity than normal, but rich and complex, with 5–10 years' aging potential.

BEAURENARD (COULON)* * * *

1981	($11.99)	84
1982	($11.99)	78
1983	($11.99)	85

I would like to score Beaurenard higher, because I sincerely enjoy the wine for its charm, soft, exuberant fruitiness and round, warm, generous flavors. However, it is a straightforward wine with little complexity. Made in a style that is clearly aimed for early consumption, Beaurenard is supple, fruity, with plenty of silky, lush flavors suggesting ripe black cherries. The 1982 is too much like a simple grapy Beaujolais, but has charm. It should be drunk over the next 2 years. The 1981 and 1983 are virtually identical in style, full-bodied, gushing with soft, round fruit, a savory, long finish, and very few tannins. However, the 1983 is a trifle more rich.

BOSQUET DES PAPES* * * * *

1985	($14.00)	91
1984	($12.00)	86
1983	($12.99)	90

The 1985 Châteauneuf-du-Pape is explosively rich, deeply colored, has oodles of blackberry fruit, a powerful presence on the palate, long, deep and quite impressive. The balance, depth and complexity are there; it will need 5–6 years. The 1984 is, along with Chante Perdrix, Vieux Télégraphe and Beaucastel, one of the best I tasted, gloriously lush and fruity and hardly the type of wine one suspects was produced from an off year. It has excellent color, a fragrant perfume of rich, chocolatey, plummy fruit, a forward personality, and soft, lush finish. Drink it over the next 5–6 years while you await the considerable pleasures of the 1983. A year and a half ago, the 1983 stood out in a big tasting of Châteauneuf-du-Papes put on for me by the growers. It continues to impress me greatly. Dark ruby in color with a gorgeous fragrance of blackcurrants, fruit, tobacco and exotic spices, it is quite rich on the palate, moderately tannic, and impeccably balanced. I would defer gratification to 1987 and beyond.

LES CAILLOUX (BRUNEL)* * * *

1980	($8.99–$11.99)	80
1981	($8.99–$11.99)	84
1983	($11.99)	87
1984	($11.99)	84

The 1980 has average color, a herbaceous, spicy, peppery, faintly fruity bouquet. On the palate it is well structured but a trifle austere and lean. It should be mature now. The 1981 has more richness and concentration, a moderately intense, peppery, spicy bouquet, medium to full body, and a good finish. It can easily be drunk now, but will get better over the next 1–2 years. The 1983 is the best of these, full-bodied, rich, with a spicebox aroma. The 1984 is a success for the vintage.

CHANTE CIGALE* * *

1978	($15.95)	88
1979	($9.95)	82
1981	($10.95)	86
1983	($11.95)	78

I always find an intensely herbal, olive-scented aroma intermingled with blackberry fruit, spices, and earthy scents in the wines of Chante Cigale. The 1978 is top-class, still big, broodingly opaque, chocolatey, herbal, peppery, and very full-bodied and rich on the palate. The wine can be drunk now, but try to keep your hands off it until 1988–89. The 1979, which the proprietor, Favier, thinks is better, is overtly herbaceous, minty and very, very peppery. It is good, but lacks the dimension of the 1978. The 1981 is closer in style to the 1978 than the 1979, rich, supple, with plenty of fruit and length on the palate. The 1983 is not a success here since it lacks some color and is rather weak on the palate.

CHANTE PERDRIX* * * *

1979	($9.99–$13.99)	86
1981	($9.99–$13.99)	86
1982	($9.49–$12.99)	80
1983	($11.99)	90
1984	($10.99)	88

Chante Perdrix produces Châteauneuf-du-Pape wines that by any standards of this appellation are huge, chewy, black ruby-colored wines loaded with viscous, blackberry, occasionally herbal-scented and flavored fruit, as well as a hefty dose of alcohol. Sometimes the wines can be overpowering, and even when well balanced Chante Perdrix is a wine to reserve for cheese. The 1982 showed very poorly at a big tasting put on for me in Châteauneuf-du-Pape in 1984, but in recent tastings it has fared much better. However, the 1984, 1983, 1981, and 1979 are authentic examples of Chante Perdrix's powerful style of Châteauneuf-du-Pape. Very deeply colored, with thick, chocolatey, herbaceous flavors, quite full-bodied and spicy, peppery, and chocolatey to smell, these big, aggressive wines are unique, and may even be too much for some people. I thought the 1981 and 1983 had an edge in complexity and balance over the 1979, but these wines are immense and chewy and will last for 5–9 years. Look out for the 1985, a great success for the vintage.

CHAPOUTIER (LA BERNARDINE)* * *

N.V. La Barbe-Rac (A Luxury Cuvée)	($30.00)	89
1978	($10.50)	70
1982	($7.50)	76
1983	($8.99)	83

Two of these Châteauneuf-du-Papes are quite mediocre. The 1982, from a mediocre to poor vintage, is shockingly better than the 1978, from a great vintage. The 1978 is tired, flat, and lacking interest. The 1982 is soft, straightforward, fruity, and charming in an innocuous way. The 1983, however, offers more flesh and muscle with much better depth of fruit. Chapoutier's limited-edition, luxury cuvée, the Barbe-Rac, is quite rich and intense, with great length.

LES CLEFS D'OR (DEYDIER)* * * *

1979	($12.95)	85
1980	($11.95)	83
1981	($12.95)	86
1982	($12.99)	82
1983	($12.95)	87

One of my favorite producers of Châteauneuf-du-Pape, the reclusive Deydier, produces an old-style, ripe, rich, full-bodied wine with a lot of extract, power, and aging potential. Even in a light year such as 1982, Deydier obtained a measure of concentration, a ripe berry, tarry fruitiness, and enough tannin to warrant 2–3 years of cellaring. The 1981 is much richer, with a deep-scented, spicy aroma, full-bodied, black cherry flavors, and firm tannins. It needs 5 more years to be at its best. The 1980 is a marriage of styles between the lighter 1982 and fuller, bigger 1981. It should be aged for 4 years. The 1979 is similar to the 1981, only a trifle less rich and more austere, but very well made and interesting. The 1983 is Deydier's best wine since his great 1978. It is a rich, very concentrated wine with at least a decade of aging potential.

CLOS DU MONT-OLIVET (SABON)* * * *

1981	($9.95)	85
1983	($12.99)	87
1984	($12.99)	85

Clos du Mont-Olivet is normally an excellent Châteauneuf-du-Pape, but it rarely comes my way. The 1978 and 1976 were especially notable, particularly the latter, in a year when the wines of the southern Rhône were notoriously irregular. Both the 1981 and 1983 are quite backward, tannic, and will probably merit a higher score in 5–6 years, when they are mature. The bouquet of oak and ripe cherries is first-class; full-bodied, tannic, and needing time, these are wines for the patient. Keep an eye out for this domaine's 1985, an astonishingly great wine that most of the local cognoscenti feel is the best of the vintage.

CLOS DE L'ORATOIRE (AMOUROUX)* * *

1978	($9.99)	83
1979	($9.99)	82
1983	($12.99)	82

One of the great names of Châteauneuf-du-Pape, the wine of Clos de L'Oratoire has changed considerably in style over recent years, moving further and further away from the big, rich, dense, traditional style to a Beaujolais-like, soft, very fruity and charming wine that is best drunk within 5–6 years of the vintage. The 1978 is such a wine, effusively fruity, with a bouquet and flavor of jammy cherry fruit. It is fully mature. The 1979 and 1983 are quite similar, only lighter, but very fruity, quite attractive, and best consumed over the next year.

CLOS DES PAPES (AVRIL)* * * * *

1980	($10.95)	84
1981	($12.99)	88
1982	($9.95)	82
1983	($12.99)	87

A highly respected estate, Paul Avril's Clos des Papes produces tannic, ageworthy wines in a very traditional manner. The 1982 is light yet very fruity and charming. The 1981, however, is a big, ripe, dense wine with excellent color, a seductive bouquet of ripe black cherries and wood, firm, full-bodied flavors, and a healthy dosage of tannin. It should be given 3–4 years of cellaring. The 1980 is a success, with a ripe, spicy, cherry-scented bouquet, and richly fruity, full-bodied flavors admirably backed by tannin. The 1983 is also very promising, with a rich black cherry, peppery bouquet and full-bodied flavors.

FONT DU LOUP (MELIA)* * *

| 1981 | ($13.99) | 89 |

| 1982 | ($12.00) | 80 |

Two very attractive wines for drinking over the next 1–2 years. The 1982 is medium ruby, with an intense aroma of strawberries. On the palate, it is easygoing, charming, and soft. The 1981 has much deeper color, a ripe aroma of peaches and oranges, a ripe Grenache smell, and is quite full-bodied, with an alcoholic kick, and soft, lush finish. It is splendidly concentrated and is a privilege to drink.

FONT DE MICHELLE (GONNET)* * * *

| 1981 | ($8.99) | 86 |

| 1982 | ($8.49) | 83 |

| 1983 | ($9.99) | 87 |

| 1984 | ($9.99) | 85 |

An up and coming estate that first began to estate bottle its wines in 1974, Font de Michelle has consistently impressed me in tastings. The 1982, one of the top wines of this difficult vintage, is loaded with attractively ripe, plummy fruit, has surprisingly good color for the vintage, and a round, richly fruity texture. Drink it over the next 2 years. The 1981 and 1983 continue their impressive tradition with rich, full-intensity bouquets of ripe fruit, black pepper, and spices. Full-bodied, generously flavored and heady, these big wines will keep for 5–8 years. The 1984 is also above average, a peppery, spicy, fruity, alluring sort of wine.

FORTIA* * * * *

| 1980 | ($11.95) | 85 |

| 1981 | ($15.95) | 88 |

| 1983 | ($15.95) | 87 |

Historically the most significant Châteauneuf-du-Pape estate, Fortia is the property of Baron LeRoy de Boiseaumarié, whose father founded the *appellation contrôlée* system in France. The wine is generally one of the best in Châteauneuf-du-Pape, almost on the level of Beaucastel or Rayas. The 1978 is a marvelous wine; 1983 rivals it. The 1981 is one of the top 1981s, rich with a ripe bouquet of raspberries and violets; this wine is big, tannic, full-bodied, and in need of 3–4 years of cellaring. The 1980 Fortia has a telltale, intense raspberry, peppery bouquet, lush, ripe flavors, and good, deep, dark color. The 1983 is even deeper and more ageworthy, very perfumed and rich, a top success for the vintage.

LA GARDINE* * *

1978	($16.00)	80
1981	($14.00)	86
1983	($14.00)	84

La Gardine produces a chunky, smoky, heavy style of wine that is impressively colored, very weighty and alcoholic, with chewy, viscous flavors. The 1978 is thick, ripe, almost portlike, and interesting, although it is hard to imagine drinking this wine with food. The 1981 is this estate's strongest effort in 5–6 years—a rich, chewy, leather-scented wine with a lot of muscle. The 1983 is much in the same style, though not so concentrated.

GRAND TINEL (JEUNE)* * * *

1979	($10.99)	85
1980	($10.99)	82
1981	($10.99)	90
1982	($11.99)	78
1983	($11.99)	87

Grand Tinel makes consistently fine Châteauneuf-du-Papes that are usually characterized by a very dark color, a ripe peach and raspberry-scented bouquet, and full-bodied, relatively rich, concentrated flavors. Most Grand Tinels need at least 5–6 years of cellaring, and are best drunk before they reach age 12. The 1979 is very full, with a complex bouquet of smoky, raspberry fruit, and rich, full-bodied flavors. It will improve for 3–5 more years. The 1980 is good, but straightforward and rather one-dimensional. The 1981 has excellent depth, is a savory, full, very attractive, big-styled wine for drinking over the next 3–5 years. The 1983, rich and full-bodied, is potentially the best of this group, a very powerful, long, deep wine made in a traditional style.

GUIGAL* * *

1979	($14.49)	84
1981	($16.49)	86
1982	($14.49)	87

Guigal's Châteauneuf-du-Papes have the house style imprinted on them. The wines are very dark in color, with ripe, rich berry aromas, solid tannic, full-bodied flavors, and good finishes. They are lush, deep, opulent wines, yet are clearly capable of aging 7–10 years in the bottle. The 1982 has the most concentration of the above trio and looks to be the best wine from this appellation, an irony given the fact that most people tend to think that the growers can do a better job in off years than a *négociant*.

HAUT DES TERRES BLANCHES (DIFFONTY)* * *

1979	($8.49)	86
1981	($8.49)	84

Rémy Diffonty produces very stylish, complex wines with plenty of flavor, tarry, earthy, almost truffle-scented bouquets and round, soft, lush textures. The 1979 is top-notch, but has quickly disappeared from the marketplace; it is better than Diffonty's 1978. The 1981 is lighter in color, less rich and fruity, but still very attractive, with plenty of peppery, berry fruit, a bouquet suggestive of caramel and spices, and soft, lush, nicely concentrated flavors. Drink the 1981 over the next 3 years, the 1979 over the next 6.

PAUL JABOULET AINÉ (LES CÈDRES)* * *

1980	($10.99)	84
1982	($10.99)	83

1983	($12.99)	82

1985	($12.99)	84

Jaboulet's Châteauneuf-du-Pape seems to get overlooked when the firm's wines are discussed. However, his Les Cèdres can be magnificent. The 1961 is still stunning, as is the 1967. The 1982 Les Cèdres will certainly be considered a success for the vintage. Fresh, fruity, with oodles of fat, supple flavors, and light tannins, this wine is destined to be drunk young, preferably within 3 years. The 1980 is slightly richer, with a big, ripe raspberry-dominated bouquet, a peppery, spicy quality, and solid, rich, ripe fruit. The 1983 and 1985 have good black cherry fruit, full body, and a long finish, though the 1985 is slightly more concentrated.

MONT-REDON* * * *

1978	($11.99)	84

1980	($10.99)	75

1981	($14.99)	86

1982	($14.99)	80

1983	($14.99)	86

For those who remember the old-style Mont-Redon wines from such vintages as 1961, 1955, and 1949, all of which remain quite lively and brilliant examples of Châteauneuf-du-Pape, the new, lighter style this estate adopted in the '70s will prove a disappointment, for it has robbed Mont-Redon of much of its character. At times the wine has resembled a sound, run-of-the-mill Côtes du Rhône, which is a tragedy to say the least. The 1978 and 1980 taste mature, fruity, soft, and very pleasant. The 1978 and 1981 should continue to drink well for 2 years; the 1980's future is now—they are clean, technically correct, but less intense than in the past. However, all this may be changing since the excellent 1981, 1983, and 1985 are clearly the finest wines this estate has made in over a decade. All three wines have a rich, smoky, raspberry-scented nose, and long, lush flavors. An estate on the rebound, I hope.

LA NERTHE* * * *

1980	($12.99)	84
1981	($12.99)	87
1983	($12.99)	86

La Nerthe can be one of the very best estates of Châteauneuf-du-Pape. La Nerthe's wine is quite full-bodied, unsually high in alcohol, with a first-class aroma of floral and ripe raspberry/blackberry scents. These tend to be powerful wines that are clearly very traditionally made and normally require 5–7 years to be at their best. Neither the 1980 nor excellent 1981 are up to the superb 1978 or 1979 La Nerthes. However, both are serious wines that clearly merit the interest of Rhône wine enthusiasts. The 1983 is full and rich in the nose. Rich, extroverted, powerful, and voluptuous, it is the best La Nerthe since 1978 and 1981.

PÈRE CABOCHE* * *

1981	($8.99)	83
1983	($9.99)	84
1981 Elisabeth Chambellan	($10.49)	85

The enthusiastic Jean-Pierre Boisson runs the Domaine Père Caboche, which makes Châteauneuf-du-Pape in a forward, rich, ripe, fruity style. Given this style, the wines are best drunk within 5–6 years of the vintage. The 1981 and 1983 wines of Père Caboche are soft, direct, quite enjoyable, fruity, medium- to full-bodied, with hardly any tannins. The best wine of this trio is the 1981 Elisabeth Chambellan, which is filled with concentrated, round, spicy, peppery, black cherry fruit. It is full-bodied, has a long, rich, lush finish, and should be drunk over the next 2 years.

JÉRÔME QUIOT* * *

1981	($7.99)	82
1982	($7.99)	80

1983	($8.99) 78

The 1981 and 1983 are extremely pleasing styles of Châteauneuf-du-Pape. Quiot has produced a fragrant, ripe, almost sweet wine, with round, generous, voluptuous, fruity flavors that show little tannin, but with a very pleasing, soft texture, and long finish. Both wines are delicious now and should be drunk over the next 2 years. The 1982 is soft, fruity, very pleasant and charming, but simple, a trifle one-dimensional.

RAYAS* * * * *

1978	($25.00) 93
1979	($25.00) 91
1981	($25.00) 90
1983	($25.00) 91

The reclusive and eccentric Jacques Reynaud oversees what some observers feel is the best wine of Châteauneuf-du-Pape. These four wines do justice to the fame Rayas has among Châteauneuf-du-Pape fanciers. The 1978 has been available for some time, but the high price has kept it from jumping off merchants' shelves, since it is certainly not lacking in quality. Still very young, very deep ruby in color, with a very concentrated, powerful, weighty feel on the palate, this big wine is simply loaded with potential. Lay it away for at least 5–6 more years. In comparison, the 1979 is actually more attractive now while being every bit as rich, full-bodied, and complex as the 1978; but the tannin is less intrusive. The 1979 should drink beautifully and improve for at least 7–10 years. The 1981 is gorgeously aromatic now, with layers of ripe, decadently rich fruit. It should drink well for 10 years. The 1983 is very forward, yet still packed with fruit and flavor, and while quite outstanding, will not have the aging potential of the other three vintages. Consumers should look for the second label of Rayas, Pignan. In vintages such as 1981 and 1983 Pignan is difficult to distinguish from Rayas.

RELAGNES* * *

1982	($12.99)	83
1983	($12.99)	85

In 1982 the Domaine des Relagnes produced a very attractive wine in a vintage that was generally unkind to the *vignerons* of Châteauneuf-du-Pape. A bouquet of ripe cherries and peppery spice is quite seductive and intense. On the palate, the wine is ready to drink, with clean, soft, very fruity flavors, and a surprisingly good, lengthy finish. The 1983, a knockout from the cask, rich, dense, spicy, and very complex, is closed in and less impressive from the bottle. This little-known estate merits much more attention.

ROGER SABON* * * *

1981	($7.49)	86
1983	($9.99)	86

The 1981 from Sabon is a classic Châteauneuf-du-Pape. This big, tightly knit wine has a firm but promising bouquet of berry fruit, black pepper, and tarry scents. On the palate, the wine is deep, rich, yet tannic and still quite youthful. The 1983 is very burgundylike, with an expansive bouquet of cherry fruit and spices—it is very seductive.

VIEUX LAZARET* * *

1981	($8.99)	83
1983	($8.99)	84

Vieux Lazaret produces very fruity, round, supple wines that are meant for immediate consumption. Both the 1981 and 1983 are quite fruity, medium- to full-bodied, with plenty of ripe berry fruit in the bouquet and flavor, a certain sweetness, and a generous, soft finish. A good, charming, rather uncomplicated style of Châteauneuf-du-Pape, both should be drunk over the next 3 years.

VIEUX TÉLÉGRAPHE* * * * *

1981	($9.49)	85
1982	($7.99)	84

1983	($9.99)	90

1984	($9.99)	86

Although Brunier has significantly lightened his style of Châteauneuf-du-Pape (the magnificent 1978 was the best of the old style), his wines remain among the most consistently well made and delicious Châteauneuf-du-Papes produced. The 1981 is a lush, full-bodied, deeply fruity wine with enough stuffing and tannin to provide enjoyable drinking over the next 5–6 years. The 1982 vies for the top wine of the appellation in that vintage. It has very good color, a big, plummy, spicy, leafy-scented aroma, fat, round, generous, sweet flavors, and little tannins in evidence. It is undoubtedly a top success in this difficult vintage and should be drunk now. The 1983 is Brunier's best wine since the 1978; it is a big, fragrant, supple and rich wine. The 1984 is well balanced, fruity, elegant, and should drink well for 4–5 years.

White Wines—Châteauneuf-du-Pape

Only a tiny amount of white Châteauneuf-du-Pape is made, but when it is vinified at cool temperatures and quickly bottled and quickly drunk, it can be quite delicious. The top producers are Beaucastel, which makes the wine that lasts the longest, Vieux Télégraphe, Clefs d'Or, Nalys, Quiot, Font de Michelle, and occasionally Père Caboche and La Nerthe. As a general rule, the 1985s and 1983s are superior to the 1984s.

Beaucastel (Perrin) 1983	($10.99–$13.95)	86

Beaucastel (Perrin) 1984	($10.99–$13.95)	83

Beaucastel (Perrin) 1985	($19.95)	90

Beaucastel's white wine, which is 80% Roussanne, is the longest-lived dry white wine of the southern Rhône. I recently tasted the 1954, 1962, and 1971, which were all in stunning condition. The 1983, while not as opulent and rich as the 1982, has an intriguing bouquet of straw, mineral scents, and pears. On the palate, it is full-bodied, admirably concentrated, and quite well balanced. It needs 2–3 years to really open up. The 1984 is light, pleasant, and crisp, but, due to the vintage, lacks some concentration. The 1985 is powerful, rich, and truly outstanding.

Les Cailloux (Brunel) 1985   ($10.95)   86

Deep, intensely fruity, ripe, long, and alcoholic, this is the best white
wine yet from Les Cailloux. It is a solid, powerful wine that has no
flaws.

Clefs d'Or (Deydier) 1985   ($12.95)   85

A highly aromatic wine with a full-blown bouquet suggesting tropical
fruit, the 1985 Clefs d'Or is an exotic wine with a bit too much alcohol
in the finish, but is ripe, full, and distinctive. Drink over the next 2
years.

Nalys 1985   ($10.99)   86

This is a delicious wine with clean, fresh, fruity aromas of light intensity, crisp acidity, and good depth. It is solid, crisp, and direct. Drink
over the next 1–2 years.

La Nerthe 1983   ($10.99)   82

La Nerthe 1985   ($10.99)   85

La Nerthe's popularity for big, rich, full-tilt red wines seems to have
carried over to the 1985 white wine, which has interesting pear and
pineapple flavors, plenty of body, and a hefty dose of alcohol. In
contrast, the 1983 has an attractive sweet cotton-candy-like bouquet,
good acidity, and despite some heady alcohol in the finish, it seems a
much better wine.

Quiot 1985   ($9.99)   82

Another fresh, very correct wine, with a plump, fat, alcoholic feel on
the palate, a slightly perfumed bouquet, and good, crisp acidity and
balance, the 1985 Quiot should be drunk over the next 2 years.

R. Ogier 1984   ($6.99–$7.99)   55

This white Châteauneuf-du-Pape could be a wine from anywhere in
the world. It is simple, lacking in flavor, high in alcohol, and just
downright poor.

Père Caboche (Boisson) 1983   ($9.49)   75

Père Caboche (Boisson) 1985   ($9.49)   84

One of the better producers of white Châteauneuf-du-Pape, Père Caboche usually makes aromatic, fresh, lively, rich wines. The 1983

showed quite an unexpected degree of mediocrity, with high acidity and average-intensity, nondescript flavors. On the other hand, the 1985 is fragrant, full-bodied, with nicely concentrated fresh fruit and floral scents and flavors. It should be drunk over the next 2 years.

Vieux Télégraphe (Brunier) 1985   ($9.99–$11.99)   90

Brunier produces only 300 cases of this white Châteauneuf-du-Pape. Made entirely from the Grenache Blanc grape, it tastes like it came from the Viognier grape. Full-bodied (13.5% alcohol), luxuriously opulent, decadently fruity, this round, silky wine has layers of fruit. Like most good white Châteauneuf-du-Papes, this wine is a perfect choice for dishes cooked over the pungent and aromatic mesquite wood.

Gigondas

The Name Gigondas has such a nice, easy ring to it that I am surprised the wines of this region—adjacent to and just slightly to the northeast of Châteauneuf-du-Pape—have not attained more success in America. Like the wines of Châteauneuf-du-Pape, they are excellent values, and contrary to what most people think, can live and improve for a decade or more when vinified traditionally. Gigondas is almost always a big, full-bodied, alcoholic wine, so it is best treated as a robust and generously flavored Châteauneuf-du-Pape.

DE GOUR DE CHAULE (BEAUMET-BONFILS)* * * *

1979	($9.99)	87
1981	($9.99)	86
1982	($9.99)	84

A sensational producer of Gigondas, these wines have bouquets of cedary, ripe fruit, and are lively, robust wines filled with aromas and flavors of black cherry and pepper. Luscious and fat on the palate, with a wonderfully rich, full, well-balanced feel, these big, complex Gigondas are as good as they come. The 1981 and 1979 are better than the 1982.

R. COMBE* * *

1982 L'Oustaou Fauquet   ($5.99–$6.49)   80

Attractive berry fruit and spicy, herbal, fennel aromas intermingle to provide a nice backdrop. On the palate, the wine is solid, medium- to full-bodied, and cleanly made. The short finish detracts from an otherwise decent effort.

GEORGES FARAUD* * * *

1981	($9.99)	85
1982	($9.99)	87
1983	($9.99)	86

This ancient winemaker produces inky-colored, very peppery, very concentrated wines that can age and improve for 10 or more years. Both his 1983 and 1982 are extremely powerful, cedary, peppery, with interest and personalities, layers of flavor, and are quite full-bodied. The 1982 is the richest of the wines. The 1981 is a little vegetal in aroma, but ripe and backward.

LES GOUBERTS* * * * *

1979	($9.99)	90
1980	($7.49)	86
1981	($9.95)	90
1983	($9.99)	83
1984	($9.99)	87

Virtually every Rhône wine observer agrees that this is an up and coming estate, meticulously run by Jean-Pierre Cartier, and fully capable of making exquisite Gigondas. His wines are nearly black in color, with a full-blown, peppery, intense blackcurrant bouquet, a dense, deep, very concentrated, chocolatey fruitiness. His 1979 and 1981 Gigondas are monumental wines, his 1983 somewhat diluted by his high standards. His 1984 is a notable success and his 1985 a smashing success which will not be released until 1988.

GUIGAL* * *

1981	($8.99)	86
1982	($9.99)	86

| 1983 | ($9.99) | 87 |

Marcel Guigal's Gigondas seem to get better with each vintage. The 1981 is loaded with peppery, rich fruit, is full-bodied, quite complex, and very long on the palate. Drinkable now, but destined to live 4–7 more years. The 1982 is loaded with peppery scents and raspberry fruit, is opulent and luscious on the palate. The 1983 is truly outstanding, long, rich, dense, with great extract and character.

PAUL JABOULET AINÉ* * *

1978	($12.00)	85
1979	($9.00)	87
1983	($8.79)	78
1985	($9.99)	84

I have seen all four of these vintages of Jaboulet's very good Gigondas on the retail shelves, and there is no doubt that the wine to get is the 1979, which is still very young, rich, and full. The 1978 is more evolved, with an attractive, gamey, raspberry fruitiness, and full body. The 1983 and 1985 are straightforward in style, peppery, spicy, and not yet as complex as either the 1979 or 1978.

LONGUE-TOQUE* * * *

| 1981 | ($6.49) | 76 |
| 1982 | ($7.99) | 84 |

Longue-Toque is a very highly regarded estate, particularly by John Livingstone Learmonth in his exquisite book, *The Wines of the Rhône*. The 1981 Longue-Toque is an above-average wine, but is hardly inspirational. A leafy, stalky aroma and high acid flavors are surprisingly austere. It is certainly an interesting wine, but nothing special in 1981. The 1982 is much fruitier, long, ripe, and supple. The unreleased 1985 looks to be spectacular in quality.

OGIER

| 1981 Luc de Mayreuil | ($5.99) | 52 |

Hot, very alcoholic, oxidized aromas are hardly the stuff that dreams or even good wines are made of. A poor wine with no resemblance to Gigondas. Avoid.

MONTMIRAIL* * *

1978	($10.99)	83
1979	($9.99)	80
1981	($9.99)	84

Montmirail produces big, chunky, densely colored wines that seem to lack complexity and for some reason are quite overpriced vis-à-vis other Gigondas wines. The 1978 is a huge, heavy wine that has plenty of power and character, but becomes a little overbearing in the glass. The 1979 is quite big, but does not have the depth of the 1978. The 1981 is big, tough, and rich. These solid, sturdy wines are certainly good, but overpriced.

LES PALLIÈRES* * * *

1979	($8.99)	85
1981	($8.99)	88
1982	($9.99)	87
1983	($9.99)	91

Difficult to find, Les Pallières is a genuine old-style Gigondas, rustic, full-flavored, big, and spicy, with gobs of cedary, earthy, ripe fruity flavors, full body, a hefty dosage of alcohol, and a long finish. Les Pallières is usually held 2½–3 years in cask before being released, and can easily age for 5–8 years. While the 1981 is excellent, the 1983 is fabulous, as is the unreleased 1985, but all of these wines are quite special for their intensity and distinctive style. The 1982 is closest to full maturity today.

RASPAIL (AY)* * * *

1981	($8.49)	86
1982	($8.49)	85
1983	($8.49)	84
1984	($8.99)	78

An outstanding producer of long-lived Gigondas, Raspail's 1964, 1966, and 1971 are wines that are still in excellent condition today. The 1981 and 1985 are the best vintages for Raspail since the excellent 1978, which is potentially the finest Raspail in two decades. Black purple, peppery, intensely concentrated, and full-bodied, these generous, plummy, deep wines can be drunk now, but five years of cellaring will add extra joy.

ST.-GAYAN (MEFFRE)* * * *

1980	($9.99)	86
1981	($9.99)	86
1982	($9.99)	85
1983	($9.99)	83

One of the best producers of Gigondas, St.-Gayan has a sumptuous style of winemaking that produces black purple wines with explosive bouquets of blackberry fruit, truffles, and smoky, hickory scents. Both the 1980 and 1981 are enormously rich, full-bodied wines with layers and layers of rich, ripe fruit, long, rich finishes and, I suspect, head-dizzying alcohol contents. Big, lusty, and intensely aromatic, both these wines will live for 5–8 more years. The 1982 is ready to drink, a little unstructured by this producer's standards, but fruity and soft. The 1983 is fat, plummy, and ripe, but dry in the finish. The unreleased 1985 is this property's best wine since 1978.

TRIGNON* * *

1983	($5.99)	84

André Roux makes an assortment of southern Rhône wines. His Gigondas is a robust yet finely balanced wine with good color, a spicy, robust fruitiness, and full body. Drink over the next 2–3 years.

Lirac and Côtes du Rhône-Villages, Rasteau, Cairanne, etc.

It is this vast wine-producing area in the southern Rhône that can offer the shrewd wine consumer the finest red wine values that exist in the world. The range of quality is enormous in the Côtes du Rhône-Villages appellations and its most noted wine-producing towns, Séguret, Vacqueyras, Sablet, Cairanne, Rasteau, Visan, and Chusclan. The high-quality Côtes du Rhônes from the area's best producers are almost always priced less than $7 a bottle and, when well chosen, offer sumptuous, rich, full-blown flavors and, far more important, immediate gustatory pleasure. Nineteen eighty-five is the best recent vintage for both red and white Côtes du Rhônes since 1978.

The following red Côtes du Rhône are listed alphabetically by the name of the estate or wine.

D'Aigueville 1985 Côtes du Rhône   ($5.49)   78

Normally a reliable producer of chunky, rustic-styled Côtes du Rhône, the 1985 is surprisingly light for d'Aigueville, but has straightforward, pleasant fruitiness and soft, easygoing texture. Drink over the next year.

Berthete 1983 Côtes du Rhône   ($5.49)   82

Another producer of high-quality Côtes du Rhône to keep an eye out for, Berthete's 1983 is moderately rich, full-bodied, fruity, and deep. It can be drunk now or aged for 2 years.

Brusset 1982 Cairanne Côtes du Rhône-Villages   ($5.99)   83

Brusset 1983 Cairanne Côtes du Rhône-Villages   ($5.99)   83

One of the best Côtes du Rhône domaines, Brusset produces full-flavored and full-bodied, deeply colored wine with a smoky, hickory-scented bouquet, rich, plummy fruit, a velvety texture, and spicy, rich finish. The 1982 is a trifle more fruity than the 1983, which has a little more aging potential. They should be consumed over the next 2–3 years.

Cabasse Réserve 1983 Séguret Côtes du Rhône-Villages ($5.99) 85

Cabasse Réserve 1985 Séguret Côtes du Rhône-Villages ($6.99) 85

Two really outstanding wines for Nadine Latour's Domaine de Cabasse, these wines have the strength, richness, and vigor of a Gigondas or Châteauneuf-du-Pape. Deep ruby/purple, with a first-class bouquet of ripe black cherry and peppery fruit, these powerful, full-bodied wines have the depth and tannin to age for at least 5 or more years. Quite impressive.

Caves des Vignerons du Rasteau 1983 Côtes du Rhône

($3.99–$4.99)   82

Caves des Vignerons du Rasteau 1985 Côtes du Rhône

($3.99–$4.99)   83

Produced from one of the best cooperatives in France, these lovely, soft, very generously flavored, spicy wines have robust, peppery, herbaceous bouquets, attractive fruit flavors, and soft, delicious, surprisingly long finishes. Drink over the next several years.

Chantegril 1982 Côtes du Rhône   ($3.99)   76

Chantegril 1983 Côtes du Rhône   ($4.99)   78

A ripe Grenache bouquet of peaches and apricots is immediately noticeable in both of these wines. On the palate, the wines are quite soft, round, and simple, but offer warm, easy to swallow flavors. Produced by the excellent Lirac estate of Saint-Roch.

Cru de Coudelet 1982 Côtes du Rhône   ($6.99)   81

Cru de Coudelet 1983 Côtes du Rhône   ($6.99)   85

Cru de Coudelet 1984 Côtes du Rhône   ($6.99)   85

Coudelet is produced by the famous Beaucastel estate in Châteauneuf-du-Pape, and its vineyard is separated from the Châteauneuf-du-Pape appellation by only a two-lane road. The Coudelet wines are big, smoky, robust, intense wines. The 1978 still needs 2–3 more years of cellaring. Both the 1983 and the surprisingly good 1984 are top-flight Côtes du Rhônes for drinking over the next 3–4 years. The 1982, from a very difficult vintage, is quite charming. Both the 1983 and 1984 are loaded with easy to drink, strawberry and raspberry fruit; these medium-bodied wines should be drunk over the next 5–7 years.

Devoy 1980 Lirac   ($3.99)   80

The wines of Lirac have yet to become well known in this country, but they are consistently good, usually better than most Côtes du Rhône, yet very, very cheap. This 1980 is quite peppery and spicy, but has oodles of blackberry fruit, some subtle herbal components, and a robust, gutsy texture. Drink over the next year.

Fonsalette 1978 Côtes du Rhône	($11.99)	85
Fonsalette 1979 Côtes du Rhône	($9.99)	89
Fonsalette 1981 Côtes du Rhône	($11.99)	86
Fonsalette 1982 Côtes du Rhône	($11.99)	87
Fonsalette 1983 Côtes du Rhône	($11.99)	87
Fonsalette 1978 Côtes du Rhône Syrah	($13.99)	90
Fonsalette 1983 Côtes du Rhône Syrah	($13.95)	90

Château Fonsalette is a likely candidate for criticism because of the unusually high prices fetched for its wines, as well as the bizarre behavior exhibited by its owner, Jacques Raynaud. However, one taste of these Côtes du Rhônes leaves no doubt that they are equal to, if not better than, 80% or more of the wines from Châteauneuf-du-Pape and Gigondas. The 1978 Côtes du Rhône is drinking beautifully now, showing a complex, cedary, plummy, savory bouquet, big, velvety complex flavors and a top-notch finish. As good as it is, the 1979, 1982, and 1983 Côtes du Rhônes are better—very fragrant with scents of cedar, violets, blackcurrants and oak, they are opulent on the palate with a wonderful texture and gorgeous peppery bouquets. They would have been the greatest Côtes du Rhônes I have tasted except for the 1978 and 1983 Côtes du Rhône Syrahs, special cuvées of 100% Syrah from old vines. Both are blockbuster wines with incredible depth and richness and black purple color; they promise to be magnificent in 10–15 years.

La Fourmone 1981 Vacqueyras Réserve du Paradis	($5.99)	83
La Fourmone 1982 Vacqueyras Réserve du Paradis	($5.49)	82

Roger Combe, the proprietor of La Fourmone, is both a winemaker and a poet. His wines from Vacqueyras (he also makes Gigondas) are always black purple in color and have a deep bouquet of blackberry fruit and spicy oak. They would appear to be heavy and viscous from their impenetrable color, yet are not. Quite manageable on the palate, with lively, plummy, ripe fruit flavors, they are usually at their best 3–4 years after the vintage. The 1982 is already quite attractive, soft, fruity, and very flavorful. The 1981 is bigger, more robust, but seems to harmoniously combine strength with elegance and ripe, rich fruit.

Goubert 1983 Côtes du Rhône	($5.99)	85
Goubert 1981 Côtes du Rhône Beaumes des Venise	($9.99)	90
Goubert 1983 Côtes du Rhône Beaumes des Venise	($9.99)	86
Goubert 1984 Côtes du Rhône Beaumes des Venise	($8.99)	85
Goubert 1981 Côtes du Rhône Sablet	($5.99)	84
Goubert 1984 Côtes du Rhône Sablet	($5.99)	84

The Domaine Goubert has quickly emerged as one of the shining superstars in the southern Rhône. The proprietor, Jean-Pierre Cartier, makes a Côtes du Rhône from the appellation of Beaumes des Venise as well as the finest Gigondas of the appellation. His wines are broodingly deep in color, with a big, spicy, hickory, earthy, smoky bouquet. These full-bodied, robust wines have impressive concentration, a long finish, and can easily handle 3–5 years of cellaring.

Guigal 1980 Côte du Rhône	($5.99)	83
Guigal 1981 Côtes du Rhône	($5.99)	85
Guigal 1982 Côtes du Rhône	($5.99)	85
Guigal 1983 Côtes du Rhône	($6.49)	86

Guigal makes lovely Côtes du Rhônes. All three have lovely, seductive, clean, pure bouquets of ripe berry fruit and peppery spices. On the palate, the wines exhibit savory, multidimensional, fruity flavors, shocking length, and good balance. The 1981 and 1982 have a little more length to them; the 1983 is excellent, opulent and rich, his best wine yet from this appellation.

P. Jaboulet 1983 Parallèle 45 Côtes du Rhône	($6.99)	83
P. Jaboulet 1985 Parallèle 45 Côtes du Rhône	($4.99–$5.99)	83

P. Jaboulet 1985 Vacqueyras Côtes du Rhône   ($4.49–$5.99)   84

The 1983 Parallèle 45 is quite plummy and fruity, with a substantial, full-bodied attack on the palate. Though it is one of the best Parallèle 45s in years, the 1983 is even better. The Vacqueyras has an intensely peppery, spicy aroma, full body, and a straightforward, plummy, briary fruitiness with considerable length.

Ogier 1979 Calandry Côtes du Rhône   ($4.49)   60

Ogier 1982 Vacqueyras Côtes du Rhône   ($4.49)   56

Ogier's wines are consistent—consistently inferior. Rarely do I find a wine nasty and unpleasant, but these two wines are abrasive on the palate and seem to have just one outstanding component to them: hot, high alcohol. Stay away.

Rabasse-Charavin 1984 Cairanne Côtes du Rhône   ($5.99)   82

Rabasse-Charavin 1985 Cairanne Côtes du Rhône   ($5.99)   84

This producer made a superb 1985 Côtes du Rhône with oodles of rich, deep, soft, lush fruit, a complex, cedary, ripe black cherry-scented bouquet, and wonderful finish. It should be drunk over the next year. The 1984 is lighter, with an intense, charming fruitiness, medium body, some hot alcohol in the finish, but it is very agreeable and fruity.

St.-Anne 1985 Cuvée Notre Dame des Cellettes   ($5.95)   85

St.-Anne 1985 Saint-Gervais Côtes du Rhône   ($5.95)   85

One of the top domaines in the Côtes du Rhône, St.-Anne has in 1985 produced firm, medium-bodied wines with good color, concentration, and firm tannins. Well structured, these stylish, well-balanced wines will be better in 6 months, although they are quite attractive now for their intense berry fruitiness and lengthy finish.

Saint-Maurice L'Ardoise 1978 Côtes du Rhône   ($3.99)   76

Very peppery, somewhat herbaceous, this medium-bodied Côtes du Rhône has a robust, chunky fruitiness and average length.

St.-Paul 1982 Côtes du Rhône   ($5.99)   75

The 1981 Caves St.-Paul Côtes du Rhône was one of the finest Côtes du Rhônes I have ever tasted. However, the 1982 is somewhat diffuse and light, but still attractively fruity, soft, supple, and ready to drink.

St.-Roch 1980 Lirac	($5.99)	80
St.-Roch 1981 Lirac	($5.99)	82
St.-Roch 1982 Lirac	($6.99)	84
St.-Roch 1982 Lirac Cuvée Ancienne Viguerie	($8.99)	84

Along with Château Ségriès in Lirac, Antoine Verda's beloved domaine called St.-Roch produces the finest wines of this appellation. His Liracs tend to have in common a big, intense perfume of apricots, peaches, and berry fruit, soft, voluptuous flavors, and a lush, almost sweet texture on the palate. The 1980 is a good wine, direct, fruity, ripe, and round, but the 1981 and 1982 are better. They are round and generous wines with oodles of sweet berry fruit. Both, like the 1980, should be drunk over the next one to two years. The 1982, a special cuvée of the estate's best lots, is more concentrated and more interesting.

Treilles 1982 Côtes du Rhône	($4.59)	81

Quite delicious, this medium ruby-colored wine has a silky, luxurious texture, a lovely ripe berry quality to its bouquet, and good concentration. It is perfect for drinking now and over the next 12 months.

Trignon 1983 Côtes du Rhone	($4.99–$5.49)	78
Trignon 1983 Rasteau Côtes du Rhône-Villages	($5.99)	83
Trignon 1983 Sablet Côtes du Rhône-Villages	($5.99)	83

André Roux is one of the most innovative producers of fine Côtes du Rhône wines. Using a carbonic maceration method that employs much higher temperatures for extraction of color and fruit, and eschewing the use of wood barrels for aging, Roux obtains wines that are remarkably fruity and supple, ready to drink young, yet having an uncanny ability to age well. The 1983 Côtes du Rhône is a good, straightforward wine with attractive berry fruit and good spice. However, for a few cents more, you should move up to the 1983 Rasteau and 1983 Sablet.

Both have a lot of ripe, tasty, peppery, blackcurrant fruit, supple, easy to appreciate flavors, and enough tannins to warrant cellaring for 3–5 years.

Vidal-Fleury 1982 Cairanne Côtes du Rhône	($4.99)	84

Vidal-Fleury 1983 Les Ronvières Côtes du Rhône	($4.99)	83

Always well made, Vidal-Fleury's Côtes du Rhône 1983 is nowhere near a match for the wonderful 1978, but it does offer charming, soft, berry fruit and adequate length. The 1982 Côtes du Rhône from the village of Cairanne is wonderfully plump, rich, ripe, long, and loaded with fruit.

La Vieille Ferme 1983 Côtes du Ventoux	($4.00)	82

La Vieille Ferme 1982 Gold Label Côtes du Rhône	($4.49–$4.99)	82

La Vieille Ferme 1983 Réserve Côtes du Rhône	($4.49)	83

La Vieille Ferme 1984 Réserve Côtes du Rhône	($4.99)	83

The best red wines from La Vieille Ferme in quite a few years. Jean-Pierre Perrin has apparently gone back to a bigger, richer style with more body and stuffing. The result is obviously a success. Rich, peppery fruit jumps from the glass. On the palate, the wines are full, lush, interesting, and very delicious to drink. The Côtes du Ventoux is a little lighter. Drink over the next 3–4 years.

Vieux Chêne 1985 Cuvée des Capucines	($6.49)	84

Vieux Chêne 1985 Cuvée Haie aux Grives Côtes du Rhône	($6.99)	85

This domaine has consistently provided me with some deliciously fruity, plump bottles of Côtes du Rhône. My favorite cuvée from Vieux Chêne has been the Haie aux Grives. The 1985 has a ripe, peach-scented bouquet, juicy, ripe fruity flavors, medium body, and a good, silky finish. It should be drunk over the next 3 years. The other Côtes du Rhône lacks the richness and extra ripeness of the aforementioned special cuvée, but is soft, fruity, easy to drink, and a very pleasing wine to drink over the next 1–2 years.

Muscat de Beaumes de Venise

These largely unknown, marvelous Rhône wines are intensely perfumed, sweet dessert wines produced from the Muscat grape. They are rich and lively wines, and despite their high alcohol content, I find them much easier to drink and fresher than the Sauternes and Barsacs. The wines are perfect for after-dinner sipping or, better yet, served with an open fruit tart. They are wines that are best drunk within 3–4 years of the vintage, when they retain their remarkable freshness, intense, exuberant fruitiness, and incredible perfume of ripe pears and peaches.

Domaine de Coyeaux 1985   ($10.99)   87

Light golden orange, with a moderate aroma of almonds, apricots, and lychee nuts, this sweet, rich, viscous wine is not heavy at all but vibrant, alive, and zesty. It is, however, heady, with a dizzying alcohol content of 16%. Drink over the next year, and serve it with fresh fruit or fruit desserts.

Domaine Durban 1985   ($10.99)   90

Domaine Durban N.V.   ($8.99)   87

The Domaine Durban has perhaps the highest reputation for Muscat de Beaumes de Venise, with ripe orange, apricot, and nut scents, and flavors of almond. The non-vintage wine is rich and concentrated on the palate, intense and decadent. The 1985 has all of these same qualities but also more acidity and a more complex bouquet.

Paul Jaboulet Aîné 1985   ($12.95)   90

A sensational bouquet of ripe tropical fruit, as well as scents of peaches, almonds, and apricots fill the nose. On the palate, this light orange-colored wine is sweet but extremely well balanced, with really crisp acidity and a lovely, lush, concentrated feel on the palate. Despite its richness and sweetness, the wine is quite easy and refreshing and never becomes cloying, heavy, or tiring to drink. A total success.

Domaine St.-Sauveur 1985   ($12.49)   85

Medium orange/gold in color with a big, ripe, intense aroma of ripe tropical fruit and floral scents; on the palate, the wine is a trifle heavy, but loaded with rich, ripe fruit.

THE SOUTHWEST

Few people are very familiar with this remote area of vineyards spread out between the Spanish border, the Correre to the north, and the Lot Valley to the south. Even for frequent tourists to France, this area is largely uncharted territory. Yet there are some very serious, very good wines produced here. For red wine enthusiasts there are plenty of wines to choose from—the fruity, light, casual wines of Bergerac, the stern, tannic, dark, remarkably cheap, long-lived red wines of Madiran, and the progressive, modern-style, supple, fruity Bordeaux-like wines of Cahors. While there is less to choose from among the white wines, crisp, dry, fruity whites are available from Bergerac, and France's most curiously named white wine, the Pacherenc du Vic Bihl, is also a delicious, crisp, lively wine.

Recent Vintages

Vintages in this vast area are hardly ever discussed or rated, but since the weather closely resembles that of Bordeaux, the years tend to be similar in style. Consequently, 1982 and 1985 stand out, closely followed by 1983, 1981, 1978, and 1979.

A GUIDE TO SOUTHWEST FRANCE'S BEST PRODUCERS

* * * * (EXCELLENT PRODUCERS)

Chateau d'Aydie-Laplace
(Madiran)
Domaine Bouscassé
Clos de Gamot (Cahors)

Clos de Triguedina Prince
Phobus (Cahors)
Château la Jaubertie (Bergerac)
Château Montus (Madiran)

*** *(GOOD PRODUCERS)*

Château Bellevue (Bergun)
Château de Cayrou (Cahors)
de Chambert (Cahors)
Clos de Triguedina (Cahors)
Haute Serre (Cahors)
Château Michel de Montague
 (Bergerac)

Château Court-Les-Mûts
 (Bergerac)
Château du Perron (Madiran)
Château de Peyros (Cahors)
Château St.-Didier Parnac
 (Cahors)

Southwest France—Today's Buying Strategy

For the light white and red wines of Bergerac, don't risk drinking anything older than 1983. Nineteen eighty-four is disappointing for this area, but 1985 is very good and is the year to search out now. For Madiran, this is a fertile hunting ground for shrewd, bargain-conscious consumers. For the moment, only a handful of importers and even fewer wine retailers have had the courage or initiative to represent a red Madiran or white Pacherenc du Vic Bihl, because the wines would have to be "hand sold," meaning that consumers would have to be convinced to try these wines; for many retailers, this is simply too great an effort. The 1982s from Madiran are very good, as are the 1983s and 1985s. The top Madirans from these vintages will last 7–10 years without any difficulty. For the rare white wine, Pacherenc du Vic Bihl, stick to the most recent vintage, 1985.

2. ITALY

The wines of Italy may be at once the most bewildering, frustrating, and sometimes fascinating group of wines to taste and evaluate. Italy produces more wine than any country in the world, and the Italians still drink more wine than anyone else, a hefty averge of 92 liters a year per man, woman, and child. If that does not seem like a lot of wine, compare that with America's annual consumption of 8.4 liters per person and you get the picture of how important production and consumption are in Italy.

The range of wines produced in Italy is staggering. There are many wines still made with nineteenth-century techniques that are, unfortunately, still exported. These wines are often oxidized, have excessive amounts of volatile acidity, and taste dirty, coarse, and sharp. On the other hand, there are also increasing amounts of wines produced in shiny, sparkling clean, stainless steel tanks, their vinification temperature regulated by computers. From the sun-drenched and baked wine regions of Sicily, Campania, Basilicata, and Calabria to the cool Alpine climates of Trentino, northern Lombardy, and Piedmont, there is a remarkable diversity of wines, winemaking styles, grape varieties, and flavors. More so than elsewhere, there is a dichotomy to Italian wines: Italy's greatest wines compete with the finest produced anywhere in the world, yet the bad wines of Italy are among the world's worst.

Following are my observations about the current state of affairs of Italian wines.

1. Italy's greatest red wines are either the product of the Nebbiolo or Sangiovese grape. There are a handful of exceptions. Nebbiolo finds its greatest heights in the wines of Piedmont, the pastoral, hilly section of northern Italy. It is here that Italy's two greatest wines are produced: the stern, tannic, rich, full-bodied Barolo and the more elegant Barbaresco. Although the Sangiovese grape is equally reputed and can reach supreme heights in the hands of careful, skilled winemakers, it most frequently yields good but rarely great Chiantis and Brunello di Montalcinos.

2. Italy's new breed of crisp, light, dry, fruity white wines made with modern technology, particularly Chardonnay, Pinot Grigio, Bianco di Custoza, Pinot Bianco, Vernaccia di San Gimignano, Orvieto, and Trebbiano, represent outstanding values and have no peers for lightness, freshness, and immediate charm in drinking, provided of course that they are vinified at cool temperatures, made in stainless steel, and bottled very early to capture their fruitiness and vivacity.

3. Italian experimentation with new styles of red wine, often aged in small oak casks as in Bordeaux and produced from various blends of Cabernet Sauvignon, Cabernet Franc, Merlot, and Sangiovese, has resulted in a number of stunning new wines that have the potential to be considered world-class red wines.

4. Italian winemakers are getting very serious about making complex, sparkling wines that can rival top French champagnes. Virtually all of the serious efforts in this area are taking place in Lombardy, where producers such as Ca Del Bosco, Bellavista, and Berlucchi are making very good, very interesting, dry sparkling wines in the *methode champenoise* manner.

5. For the most part, Italy's serious red wines spend too much time aging in wood containers. From the smell of some of them, I'd guess the wood is also not terribly clean. The result is far too many oxidized, dried-out wines deficient in the ripe fruit that they once had. Gradually, some of the winemakers are seeing the folly of their ways, but shorter aging periods—1–3 years rather than 3–10 years in some instances—would render wines richer in fruit and less prone to oxidation. Bottling the entire crop at the same time, à la Bordeaux, would also be a welcome change and would elimi-

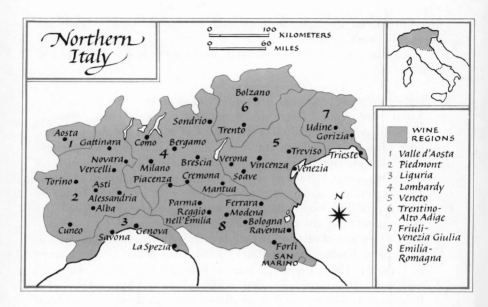

Northern Italy

0 — 100 KILOMETERS
0 — 60 MILES

Bolzano
6
Sondrio
Trento
7
Udine
Gorizia
Aosta 1 Gattinara Como Bergamo 5 Treviso Trieste
Novara 4 Brescia Verona Vincenza Venezia
Vercelli Milano Cremona Soave
Torino Piacenza Mantua
Asti
2 Alessandria Parma Ferrara
Alba Reggio Modena
nell'Emilia 8 Bologna
Cuneo 3 Genova Ravenna
Savona
La Spezia Forli
SAN
MARINO

N

WINE
REGIONS

1 Valle d'Aosta
2 Piedmont
3 Liguria
4 Lombardy
5 Veneto
6 Trentino-
   Alto Adige
7 Friuli-
   Venezia Giulia
8 Emilia-
   Romagna

Southern Italy

San Severo
Manfredonia
Benevento Foggia
Napoli 2 Bari
Salerno Matera Ostuni
1 Rionero Brindisi
Potenza Taranto
Metaponto
3 Gallipoli
TYRRHENIAN
Cetraro Ciro
SEA Paola Cosenza
4
Catanzaro
Caraffa
Messina
Palermo Reggio di
Trapani Calabria
Marsala Taormina
5 Catania
Agrigento
Siracusa
Ragusa

N
W   E
S

WINE
REGIONS

1 Campania
2 Puglia
3 Basilicata
4 Calabria
5 Sicily

0 — 60 MILES
0 — 100 KILOMETERS

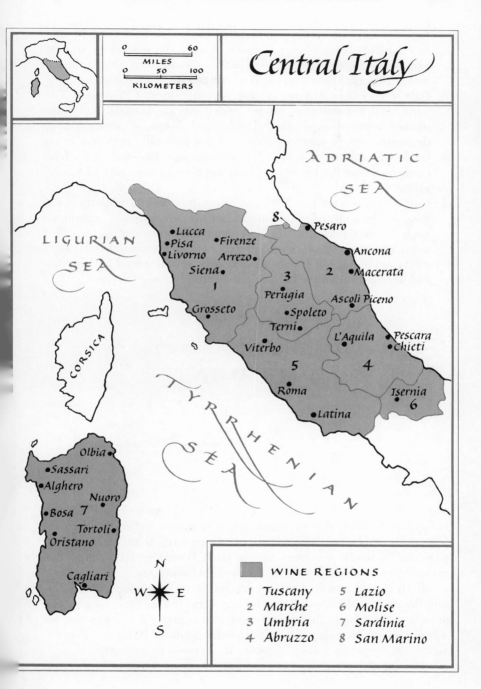

Central Italy

MILES
0   60

KILOMETERS
0   50   100

ADRIATIC
SEA

LIGURIAN
SEA

TYRRHENIAN
SEA

CORSICA

Lucca
Pisa
Livorno
Firenze
Arrezo
Siena

1

Grosseto

8

Pesaro
Ancona
Macerata

2

Perugia

3

Spoleto
Terni
Viterbo

Ascoli Piceno

L'Aquila
Pescara
Chieti

5

Roma

4

Latina

Isernia

6

Olbia
Sassari
Alghero
Nuoro
Bosa   7
Tortoli
Oristano

Cagliari

N
W   E
S

WINE REGIONS

1 Tuscany	5 Lazio
2 Marche	6 Molise
3 Umbria	7 Sardinia
4 Abruzzo	8 San Marino

nate the extreme bottle variation that now exists between a producer's Chianti bottled after 3 years of aging in wood vats and the same wine bottled after 6 or 7 years in wood vats. This results in totally different wines and is confusing to the wine consumer.

6. Italy's red wines, at least the big, serious wines of Piedmont, Tuscany, and a handful of others from Umbria, Abruzzi, and Campania, require, as a general rule, 1–2 hours of aeration after decanting into a clean container. I am generally opposed to extended breathing of wines, but my tastings time and again have confirmed that the big reds of Italy improve significantly with some airing.

7. Italy's wine scandal of 1986, involving the criminal adulteration of wine by the addition of potentially harmful, even deadly, chemicals such as methanol and diethylene glycol, significantly tarnished many great winemakers who merely also make wine in Italy. Only a tiny percentage of Italy's winemakers were involved in this criminal activity, and none of their wines are reviewed herein.

PIEDMONT

Italy's Finest Wine Region

One will get no arguments from this writer that Piedmont is not Italy's greatest wine region and that Barolo and Barbaresco are frequently Italy's two best red wines. The great intellectual and rich, powerful, sensory pleasures that a great Barolo or Barbaresco can provide have been well established in wine literature.

Both Barolo and Barbaresco are produced in a bucolic, hilly terrain that serves double duty as the white truffle kingdom of Italy. The drab town of Alba is the closest thing to a commercial city center for this viticultural region, which has the sharp hills of Barolo to its south and the more gently rolling slopes of Barbaresco to its northeast.

Part of the reluctance on the part of many wine enthusiasts to jump at the opportunity to purchase many of the exquisite Barolos and Barbarescos on the market is that these big, brawny wines are often forbidding and savage in their youthful rawness. Certainly Barbaresco is the tamer of the two, but the grape they are made from, the afore-mentioned Nebbiolo, is quite capable of rendering furiously tannic, unyielding wines that beg for ten years' aging to reveal their complex aromas of peppery spices, rich truffle-scented fruit, leather, tar, and tobacco. Barbaresco has the reputation of being the most approacha-ble in its youth and is less robust and less tannic, but such generali-zations fall short of doing justice to the divergent styles of wine found in these two regions, as well as the different soils and microclimates that will affect the style, texture, taste, and personality of the wines.

With respect to Barolo, it is Italy's most robust, powerful, full-bodied, tannic, and by most accounts, memorable wine. However, there are different schools of winemaking in Barolo that result in quite differently styled wines. Barolo enthusiasts will add that the style of many Barolos can also be predicted from the vineyard in which the grapes are grown. Certainly, one of the most obvious trends over the recent decade has been the emergence of single-vineyard-designated Barolos. This trend is also very obvious in Barbaresco. However, in Barolo and Barbaresco, like Burgundy in France, different growers often use grapes from the exact same vineyard, yet vinify and handle the wines in different manners. Consequently the consumer is often confronted with wines from the same vineyard and vintage that taste totally different. At present, virtually everyone agrees that the top Barolo vineyards are Marcenasco, Monprivato, Villero, Bussia So-prana, Cannubi, Brunate, Rocche, Monfortino, Monfalletto, Lazzar-ito, and Rionda. However, just knowing the vineyards is not enough. One must also know the winemaking styles of the top Barolo and Barbaresco producers.

If Barolo and Barbaresco are two of Italy's greatest wines, then the smooth, fruity Dolcetto is one of that country's most delicious but misunderstood wines. It is not sweet, as many wine enthusiasts think, but quite dry, though in top vintages like 1985 it is intensely fruity, lush, and oozing with plummy fruit.

Wines called Nebbiolo d'Alba are sometimes a producer's declas-sified Barolo or Barbaresco, but are almost always good values. Bar-bera d'Alba, Grignolino, and Freisa are Piedmont's weakest wines. The first, often abhorrently sharp and acidic except in the hands of a producer such as Vietti, Giacosa, or Pio Cesare, the second, innocu-ously light and bland, and the third, a totally repugnant wine (at least to American palates), of something that is frothy, sweet, and acidic.

North of Alba and the famous Barolo/Barbaresco zone, in full view of the Alps, are several other red wine regions of Piedmont. Carema, Gattinara, Spanna, Ghemme, and Donnaz are the best of these wines, all bred from the Nebbiolo and all capable of producing very good wines in the hands of the best producers.

PIEDMONT
QUICK VINTAGE GUIDE

1985—Gaja, Ceretto and their peers are already calling it one of the greatest vintages this century. I believe they said the same thing about 1982, 1978, and 1971. Nevertheless, broker Neil Empson claims it is better than either 1982 or 1978, which is difficult for me to imagine, given the superlative quality of the latter two years. Unfortunately, no one will see a bottle of the best red wines until 1988, with most *riservas* not reaching the market until 1990–1992. Since top Barolos and Barbarescos need 12–15 years of cellaring, the best wines of 1985 won't be ready until 2000–2010. Will you have the discipline to wait?

1984—Maligned by the press corps (as was the case everywhere in Europe), this vintage in Piedmont is claimed to be average in quality with the wines light yet forward and flavorful.

1983—A good vintage of rather tannic, stern wines, the 1983s may turn out to be similar to the unyielding but overall potentially good 1974s.

1982—A very great vintage. The wines are loaded with ripe, rich fruit, have plenty of tannins, full body, and real alcoholic punch to them. They are tasting surprisingly forward, and since most great vintages of Barolo and Barbaresco need 10–15 years of bottle age to mature, this might be the rare opportunity to enjoy a rich, dense, ripely fruity Barolo or Barbaresco before the age of 10. Despite the accessible nature of this vintage, the top wines should keep 25 or more years. A year to buy.

1981—Rain during September ruined what could have been a very good year. Many of the best growers declassified their entire crops. My initial tastings have turned up fruity, compact, short wines that are rather plain.

1980—Somewhat of a sleeper vintage, the 1980s are medium-bodied, rather light wines, but the good growers have produced wines with plenty of fruit, soft tannins, and charm. It is a vintage to drink over the next 4–5 years. If priced right, 1980 is worth considering.

1979—One of the best vintages for current drinking. Elegant, ripe, fruity wines were produced. They may lack the muscle, power, and great concentration of a vintage such as 1978 or 1982, but they offer plenty of finesse and complexity. Not to be overlooked.

1978—This is a great vintage of very long-lived wines, huge in structure, very tannic, very concentrated, but the best of them are still a good 10 years away from maturity. The crop size was small, the style of the wines aggressive, rich, and tough. They have developed very slowly, causing impatient critics to downgrade them. The 1982s show more ripe, intense fruit than the 1978s did at a similar stage, but this is a great vintage that just needs plenty of time.

1977—A horrendous year of rain and cold weather. Most good growers declassified their entire crops.

1976—Another bad year; the wines lacked ripeness, had excessive tannins, and are now drying out.

1975—The first of a trio of consecutive poor vintages, the 1975s I have tasted have had aromas of tea, light-intensity flavors, and shallow personalities.

1974—This is a highly rated vintage, but one I find overrated; the wines are too hard and tannic, and lacking in ripeness and richness. Perhaps time will prove me wrong, but most of the Piedmont wines from 1974 lack length, grace, and charm.

1973—Relatively easy to drink, soft, pleasant, light wines were produced in 1973. All should have been drunk by now.

1972—As in most of Europe's viticultural regions, rain was the ruination of this vintage.

1971—Until the advent of the remarkably promising 1982s, the 1971s had been what I consider a classic Piedmont vintage. Rich, perfumed, and deeply concentrated, these wines are now entering their plateau of maturity, which should easily last for another 10–15 years. A great vintage.

Older Vintages

The 1970s are very good, eclipsed in stature by the admittedly greater 1971s; the 1969s are average in quality and best drunk up. The 1968s are disastrous; the 1967s very good, but now beginning to slip; the 1966s and 1965s below average to poor; and the 1964 another great vintage. Well-stored bottles of 1964 Piedmontese wines are gloriously rich and scented.

A GUIDE TO PIEDMONT'S BEST PRODUCERS

* * * * * (OUTSTANDING PRODUCERS)

Bruno Ceretto (Barolo/
   Barbaresco)
Angelo Gaja (Barbaresco)

Bruno Giacosa (Barolo/
   Barbaresco/Arneis)
Renato Ratti (Barolo/Dolcetto)

* * * * (EXCELLENT PRODUCERS)

Castello di Neive (Barbaresco)
Clerico (Barolo)
Pio Cesare (Barolo/Barbaresco)
Cogno-Marcarini (Barolo)
Aldo Conterno (Barolo/Dolcetto)
Giacomo Conterno (Barolo)
Fontanafredda (Barolo)
Marchesi di Gresy (Barbaresco)

G. Mascarello (Barolo)
Produttori di Barbaresco
   (Barbaresco)
Francesco Rinaldi (Barolo)
L. Sandrone (Barolo)
Valentino (Barolo/Dolcetto)
Vallana (Spanna/Gattinara)
Vietti (Barolo/Dolcetto)

* * * (GOOD PRODUCERS)

Mario Antoniolo (Gattinara)
Brovia (Barolo)
Carretta (Barolo)
Dessilani (Gattinara, Spanna,
   Ghemme)
Dosio (Barolo)
Luigi Einaudi (Barolo)
Giovannini Moresco
   (Barbaresco)

Pasquero-Secondo (Barbaresco)
Pelissero (Barbaresco)
Prunotto (Barolo)
Ravizza (Gattinara)
Giuseppe Rinaldi (Barolo)
Roagna (Barbaresco)
Scarpa (Barolo)

* * (AVERAGE PRODUCERS)

Borgogno (Barolo)
Agostino Brugo (Gattinara)
Damilano (Barolo)
Deforville (Barbaresco)

Franco-Fiorina (Barolo)
Elli Giacosa (Barolo)
Spinona (Barbaresco)
Travaglini (Gattinara)

* (OTHER PRODUCERS)

Guido Barra (Gattinara)
Bersano (Barolo)
Bil Colle (Barbaresco)
L. Caldi (Barolo)

Kiola (Barolo)
Marchesi di Barolo (Barolo)
Oddero (Barolo)
A. Scavino (Barolo)

Piedmont—A Buying Strategy

To the extent that you can still find some of the outstanding 1978s on the shelves of retailers, they should be gobbled up—not for drinking now, but for cellaring until 1990. This is particularly true for the best Barolos and Barbarescos from top producers. Nineteen seventy-nine is the best vintage for current consumption, and the 1982s, destined to be great classics, will be arriving over the next several years and, of course, merit significant interest. As for the white wines of Piedmont, look for the excellent 1985s and avoid older vintages, which are now showing signs of losing their fruit.

MARIO ANTONIOLO (GATTINARA)* * *

1974 Gattinara	($12.50)	78
1975 Gattinara	($10.50)	60
1978 Gattinara Osso San Grato	($12.00)	86
1979 Gattinara Osso San Grato	($12.00)	84
1974 Gattinara San Francesco	($12.50)	81
1976 Gattinara San Francesco	($12.00)	75
1978 Gattinara San Francesco	($12.00)	85
1979 Gattinara San Francesco	($12.00)	85

One of the best producers of Gattinara, the wines of Antoniolo are widely available in America. His best wines come from two specific vineyards, Osso San Grato and San Francesco, and are so called on the label. I was disappointed in the 1974s from Antoniolo, but his 1978s and 1979s are quite good.

Both 1974s display complex, leathery, earthy aroma and decent fruit, but finish short and have excessive tannin levels, making further aging a gamble. The 1976 is austere and severe and going nowhere. The 1975 has some spicy, leathery, earthy fruit in the nose, but tastes bitter and clumsy on the palate. The 1978s are rich and fruity, show a sweet ripeness and good tannic backbone. They can be drunk now or cellared for another 2–3 years. The 1979s are a shade less powerful than the 1978s, but are medium-bodied, elegant, spicy, attractive wines for drinking over the next 1–2 years.

GUIDO BARRA (GATTINARA)*

1974 Gattinara	($9.99)	82
1979 Gattinara	($8.99)	74
1978 Spanna	($6.99)	72
1981 Spanna	($6.00)	78

I have not had a great deal of tasting experience of Barra's wines. Those I have tasted have been rather old-style, coarse, somewhat oxidized wines that lacked fruit and complexity. The best Barra wine I have tasted is the 1974 Gattinara, which is fully mature, spicy, and aromatic. The other three wines are deficient in fruit.

AGOSTINO BRUGO (GATTINARA)* *

1975 Gattinara	($9.00)	76
1976 Gattinara	($9.00)	82
1979 Gattinara	($9.00)	85
1975 Spanna	($6.00)	83
1976 Spanna	($6.00)	78

Brugo's wines are generally robust, soundly made, and flavorful. They are usually rustic in style and, though lacking in finesse and elegance, are nevertheless good, rich, savory wines. Brugo produces wine under the Gattinara, Ghemme, and Spanna labels. Among the Spannas, the 1976 is ready to drink, spicy, tarry, medium-bodied, and robust. The 1975 has more richness and fruit, a pungent, earthy, tarry bouquet. It can age for 1–3 more years. Of the Gattinaras, the best is the 1979, which has a medium ruby color, a richly scented bouquet of cherry fruit and fresh leather, medium body, and good length. It should keep well for 2–3 years. The 1975 is lean and somewhat dry and tannic, whereas the 1976 is plump, simple, but quite satisfying in a robust, savory way.

CARRETTA (BAROLO)* * *

1978 Barolo Cannubi	($14.00)	87
1979 Barolo Cannubi	($12.00)	85
1978 Nebbiolo d'Alba	($6.00)	83
1980 Nebbiolo d'Alba	($5.59)	75

Carretta is a fine producer who seems to get overlooked in discussions of top Barolo producers. Perhaps it is because his wines tend to be savagely tannic and backward when young, and it is nearly impossible to judge if they have sufficient fruit to outlast the huge, raw tannins. Certainly his 1970 and 1971 were brilliant examples of Barolo when tasted in 1985 in a comparative tasting of these two vintages. I regard his 1970 as the best Barolo produced in that vintage.

True to form, Carretta's new releases, 1978 and 1979, are both 8–10 years away from maturity. That alone will, I suspect, be enough to deter most interested parties. Carretta's Nebbiolo d'Alba is also considered to be among the best; it, too, takes at least 7–8 years of cellaring to reach drinkability. The 1978 Barolo, for example, will last 25–40 years. I cannot see it reaching its peak before 2000. It is loaded with fruit but brutally tannic and really unpleasant on the palate, although those accustomed to judging young wine will see its immense potential. The 1979 is similarly styled, but not as concentrated. It needs until 1992–1995 to reach its peak. Both the white wines are for consumption now.

CASTELLO DI NEIVE (BARBARESCO)* * * *

1978 Barbaresco Santo Stefano	($12.00)	87
1979 Barbaresco Santo Stefano	($12.00)	85
1981 Barbaresco Santo Stefano	($6.49)	75
1983 Dolcetto Basarin	($6.50)	85
1985 Dolcetto Messoirano	($7.50)	84

1983 Dolcetto Messoirano	($6.50)	78

This is an excellent producer of Piedmontese wine that rarely seems to get the publicity it deserves. The wines are rich, fragrant, deep, and concentrated, without the excess of tannin so commonly found in many wines of this region. The Barbaresco Santo Stefano is usually the top wine here. Santo Stefano is one of the great vineyards of Piedmont. The 1978 Santo Stefano is drinkable now but ideally should receive another 4–5 years of cellaring. It has a rich, full-intensity bouquet of cedar, ripe cherries, spices, and leather. Ripe and full-bodied, still quite tannic and youthful, it is an excellent wine that may with time become outstanding. The 1979 Santo Stefano is a less tannic, slightly less full-bodied version of the 1978. It has a full-blown bouquet of spicy, leathery, tarry fruit and deep flavor. Among the Dolcettos, the 1983 Basarin is a textbook wine, rich, plummy, fleshy, and very fruity. It is delicious for drinking now. The 1985 Messoirano is more tannic and robust, with significant lushness. The 1983 Messoirano is herbaceous with the scent of ripe tomatoes and plenty of tannin and acidity. It lacks the charm of the other two Dolcettos.

BRUNO CERETTO (BAROLO/BARBARESCO)* * * * *

1982 Barbaresco Asij	($20.00)	88
1979 Barbaresco Bricco Asili	($30.00)	90
1980 Barbaresco Bricco Asili	($25.00)	86
1982 Barbaresco Bricco Asili	($35.00)	92
1983 Barbaresco Bricco Asili	($35.00)	88
1980 Barolo Brunate	($16.00)	78
1982 Barolo Brunate	($20.00)	89
1979 Barolo Prapo	($16.00)	89
1980 Barolo Prapo	($16.00)	75
1982 Barolo Prapo	($25.00)	89

1982 Barolo Bricco Rocche	($100.00)	91
1980 Barolo Rocche	($20.00)	81
1979 Barolo Zonchetta	($16.00)	88
1982 Barolo Zonchetta	($25.00)	87
1985 Dolcetto d'Alba	($8.00)	86
1982 Nebbiolo d'Alba	($7.00)	84

The Cerettos are justifiably proud of their wines, particularly their Barolo, which comes from specific vineyards called Prapo, Brunate, Rocche, and Zonchetta, and their Barbaresco, from a highly regarded vineyard called Bricco Asili. The style of wines is classic, relying on modern equipment and facilities to produce wine full of fruit yet with no excess of tannin or suggestion of oxidation. I find the wines among the most accessible and easy to drink when young, since they possess a core of very good fruit that, along with their very aromatic character, is one of their personality traits. I cannot assess how they age because I have not tasted anything older than 1978, but they have good balance and sufficient fruit. Interestingly, Ceretto's 1979s seem more success-ful than his 1978s.

All of the 1982s are very, very successful, led by the sublime, gorgeously scented, rich, supple 1982 Barbaresco Bricco Asili and absurdly priced, yet rare 1982 Barolo Bricco Rocche. Both will im-prove for another 5–10 years. The 1982 Barbaresco Asij and Barolo Brunate offer contrasting styles, the Barbaresco rich, velvety, and deep, yet very accessible, the Barolo backward, very rich, and full, but in need of 7–8 years of cellaring. Both the excellent 1982 Barolo Zonchetta and Prapo need 7–10 more years. The 1979 Barbaresco Asili, the 1979 Barolo Prapo, and 1979 Barolo Zonchetta are delicious to drink now, ripe, very fragrant, rich, quite well balanced. The aro-mas of ripe cherries and leather and the seductively lush, almost sweet, ripe fruit palate sensations are top-notch. Less profound but very good is the 1980 Barbaresco Bricco Asili. The 1980 Barolo Prapo is a trifle too hard, tannic, and slightly vegetal. The 1982 Nebbiolo d'Alba is easy to drink, fruity, direct, rather soft, and quite pleasant. Of recent releases, the 1985 Dolcetto d'Alba is gloriously fruity, fat, soft, and loaded with character. The famed 1983 Barbaresco Bricco Asili continues the tradition of excellent wines from this vineyard.

PIO CESARE (BAROLO/BARBARESCO)* * * *

1974 Barbaresco Riserva	($14.99)	75
1978 Barbaresco Riserva	($17.49)	88
1979 Barbaresco Riserva	($16.49)	84
1980 Barbaresco Riserva	($16.49)	70
1978 Barolo Riserva	($16.69)	86
1979 Barolo Riserva	($16.49)	87

For years this firm in Alba produced very traditional, old-style wines fermented at hot temperatures for very long periods in old wooden vats. Now stainless steel has replaced the wood and temperature control is observed. If anything, these changes have been for the better. The wines are still big, well-proportioned, potentially long-lived examples of their type. I find the weakness of this firm shows in off vintages where the wines sometimes do not turn out as well as might be expected. Certainly in top vintages such as a 1978, Pio Cesare does not miss the mark. Unlike many other producers in Piedmont, Pio Boffa, the administrator of the firm, does not believe in single-vineyard wines, preferring to blend wines from different vineyards, claiming that this is what gives a wine balance. The top-rated wines, the 1978 Barbaresco Riserva and 1979 Barolo Riserva, have classic Nebbiolo scents of tar, leather, earth, and ripe bing cherries. Both show surprisingly rich, supple fruit, good length, and further aging potential of 6–8 years. The 1978 Barolo Riserva exhibits good richness and, though it won't be fully mature before 1990, already tastes well, with plenty of ripe fruit, spice, leather, and tobacco. The 1979 Barbaresco Riserva is light but tasty and ready; the 1974 Barbaresco is quite harsh and severe and just seems to lack fruit. The 1980 Riserva may be in a dumb stage, but it too tastes short and deficient in fruit and is entirely too tannic.

CLERICO (BAROLO)* * * * *

1980 Barolo Bussia	($10.00)	87
1982 Barolo Bussia	($14.00)	90

1982 Barolo Ginestra   ($14.00)   90

This small producer makes outstanding Barolo from the Ginestra and Bussia vineyards. The 1980 Barolo Bussia is a very good wine from this rather mediocre vintage. The 1982s need 10–15 years of cellaring, but they are explosively rich, intense wines with exceptional concentration, length, and balance. The Ginestra is a touch more supple than the Bussia, but both should prove to be fabulous wines with a decade or more of cellaring potential.

COGNO-MARCARINI (BAROLO)* * * *

1980 Barolo Brunate   ($14.59)   83

1980 Barolo La Serra   ($14.59)   81

This producer is quite highly regarded, but I have always found the wines somewhat light and a trifle diluted rather than delicate, elegant, and suave. His 1971 is over the hill and his 1978s were a disappointment, particularly in view of the excellence of the vintage; so one wonders, why all the acclaim? These two 1980s are decently made, fruity, soft, with pleasant cherry fruit flavors and some spice. They are supple and ready to drink. The Brunate has more fruit, depth, and length.

ALDO CONTERNO (BAROLO/DOLCETTO)* * * *

1980 Barolo Colonnello   ($16.49)   86

1985 Dolcetto d'Alba   ($6.00)   85

Only Ratti produces a better Dolcetto than Aldo Conterno. However, it is Conterno's Barolos for which he is most famous. I recall vividly his 1971 Barolo Bussia Colonnello, tasted only once, but what a gorgeously proportioned wine, and how it oozed with fruit! For some reason, his wines are hard to find. I felt when I last visited Conterno that his obsession with the modern style of winemaking had gone a little far, since the 1978s tasted surprisingly fruity and did not seem to have sufficient tannin for 8–10 years of cellaring. However, more recently tasted wines have all shown well. The 1980 Barolo Colonnello is a top success for this rather maligned vintage. It is quite rich with a tarry, plummy, supple fruitiness. It should be drunk over the next 2–3 years. His 1985 Dolcetto d'Alba is a stunningly lush, richly fruity wine that is about as good a Dolcetto as one can find.

GIACOMO CONTERNO (BAROLO)* * * *

1979 Barbera d'Alba	($8.95)	79
1971 Barolo Monfortino	($25.00)	92
1974 Barolo Monfortino	($35.00)	78
1978 Barolo Monfortino	($40.00)	92
1971 Barolo Riserva	($25.00)	90
1973 Barolo Riserva	($15.00)	75
1979 Barolo Riserva	($20.00)	82

Giovanni Conterno, who runs this firm, is probably Piedmont's most traditional and stubborn winemaker. His nineteenth-century winemaking philosophy produces some of this region's most dramatic wines, but his inflexibility and blind commitment to tradition can also result in some oxidized, overly tannic wines with little charm and fruit. Unlike his brother Aldo, who bottles his Barolo after two years of aging, Giovanni rarely bottles before ten—yes, ten—years of cask aging. He is a perfectionist when it comes to quality, never hesitating to produce no wine in years when the grapes don't measure up. His predilection for keeping some of his lots of wine a decade or more in wood has caused some wines to taste dry, volatile, or oxidized. Conterno's best wine is the special Barolo called Monfortino, unquestionably Barolo's single greatest and most dramatic wine. The classic vintages for Monfortino are 1964, 1967, 1971, and 1978. I have not been impressed with the 1974 Monfortino; its mouth-searing tannins seem entirely too excessive for its fruit. His Barolo Riservas, aged only a mere 4–6 years in wood, can also be excellent. The 1971 is superb, chewy, intense, and extremely full-bodied. In Conterno's Barolos one finds the essence of Barolo: scents of tar, leather, tobacco, ripe fruit, a massive, chewy texture, and gobs of tannins. The 1971 Riserva needs 5–8 more years of cellaring, the 1971 Monfortino and the 1978 Monfortino a decade.

DEFORVILLE (BARBARESCO)* *

1980 Barbaresco	($12.95)	87
1983 Dolcetto d'Alba	($6.50)	83

1983 Grignolino d'Asti	($5.50)	60

This producer's best wines are his fleshy, deeply colored 1983 Dolcetto and stylish Barbarescos. The 1980 Barbaresco is a real sleeper, rich, supple, fully mature, with an expansive, tarry, smoky, ripe fruity bouquet, and lush flavors.

DESSILANI (GATTINARA/SPANNA/GHEMME)* * *

1978 Caramino Riserva	($6.49)	84
1974 Gattinara Riserva	($8.49)	85
1979 Gattinara Riserva	($8.49)	83
1978 Ghemme Riserva	($6.75)	84
1982 Spanna	($3.99)	80

Dessilani's wines offer good value, are generally direct, robust, deeply fruity wines that lack finesse but more than make up for that deficiency with richness and unabashed fruitiness. On occasion, one seems to find a dirty, flawed wine. These are not cerebral wines, but drinking wines. The 1982 Spanna is robust, full-bodied with mushroom scents and flavors of black cherries. The 1978 Caramino has rich, chocolatey fruit, smoky flavors, and an intense concentration of fruit. Let it breathe for 1–2 hours, to allow some barnyard aromas that appear initially to blow off. The 1978 Ghemme is another rustic, large-scaled wine oozing with tarry, plummy, rich aromas and full-bodied flavors. The 1974 Gattinara is a more elegant, complex wine. It has rich, tarry, ripe, fruity flavors complemented nicely by the smell of damp earth and flowers. The 1979 Gattinara is similar, a touch lighter, but well made.

DOSIO (BAROLO)* * *

1971 Barolo Riserva	($24.00)	82
1974 Barolo Riserva	($15.00)	77
1978 Barolo Riserva	($19.95)	87
1979 Barolo Riserva	($12.00)	79

| 1981 Dolcetto d'Alba | ($5.99) | 80 |

| 1983 Dolcetto d'Alba | ($5.99) | 82 |

I have had plenty of experience tasting Dosio's wines. I find them good, sometimes irregular, but generally fairly priced. The best Dosio wine I have tasted is the 1978 Barolo, a rich, deep but forward wine that can be drunk now or cellared for another 3–7 years. Dosio's Dolcetto d'Alba is usually a soundly made wine. Both the 1981 and 1983 have the requisite lush, plummy fruit that makes this wine easy to drink.

LUIGI EINAUDI (BAROLO)* * *

| 1980 Barolo | ($15.49) | 85 |

| 1981 Barolo | ($14.99) | 80 |

| 1983 Dolcetto | ($6.59) | 82 |

Einaudi's style of Barolo is one that provides plenty of body, very good color, and rich, ripe, rather soft, fruity flavors. The 1980 Barolo is delicious now, and shows good depth for this vintage. The 1981 is fruity but lighter. His Dolcetto is always made in a big, ripe, soft style. The 1983 merits interest.

FONTANAFREDDA (BAROLO)* * * *

| 1978 Barolo Bianca | ($13.00) | 85 |

| 1978 Barolo Delizia | ($13.00) | 88 |

| 1978 Barolo Gattinara | ($13.00) | 86 |

| 1978 Barolo Lazzarito | ($13.00) | 88 |

| 1978 Barolo La Rosa | ($13.00) | 87 |

This modern winery perched in the hills of Barolo makes very good Barolo that can be applauded for its reasonable prices as well as high quality. The style of Fontanafredda's Barolos is classic—the wines take a good 8–10 years of cellaring *after* release to shed sufficient tannins. Somewhat confusing for the consumer is that Fontanafredda produces at least six different single-vineyard Barolos in top years such as 1978. The differences in taste are marginal, at least at this early stage of their lives. All the 1978s of Fontanafredda are dark in color, with full body, gobs of hard tannins, excellent concentration, and tarry, rich, spicy bouquets. The difference in scores is negligible and largely attributable to the higher ranked wines having more complex aromas. I would suggest cellaring them until at least 1992–1995. They will last for 10 years.

ANGELO GAJA (BARBARESCO)* * * * *

1979 Barbaresco	($16.00)	85
1982 Barbaresco	($25.00)	87
1979 Barbaresco Costa Russi	($35.00)	85
1982 Barbaresco Costa Russi	($65.00)	93
1979 Barbaresco San Lorenzo	($45.00)	86
1982 Barbaresco San Lorenzo	($65.00)	90
1979 Barbaresco Sori Tilden	($35.00)	90
1982 Barbaresco Sori Tilden	($65.00)	95
1982 Cabernet Sauvignon Darmagi	($25.00)	84

I have on occasion been criticial of Gaja's pricing policy, but I am a great admirer of this man who has done so much to bring attention to the top Italian wines. His wines remain expensive; one must remember that they are rare items and it only takes one visit to his modern winery in Barbaresco to see that Gaja spares no expense in making wine. He is a pioneer in small cask aging (as practiced in Bordeaux) of his best wine, a practice that has been criticized by some but in general has had a major impact on some of Italy's best winemakers. He is at the forefront of his profession, and while it may take a decade to see if his small barrel-aging methods are best for Italy's top red wines, Gaja's results to date speak for themselves. His wines are grandiose examples of winemaking at its best and most adventurous. Gaja's 1982 Barbarescos are to me his greatest wines to date; his new experiments with Chardonnay and Cabernet Sauvignon in the foothills of Piedmont look promising—as well as disconcerting to his neighbors. His 1979 regular Barbaresco can still be found on the market at $16–$18 a bottle, a good $8–$10 less than the 1982. The 1979 regular bottling is drinking well now and is a good introduction to the Gaja winemaking style. As for the 1982s, the Barbaresco is quite impressive, with a rich, ruby color, a toasty vanillin, oaky scent to the bouquet, some of the telltale tarry character of Nebbiolo, and excellent length. There is plenty of tannin to this full-bodied wine, so give it 8–10 years of cellaring. The San Lorenzo is a denser wine than the regular Barbaresco, has even more depth and tannin, an outstanding aroma of ripe fruit and new oak, and 10–20 years of evolution ahead of it. The most forward wine is the Costa Russi, a rich, very concentrated wine with an intense perfume of plummy, ripe fruit and oak. It has a good lashing of tannin but a more velvety, unctuous texture. It is a great Barbaresco that can use 6–8 years of cellaring. Lastly, the Sori Tilden has awesome potential, provided one can wait a minimum of 10 or more years. Very dark, very backward, but oh, so promising, this spectacular wine has layers of concentrated fruit, ripe tannins, a powerful, long finish, and a dramatic personality. The single-vineyard Barbarescos are rare (approximately 1,000 cases of each were produced). The regular Barbaresco has good availability. Gaja also produces a Cabernet Sauvignon that is quite overpriced, but well made, fruity, too obviously oaky, but encouraging.

BRUNO GIACOSA (BARBARESCO/BAROLO/ARNEIS)* * * * *

1983 Barbaresco Gallina	($15.00)	87
1978 Barbaresco Santo Stefano	($35.00)	95
1979 Barbaresco Santo Stefano	($20.00)	90
1980 Barbaresco Santo Stefano	($17.00)	89
1982 Barbaresco Gallina	($25.00)	88
1978 Barolo Bussia	($25.00)	88
1979 Barolo Bussia	($25.00)	90
1978 Barolo Rocche	($35.00)	90
1980 Barolo Rocche	($13.00)	89

1978 Barolo Rionda Serralunga	($55.00)	94
1978 Barolo Villero	($18.00)	88
1979 Barolo Villero	($18.00)	90
1980 Barolo Villero	($15.00)	87
1980 Barolo Rionda	($25.00)	84

When I first wrote about Bruno Giacosa I called him "Piedmont's best kept secret." I have continued to follow his wines with an obsession befitting a man with the genius touch he has. He owns no vineyards, preferring to purchase his grapes from Piedmont's best vineyards in the top vintage years; in lesser years, he simply makes no wine. The quality of the wines is extraordinary; I have never tasted anything less than a fine wine from Giacosa. They are wonderfully opulent, highly aromatic, complex wines with layers and layers of ripe fruit and good, but not excessive, tannic backbones. If I said his top Barbarescos and Barolos can rival a great vintage of Pétrus for richness and complexity, few, I suspect, would believe it. However, Giacosa's wines are on that level; though hard to find and expensive, Giacosa's best wines are undoubtedly his Barbarescos from the Santo Stefano, Montefico, and Gallina vineyards. I know of no Barolo producer who is able to get such a voluptuous richness to his wines as he somehow does. His Barolos from such single vineyards as Bussia, Le Rocche, and Villero are sensational wines. His 1978 Barolo Serralunga from the Rionda vineyard is one of the greatest Barolos ever produced and is destined to live and improve for 15–25 years. Italy's greatest winemaker? For me, yes. His 1971 and 1978 Barbaresco Santo Stefanos are still the greatest Italian wines I have ever tasted.

All the wines above are available in small quantities. Because of his winemaking style, his wines can be drunk young but improve for 10–15 years after their release.

MARCHESI DI GRESY (BARBARESCO)* * * *

1979 Barbaresco Martinenga	($10.99)	84
1980 Barbaresco Martinenga	($12.00)	84
1982 Barbaresco Martinenga	($25.00)	85

1979 Barbaresco Martinenga Camp Gros	($24.00)	89
1982 Barbaresco Martinenga Camp Gros	($28.00)	88
1982 Barbaresco Martinenga Gaiun	($28.00)	90
1984 Martinenga	($10.00)	82

I have only tasted three vintages of the di Gresy wines, but have been impressed by their harmony and elegance. They are not as rich and powerful as those of Bruno Giacosa, Gaja, or Castello di Neive, but lean stylistically toward the Barbarescos produced by Ceretto from his Bricco Asili vineyard. Gresy produces his Barbarescos from a vineyard called Martinenga. Within that vineyard he separately vinifies two choice lots called Camp Gros and Gaiun. All the wines offer high quality and surprising complexity and finesse. Curiously, I thought the 1979 Martinenga Camp Gros, with its rich cherry fruit, spicy, leather-scented bouquet, and ripe flavors, a worthy rival of the 1982s, the latter of which are from a much more highly touted vintage. Top marks did, however, go to the 1982 Martinenga Gaiun, a beautifully made wine that needs 5–6 years to soften and shed its tannins, but has a super bouquet of ripe cherry fruit, spicy oak, and tobacco. The 1982 Martinenga Camp Gros is similarly styled, only more backward and closed, but rich and elegant. I liked the 1982 Martinenga quite a bit, but it does not have the concentration of the aforementioned wines; it should be ready by 1990–1992. For current drinking, in addition to the 1979 Martinenga Camp Gros, the regular 1979 Martinenga Barbaresco is supple, fragrant, and tasting quite good. The 1980 Martinenga is equally good, a trifle firmer and more compact, but very well made. Lastly, the intensely fruity and elegant 1984 Martinenga is light but smells of cherry jam and is delicious on the palate. These are impressive Barbarescos.

G. MASCARELLO (BAROLO)* * * *

1978 Barbaresco Bernadotti	($14.00)	85
1979 Barbaresco Chirella	($11.95)	83
1979 Barbera Ginestra	($6.49)	84

1978 Barolo Monprivato	($15.00)	90

1979 Barolo Monprivato	($15.00)	87

1978 Barolo Villero	($14.00)	87

1979 Barolo Villero	($15.00)	84

1982 Dolcetto Boscarello	($6.50)	78

Mascarello's wines are among the deepest colored, richest, and most tannic produced in Barolo. One suspects that if Giacomo Conterno bottled his Barolo after 4 or 5 years rather than 10, it would look as ruby/purple and be as dense and backward as those of G. Mascarello. His best wine is the Barolo from the Monprivato vineyard, which in vintages such as 1978 will last 30–40 years and not be drinkable until 1995 or later. It is a monumental wine. The 1979 Monprivato is only a shade lighter and should be mature by 1990. The other Mascarello wines are cut from the same cloth, dark, rich, rather boldly styled, and very tannic. Mascarello's 1979 Barbera from the Ginestra vineyard, normally a variety I find too acidic and austere, is quite good in this instance. Before you rush out to buy a Mascarello wine, be sure you have the requisite patience to wait for it to mature, especially the Barolos and Barbarescos.

GIOVANNINI MORESCO (BARBARESCO)* * *

1978 Barbaresco Pajore	($18.95)	85

1979 Barbaresco Pajore	($18.95)	86

To my knowledge, Moresco produces only Barbaresco. The three vintages I have tasted have been good—elegant, spicy, clean wines that in style resemble those of di Gresy and Ceretto. Moresco's Barbaresco comes from a single vineyard, Podere de Pajore. The 1967, tasted in 1985, seemed more like a great burgundy than a Barbaresco. His 1978, acclaimed in his native Piedmont, is good, and certainly flavorful, with ripe cherry fruit in evidence. The 1979 shows more concentration and perfume than the 1978, and the promise of complexity and a velvety richness if cellared to 1987–88. Given the three wines of Moresco that I have tasted, I question his exalted status among Barbaresco's elite winemakers.

PASQUERO-SECONDO (BARBARESCO)* * *

1979 Barbaresco d'Paytin	($14.00)	76
1980 Barbaresco d'Paytin	($14.00)	75
1982 Barbaresco d'Paytin	($14.00)	86

This tiny producer produces gentle, supple, medium-weight Barbarescos of which the best come from the Sori d'Paytin vineyard. His 1978 is excellent, a benchmark standard for the more elegant, less robust and muscular style of Barbaresco that is most consistently practiced by di Gresy and Ceretto. Since 1978, his wines have been good but hardly inspiring, although the 1982 Sori d'Paytin is very promising. It is supple, deeply fruity, with ripe, very fleshy, forward flavors of ripe black cherries, medium to full body, and a good, long finish. It should be ready by 1989–90. Neither the 1980 nor the 1979 exhibit sufficient fruit to warrant interest. Both are dry, rather lean, austere wines.

PELISSERO (BARBARESCO)* * *

1978 Barbaresco	($12.00)	84

The only vintage I have tasted is 1978: a powerful, very full-bodied, broodingly backward, dark and tannic wine. Its cherry, ripe, sweet fruit more than balances out the huge tannic clout; however, I wouldn't dare drink it before 1990–1992.

PRODUTTORI DI BARBARESCO (BARBARESCO)* * * *

1979 Barbaresco Asili	($12.00)	89
1979 Barbaresco Moccagatta	($12.00)	87
1979 Barbaresco Ovello	($12.00)	85
1979 Barbaresco Pora	($12.00)	85
1979 Barbaresco Rabaja	($12.00)	87
1979 Barbaresco Rio Sordo	($12.00)	85

Many wine enthusiasts take a dim view of cooperative-produced wines. There are indeed growers' cooperatives that are poorly run, but this cooperative of upwards of 50 Barbaresco growers is considered by many to be one of the finest in the world. Should you find any of Produttori's 1978 Barbarescos still languishing on the shelves, don't hesitate to grab the Moccagatta, Pora, Montefico, and Rabaja vineyard-designated Barbarescos. All could use cellaring until 1990–1995. As for the 1979s, they are an impressive group as well, though marginally less concentrated and tannic than the 1978s. While none is fully mature, they all have such ripeness of fruit that they are accessible. The Asili has a striking bouquet of rich cherry fruit, saddle leather, and flowers. Rich and supple with layers of fruit, it is the standard bearer for the class of 1979 Produttori wines. The Rabaja is dark and rich, more muscular and closed; it needs until 1990 to reach its peak. The Ovello, Pora, Rio Sordo, and Moccagatta are still quite youthful, closed, and young. Of these four wines, the Moccagatta looks to be the most impressive. I would keep an eye out for the 1982s when they are released as these wines represent outstanding value.

PRUNOTTO (BAROLO)* * *

1978 Barolo	($12.00)	78
1979 Barolo	($9.00)	82
1978 Barolo Bussia	($14.00)	84
1979 Barolo Bussia	($11.99)	85
1978 Barolo Cannubi	($15.00)	80
1979 Barolo Cannubi	($11.99)	83
1978 Barolo Ginestra	($14.00)	86
1979 Barolo Ginestra	($11.99)	86

A very traditional producer of Piedmontese wines, Prunotto's wines tend to be hard, very dry and tannic, and sometimes coarse. I was not fond of the firm's 1974s and even the 1971s were less successful than other producers'. All the grapes for Prunotto wines are purchased, and the wine is aged for a long time in large oak casks. The wines are dense and chewy, and those who like this rough and tumble, macho style of Barolo may score them higher than I do. Curiously, I thought Prunotto's 1979s more fruity and successful than his 1978s, an overall better vintage. In both vintages, I preferred the Ginestra because of

its extroverted, rich, chewy, fruity character. And it has plenty of
tannin. The 1978s should peak between 1990–2005, the 1979s between
1987–1995.

RENATO RATTI (BAROLO/DOLCETTO)* * * * *

1979 Barolo	($8.00)	78
1978 Barolo Marcenasco	($20.00)	90
1979 Barolo Marcenasco	($16.00)	85
1985 Dolcetto Colombe	($9.00)	85
1981 Barolo Marcenasco Conca	($16.00)	84
1979 Barolo Marcenasco Rocche	($16.00)	87
1980 Barolo Marcenasco Rocche	($16.00)	85
1981 Barolo Marcenasco	($16.00)	86

Ratti's sensibly made wines combine richness with lushness, power
with finesse, and at a consistently high level of quality, even in difficult
vintages such as 1980 and 1981. There is almost a sweetness to his
wines as a result of picking his grapes at a very high level of maturity.
His wines are produced in temperature-controlled stainless steel vats
and aged in casks only for the minimum time mandated by Italian law.
Unlike some of his peers, who appear to have gone too far with their
compromises to the modern taste for soft, ready to drink wines, Ratti's
wines are not wimpish but rich, full-bodied, intense wines with 10–15
years' aging potential in the top vintages. However, since he retains
such a marvelous balance and depth of fruit to the wines, they are
approachable when young. His Barolos are wines to search out, particularly the special Marcenasco Vineyard wines that occasionally list
the subsections of that vineyard, Conca and Rocche, as well. His
1978s can be drunk now, but need another 4–5 years of cellaring. His
1979s are fully mature, his 1980s almost mature, and his 1981s great
successes for the vintage. His Dolcetto from the Colombe vineyard is
the benchmark standard for all other Dolcettos in Piedmont. Unfortunately, too little of it is available—it is a captivating, lush, fruity wine
that is a joy to drink.

GIUSEPPI RINALDI (BAROLO)* * *

1982 Barbera d'Alba	($5.99)	65
1970 Barolo Brunate	($29.00)	72
1971 Barolo Brunate	($32.00)	88
1974 Barolo Brunate	($26.50)	86
1978 Barolo Brunate	($24.95)	87
1979 Barolo Brunate	($20.00)	78
1980 Barolo Brunate	($12.99)	75
1982 Barolo Brunate	($28.00)	88

One taste of this man's wine reveals a very traditional approach to Barolo winemaking. These are rather huge, intense, very aromatic, very chewy, very tannic, and very large-scaled wines that may well intimidate neophyte tasters. The three stars are the 1978, 1974, and 1971. The surprise is the 1974, a vintage that the Piedmontese cognoscenti hold in high regard, but in which the reality often is far less encouraging. Rinaldi's 1974 is almost mature; rich, chocolatey, smoky, tarry notes are pervasive in its bouquet. Rich, deep, and full-bodied, it should age well for another 4–5 years. The 1971 is at its peak: rich, chewy, lush flavors, an altogether overwhelming array of aromas ranging from mushrooms to road tar to spring flowers. Massive on the palate, with some volatile acidity present, it is a textbook, big, old-style Barolo. Both the 1978 and 1982 may turn out, circa 1995–2000, to be the best wines. Both have layers of ripe, dense fruit, huge body, and mouth-searing tannins. The 1970 was totally oxidized and could not be judged, the 1979 bitterly tannic, and the 1980 excessively volatile. G. Rinaldi looks to be a hit-and-miss producer, but in the top vintages he seems right on target.

ROAGNA (BARBARESCO)* * *

1982 Barbaresco	($15.00)	78
1979 Crichet Pajè	($12.00)	86

| 1982 Crichet Pajè | ($14.00) | 80 |

| N.V. Opera Prima | ($12.50) | 60 |

I have enjoyed Roagna's wine, so I was surprised to see recent releases do so poorly. The 1979 Crichet Pajè is an extremely elegant Barbaresco for drinking now. Loaded with spicy vanillin oak and ripe cherry fruit, this wine has excellent balance and a surprising measure of finesse. However, the 1982 Barbaresco is lean, quite short and insubstantial on the palate, and really atypical for the vintage. The 1982 Crichet Pajè should, given the vintage, be a bigger, richer, better wine than the 1979. It is not. It tastes lean and, while it has a nice, attractive bouquet, seems disappointing for Roagna and the vintage. The new non-vintage Opera Prima, vinified and aged in small oak casks, tasts sour, with the new oak totally obliterating any trace of Nebbiolo fruit. It is an experiment that seems to have missed its mark.

L. SANDRONE (BAROLO)* * * *

| 1980 Barolo | ($12.00) | 84 |

| 1981 Barolo | ($12.00) | 82 |

| 1982 Barolo | ($15.00) | 90 |

| 1985 Dolcetto d'Alba | ($6.99) | 85 |

| 1984 Dolcetto d'Alba | ($6.50) | 80 |

Sandrone is a very small producer of both Barolo and Dolcetto. His wines are very dark in color, quite rich, robust, and, in the case of his Barolo, a very tannic, potentially very long-lived wine. The superstar is the 1982 Barolo, a chewy, very concentrated, full-bodied wine exuding scents of chocolate, leather, and road tar. It is explosively rich and deep, lingers and lingers, and should be quite a stunning Barolo circa 1995–2000. Don't miss the 1985 Dolcetto either.

VALENTINO (BAROLO/DOLCETTO)* * * *

| 1978 Barolo | ($12.00) | 89 |

| 1979 Barolo | ($12.00) | 87 |

1980 Bricco Manzoni	($8.00)	85

1985 Dolcetto d'Alba	($6.99)	84

An excellent producer whom I have only followed since 1978, but whose wines show top-flight winemaking skills. Furthermore, the prices are extremely reasonable. His blended wine, Bricco Manzoni, is ripe, earthy, quite delicious, and full-bodied. It is meant to be drunk over the next 3–4 years. The 1978 and 1979 Barolos are rich, smoky, tarry-scented wines, quite full-bodied, very cleanly made, with broad, ripe flavors. The 1979 is for drinking now and over the next 5–6 years; the 1978 for cellaring until 1990 and then enjoying for the next decade. Don't overlook the exuberant, intense, very fruity, rich, blackberry-scented and flavored Dolcetto. It is ideal for drinking over the next few years.

VALLANA (SPANNA/GATTINARA)* * * *

1978 Barbera	($4.25)	83

1978 Boca	($7.25)	74

1980 Bonarda	($4.25)	73

N.V. Bucciarossa	($3.50)	81

1979 Gattinara	($9.50)	85

1966 Spanna Montalbano	($14.50)	89

1967 Spanna Montalbano	($14.50)	85

1969 Spanna Montalbano	($11.50)	86

1974 Spanna Montalbano	($9.00)	85

1977 Spanna Montalbano	($7.50)	84

1966 Spanna Piemonte	($16.00)	87

1968 Spanna Piemonte	($12.50)	85

1974 Spanna Piemonte	($9.00)	86
1976 Spanna Piemonte	($9.00)	85
1978 Spanna Piemonte	($8.50)	87
1967 Spanna Traversagna	($14.50)	86
1977 Spanna Traversagna	($7.50)	82

One of the most unique individuals I have ever met was Vallana. I can vividly remember him telling me that if he could hold a glass of wine parallel with his abdomen and smell its bouquet, the vintage was great. Some of his wines have been among the finest Italian red wines I have ever drunk. His 1958, 1961, and 1964 Spannas Campa Raudii were superb wines that are still evolving and continue to be outstanding today. Vallana's peers in Piedmont always accused Vallana of illegally blending in juice from southern Italy, an allegation that was never proven, and whether it is true or not, the bottom line was that no one in Gattinara or Spanna (and few in Barolo or Barbaresco) have produced such majestic wines. Reports are that Vallana and his wines have slipped, but as the scores above attest, his 1978 Spanna is excellent and 1979 Gattinara better than any his winemaking rivals in Gattinara have produced. His wines are not very elegant, but rather very rich, dense, powerful, deeply colored, somewhat rustic wines that age beautifully for 15–25 years.

Of the above wines, all are quite ready to drink except for the 1979 Gattinara, which is quite dark in color, rich, chewy, robust, and quite tannic. It should hit its peak between 1990–2000. The 1978 Spanna is excellent, with a rich, intense bouquet of cedar, tobacco, chocolate, and smoky, tarry fruit. It has layers of fruit and will improve for at least another 4–5 years. Both 1977 Spannas are good, particularly in view of the horrible vintage conditions. Among the older wines, the 1974, 1969, 1967, and 1966 Spanna Montalbanos are lush, rich, very aromatic wines with bouquets of sweet cedar, smoke, coffee, and ripe, tarry fruit. Only the 1966 Spanna Piemonte smells a little odd at first, but with 2–3 hours of breathing, cleans up and becomes intensely perfumed with scents of tar, hickory, fennel, and ripe, plummy fruit. It is very rich and concentrated on the palate. Vallana's wines are among the most individualistic produced. They are very old-style, rich, chewy, unfiltered wines that must be rested and decanted 1–2 hours before serving.

VIETTI (BAROLO/DOLCETTO)* * * *

1982 Barbaresco	($15.00)	82
1981 Barbaresco Masseria	($12.00)	80
1982 Barbaresco Masseria	($14.00)	86
1980 Barbera Rocche	($4.75)	78
1978 Barolo Briacca	($14.00)	87
1980 Barolo Briacca	($8.95)	81
1978 Barolo Rocche	($14.00)	88
1980 Barolo Rocche	($8.95)	80
1982 Barolo Rocche	($17.00)	90
1985 Dolcetto	($6.95)	85
1985 Dolcetto Disa	($6.95)	85
1982 Dolcetto San Giorgio	($4.95)	86
1982 Fioretto	($7.00)	78
1982 Nebbiolo d'Alba	($4.95)	84

Alfredo Currado is the proprietor and winemaker of the Vietti winery and in addition to being one of the most respected talents of the region is a remarkably gentle and gracious man. He continues to increase the number of different bottlings of wine, preferring to vineyard designate everything on his distinctive artistic labels. His best wines are his Barolos, which usually need 10–15 years of cellaring. In all of Vietti's wines, he achieves a dense, rich color and avoids excessive cask aging that can lead to oxidation and volatile acidity problems. His 1971 Briacca was still not fully mature when tasted in October 1985. His 1971 Rocche is just now entering its plateau of maturity. His 1978 Barolos are outstanding successes and his 1982s perhaps his finest wines to date, particularly the fabulously rich, full-bodied, dense Rocche. His Dolcettos are usually quite deeply colored and fruity. The 1982 Dolcetto San Giorgio is as good as Dolcetto can get: plummy, soft, decadently fruity and opulent. The 1985s are also gorgeously fruity and supple and significantly better than his disappointing 1984 Dolcettos. The Fioretto, a blended wine that Vietti has introduced, is impressively dark in color, but rather dull and flat on the palate and clearly in need of some acidity. His 1982 Barbaresco is forward but supple, very fruity, and deep, with at least a decade of cellaring potential. His 1982 Barolo Rocche is the best Barolo I have yet tasted from Vietti—a profound wine.

Piedmont's White Wines

Piedmont does produce a handful of interesting white wines. Of course, the region also makes an ocean of Asti Spumante, the ever popular, sweet, sparkling wine that can be good but has lost favor among serious wine enthusiasts because so much of it is cloyingly sweet, dull, and heavy. The serious dry white wines of Piedmont are the Gavi white wines made from the Cortese grape and the Arneis white wines produced from the grape of the same name. There are also experimental plantings of Chardonnay, with Angelo Gaja's being the most promising, and a very low alcohol, delicious, fresh, very fragrant, slightly sparkling Muscat-based wine called Moscato d'Asti, which in the hands of producers such as Vietti, Giacosa, and Vignaioli St. Stefano of Ceretto puts any Asti Spumante to shame.

ARNEIS DEI ROERI

1985 Castello di Neive	($12.00)	87
1985 Giacosa	($14.00)	88
1985 Rabino S. Vittoria	($4.99)	82
1984 Vietti	($10.00)	75
1985 Ceretto	($15.00)	86

Arneis is a wine with historical reputation and with perhaps as much potential as any white grape yet planted in Piedmont. The quantities produced to date have been very small. Both Castello di Neive and Giacosa produced very fine 1983, 1984, and 1985 Arneis wines. Giacosa's is lighter and more elegant, Castello di Neive's richer, fatter, and a more powerful wine. Vietti also produces Arneis, which is quite dry, with a taste and scent of almonds, good body, and loads of fresh fruit. I have not been impressed by it. The famous red wine producer Ceretto made an Arneis in 1985, and it is excellent, fresh, loaded with fruit, but requires drinking over the next 1–2 years.

GAVI AND CORTESE DI GAVI

1983 Broglia Fasciola	($10.99)	85
1983 Pio Cesare	($8.49)	85
1984 Pio Cesare	($8.99)	82
1985 Pio Cesare	($11.99)	85
1984 Contratto	($7.49)	84
1984 Gallo d'Oro	($8.99)	84
1983 La Scolca	($18.00)	84
1984 Villa Sparina	($10.99)	84

Gavi white wines have gotten considerable acclaim but, while generally pleasant, dry, austere wines, they are considerably overpriced when looked at with respect to what is available elsewhere from Italy. In style, they have an austerity and a bone dry, almost severe character that is vaguely reminiscent of a French Chablis that has been tank fermented and not exposed to any aging in wood casks. The 1983s are still on the shelves and are better wines from a fruitier, riper, richer vintage than the new releases. The 1984s are by and large ungenerous and too severe. The 1985s are excellent, but are just now coming on the market. Certainly, Pio Cesare's Cortesi di Gavi confirmed the vintage's fine reputation. Should you still be interested, I recommend the above wines, keeping in mind that the 1983 is better as a general rule than the 1984, and 1985 potentially the best yet.

MOSCATO D'ASTI

1985 Ceretto Santo Stefano	($6.49)	87
1985 Dogliotti Caudrine	($4.99)	84
1985 B. Giacosa	($6.99)	85

1985 Rivetti	($6.99)	87

1985 Vietti	($6.49)	85

These exquisitely scented, moderately sweet Muscats are very low in alcohol (5–7% is normal), have intense bouquets of apricot, peaches, and other summer fruit, are light in body, and slightly sparkling. They are so fresh and youthful that they are a joy to drink either as an apéritif or with a fruit dessert. Fresh, vivacious, and lively, I recommend the above producers highly. These wines must be drunk within two years of their vintage; they will not keep.

TUSCANY

Tuscany's Red Wines

The red wines of Tuscany are even more famous than the red wines of Piedmont. The diversity in winemaking styles, not to mention the range of quality, is enormous. The highly touristed region is of course most famous for its Chianti, the light to medium ruby-colored wine of which I find the great majority frail, pale, and quite insipid. However, there is top-quality Chianti wine made. Monsanto, Capannelle, Monte Vertine, Badia a Coltibuono, Ruffino, Castello di Rampolla, and Isole e Olena are a handful of producers who make world-class, serious wines of flavor and character.

Tuscany is also the home base for Italy's most expensive red wine, Brunello di Montalcino. This is an interesting wine, and usually overoaked because of the ridiculous law that requires a minimum of 3½ years in wood. There are a lot of underachievers in Brunello with famous names and expensive wines. Ironically, some of the best producers of Brunello di Montalcino are some of the least known and least publicized.

Other Tuscan red wines to take note of include a wine called Carmignano, in taste not distinguishable from a Chianti, and Vino Nobile di Montepulciano, another legendary Tuscan wine that only rarely lives up to its historical reputation of quality.

Yet the most interesting wines being produced in Tuscany may well turn out to be wines made outside the Italian wine laws and not entitled to appellation status. Over the last decade, many top producers inspired by oenological practices in Bordeaux, and also by Piero Antinori of Tuscany and Angelo Gaja in Piedmont, have been making more and more wines that are either 100% Sangiovese (the basic red grape of Chianti and Brunello) or Sangiovese/Cabernet blends. These wines, often aged à la Bordeaux in small new oak casks, have proved to be exceptionally good, ageworthy and, despite double-digit price tags, very popular with wine enthusiasts. Most of them are infinitely better, richer wines than the great majority of Chiantis. At present, I am most impressed by such wines as Monte Vertine's Le Pergole Torte, Il Palazzino's Grosso Senese, Castello di Volpaia's Coltassaia, Antinori's Tignanello, Villa Cafaggio's Solatio Basilica, Avignonesi's Grifi, San Guido's Sassicaia, Castello di Rampolla's Sammarco, Berardenga's Fontalloro, Fontodi's Fiaccianello, and the Monte Antico. Given the high quality of many of these wines and the enthusiastic reaction they have received from consumers, one can expect many more like them to appear on the market, even though they can legally only be called "Vino da Tavola." These revolutionary new wines are, however, not cheap—expect to pay $10–$20 a bottle for them.

TUSCANY
QUICK VINTAGE GUIDE

1985—As in Piedmont, there is great enthusiasm for this vintage. No one yet has said it is the vintage of the century, but it is expected to be one of the very best vintages in the last 20–25 years. It was a hot, drought year.

1984—A dreadful year, much worse in Tuscany than in Piedmont to the north. Rain and a paucity of sunshine were the culprits. No doubt the trade will say the wines are light and commercial, but at this point this looks to be a vintage to pass up.

1983—Quite highly regarded, Tuscany had weather conditions similar to those experienced in Bordeaux hundreds of miles to the west. A drought year of intense heat caused sugars and the consequent alcohol level to skyrocket in the grapes. The reports are that the wines are ripe, alcoholic, fat, low in acidity, and jammy, with deep layers of fruit.

1982—Considered more "classic" than 1983, which I suppose means less powerful and less opulently fruity and rich wines. Certainly a very good vintage with firm tannins, good depth, and ripeness. My tasting notes indicate that the vintage is the best since 1975, maybe 1971. A year to be taken seriously. For Brunello di Montalcino, it is the best vintage since 1970.

1981—An average vintage of light, pleasant, rather frail wines. Most are fully mature. Only a handful will get better.

1980—An average vintage of light, soft, easy to drink wines. They require drinking up.

1979—A good vintage of wine with more flesh and stuffing than either 1980 or 1981. As in most of Europe, a gigantic crop was harvested.

1978—Rather highly regarded, but I have never found the wines to be terribly exciting, either in Brunello or Chianti.

1977—Rather successful, particularly in view of the negative publicity surrounding this vintage in Europe. Most Brunellos and Chiantis have more fruit and character than the more highly rated wines of 1978.

1976—For Tuscany, a disastrous vintage because of heavy rains that diluted the grapes.

1975—A very good vintage, 1975 was initially claimed by the producers of Chianti and Brunello to be a great vintage, but it is not. All of the wines are fully mature and should be drunk up over the next several years.

1974—An average year of pleasant but rather charmless wines that have lacked flesh and fruit. Most are now too old to drink.

1973—It has been a good five years since I last tasted a 1973 Chianti or Brunello. The wines were never very attractive, were excessively light and feeble, and I would suspect are now totally decrepit.

1972—Like most of Europe, a wet, cold summer precluded the grapes from reaching maturity. Most of the better producers did not declare a vintage, preferring to declassify their entire crop. A disaster.

1971—Arguments among Chianti-lovers have long raged as to which was a greater vintage, 1971 or 1970. The 1971s, rich, alcoholic, sumptuous wines, drank well young but are now tiring. They can, where well stored, be delicious, voluptuous, rich wines that are full of fruit, but even the best preserved examples of this vintage should be drunk immediately.

1970—Unquestionably a greater vintage for Brunello di Montalcino than 1971, but in Chianti most observers have given 1971 the edge. However, the 1970 Chiantis, less flashy and flamboyant in their youth, have opened and blossomed in aging. The Chiantis from this vintage, overshadowed by the 1971s, can offer many surprises. The best Brunellos are sensational and will last at least another decade.

A GUIDE TO TUSCANY'S BEST PRODUCERS OF CHIANTI, BRUNELLO, VINO NOBILE DI MONTEPULCIANO

* * * * * (OUTSTANDING PRODUCERS)

Altesino (Brunello)
Campogiovanni (Brunello)
Constanti (Brunello)
Il Poggione (Brunello)

Monsanto (Chianti)
Pertimali (Brunello)
Castello di Rampolla (Chianti)

* * * * (EXCELLENT PRODUCERS)

Antinori (Chianti)
Avignonesi (Vino Nobile)
Badia a Coltibuono (Chianti)
Berardenga (Chianti)
Boscarelli (Vino Nobile)
Capannelle (Chianti)
Carparzo (Brunello)
Castello de Castellina (Chianti)
Fontodi (Chianti)

Il Palazzino (Chianti)
Isole e Olena (Chianti)
Lisini (Brunello)
Monte Antico (Tuscany)
Monte Vertine (Chianti)
Ruffino (Chianti)
San Guido (Tuscany)
Castello di Volpaia (Chianti)

* * * (GOOD PRODUCERS)

Barbi (Brunello)
Biondi Santi (Brunello)
Ca' del Bosco (Brunello)
Camigliano (Brunello)
Capezzano (Vino Nobile)
Caprili (Brunello)
Fanetti (Vino Nobile)
Fassati (Vino Nobile)
La Fortuna (Brunello)

Montesodi (Chianti)
Castello di Nipozzano (Chianti)
Nozzole (Chianti)
Riecine (Chianti)
San Filippo (Brunello)
Savignola Paolina (Chianti)
Villa Cafaggio (Chianti)
Villa Selvapiana (Chianti)

ITALY: NEW BREED REDS—A LIST OF THE 20 BEST
A Quick Reference Guide to the Best
Sangiovese- or Cabernet-Based Wines

Borro Cepparello (Isole e Olena) Chianti
Brusco di Barbi (Barbi) Brunello
Ca del Pazzo (Carparzo) Brunello
Capannelle Rosso (Capannelle) Chianti
Coltassala (Castello di Volpaia) Chianti
Flaccianello Della Pieve (Fontodi) Chianti
Fontalloro (Felsina) Chianti
Grifi (Avignonesi) Vino Nobile
Grosso Senese (Il Palazzino) Chianti
Il Sodaccio (Monte Vertine) Chianti

Le Pergole Torte (Monte Vertine) Chianti
Sangioveto Grosso (Monsanto) Chianti
Monte Antico (Monte Antico) Tuscany
Palazzo Altesi (Altesino) Brunello
Sammarco (Castello di Rampolla) Chianti
San Giorgio (Lungarotti) Umbria
Sassicaia (Antinori) Tuscany
Solaia (Antinori) Tuscany
Solatia Basilica (Villa Cafaggio) Chianti
Tignanello (Antinori) Chianti

Tuscany—A Buying Strategy

The buying strategy for Tuscany is simple—buy without hesitation the 1983s and 1982s, this area's best overall vintages since 1970 and 1971. Chiantis are deeply fruity, ripe, rich wines that will give great pleasure for most of the next 5 years. The top Brunellos and new breed Sangiovese- or Cabernet-based wines will provide fascinating drinking for at least the next decade. As for Chianti, unless you are buying wine from a great producer like Monsanto in a great vintage, you are best advised to steer clear of anything older than 4–5 years for the simple reason that Chianti is a notoriously short-lived wine. In short, your first choice should be the 1982s from Tuscany and second choice the 1983s. For Tuscany's white wines, the 1985s are vastly superior to the 1984s.

ANTINORI* * * *

1980 Tignanello	($13.00)	83
1981 Tignanello	($18.00)	88

1982 Tignanello   ($20.00)   90

Tignanello, a blend of roughly 80–85% Sangiovese and 15–20% Cabernet, is one of the most successful new breeds of Italian wines. Unfortunately, its price continues to escalate. The 1982 and 1981 are the best Tignanellos released yet. Both have sweet, oaky, ripe, fruity, complex bouquets, supple but firm, deep flavors, and medium to full body. The 1981 can be drunk now but will likely improve for 4–5 years. The 1982, a richer, more tannic wine, ideally needs 3–4 year. The 1980 is less opulent and charming, with a more compact feel on the palate, but still flavorful and attractive. I would drink the 1980 over the next 2–3 years.

AVIGNONESI* * * *

1981 Grifi   ($12.00)   87

1982 Grifi   ($12.00)   86

1983 Grifi   ($12.00)   88

This wine is the product of the fine Avignonesi winery. It is also a blend of Sangiovese and Cabernet with the Sangiovese representing 70–75% of the total. The three vintages released to date have all been very impressive yet differently styled. The 1981 is rich but very elegant. It exhibits cherry fruit, oak, flowers, and vanillin in its bouquet. Lush and rich on the palate, it should continue to drink well for 4–5 years. The 1982 is reputedly better, but in two separate tastings it had plenty of potential, a deeper, richer looking color, more tannin and oak, but just does not "sing" as my English counterparts would say. It definitely needs 2–3 years more of bottle age. At present, the most impressive wine of this trio is the 1983. It has a very complex bouquet of cigar box spices, ripe, rich bing cherry fruit, and noticeable oak; this is a full-bodied, tannic wine with plenty of rich, supple fruit and an alcoholic clout to its finish. It should age well for upwards of a decade.

CAPEZZANO* * *

1980 Ghiail Della Furba   ($15.00)   86

From the best producer of Carmignano in Tuscany, Capezzano also produces a tiny amount of this wine, a 70% Cabernet Sauvignon, 30%

Merlot blend. The 1980 has a textbook blackcurrant, cedary, olive-scented bouquet, good firm tannins and medium body.

CARPARZO* * * *

1982 Ca del Pazzo	($15.00)	82

1983 Ca del Pazzo	($20.00)	86

Produced by the excellent Brunello producer Carparzo from a 50-50 blend of Cabernet Sauvignon and Sangiovese, the 1982 has dark ruby color, good depth and ripeness of fruit, but lacks complexity and tastes a bit dull and one-dimensional. The 1983 seems to show greater depth, richness, and more complexity in its bouquet. Both should age for 5–7 years.

CASTELLARE DI CASTELLINA* * * *

1982 I Sodi di S. Niccolo	($15.00)	87

A 100% Sangiovese wine, the 1982, the only vintage I have tasted, was quite impressive.The bouquet suggests very ripe black cherries and chestnuts. Medium- to full-bodied, long, with good richness and length, this wine should continue to improve for at least 4–6 more years.

FONTODI* * * *

1982 Flaccianello Della Pieve	($14.99)	89

The 1982 Flaccianello should provide convincing evidence that 100% Sangiovese wines offer considerably more in flavor interest and complexity than regular Chiantis. This wine is excellent, deep in color, with an explosive bouquet of plums, new oak, and chocolate. On the palate, the wine is smoky, ripe, lush, yet seems to need 2–3 more years to resolve its tannins. A very impressive wine, it should be drunk between 1987 and 2000.

IL PALLAZZINO* * * *

1982 Grosso Senese	($12.00)	88

A 100% Sangiovese wine from the excellent Chianti producer Il Pal-lazzino, this wine is aged in small oak casks. Explosively rich on the palate with big, rich, fat, cherry and strawberry flavors wrapped in spicy, toasty oak, this is a rather voluptuous wine, full-bodied, rather heady and high in alcohol, but loaded with flavor and character. Drink over the next 3–4 years.

ISOLE E OLENA* * * *

| 1982 Cepparello | ($10.50) | 85 |

A 100% Sangiovese wine with a very Bordeaux-like personality, the 1982 Cepparello has a dark ruby, deep color, spice-box, rich, fruity bouquet, moderate levels of tannin, excellent aging potential of 5 more years, and a clean, well-balanced feel. A young, promising wine.

MONSANTO* * * * *

| 1974 Sangioveto Grosso | ($16.00) | 75–85 |

Tasted twice, this 100% Sangiovese from Chianti's finest producer proved disappointing once and very good a second time. From the good bottle, the wine smelled like a textbook Graves, with a tobacco-scented, smoky, earthy bouquet. On the palate, the wine was rich, alcoholic, and quite big and aggressive. Will the real Sangioveto Grosso please come forth?

MONTE ANTICO* * * *

1981	($5.99)	86
1978 Riserva	($6.99)	86
1979 Riserva	($6.99)	84
1980 Riserva	($6.99)	87
1981 Riserva	($6.99)	87
1983	($5.99)	86

This Tuscan wine is one of today's great values in complex, rich, savory wines. It is made from 100% Sangiovese grapes grown on a vineyard adjacent to Brunello di Montalcino. In quality it challenges and even surpasses many $20–$25 Brunellos and virtually all of the $8–$10 Chianti Classicos. Both the 1978 and 1979 Riservas are quite mature with rich, sweet, broad flavors, full-intensity bouquets of oriental spices, rich, berry fruit, smoked meats, and cinnamon. Both have a good deal of sediment and are obviously unfiltered wines, so care must be taken to decant them. The 1980 Riserva is similar, only darker in color, a little firmer on the palate, but complex and aromatic, with sweet, ripe fruit displayed in abundance. The 1981 and 1983 ($6) are, for their complexity and quality, among the greatest Italian red wine values on the market. Both have complex, cedary, roasted chestnut, spicy bouquets, long, deep, soft lush flavors, and 1–2 more years of evolution ahead of them. The 1981 Riserva is styled similarly to the 1981 regular, perhaps a trifle less expansive on the palate, and capable of evolving 4–5 years.

MONTE VERTINE* * * *

1982 Il Sodaccio	($18.00)	83
1979 Le Pergole Torte	($20.00)	87
1980 Le Pergole Torte	($18.00)	84
1982 Le Pergole Torte	($14.00)	87

Virtually anything produced by this grower in Tuscany is of high quality, from his Chianti Classicos to the limited bottlings of 100% Sangiovese Le Pergole Torte and Il Sodaccio. The best two vintages of Le Pergole Torte to date have been the 1979 and 1982. The 1979 is a delicious wine with an uncanny resemblance to an intensely fruity, spicy Zinfandel. It is richly scented and just now reaching its plateau of maturity. The 1980 is good, but has less length and dimension than the other vintages. The 1982, the new release, is quite exciting, with a toasty new oak bouquet filled with the scents of ripe cherry fruit. The impression on the palate is one of balanced richness, moderate tannins, and 4–5 years of further evolution. The 1982 Il Sodaccio is good but rather light and lacks the richness and dimension of the 1982 Le Pergole Torte.

CASTELLO DI RAMPOLLA* * * *

1980 Sammarco	($18.00)	86
1981 Sammarco	($18.00)	88
1982 Sammarco	($20.00)	90

A blend of 75% Cabernet Sauvignon and 25% Sangiovese, the 1980 is a rather forceful, rich, aggressive wine that exhibits a lot of character and richness, has medium to full body, and a tannic finish. It needs 2–4 more years to develop. The 1981 is richer, with a rounder, lusher texture. It has immense appeal and should develop well for at least 4–7 years. The 1982 is a profound wine, rich, intense, with great length, depth, and 10–15 years of aging potential.

SAN GUIDO* * * *

1980 Sassicaia	($16.00)	86
1981 Sassicaia	($22.00)	91
1982 Sassicaia	($30.00)	91

This wine, which has gained something of a cult following, is a blend of 95% Cabernet Sauvignon and 5% Cabernet Franc. It is an excellent wine, to date the finest Cabernet wine made in Italy. It is also very long-lived. A vertical tasting of the 1982, 1981, 1980, 1979, 1978, 1976, 1975, and 1971 I attended in January, 1986, proved quite conclusively that the 1981 and 1982 are the finest Sassicaias to date. Both are stunningly rich wines, not unlike great Médocs; both need 10–12 years of cellaring to peak. Following the 1981 and 1982, the 1978 and 1975 stand out. The 1980, which is widely available, can be held 5–6 years, is dark ruby, elegant, and showing well already. It does not have the concentration and depth of the 1981, 1978, or 1975. Sassicaia remains hard to find and quite expensive.

VINATTIERI ROSSO

1983	($12.50)	83

The bouquet is richly fruity, oaky, and interesting. On the palate, the wine is medium-bodied but rather short in the finish and somewhat lacking in the mid-range. A blend of Sangiovese and Cabernet that just misses the mark (perhaps made from young vines).

CASTELLO DI VOLPAIA* * * *

1981 Coltassala	($14.00)	84
1982 Coltassala	($14.00)	87

The Volpaia estate makes good Chianti and the Coltassala is the name of their 100% Sangiovese, small cask-aged Tuscan wine. The 1981 is a very good wine, oaky with plenty of black cherry fruit present, medium-bodied, rather graceful, with a supple, lush finish; it can be drunk now or aged 2–4 more years. The 1982 is altogether a bigger, denser, deeper wine, medium to dark ruby with a ripe cherry, spicy, oaky bouquet, tannin, and medium- to full-bodied flavors. The 1982 needs 3–5 more years to reach its zenith.

Brunello di Montalcino and Rosso di Montalcino

Tuscany's and Italy's most expensive red wine is, in reality, rarely worth its stiff price. That is not to suggest that good Brunello cannot be found, but the romantic and historical accounts of this wine seem to have more to do with its legendary status than the reality of its flavor depth, dimension, and complexity. I have tasted a lot of Brunello di Montalcino and can remember only four great bottles ever tasted: the 1970 Constanti, 1970 Il Poggione, 1970 Barbi, and 1975 Altesino. That is a rather pitiful percentage for a great wine, yet it confirms the fact that Brunello di Montalcino is the Chambertin of Italy—always outrageously priced and overrated, but rarely great. The most famous producer, Biondi Santi, gets prices of $50–$150 for recent vintages of his wines and they are among the most disappointing wines of this region. From a consumer's perspective, I would advise strongly to boycott these wines unless you can find the top wines of Brunello, which unfortunately are among the hardest to find since four of the top six producers, Altesino, Pertimali, Constanti, and Campogiovanni have very limited quantities to sell. Two excellent producers with good distribution in America are Carparzo and Il Poggione.

ALTESINO* * * * *

1979	($15.00–$20.00)	89

1980	($15.00–$20.00)	85

The only difference in these two wines is that the 1979 tastes richer, more intense, and has a more complex bouquet. The 1980 is rather light for Altesino, but quite supple, very fruity, with smoky, ripe plummy fruit, medium body, and a good finish. The 1979 is quite rich and full-bodied, deep with layers of tarry, smoky fruit, and 5–8 more years of improvement ahead of it. Altesino also produces an excellent single-vineyard-designated Brunello that I have not tasted since 1975.

BARBI* * *

1977	($25.00)	85
1978	($18.00)	78
1979	($18.00)	80
1978 Riserva	($25.00)	83

This producer was my benchmark Brunello producer before I discovered the likes of Il Poggione, Altesino, and Carparzo. Some of the older vintages are excellent. The 1964, 1971, and fabulous 1970 are memorably good Brunellos. Since the mid-'70s, the style of wine here has been lightened up and, while Barbi used to be one of the best, they are now in the second tier of Brunello producers. Perhaps this is only a temporary thing. Of the above wines, the 1979 and 1978 regular bottlings are pleasant, light, rather straightforward wines. They lack richness and depth. The 1978 Riserva shows some potential, but again does not have much of a finish or depth. The best current vintage is the regular 1977, which has an expansive, burgundian, earthy, richly fruity bouquet, medium body, and lush fruit.

BIONDI SANTI* * *

1977	($25.00)	82
1978	($25.00)	77
1979	($25.00)	70
1970 Riserva	($110.00)	86
1971 Riserva	($90.00)	85
1975 Riserva	($85.00)	87
1977 Riserva	($55.00)	80

This estate is an easy target for criticism. Prices for their wines are quite absurd, and while the wines are not bad (in fact the 1975 Riserva is very good), there are far too many mediocre wines. Not once have I tasted a great wine from Biondi Santi, although cask samples of the

1982 and 1985 looked superb. At a blind tasting several years ago, Biondi Santi vintages in the '60s and early '70s did not fare well against the competition. Of course, much is made of the fact that these wines need 2–24 hours of aeration, but I have done that only to find that they get more astringent and bitter in the glass, not better. For me the problem with these wines (forgetting the high prices) is that they are far too tannic and the tannins too often are dry and bitter. In short, the wines are unpleasant to drink and one wonders how the wine can command the price it does. Of the above vintages opened and examined over a 48-hour period, only one wine improved in the glass—the 1975 Riserva—and it was very good when it was first poured. The 1979 and 1978 are deficient in fruit. The 1977 is spicy with scents of minerals and leather and decent fruit, although not very deep or concentrated. The 1975 Riserva needs 6–10 years, but shows good color and sufficient fruit to balance out the tannin. The 1971 Riserva is quite good, the 1970 Riserva richer and more powerful. It is dark in color, and seems to have reached full maturity. Only about 1,200 cases of Riserva are made and 3,200 cases of regular Brunello, so the limited availability no doubt keeps the prices for these wines extremely high.

CA' DEL BOSCO* * *

| 1979 | ($18.00) | 84 |

This looks to be a well made Brunello, quite backward, dark in color, very spicy with the telltale aroma of saddle leather. The 1979 Del Bosco needs 6–10 years of cellaring as the tannins are immense at the moment. Hard, tough, and inaccessible, it may ultimately merit a higher score.

CAMIGLIANO* * *

1974 Riserva	($12.00)	65
1978 Riserva	($12.00)	85
1980 Riserva	($10.00)	82
1983 Rosso	($6.00)	82
1984 Rosso	($6.00)	55

This producer can be a good choice for inexpensive Brunello; however, as the scores demonstrate, consistency is often a problem. The

1975 is the best Camigliano Brunello I have tasted and still needs another 3–4 years of cellaring. The 1980 and 1978 have good, smoky, ripe, pleasant fruit and are ready for drinking. The 1983 Rosso is a good value: smoky, ripe, supple wine with plenty of cherry fruit. Otherwise, the 1984 Rosso is thin, acidic, and bitter. The 1974 has a flawed, musty, cheesy aroma that does not blow off.

CAMPOGIOVANNI* * * *

1979 Brunello di Montalcino	($18.95)	90

An up and coming star in Brunello, Campogiovanni's recent vintages have all been exceptional. The 1979 is deeply colored and still very youthful; this wine has an intense bouquet of smoky nuts, tobacco, and rich fruit, and is not unlike a fine Graves. Full-bodied, rich and still quite tannic, there is a lot of wine here. Drinkable now, I think cellaring of 4–6 years will reveal even more.

CAPRILI* * *

1979	($18.00)	86
1981	($18.95)	86

Both wines are similar: very tannic yet quite impressive Brunellos that seem to have all the depth and ripe fruit to carry the tough tannins that are present. The bouquets are quite intense with chocolate and smoky, earthy scents; the wines are quite full-bodied and rich, but 6–10 years away from maturity.

CARPARZO* * *

1978	($16.00)	85
1980	($19.00)	82
1981	($20.00)	86
1979 La Casa	($30.00)	90
1980 La Casa	($30.00)	89
1979 Riserva	($25.00)	86

1981 Rosso	($5.00)	76

1982 Rosso	($5.00)	80

This is a reliable producer of very good, and if the 1979 and 1980 La Casas are any indication, potentially great, Brunello di Montalcino. The 1979 La Casa has a stunning bouquet of rich, tarry fruit and fresh saddle leather, with some oriental spices intermingled. On the palate it explodes with a deep, rich fruitiness. Quite full-bodied and long, it was the number one Brunello in several tastings. It can be drunk now but promises to be better in 4–6 years. The 1980 La Casa is a shade less concentrated but has the same rich, smoky, complex, broadly flavored character. The 1979 Riserva is also impressive, but the tannins are quite pronounced; yet the rich, dense fruit and concentration of this wine suggests a higher-rated wine than I have scored it, provided one can wait 5–8 more years. The 1978 regular bottling is quite tarry, stemmy, and ready to drink. The 1981 shows considerably more depth and length. The two Rossos are supple, easy to drink, and very pleasant.

CONSTANTI* * * * *

1979	($25.00)	89

1980 Riserva	($40.00)	88

In 1985 I tasted this producer's 1970, a superb Brunello that did justice to the historical reputation this region's wines have. The two current releases both have considerable merit. Both of these vintages are less tannic and backward than normal. The 1980, along with the Pertimali, is one of the leading Brunellos of that vintage. Sweet, ripe, intense aromas of leather, tar, and tobacco gush from the glass. On the palate the wine is fat, quite round, and supple. It should drink well for 5–6 years. The 1979 is similarly styled, more obviously fruity and perhaps less smoky-scented in its bouquet, but still very attractive for drinking over the next 4–6 years.

LA FORTUNA* * *

1979	($15.00)	85

This is a very good Brunello. It has the characteristic harshness and aggressive tannins present, but the bouquet exhibits some tarry, ripe, earthy scents and the palate impression is one of richness, heavy tannins, and clean winemaking. Cellar until 1990–1992.

IL POGGIONE* * * * *

1979	($20.00)	88
1977 Riserva	($20.00)	89
1978 Riserva	($25.00)	89
1982 Rosso	($6.79)	85

One wishes there were more Brunellos like those of Il Poggione. Rich, intense, broadly flavored wines with balance, complexity, and character, this producer seems to extract flavor and interest out of his grapes even in the most difficult vintages. The 1982 Rosso is a forward, relatively rich, spicy, robust wine for drinking over the next 3–4 years. It is one of the best Rossos I have ever drunk. The 1979 Brunello exhibits exotic, ripe, rich, lush fruit, medium to full body and a well-developed, complex bouquet of tar, smoked nuts, and ripe fruit. The 1978 and 1977 Riservas are two of the finest Brunellos of their respective vintages. Both have full-intensity, ripe, smoky, tarry, deep bouquets, full body and surprisingly rich, lush, fruity flavors, and excellent length. The 1978 is deceptively easy to drink and seems close to maturity, although there are good, ripe tannins in the finish. Il Poggione is one of the best of the Brunello producers.

LISINI* * * *

1977	($25.00)	84
1978	($25.00)	82

This estate was one of my favorite producers, having made excellent Brunellos in 1975, 1971, 1970, and even in 1973, a difficult vintage. The 1977 is a good Brunello, but not a great wine. It is full-bodied, ripe, and impressively colored, but hard and bitter in the finish. I find it awkward and lacking grace and finesse. Perhaps 5–6 years of cellaring will be beneficial. The 1978 is plump, rather forward, with a moderately intense bouquet of tobacco and earthy fruit. It is an above-average wine, but not special.

PERTIMALI* * * * *

1979   ($25.00)   88

1980   ($25.00)   86

This small, excellent producer's wines are well worth seeking out.
They seem to be made in a more sensible modern style without excessive oak aging and consequently retain much more fruit and richness
than other Brunellos. Both vintages of Pertimali offer a deep, dark
color (among the darkest in color of any Brunello), rich, hickory,
smoky-scented bouquets, full body, deep, concentrated flavors, and
plenty of tannin. The wines are very cleanly made and need 5–7 years
of cellaring. The 1979 tastes a trifle more concentrated.

SAN FILIPPO* * *

1980   ($17.49)   85

Dark ruby with a ripe, tarry fruit, leather-scented, spicy bouquet, this
wine has a supple, accessible richness, good length, and complexity.
Not a great Brunello, but certainly a very good wine that can be drunk
now and over the next 4–5 years.

VILLA BANFI

1979   ($18.00)   74

1980   ($18.00)   75

There are great hopes for the huge fortunes invested in this estate,
but at present the vineyard is very young and the wines no doubt show
the effect. The 1980 is very dry and lacks mid-range and length. It is
a compact, rather simple wine. The 1979 is similarly styled, pleasant
and innocuous with less tannin than the 1980.

Chianti

There are hundreds of producers of Chianti. It is Italy's best-
known wine (along with the ubiquitous Lambrusco and Asti Spumante), though sadly only on occasion delicious and sublime. More
often than not, it is pale in color, diluted in flavor, and possessed of
not more than 2–3 years of bottle life. While not expensive at $5–$7 a
bottle, neither is it a good value. However, in the hands of a handful
of producers, Chianti can be an excellent wine. However, producers

who make fine Chianti charge a lot for it, so top-quality Chianti is not the value it is perceived to be.

I have tasted several hundred Chiantis and have found the quality to be generally average to below average. Moreover, I have tasted only three Chiantis in my life that I would call great: the 1970 and 1971 Monsanto Il Poggio Chianti and Berardenga 1970. Out of several hundred producers, that is a very poor record of quality. Who are the best Chianti producers? In order of my findings, Monsanto stands in a class by itself, followed by Ruffino's Gold Label Riserva Ducale, Cappannelle, Il Palazzino, Berardenga, Monte Vertine, Badia a Coltibuono, and Castello di Rampolla.

Here are my notes on the current releases from the top eight estates.

BADIA A COLTIBUONO* * * *

1974 Riserva	($14.95)	75
1978 Riserva	($9.50)	85
1979 Riserva	($13.95)	82

Coltibuono produces rather rustic Chiantis, lacking a touch in finesse, sometimes a little inconsistent, but usually intense and rather dramatic. The 1974 is tired and has an annoying bitterness and musty character that is off-putting. The 1979 is above average, a trifle too tannic and surprisingly orange at the rim. The winner is the 1978. A robust, rustic, slightly earthy, herbaceous bouquet is followed by a wine that is rich, rather alcoholic, and powerful for a Chianti. It finishes long in the mouth.

BERARDENGA FATTORIA DI FELSINA* * * *

1977	($8.95)	80
1981	($5.99)	84
1970 Riserva	($17.95)	90
1974 Riserva	($11.95)	84
1975 Riserva	($14.95)	85

| 1979 Riserva | ($7.50) 75 |

With the exception of the 1979 Riserva, which has an attractive bouquet but tasted a little tart on the palate, these were all elegant, ripe, round Chiantis with a prominent raspberry-scented fruitiness and medium body. The 1970 is a stunning, great wine and, given its great concentration and depth, one cannot help but wonder if Berardenga has lightened the style in recent vintages. The 1970 is available and will last at least another 4–5 years. Both the 1974 Riserva and 1975 Riserva are fully mature, nicely scented, cleanly made wines with good fruit, medium body, and elegance. The 1977 is supple, but short on the palate. No doubt because of the raspberry fruitiness of these wines, I find a vague resemblance to burgundy.

CAPANNELLE* * * *

| 1975 Riserva | ($15.00) 85 |

| 1977 Riserva | ($15.00) 86 |

| 1980 Riserva | ($15.00) 85 |

| 1982 Riserva | ($15.00) 84 |

The Capannelle Chiantis are among the best wines produced, and perhaps the most expensively packaged—in heavy glass bottles with very stylish labels. I have even seen a limited-edition bottle with a solid silver label. The wines, while expensive, do indeed deliver clean, rich, cherry and strawberry fruit, rich, toasty, spicy, oaky aromas, and good length. The 1975 Riserva is still a lovely mouthful of Chianti. Nineteen seventy-seven is even better: sweet, savory, lush, and quite seductive. The 1980 is not as expansive or as deeply fruity as the 1977, but offers a very good introduction to the top class of Chianti. The 1982 is good, but given the vintage less impressive than one might have expected.

IL PALAZZINO* * * *

| 1981 | ($6.99) 84 |

| 1982 | ($6.99–$7.99) 85 |

1982 Riserva   ($7.99–$8.99)   86

The only three Chiantis I have tasted from this estate have been very good. It is a relatively new estate that also makes the 100% Sangiovese wine, Grosso Senese. The style of Chianti produced is marked by the smell of new oak barrels, a ripe, rich, cherry fruitiness, good firm tannins, and very clean, well-delineated flavors. They are impressive Chiantis with color and flavor, to be drunk between age 4 and 8.

MONSANTO* * * * *

1975 Il Poggio   ($18.00)   86

1977 Il Poggio   ($17.00)   87

1978 Il Poggio   ($16.00)   80

1979 Il Poggio   ($13.00)   85

1981   ($9.99)   85

At present, the Monsanto estate is at the head of the pack in Chianti. The 1970 and 1971 Monsanto Chiantis from the Il Poggio vineyard continue to represent truly great wine, but I have seen nothing from Monsanto since then that appears capable of equaling them. The 1973 and 1974 Il Poggios were certainly uninspiring. More recently, the 1975 is quite good, still young but with a rich, smoky, mineral-scented bouquet, a lovely sweetness of fruit and firm tannins backing up a medium- to full-bodied texture. The 1977 is also quite young, but has impressive credentials, though I would be surprised if it equals the 1970 or 1971. Dark ruby with a big, smoky, tobacco-scented bouquet, tannic, full-bodied flavors and very good length, it needs 1–3 years of cellaring. The 1978 is dark in color, but dull and slightly bitter and astringent. If it is going to get better, it needs another 3–4 years of cellaring. The 1979 is neither as hard and astringent as the 1978 nor as promising as the 1977. Nevertheless, it is forward, with Monsanto's telltale, smoky, earthy, ripe bouquet, medium body, and soft finish. It should be drunk over the next 3–4 years. The 1981, not from the Il Poggio vineyard, is a deeply colored and broadly flavored wine with character.

MONTE VERTINE* * * *

1982   ($14.00)   83

1981 Riserva   ($12.00)   85

Monte Vertine is a very reputable producer of Chianti as well as of
two single-vineyard wines called Le Pergole Torte and Il Sodaccio.
The 1981 Riserva Chianti is drinking well today and should continue
to hold well for several years. It has spicy vanillin oak and ripe berry
fruit abundantly displayed in a medium-bodied, softly textured format. The 1982 regular bottling is fruity, soft, easy to drink, but lighter
and less deep than the 1981 Riserva.

CASTELLO DI RAMPOLLA* * * *

1979 Riserva   ($7.99)   85

1980 Riserva   ($7.99)   85

1981 Riserva   ($7.49)   86

1982 Riserva   ($7.99)   86

1983 Riserva   ($7.99)   85

This is one of my favorite Chianti producers, whose wines represent
the new school of winemaking in Chianti. The wine is partially aged
in small barrels and small percentages of Cabernet Sauvignon are
blended in. All of these vintages above are strong efforts with plenty
of flavor interest, body, and character. Unlike most pale-colored
Chiantis, the Rampolla wines have good color. The 1981 and 1982 are
the most ageworthy of the above wines. Both can use 2–4 years of
cellaring, but have a rich, cedary, spicy, fruity nose, good color, medium body, and firm tannins. The 1980 and 1983 are more open and
aromatic, with good, ripe fruit, some spicy oak in evidence, and good
length. The 1979 is slightly herbaceous, but ripe and cedary, medium-
bodied, and is now mature.

RUFFINO* * * *

1978 Gold Label	($14.49) 86

1979 Gold Label	($13.99) 83

One of the most famous producers, Ruffino's Gold Label (their best wine) can be found easily and older vintages frequently show up. The 1979 is fat and supple, with easy to drink flavors and some high alcohol showing through in the finish. The 1978 tastes like many a Brunello. It has a big, ripe, rich, leather-scented bouquet. Full-bodied, heady and rich, it is a rather big proportioned Chianti for drinking over the next 5–6 years.

THE SIX BEST VALUES IN CHIANTI

While these six firms do not produce Chianti on as sublime a level of quality as that of the aforementioned eight growers, their wines have consistently demonstrated a very high rapport in quality/price. They are the best values for Chianti and the wines generally sell for less than $6 a bottle. Look for the 1982s and 1983s from these producers:

Castello di Volpaia	Dr. Gracciano
Fontodi	Di Pancole
Fossi	Villa Cafaggio

Other Tuscan Red Wines
(Vino Nobile di Montepulciano, Carmignano)

Brunello di Montalcino may be Tuscany and Italy's most expensive and overrated wine, and Chianti may be Tuscany and Italy's best-known red wine, but there are several other red wines of merit produced there. Carmignano is not terribly well known but can be a good wine. It is made, as are most Chiantis, from a blend of red wine grapes (Sangiovese, Canaiolo Nero, and Cabernet Sauvignon), as well as white grapes. The top producer is Capezzana. The other red wine of importance is Tuscany's Vino Nobile di Montepulciano. There are four good producers of this Chianti-like, tasty wine—Avignonesi, Boscarelli, Fanetti, and Fassati. I have read excellent things about Buonsignori, but I have never seen a bottle of his wine.

Both Carmignano and Vino Nobile, when well made, taste like very good Chiantis. Neither wine is a particularly good value. In my tastings, three wines stood above the rest—the 1983 and 1982 Avignonesi Vino Nobile di Montepulciano, the 1981 Carmignano Riserva from Capezzana, and the 1983 Boscarelli.

AVIGNONESI* * * *

| 1982 Vino Nobile di Montepulciano | ($16.00) | 87 |

| 1983 Vino Nobile di Montepulciano | ($12.00) | 86 |

I find this producer's wines consistently very good, and both of these wines are well made. The 1982 is more powerful, with very good color, enough stuffing and tannin to age 7–8 years, and plenty of ripe black cherry fruit. It is one of the best Vino Nobiles I have ever tasted. The 1983 is a less powerful version of the 1982, stylish, graceful, ripe, and medium- to full-bodied. Both are serious wines that should improve for 7–8 years.

BOSCARELLI* * * *

| 1983 Vino Nobile di Montepulciano | ($13.50) | 87 |

An impressive yet youthful wine, the 1983 Boscarelli has a rather spicy, raspberry-scented bouquet, loads of concentrated fruit, a healthy dosage of tannin, a balanced, good finish and medium body. Drink between 1988 and 1995.

CAPEZZANA* * *

| 1981 Carmignano Riserva | ($11.00) | 85 |

Approachable now, this wine has a complex, sweet, cedary, ripe, fruity bouquet. Quite cleanly made, fruity, and medium-bodied, this is a very attractive wine for drinking over the next 3–4 years.

FASSATI* * *

| 1979 Vino Nobile de Montepulciano | ($9.00) | 84 |

| 1980 Vino Nobile de Montepulciano | ($7.00) | 83 |

These are two good wines, although not quite on the level of those of Avignonesi. The 1980 has a chocolatey, ripe, spicy nose, good color, some attractive, sweet fruit in the flavor, and a soft, medium-bodied texture. It should be drunk over the next 2–3 years. The 1979 is slightly more concentrated, with an aroma of ripe cherries, spicy oak, and firmer, more aggressive tannins noticeable on the palate. It needs 2–3 years before consumption since it is relatively unevolved.

Tuscany's White Wines

Over recent years, much has been made of the new Tuscan white wines. There is the Pomino from Frescobaldi, the Galestro of Antinori, the inexpensive Bianco di Pitigliano, and of course, numerous white wines usually made from Trebbiano by the Chianti producers. Italy does indeed make lovely white wines today, but none of the aforementioned Tuscan whites are any more exciting than the domestic jug wines that Americans can obtain at lower prices. The only Tuscan white I can stand behind and recommend enthusiastically is the Vernaccia di San Gimignano. Thankfully, it is not made from the bland, tart Trebbiano grape, but rather from the Vernaccia grape, and it comes from the remarkable medieval fortified hill town of San Gimignano. All the Vernaccias today are made in stainless steel, temperature-controlled tanks and the results are refreshingly crisp, light yet flavorful, dry wines that seem to perfectly match, and are easy to drink with, fish and chicken. Nineteen eighty-three was an excellent vintage for Vernaccia, but most 1983s should be drunk up. The vintage in 1984 was not so good, but the 1984 Vernaccias, if not as fruity and solid as the 1983s, were still extremely enjoyable wines. The 1985s are better than the 1983s. The best Vernaccias, year in and year out, are the wines from Falchini, Ponte a Rondolino, Strozzi, di Pancole, and Pietraserena. Of these five excellent producers, I find Strozzi's the fruitiest, Falchini's and di Pancole's the lightest, and Ponte a Rondolino and Pietraserena the fullest. A double pleasure about Vernaccia di San Gimignano is the price—it costs no more than $6 a bottle.

1985 Falchini Vernaccia di San Gimignano	($4.99)	85
1985 di Pancole Vernaccia di San Gimignano	($3.99)	84
1985 Pietraserena Vernaccia di San Gimignano	($5.99)	84
1985 Ponte a Rondolino Vernaccia di San Gimignano	($4.99)	85
1985 Strozzi Vernaccia di San Gimignano	($4.69)	86

OTHER SIGNIFICANT RED WINES OF ITALY

Italy's Least-known Great Red Wines

Piedmont and Tuscany are not the only serious red wine regions of Italy. Following are reviews of the best red wines from several other regions of Italy that are available commercially in America. But first, here are some observations. The red wine of Campania called Taurasi from Mastroberardino is probably Italy's most famous and renowned wine produced outside of Tuscany and Piedmont, but it is not, in my opinion, the best. In the hilly, pastoral province of Umbria, Giorgio Lungarotti produces three red wines that rival the greatest reds made in Italy. The Rubesco, the Rubesco Riserva from the vineyard Monticchio, and the San Giorgio Cabernet Sauvignon are not only better than the highly publicized Taurasi, but are truly world-class wines. In the wild and primitive province of Abruzzi, just to the south of Umbria, two men, Edoardo Valentini and Emilio Pepe, produce uncommonly rich and powerful red wines called Montepulciano d'Abruzzo. In the southern provinces of Italy there are a number of great wines. In Apulia, the Salice Salentino of Dr. Cosimo Taurino is first-rate. In Basilicata, on the slopes of Mount Vulture, the robust, fleshy, Aglianco del Vulture is made. Even in the wilderness of Sicily, a red wine called Regaleali from Giuseppe Tasca d'Almerita is a rich, classy, powerful wine. Also, the much-maligned Valpolicella, in the hands of a grower such as Quintarelli, can become an expansive, rich, flavorful wine. There are others, but these grand reds compete with and in many cases surpass the best wines that Italy can produce in the famous regions of Piedmont and Tuscany.

GIUSEPPE TASCA D'ALMERITA (SICILY)* * *

1981 Regaleali   ($14.99)   85

What this wine lacks in finesse, it compensates for in richness, power and full body. Dark ruby and very fleshy, on the palate the wine is fat, rich, alcoholic, and loaded with clean, plump, black cherry fruit flavors. Although not complex, it is rather substantial. It is quite drinkable now, but given its hefty constitution, will last at least another 4–6 years.

D'ANGELO (CAMPANIA)* * * *

1981 Aglianco del Vulture   ($8.99)   88

1982 Aglianco del Vulture   ($9.79)   87

While the southern Italy winery of Mastroberardino gets all the good press, D'Angelo may be an even better winemaker. Two vintages that Mastroberardino claims are top-notch, 1983 and 1980, were declassified by D'Angelo, who says they are inferior. His 1981 is an excellent wine, deep in color, rich in its aroma with scents of chocolate, coffee and leather. On the palate it is quite velvety, full-bodied with a broad, lush finish. The 1982 is quite similarly styled, only more tannic and seemingly a trifle more muscular and alcoholic. Both wines stood out in my series of Italian red wine tastings.

LUNGAROTTI (UMBRIA)* * * *

1978 Rubesco   ($7.49)   85

1979 Rubesco   ($7.49)   83

1975 Rubesco Riserva Monticchio   ($17.49)   90

1978 San Giorgio   ($18.00)   86

1979 San Giorgio   ($18.00)   89

The San Giorgio Cabernet, produced from a vineyard planted in 1971, seems to get better with each passing vintage. The 1978, not yet mature, is impressively dark ruby in color, with a moderately intense, blackcurrant, subtle, herbaceous bouquet, medium to full body, and firm tannins. It should peak between 1988–1992. The 1979 is better and much more forward. It is every bit as concentrated as the 1978, but more accessible, with blackcurrant fruit, rich tobacco and smoky scents intertwined in a complex, fragrant bouquet. Full-bodied, rich and moderately tannic, the 1979 San Giorgio is the best Cabernet produced yet from Lungarotti, and rivals the legendary Sassicaia. As for the Rubescos, the 1978 is mature, has ripe, rich, supple, spicy, earthy fruit, medium-full body, good length, and a Bordeaux-like bouquet. The 1979 is similarly proportioned but less evolved and is unready to drink. The superstar here is the single-vineyard 1975 Monticchio Rubesco; few wine enthusiasts seem to realize how fine this wine is. Already 11 years old, it needs another 5 to be fully mature and will last another 10–20 years. Intense with black cherry scents, this intense, opulent, full-bodied wine is extremely impressive and potentially a great wine.

MASTROBERARDINO (CAMPANIA)* * * *

1981 Taurasi	($9.00)	84
1982 Taurasi	($11.00)	82
1968 Taurasi Riserva	($75.00)	90
1971 Taurasi Riserva	($45.00)	82
1973 Taurasi Riserva	($40.00)	84
1977 Taurasi Riserva	($30.00)	80
1978 Taurasi Riserva	($24.49)	78
1979 Taurasi Riserva	($20.00)	84
1980 Taurasi Riserva	($13.00)	86

This wine is generally considered one of Italy's half-dozen best red wines. I wonder if the greatness of the 1968 Taurasi has caused some to have an overinflated view of this wine, or whether recent vintages have not been as successful. Or has the style of vinification lightened up? Whatever the reason, in tasting through these wines, the common element was an earthy, cheesy nose that I suspect most tasters would find a little unusual. Curiously, it was missing in the superb 1968. The 1968 remains relatively young, but is splendidly rich with a deep, ripe, complex bouquet, long, dense flavors, and fine balance. The 1980 and

1979 Riservas show promise for good (not great) drinkability in 7–8 years since their tannin level is quite aggressive at the moment. The 1977 is reputedly excellent, but the wine had a rather stewed, baked nose, very high acidity, and a hard, lean texture with little charm. The 1978 tasted one-dimensional except for a cheesy, farm-like nose. The 1973 showed a lovely, moderately intense cherry fruit, medium body, and some hard tannins in the finish. It should be drunk over the next 5–6 years. The 1971 had an interesting earthy nose, rather light to medium color, but tasted off in the mouth, with plenty of tannin left. The 1981, not a *riserva*, was youthful, clean, with plenty of ripe cherry fruit in a medium-bodied format. The same thing could be said for the rather compact, straightforward 1982.

EMILIO PEPE* * *

1974 Montepulciano d'Abruzzo	($20.00)	86
1978 Montepulciano d'Abruzzo	($20.00)	72

Pepe produces a deep, aromatic, ripe, full-bodied Montepulciano d'Abruzzo. The 1974 has a spicy, cigar box bouquet, deep, full-bodied, rustic feel on the palate, with exceptional richness. It is ready to drink now but will hold. The 1978 is impressively dark, but flawed from excessive volatile acidity.

QUINTARELLI* * *

1979 Rosso Ca Del Merlo	($6.99)	85
1980 Valpolicella	($7.99)	86

One has never tasted Valpolicella until he has tried one produced by Quintarelli. His Valpolicella is loaded with velvety, ripe cherry flavors, has good length and depth, and a spicy, berry-scented bouquet. It is ideal for drinking now and over the next 1–3 years. The 1979 Rosso Ca Del Merlo is also ripe, fat, supple, and deliciously fruity. Both wines are very cleanly made, stylish, and very good values.

DR. COSIMO TAURINO* * * *

1975 Patriglione Rosso   ($8.99)   ?

1979 Salice Salentino Riserva   ($5.49)   84

This man produces the best Salice Salentino and it is a great value. The 1979 Riserva is a straightforward, robust, ripe cherry-scented wine with good fruit, a medium- to full-bodied texture, and decent finish. On the other hand, the 1975 Patriglione is extremely high in alcohol, tastes like an overblown, heavy-handed Amarone, and is so viscous that it is almost sickening to drink.

EDOARDO VALENTINI* * * *

1974 Montepulciano d'Abruzzi   ($16.95) 86

1975 Montepulciano d'Abruzzi   ($14.95) 88

For the first time, Valentini's wines are now available in America. A young man who left the practice of law to pursue making wine, he is considered the finest producer of Montepulciano d'Abruzzo. Valentini obviously believes in rich, unfiltered, intense wines that need a decade of aging to reveal their multidimensional personalities. Both the above wines remain relatively young, especially in view of their age. They are rich, alcoholic, viscous wines that, despite their size, have very good balance and complex bouquets of hickory wood and bing cherries. Both still have a good measure of tannin, but because of low acidity are very enjoyable now. Valentini's wines are very rare but worth a search to find.

OTHER
SIGNIFICANT
WHITE WINES OF
ITALY

Friuli-Venezia Giulia:
Italy's Best Made and Most Delicious
White Wines for $5—$9

White wines are made everywhere in Italy, but for today's modern taste, the crisp, light, fruity, fresh whites of Friuli-Venezia Giulia are, in my opinion, Italy's most enjoyable white wine resource. Modern technology is abundant here and what one usually gets for less than $8 a bottle is a deliciously vibrant wine, dry yet lively, fruity and often with just a trace of effervescence from some CO_2 intentionally left in. Pinot Grigio, Tocai, Pinot Bianco, Malvasia, Chardonnay, Müller-Thurgau, Sauvignon, Ribolla, and Riesling Renano are never great, profound, complex white wines, but in the hands of the best producers are among the most easy to drink and refreshingly light wines produced on the face of the earth. Picolit, the ultra-rich, sweet dessert wine, is supposedly this area's challenge to the Barsacs and Sauternes of France. In fact, it is an outrageously overpriced mediocrity that I urge you to bypass without hesitation. Friuli-Venezia Giulia produces light, fresh red wines. The Cabernet is always fruity but also invariably herbaceous and vegetal. Better bets are the soft, light, fruity Merlot made here and the native Refosco.

THE BEST PRODUCERS IN FRIULI-VENEZIA GIULIA

Abbazia di Rosazzo—An outstanding producer of crisp, fresh, technically flawless white wines. The 1983s and 1985s are excellent across-the-board. The 1984s, like most producers' wines, are more lean, acidic and tart, but good. The Ridge-like label is controversial. Best wines: Pinot Bianco, Tocai, Ronco Acacie, Sauvignon.

Borgo Conventi—Vibrant, fresh, delicious wines that are light, very cleanly made, and still flavorful are commonly found with this producer. Nineteen eighty-threes are richer, fuller than the lean 1984s. Best wines: Pinot Grigio, Tocai, Pinot Bianco.

Bortoluzzi—Of all the 1984 Friuli wines, Bortoluzzi's were clearly the best. I never tasted his 1983s, but can enthusiastically recommend the fresh, surprisingly rich, crisp 1984s and his rich, multiflavored 1985s. Best wines: Pinot Grigio, Foian Blanc, Chardonnay, Riesling Renano.

Enofriulia—I did not see the 1984s, but both the 1983s and 1982s were excellent. Light, deliciously fruity, crisp, vibrant wines with style and character. Best wines: Müller-Thurgau, Pinot Bianco, Pinot Grigio.

Livio Felluga—Felluga is a very well-known producer who makes good but generally expensive wine from Friuli. Best wines: Pinot Grigio, Tocai, and perhaps the only Picolit to merit some acclaim.

F. Furlan—Among the richest wines, the wines of Furlan are intense, sometimes a trifle low in acidity, but always among the most distinctive of this region. Best wines: Ribolla Gialla, Pinot Grigio, Tocai, and Malvasi. The 1985s and 1983s are superior to the 1982s.

Ronco del Gnemiz—A tiny producer with an impeccable reputation. The 1983s from Gnemiz were stunningly fresh, fruity, and stylish. The 1984s were the best tasted after those of Bortoluzzi and his newly released 1985s exceptionally good. Best wines: Pinot Grigio, Müller-Thurgau, Tocai Friulano, Chardonnay.

Ronchi di Fornaz—The Tocai and Pinot Bianco are delicious here, particularly the 1985s.

The Whites of Lombardy and Trentino: Italy's Most Serious Sparkling Wines and Santa Margherita

Lombardy and Trentino both produce good red wines. In fact, some are excellent. The Teroldego Rotaliano of the Baron de Cles and the new Cabernet-based wines of Bellavista come to mind immediately. And of course, there is the famous Giorgio Gray, a mystical, reclusive oenologist from Bolzano who is reputed to produce a superlative array of wines. However, it is the white wines that merit most attention from this area, particularly the sparkling wines from Ca' del Bosco and Bellavista and the exceptional white wines of Santa Margherita. The following are my notes on their wines.

BELLAVISTA* * *

1984 Chardonnay Uccellanda	($14.00)	84

N.V. Cuvée Brut	($9.00)	86

1982 Franciacorta Cuvée Brut	($14.00)	85

1981 Gran Cuvée Pas Opere	($19.00)	86

This luxurious estate in Lombardy specializes in sparkling wines, Cabernet Sauvignon aged in small casks, and oak-aged Chardonnay. The results are impressive. The sparkling wines are a match for the Ca' del Bosco wines that have long set the benchmark for high-quality Italian sparklers. The Non-Vintage Cuvée Brut is very French-like, with a crisp, clean, yeasty aroma, elegant flavors, and good finish. I liked it at least as much as the vintage-dated, more expensive bottlings. The 1982 Franciacorta Cuvée Brut is fuller, more austere, quite dry, medium-bodied, and very well made. The 1981 Gran Cuvée is a very yeasty, austere sparkling wine with considerable finesse. It comes in a bottle very reminiscent of the Krug champagnes of France. The single-vineyard Chardonnay Uccellanda is a good beginning. It is quite oaky, but shows good applelike fruit with a suggestion of butter.

BERLUCCHI* * *

1981 Brut Cuvée Imperiale	($15.69)	86

N.V. Brut Cuvée Imperiale	($11.75)	80

N.V. Pas Dose Cuvée Imperiale	($11.75)	78

N.V. Rose Cuvée Imperiale	($11.75)	80

Berlucchi is a very highly respected producer of sparkling wines. The star here is the 1981 Vintage Brut that surpasses in complexity, finesse, and quality many a French champagne. It has a yeasty bread dough-scented bouquet, very good effervescence, tiny bubbles, and a crisp, fresh, lively finish. How good it is to see Italian sparkling wine of this quality level.

CA' DEL BOSCO* * *

N.V. Brut Spumante Non-Vintage   ($18.00)   84

This producer can make excellent sparkling wine on a par with very
good French champagne. It used to have no competition, but the
Bellavista winery is now also doing special things. The above non-
vintage Brut is yeasty and toasty, with clean, fresh, medium-bodied
flavors, good effervescence, and small, lingering bubbles. The wine is
dry and very cleanly made.

SANTA MARGHERITA* * *

1985 Chardonnay   ($10.99)   86

1984 Chardonnay   ($10.99)   85

1985 Luna dei Feldi   ($14.00)   86

1985 Pinot Grigio   ($11.49)   85

1984 Pinot Grigio   ($10.00)   84

This estate in Trentino produces a considerable amount of wine. However, the white wines of Santa Margherita are the most striking examples I have tasted of the new breed of Italian whites, richly fruity,
very crisp, impeccably clean, stylish wines that have just enough
varietal character. Perhaps their greatest attribute is the one that is
impossible to articulate properly—you just want to keep drinking
them. The 1984s are among the most successful white wines I tasted
in this difficult vintage. The Luna dei Feldi is excellent, dry, so fresh
and vibrant, yet so fruity and tasty. The 1985s are richer, fuller wines
that continue to drink beautifully today. If you want a quality benchmark for Italian white wines, these are your reference point. But be
warned, prices have jumped considerably in the last several years.

Other Recommended Italian White Wines
(The Best of the Rest)

ANSELMI* * * *

| 1985 Soave Anselmi | ($6.99) | 85 |

| 1985 Soave Capital Foscarino | ($8.99) | 85 |

If you are like me, you probably think of Soave as a watery, thin, inoffensive wine. Well, these two Soaves are the finest two I have ever drunk. Both are dry but have plenty of fresh fruit, a lot of flavor, medium body, crisp acidity, surprising ripeness and length, and outstanding balance. For Soave, these are as perfect a wine as one can get. They are vibrant, refreshing, and a treat to drink.

BIGI* * *

| 1985 Orvieto Classico | ($4.99) | 84 |

I had always preferred to remember this beautiful town for its lovely cathedral and breathtaking situation atop an outcropping of rocks rather than as a place for interesting white wine. The 1985 Bigi Orvieto may cause me to take the wines seriously. It is a crisp, quite dry and fruity, vibrant wine that should be drunk over the next year.

MACULAN* * * *

| 1985 Breganze di Breganze | ($8.99) | 86 |

| 1985 Breganze Bianco Canzio | ($8.99) | 87 |

| 1985 Chardonnay | ($8.99) | 85 |

| 1983 Torcolato | ($25.00) | 90 |

This winery in Veneto is emerging as a real star, particularly for the excellent white wines made by Fausto and Franca Maculan, a young brother-and-sister team. Maculan may be Italy's largest purchasers of new oak barrels for aging both their red and white wines. I prefer the whites to the reds here. His 1985 whites look extra special. The Breganze di Breganze is a wonderfully fresh, exuberant white wine that flows with crisp fruit, has good body, and with pasta and fish is an undeniably alluring wine. Even better is the 1985 Breganze from the vineyard Canzio that is aged six months in oak barrels. It has a fine

Chablis-like character and is complex, spicy, loaded with fruit and quite dry. The 1985 Chardonnay is very good, a trifle oaky and toasty, but has crisp, well-defined fruit. The Torcolato is the best sweet wine I have tasted from Italy and seems to resemble a fine Suduiraut from Sauternes. It is very rich, sweet and full-bodied, but has excellent acidity. Remember the name Maculan—I predict you will be hearing many good things about this winery.

MASTROBERARDINO* * * *

1985 Greco di Tufo	($9.99)	83

1985 Fiano di Avellino	($18.49)	86

I was not at all happy with the 1984s from this famous producer in Campania. However, the 1985s show much more fruit, style and flavor authority. The Greco di Tufo has plenty of citrusy, floral fruit, good, crisp acidity, and is a delightful wine to drink. The Fiano di Avellino has some unreleased CO_2, lively, lush, crisp, well-delineated, lemony, fruity flavors. I enjoyed both of these wines, but even knowing that the production is tiny, I have a great deal of trouble justifying the high prices for the Fiano. I understand that Mastroberardino has a single-vineyard Fiano called Vignadora that is even better and more expensive. The prices are high.

MASO POLI* * *

1985 Chardonnay	($6.99)	84

1985 Pinot Grigio	($5.99)	85

The 1985 Pinot Grigio has surprising richness, ripeness, and character, and is an excellent bargain as well. Spicy, richly fruity, and medium-bodied, this wine will drink very well for at least another 12 months. The Chardonnay is lighter, more delicate and very pleasant in an understated way.

MIRAFIORE* * *

1985 Soave	($4.49)	83

Until I tasted the Anselmi Soaves reviewed above, I thought this was the best Soave on the market. It remains a deliciously alive, tasty wine with surprising character.

GUERRIERI RIZZARDI* * * *

1985 Soave Costeggiola	($5.99)	84

1985 Dogoli	($6.69)	85

The Dogoli is an elegantly wrought wine. It is a delicious, very aromatic, flowery-scented, vivacious, fruity wine that begs for attention because of its charm and freshness. Medium-bodied, exuberant, and just plain delicious to sip, this wine should go handsomely with broiled or steamed fish. The 1985 Soave Costeggiola is an impressive, fragrant, crisp, delicious, dry white wine with a vibrant personality.

CASTEL SCHWANBURG* * * *

1985 Chardonnay	($6.99)	86

1985 Pinot Bianco	($6.99)	85

This estate draws its grapes from the Alto Adige and the 1985s are delicious—rich and fruity, impeccably clean and crisp, with good varietal character and plenty of pure ripe fruit. They should be drunk over the next 2–3 years.

J. TIEFENBRUNNER* * * *

1985 Rhine Riesling	($4.99)	76

1984 Pinot Grigio	($4.89)	74

1985 Pinot Grigio	($5.99)	86

1985 Chardonnay	($5.99)	86

1985 Gewürtztraminer	($4.99)	86

Forget the lean, citric, deficient 1985 Riesling, and the flabby, loosely knit, oxidized 1984 Pinot Grigio. However, the other three Tiefenbrunner wines represent excellent values and are extremely attractive wines. The 1985 Pinot Grigio is a serious wine with broad, lush fruit, a fresh, lively feel and good finish. The 1985 Chardonnay is intensely fruity, long and ripe in the mouth with good acidity. The 1985 Gewürztraminer is lovely, delicate, quite flavorful and really impressive.

VALENTINI* * * *

| 1982 Trebbiano d'Abruzzo | ($14.50) | 88 |

The finest dry Italian white wine I have ever tasted, this rich burgundian imitation is produced from a grape I usually despise—the ubiquitous Trebbiano. However, in the hands of Signori Valentini the wine has an uncommon power, richness, and depth of character that I had heretofore believed was reserved for only the best French white burgundies. This is a fascinating wine that is still quite young and potentially can get even better. Very rare, unfortunately.

VILLA BANFI* *

| 1985 Pinot Grigio San Angelo | ($8.99) | 82 |

| 1984 Chardonnay Fontanelle | ($9.99) | 82 |

| 1985 Gavi Principessa | ($10.49) | 70 |

The Gavi is virtually tasteless except for a pronounced citrusy character. Most 3-dollar jug wines have more character and fruit. The other two offerings show some style and flavor interest. The Pinot Grigio is also a touch citrusy, but has good fruit present, is very fresh and quite charming in a simple way. The Chardonnay is lemony, light- to medium-bodied, fresh, cleanly made and the perfect "food" wine.

3. GERMANY

It is rather sad that Germany's finest wine producers are rarely accorded the recognition and respect in American wine circles that their peers in Bordeaux or Napa Valley receive. There appear to be a multitude of reasons why this is the case. First, German wine laws and the hierarchy of quality are extremely difficult to understand. Second, the German language itself is more troublesome to comprehend and read for Americans than either French or Italian. Third, German wine labels are overzealous—there is simply too much information on them, which only complicates matters for the consumer. Finally, there is the prevailing image—or should I say myth—that German wines are cloyingly sweet and therefore fattening and simply not serious enough to merit attention.

Unfortunately, none of these preconceptions that afflict most American wine drinkers about German wines are likely to change. Despite the tremendous national publicity for Germany's outstanding 1983 vintage, few wine drinkers other than the hard-core German wine enthusiasts jumped at the opportunity to purchase what are excellent wines at amazingly reasonable prices. Nevertheless, consider the following points and comments and try to taste at least a half-dozen of the 1983 or excellent 1985 Rieslings from the best producers. Perhaps

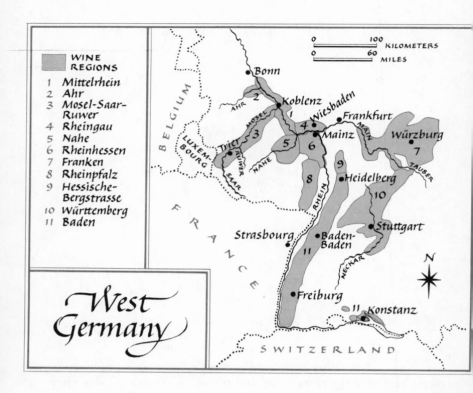

West Germany

WINE REGIONS

1 Mittelrhein
2 Ahr
3 Mosel-Saar-Ruwer
4 Rheingau
5 Nahe
6 Rheinhessen
7 Franken
8 Rheinpfalz
9 Hessische-Bergstrasse
10 Württemberg
11 Baden

Rheingau

Bereich Johannisberg

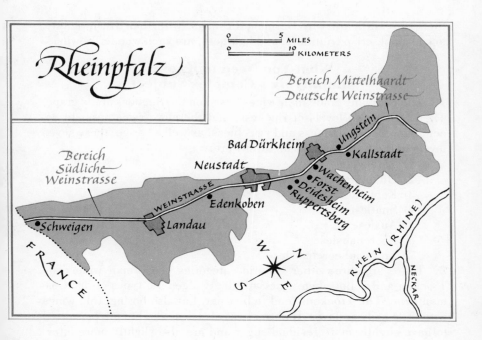

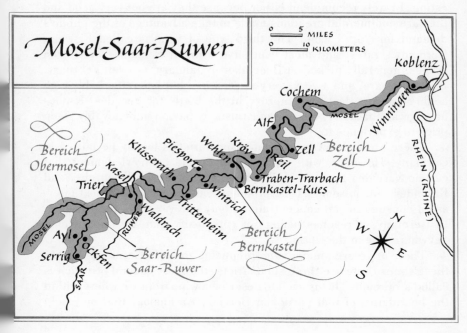

then you will learn why German Rieslings, with their fresh acidity, low alcohol, crisp fruitiness, and lightness, are such wonderful wines.

What You Need to Know:
Simplifying a Complex Subject

1. The Germans grade their wines based on the ripeness of the grape. There are seven levels of ripeness, and therefore sweetness. In ascending order of ripeness and sweetness, as well as price, these seven levels in the German wine hierarchy are:

1) Tafelwein
2) Qualitätswein (QbA)
3) Kabinett
4) Spätlese
5) Auslese
6) Beerenauslese
7) Trockenbeerenauslese

2. There are three other generic categories of German wine. The Trocken and Halbtroken wines are the two generic types of dry German wine. The Trockens tend to be drier, but also boring, thin wines with little body or flavor. Halbtrockens also taste dry but are permitted to have slightly more residual sugar and are also slightly more interesting. I rarely recommend either because they are not very good and they are commercial creations made to take advantage of the public's demand for "dry" wine. The third type of wine is called Eiswein, Germany's rarest and most expensive wine. It is made from frozen grapes, generally picked in December or January, or even February. It is quite rare, and a very, very sweet wine, but has remarkably high acidity and can last and improve in the bottle for decades. It does have great character, but one must usually pay an unbelievably steep price to experience it.

3. There are at least two dozen grape varieties legally permitted in Germany. However, with all due respect and acknowledgment that certain varieties such as Müller-Thurgau, Silvaner, Scheurebe, and Rulander can, in some cases, produce something special, most interested consumers can concentrate on only one varietal—the Riesling. In Germany, it reaches heights of complexity that are unparalleled anywhere else in the world.

4. There are eleven major wine-producing zones in Germany. Within these zones there are three subdistricts, the most general of which is called a Bereich. This is used to describe a wine from anywhere within the boundaries of that particular Bereich. An analogy that may help facilitate this distinction would be the closest French equivalent, a wine entitled to Appellation Bordeaux Contrôlée or Appellation Bourgogne Contrôlée. Within the Bereich there are more specific boundaries called Grosslagen, to which the closest French equivalent would be the generic appellation St.-Julien Contrôlée or Appellation Morey-St.-Denis Contrôlée. These would be wines that are not from a specific château or specific vineyard but from a specific region or collection of sites for vineyards. There are 152 different Grosslagen in Germany. The most specific zone in Germany is called an Einzellage, which is a specific site or vineyard. There are 2,600 of them in Germany and again, by analogy, the closest French equivalent would be a specific St.-Julien château such as Ducru-Beaucaillou, or a specific Premier Cru or Grand Cru Burgundy vineyard in Morey-St.-Denis such as Clos des Lambrays. Perhaps this will help one to understand the breakdown of the German wine zones. However, few people have the patience to memorize the best Einzellagen or Grosslagen, so it is much more important to try to remember the names of some of the best producers.

5. The majority of the best producers in Germany are located in four of the eleven German wine zones. They are the Mosel-Saar-Ruwer, the Rheingau, the Rheinhessen, and the Rheinpfalz. While there are certainly good wines, even some outstanding wines, made in the other seven German wine zones, far and away the great majority of the finest German wines are produced in these four regions, with the Mosel-Saar-Ruwer being the very best region in all of Germany.

6. The best German wines are those produced at the Kabinett, Spätlese, Auslese, Beerenauslese, and Trockenbeerenauslese levels of ripeness and sweetness. Most consumers tasting a Kabinett wine would not find it particularly sweet, although there is residual sugar in the wine. Because of the high natural acidity found in German wines, a Kabinett generally tastes fresh, fruity, but not sweet to most palates. However, most tasters will detect a small amount of sweetness in a Spätlese, and even more with an Auslese. All three of these types are ideal wines for having as an apéritif or with food, whereas the wines entitled to Beerenauslese and Trockenbeerenauslese designations are clearly dessert wines, very rich and quite sweet. One should keep in mind that the alcohol level in most German wines averages between 7–9%, so one can drink much more of this wine without feeling its effects. One of the naïve criticisms of German wines is that they do not go well with food. However, anyone who has tried a fine Kabinett, Spätlese, or Auslese with Oriental cuisine, with roast pork, or even with certain types of fowl such as pheasant or turkey can tell you that these wines work particularly well, especially Spätlese and Auslese.

7. The best German wines age like fine Bordeaux. In great vintages, such as 1983, one can expect a Kabinett, Spätlese, or Auslese from a top producer to evolve and improve in the bottle for 5–10 years. A Beerenauslese or a Trockenbeerenauslese has the ability in a great vintage to improve for two or three decades. This is a fact, not a myth, to which those who have recently tasted some of the great Ausleses from 1959 can easily attest. German wines at the top levels, from the top producers, do indeed improve remarkably in the bottle, though the trend among consumers is to drink them when they are young, fresh, and crisp.

QUICK VINTAGE GUIDE

1985—The German wine trade has touted this year rather highly, but except for a handful of areas it in no way compares to the outstanding 1983 vintage. Nevertheless, it is a good to very good year with a moderate production of wines with good acidity and more typical textures and characteristics than the opulent, rather richly fruity, yet sometimes overblown 1983s. Like 1983, the dryness during the summer and fall prevented the formation of Botrytis cinerea. The Rieslings in many cases can be very good, but will be firmer and slower to evolve and less open than the more precocious, overt, fruity 1983s. Overall, the 1985s should be at their best between 1988 and 1995. Reports indicate that the top successes were in the Middle Mosel, with potentially great wines from villages such as Urzig and Erden.

1984—Fresh, light, very pleasant, straightforward wines that are neither green nor too acidic were produced in this vintage of average quality, and below-average quantity. They will not keep, so drink the 1984s over the next 3–4 years. The Mosel estate of Dr. F. Weins-Prüm Erben made excellent wines in 1984, as did Monchof.

1983—This vintage has received the most publicity since the 1976 vintage. Most growers seem to feel that it is certainly the best since the 1976. It was a very large crop throughout all viticultural areas of Germany, but it was especially large and exceptional in quality in the Mosel-Saar-Ruwer region. The wines have excellent concentration, very fine levels of tartaric rather than green malic acidity, and a degree of precocious ripeness and harmonious roundness that gives the wines wonderful appeal now. However, because of their depth and overall balance, they should age well for at least 10 or more years. The vintage seemed strongest at the Spätlese level, since there were very little Auslese, Beerenauslese, and Trockenbeerenauslese wines produced. Nineteen eighty-three is also a great year for Eiswein where, as a result of an early freeze, above-normal quantities of this nectarlike, opulent wine were produced. However, despite larger quantities than normal, the prices are outrageously high for the Eisweins but very realistic and reasonable for the rest of the wines.

1982—In 1982 the Germans harvested a record crop of wine. The wines are ready to drink, fruity, somewhat soft, and on occasion, somewhat diluted because of the huge crop, but are very cleanly made and fresh. Very few wines at the Auslese level and above were produced. Overall, 1982 is a big, commercial vintage with plenty of appeal, and is priced quite reasonably.

1981—The Mosel was particularly blessed in 1981 with a number of excellent Kabinett and Spätlese wines. There was a little bit of Eiswein produced in the Rheingau of outstanding quality.

1980—A somewhat maligned vintage but, as in the rest of Europe, there are many successful wines, though few great ones. Certainly the Mosel and Rheingau seem to have produced better wines than elsewhere in Germany. These wines are now fully mature and should be drunk before the end of the decade.

1979—Between 1976 and 1983, this is certainly the most successful overall vintage for all of Germany. The quality in the Mosel was very good, even excellent, and the wines extremely well balanced with very good acidity and wonderfully fresh, nicely concentrated fruit flavors that are rounding into the full bloom of maturity at the moment. The top Rieslings are fully mature and should be drunk before the end of this decade.

Older Vintages

The great vintage that can still be found in the marketplace is 1976, a vintage that, by German standards, produced incredibly ripe, intense, opulent wines, with a significant amount of wine produced at the Auslese and Beerenauslese levels. These tend to be very sweet and are drinking sensationally well at the moment. The top wines should continue to last for another 5–8 years. Some critics have disputed the greatness of this vintage, saying that the 1976s are low in acidity, but that seems to be a minority point of view. The wines remain reasonably priced at the Auslese level, but the Beerenausleses and Trockenbeerenausleses from this vintage are soaring into the stratosphere in price. The 1977 vintage should be avoided, and 1978, unlike in France, was not a particularly successful year in Germany. Well-kept 1975s can provide great enjoyment, as can the wines from another great vintage, 1971. I would avoid the wines from 1972, and, of course, the 1973s, which were good in the mid-'70s, but are now tiring quite a bit.

A GUIDE TO GERMANY'S BEST PRODUCERS

***** (OUTSTANDING PRODUCERS)

F. W. Gymnasium (Mosel-Saar-Ruwer)
Monchof (Mosel-Saar-Ruwer)
Egon Müller (Mosel-Saar-Ruwer)

J. J. Prüm (Mosel-Saar-Ruwer)
Von Schubert (Mosel-Saar-Ruwer)
Geltz-Zilliken (Mosel-Saar-Ruwer)

**** (EXCELLENT PRODUCERS)

Adelmann (Württemberg)
Aschrottsche Erben (Rheingau)
A. Babach Erben (Rheinhessen)
Bassermann-Jordan (Rheinpfalz)
Bischofliches Konvikt (Mosel-Saar-Ruwer)
Bischoflishes Priesterseminar (Mosel-Saar-Ruwer)
H. Braun (Rheinhessen)
Brentano (Rheingau)
Dr. Burklin-Wolf (Rheinpfalz)
Christoffel-Berres (Mosel-Saar-Ruwer)
Hans Crusius (Nahe)
Deinhard (Mosel-Saar-Ruwer and Rheinpfalz)
O. Dunweg (Mosel-Saar-Ruwer)
G. Siben Erben (Rheinpfalz)
Eser (Rheingau)
Dr. Fischer (Mosel-Saar-Ruwer)
Forstmeister-Geltz-Erben (Mosel-Saar-Ruwer)
Freiherr von Heddesdorff (Mosel-Saar-Ruwer)

Graf zu Hoensbroech (Mosel-Saar-Ruwer)
F. Haag (Mosel-Saar-Ruwer)
F. Heyl (Rheinhessen)
Hohe Domkirche (Mosel-Saar-Ruwer)
Koehler-Ruprecht (Rheinpfalz)
Landgraf von Hessen (Rheingau)
Lauerburg (Mosel-Saar-Ruwer)
Licht-Bergweiler (Mosel-Saar-Ruwer)
Licht-Kilburg (Rheingau)
Dr. Loosen (Mosel-Saar-Ruwer)
Milz-Laurentiushof (Mosel-Saar-Ruwer)
Dr. R. Muth (Rheinhessen)
Dr. Nagler (Rheingau)
A. S. Prüm-Erben (Mosel-Saar-Ruwer)
Pleffingen (Rheinpfalz)
E. Reverchon (Mosel-Saar-Ruwer)
Ruetter Kunz (Mosel-Saar-Ruwer)

Schloss Johannisberg (Rheingau)
Schloss Plettenberg (Nahe)
Dr. A. Senfter (Rheinhessen)
St. Johannishof (Rheingau)
Staatlichen Weinbaudomanen (Mosel-Saar-Ruwer)
Staatsweinguter Eltville (Rheingau)
J. H. Strub (Rheinhessen)
Vereinigte Hospitien (Mosel-Saar-Ruwer)

von Hoevel (Mosel-Saar-Ruwer)
von Kanitz (Rheingau)
von Kesselstatt (Mosel-Saar-Ruwer)
von Mummisches (Rheingau)
von Simmern (Rheingau)
Dr. Heinz Wagner (Mosel-Saar-Ruwer)
Weins-Prüm Erben (Mosel-Saar-Ruwer)
H. Wirsching (Franken)
Dr. Zenzen (Mosel-Saar-Ruwer)

* * * *(GOOD PRODUCERS)*

S. Adler (Baden)
F. Altenkirch (Rheingau)
P. Anheuser (Nahe)
Bergweiler-Prüm (Mosel-Saar-Ruwer)
F. Baumann (Rheinhessen)
Graf von Neippergsches (Württemberg)
L. Guntrum (Rheinhessen)
Johann Hart (Mosel-Saar-Ruwer)
D. Hermann (Mosel-Saar-Ruwer)
Irsch-Ockfen (Mosel-Saar-Ruwer)
Josefinegrund (Mosel-Saar-Ruwer)
Josephshof (Mosel-Saar-Ruwer)
Jostock-Thul (Mosel-Saar-Ruwer)
J. Kock (Mosel-Saar-Ruwer)
Kurfurstenhof (Rheinhessen)
D. Hermann (Mosel-Saar-Ruwer)
Lehneit-Veit-Erben (Mosel-Saar-Ruwer)
Max Markgraf (Baden)

Oekonomierat Piedmont (Mosel-Saar-Ruwer)
Oekonomierat Rebholz (Rheinpfalz)
F. Reh (Mosel-Saar-Ruwer)
P. Scherf (Mosel-Saar-Ruwer)
Schloss Groenesteyn (Rheingau)
Schloss Reinhartshausen (Rheingau)
Schloss Vollrads (Rheingau)
F. Schmitt (Rheinhessen)
R. Schmitt (Franken)
Schumann-Nagler (Rheingau)
B. Simon (Mosel-Saar-Ruwer)
Studert-Prüm (Mosel-Saar-Ruwer)
H. Taprich (Mosel-Saar-Ruwer)
Erbhol Tesch (Nahe)
Dr. Thanisch (Mosel-Saar-Ruwer)
Usinger-Gunderlach (Rheinhessen)
Van Volxem (Mosel-Saar-Ruwer)
von Buhl (Rheinpfalz)
von Hessisches (Rheingau)

von Prittwitz (Mosel-Saar-   Würzburg Staalichen Hofkeller
   Ruwer)   (Franken)
R. Weil (Rheingau)   W. Zahn (Mosel-Saar-Ruwer)
S. Weiland (Mosel-Saar-Ruwer)

Today's Buying Strategy

There are plenty of bargains at the Kabinett and Spätlese levels from the good producers for the two most recent exciting vintages, 1983 and 1985, ranging in price from $6–$10 a bottle for Kabinett and $6–$12 a bottle for Spätlese. At the level of Auslese, the prices start at $9–$10 and can go as high as $16–$20 for some wines. Therefore, the best Spätleses and Kabinetts from 1983 and 1985 represent the best values. The 1984s are not bad wines, but are simply overshadowed by the two surrounding vintages. The 1982s can be good if well stored, but again, the best of them are not as good as the 1983s and 1985s. Should you want to indulge in a great, nectarlike Beerenauslese, Trockenbeerenauslese, or Eiswein from recent vintages such as 1971, 1981, 1983, or 1985, expect to pay from $50 to more than $100 for *one* bottle.

4. PORTUGAL

DRY RED TABLE WINES

Except for the unctuous, rich, almost decadent joys of vintage port, Madeira, and one of the greatest nectars of all, Muscatel de Setubal, the potential for fine wine from Portugal has yet to be discovered by most wine enthusiasts. Of course, the ubiquitous, spritzy, rather sweet Portuguese rosés are known the world over and are what many consumers first drink when they deem themselves too old or too sophisticated for soda pop. But Portugal produces some good red wines that could even be superb if winemaking was not still adhering to nineteenth-century practices, as well as a few lively, crisp, tart white wines, the best of which are the *"vinho verdes."* For dry red wine, the best are from such regions as Dão, Bairrada, and the Dour.

QUICK VINTAGE GUIDE

Vintages in Portugal seem to have relevance only to the port trade. For the dry red table wines, none of the wineries seem to think vintages matter a whole lot, but certainly 1983, 1982, 1980, and 1977 would be recent years in which grapes were reputed to ripen evenly and reach perfect maturity.

A GUIDE TO PORTUGAL'S BEST PRODUCERS OF DRY RED TABLE WINE

* * * * (EXCELLENT PRODUCERS)

Carvalho, Ribeiro, Ferreira   J. M. da Fonseca (Periquita)
(Dão, Serradayres, Garrafeira)   João Pires (Cabernet and
Ferreira (Barca Velha)   Muscat)

* * * (GOOD PRODUCERS)

Caves Alianca (Vinho Verde)   Grao Vasco (Dão)
Caves St. Jão (Garrafeira)   Quinta da Aveleda (Vinho
Caves Velhas (Dão, Romeira)   Verde)

A Buying Strategy

First, the intense, rich, full-bodied Barca Vehlas from Ferreira are expensive at $12 a bottle. However, they compete with the elegant, seductive, voluptuous Periquitas of Fonseca for honors as Portugal's top dry red table wine. The Periquitas cost about $8 a bottle. The excellent firm of Carvalho, Ribeiro, and Ferreira produces three fine reds, all selling for under $8 a bottle. Their supple, generously fla-vored Dão from Conte de Santar, their claretlike, stylish Serradayres, and old, robust, yet sometimes coarse Garrafeira are all worth a try. Lastly, the Quinta de Bacalhoa near the famous Sintra castle makes modern-style, Bordeaux-inspired Cabernet Sauvignon for a modest $6 a bottle.

For white wines, the tart, light, exuberant Vinho Verde—if drunk within two years of the vintage from producers such as Quinta da Aveleda and Carvalho, Ribeiro, Ferreira—is a refreshingly crisp, lively wine for around $4 a bottle. Lastly, if you are able to find any, the Muscat from João Pires is a lovely wine: dry, flowery and deli-ciously fruity.

PORT

The pleasures of port are justifiably legendary. Good vintages are said to need 10, even 15, years of cellaring before they can be drunk. However, the truth is that vintage port is terribly appealing even when consumed in its youth, though port fanatics would consider that infanticide. The major port houses all have their specific styles and the level of quality of these houses is remarkably high. In addition to vintage port, which seems to be declared in only three to four vintages a decade, there are other types of port, the best of which is old tawny port. I find ruby port rather one-dimensional, late-bottled port lacking character, and white port a rather grotesque aberration.

For me, it is vintage port and tawny port, or nothing, and consequently that is what I shall write about.

QUICK VINTAGE GUIDE

The great recent vintages for port are 1963, 1970, 1977, and 1983. Other years have been declared and are quite good, such as 1982, 1980, 1975, and 1966, but they do not have the level of sheer intensity and richness of the first four referenced vintages, nor do they have the aging potential.

A GUIDE TO PORTUGAL'S BEST PRODUCERS OF PORT

* * * * * (OUTSTANDING PRODUCERS)

Dow	Graham
Fonseca	Taylor Fladgate & Yeatman

* * * * (EXCELLENT PRODUCERS)

Cockburn	Quinta do Noval
Croft	Sandeman
Ferreira	Warre

* * * (GOOD PRODUCERS)

Calem	Offley Forrester
Delaforce	Poças Junior
Gould Campbell	Ramos-Pinto
Martinez	Smith-Woodhouse

Port—A Buying Strategy

Since the port producers do not release their production figures, and since most of them rarely declare a vintage more than four times a decade, quantities of vintage port are believed to be rather small. Prices for port usually do not begin to become expensive until the wine reaches its tenth birthday, the time when port-fanciers begin to seriously imbibe a given vintage. Demand for vintage port continues to grow at a rapid pace and my advice is to stock up on the remaining 1977s that exist, because this is the greatest vintage since 1963, though the 1983s are not far behind in quality. As for the 1983s, I would take a serious look at them. At the moment they are priced very reasonably, but their prices can only go up once the quality of the vintage is more widely known. The 1963s and 1970s are very expensive, but the 1975s, forward, lighter weight wines that are delicious now, are somewhat undervalued in the scheme of things.

The other type of port I would not hesitate to try would be the mellow, fully mature, old tawny ports offered by the better houses. Tawny ports are aged 10, 20, sometimes 30 or 40 years in cask and have a very complex, mellow, savory, nutty, berry fruit character. Many cheaply made, blended tawny ports have given this type of port a bad name, but the old authentic tawny ports from firms such as Dow, Graham, Ferreira, Taylor Fladgate & Yeatman, and Quinta do Noval are truly superb.

COCKBURN* * * *

1963	($45.00)	86
1970	($40.00)	87
1975	($20.00)	82
1983	($15.00)	88

This house tends to produce quite full-bodied, rich, alcoholic, spirity vintage ports that never have a great deal of complexity or finesse but offer meaty, chocolatey, spicy, full-bodied, alcoholic flavors at the expense of elegance. The 1977 has always tasted a bit awkward but shows enormous depth, power, and richness. One should wait until the end of this century before drinking it. The 1975 is light, a little alcoholic, and not terribly distinguished. The 1970 is big and powerful and just now reaching maturity. The 1963 is fully mature, spicy, with a chocolatey, meaty texture and somewhat hot, short finish.

CROFT* * * *

1963	($60.00)	86
1966	($30.00)	87

1970	($35.00)	85

1975	($15.00)	87

1977	($20.00)	88

1982	($20.00)	90

Croft never seems to get much publicity since the wines, while always very good, sometimes even excellent, never quite reach the superb level of the top houses in Oporto. However, Croft seems to do surprisingly well, often rivaling the top ports in the less glamorous vintages such as 1975 and 1966. The 1975 is almost as good as Croft's 1977. Both are rich, creamy, intense ports that should be fully mature within 10–12 years, relatively soon for a vintage port. The 1970 is quite good, but in the context of the vintage, marginally disappointing. The 1966 is a sleeper: complex, rich, very aromatic, with long, deep flavors. The 1963, one of the great vintages for port, is good but unexciting. However, the 1982 is superb, a powerful, broadly flavored wine with exhilarating depth and richness on the palate and at least 25 years of life ahead of it.

DELAFORCE* * *

Eminence's Choice 16-year-old Tawny Port	($12.00)	85

1966	($45.00)	86

1970	($40.00)	84

1975	($22.00)	82

1978 Quinta da Corte	($25.00)	85

1982	($18.00)	85

This house tends to make good port and sell it at rather reasonable prices. The 16-year-old tawny is soft and pleasant but lacks a bit of character. The 1978 single-vineyard port, Quinta da Corte, is straightforward and chunky, with good length but not much complexity; the same can be said for the 1975 and 1970, both of which are fully mature. It has been several years since I have tasted a 1966, but my recollection is that it is the best Delaforce port I have had.

DOW* * * * *

Boardroom 15-year-old Tawny	($12.00)	87
Gold Label 30-year-old Tawny	($32.00)	90
1963	($60.00)	92
1966	($35.00)	88
1970	($45.00)	86
1975	($20.00)	85
1977	($45.00)	93
1980	($20.00)	88
1983	($25.00)	90

This is an extraordinary house that seems to have been particularly successful with its vintage ports since 1977. Of course, the 1963 is a classic, a monumental, rich, still tannic wine that will last at least another 30 years. The 1966 is also a top success for that vintage; in fact, it would be hard to find a better port that year. The 1970 is good, but for some reason has never blossomed and developed any complexity, and the same can be said for the fully mature, fruity, soft 1975. However, starting with the 1977 Dow has hit its stride. The 1977, still a baby, is fabulously scented, very rich and concentrated, and has a potential longevity of at least another 30–50 years. The 1980 is very, very good and certainly better than what this house produced in 1975 and 1970. It should mature relatively fast and be ready to drink by 1992. The newest vintage port, the 1983, is rich, concentrated, very fruity, and magnificently perfumed, suggesting that it is going to mature early, long before the 1977. As for the tawny ports from Dow, they can also be superb. The 30-year-old tawny has a scent of sweet saddle leather, hazelnuts, and rich fruit. The 15-year-old tawny, for ⅓ the price, is a somewhat lighter but no less interesting version.

FERREIRA* * * *

Duque de Bragança 20-year-old Tawny	($20.00)	88
1970	($45.00)	85
1975	($18.00)	86
1977	($28.00)	87
1980	($18.00)	85
1983	($20.00)	88

This house is terribly underrated when top ports are mentioned. Their vintage ports tend to lack a bit in complexity and majesty of aromas, but do offer rich, robust, concentrated flavors of chocolate, spices, and deep, plummy fruit. However, their 20-year-old tawny, Duque de Bragança, must certainly be one of the top tawny ports made in Portugal and is well worth seeking out by those who want something to drink immediately.

FONSECA* * * * *

Bin 27	($10.00)	84
Fonseca 10-year-old Tawny	($15.00)	86
1963	($65.00)	96
1966	($50.00)	88
1970	($45.00)	93
1975	($18.00)	89
1977	($38.00)	93
1980	($30.00)	87
1983	($25.00)	92

Fonseca is one of the great port lodges. It produces the most exotic and most complex port. If Fonseca lacks the sheer weight and power of a Taylor, Dow, or Warre, or the opulent sweetness and intensity of a Graham, it excels in its magnificently complex, intense bouquet of plummy, cedary, spicy fruit and long, broad, expansive flavors. One might call it the Pomerol of vintage ports, with its lush, seductive character. When it is young, it often loses out in blind tastings to the heavier, weightier, more tannic wines, but I always find myself upgrading my opinion of Fonseca after it has had 7–10 years of age. If there is a disappointment for me, it is their Bin 27, a huge commercial success; it is rather straightforward and simple. However, for vintage ports, the newly released 1983 is magnificently scented, full-bodied, creamy, rather forward, but showing great length and character. The 1980 is very good, possibly excellent, but tasted lighter than some of the best ports from that vintage. The 1977 has developed magnificently in the bottle, and while it clearly needs another decade to reach its summit, it is the best Fonseca since the 1970 and 1963. Fonseca's 1975, which is fully mature, shows just how good this house can be; it is a port to seek out since the vintage does not have the reputation or the price tag that 1977 and 1970 do. It should drink magnificently for another decade or more. The 1970, of course, is a powerful Fonseca, with an exotic bouquet and lush, creamy, multidimensional flavors. The 1966, a top success as well, is fully mature, but will hold for 15 or more years, and the 1963, one of the great modern-day classics of vintage ports, is an incredibly aromatic, sublime, majestic port that simply defines Fonseca's style perfectly.

GOULD CAMPBELL* * *

1977	($23.00)	84
1980	($15.00)	85
1983	($16.00)	82

My experience with this house is limited, but I have found the 1980 and 1983 rich, full-bodied, well colored, and complex. One rarely sees this brand stateside.

GRAHAM* * * * *

Emperor Tawny 20-year-old	($12.00)	85
Prince Regent's 10-year-old Tawny	($26.00)	88

1963	($65.00)	92
1966	($40.00)	88
1970	($60.00)	93
1975	($22.00)	80
1977	($45.00)	96
1980	($25.00)	88
1983	($25.00)	95

Graham is another great port house, producing one of the deepest colored and sweetest styles in vintage port. Along with Taylor and Fonseca, Graham has probably been the most consistent producer of great port in the post-World War II era. Their tawnys are quite good rather than exceptional, but their vintage ports are truly sublime and sumptuous. The 1983, like most vintage ports, seems more forward than normal, but has a great depth of very ripe, viscous, unctuous, plummy, tarry fruit and significant tannin in its very long finish. It is black purple in color. I doubt that it will be as profound or as long-lived as the great 1977, but it is certainly one of the top two or three ports of that vintage, and better than the excellent 1980 that Graham produced. The 1970 is a monumental vintage port and one of the greats of that vintage. It begs to be drunk now, although it will last for at least another two decades. The 1966, which I initially thought rather mediocre, has developed beautifully in the bottle and is a much finer vintage port than I suspected. It should be drunk now since it is not likely to get any better. The 1975 is the only recent vintage of Graham that I find disappointing. It is rather light in color, finishes very short on the palate, and obviously lacks depth and ripeness.

MARTINEZ* * *

1963	($30.00)	78
1967	($19.00)	85
1975	($25.00)	86

1982	($15.00)	84

This house is rarely seen in the United States and I was unimpressed with the example of the 1963 that I once had in a comparative tasting. However, the two most recent notes I have are for the 1967 and 1975; both were good, medium-weight, tarry, plummy ports without a lot of character, but with good ripeness and clean winemaking.

OFFLEY FORRESTER* * *

1970	($30.00)	86
1972	($15.00)	83
1977	($22.00)	86
1980	($17.50)	83
1983	($15.00)	85

Offley Forrester produces medium-weight ports that, given their reasonable price, offer value rather than great complexity and richness. Curiously, the 1972, a vintage not declared by most port shippers, produced a very good wine and I have good notes on the 1970, 1977, and 1983.

QUINTA DO NOVAL* * * *

1963	($65.00)	82
1970	($50.00)	84
1975	($24.00)	85
1978	($25.00)	84
1982	($25.00)	87

The beautiful Quinta do Noval is undoubtedly the most famous port producer, largely because their 1931 and 1927 were to vintage port what the 1947 Cheval Blanc and 1945 Mouton-Rothschild were to the Bordeaux trade—divine, monumental wines of extraordinary depth of flavor. Also, the Quinta do Noval produces a rare vintage port from a small vineyard of ungrafted, pre-phylloxera vines called Nacional. It is so rare that I have never seen, much less tasted, a bottle of what is supposedly a great port. However, the truth of the matter is that recent vintages of Quinta do Noval have not been nearly as impressive as they should be. Commentators have described the wines as light, elegant, and charming when in fact they lack richness and depth of flavor. The 1963 and 1970, two great vintages for port, are disappointing. The 1975 has turned out charming, fruity, and actually better than the 1970 or 1963, which is inexplicable. The two most recent vintages, 1978 and 1982, two vintages not declared by most port houses, have shown more richness of flavor and character in bouquet and aroma.

RAMOS-PINTO* * *

Quinta da Bom Retiro Tawny 20-year-old	($22.00)	86
Quinta da Ervamoira Tawny 10-year-old	($12.99)	85
1970	($22.00)	86
1980	($11.99)	84
1983	($15.00)	85

I know little about this firm other than that both their tawnys are excellent and offer considerable value, and that the two vintage ports currently on the market show a style not unlike that of Fonseca, a lush mellowness and complex, plummy, chocolatey bouquet. Their 20-year-old tawny, the Quinta da Bom Retiro, is really quite sumptuous.

SANDEMAN* * * *

Founder's Reserve	($12.00)	80
N. V. Royal Tawny	($15.00)	83
1970	($45.00)	84
1975	($27.00)	84
1977	($30.00)	87
1980	($22.00)	82

1982   ($18.59)   87

Sandeman is one of the biggest and most conspicuous of the port
houses, with extensive interests in the sherry business as well. They
advertise significantly and their products are well represented in virtually every American marketplace. The quality is quite good given
the quantity of wine produced, but rarely does a Sandeman tawny or
vintage port hit the true heights that a Dow, Fonseca, Taylor, or
Graham will. Their Royal Tawny has an attractive, nutty, ripe black
cherry character. Their Founder's Reserve, which is highly publicized, is good, inexpensive, straightforward port of little complexity
but with plenty of mellow, savory, sweet flavors. Their vintage ports
have been a bit light, but the 1977 and 1982 show considerable
strength and richness. However, the 1980, 1975, and 1970 are good
rather than exciting in quality.

SMITH-WOODHOUSE* * *

1980   ($16.00)   85

My experience with Smith-Woodhouse is limited, but I was impressed
with a 1980 vintage port that showed a lovely, supple, ripe, rich, fruity
character in an early-maturing style. Their tawnys are very good but
rarely seen in the marketplace.

TAYLOR FLADGATE & YEATMAN* * * * *

N.V. Tawny   ($10.00)   85

10-year-old Tawny   ($18.00)   87

20-year-old Tawny   ($32.00)   90

30-year-old Tawny   ($45.00)   87

1963   ($70.00)   95

1966   ($50.00)   88

1970   ($45.00)   96

1975   ($22.00)   87

1977	($40.00)	96

1980	($20.00)	89

1983	($24.00)	94

This house must certainly be the Latour of Portugal. Their ports are remarkably backward yet still impressive when young. Of all the vintage ports, those of Taylor need the longest time to mature and even when fully mature seem to have an inner strength and firmness that keep them going for decades. Their tawnys are also among the very best, though somewhat expensive. For current drinking, the 20-year-old tawny is a wonderfully fragrant, nutty-scented wine of great character and complexity. Among their vintage ports there has not been an unsuccessful year since 1963. The 1963 is quite fabulous yet still seemingly capable of developing for another decade or more. The 1966 is drinking well now and is a very good rather than exceptional Taylor. The 1970 is fabulous, a broodingly dense-colored, backward port that has all the signs of future greatness, provided one is willing to cellar it until the early 1990s. The 1975 has turned out richly fruity, supple, and offers delicious drinking for the near future. The 1977 has consistently been at the top of my list of vintage ports in this great vintage, although the Dow, Graham, and Fonseca are equally splendid. It is a mammoth, opaque, statuesque vintage port of remarkable depth and power, but it should not be touched before 2000. The 1980 is probably the best port of the vintage, and the 1983 is wonderfully aromatic and so perfumed (a characteristic of this charming vintage), yet powerful, long, and deep on the palate. It gives every indication of being an early-maturing Taylor, but I wouldn't want to drink it before 1995.

WARRE* * * *

Nimrod Tawny	($15.00)	85

1963	($65.00)	87

1966	($50.00)	86

1970	($50.00)	87

1975	($23.00)	86

| 1977 | ($37.00) | 92 |

| 1980 | ($22.00) | 88 |

| 1983 | ($19.00) | 90 |

This house makes rather restrained yet rich, flavorful vintage port and a very good tawny called Nimrod. Their vintage ports seem slow to develop, and while they never have quite the voluptuous richness of a Dow, Graham, or Fonseca, they have their own unique mineral-scented character that gives them their own complexity and style. The 1983 is richly perfumed and fragrant, which is so typical of the ports from this vintage, and is seemingly more forward than normal. The 1980 is backward, firm, and has yet to reveal its true personality; the 1977 is quite powerful, very deep and intense, particularly for Warre; and the 1975 is soft, supple, and clearly mature. Of the older vintages, the 1970 remains rather unyielding but still impressive, the 1966 fully mature and good but not exciting, and the 1963 very, very good and now fully mature.

5. SPAIN:
AN AWAKENING GIANT

RED WINES

Ask a French wine producer in Bordeaux what wine region in the world has the best chance of competing qualitatively with his, and the answer will not be California's Napa Valley, but Spain.

The potential for great red wine in Spain's top three viticultural regions, the Rioja, Penedès, and Ribera del Duero, all in northern Spain, is considerable. Yet most wine enthusiasts probably think of inexpensive sparkling wines and sherry rather than fine red table wines when the topic of Spanish wine production comes up.

Admittedly, the high-quality sherries made in the hot, arid southern region of Jerez la Frontera offer considerable diversity in style and appeal, but for centuries little has changed in the making of sherry. In the red wine regions, however, there is a considerable revolution in winemaking and growers and producers are committed to making fine wine; I predict that they will have a significant positive impact on the future and image of Spain's red wine.

The consumer should remember that there are three constant conditions that exist for Spanish red wines: First, an obviously sweet, oaky taste, what the Spanish palate adores, that many Americans

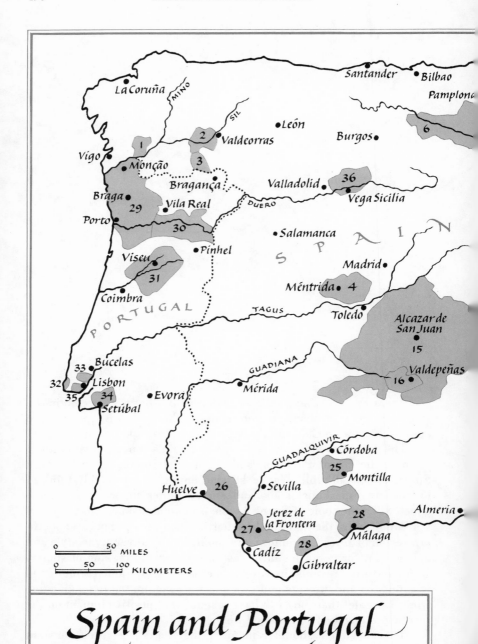

Spain and Portugal

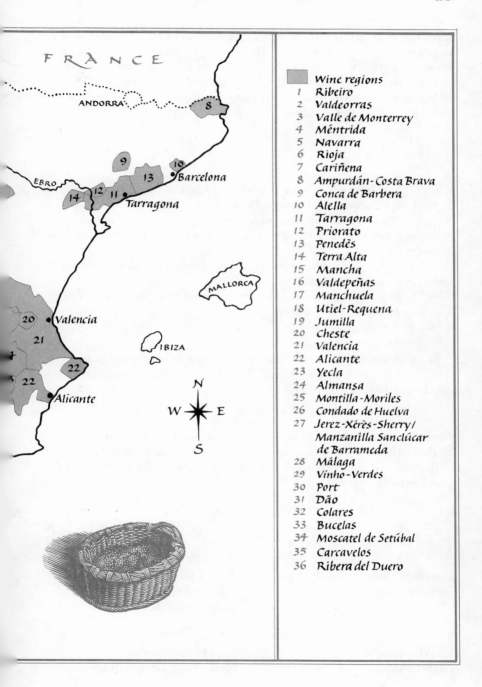

Wine regions
1   Ribeiro
2   Valdeorras
3   Valle de Monterrey
4   Méntrida
5   Navarra
6   Rioja
7   Cariñena
8   Ampurdán- Costa Brava
9   Conca de Barbera
10 Alella
11 Tarragona
12 Priorato
13 Penedès
14 Terra Alta
15 Mancha
16 Valdepeñas
17 Manchuela
18 Utiel- Requena
19 Jumilla
20 Cheste
21 Valencia
22 Alicante
23 Yecla
24 Almansa
25 Montilla- Moriles
26 Condado de Huelva
27 Jerez-Xérès-Sherry/
    Manzanilla Sanclúcar
    de Barrameda
28 Málaga
29 Vinho- Verdes
30 Port
31 Dão
32 Colares
33 Bucelas
34 Moscatel de Setúbal
35 Carcavelos
36 Ribera del Duero

have come to appreciate as well. Second, except for a handful of very expensive wines, Spain offers the very finest rapport in quality/price of any red wine produced today. Third, the usual practice in Spain is that the wineries release their wines when they are ready to drink. All of Spain's wines are relatively mature when released, but the best of them keep well in the bottle.

QUICK VINTAGE GUIDE

1985—Virtually every wine-producing region of Spain reported 1985 to be a very successful, high-quality vintage.

1984—This vintage has a terrible reputation because of a poor, cool European summer, but the wines of Spain may turn out to be the best made in Europe.

1983—A hot, dry year caused some problems, but early reports indicate a very good year.

1982—For Rioja and Ribera del Duero, the finest vintage since 1970, and largely regarded as a great year.

1981—A very good vintage.

1980—An average-quality year.

1979—A good year in the Penedès area, but only average in Rioja.

1978—For Rioja, Penedès, and the Ribera del Duero, the best overall vintage between 1970 and 1982.

Older Vintages

Nineteen seventy was a great vintage for most of northern Spain. Prior to that, 1964 was another superb vintage. Well-kept bottles of 1970 and 1964 red wines from Rioja and the Ribera del Duero can be excellent examples of Spanish red wines.

A GUIDE TO SPAIN'S BEST PRODUCERS

* * * * * (OUTSTANDING PRODUCERS)

Pesquera (Ribera del Duero)   Torres Black Label Coronas
La Rioja Alta (Rioja)   (Penedès)
                                          Vega Sicilia (Ribera del Duero)

* * * * (EXCELLENT PRODUCERS)

CVNE (Rioja)   Jean León (Penedès)
Laserna (Rioja)   Marqués de Grinon (Rueda)

Muga (Rioja)   Torres Gran Coronas (Penedès)
Remelluri (Rioja)

*** *(GOOD PRODUCERS)*

Bilbainas (Rioja)   Marqués de Murrieta (Rioja)
Campo Viejo (Rioja)   Marqués de Riscal (Rioja)
Castillo de Tiebas (Navarra)   Mont Marcal (Penedès)
Faustino Martinez (Rioja)   Olarra (Rioja)
Lar de Barros (Tierra de Barros)   Rioja Vega-Muerza (Rioja)
Lopez de Heredia Vina   Señorio de Sarria (Navarra)
  Tondonia (Rioja)   Torres Gran Sangre de Toro
Marqués de Caceres (Rioja)   (Penedès)

** *(AVERAGE PRODUCERS)*

Age-Unidas (Rioja)   Gran Condal-Bodegas Santiago
Masia Bach (Penedès)   (Rioja)
R. Barbier (Penedès)   Lan (Rioja)
Berberana (Rioja)   Montecillo (Rioja)
Beronia (Rioja)   Federico Paternina (Rioja)
Franco Españolas (Rioja)   Priviligio Pedro Domecq (Rioja)
                                                Vina Pedrosa (Ribera del Duero)

Today's Buying Strategy

For the most part, Spanish wines are aged in oak vats but also in
bottle a long time before release. The Spaniards like to buy and drink
their wine when it has mellowed and is close to maturity. Consequently, most Spanish wines are ready to drink when released, although they may not yet be fully mature. Prices over recent years
have been remarkably stable as the best of these wines continue to
represent great bargains in mature red wines. Except for a handful of
the rarer, more sought after Spanish red wines, the Vega Sicilia,
Pesquera, and Torres Black Label Gran Coronas, I buy Spanish wines
not to cellar, but to drink immediately. Keep in mind that 1978, 1981,
and the great 1982 are the three best recent vintages. Most of the top
1982s are just now coming on the market and these three vintages
would be those on which I would concentrate.

A Comment on Spanish Sparkling Wines

The large Spanish sparkling wine business is best at producing
solid, reliable, unexciting, sparkling wines at remarkably low prices.
If they do not provide inspiring drinking, they are certainly adequate
and, most important, cheap. The best producer of sparkling wine is

Juve and Champs, followed by Cordorníu, Freixenet, Penelada, and Segura Viudas. Over 90% of the Spanish sparkling wine is produced in Penedès and the two largest firms, Codorníu and Freixenet, account for the great majority of the sparkling wine produced in Spain.

Following are my notes for all the top producers of Spain's red wine-producing regions.

AGE-UNIDAS (RIOJA)* *

1981 Siglo	($3.99)	65

This winery can produce good wine, but most consumers will probably remember the wines more for the burlap bag in which the wine bottle is encased. The best vintage I ever tasted was the 1961, which was soft and fruity and held for a number of years. The 1981 is quite light and a little stale-tasting.

RENÉ BARBIER (PENEDÈS)* *

1978 Cabernet Sauvignon	($5.99)	78
1983 Red Wine	($3.99)	80
1983 Reserva	($5.99)	75

René Barbier produces rather straightforward, fruity, medium-bodied wines that are meant to be drunk young. The prices are reasonable, but the wines often lack a focal point of interest, as is the case for the three selections above.

BERBERANA (RIOJA)* *

1981 Carta de Oro	($4.79)	82
1975 Gran Reserva	($7.49)	80
1978 Gran Reserva	($5.99)	83
1980 Reserva	($5.49)	78

The Riojas are all average to slightly above average quality wines as well as fully mature. The 1981 Carta de Oro is light ruby with a moderately intense, oaky, strawberry and cherry-scented bouquet and light flavors. The 1980 Reserva is light, with a cardboard-type aroma and decent flavors. Between the other two Reservas, the 1978 is spicy with nice cherry fruit, medium body, and decent length. The 1975 is just beginning to dry out in fruit and should be drunk up. These are decent, rather lightweight Riojas.

CAMPO VIEJO (RIOJA)* * *

1975 Gran Reserva	($7.99)	85
1970 Gran Reserva Villamagna	($16.00)	86
1973 Gran Reserva Villamagna	($13.75)	85

All three of these Riojas showed quite well in my tastings. They have good color, plenty of richness and length, mature, well-developed bouquets, and good character. The 1975 has a rich, intense bouquet of coffee, spices and leather, medium body, soft, generous flavors, and a good finish. The 1973 has an aged Rioja smell of sweet, oaky aromas, and soft, cherryish fruit. It is a medium-bodied, mellow, rather good Rioja. The 1970, from a great vintage for the area, has a deep color, a spice box, cedary, sweet, oaky bouquet, rich, fleshy flavors that have a round, plump texture, and good finish. These are attractive, well-made, interesting Riojas.

CVNE (RIOJA)* * * *

1982 Clarete	($4.49)	84
1978 CVNE	($4.99)	80
1975 Reserva Imperial	($8.99)	84
1976 Reserva Imperial	($8.99)	83
1980 Vina Real	($4.49)	82
1975 Vina Real Gran Reserva	($8.99)	84

This producer is still among the top Rioja houses. The 1982 Clarete is supple and loaded with fruit. One can only anticipate with great desire just how good the 1982 Reserva Rioja will be, given the success of this lighter-styled Clarete. The 1980 Vina Real has good color, a spicy, plum fruitiness, bigger body but not the charm of the 1982. The 1978 CVNE has a spicy, fruity, complex bouquet, medium body, but finishes short. The 1975 Vina Real (in the burgundy-shaped bottle) is a rich, medium- to full-bodied wine with good concentration, a round texture, and good length. The 1976 Reserva Imperial (in the Bordeaux-shaped bottle) is more angular, lean, and lacks the richness of the 1975 Vina Real. The 1975 Reserva Imperial is better than the 1976, and has more body, depth, and richness of fruit. It is fully mature and should keep well for 2–5 years.

FAUSTINO-BODEGA MARTINEZ (RIOJA)* * *

1970 Faustino	($11.99)	85
1976 Faustino	($5.99)	84

I have tasted a range of older Rioja Reservas from this firm that were well made, not terribly complex or profound, but spicy, fruity, soft, velvety wines that exhibited quality winemaking. The 1976 Faustino, the vintage currently available, is quite an alluring wine. A moderately intense bouquet of sweet oak and ripe cherry fruit is pleasant. On the palate, the wine is supple, lush, and fully mature. The 1970, which is still commercially available, is slightly richer, with a deep, more complex bouquet.

GRAN CONDAL-BODEGAS SANTIAGO (RIOJA)* *

1976 Reserva Rioja	($5.99)	76
1978 Reserva Rioja	($5.99)	72
1983 Rioja	($3.49)	75
1984 Rioja	($3.49)	78

All four of these wines are light, insubstantial, and fairly bland. The 1984 is the most appealing, with a charming, light-intensity strawberry fruitiness. The 1978 Reserva has an aged maturity but short, thin finish. The 1976 Reserva has a decaying, leafy, vegetal smell and short, light flavors.

LAR DE BARROS (TIERRA DE BARROS)* * *

1982 Tinto Reserva	($5.99)	85

To date, this is the best red Spanish wine I have tasted outside of the famous viticultural areas of Rioja, Penedès, Navarra, Ribera del Duero, and Rueda. It is a very good wine with an exotic bouquet suggesting chocolate cherry candy and has the texture of a lush Pomerol, with a smooth, velvety finish.

VINÍCOLA LASERNA (RIOJA)* * * *

1975 Contino	($8.99)	87
1978 Contino	($8.99)	88
1980 Contino	($8.99)	86

This is one of the few estates to use a specific vineyard for its wine. The winery is largely unknown, but the quality of the wines is among the best in Spain and the potential enormous. All of these wines have very good color, very fragrant, oaky, voluptuous, deep, intense bouquets, loads of fruit and concentration, and long finishes. The wines have the sweet oakiness so common in Spanish red wines as well as a lush Pomerol fruitiness. An estate to watch carefully.

JEAN LEÓN (PENEDÈS)* * * *

1978 Cabernet Sauvignon	($5.99)	86
1979 Cabernet Sauvignon	($5.99)	86

This winery continues to turn out very fine Cabernets at very modest prices. However, despite their prices, these wines need cellaring since they are made in a very rich, deep, tannic, full-bodied style. For example, older vintages such as the 1974 and 1975 are still not fully mature. The 1978 and 1979 are deeply colored, medium- to full-bodied wines loaded with aromas and flavors of toasty new oak, blackcurrants, and exotic spices. Both can be drunk now, but given their structure and depth, I would imagine 5–6 years of cellaring might just yield some shockingly complex, rich wines.

LOPEZ DE HEREDIA VIÑA TONDONIA (RIOJA)* * *

1978 Viña Tondonia	($5.99)	80
1979 Viña Tondonia	($4.99)	75

This winery makes two styles of wine, a Viña Tondonia in a Bordeaux-shaped bottle and a more robust, richer Viña Bosconia in a burgundy-shaped bottle. Older vintages from the '50s and '60s were beautiful examples of Rioja at its best; however, recent vintages have a tendency to be fruity, soft, light and rather straightforward in style, as typified by the above examples.

MARQUÉS DE CÁCERES (RIOJA)* * *

1975 Reserva	($8.49)	84

1981 Tinto	($4.49)	82

The Cáceres style of Rioja represents the very modern style that draws its inspiration from Bordeaux. The wines are fruity, supple, straightforward and not oaky. Both of these wines, while lacking a little depth and character, are still good wines with clean, soft, generous, ripe cherry flavors, medium body, and pleasant finishes. Both should be drunk over the next several years.

MARQUÉS DE GRIÑON (RUEDA)* * * *

1982 Tinto de Crianza	($7.49)	87

1983 Tinto de Crianza	($7.99)	85

The inspiration for this wine from Rueda is Carlos Falco, an agricultural engineer and graduate of the University of California at Davis. His 1982 is 90% Cabernet Sauvignon and 10% Merlot, aged 2 years in American oak. (The famous Professor Peynaud and Alexis Lichine are consultants here.) The 1982 is a rich, deeply flavored wine with a complex bouquet of cedarwood and ripe plums. On the palate, the wine is rich, supple, quite drinkable now, but shows every indication of being able to live for 5–10 years. It is extremely impressive. The 1983 is very similar in style but slightly less fat and deep. Both are excellent examples of the newer styles of Spanish red wines.

MARQUÉS DE MURRIETA (RIOJA)* * *

1978	($6.99)	82

1978 Castillo de Ygay	($10.99)	85

The Marqués de Murrietta is one of the oldest Bodegas in Spain. The winery has an excellent reputation, although I have found the quality of the wines to be rather spotty and inconsistent. The above two wines are both fully mature, show a great deal of oak aging, and have round, soft, supple flavors. Neither is likely to improve any further and should be drunk up.

MARQUÉS DE RISCAL (RIOJA)* * *

1978	($5.99)	82
1980	($5.99)	74
1981	($5.99)	78

The Marqués de Riscal is one of Rioja's most famous wineries, from which I have had some wonderfully rich, complex, old vintages. However, recent wines have not shown nearly as well and have tasted significantly lighter than some of the older vintages. However, should you come across any of their Gran Reservas, which usually have a hefty portion of Cabernet Sauvignon added in, they are worth a try. I have not seen any recent vintages of these in the marketplace.

MONT MARCAL (PENEDÈS)* * *

1982 Cabernet Sauvignon	($8.00)	?
1981 Tinto Reserva	($8.00)	?

There are some attractive components to these wines, but also some disturbing flawed qualities. The 1982 Cabernet has a slight barnyard aroma that spoils a wine that otherwise has a lovely, lush, rich texture and deep fruit. The 1981 Tinto Reserva has an aroma of overripe black cherries and sweaty leather and seems rather unstable in the bottle. Neither is worth a gamble.

MONTECILLO (RIOJA)* *

1981 Cumbrero	($3.95)	80
1978 Monty	($6.95)	82

This winery produces Rioja in the very modern, fruity, soft style that eschews excessive amounts of wood aging. The wines are straightforward, fruity, soft, and cleanly made.

MUGA (RIOJA)* * * *

1982 Muga	($4.49)	84
1978 Prado Enea	($8.99)	86

This is one of my favorite Bodegas in Rioja. Their wines are very traditionally made, tend to be quite oaky and light in color, but are very aromatic, with sweet, long, ripe flavors. The 1982 Muga has ripe, plummy fruit and a generous bouquet of expansive, spicy oak and rich fruit. The 1978 Prado Enea is deeper, more complex, and certainly one of the finest Riojas on the market. Both are ready to drink now.

OLARRA (RIOJA)* * *

1980 Cerro Añon	($4.49)	82
1982 Cerro Añon	($4.99)	75
1978 Cerro Añon Reserva	($9.29)	78
1981 Tinto	($4.99)	80
1975 Tinto Gran Reserva	($9.79)	82
1978 Tinto Reserva	($6.49)	83

Several years ago, in tasting through the Olarra wines, I was very impressed with their quality and reasonable prices; certainly these wines have enjoyed and deserved a great deal of success. But more recent offerings have been only average in quality, and seem less impressive than those first tasted 4–5 years ago. All of the above wines are soundly made but rather dull.

FEDERICO PATERNINA (RIOJA)* *

1964 Gran Reserva	($19.95)	65
1966 Gran Reserva	($19.95)	67
1968 Gran Reserva	($16.00)	62
1970 Gran Reserva	($10.00)	75

The Paternina Bodega is certainly one of the Rioja's most famous names. In fact, I can remember some grand old wines from vintages in the '50s and early '60s. However, the 1964, 1966 and 1968 Gran Reservas all suffered from the same problem: an objectionable cardboard smell I associate with filter pads. However, I would think that given the 8–10 years these wines spent in oak, they hardly needed to be filtered for clarity. Whatever the reason, the wines tasted short, were terribly deficient in fruit on the palate, and were rather dried out. The 1970 had some fruit left to it. What a shame for this fine old Bodega to release such inferior wines.

PESQUERA (RIBERA DEL DUERO)* * * * *

1975 Pesquera Reserva	($39.95)	92
1982 Pesquera	($11.99)	92
1982 Pesquera Reserva	($25.00)	95
1983 Pesquera	($11.99)	90
1984 Pesquera	($11.99)	85

The new star in Ribera del Duero is the Pesquera of Alejandro Fernandes. With vineyards next to Vega Sicilia, this wine is aged only 2–2½ years in cask (à la Bordeaux) and then bottled. The results are stunning. Both the 1982s are staggeringly immense wines, rich, unctuous, with the depth and texture of a great Pomerol such as Pétrus or L'Evangile, plenty of ripe, round tannins, the sweet oaky smells that typify a Spanish red, and unbelievable length. The 1983 is identical, but slightly less open and opulent; the 1984 is just a shade lighter and less concentrated. The 1975, just released, is another fine effort, very rich, and despite its luxurious texture, it has the depth and harmony to improve for another two decades. A 1972 Pesquera tasted last month was sublime. Pesquera's wines must be tasted to be believed. They should last 5–15 years, but because of their massive fruit can be drunk young. The Pétrus of Spain?

PRIVILIGIO PEDRO DOMECQ (RIOJA)* *

1976	($5.99)	70
1980	($3.99)	70

This winery makes inexpensive but soft, fruity, light-bodied wines for drinking upon release. They show no evidence of any ability to improve within the bottle.

REMELLURI (RIOJA)* * * *

1979 La Bastida de Alava	($6.99)	86

1980 La Bastida de Alava	($6.99)	85

1982 La Bastida de Alava	($6.99)	87

Remelluri is one of only a handful of Rioja estates to produce and estate bottle their wines from their own vineyards. The proprietor, Don Jaime Rodriquez Salis, believes in elegant, complex wines, and that is what one finds—wines with a refined fragrance and gentle suppleness and lushness that are more akin to burgundies than Bordeaux. His wines are aged 3–4 years in oak casks and then bottled. This is a very serious estate and, after the Bodegas La Rioja Alta in Haro, perhaps the region's second best producer. All three of these wines are similarly styled—medium-bodied, graceful, stylish wines with smooth, harmonious, generous flavors. The 1982, Rioja's first great vintage since 1970, is more concentrated but ready to drink. The 1980 is slightly lighter but has a lovely bouquet of ripe berry fruit and sweet oak. The 1979 is virtually identical in style, but I thought it just a bit longer on the palate. I am not sure whether these wines will improve in the bottle, but they will keep easily for 3–5 years.

LA RIOJA ALTA (RIOJA)* * * * *

1970 Reserva 890	($19.99)	90

1973 Reserva 904	($14.99)	89

1983 Viña Alberdi	($4.49)	75

1978 Viña Ardanza	($7.49)	84

1976 Viña Ardanza	($8.49)	86

This is the top Rioja winery, and the demand for its products, and consequently the prices, reflect it. However, I know of no one who has ever tasted these wines to complain about the price—they are that good. La Rioja Alta is a practitioner of the old school of Rioja winemaking. The wines are kept 6, 8, even 10 years in cask and only released when the winery deems them ready. The 1983 Viña Alberdi is quite undistinguished, but the other wines certainly have plenty to offer. I marginally prefer the 1976 to the 1978 Viña Ardanza only because the 1978 is still a little tannic. Both are spicy, rich in fruit, medium-bodied, with cedary aromas and excellent balance. The top of the line cuvées, the 1973 Reserva 904 and 1970 Reserva 890, are both quite exceptional. The Reserva 904 is fully mature, light in color, and has a gorgeous fragrance of ripe, rich fruit and smooth, complex, almost Volnay-like flavors. It will keep for 4–5 years, but I know of nowhere in the world where you can find this level of mature, sublime complexity for $15. The 1970 Reserva 890 is altogether outstanding— from its full-intensity bouquet that suggests roasted chestnuts, to-bacco, and a fine Graves, to its long, rich, smooth, medium- to full-bodied flavors that linger and linger on the palate.

RIOJA VEGA-MUERZA (RIOJA)* * *

1975 Reserva	($8.95)	84
1978 Reserva	($4.95)	84
1981 Tinto	($3.99)	80

This winery has in recent years consistently provided good wine at rather low prices. Of the three current releases, the 1981 is a little dull and one-dimensional, but for the price no one will complain about the quality. Both the 1978 and 1975 are a big step upward. The 1978 is light ruby in color, has a moderately intense, rather seductive rasp-berry-scented bouquet, soft, supple flavors, and nice balance. It is ready to drink. The 1975 is a more serious wine, but more tannic, with a sterner, rougher framework, and is slightly less charming. If you prefer charm, try the 1978; if you like power, the 1975.

SEÑORIO DE SARRIA (NAVARRA)* * *

1982	($2.99)	80
1973 Reserva	($7.99)	85
1978 Tinto	($5.99)	84
1978 Viña del Lerdon	($5.99)	85

This well-run Navarra winery produces rather light-colored wines, but don't let that mislead you. They are spicy, fragrant, and redolent with scents of sweet oak, cherries, and flowers. The 1982 is light, fruity, supple and a very attractive value. Both 1978s have more richness, medium body, supple, elegant textures. The Viña del Lerdon tasted longer on the palate. The 1973 Reserva is beginning to tire a bit (at least the bottle I tried was fatigued), but is still a delicious mouthful of savory, oaky, fruity, easy to drink yet complex and elegant Spanish wine.

TORRES (PENEDÈS)* * * *—* * * * *

1982 Coronas	($3.49)	83
1979 Gran Coronas Reserva	($6.79)	87
1981 Gran Coronas Reserva	($6.49)	88
1982 Gran Coronas Reserva	($6.99)	89

At $3.99, the 1982 Coronas is one of the great red wine values in today's market. It is remarkably consistent from bottle to bottle. A moderately intense, black cherry bouquet intermingled with scents of spice is very appealing. Round and generously flavored, this medium-bodied, dry wine has soft tannins, good concentration, and character. Serve it blind and most tasters will think it is a $10 bottle of wine. The 1982, 1981, and 1979 Gran Coronas Reservas are astonishing bargains. The rich, complex bouquets of ripe plums, spicy oak, and vanillin are top-flight. On the palate, they are full-bodied, deep, savory, and quite long, with layers of fruit. A Spanish Lynch-Bages? Perhaps. Each should drink and improve for at least 5–6 more years. They are blends of 60% Cabernet Sauvignon and 40% Tempranillo, the dominant red wine grape of Penedès and Rioja.

1981 Sangre de Toro	($3.29)	79
1982 Sangre de Toro	($3.99)	83
1978 Sangre de Toro Reserva	($4.99)	85

I suspect more Spanish restaurants use the Sangre de Toro in their Sangria than any other wine. In a way it does a disservice to the wine. For $4 a bottle, it offers plenty of rich, chunky, supple fruit and is similar to a good generic Côtes du Rhône. The 1981 is chunky, deep in color, but one-dimensional. For the extra $2, I would go for the 1978 Reserva, which has a fragrant, ripe, spicy bouquet, big, rich flavors and a long, supple finish. It's a fleshy, rich wine made from

65% Grenache and 35% Carignane. It is Spain's answer to a good Châteauneuf-du-Pape.

1977 Gran Coronas Black Label	($13.00)	90
1978 Gran Coronas Black Label	($16.00)	92
1981 Gran Coronas Black Label	($18.00)	90

The 1978 is the first Black Label to be 100% Cabernet Sauvignon. These are truly extraordinary wines and among the world's greatest. Their prices are, quite frankly, unbelievable and not likely to remain low once the wine-consuming public realizes how great these wines can be. The 1977 has a wonderful bouquet of toasty vanillin oak, ripe blackcurrants, and leather. On the palate, it is velvety, supple, deeply flavored, and oh, so long. It should be drunk over the next 5–6 years. The 1978 is, I think, the greatest Black Label yet produced. One hundred percent Cabernet Sauvignon, the bouquet explodes from the glass with complex aromas of oak, cassis, coconuts, violets, truffles, and leather. Very concentrated, moderately tannic, fleshy and deep, it has the concentration and texture of a great vintage of Pétrus. Yes, the score is correct; I feel there are few red wines in the world from the 1978 vintage that can top this marvelously balanced, impeccably vinified wine. It should develop and last for at least 8–10 years. The newly released 1981 continues the splendid line of successes from Torres. It is reminiscent in style of the 1977, but has slightly more richness and fragrance.

1975 Gran Coronas Reserva	($7.99)	83

This new release, a commemorative bottling, is showing a spicy, tobacco and earthy bouquet, rather tannic, hard flavors, and an angular personality. I prefer the recent Gran Coronas Reservas to this older vintage.

VEGA SICILIA (RIBERA DEL DUERO)* * * * *

1960 Unico Reserva	($60.00)	87
1965 Unico Reserva	($45.00)	80
1966 Unico Reserva	($45.00)	92

1972 Unico Reserva	($37.95)	90
1976 Valbuena	($23.00)	85
1978 Valbuena	($23.00)	88
1979 Valbuena	($23.00)	89
1980 Valbuena	($16.00)	87
1982 Valbuena	($25.00)	82

Vega Sicilia is reputed to produce Spain's greatest red wines. Because of the high prices charged, the estate has been a target for criticism. However, the wines I tasted, except for the 1965 Vega Sicilia, ranged from excellent to superb. The top wine is the Vega Sicilia Unico Reserva; it is expensive and produced in very limited quantities. Given their quality, age, and rarity, the price is not unfair. The 1960 has a full-intensity, sweet, oaky bouquet dominated by the smell of rich, plummy fruit on the palate. The wine is expansive, lush and flowing, like a great old Pomerol. It is very concentrated and so well balanced. Since the Vega Sicilias are kept at least 10 years in cask prior to release, I doubt much aging takes place in the bottle. The 1965 is awkward, rather compact, and lacking in personality. I tasted it twice and was left surprised by its rather mediocre character. The 1966 is fabulous: a rich, spicy, sweet, oaky bouquet with rich, opulent, voluptuous flavors, an incredible finish, and remarkable complexity. It can hardly get any better. The newest Unico Reserva is the 1972, another rather profound wine with the telltale sweet, oaky, richly fruity, full-blown bouquet and ripe, voluptuous, opulent flavors and length. The wine is all the more remarkable for the fact that 1972 was a terrible vintage in Europe.

Before you invest $40–$60 in a Vega Sicilia Reserva, an excellent introduction to the style of this winery is its Valbuena, which spends "only" 5 rather than 10 years in oak. It is very similarly styled, with the same lush, intense opulence of fruit, fragrant, sweet, oaky smells, and easy to drink yet very complex style. The 1980, 1979, and 1978 are all excellent, the 1976 less concentrated, a trifle too oaky. The wines of Vega Sicilia are exotic, dramatic, and intensely rich.

VIÑA PEDROSA (RIBERA DEL DUERO)* *

1983 Tinto Pedrosa	($8.99)	78
1982 Tinto Reserva Pedrosa	($12.99)	84
1985 Viña Pedrosa	($5.99)	83

The best wine I tasted from Pedrosa was the 1985 Viña Pedrosa, a rich, supple, explosively fruity wine that must be Spain's answer to Italy's Dolcetto or France's Beaujolais. It is meant to be drunk young and it is quite delicious. The 1983 Tinto had a fine dark color but rustic, coarse texture. The 1982 Tinto exhibited more charm and character.

THE WINES OF NORTH AMERICA

California
Oregon
Other American
Viticultural Regions

6. CALIFORNIA

Just when I began writing about wine (in 1978), European wine prices, particularly those of France, were exceptionally high. California wines in comparison looked much the better value and, in many cases, much the better wine. France and most of Europe had just been through a succession of generally mediocre vintages: a horrible 1972, below-average years in 1973 and 1974, a spotty 1975, a good 1976, but bad 1977. To make matters worse, the dollar was very weak. California, on the other hand, was in what looked to be its glory days. The rich, lusty, powerful wines of 1973 and 1974 were performing to raves across the country. The 1975, 1976, and 1977 vintages, though less publicized, were all successful in very different ways for California's wine producers. In addition, the vintners were still basking in the adulatory international publicity surrounding the much ballyhooed Steven Spurrier Paris tasting, wherein California Chardonnays and Cabernets thoroughly trounced some of the finest wines from Bordeaux and Burgundy. In 1978, California wines dominated the marketplace as well as the wine press. Even national news magazines *(Time, Newsweek, Forbes)* got into the act, going so far as to predict a "golden age" for California's wine industry.

However, wine-buying patterns are cyclical, and California's star-

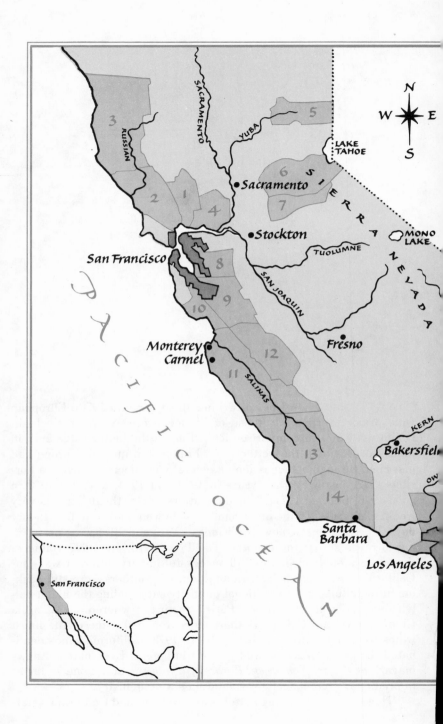

California

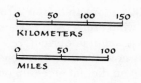

NEVADA

MOJAVE DESERT

San Bernardino

16

SALTON SEA

COLORADO

San Diego

17

18

MEXICO

■ Wine regions
1 Napa Valley
2 Sonoma
3 Mendocino
4 Solano
5 Sierra Foothills
6 El Dorado
7 Amador
8 Alameda
9 Santa Clara
10 Santa Cruz
11 Monterey
12 San Benito
13 San Luis Obispo
14 Santa Barbara
15 Los Angeles
16 Riverside
17 San Diego
18 Imperial Valley

| 0 | 50 | 100 | 150 |
KILOMETERS

| 0 | 50 | 100 |
MILES

dom held center stage for only a few short years. By 1981 the dollar was beginning to flex its muscles and giving the European currencies a beating. The poor series of vintages in Europe ended in 1978 with the English wine writer Harry Waugh dubbing 1978 the "miracle vintage." That year was followed by a series of big, abundant, European grape crops of at least high quality, and in some cases, extraordinary quality. Prices for European wines dropped and consumer and press attention turned to Europe. One's credibility was being stretched to the limit to believe that so many different viticultural regions of Europe could be having so many wonderfully fine, quality bumper crops of grapes. But the fact of the matter was that it was true. A further enticement to the wine consumer was the price of European wines, which declined considerably in the early '80s as the dollar surged in strength, setting record highs that had not been seen in over two decades. California wines, so glamorous and sexy, and on allocation virtually everywhere in 1978, became less fashionable, and unfortunately, less interesting. The great textbook vintages of 1970, 1973, and 1974 were replaced by good but often problematic years where there was either too much heat, or rain, or both. To exacerbate things further, many California vintners were in search of more finesse and elegance in their wines and became convinced that bland, innocuous, technically perfect, squeaky clean wines that had perfect pHs, perfect acidity, and just the right amount of alcohol, but little flavor, would somehow be considered more elegant and satisfying than wines with dynamic and distinctive regional characters and personalities. In short, many California wines began to resemble a multinational corporation salesperson: they began to look alike and taste alike.

If these wines lacked boldness, character, and personality, their winemakers, many of them recent graduates of the University of California at Davis, assured us that, unlike the "dirty, defective, high pH French wines," these wines were flawless and perfect with food. It was this image of wine as a boring, bland, standardized product akin to beer or liquor that in the long run has hurt California wine sales in the 1980s more than the strong dollar and the succession of high-quality wine crops from France, Germany, Italy, and Spain. However, change is again underfoot.

It is now 1987, and the boom period for buying European wines is over. If you did not stock up on the marvelous wines from Europe that were sold at bargain prices the last several years, you can only blame yourself. Today, several things stand out.

1. European, particularly French, wine prices have again gotten out of hand. Burgundy is the worst example, but the glamor châteaux of Bordeaux are also soaring in price because of higher and higher demand for their wines and a dollar that has dropped significantly in value.

2. California has had its best back-to-back vintages, 1984 and 1985, since 1973 and 1974. Its two wine stars, Chardonnay and Cabernet Sauvignon, look awfully impressive and they appear to be priced very fairly. Furthermore, it seems that the more intelligent wine-makers have abandoned their misconceived flirtations with innocuous, bland, sterile wines. There has been a slight trend to letting the raw materials from these two top vintages receive minimal handling in the wine cellar and to permit the quality of the grapes to shape the personality of the wine rather than having the centrifuge and filtering take the flavor and complexity out of it. In addition, there are still many good wines from 1982 that are hard to ignore. For certain, California is in an excellent position to regain control of the marketplace for fine wine.

An Overview of the Major California Varietals

White Wine Varietals

Chardonnay—The great superstar of the white wines, Chardonnay at its best can produce majestically rich, buttery wines with layers of flavors suggesting tropical fruits, apples, and peaches. It flourishes in all of California's viticultural districts. The trend in the '80s in California has been to pick the grapes earlier to achieve higher natural acidities. Even though Chardonnay definitely produces California's finest white wines, far too many, though technically flawless, tend to lack character and taste like imitations of one another. This may change as winemakers and owners become more confident. Chardonnay is generally aged in oak barrels for several months to a year. They can be long-lived wines in the hands of a producer such as Trefethen, Sonoma-Cutrer, Stony Hill, Mayacamas, or Kalin, but the great majority of these wines require drinking up before they turn 5 years old. Anyone who tells you anything different clearly does not have your best interests in mind. One trend to pay particular attention to is the bevy of top-quality, low-priced Chardonnays that have appeared on the market. Labels to look for are Glen Ellen, Stratford, and Liberty School, which consistently produce good Chardonnays for under $7.

Chenin Blanc—This maligned, generally misunderstood grape can produce lovely apéritif wines both dry and slightly sweet, but in either style, fruity, delicate, perfumed, and light-bodied. However, sagging sales have caused many premium wineries to abandon it. Dry Creek, Chappellet, Preston, Alexander Valley, and Hacienda make some of the best.

French Colombard—Like the Chenin Blanc, another varietal that is rarely accorded respect by consumers. Its charm is its aromatic character and crisp, light-bodied style. Parducci and Chalone consistently prove its credentials.

Gewürztraminer—Highly promoted and encouraged by the California wine press, this varietal, made in the dry, slightly sweet, and late-harvest (very sweet) style, is to my palate a watery, vague resemblance to the spicy, exotic, flamboyant Gewürztraminers made in Alsace, France. Wineries that have captured some authentic Gewürztraminer character in their wines are Evensen (Napa), Joseph Phelps (Napa), and Chateau St. Jean (Sonoma).

Muscat—This is a terribly underrated and underappreciated varietal that produces at the top levels slightly sweet, remarkably fragrant, perfumed wines that are usually loaded with tropical fruit aromas and flavors. Robert Pecota, Louis Martini, and Bonny Doon all achieve special results with this grape.

Pinot Blanc—Often indistinguishable from Chardonnay in a blind tasting, Pinot Blanc is usually a more steely, crisper, firmer wine than Chardonnay. Chalone makes the best Pinot Blanc in California, followed by Congress Springs, Mirassou, and Bonny Doon.

Sauvignon Blanc—In the last several years, the trendy California wine scene made this grape the "great white hope," and now that wineries have taken up its cause, it seems to be falling out of fashion. It is often called Fumé Blanc. It is a crisp wine with a subtle earthy, herbaceous quality that in many examples becomes grotesquely vegetal, although examples of blatantly vegetal wines are much less common today than several years ago. It is a remarkably flexible wine with an assortment of foods and the level of quality across-the-board is quite high. Yet, rather unfortunately, far too many wineries aim for the middle-of-the-road, safe style of wine and, as with Chardonnay, one finds an excessive number of fairly neutral, bland, innocuous examples of this wine. Sauvignon Blanc is often blended with Semillon to give it more body and a creamy character. Some of California's best Sauvignon or Fumé Blancs are produced by Robert Mondavi, Dry Creek, Kalin, Matanzas Creek, Chateau St. Jean, Spottswoode, and Glen Ellen.

Semillon—This is clearly one of the up and coming white varietals of California. It is the perfect partner when added to the crisp, lean, acidic Sauvignon Blanc because it seems to always have plenty of body and a creamy richness. It is difficult to handle entirely by itself, but Kalin Cellars of Marin County has produced a ravishing string of Semillons from old vines planted in Livermore, and Beringer has produced a decadently sweet dessert wine from this varietal.

White Riesling or **Johannisberg Riesling**—With over 8,000 acres of this varietal planted in California, the wine industry is not likely to tear out the vines; nevertheless, except for the world-class, late-harvest sweet Rieslings made by Joseph Phelps, Chateau St. Jean, Raymond and a handful of other wineries, the attempts at making dry Kabinett or Spätlese-styled Rieslings have generally produced dull, heavy wines with little character whatsoever. The simple truth of the matter is that most of the Riesling is planted in areas where the soil is too rich or the climate too hot. With only a few exceptions—Jekel, Kendall Jackson, Chateau St. Jean are three that come to mind—the conditions are only suitable for great, sweet, dessert-style Rieslings. No one wants to hear it, but its drier versions have largely been failures.

Red Wine Varietals

Cabernet Franc—Now being used by more and more wineries to give complexity to their wines' bouquet, Cabernet Franc is a cedary, herbaceous-scented wine that is much lighter in color and body than either Cabernet Sauvignon or Merlot. It rarely can stand by itself, but used judiciously in a blend, it can provide an extra dimension. Two great California wines with significant proportions of Cabernet Franc that have stood the test of time are the 1971 Robert Mondavi Reserve Cabernet and the 1977 Joseph Phelps Insignia red wine. The Santa Cruz winery of Congress Springs has recently demonstrated success with this varietal.

Cabernet Sauvignon—This great red wine grape has found a hospitable home in many areas of California. It reaches its heights in Napa, the Santa Cruz Mountains, and Sonoma. It renders wines dense in color, with high tannins and a rich blackcurrant-scented and flavored fruitiness often intertwined with subtle, spicy, herbaceous scents. While wines made from Cabernet Sauvignon can be remarkably long-lived—15–20 years in a few instances—most California Cabernets should be drunk before they attain the age of 8. However, wines from the top wineries can certainly last 12–15 years before fading. But beware. Many California Cabernets, primarily those made from grapes in Santa Barbara, San Luis Obispo, Monterey, and Lake counties, have extremely vegetal aromas and flavors. This defect even afflicts certain Sonoma and Napa Cabernets. Don't let anyone tell you this is a peculiar personality trait of California Cabernet. It is a major defect, and many wineries have to face the fact that their vineyards are planted in improper soils and regions—a fact hard to accept when it costs upwards of $30,000 an acre to purchase, clear, and plant a vineyard.

Merlot—The higher alcohol, fleshier, more supple stablemate of Cabernet Sauvignon, Merlot can stand by itself and be enjoyed for its opulence, or blended with Cabernet Sauvignon to provide a softer, lusher texture. Some wineries are now offering Merlot on its own, and the results have generally been quite good.

Petite Sirah—Unfortunately, this varietal has fallen from grace. Though not the true Syrah, it can produce richly colored, very tannic, intense wines with peppery, cassis-scented bouquets. The Ridge and Freemark Abbey Petite Sirahs from Napa's York Creek Vineyard prove the outstanding potential of this grape when planted in the proper soils and grown and vinified with care.

Syrah—The great red grape of the Rhône Valley. Few California wineries have toyed with this varietal, which may be more suitable for the climate and soils of more California viticultural districts than any other varietal. Joseph Phelps produces a Syrah in a light, fruity, Beaujolais style, but Bonny Doon in the Santa Cruz Mountains has made exquisite wines from Syrah in 1983, 1984, and 1985. Qupé is another pioneer with this varietal. Perhaps these wineries will finally prove that outstanding wines from this varietal can be made in California.

Pinot Noir—Largely a failure in California's North Coast regions, the Pinot Noir has probably broken more winemakers' hearts than anybody or anything else. Grapes grown in the cool Carneros region have consistently shown promise, as have grapes grown in Monterey and other areas of the Central Coast. One must always approach California Pinot Noir with the greatest degree of caution, for the bad, or should I say bad and bizarre, examples of this wine are repugnant. Yet progress continues to be made. In the north, Robert Mondavi, Acacia, Hanzell, and the two emerging superstars, Saintsbury and Kalin, have somehow found the secret. South of San Francisco, Chalone, Calera, Thomas Fogarty, Edna Valley and a handful of other wineries have also found the elusive formula for good Pinot Noir.

Zinfandel—The perennial whipping boy of the wine press, Zinfandel all but disappeared from the popularity charts in the late '70s and early '80s. It can be a remarkably satisfying wine, rich, bold and dramatic. It can also cause rampant confusion since it appears in so many different styles—from light, zesty Beaujolais-inspired wines to heavy, portlike, late-harvest monsters. The best Zinfandels have properly balanced richness and harmony. The two best practitioners, Ridge and Ravenswood, continue to be in a class by themselves.

QUICK VINTAGE GUIDE

1985—On overall balance, the finest vintage for California Cabernet Sauvignon, Chardonnay, and Sauvignon Blanc since 1974. A perfect growing season preceded near-perfect conditions for harvesting. Napa and Sonoma look to be the best, Santa Cruz and Mendocino just behind in quality. The Cabernets should be both rich and long-lived, less extroverted and opulent in their youth than the 1984s, but certainly longer-lived. This could prove to be the best overall vintage since 1970.

1984—An excellent year, somewhat overshadowed by 1985, 1984 was one of the hottest years on record, with temperatures soaring over 100° F frequently during the summer. An early flowering and early harvest created problems because many grape varietals ripened at the same time. The style of the Chardonnays and Cabernets is one of very good to excellent concentration, an engaging, opulent, forward fruitiness that gives the wines appeal in their infancy and good overall balance. Mendocino is less successful than elsewhere, but the ripe, rich, forward character of the wines of this vintage gives them undeniable charm and character. The majority of winemakers call 1985 a more classic year, 1984 a more hedonistic year. Certainly 1984 and 1985 are California's best two back-to-back vintages since 1973 and 1974.

1983—An average year for most of California's viticultural regions, though the Chardonnays from Napa are very good, even excellent. The Cabernets are medium-bodied, rather austere, and lack the flesh and richness found in good years. Nevertheless, some stars are to be found, but overall the quality of Napa and Sonoma Cabernets is disappointing. The white wines should be drunk before the end of 1987; the red wines will keep for at least another 4–6 years.

1982—The growing season was plagued by heavy rains, then high temperatures. The press seemed to take a cautionary approach to the vintage, and as it turns out, justifiably so. Sonoma is more consistent than Napa, and Santa Cruz is surprisingly weak in 1982. The Sonoma red wines are ripe, rich, very forward, and much more interesting than those of Napa, which range in quality from outstanding to out of balance. Chardonnays are mediocre, diluted, and lacking depth and acidity. They should have been drunk up by now.

1981—Like 1984, a torridly hot growing season that had all varietals ripening at once and the harvest commencing very early. Many fine, ripe, rich, dramatic Chardonnays were produced, but they should have been drunk by now. The Cabernets are good rather than exciting, with the best of them having a decade of life. Most 1981 Cabernets, because of their forward character, should be drunk before 1991–1992.

1980—A relatively long, cool growing season had wineries predicting a classic, great vintage for both Chardonnay and Cabernet. As the wines have matured, the Chardonnays were indeed excellent, but not as good as in 1984 and 1985. The Cabernets are very good, but hardly great. The Cabernets do however have good acidity levels and seem by California standards to be evolving rather slowly. A vintage that has a top-notch reputation but in reality appears to be a very fine rather than monumental year.

Older Vintages

Since I fervently believe that California's Chardonnays and Sauvignon Blancs rarely hold their fruit or improve after 4–6 years, older vintages are of interest only with respect to California red wines, principally Cabernet Sauvignon.

1979—This year produced a good vintage of tannic, well-endowed wines that are now fully mature.

1978—An excellent vintage from a hot year that produced very concentrated, rich, plummy, dense wines that have aged quite quickly. In all but a few cases, they should be drunk up before the end of this decade.

1977—An above-average vintage that rendered elegant, fruity, supple wines that are now just beginning to tire a bit.

1976—A hot, drought year in which production yields per acre were very small. The wines are very concentrated and tannic, sometimes out of balance. Nevertheless, the great examples from this vintage (where the level of fruit extract matches the ferocity of the tannins) should prove to be among the longest-lived Cabernets of this generation.

1975—After the great vintage of 1974, few people wanted to believe California could have another good vintage. The wines, noticeably lighter and less alcoholic and opulent than the 1974s, are all fully mature now. They are refined, fruity, very well-balanced Cabernets, but they should be drunk up.

1974—A great vintage of very rich, very big, deep, dramatic, intense wines that have shown well from their first release. Some of the lesser stars have started to fade, and even the greatest wines from this vintage are not likely to get much better. And yet, 1974 offers wine enthusiasts flamboyant, rich, intense wines that should continue to drink seductively and well for at least another 5–6 years.

1973—A very fine vintage of classically structured Cabernet with plenty of fruit, some finesse, and 10- to 12-year life lines. These wines should be drunk up.

1972—A rain-plagued, terrible year except in the Santa Cruz area, which produced a bevy of fine wines.

1971—A mediocre year, although Mondavi's Reserve and the Ridge Montebello are two of the greatest Cabernets I have ever tasted.

1970—Along with 1968, 1974, 1984, and 1985, one of California's most successful vintages. The top 1970s are still in great form, with a decade of life left in them at the top levels.

1969—A good vintage, but the wines did not have the stamina or extract to last more than 10 years. I know of nothing from this vintage that should not have been drunk up by now.

1968—A great vintage: powerful, rich, deep, dense wines that when stored well are close to perfection today.

A GUIDE TO CALIFORNIA'S BEST PRODUCERS OF CABERNET SAUVIGNON, MERLOT, OR BLENDS THEREOF

* * * * * (OUTSTANDING PRODUCERS)

Beaulieu Private Reserve Georges de Latour (Napa)
Carmenet (Sonoma)
Caymus Special Selection (Napa)
Diamond Creek (Napa)
Dominus (Napa)
Duckhorn Three Palms Vineyard Merlot (Napa)
Dunn Howell Mountain (Napa)
Forman (Napa)
Groth (Napa)

Heitz Martha's Vineyard (Napa)
William Hill Reserve (Napa)
Lyeth (Sonoma)
Mayacamas (Napa)
Robert Mondavi Reserve (Napa)
Chateau Montelena (Napa)
Opus One (Napa)
Joseph Phelps Eisele (Napa)
Ridge Monte Bello (Santa Cruz)
Silver Oak (Napa)
Spottswoode (Napa)
Stag's Leap Cask 23 (Napa)

* * * * *(EXCELLENT PRODUCERS)*

Aquila Merlot (Marin)
Beringer Private Reserve (Napa)
Buehler (Napa)
Burgess (Napa)
Chappellet (Napa)
Conn Creek (Napa)
Durney (Monterey)
Girard (Napa)
Inglenook Reserve (Napa)
Jaeger (Napa)
Johnson-Turnbull (Napa)
Kistler (Sonoma)
Laurel Glen (Sonoma)

Long (Napa)
Matanzas Creek Merlot
  (Sonoma)
Monticello (Napa)
Mount Eden (Santa Cruz)
Joseph Phelps Insignia (Napa)
Ravenswood (Sonoma)
Ritchie Creek (Napa)
Rubicon (Napa)
Santa Cruz Mountains (Santa
  Cruz)
Sattui (Napa)

* * * *(GOOD PRODUCERS)*

Alexander Valley (Sonoma)
Baldinelli (Amador)
Beringer (Knight's Valley)
Boeger (El Dorado)
David Bruce (Santa Cruz)
Cakebread (Napa)
Carneros Creek (Napa)
Cassayre-Forni (Napa)
Chateau Chevre (Napa)
Clos du Bois (Sonoma)
Clos du Val Reserve (Napa)
Congress Springs (Santa Clara)
Cuvaison (Napa)
Dehlinger (Sonoma)
Dry Creek (Sonoma)
Eberle (Paso Robles)
Fetzer (Mendocino)
Fisher (Sonoma)
Flora Springs (Napa)
Franciscan (Napa)
Glen Ellen (Sonoma)
Gundlach Bundschu (Sonoma)
Grgich Hills (Napa)
Harbor (Yolo)
Jordan (Sonoma)
La Jota (Napa)

Robert Keenan (Napa)
Kenwood (Sonoma)
Charles Krug (Napa)
Charles Lefranc (San Benito)
Louis Martini (Napa)
Montevina (Amador)
Mount Veeder (Napa)
Newton (Napa)
Pine Ridge (Napa)
Quail Ridge (Napa)
Raymond (Napa)
Roudon Smith (Santa Cruz)
Round Hill (Napa)
Rutherford Hill (Napa)
Sebastiani (Sonoma)
Sequoia Grove (Napa)
Shafer (Napa)
Silverado (Napa)
Simi (Sonoma)
St. Clement (Napa)
Stelzner (Napa)
Sterling (Napa)
Stonegate (Napa)
Sullivan (Napa)
Trefethen (Napa)
Tudal (Napa)

Vichon (Napa)
Villa Mt. Eden (Napa)

Whitehall Lane (Napa)
Stephen Zellerbach (Sonoma)

* * *(AVERAGE)*

Cain (Napa)
Christian Brothers (Napa)
Clos du Val (Napa) (since 1979)
Cronin (San Mateo)
Far Niente (Napa)
Freemark Abbey (Napa) (since 1974)
Gallo (Stanislaus)

Guenoc (Lake)
Lakespring (Napa)
Paul Masson (Monterey)
McDowell (Mendocino)
Parducci (Mendocino)
Rombauer (Napa)
Spring Mountain (Napa)
Tulocay (Napa)

A GUIDE TO CALIFORNIA'S BEST PRODUCERS OF CHARDONNAY

* * * * * *(OUTSTANDING PRODUCERS)*

Chalone (Monterey)
DeLoach (Sonoma)
Forman (Napa)
Hanzell (Sonoma)
Kalin (Marin)
Long (Napa)
Matanzas Creek (Sonoma)

Robert Mondavi Reserve (Napa)
Chateau Montelena (Napa)
Mount Eden (Santa Clara)
Sonoma Cutrer (Sonoma)
Stony Hill (Napa)
Trefethen (Napa)

* * * * *(EXCELLENT PRODUCERS)*

Acacia (Napa)
Anderson (Napa)
Clos du Bois (Sonoma)
Congress Springs (Santa Clara)
Cronin (San Mateo)
Edna Valley (San Luis Obispo)
Flora Springs (Napa)
Girard (Napa)
Grgich (Napa)
Groth (Napa)

Monticello (Napa)
Morgan (Monterey)
Newton (Napa)
Raymond (Napa)
Ritchie Creek (Napa)
Château St.-Jean (Sonoma)
Saintsbury (Napa)
Simi (Sonoma)
Talbott (Monterey)
ZD (Napa)

* * * *(GOOD PRODUCERS)*

Alderbrook (Sonoma)
William Baccala (Mendocino)
Balverne (Sonoma)
Beringer (Napa)
Chateau Bouchaine (Napa)
David Bruce (Santa Cruz)
Buena Vista (Sonoma)
Burgess (Napa)
Chappellet (Napa)
Concannon (Santa Clara)
La Crema (Sonoma)
Cuvaison (Napa)
Dolan (Mendocino)
Dry Creek (Sonoma)
Eberle (Paso Robles)
Far Niente (Napa)
Fetzer (Mendocino)
Fisher (Sonoma)
Thomas Fogarty (Monterey)
Folie à Deux (Napa)
Fritz (Sonoma)
Gainey (Santa Barbara)
Glen Ellen (Sonoma)
Guenoc (Lake)
Gundlach Bundschu (Sonoma)
Hacienda (Sonoma)
Haywood (Sonoma)
William Hill (Napa)
Inglenook (Napa)
Jekel (Monterey)
Robert Keenan (Napa)

Kendall-Jackson (Lake)
Kistler (Sonoma)
Landmark (Sonoma)
Domaine Laurier (Sonoma)
Leeward (Central Coast)
Charles Lefranc (San Benito)
Manzanita (Napa)
Mayacamas (Napa)
Merry Vintners (Sonoma)
Milano (Mendocino)
Mount Veeder (Napa)
Neyers (Napa)
Perret (Napa)
Joseph Phelps (Napa)
R. H. Phillips (Yolo)
Pine Ridge (Napa)
Quail Ridge (Napa)
Martin Ray (Santa Clara)
Rutherford Hill (Napa)
Sanford (Santa Barbara)
Sausal (Sonoma)
Shafer (Napa)
Smith-Madrone (Sonoma)
St. Andrews (Napa)
St. Clement (Sonoma)
Stag's Leap (Napa)
Sterling (Napa)
Stratford (Napa)
Vichon (Napa)
Zaca Mesa (Santa Barbara)

* * *(OTHER PRODUCERS)*

Bargetto (Santa Cruz)
Clos du Val (Napa)
Conn Creek (Napa)
Firestone (Santa Barbara)
Freemark Abbey (Napa) (since
   1978)
Gallo (Central Coast)
Jordan (Sonoma)

Lambert Bridge (Sonoma)
J. Lohr (Monterey)
Lords and Elwood (Napa)
Michton (Sonoma)
Pellegrini (Sonoma)
Schug (Napa)
Rodney Strong (Sonoma)
Sebastiani (Sonoma)

A GUIDE TO CALIFORNIA'S BEST PRODUCERS
OF SAUVIGNON BLANC AND SEMILLON

***** *(OUTSTANDING PRODUCERS)*

Kalin (Marin)

Lyeth (Sonoma)

Matanzas Creek (Sonoma)

Robert Mondavi Reserve (Napa)

**** *(EXCELLENT PRODUCERS)*

Acacia (Napa)

Beaulieu (Napa)

Dry Creek (Sonoma)

Duckhorn (Napa)

Glen Ellen (Sonoma)

Karly (Amador)

Simi (Sonoma)

Spottswoode (Napa)

St. Clement (Napa)

Château St. Jean (Sonoma)

Sterling (Napa)

*** *(GOOD PRODUCERS)*

Alderbrook (Sonoma)

Amizetta (Napa)

Beringer (Napa)

Château Bouchaine (Napa)

Carmenet (Sonoma)

Congress Springs (Santa Cruz)

Fetzer (Mendocino)

Flora Springs (Napa)

Fritz (Sonoma)

Frog's Leap (Napa)

Gallo (California)

Kenwood (Sonoma)

Parducci (Mendocino)

Robert Pecota (Napa)

Joseph Phelps (Napa)

R. H. Phillips (Yolo)

Preston (Sonoma)

Stag's Leap (Napa)

Stratford (Napa)

A GUIDE TO CALIFORNIA'S BEST PRODUCERS OF PINOT NOIR

***** *(OUTSTANDING PRODUCERS)*

Calera (San Benito)

**** *(EXCELLENT PRODUCERS)*

Bonny Doon (Santa Cruz)

Calera (San Benito)

Chalone (Monterey)

Edna Valley (San Luis Obispo)

Hanzell (Sonoma)

Kalin (Marin)

Saintsbury (Napa)

Santa Cruz Mountain (Santa Cruz)

Sea Ridge (Sonoma)

*** *(GOOD PRODUCERS)*

Acacia (Napa)
Beaulieu (Napa)
Belvedere (Sonoma)
Kistler (Sonoma)
Robert Mondavi (Napa)
Monticello (Napa)
Mount Eden (Santa Cruz)
Qupé (Santa Barbara)

Richardson (Sonoma)
Sanford (Santa Barbara)
Soleterra (Napa)
Robert Stemmler (Sonoma)
Joseph Swan (Sonoma)
Trefethen (Napa)
Tulocay (Napa)

A GUIDE TO CALIFORNIA'S BEST PRODUCERS OF ZINFANDEL

***** *(OUTSTANDING PRODUCERS)*

Ravenswood (Sonoma)   Ridge (Santa Cruz)

**** *(EXCELLENT PRODUCERS)*

Calera (San Benito)
H. Coturri (Sonoma)
Edmeades (Mendocino)
Grgich (Napa)
Lytton Springs (Sonoma)
Chateau Montelena (Napa)
Monterey Peninsula (Monterey)

Joseph Phelps Alexander Valley
   (Sonoma)
Rafanelli (Sonoma)
Richardson (Sonoma)
Sausal (Sonoma)
Shenandoah (Amador)
Storybook Mountain (Napa)
Joseph Swan (Sonoma)

*** *(GOOD PRODUCERS)*

Baldinelli (Amador)
Burgess (Napa)
Caymus (Napa)
DeMoor (Napa)
Dry Creek (Sonoma)
Fetzer (Mendocino)

Guenoc (Lake)
Montevina (Amador)
Preston (Sonoma)
Story (Amador)
Sullivan (Napa)
Sutter Home (Amador)

Today's Buying Strategy

In devising an intelligent buying strategy for California wine, it is obviously to your advantage to know the finest producers of each major varietal. However, there are several other factors that are also important. California excels in making lusciously fruity, crisp, lively white wines from Chardonnay and Sauvignon Blanc. Vintages do differ in quality, but rarely is there a complete disaster. With few exceptions, all of California's white wines are best drunk within 3–4 years of the vintage. Their winemakers don't like to admit such things, but who really cares? The quality level of Chardonnay and Sauvignon Blanc is very high, and since they drink so well young, why should anyone worry if they are not long-lived? The cardinal rule then is to concentrate on buying white wines from the best two recent vintages, 1985 and 1984, and generally avoid anything older.

For California's rosé or blush wines, Chenin Blancs, and dull, generally poor Rieslings, the rule is even more strict—buy and drink immediately the 1986s and 1985s and avoid anything older. The only exception would be the sweet, nectarlike, late-harvest Rieslings from top producers such as Chateau St. Jean, Joseph Phelps, Austin Cellars, Raymond, and Milano, which exhibit the potential to last and improve in the bottle for 5–8 years, perhaps longer.

As for the red wines produced in California, one generally has a great deal more flexibility. The attraction of many California red wines is their grapy, exuberant, fleshy, forward character. Even though they may not be fully mature or have developed secondary bouquets, most California red wines are undeniably attractive to drink young. For California Pinot Noir, the good ones should be drunk within 5–6 years of the vintage. Concentrate on the 1984s and 1985s, which are splendidly ripe and opulent, and the 1983s of Chalone and Calera.

For Zinfandels, these again are wines to drink within the first 5–7 years of the vintage. The principal exceptions are the wines produced by Ridge, which can last in the bottle for 8–10 years with no difficulty. The two vintages to get excited about for Zinfandel are 1984 and 1985.

For the Cabernet Sauvignon, Merlot, and proprietary blends thereof, the two best vintages are 1984 and 1985. The 1984s are more forward, supple, richly fruity, velvety wines that have enough backbone to insure their longevity for 8–12 or more years, but they are also wines that have great appeal in their youth. Nineteen eighty-five's best Cabernets are not likely to appear on the market until 1988–1989, but this is unquestionably the year with the greatest potential for California Cabernet since the outstanding 1970s and 1974s. The 1985s will be less accessible and opulent in their youth than the 1984s, but they should prove to be relatively long-lived by California standards. As for 1983 and 1982, both vintages produced many fine wines, but they are very irregular in quality (especially 1983), and neither year can pretend to have either the peaks or the consistency of 1984 or 1985.

Prices should remain fairly stable for California wines. During the sluggish years of 1980 to 1985, when European wines dominated the marketplace, many producers in California learned that the increasingly intelligent American wine consumer shops wherever the best values in wine are to be found. There is no loyalty to any one wine region of the world, and there should not be. Shrewd consumers' shopping patterns follow excellence and value—wherever they might be found. Now, however, European wine prices have jumped again, and California's producers, rather than raising prices, seem to be content just to get a tighter grasp on the marketplace before inaugurating price hikes for their wines. Stability in domestic wine prices should be the rule for the next 12 to 24 months, with perhaps slightly higher prices for Chardonnays.

ACACIA (NAPA)

1985 Chardonnay	Napa	($12.50)	83
1985 Chardonnay Carneros	Napa	($15.00)	86
1985 Chardonnay Marina Vineyard	Napa	($16.00)	87
1985 Chardonnay Winery Lake Vineyard	Napa	($18.00)	87
1983 Pinot Noir Iund	Napa	($15.00)	83
1983 Pinot Noir Lee Vineyard	Napa	($15.00)	80
1983 Pinot Noir Madonna	Napa	($15.00)	85
1983 Pinot Noir St. Clair	Napa	($15.00)	84
1983 Pinot Noir Winery Lake	Napa	($15.00)	84
1985 Sauvignon Blanc	Napa	($10.00)	86

Acacia was sold in 1986 to Chalone, so the level of quality should remain quite high. This winery, which made its first wine in 1979, quickly gained a strong following for its vineyard-designated, stylish yet flavorful Chardonnays and interesting, sometimes good Pinot Noirs. In 1984, Sauvignon Blanc and tiny quantities of Merlot were added to its stable, and the former has proved to be among the best made in California. As for the Chardonnays, the 1985s show the very forward, lush ripeness of the vintage, with the Winery Lake and Marina showing deeper, richer fruit than the other offerings. As for the Pinot Noirs, the 1984s promise to be better than the 1983s, but of the

1983s the Madonna and St. Clair are certainly the best picks at this moment. In tracing this winery's performance in Pinot Noir over the last few years, the Winery Lake tends to be the most French in style and the Madonna and St. Clair the two densest and richest in extract. As for the Sauvignon Blanc, it is wonderfully filled with ripe, fresh, subtly herbaceous fruit, a touch of oak, and a lot of depth and character. Acacia, in its short history, has a proven track record of fine winemaking.

ADLER FELS (SONOMA)

1984 Chardonnay Nelson Vyd.	Sonoma	($10.99)	56
1985 Fumé Blanc	Sonoma	($8.99)	69

This winery stresses the two major white varietals of California, Chardonnay and Fumé Blanc, aiming for a light, understated style of wine. The wines have been cleanly made but often lack intensity and varietal character. The two offerings above proved to be among the most disappointing wines yet released by this winery, founded only in 1980.

ALDERBROOK (SONOMA)

1984 Chardonnay	Sonoma	($8.99)	86
1984 Sauvignon Blanc	Sonoma	($7.50)	84
1984 Semillon	Sonoma	($7.99)	85

This new winery, founded in 1982, is stressing white wine and to date the wines have looked strikingly good, with a rich, opulent fruitiness, plenty of varietal character, and good acidity for balance. Prices are modest given the quality level this winery is achieving; this should be a name to follow as their production increases.

ALEXANDER VALLEY VINEYARD (SONOMA)

1982 Cabernet Sauvignon	Alex. Vly.	($10.99)	86
1984 Cabernet Sauvignon	Alex. Vly.	($11.99)	88
1984 Merlot	Alex. Vly.	($11.99)	87
1984 Chardonnay	Alex. Vly.	($11.00)	83

1985 Chardonnay	Alex. Vly.	($11.00)	86

1985 Chenin Blanc	Alex. Vly.	($6.00))	84

The Alexander Valley Winery in Sonoma County rarely seems to get the publicity it clearly merits for its very reasonably priced, well-made wines. Its Chenin Blanc is always made with a lot of appeal—a fruity, soft wine with good acidity. Its Chardonnays can range from some of the best to merely adequate. The 1985 looks to be excellent, with the right amount of oak in its character. The 1984, for whatever reason, has always tasted rather lean and delicate when in fact this winery is known for rather bold, toasty, buttery Chardonnays. Of the recent Cabernets, the 1982 is a clear standout, with plenty of ripe berry fruit, full body, and a lush texture. The 1983 is similarly styled, but lacks the depth and richness of the 1982. However, both the 1984 Cabernet and 1984 Merlot, both with fabulous richness, appear to be the best red wines yet made here.

AMIZETTA (NAPA)

1984 Sauvignon Blanc	Napa	($9.49)	84

1985 Sauvignon Blanc	Napa	($9.49)	85

This tiny winery, which produces Sauvignon Blanc and a yet to be released Cabernet Sauvignon, has gotten off to a good start with these two Graves-like Sauvignons. The 1984 is a deeper colored wine, slightly fuller in body and longer in the finish, flavorful, and concentrated. The 1985 is a vibrant, fresh, very lively wine with a stony, mineral-scented fragrance, crisp acidity, good flavors, and zesty finish. A noteworthy pair of new releases.

S. ANDERSON (NAPA)

1983 Blanc de Noirs Sparkling Wine	Napa	($16.00)	75

1983 Chardonnay	Napa	($15.00)	85

1984 Chardonnay	Napa	($15.00)	89

1983 Chardonnay Proprietor's Selection	Napa	($15.99)	90

This small winery produces just over 3,000 cases of Chardonnay and sparkling wine. The Chardonnays are excellent, rich, medium- to full-bodied wines with toasty oak and tropical fruit, as well as good acidity for balance. While the regular bottling of 1983 is good, the 1983 Proprietor's Selection is exceptional—rich, deep, and profoundly flavored. The 1984 may turn out to be as good. It is lusciously fruity, quite well balanced, a big Chardonnay adroitly balancing power and finesse. The 1983 sparkling wine is like the preponderance of California sparklers: lean, tart, and severe, with little flavor interest.

AQUILA (MARIN)

1981 Merlot	California	($22.50)	87

The tiny production (a scant 500–600 cases) of this wine made by Sean H. Thackrey is available only in limited quantities, but it is wonderfully interesting yet firmly structured Merlot with plenty of fruit, spices, and subtle mint in its character.

ARTISAN WINES (NAPA)

This firm was formed in 1984 as another broker specializing in buying lots of wine and blending it together. The names of the wines, such as Michael's Cabernet Sauvignon, Ultravino Chardonnay, or La Cruvinet Chardonnay, are a little cute, but the quality of the first releases, the 1982s and 1983s, was at least average.

WILLIAM BACCALA (MENDOCINO)

1984 Chardonnay	Mendocino	($10.99)	85
1985 Chardonnay	Mendocino	($11.99)	85

This winery has obtained a quick reputation for its style of lush, reasonably priced Chardonnays. Both the 1984 and 1985 Chardonnays showed liveliness, fragrance, and crisp acidity with moderately intense, well-focused, varietal fruit. Both are the type of Chardonnays that beg to be drunk within the first 3 years of their lives. Production has averaged 15,000 cases.

BALDINELLI (AMADOR)

1980 Cabernet Sauvignon	Amador	($7.99)	86
1981 Cabernet Sauvignon	Amador	($7.99)	86

Baldinelli, located in Amador County, makes a little bit of Zinfandel and an especially rich, robust, intense Cabernet Sauvignon from vines

grown in the Shenandoah Valley. The prices seem remarkably fair for
the quality of this Cabernet, which is made in the extroverted, intense,
chewy style that often resembles the California Cabernets famous in
the mid-'70s. It is the type of wine that seems to suggest it will last for
10 years, though it is hard to resist its intense, forward, lush character
now. An underrated winery.

BALVERNE WINERY (SONOMA)

1984 Chardonnay	Sonoma	($14.00)	84
1984 Sauvignon Blanc	Sonoma	($9.99)	82

This winery, founded in 1979, produces well-balanced, clean, undramatic examples of Sauvignon Blanc and Chardonnay that are technically correct but beg for a little more personality. The Chardonnay
tends to have just the right amount of oak, a lemony, citrusy, varietal
fruitiness, and medium body. The Sauvignon Blanc is crisp, with a
suggestion of lushness from a small amount of added Semillon. A good
winery that charges rather high prices for its wine.

BARGETTO (SANTA CRUZ)

1983 Chardonnay	Tepusquet	($9.99)	75
1984 Chardonnay Cypress Vyd.	Santa Maria	($9.99)	84

The little experience I have had with this 40,000-case winery has left
me unmoved. The wines are decent, straightforward, pleasant yet
uninspiring wines. The emphasis in winemaking seems to be on the
fresh, fruity aspect of the wine. The winery also produces Riesling,
Chenin Blanc, and some Cabernet Sauvignon and Zinfandel.

BEAULIEU (NAPA)

1982 Cabernet Sauvignon Beau Tour	Napa	($8.49)	82
1980 Cabernet Sauvignon Private Reserve	Napa	($20.00)	90
1981 Cabernet Sauvignon Private Reserve	Napa	($20.00)	85
1982 Cabernet Sauvignon Private Reserve	Napa	($20.00)	90
1984 Chardonnay Beaufort	Napa	($11.00)	84

| 1984 Chardonnay Los Carneros | Napa | ($15.00) | 85 |

| 1984 Sauvignon Blanc | Napa | ($8.99) | 86 |

Beaulieu has a deserved reputation for being one of California's greatest wineries. Its fame is largely based on its remarkable Private Reserve Cabernet Sauvignon, which has never strayed from its style of great ripeness and opulence marked by the significant amount of time it spends aging in new American oak barrels. Certain vintages have been monumental wines—1968, 1970, 1976, and more recently 1980, 1982 as well as the unreleased 1984. Other vintages have sometimes been curiously light and underwhelming—1977 and 1978 for example. The lighter Cabernet Sauvignon is represented by the Beau Tour, made to be drunk young, and the Rutherford, which tends to be a bit richer than Beau Tour but, to my taste, no more interesting. Both of the lower-level Cabernets are distinctly different from the Private Reserves. The 1980 and 1982 Private Reserves will easily last 10–15 years, but the 1981 seems tannic and closed, and somewhat disappointing given the great reputation this wine has. As for the Chardonnays, the winery seems to be making increased quality efforts. The 1984 Los Carneros as well as the 1983 Los Carneros are two of the best Chardonnays that the winery has released in almost a decade. Beaulieu's Sauvignon Blanc is always excellent: fruity, crisp, with a subtle herbaceousness in the background. Another wine to look for, which is made in very limited quantities, is B.V.'s Special Pinot Noir from Los Carneros, which never reminds me particularly of Pinot Noir, but which I nevertheless enjoy immensely.

BELVEDERE WINE CO. (SONOMA)

The Belvedere Wine Co. has put together a list of independent wine producers who supply grapes to this company and have their wines vineyard designated. To date the most successful wines have been the Winery Lake Pinot Noir from Napa Valley which sells for $11–$12 and the Bacigalupi Pinot Noir from Sonoma. I have found the Cabernets from the Robert Young Vineyard and York Creek Vineyard less interesting and the Chardonnays from the Winery Lake Vineyard in Napa and the Bacigalupi Vineyard in Sonoma to be inconsistent. The winery also produces very inexpensive wines under the "Wine Discovery" label that tend to be dull, thin, and uninteresting. Belvedere can turn out some splendid wines—the 1981 Winery Lake Pinot Noir and several of the Winery Lake Chardonnays have been top-notch—but there has been little consistency and the wines have occasionally been marked by too much aging in new oak barrels.

BERINGER (NAPA)

1982 Cabernet Sauvignon Knight's Valley		($9.00)	82
1981 Cabernet Sauvignon Private Reserve		($20.00)	86
1980 Cabernet Sauvignon Private Reserve	Lemmon-Chabot	($20.00)	90
1984 Chardonnay Gamble Ranch	Napa	($12.99)	85
1984 Chardonnay	Napa	($8.99)	80
1983 Chardonnay Private Reserve	Napa	($16.00)	86
1984 Fumé Blanc	Napa	($6.99)	83

This famous old winery, located in the heart of Napa Valley, tends to produce a consistently good range of wines; its two best wines, the Private Reserve Cabernet and Chardonnay, are particularly intense and marked by long aging in oak barrels. The Fumé Blanc is herbaceous, fruity, and an above-average rather than an exciting example of its type. The 1980 Private Reserve Cabernet Sauvignon from the Lemmon-Chabot ranch is outstanding: a rich, dense, ripe wine that should mature early because of low acidity. The 1981 Private Reserve does not have quite the richness of the 1980, but does have the typically rich, chocolatey, spicy flavors that one finds in many of the Beringer Private Reserve Cabernets. The 1982 Knight's Valley Cabernet tends to be much softer and much lighter in style, but is straightforward and well made. Of the Chardonnays, the barrel-fermented Gamble Ranch Napa can often resemble an oaky, buttery, French Meursault. The Private Reserve always seems to have the better balance, is well marked by oak, made in a big, rich style, and is typically Californian in its proportions. Visitors to the winery should also ask if any of the limited production, splendidly sweet, Semillon-based wine made by retired yet still active winemaker Myron Nightingale is available. The 1980 and most recent vintage, 1983, are wonderfully rich wines not unlike an excellent sweet wine from the Sauternes region of France.

BOEGER WINERY (EL DORADO)

1984 Merlot	El Dorado	($10.99)	85
1985 Sauvignon Blanc	El Dorado	($7.50)	84

This small winery produces straightforward wines that include several generic wines curiously called "Hangtown Red" and "Hangtown White." Their best two wines for me have been the Sauvignon Blanc, which is round and richly fruity with good varietal character, and their Merlot, which offers plump, lush, plummy flavors and the prospect of early maturity.

JEAN CLAUDE BOISSET (NAPA)

This venture by a Burgundy *négociant* was begun in 1980. The wines tasted to date have been made in a straightforward, commercial style that exhibits little character or depth of flavor. The production of 10,000–12,000 cases has included fairly priced but one-dimensional Chardonnay, Cabernet Sauvignon, and Sauvignon Blanc.

BONNY DOON VINEYARD (SANTA CRUZ)

1983 Cabernet Sauvignon Anderson Valley	($13.99)	85
1984 Le Cigare Volant	($11.99)	87
1985 Pinot Blanc Monterey	($8.99)	85
1983 Pinot Noir Bethel Heights Oregon	($18.00)	87
1985 Pinot Noir Bethel Heights Oregon	($18.00)	88
1983 Syrah	($10.99)	86
1984 Syrah	($10.99)	88
1985 Vin Gris de Grenache	($6.99)	85

This is one of the most distinctive and unique winery operations in all of California. Winemaker Randall Graham clearly marches to the beat of a totally different drummer. In search of the secret for making wines modeled after the great Rhône classics of France (Châteauneuf-du-Pape, Hermitage, and Côte Rôtie), Graham is producing this country's finest Syrah-based wine and his interpretation of Châteauneuf-du-Pape, the historic 1984 Le Cigare Volant, shows wonderfully rich, raspberry, peppery fruit and remarkable character. Virtually everything from this winery is of great interest, including the late-harvest, rich Muscat dessert wine that resembles a Beaumes de Venise from the Rhône and the remarkable rosé called Vin Gris of Grenache that is remarkably similar to a Tavel. Graham's talent are obvious, yet he rarely seems to get the publicity and accolades his considerable winemaking skills deserve. Even his Pinot Noir, which he buys from the excellent Bethel Heights Vineyard in Willamette Valley, Oregon, is among the finest made in California, though not in truth a California wine. Bonny Doon's wines should be sought after by any wine enthusiast for their distinctive, unique qualities.

BRANDER VINEYARDS (SANTA BARBARA)

1984 Sauvignon Blanc	Santa Ynez	($8.99)	85

This winery seems to do its best job with Sauvignon Blanc. Surprisingly, it does not have the intense vegetal character I associate with Sauvignons from Santa Ynez Valley. The 1984 shows wonderfully crisp, clean, excellent varietal character.

DAVID BRUCE WINERY (SANTA CRUZ)

1982 Cabernet Sauvignon	California	($12.00)	82
1983 Chardonnay	California	($12.00)	72
1984 Chardonnay	California	($12.00)	78

Older vintages from David Bruce seemed to represent hit-or-miss propositions, often fabulously rich, intense, full-bodied wines that, while never lacking character, had as many virtues as flaws. Recent vintages have gone a hundred and eighty degrees in the other direction; they have shown remarkable restraint, to the point that they lack interest. The 1982 Cabernet seems remarkably tannic and lean on the palate. The 1983 and 1984 Chardonnays seem to be rather thin on the palate. The 1983 in fact is rather flat and out of balance, whereas the 1984 has a toasty, pineapple-scented, tropical fruit bouquet but seems to fade in the glass with a rather watery, tart, high-acid finish. One wishes for a return to the old style practiced here.

BUEHLER VINEYARDS (NAPA)

1982 Cabernet Sauvignon	Napa	($12.00)	90
1983 Cabernet Sauvignon	Napa	($12.00)	87
1984 Cabernet Sauvignon	Napa	($12.00)	89
1985 Pinot Blanc	Napa	($8.00)	85

This tiny winery, which only began to produce wine in 1978, makes full-blooded, intense, smoky, rich, almost exotic Cabernet with layers of flavors that fanciers of big, lush, rich wines find stunning but those who prefer lightness find overwhelming and exaggerated. Nevertheless, these are bold expressions of California winemaking and I for one applaud what John Buehler is doing. His 1982, despite some bottle variation problems I have had, is a fabulous wine which now appears to be equaled by a similarly styled, lush, intense, very rich 1984. His Pinot Blanc gets less attention, but it is a very well-balanced, clean, well-defined wine that should be drunk within two years of the vintage. Buehler also makes an excellent blush wine, but only the most recent vintage should be considered for drinking.

BUENA VISTA (SONOMA)

1981 Cabernet Sauvignon Special Selection	Sonoma	(18.00)	85
1983 Chardonnay	Sonoma	($10.00)	75
1984 Chardonnay	Sonoma	($10.00)	80
1985 Fumé Blanc	Lake	($8.99)	84

This winery, with a significant production in excess of 100,000 cases, has been German-owned since 1979. Its colorful history goes back to the middle of the nineteenth century (it is California's oldest winery). The wines tend to be straightforward, commercial examples of their type, which rarely disappoint but are not exciting either. The Chardonnays tend to be lean, compact, varietal examples without much depth of character. The Cabernets tend to be rather tannic and dark and show little charm, although the 1981 Special Selection has the best depth and complexity I have experienced from Buena Vista Cabernet. The winery made a delicious, soft, intensely fruity Fumé Blanc in 1985. My gut feeling is that this winery could do better if it wanted to be more creative.

BURGESS CELLARS (NAPA)

1981 Cabernet Sauvignon Vintage Selection	Napa	($16.00)	84
1982 Cabernet Sauvignon Vintage Selection	Napa	($16.00)	88
1983 Chardonnay Vintage Reserve	Napa	($12.99)	72
1984 Chardonnay Vintage Reserve	Napa	($12.99)	86

Tom Burgess, the owner of this medium-sized winery that produces 30,000 cases of wine per year, seems to be content to do his job quietly but steadily. His Cabernets have ranged from among the best in California to merely good. His 1974, 1976, 1978, and more recently the 1982, certainly have been among the top several dozen Cabernets made in those vintages. His Cabernets tend to be tannic and backward, but the 1982 shows a very accessible, charming, lush quality, even though it has a decade of life ahead of it. The Chardonnays at Burgess started off in the mid-'70s as huge, oaky, alcoholic wines that seemed to fall apart after a couple of years. The more recent examples have shown remarkable restraint, crisp acidity, and a much lighter touch with the oak, with the 1984 the best of the current offerings. Perhaps they lack the drama and flamboyance of the earlier Chardonnays, but they are better balanced and better examples of this type of wine. Burgess wines may not be expensive, but they are generally quite well made. The winery also makes a good, rather tannic, deeply colored Zinfandel.

BYRON (SANTA BARBARA)

1984 Chardonnay	Central Coast	($8.00)	86
1984 Sauvignon Blanc	Santa Barbara	($7.49)	85

A brand new performer on the California wine scene, the first two releases exhibited excellent winemaking, plenty of varietal character, and a very intelligent pricing policy. Perhaps this is a name to watch.

CAIN CELLARS (NAPA)

Founded in 1981, this young winery seems to be doing a better job with its white varietals, Chardonnay and Sauvignon Blanc, than with its tart, weedy Merlot. Cabernet Sauvignon is to be offered as well. First releases did not inspire confidence in this winery.

CAKEBREAD CELLARS (NAPA)

1981 Cabernet Sauvignon	Napa	($12.99)	84
1982 Cabernet Sauvignon	Napa	($16.59)	85
1983 Chardonnay	Napa	($13.99)	82
1984 Sauvignon Blanc	Napa	($10.99)	84

Cakebread Cellars produces generally good, straightforward wines that lean toward being austere and compact in texture. My major objection is that their prices seem out of line with the quality level. The Sauvignon Blanc tends to be the most interesting wine, with a dry, subtle, herbaceous character and lean framework. The Cabernets are also rather backward and hard, with little charm, and aging seems to provide more disappointments than benefits. The Chardonnay tries to out-Chablis Chablis and fails to do so. The potential seems to be here, but the wines remain overpriced given the quality level.

CALERA WINE CO. (SAN BENITO)

1985 Chardonnay Santa Barbara	($12.00)	84
1982 Pinot Noir Jensen	($25.00)	86
1983 Pinot Noir Jensen	($22.00)	87
1984 Pinot Noir Reed	($25.00)	90
1983 Pinot Noir Reed	($22.00)	84
1982 Pinot Noir Santa Barbara	($10.00)	74
1983 Pinot Noir Santa Barbara	($10.00)	72

| 1982 Pinot Noir Selleck | ($25.00) | 88 |

| 1983 Pinot Noir Selleck | ($23.00) | 86 |

| 1984 Pinot Noir Selleck | ($25.00) | 90 |

At present, the tiny Calera Winery is making California's best and most intriguing Pinot Noirs. They are rich, aromatic, rather intense, unique wines. The production is tiny, the costs of production high, so the prices for the final product look expensive. However, you are not likely to be disappointed, particularly if you are in search of flamboyant and intense, exotic Pinot Noirs. The 1982s are intensely smoky, spicy, fragrant, rich wines that some might call the Chambertins of California. They are unfiltered and, whether for that reason or not, seem to swell and develop in the glass as they sit. Usually the Selleck is the most evolved and the Reed and Jensen the most tannic and presumably ageworthy. All three of the 1982 wines can be drunk now for their extroverted, full-intensity, complex bouquets, although they show the potential to improve for several more years. The 1982 Santa Barbara, made from purchased grapes, is very weedy and vegetal, and not to my liking. The 1983s continue the success this winery has had with this fickle varietal. They are similar to the 1982s, perhaps slightly less exuberant and intense, but are immensely interesting wines. The Selleck again is the most advanced and the Reed and Jensen more backward, with spicy, leathery, exotic bouquets. Of the three, the Jensen looks to be the star. Again, the Santa Barbara, made from purchased grapes, is excessively vegetal and of little interest. The 1984 Selleck and Reed exhibited flamboyant, spicy, fragrant Pinot Noir character and layers of flavor. Calera also makes an inexpensive Zinfandel that can be very good—although my experience is that it is inconsistent from vintage to vintage—and a sound, fruity, straightforward chunky Chardonnay.

CALLAWAY VINEYARDS (RIVERSIDE)

| 1984 Chenin Blanc | Temecula | ($5.99) | 65 |

| 1984 Sauvignon Blanc | Temecula | ($7.99) | 68 |

| 1985 Chardonnay Calla-lees | Temecula | ($9.49) | 85 |

This winery was sold in 1982 to the big spirits company, Hiram Walker. The quality has been uninspiring and the wines often very unusual and bizarre-tasting. Apparently, the new company will specialize in white wines, but the first releases, except for the fine 1985 Chardonnay, left me wondering what their future is.

CAPARONE WINERY (ST. LUIS OBISPO)

1981 Merlot	Tepusquet	($12.99)	55
1982 Merlot	Tepusquet	($9.99)	62

This tiny winery produces 3,000 cases of apparently only red wines, but the owners intend to promote several Italian wine varieties such as the Sangiovese and Nebbiolo. I hope they have more success with these wines than they have had with their Cabernet Sauvignon and Merlot, which have tasted excessively vegetal and unpleasant.

CARMENET VINEYARD (SONOMA)

1983 Sauvignon Blanc	Edna Vly.	($9.99)	86
1984 Sauvignon Blanc	Edna Vly.	($9.99)	82
1982 Sonoma Red Table Wine		($18.00)	87
1983 Sonoma Red Table Wine		($16.00)	84
1984 Sonoma Red Table Wine		($16.00)	90

Carmenet is the new winery that the famous Chalone corporation constructed; its first several wines, a Sauvignon Blanc and proprietary blend of Cabernet Sauvignon, Cabernet Franc, and Merlot, have been instant successes. The Sauvignon in 1983 showed intense, exotic, herbaceous-scented fruit and loads of flavor. The 1984 seemed to border on being excessively vegetal, but was nevertheless interesting. The great successes appear to be their red wines. The 1982, the first vintage, has developed a rich, fragrant, ripe plummy bouquet, deftly married with spicy oak. It still shows a great deal of tannin, but has an excellent concentration and length and should be a good candidate for at least 7–10 more years of aging. The 1983 is equally dense, but quite closed and tannic and at present showing less of its potential. The 1984 looks to be the best wine yet from Carmenet, a rich, opulent, intense wine with loads of fruit, plenty of body, and at least a decade of life ahead of it. Prices are moderately high here, but quality is clearly present.

CARNEROS CREEK WINERY (NAPA)

1981 Cabernet Sauvignon	Napa	($12.00)	84
1982 Cabernet Sauvignon	Napa	($12.00)	83
1983 Cabernet Sauvignon	Napa	($12.00)	78
1983 Chardonnay	Napa	($10.00)	79
1984 Chardonnay	Napa	($10.00)	83
1982 Merlot	Napa	($10.00)	72
1983 Pinot Noir	Napa	($16.00)	84

The smallish winery of Carneros Creek began production in 1971 and left many critics immensely pleased with the excellent Cabernet Sauvignons, Zinfandels, and occasionally delicious Chardonnays. In 1977, Carneros Creek made a truly outstanding Pinot Noir that had heads buzzing. Nevertheless, the great promise that this winery showed in the early '70s has not been fulfilled in the '80s, for reasons that are yet to be identified. Certainly the quality remains average to above average, but in recent vintages the wines have shown much less intensity and character and seem to be made in a very commercial style aimed at offending the least number of people. The rich, intense, dramatic Cabernets have given way to a lighter, rather innocuous style, as have the Chardonnays. The great success of the 1977 Pinot Noir has been followed by rather mediocre wines of little interest, with the possible exception of the 1983. This is all rather unfortunate.

CARTLIDGE, MOSER AND FORSYTH-STRATFORD LABEL (NAPA)

1984 Chardonnay	California	($10.00)	85
1985 Chardonnay "Canterbury"	California	($6.50)	86
1983 Merlot	California	($10.00)	84
1985 Sauvignon Blanc	Napa	($9.00)	85

This team of wine brokers, who sell their wine under the Stratford label, began business in 1980 and have quickly built an impeccable track record for offering very good quality wines at reasonable prices.

The wines show ripe yet well-balanced flavors and a forward, accessible fruitiness. They have been the pacesetters for the new breed of wine brokers who purchase grapes from all over California. The 1985 Chardonnay (Canterbury) offers amazing value. The quality has remained high and the prices are remarkably reasonable. If you are searching for a good value in California Chardonnay, Sauvignon Blanc, or Merlot, Stratford is a name to seek out.

CASSAYRE-FORNI (NAPA)

1981 Cabernet Sauvignon	Napa	($10.99)	85
1984 Chenin Blanc	Napa	($6.00)	82
1982 Zinfandel	Sonoma	($7.99)	74

This tiny winery, located near Rutherford, has consistently produced black ruby-colored Cabernets with plenty of tannin and intensity that have held up well in the bottle. Their 1978 is still evolving while some of the more famous Cabernets from that vintage are fully mature. They also produce Zinfandel, about which I have lukewarm feelings, and good Chenin Blancs. The 1984 Napa is dry, crisp, quite lively, and one of the better examples of its type. Overall, this is a winery worth taking a look at, even though their wines are hard to find and the production of under 7,000 cases makes it unlikely that they will be well distributed in national markets.

CAYMUS VINEYARD (NAPA)

1981 Cabernet Sauvignon Grace Family Vyds.	Napa	($35.00)	91
1982 Cabernet Sauvignon Grace Family Vyds.	Napa	($35.00)	90
1981 Cabernet Sauvignon	Napa	($15.00)	87
1982 Cabernet Sauvignon	Napa	($15.00)	87
1983 Cabernet Sauvignon	Napa	($15.00)	85
1980 Cabernet Sauvignon Special Selection	Napa	($35.00)	90
1981 Cabernet Sauvignon Special Selection	Napa	($35.00)	88

| 1984 Chardonnay | Napa | ($10.00) | 84 |

| 1984 Sauvignon Blanc | Napa | ($9.99) | 84 |

The Caymus Winery, owned and run by Charles Wagner and his son, has been one of the great success stories of California. The production remains under 40,000 cases and the quality of their wines across-the-board ranges from at least good to extraordinary in the case of their Cabernet Sauvignons. Their secondary label, the Liberty School, is one to seek out for good values, particularly in Cabernet Sauvignon and Chardonnay. Caymus also produces some Pinot Noir that I do not find up to the level of quality of their other wines, and Zinfandel that tends to be rich, spicy, and loaded with berry fruit. If the winery has room for improvement, it is probably with their Chardonnay and Sauvignon Blanc, which are good examples of their types, but rarely have the character, sheer intensity, and flavors of their red wines. The 1984 Chardonnay and Sauvignon Blanc are attractive examples, easy to drink, easy to like, and satisfying. Their regular Cabernets tend to be rich, supple, loaded with blackcurrant fruit, quite concentrated, and always made with enough backbone to age for 7–10 years. They are consistently among the best Cabernets produced in California. At the top echelon of quality are the two luxury Cabernets produced by Caymus—the Special Selection, a monumental Cabernet aged 3½ years in small oak barrels, and the Grace Family Vineyard Cabernet, made in exactly the same manner by Caymus in very limited quantities. Both of these wines show remarkable concentration and surprisingly are not as oaky as one would suspect from their long sojourn in barrels. They represent the pinnacle of quality of what one can find in California; certainly the 1982 and 1981 Grace Family Vineyard and 1980 and 1981 Special Selection Cabernets are worthy additions to anyone's cellar. Older great vintages of the Caymus Special Selection Cabernet are the 1979, 1978, 1976, and 1975.

CHALONE VINEYARDS (MONTEREY)

| 1983 Chardonnay | California | ($18.99) | 84 |

| 1984 Chardonnay | California | ($20.00) | 90 |

| 1985 Chardonnay | California | ($20.00) | 91 |

| 1983 Chardonnay Reserve | California | ($25.00) | 90 |

1984 Chardonnay Reserve	California	($25.00)	92
1983 Pinot Blanc	California	($14.99)	83
1984 Pinot Blanc	California	($14.95)	87
1985 Pinot Blanc	California	($15.95)	88
1981 Pinot Noir	California	($15.00)	87
1982 Pinot Noir	California	($15.00)	85
1983 Pinot Noir	California	($15.00)	86
1981 Pinot Noir Reserve	California	($25.00)	88

The tiny Chalone Vineyard, which produces less than 15,000 cases of wine, is located in the remote Gavilan Mountains about a 40-minute drive from Soledad, California. The wines here have been distinctive, rich, original expressions of the winemaking art at its best. The Chardonnays have, in certain vintages, been perhaps the single best white wines produced in California. The Pinot Noirs are smoky, rich, intense and always interesting, and the Pinot Blancs pacesetters as well. As production increased, the Chardonnays and Pinot Blancs at first seemed to have taken on a slightly lighter style, with the reserve bottlings seeming to get the best juice from the oldest vines. Both the 1983 Chardonnay and Pinot Blanc were good wines, but disappointing by the high standards of Chalone. Certainly, the 1984s and 1985s were a return to the style one expects from Chalone, which is barrel-fermented, oaky, buttery, intense, complex wines with great depth of flavor. The Reserve wines are among the finest in California, but one must get on Chalone's private mailing list to be able to reserve a few bottles of them. The Pinot Noirs have been brilliant, a fabulous 1978 that is still drinking well, and a 1980 that is still not mature; both are among a handful of great Pinot Noirs made in the last decade in California. Of recent vintages that are still available commercially, the 1981, 1982, and 1983 are very, very good, and the unreleased 1984 a superstar Pinot Noir. The Pinot Noir reserves are simply richer and more ageworthy. This is a great winery that has had remarkable success throughout the country for its unwavering commitment to quality wines. One would like to see more California wineries emulating the style of Chalone Vineyards. The prices for their wines are high, but I have yet to hear of anyone being disappointed with what they have found in a bottle of Chalone wine.

CHAPPELLET VINEYARD (NAPA)

1980 Cabernet Sauvignon	Napa	($18.00)	88
1982 Cabernet Sauvignon	Napa	($18.00)	87
1983 Chardonnay	Napa	($14.95)	85
1984 Chenin Blanc	Napa	($7.99)	84

This lovely winery, tucked away in the hills east of Rutherford, produces on average just under 30,000 cases of wine, all of which can be recommended with enthusiasm. The Chenin Blanc is among the best made in California, as well as among the most expensive. Most consumers turn their noses up at Chenin Blanc, but one taste of Chappellet's reveals just how fresh, exuberant, and satisfying this wine can be as an apéritif. The Chardonnay is always a graceful, stylish, elegant wine that has good, crisp acidity and an understated character but always enough flavor interest to keep one going back for another glass. The 1983 looks to be one of the better Chardonnays that Chappellet has made in the last several years. The pride of this house, and rightfully so, are the ageworthy Cabernets, which are deep in color, somewhat austere in the beginning of their lives, but attractive, well-made, elegant wines with plenty of flavor. The 1980, a long-time favorite, is still not fully mature; the 1982 is a lusher, more forward, accessible version of the 1980. Prices for Chappellet's wines are on the high side, but then so is the quality.

CHÂTEAU BOUCHAINE (NAPA)

1983 Chardonnay	Napa	($12.00)	78
1984 Chardonnay	Napa	($12.00)	75
1983 Chardonnay	Carneros	($15.00)	86
1984 Chardonnay Winery Lake	Carneros	($15.00)	85
1983 Pinot Noir	Carneros	($12.50)	72

1983 Pinot Noir Winery Lake	Carneros	($15.00)	80

1984 Sauvignon Blanc	Napa	($8.99)	84

The Château Bouchaine Winery always seems to play it safe, preferring middle-of-the-road, good wines to dramatic artistic expressions of Napa viticulture. Their Chardonnays tend to be their best wines, no doubt because if you get good grapes there is little harm (given competent winemaking, of course) that you can do to them. Both the 1983 and 1984 Chardonnay Carneros merit interest for their satisfying, straightforward varietal character, good length, and likeable format. The Sauvignon Blanc tends to be a bit grassy to my taste and I would like to see that aspect toned down, but it is a decently made, interesting wine. The Pinot Noirs, which this winery has touted from the beginning, seem to be made with the restaurant trade in mind—squeaky clean, overly filtered wines that are totally predictable; nevertheless, they are clean, with a little bit of cherry fruitiness, a little bit of oak, and a pleasant finish. One wishes they would take a little bit more risk here rather than settling for something that is good, but hardly exciting.

CHÂTEAU CHEVRE WINERY (NAPA)

1980 Merlot	Napa	($10.99)	83

1981 Merlot	Napa	($12.99)	84

1984 Merlot	Napa	($13.99)	85

This converted goat barn has specialized only in Merlot, which has tended in vintages such as 1980 and 1981 to be dense in color, rich in extract, and high in tannins. Whether these two wines age into harmonious, complex, interesting wine remains to be seen, but the extract and potential look to be there. The 1984 is fully mature, rich, savory, and quite seductive.

CHÂTEAU MONTELENA (NAPA)

1980 Cabernet Sauvignon	Napa	($16.99)	87

1982 Cabernet Sauvignon	Napa	($16.99)	92

1982 Cabernet Sauvignon Silverado	Napa	($9.99)	84

1983 Chardonnay	Alexander Vly.	($15.95)	87
1984 Chardonnay	Alexander Vly.	($15.99)	87
1983 Chardonnay	Napa	($16.99)	88
1984 Chardonnay	Napa	($16.99)	89
1982 Zinfandel	Napa	($10.00)	86

This Calistoga-based firm, with its fortresslike winery, is one of California's most consistent producers of top-quality wines across-theboard. Their Chardonnays, always exuberantly rich and oaky, are brilliant expressions of California winemaking. Their Zinfandel remains one of the best of its type: a rich, intense, briary, full-bodied wine with plenty of extract and flavor. And their Cabernet Sauvignons have emerged since the late '70s as among the very best in all of California. One wishes that there were more than 25,000 cases produced here since the wines are hard to find in certain marketplaces. Of the recent Chardonnays, both the 1984 and 1983 are excellent, the Alexander Valley having a slightly lusher, more accessible, buttery style than the more firmly structured Napa. The 1982 Zinfandel is a powerful, rich, lush, intense wine with great flavor. Their second label, Silverado Cellars, in 1982 produced a wonderfully rich, supple, fat Cabernet for early drinking. And of course both the 1982 and 1980 Montelena Cabernets show plenty of tannin, great concentration, and at least 8–10 years of aging potential. Prices are on the high side, but the quality here seems to get better with each passing vintage.

CHÂTEAU ST. JEAN (SONOMA)

1983 Chardonnay Belle Terre	Alexander Vly.	($16.00)	82
1984 Chardonnay Belle Terre	Alexander Vly.	($16.00)	84
1983 Chardonnay Frank Johnson	Alexander Vly.	($16.00)	84
1984 Chardonnay Frank Johnson	Alexander Vly.	($16.00)	84
1983 Chardonnay Robert Young	Alexander Vly.	($18.00)	83
1984 Chardonnay Robert Young	Alexander Vly.	($18.00)	87

1983 Chardonnay	Sonoma	($12.00)	78
1984 Chardonnay	Sonoma	($12.00)	81
1984 Fumé Blanc La Petite Etoile	Sonoma	($10.99)	82
1985 Fumé Blanc	Sonoma	($8.99)	82
1985 Gewürztraminer	Sonoma	($8.99)	82
1984 Selected Late-Harvest Semillon-Sauvignon	St. Jean Vyds.	($20.00)	90

From the very beginning Chateau St. Jean has produced a bevy of high-quality white wines ranging from intensely herbaceous, grassy Fumé Blancs that have become more subtle as their winemaking evolved, to rich, intense, vineyard-designated Chardonnays, of which the best consistently have been the Robert Young, Belle Terre, and Frank Johnson. The winery also makes a fairly bland Gewürztraminer, a good value in its "Vin Blanc" generic wine, and every once in a while a bit of Cabernet that tends to be rather rich but heavy-handed and excruciatingly tannic. Perhaps the best wine made by St. Jean is its late-harvest, decadently rich Riesling from both the Belle Terre and Robert Young vineyards. The 1978 was a rich Trockenbeerenauslese-styled wine. The 1982s were also remarkably hedonistic in their nectarlike richness and sweetness. In 1984, an impressive Sauternes-like, sweet, late-harvest Semillon/Sauvignon Blanc was added to the lineup. Chateau St. Jean has also gotten involved in the production of sparkling wines, which have been incredibly overpriced and rather bland, tart, neutral-tasting wines that I cannot recommend. Fortunately, the lofty debut price of $20 a bottle has dropped to $10. In 1984 the winery was sold to the Japanese group Suntory and reports are that the quality will continue at the present level. Of the current releases, the 1984 vintage was a much greater success than the 1983. The 1983 wines here, particularly the Chardonnays, lacked richness and length, but the 1984s are filled with ripe aromas and flavors of tropical fruits with a touch of spicy oak and are very flavorful. The Fumé Blancs have taken on a less grassy character and now are better made than ever. For all the success Chateau St. Jean has had with its white wines, with the exception of the late-harvest Rieslings that seem to have a 10-year life potential, the Chardonnays and Fumé Blancs are best drunk within the first 3–4 years of their lives since they have rarely shown the ability to age and retain their fruit beyond that period. (The 1980 and 1982 Robert Young Chardonnays, for example, both intense and delicious when released, are now drying out, with the alcohol becoming more and more noticeable.) Prices are on the high side.

CHRISTIAN BROTHERS WINERY (NAPA)

1980 Cabernet Sauvignon	Napa	($8.99)	76
1982 Chardonnay		($9.00)	75
1980 Zinfandel		($6.00)	70

The huge Christian Brothers Winery, which produces in excess of one million cases a year, has a wonderful location in the Napa Valley, but the quality of the wines is hardly inspiring. In a positive sense, one can say that they are inexpensive, modestly priced, and never bad examples of their types. But they rarely have much varietal character and sometimes seem watery in taste. Despite their modest prices, there are no values to be found here.

CLOS DU BOIS WINERY (SONOMA)

1981 Cabernet Sauvignon	Alexander Vly.	($9.99)	84
1980 Cabernet Sauvignon Briarcrest	Alexander Vly.	($12.99)	77
1981 Cabernet Sauvignon/ Merlot Marlstone	Alexander Vly.	($15.00)	86
1984 Chardonnay Barrel Fermented	Alexander Vly.	($9.00)	80
1983 Chardonnay Calcaire	Alexander Vly.	($15.00)	85
1984 Chardonnay Calcaire	Alexander Vly.	($15.00)	87
1983 Chardonnay Flintwood	Dry Creek	($11.99)	90
1984 Chardonnay Flintwood	Dry Creek	($15.00)	90

| 1984 Chardonnay | | | |
| Proprietor's Reserve | Alexander Vly. | ($18.00) | 88 |

| 1983 Merlot | Sonoma | ($9.99) | 82 |

| 1980 Pinot Noir | | | |
| Proprietor's Reserve | Sonoma | ($8.99) | 75 |

| 1982 Pinot Noir | Sonoma | ($8.99) | 70 |

| 1985 Sauvignon Blanc | | | |
| Barrel Fermented | Alexander Vly. | ($8.99) | 85 |

Clos du Bois prides itself on having won more medals than any other California winery. With a production in excess of 100,000 cases, this winery has achieved a high degree of success due to both the quality of its wines and its remarkable owner, Frank Woods. The wines, which have been produced here since 1974, have a good reputation, though my tasting notes always show the Chardonnays to be the best wines of the Clos du Bois stable, particularly the Flintwood and Calcaire Vineyards, and Proprietor's Reserve. The Flintwood is always more austere, but oozing with character, and the Calcaire is a very California-style Chardonnay, with plenty of tropical fruit and toasty oak. As for the Cabernets, they tend to be good rather than exciting, although the luxury proprietary blend of Cabernet Sauvignon, Merlot, and some Cabernet Franc, Marlstone (in 1981) is the best I have tasted yet from Clos du Bois. The other Cabernets come under such vineyard names as Woodleaf and Briarcrest, and they tend to be very forward, soft, rather ripe wines that are surprisingly herbaceous but always fruity and supple. The Pinot Noirs have, to my mind, been disappointing and typical of many California Pinot Noirs in that they are overly vegetal, sometimes minty, but hard and lacking charm. The winery also produces a relatively sweet, decent Gewürztraminer and a dull Johannisberg Riesling, but with each vintage has shown more and more progress with its barrel-fermented Sauvignon Blanc, which was excellent in 1985.

CLOS DU VAL WINE CO. (NAPA)

| 1982 Cabernet Sauvignon | Napa | ($13.99) | 67 |

| 1981 Cabernet Sauvignon | Napa | ($12.00) | 76 |

1982 Chardonnay	Napa	($12.00)	74
1983 Chardonnay	Napa	($12.00)	82
1984 Chardonnay	Napa	($12.00)	80
1983 Merlot	Napa	($11.99)	75
1984 Semillon	California	($8.00)	84

Clos du Val has been another California success story since its first vintage. Its Bordeaux-trained winemaker, Bernard Portet, has captured the hearts of many California wine enthusiasts and comes from a Bordeaux family famous for its expert winemaking. The wines of Clos du Val seem to get much greater reviews on the West Coast than I have been able to give them. Why the difference? For one, this winery seems, in my opinion, to excel in producing basically bland, straightforward, undramatic wines that seem overly filtered and lacking character. This was not always the case, for the Cabernets in the period 1972–1978 had both flavor and character. More recently, the only exceptions to blandness have been the 1983 Chardonnay, the best Chardonnay this winery has produced in almost a decade, and the very good Semillon, which Clos du Val seems to routinely produce. The Cabernets since 1978 have been clean, technically correct, but largely devoid of character and personality. Perhaps the 1984s and 1985s will see a return to the style of Cabernets made in 1974 and 1975, which are still in good condition today. Sometimes I even pick up the smell of cardboard, which suggests an overzealous use of filter pads. I am at a loss to understand why I seem to be in a minority, but having had these wines many times, I will stand by my opinion that while this is one of California's most successful wineries, it remains a very overrated producer of fine wines.

CONCANNON VINEYARD (ALAMEDA)

1984 Chardonnay		($10.99)	85
1984 Sauvignon Blanc	Livermore	($8.99)	84

With a production in excess of 115,000 cases, I would expect to see more of Concannon's wines on the market than I have to date. The winery has long been known for its quality Petite Sirahs, which are rather intense, aggressive, but uncomplex wines. Recently, however, the winery has turned out remarkably crisp, medium-bodied, very fresh, lively Chardonnays and Sauvignon Blancs that have plenty of varietal character but are easy to drink in the lighter style. Prices here seem moderate and not out of line with the quality of the wines.

CONGRESS SPRINGS VINEYARD (SANTA CLARA)

1984 Cabernet Franc	Santa Cruz	($11.99)	86
1984 Cabernet Sauvignon	Santa Cruz	($12.00)	85
1982 Cabernet Sauvignon	Santa Cruz	($12.00)	78
1985 Chardonnay Private Reserve	Santa Cruz	($20.00)	90
1984 Chardonnay Private Reserve	Santa Cruz	($20.00)	91
1984 Chardonnay	Santa Clara	($12.00)	86
1985 Chardonnay	Santa Clara	($12.00)	88
1985 Pinot Blanc	Santa Clara	($9.00)	84
1984 Pinot Noir	Santa Cruz	($15.95)	84

Located in the mountains near Saratoga, this winery, with a relatively tiny production of 6,500 cases, seems to produce very interesting, distinctive wines whether they be Cabernet, Chardonnay, or Pinot Noir. The Chardonnays are marked by plenty of time spent in oak, but they are also loaded with wonderful aromas of tropical fruit and have a creamy, rich, luxurious palate impression. They are not timid wines by any means. The Private Reserve bottlings from Santa Cruz seem to have more of the buttery, butterscotch flavors than the straight Santa Clara bottlings. The 1985 and 1984 Reserves are fabulous, two of the great Chardonnays made in California. The winery's Cabernets tend to show a great deal of oak with rather uncomplicated fruit flavors, but demonstrate good winemaking and lush, ripe fruit. They are clearly wines to be drunk within their first 6–7 years of life. The 1984 is particularly good. The 1984 Pinot Noir had plenty of smoky, ripe Pinot fruit, but it just missed the mark because of too long a sojourn in oak barrels, which gave it an overly woody character. Nevertheless, this winery, which also makes a fine Semillon, Pinot Blanc, and one of the best Cabernet Franc-based wines in California (try the 1984), is worth searching out for the quality of all its wines, particularly its Chardonnays, among the very finest in California.

CONN CREEK WINERY (NAPA)

1980 Cabernet Sauvignon	Napa	($15.00)	87
1981 Cabernet Sauvignon	Napa	($15.00)	85
1982 Cabernet Sauvignon	Napa	($12.00)	75
1982 Chardonnay Chateau Maja	Napa	($8.00)	72
1983 Chardonnay Chateau Maja	Napa	($8.00)	82
1984 Chardonnay Chateau Maja	Napa	($9.99)	75

Conn Creek first burst on the scene with a fabulous 1974 Cabernet Sauvignon made from grapes that were grown in the famous Milton Eisele Vineyard near Calistoga. Since that time the winery quickly developed an excellent reputation for its rich yet oaky, intense, tannic, long-lived Cabernet Sauvignons. The 1974 was followed by top-notch successes in 1976, 1978, and 1980. The Chardonnays have been a different animal altogether, always rather flabby, unstructured, and lacking character. The winery has also produced from time to time a very alcoholic, big, rich, husky Zinfandel that seems appropriate for drinking with cheese at the end of a meal. The winery was sold in 1985 and hopefully the fine Cabernets that have been a permanent asset of this winery will continue uninterrupted.

CORBETT CANYON VINEYARDS (SAN LUIS OBISPO)

1982 Cabernet Sauvignon Coastal Classic	($7.99)	78
1984 Chardonnay Coastal Classic	($6.99)	82
1984 Sauvignon Blanc Coastal Classic	($7.99)	83

This winery has ex-Montevina winemaker Cary Gott as its head wine-maker and has introduced a budget-priced line of liter bottles of Chardonnay, Sauvignon Blanc, Cabernet, and a rosé (or blush) wine. The quality has been consistently above average and the prices quite reasonable. This is definitely a winery to seek out for its white varietals,

Chardonnay and Sauvignon Blanc, since they offer inexpensive, attractive drinking.

H. COTURRI AND SONS (SONOMA)

1982 Cabernet Sauvignon	Sonoma	($12.00)	?
1983 Zinfandel Cooke Vineyards	Sonoma	($8.99)	85
1983 Zinfandel Les Vignerons	Sonoma	($8.99)	86
1984 Zinfandel Cooke Vineyards	Sonoma	($8.99)	88

I truly admire this winery that is making wines in a very organic method (no preservatives, fining, or filtration). If they can succeed, it is the best way of insuring that the full flavor of the grape makes it into the bottled wine, but to date their record has been one of rather spotty performances. The Zinfandels are remarkably rich, distinctive, complex wines with intense, smoky, earthy aromas and flavors and would appear to be capable of aging for 8–10 years. The Cabernet seems to need 24 hours of breathing before it displays its varietal character and throws off the earthy character in the nose. These are wines for the adventurous, but one feels an obligation to support a tiny winery (less than 3,000 cases) that is trying to make wine in the authentic, traditional manner. It has been my experience with the Coturri wines that they throw a lot of sediment, which is a good sign, and that decanting the wines several hours before serving them is essential. I am generally not a great believer in the idea that breathing improves a wine, but with these traditionally, very naturally made wines, some of the unusual aromas that accompany uncorking the wine blow off to reveal very complex, interesting, pleasurable scents.

CRONIN VINEYARDS (SAN MATEO)

1983 Cabernet Sauvignon	Napa	($12.00)	74
1982 Cabernet Sauvignon Stag's Leap	Napa	($13.00)	82
1984 Chardonnay	Alexander Vly.	($14.00)	90
1984 Chardonnay	Napa	($14.00)	86

| 1984 Chardonnay Ventana Vyds. | Monterey | ($14.00) | 86 |

This tiny winery reaches out to Napa, Sonoma, and Monterey for the grapes used in its wines. The production is minuscule (less than 1,000 cases), but in just the six short years since this winery first offered a wine they have built a strong cult following for their excellent Chardonnays. Their Cabernets are certainly decent, clean, fruity, soft and straightforward, but the Chardonnays have oodles of varietal fruit and a wonderful opulence. Their 1983s were a success, but the 1984s were even better, led by the 1984 Alexander Valley, a wine that has great depth, wonderful tropical fruit, toasty oak aromas and flavors, and plenty of muscle on the palate. The 1984 Ventana Vineyards has the same type of ripe, sweet, tropical fruit aroma, with rich, big, lush flavors, high acidity, and slightly less power on the palate. The most closed of the three Chardonnays is the Napa, which is more subtle, more tightly knit, and should evolve nicely for 1–3 more years. The wines of Cronin are available only in California, but it's a name to keep in the back of your mind should you come across one of their Chardonnays.

CUVAISON (NAPA)

1981 Cabernet Sauvignon	Napa	($12.00)	77
1982 Cabernet Sauvignon	Napa	($12.00)	84
1983 Chardonnay	Napa	($12.00)	85
1984 Chardonnay	Napa	($12.00)	84

Cuvaison, located in the northern end of Napa Valley near Calistoga, has a relatively large production of around 32,000 cases of wine divided between Chardonnay and Cabernet Sauvignon with a tiny bit of Zinfandel. The style of the Cuvaison wines in the late '70s was one of immense power and richness that often went too far in the pursuit of high-extract, tannic, exaggerated wines. Since then the style has lightened up, yet the wines are still flavorful. The 1983 Chardonnay is a rich, well-made, buttery, slightly toasty wine with a lot of flavor. The 1984 is a little bit lighter but shows nice elegance and good varietal character and length. Of the Cabernets, some of the old ones could be fabulously rich, particularly the 1978, but the 1981 was excessively tannic, with little fruit to be found, and the 1982 a lusher, softer wine, but rather one-dimensional in character.

DE LOACH VINEYARDS (SONOMA)

1985 Chardonnay Reserve (O.F.S)	Sonoma	($18.00)	90
1984 Chardonnay Reserve (O.F.S.)	Sonoma	($18.00)	89
1984 Chardonnay Russian River	Sonoma	($12.00)	85
1985 Chardonnay Russian River	Sonoma	($12.50)	89
1982 Pinot Noir	Sonoma	($12.00)	82
1983 Pinot Noir	Sonoma	($10.00)	78
1983 Zinfandel Russian River	Sonoma	($7.99)	80

De Loach Vineyards is making excellent white wines and adequate red wines. The Chardonnays tend to be the best product from this moderately sized winery in Santa Rosa, California. They have such wonderful opulence and ripeness that some have accused them of being slightly sweet. They are very seductive, lush wines and both the 1984s and the 1985s are deliciously succulent, lush, buttery, appley, rich, ripe Chardonnays that have immense crowd appeal. These wines are meant to be drunk within 2–3 years of the vintage. The Pinot Noirs are adequate, with little varietal character, but as red wines are pleasant and drinkable. The Zinfandels here tend to be high in alcohol with plenty of briary, berryish fruit, but again lack complexity and seem overly one-dimensional. The winery also makes one of California's best blush wines, a white Zinfandel of which the 1985 is a classic —richly fruity, fresh, lively, and altogether quite good. My advice is to stick to the Chardonnays and blush wines and wait for the reds to improve in quality.

THE JOHN DANIEL SOCIETY (NAPA)

1983 Dominus	($35.00)	93
1984 Dominus	($35.00)	91

One of the hottest new winemaking ventures in all of California is this partnership between Christian Moueix, the co-proprietor of a bevy of Bordeaux châteaux, the most famous of which is Pétrus, and the two daughters of the late, legendary John Daniel, Marcia Smith and Robin Lail. Making a proprietary luxury blend of Cabernet Sauvignon, Cabernet Franc, and Merlot from old, established vineyards in the valley. The first release was the 1983 Dominus, a monumental wine that is rich yet firmly structured and remarkably complex. The 1984 is a more opulent, lusher example of the 1983 and should mature sooner. Dominus is a great wine, made by one of the most talented winemakers of our day; moreover, Dominus is a brilliant example of using California's superb raw materials and applying the traditional winemaking philosophy of Bordeaux to them. Production is expected to grow to an excess of 5,000 cases, but despite their high prices, these wines will be eagerly snapped up by anyone who calls himself a connoisseur of wine.

DEHLINGER WINERY (SONOMA)

1982 Cabernet Sauvignon	Sonoma	($11.00)	85
1983 Cabernet Sauvignon	Sonoma	($11.00)	80
1984 Chardonnay Russian River	Sonoma	($10.00)	82
1985 Chardonnay Russian River	Sonoma	($12.00)	86
1982 Pinot Noir Russian River	Sonoma	($10.00)	70
1985 Pinot Noir Russian River	Sonoma	($10.00)	86

This small winery in Sonoma seems to do a very fine job with Cabernet Sauvignon, but is less successful with other varietals. The Chardonnays tend to be refined and polite, but one wishes there was more intensity of flavor and character. I must admit to being impressed with the 1985. While the 1982 Pinot Noir had more in common with a rich yet clumsy Zinfandel, the 1985 Pinot Noir had remarkable character, finesse and charm and is a clear success. The winery can make good Zinfandel that is often blended with a percentage of Petite Sirah. It tends to be peppery, tannic, ripe, and intense. The winery's best recent efforts, in addition to the 1985 Pinor Noir, have been the 1985 Chardonnay and the 1982 Cabernet Sauvignon, which has a slightly herbaceous, oaky aroma, but is a deeply fruity wine with plenty of richness, length, and depth.

MAISON DEUTZ (SANTA BARBARA)

N.V. Brut Cuvée	Santa Barbara	($15.00)	80

The fine French champagne house Deutz is another gambler taking a shot at making sparkling wine in California. This is the debut release and is a mild-mannered, rather lean wine with some fruit but not much depth or body. However, it is cleanly made and if more flavor depth can be attained in future releases, it will merit a more generous review.

DIAMOND CREEK VINEYARDS (NAPA)

1982 Cabernet Sauvignon Gravelly Meadow	Napa	($20.00)	87
1983 Cabernet Sauvignon Gravelly Meadow	Napa	($20.00)	86
1984 Cabernet Sauvignon Gravelly Meadow	Napa	($25.00)	90
1982 Cabernet Sauvignon Red Rock Terrace	Napa	($20.00)	88
1983 Cabernet Sauvignon Red Rock Terrace	Napa	($20.00)	85
1984 Cabernet Sauvignon Red Rock Terrace	Napa	($25.00)	90
1982 Cabernet Sauvignon Volcanic Hill	Napa	($20.00)	88
1983 Cabernet Sauvignon Volcanic Hill	Napa	($20.00)	85
1984 Cabernet Sauvignon Volcanic Hill	Napa	($25.00)	92

This small winery in the hills south of Calistoga produces some of California's greatest Cabernet Sauvignons from three separate vineyard locations. The production runs between 1,800–2,500 cases for each vintage, so there is not much to go around and knowledgeable connoisseurs for years have been snapping up these very rich, unfiltered, intense wines that seem to have no trouble aging and improving for 10–12 years. The 1982s are very forward by Diamond Creek standards but wonderfully lush, rich, and loaded with blackcurrant fruit and spicy oak. The Red Rock Terrace and Volcanic Hill are the two best in 1982 since the Gravelly Meadow seems slightly less concentrated. Nineteen eighty-three was not one of this winery's top vintages, but the wines are certainly well made, just overshadowed by the excellent 1982s and superb 1984s. Of the 1983s, the Gravelly

Meadow seems to have more depth than the other two wines. In 1984 all three wines were superb and owner/winemaker Al Brounstein thinks they are the finest wines he has ever made. They are all wonderfully opulent, rich, intense, majestic wines with explosive bouquets and plenty of tannic backbone and spine for at least 8–10 years aging potential. Despite what looks to be high prices, these are the kind of Cabernets that make California's reputation for producing world-class wine well justified.

DOLAN VINEYARDS (MENDOCINO)

1982 Cabernet Sauvignon	Mendocino	($12.95)	80
1984 Chardonnay	Mendocino	($12.99)	84

The name Dolan Vineyards comes from winemaker Paul Dolan, who has his own small wine operation of several thousand cases, though his fame is with the Fetzer Winery since he does much of the winemaking there. His Chardonnay tends to be the best wine, well marked by toasty, spicy oak with ripe fruit, good acidity, and quite tasty. Each vintage has been successful since the first in 1980. His Cabernet on the other hand is average to above average in quality, somewhat herbaceous with fat, ripe, long flavors that are lacking complexity.

DOMAINE CHANDON (NAPA)

N.V. Blanc de Noirs	($13.00)	84
N.V. Brut Napa	($13.00)	84
N.V. 10th Anniversary Reserve	($17.00)	85

With a production close to 400,000 cases, this operation, which was founded in 1973 by the French company Moët-Hennessy, has inspired a plethora of other sparkling wine operations in California. Yet, to date, Domaine Chandon sparkling wines still remain the best, though they hardly compete with the top level of French champagne. So far the wines have been light in body, easy to drink, crisp, but somewhat austere and acidic, as are many of their California competitors. The Blanc de Noirs is generally my favorite of their less expensive wines, with a light salmon color and yeasty bouquet. Their special Anniversary Reserve has a bit more complexity and roundness since it was aged longer on its lees. These are good sparkling wines, but they have yet to reach the class of the top echelon of non-vintage or vintage champagnes from France. Domaine Chandon also makes a tiny quantity of an apéritif liqueur called Panache, which is pleasant and enjoyable before a meal.

DOMAINE LAURIER (SONOMA)

1983 Cabernet Sauvignon	Sonoma	($12.99)	80
1983 Chardonnay	Sonoma	($13.59)	80
1984 Sauvignon Blanc	Sonoma	($9.99)	74

This tiny winery produces just over 10,000 cases of wine. The style that has obviously been chosen aims at lean, austere, crisp, understated wines that are called "elegant." However, all three varietals I have tasted lack richness, intensity, and are somewhat light in varietal character. They are refreshing and crisp, but for the prices charged one can do much better elsewhere.

DONNA MARIA VINEYARD (SONOMA)

1981 Cabernet Sauvignon Chalk Hill		($6.00)	74
1984 Chardonnay Chalk Hill		($10.00)	83
1984 Sauvignon Blanc Chalk Hill	Sonoma	($7.00)	80

The Chalk Hill wines made by the Donna Maria Winery tend to be realistically priced and offer straightforward, crisp, clean, varietal fruit in a medium-bodied format. The Chardonnays are the best wines produced to date, although their inexpensive Pinot Noirs, particularly the 1981, are certainly good values.

DRY CREEK VINEYARD (SONOMA)

1983 Cabernet Sauvignon	Sonoma	($8.99)	83
1984 Cabernet Sauvignon	Sonoma	($9.99)	84
1985 Chardonnay	Dry Creek	($9.99)	84
1985 Chenin Blanc	Dry Creek	($6.49)	83
1985 Fumé Blanc	Dry Creek	($8.50)	86

1984 Fumé Blanc	Dry Creek	($8.50)	85

1982 David Stare Reserve	Dry Creek	($15.00)	87

1983 David Stare Reserve	Dry Creek	($15.00)	77

The jovial David Stare has been making wine at Dry Creek since 1972 and was one of the first, along with Robert Mondavi, to promote and believe in the quality of the Sauvignon Blanc grape. It is called Fumé Blanc here and it is one of the best made in California, always crisp, subtly herbaceous, medium-bodied, and one of the few that seems capable of aging beyond 3–4 years, though I still prefer to drink it young. Stare often produces 30,000+ cases of this wine and that in itself is a remarkable achievement, particularly in view of the fact that he sells it all. His 1984 and 1985 are two of the best vintages yet. He also makes a dry, fruity, soft Chenin Blanc that is one of the better examples of its type. His Chardonnay tends to be straightforward in style but attractive and easy to drink. If this house has a weakness, it is their Cabernet Sauvignons, which tend to be a bit mixed and lack real complexity and character, though the 1982 David Stare Reserve (which was primarily a Merlot wine) had incredible flavor extract and a wonderfully lush, opulent texture reminiscent of a fine Pomerol. The 1984 tasted herbaceous, fruity, and fairly alcoholic. Stare's wines have always been modestly priced.

DUCKHORN VINEYARDS (NAPA)

1982 Cabernet Sauvignon	Napa	($14.95)	83

1983 Cabernet Sauvignon	Napa	($20.00)	88

1984 Cabernet Sauvignon	Napa	($20.00)	86

1982 Merlot	Napa	($14.95)	85

1983 Merlot	Napa	($18.00)	80

1984 Merlot	Napa	($18.00)	84

1983 Merlot Three Palms Vyd.	Napa	($22.00)	86

1984 Merlot Three Palms Vyd.	Napa	($22.00)	88

It is hard to believe that this winery was founded in 1976 and produced its first wines in 1978. The quality of their wines from the beginning has been very good to exceptional. The 1978 Cabernets and Merlots were outstanding, followed by equal successes in 1979 and 1980. Of the recent releases, the 1982s are good but exceptionally tannic and hard and not quite as successful as other vintages for Duckhorn. However, 1983, generally a less successful vintage in Napa than 1982, is a clear-cut success for two of the three red wines made by Duckhorn. The tiny production of Merlot from the Three Palms Vineyard is a broad and rich but still tannic, young wine, and the 1983 Cabernet is one of the top Cabernets from Napa in this vintage. Both wines need an additional 2–4 years of aging to round out, as do most of the Duckhorn wines, which seem to have the potential to last 10 or more years in the bottle. The 1984s all show considerable amounts of tannin, including the Merlot and Cabernet Sauvignon. The wine to get in line for should be the Merlot from the Three Palms Vineyard, which has exceptionally broad, deep flavors and also plenty of tannin. The 1984s can use 3–5 years of aging. The production at Duckhorn Winery is around 10,000 cases and the wines are sold out and on allocation each vintage. Since they are dealing with mostly purchased grapes, one wonders if they can continue their great success by simply buying the top grapes each year. The winery introduced Sauvignon Blanc in 1982 and the recent vintages, 1984 and 1985, have shown that their magical touch with red wine can be equally applied to white wine.

DUNN VINEYARDS (NAPA)

1981 Cabernet Sauvignon	Napa Howell Mountain	($18.00)	90
1982 Cabernet Sauvignon	Napa Howell Mountain	($20.00)	92
1982 Cabernet Sauvignon	Napa	($12.50)	85
1983 Cabernet Sauvignon	Napa Howell Mountain	($18.00)	87

After learning his trade as the full-time winemaker at Caymus, Randy Dunn left there in 1984 to concentrate his efforts on his own tiny vineyard on Howell Mountain. He produces only a dense, incredibly concentrated, broodingly dark, potentially superb Cabernet. His first vintages were sold out to connoisseurs yearning for the old-style

Cabernet—unfiltered, dramatically rich, and flamboyant. The early vintages, 1980 and 1981, were both superb; the 1982 Howell Mountain, another fabulous wine, is arguably the best Cabernet made in California in that vintage. Upcoming vintages, including the excellent 1983 and 1984, look equally successful. The production has averaged around 1,000 cases, so there is little to go around. However, there is no doubt that this is one of the great Cabernets made in California. Most vintages to date seem to suggest that 10 years of cellaring is required.

DURNEY VINEYARD (MONTEREY)

1981 Cabernet Sauvignon	Monterey	($12.99)	84
1982 Cabernet Sauvignon	Monterey	($12.99)	85
1983 Cabernet Sauvignon	Monterey	($12.99)	86

A smallish vineyard (15,000-case production), Durney makes several white wines with which I have never been terribly impressed. However, the glories here are the rather rich, densely colored, tobacco and chocolate-scented Cabernet Sauvignon that shows well young but seems to have the potential to last 8–9 years. I have always found the Cabernets from Monterey to have an intense vegetal character that flawed them, but this winery seems to have found the proper formula for avoiding this in their wines. The prices, given the quality level, are quite reasonable.

EBERLE WINERY (PASO ROBLES)

1982 Cabernet Sauvignon	($9.99)	86
1984 Chardonnay	($9.99)	86

A young winery (founded in 1979), Eberle's wines show good, fleshy fruit and substance, medium to full body, and plenty of flavor authority. The deep, dark Cabernet is rich, jammy, and ideal for drinking over the next 2–4 years. The Chardonnay shows a judicious use of oak, good applelike, buttery flavors, and a crisp finish. Both wines offer good value.

EDMEADES VINEYARDS (MENDOCINO)

1982 Zinfandel Ciapusci	Mendocino	($9.29)	87
1982 Zinfandel Dupratt	Mendocino	($9.59)	86

While this winery has a fairly significant production in excess of 20,000 cases and tends to make straightforward, fruity white wines such as Chardonnay and Riesling as well as a little bit of Cabernet Sauvignon, the winery's best product is its vineyard-designated Zinfandels, which are among the top half-dozen or so wines from this varietal made in California. The 1982s are particularly strong efforts, with rich, briary, berryish fruit flavors, and are very ripe, fleshy, and high in alcohol.

EDNA VALLEY VINEYARDS (SAN LUIS OBISPO)

1984 Chardonnay	Edna Valley	($12.50)	87
1985 Chardonnay	Edna Valley	($13.00)	89
1982 Pinot Noir	Edna Valley	($13.00)	86
1983 Pinot Noir	Edna Valley	($15.00)	86
1981 Pinot Noir Reserve	Edna Valley	($18.00)	87

The Edna Valley Vineyard is part of the Chalone Vineyard's empire and produces wines similar in style to those of Chalone—that being intense, full-bodied, highly extracted wines with great character and flamboyance. The Chardonnays have been the stars to date, and are made in a big, rich, toasty, buttery, broadly flavored style that makes splendid drinking in the first 2–3 years of their lives. The Pinot Noirs have not yet competed with those from Chalone, but are well-made, rich, intense wines with explosive bouquets of smoky, earthy, ripe, Pinot Noir fruit. The winery also produces small amounts of Reserve Pinot Noir that are generally unavailable unless one is on their mailing list.

FAR NIENTE (NAPA)

1982 Cabernet Sauvignon	Napa	($25.00)	82
1983 Cabernet Sauvignon	Napa	($25.00)	82

1982 Chardonnay	Napa	($21.00)	85

1983 Chardonnay	Napa	($21.00)	87

1984 Chardonnay	Napa	($21.00)	82

1985 Chardonnay ·	Napa	($22.00)	84

There is no question that Far Niente Winery has high aspirations. The prices asked for the wines, given the up-and-down performance record, are somewhat ridiculous, but one look at the packaging and you will see that much of the promotion here is on the surface. The Chardonnays have ranged from excellent to mediocre, with the 1985 and the 1983 being the best Chardonnays yet from this winery, which was founded in 1979. Recently, Far Niente has added Cabernet Sauvignon to its stable of wines and has priced it at $25 a bottle, about three times its real value given the average to above-average quality level. Both the 1982 and 1983 show a dense color but have very weedy, blackcurrant fruit and a very high, tart acidity. They do not seem capable of improving and are not particularly attractive at the moment. This is an estate that apparently lives by the motto "Why pay less?" Their Chardonnay is worth a try in certain vintages, if you don't mind spending 20+ dollars a bottle.

GLORIA FERRER (SONOMA)

N.V. Brut Cuvée Emeralda	($11.99)	84

The famous Spanish sparkling wine producers, Freixenet, have set up shop in Sonoma County and in 1986 released their first non-vintage sparkling wine. I have never been a great believer in the potential for high-quality sparkling wines from California, but their debut non-vintage Brut showed every bit as much character as Domaine Chandon, which to me has set the most consistent standards for sparkling wine in California. It is crisp, dry, fruity, with some character as well as some flavor. I hope this is a positive sign for future releases.

FETZER VINEYARD (MENDOCINO)

1982 Cabernet Sauvignon Home Vyd.	Mendocino	($12.00)	84

1983 Cabernet Sauvignon	Lake	($6.49)	67

1983 Cabernet Sauvignon	Mendocino	($7.50)	83
1984 Chardonnay Barrel Select	Mendocino	($9.00)	85
1985 Chardonnay Barrel Select	Mendocino	($9.00)	85
1985 Chardonnay Sundial	Mendocino	($7.99)	85
1985 Chenin Blanc	Mendocino	($5.99)	80
1985 Fumé Blanc	Valley Oaks	($6.49)	85
1985 Gewürztraminer	Mendocino	($6.00)	84
1985 Sauvignon Blanc	Mendocino	($6.99)	84
1983 Zinfandel Ricetti Vyd.	Mendocino	($11.00)	82

The Fetzer Vineyard, with a production now in excess of 600,000 cases, has retained a strong following for the quality/price rapport that its wines have always represented. The philosophy here has been to bottle the white wines as quickly as possible and get them on the market. It has emphasized the fresh, fruity character of each varietal. One can hardly fault that strategy since all the Chardonnays, from the crisp, non-oak-aged, wonderfully fresh, lemony, citrusy Sundial Chardonnay to the barrel-fermented, rich, oaky, toasty, buttery Barrel Select Chardonnay, are fairly priced and consistently successful regardless of vintage. The Sauvignon Blanc is herbaceous but fresh and fruity, the Gewürztraminer, Chenin Blanc, and Riesling rather simple, fruity, and pleasant. Among the reds, the Lake County Zinfandels and Cabernets often represent good values, though the 1983s seemed rather disappointing for this quality-conscious winery. The Cabernet from Fetzer, both 1982 and 1983 Mendocino, has always represented very good value, with supple, easy to drink and easy to understand blackcurrant fruit well displayed. The Zinfandels have ranged from the lighter style in Lake County to the intense, rich, tannic monsters and vineyard-designated Zinfandels of Ricetti and, in years past, Scharffenberger, Lolonis, and more recently, the Home Vineyard Zinfandel. Fetzer is still one of the better Zinfandel producers in California, though the quality level of their Zinfandels does not match what it was in the late '70s. The winery also produces a rather vegetal Pinot Noir that they like much more than I do, and one of California's better Petite Sirahs, a peppery, rich, ripe, interesting wine that at $7–$8 a bottle is always worth considering. The wines under their secondary label, Bel Arbres are good values, particularly the blush wines.

FIRESTONE VINEYARDS (SANTA BARBARA)

1977 Cabernet Sauvignon	Santa Ynez	($10.00)	55
1982 Cabernet Sauvignon	Santa Ynez	($7.50)	70
1978 Cabernet Sauvignon Reserve	Santa Ynez	($10.49)	59
1979 Cabernet Sauvignon Reserve	Santa Ynez	($10.49)	69
1984 Chardonnay	Santa Ynez	($11.99)	50
1981 Merlot	Santa Ynez	($8.99)	70
1979 Pinot Noir	Santa Ynez	($8.25)	55
1980 Pinot Noir	Santa Ynez	($6.99)	65
1983 Sauvignon Blanc	Santa Ynez	($7.49)	62
1984 Sauvignon Blanc	Santa Ynez	($7.49)	80

This large winery, with a production in excess of 75,000 cases, is jointly owned by the Japanese Suntory Group and the Firestone family of tire fame and fortune. The quality record here borders on dismal and unfortunately things seem to be in need of a major overhaul if this winery is to compete in an ever increasingly competitive and quality-conscious wine business. The white wines have lacked varietal character as well as fruit and concentration. The red wines are even worse, with many of them showing both excessive vegetal characteristics and jammy, thick, overripe fruity characters. It is a shame, because the prices seem fair and the owners certainly pleasant, but the quality is just not in the bottle.

FISHER VINEYARDS (SONOMA)

1982 Cabernet Sauvignon	Sonoma	($12.99)	80
1983 Chardonnay	Sonoma/Napa	($12.00)	85

1984 Chardonnay	Sonoma/Napa	($12.00)	85
1983 Everyday Cabernet	Sonoma	($8.99)	74
1984 Everyday Chardonnay	Sonoma	($9.00)	78

If I ever wanted to own a winery it would be situated in the gorgeous setting that Fred Fisher and his wife have in the Mayacamas Mountains right on the Napa–Sonoma boundary line. To my thinking, there cannot be a more gorgeous setting. The Everyday Chardonnay, a cutely named wine meant for easy and inexpensive consumption, is straightforward but somewhat dull. The regular Chardonnays here, including the excellent 1983 and 1984, have been nicely balanced between oak and ripe, buttery fruit in medium- and full-bodied formats. They are always worth trying. The Cabernets should be better. The Everyday Cabernet is just a bit too tame and tart and the regular Cabernet, technically flawless and very clean, has a touch of oak, a touch of blackcurrants, and a little bit of tannin, but otherwise little character or personality. I'm convinced there is more potential here than is evidenced in the wines.

FLORA SPRINGS WINE CO. (NAPA)

1982 Cabernet Sauvignon	Napa	($11.99)	81
1983 Cabernet Sauvignon	Napa	($11.99)	78
1984 Chardonnay	Napa	($11.00)	86
1983 Chardonnay Barrel Fermented	Napa	($18.00)	90
1984 Chardonnay Barrel Fermented	Napa	($18.00)	90
1985 Sauvignon Blanc	Napa	($8.00)	85

This small winery with a 15,000-case production has, since its opening in 1978, excelled with its two white wine varietals, Chardonnay and Sauvignon Blanc. The regular Chardonnay is very fruity and well structured, but the barrel-fermented takes on the character of a fine Puligny-Montrachet, with wonderful structure and toasty oak integrated into gobs of Chardonnay fruit. The 1985 Sauvignon Blanc continues the success that Flora Springs has enjoyed with this varietal, with a crisp austerity but plenty of character and freshness. Both the

1982 and 1983 Cabernet Sauvignons are rather lean and unyielding with rather tough, tannic, austere flavors. However, the launching in 1983 of the new proprietary wine, Trilogy, a Cabernet Sauvignon, Merlot, Cabernet Franc blend (33% of each), will propel this winery into the elite of red wine producers in California. There is a real quality effort being made here and this is undoubtedly a winery to keep an eye on.

THOMAS FOGARTY WINERY (SAN MATEO)

1984 Chardonnay Monterey	($15.00)	87
1983 Chardonnay Winery Lake	($15.00)	84
1984 Chardonnay Winery Lake	($15.00)	87
1982 Pinot Noir Ventana Vyds.	($8.00)	72
1982 Pinot Noir Winery Lake	($12.00)	75
1983 Pinot Noir Winery Lake	($12.00)	84

This winery's production is inching up toward 7,000 cases and Dr. Thomas Fogarty continues to show signs that he knows exactly what he wants to do with both Chardonnay and Pinot Noir. The performance record here has been a bit spotty, but the successes have been too good to ignore, so one is tempted to keep coming back to see what is next in the lineup of this winery. Fogarty's 1981 Winery Lake Pinot Noir was a classic from this temperamental varietal, but he has yet to equal that success, though the 1983 Winery Lake has the fragrant bouquet and the lovely, spicy, ripe berry fruitiness and broad flavors that make Pinot Noir so attractive. His Chardonnays have tended to be produced in the barrel-fermented, big, oaky, rich style and yet they have had in most cases sufficient fruit to carry the oak. So far, I have liked what I have seen from this winery and will continue to pay close attention to future endeavors.

FOLIE À DEUX WINERY (NAPA)

1983 Chardonnay	Napa	($12.00)	84
1984 Chardonnay	Napa	($12.00)	87

This winery is producing between 2,000–3,000 cases, the star to date being a Chardonnay. The 1983 was stylish, with a citrusy, buttery, toasty character and good lively finish, although it lacked authoritative depth of flavors. The 1984 was even better, with a more open, accessible, ripe, lemony, appley, buttery fruitiness with a nice touch of toasty oak. Prices of $12 a bottle seem quite realistic given the quality.

LOUIS FOPPIANO WINE CO. (SONOMA)

1981 Cabernet Sauvignon	Sonoma	($7.50)	83
1982 Cabernet Sauvignon	Sonoma	($7.50)	85
1981 Cabernet Sauvignon Fox Vyd.	Sonoma	($12.00)	85
1983 Chardonnay	Sonoma	($7.50)	83
1984 Chardonnay	Sonoma	($7.50)	84
1984 Sauvignon Blanc	Sonoma	($6.00)	84

For whatever reason, the Foppiano Winery never seems to get the accolades it deserves for offering the wine consumer well-made, fresh, fairly interesting wines that are easy to drink young and have both character and quality. The prices remain among the most reasonable in California and with a production in excess of 150,000 cases, the wine is widely available. Virtually everything I have tasted from Foppiano has seemed well made and a good value, from the crisp, fruity, lemony, citrusy Chardonnays to the tart, slightly herbaceous, fruity, medium-bodied Sauvignon Blancs. Even the reds are well made, with lush, medium-bodied, supple flavors, particularly the 1982 Cabernet Sauvignon (which for $7.50 is quite a bargain). The 1981 Cabernet from the Fox Vineyard is more ageworthy and can be drunk or held for another 5–6 years. The secondary label of Foppiano, Riverside Farm, produces wines that also offer good value, although they are very straightforward in style.

FORMAN WINERY (NAPA)

1983 Cabernet Sauvignon	Napa	($16.00)	90
1984 Cabernet Sauvignon	Napa	($16.00)	90
1984 Chardonnay	Napa	($16.00)	90

| 1985 Chardonnay | Napa | ($16.00) | 88 |

Ric Forman has had numerous winemaking jobs over the last decade; he was the winemaker behind the fabulous string of Sterling Cabernets and Merlots between 1973 and 1976, wines that are still drinking beautifully today as well as being great expressions of California's winemaking art. He has now settled into his own winery and the debut releases, a barrel-fermented, rich, toasty, buttery 1984 Chardonnay and classically structured, rich, tannic, beautifully made 1983 Cabernet Sauvignon, show just how much talent Mr. Forman continues to display. His second releases, the 1985 Chardonnay and 1984 Cabernet Sauvignon, are no less impressive. His Chardonnays are oak influenced and show wonderful buttery, pineapple fruit, a medium- to full-bodied format, and impeccable balance. His Cabernets are much like the ones he made at Sterling in the mid-'70s—rich, tannic, very ageworthy wines with impeccable balance and plenty of character. This is an up and coming star in the California wine world.

FRANCISCAN VINEYARDS (NAPA)

1980 Cabernet Sauvignon	Napa	($8.99)	84
1983 Chardonnay	Alexander Vly.	($10.99)	85
1983 Chardonnay Reserve	Napa	($12.00)	86
1981 Merlot Estate	Napa	($9.99)	84

The Franciscan Winery has changed ownership so many times that that probably accounts for the fact that no one seems to know the direction in which the winemaking is going. Nevertheless, recent releases, as well as some of the older releases, have consistently shown good quality. The winemakers who have passed through here over the last decade have included the likes of Justin Meyer, who is now at Silver Oak making exquisite Cabernet, and Tom Ferrell, who was at Inglenook before he came to Franciscan and then left to go to Sterling Vineyards. The Chardonnays have shown an emphasis on lush, ripe, intense fruit married with a good deal of toasty oak. The wines have shown well in my tastings and are not outrageously priced. The Cabernets have tended to be marked also by plenty of oak but have ripe, supple textures and plenty of fruit and body. They don't appear to be very ageworthy and may be released late onto the market, after they have already hit their plateau of maturity. But they are tasty and worth considering (and they rarely cost more than $12 a bottle). One would like to see this winery settle into some consistency under its new German owners since they seem to have the requisite vineyard sources for high-quality wines. Franciscan also continues to make Cask 321 Burgundy, which represents good value in a straightforward-style red wine.

FREEMARK ABBEY (NAPA)

1981 Cabernet Sauvignon Bosché	Napa	($18.00)	82
1982 Cabernet Sauvignon Bosché	Napa	($18.00)	78
1983 Chardonnay	Napa	($10.00)	78
1984 Chardonnay	Napa	($10.00)	82
1982 Edelwein Gold	Napa	($35.00)	88

Freemark Abbey is one of the older California wineries, having been founded in 1967. Production has been maintained at a modest 30,000 cases a year and the winery specializes in four wines—an oaky, rich Chardonnay, a late-harvest, decadently sweet Johannisberg Riesling called Edelwein Gold, a regular Cabernet Sauvignon, and a single-vineyard Cabernet Sauvignon from the famous, highly respected Bosché Vineyard near Rutherford. (They also make a Petite Sirah from the York Creek Vineyards in Napa Valley that is generally peppery, rich, and one of the better of its type.) The older vintages of Freemark Abbey, the 1960s and early 1970s, included some wonderful wines, but I have found recent vintages rather dull and more disappointing than pleasing. The 1983 Chardonnay is a bit flat and overly oaky. The 1982 Cabernet Sauvignon Bosché is straightforward and medium-bodied, with a slightly vegetal bouquet, and lacks richness and depth, relying more on its one-dimensional fruit than any kind of complexity that the price suggests it should have. The 1981 Bosché is a bit better, with more fruit and a bit more complexity. Given the wonderful wines this vineyard produced for Freemark Abbey in the late '60s and early '70s, it appears to be only a shadow of its former self.

FRICK WINERY (SANTA CRUZ)

1980 Pinot Noir	Monterey	($12.00)	82
1981 Pinot Noir	California	($12.00)	78

One of the smaller California wineries, with a production of only 3,500 cases, Frick Winery produces a little bit of Chardonnay and Petite Sirah, but their reason for existence has been to produce Pinot Noir. The 1981 Pinot Noir was a simple, spicy, fruity wine without much character. On the other hand, the 1980 has a very complex, penetrating, smoky, earthy, ripe, expansive bouquet that is very burgundian; but despite all the promises in the nose, it does not deliver the intensity of flavors one would expect. It finishes short and tart on the palate. If bouquet were everything, it would be a great wine.

FRITZ CELLARS (SONOMA)

1984 Chardonnay	Sonoma	($9.99)	85
1985 Fumé Blanc	Sonoma	($7.99)	85

This winery has toyed around with some Cabernet Sauvignon, Pinot Noir, and Zinfandel, but its major successes to date have been its Chardonnays, made in the lemony, citrusy style with just a touch of toasty oak for complexity, and a crisp, stylish Fumé Blanc. The production has inched up toward 20,000 cases; the prices are quite reasonable for the quality of the wines.

FROG'S LEAP WINERY (NAPA)

1983 Cabernet Sauvignon	Napa	($9.99)	85
1984 Cabernet Sauvignon	Napa	($9.99)	83
1984 Sauvignon Blanc	Napa	($9.99)	82
1985 Sauvignon Blanc	Napa	($9.99)	83

Frog's Leap Winery has enjoyed its name and created an interesting label as well as several catchily named wines with the frog theme well displayed. The winery has promoted its Sauvignon Blanc as its pride and joy; it has been a good wine, herbaceous, spicy, with good varietal character though sometimes a little overdone in its herbaceousness. The winery introduced a Cabernet Sauvignon in 1982, and the 1983 and 1984 vintages were actually better wines than the more promoted Sauvignon Blanc. Both the 1983 and 1984 have good Cabernet fruit with weedy, blackcurrant scents, lush textures, and soft tannins. They are obviously made to be drunk within the first 3–4 years after they are released. (The winery also produces a small amount of Chardonnay, which I have not tasted.) Production is inching up toward 9,000 cases.

GAINEY VINEYARDS (SANTA BARBARA)

1982 Cabernet Sauvignon	Santa Ynez	($9.99)	85
1984 Chardonnay	Santa Ynez	($8.00)	84
1985 Johannisberg Riesling Late Harvest		($12.00; 375 ml)	90
1984 Sauvignon Blanc	Santa Ynez	($7.99)	55

Gainey is a sparkling new winery that opened in 1984 and plans on producing an average of 10,000 cases for the next several years. My only experiences with the wines are those mentioned above, all of which showed good winemaking and good value. The 1984 Chardonnay is made in a lemony, crisp, tart style and while not complex, showed skilled winemaking, plenty of fruit, and a deft touch of toasty oak. The Sauvignon Blanc had an excessive herbaceous character and vegetal flavors. The 1985 nectarlike Riesling is exceptional, with a huge bouquet of tropical fruit and remarkable richness and Trockenbeerenauslese sweetness. The Cabernet Sauvignon was an even bigger surprise—lush, ripe, with plenty of blackcurrant fruit and none of the vegetal character often found in wines from this particular area. It should drink well for 3–4 years. Given their prices, most of the Gainey wines seem to be good values for the quality offered.

E. & J. GALLO WINERY (MODESTO)

1978 Cabernet Sauvignon	($7.99)	78
N.V. Chablis Blanc	($1.99)	79
N.V. Chardonnay	($4.49)	76
N.V. Chenin Blanc	($2.99)	72

N.V. Hearty Burgundy		($2.99)	77

N.V. Sauvignon Blanc		($2.79)	75

1984 Sauvignon Blanc Special Release		($4.49)	84

Gallo, with a production of a mere 60,000,000+ cases a year, or as they advertise, 250,000 cases a day, is a remarkable success story. Wine enthusiasts tend to turn up their noses when Gallo wines are mentioned, but quite honestly, no winery, given this kind of production, is more consistent in quality than Gallo. No, the wines are not the complex or sublime renditions that some of the smaller wineries can turn out but, for the value, the Hearty Burgundy and the Chablis Blanc are really quite remarkable wines when one considers their prices. The varietal wines range from a fairly dull, flat Chenin Blanc to a decent yet uninspired non-vintage Sauvignon Blanc and Chardonnay, a supple, fruity 1978 Cabernet Sauvignon, and a very good Loire Valley-inspired 1984 Sauvignon. If you haven't tried Gallo's Hearty Burgundy or Chablis Blanc for under $3, you might be surprised. Of course, the winery does much more than this, producing a line of wines called Polo Brindisi, a number of sparkling wines under the André label that are cloyingly sweet, fat, and to my taste rather unpleasant, and the very soundly made Carlo Rossi wines. Gallo also produces a full line of sherries and ports that are heavy but adequate.

GEYSER PEAK (SONOMA)

1981 Cabernet Sauvignon	Sonoma	($7.50)	75

1982 Cabernet Sauvignon	Sonoma	($7.50)	80

1984 Chardonnay	Sonoma	($7.50)	78

1985 Chardonnay	Sonoma	($7.50)	82

1984 Fumé Blanc	Sonoma	($6.29)	72

1985 Fumé Blanc	Sonoma	($6.59)	76

1985 Pinot Noir Blanc	Sonoma	($5.99)	80

Geyser Peak is one of the larger California wineries, producing a million and a half cases of wine. It was recently sold by its owner, the Schlitz Brewing Co., to a Santa Rosa resident and millionaire. The quality of the wines has been at least average and every once in a while an above-average-quality wine is produced. The Chardonnays in particular have tended to be more consistent than the other varietals, although the 1985 blush wine, the Pinot Noir Blanc, is wonderfully fruity and exuberant with good freshness. The Chardonnays have good fruit, a touch of oak, and at their prices of $7–$8 are good values. The Cabernet Sauvignons have been a bit nondescript, supple, and fruity, but somewhat tiring and boring. The 1982, with its rich berry fruit and soft texture, has the best character of recent offerings. This winery also produces a rather dull Chenin Blanc, an unusual, herbaceously scented Gewürztraminer, and a heavy, flawed Riesling.

GIRARD WINERY (NAPA)

1982 Cabernet Sauvignon	Napa	($12.00)	86
1983 Cabernet Sauvignon	Napa	($12.00)	75
1984 Cabernet Sauvignon	Napa	($12.00)	86
1984 Cabernet Sauvignon Reserve	Napa	($20.00)	90
1982 Chardonnay	Napa	($12.00)	80
1983 Chardonnay	Napa	($12.00)	?
1984 Chardonnay	Napa	($12.00)	87
1984 Sauvignon Blanc	North Coast	($8.00)	84

The Girard Winery started off strongly this decade with several outstanding releases, particularly the 1981 Chardonnay. That has been followed up by increasing the quality of its Cabernet Sauvignon each vintage. At present, the three major wines in the Girard lineup are all at least very good and in certain cases outstanding. The 1983 Chardonnay, while not quite up to the great 1981, is still a wonderfully intense Chardonnay with a fragrant bouquet of toasty oak, butter, apples, and lemons. The 1984 is suspiciously odd. The Sauvignon Blancs tend to be rather opulent and aggressively herbaceous, but are loaded with fruit. Of the Cabernet Sauvignons, the 1982 was a wonderful start for Girard followed by an austere, thin 1983, and two excellent wines in 1984, particularly the Reserve, which is Girard's finest Cabernet to date—a backstrapping, rich, intense, tannic yet beautifully structured wine for aging 10 or more years. Prices are moderately high, but the quality here has generally been consistently excellent since the beginning. The production has inched up toward 15,000 cases. (The winery also makes a little bit of Chenin Blanc, which I have never tasted.) Its secondary label is called Stephens.

GLEN ELLEN (SONOMA)

1983 Cabernet Sauvignon Prop. Reserve	Sonoma	($5.99)	80
1984 Cabernet Sauvignon Prop. Reserve	Sonoma	($5.99)	82
1984 Chardonnay Estate	Sonoma	($9.49)	85
1984 Chardonnay Prop. Reserve	Sonoma	($5.99)	78
1985 Fumé Blanc Estate	Sonoma	($8.99)	86

It's hard to believe that the Glen Ellen Winery was founded only in 1981. The owners, the Benziger family, took a bold stand with their Proprietor's Reserve Chardonnay and Cabernet Sauvignon by producing wines easy to drink and easy to understand at a remarkably high level of quality for only $6 a bottle. They have had astounding success with these two wines, which has forced as well as inspired other wineries to lower their prices as well. Today the Glen Ellen Proprietor's Reserve Cabernet Sauvignon at $6 is still one of the best buys on the market, and the Chardonnay Proprietor's Reserve, while not quite as interesting as the Cabernet, is nevertheless a fruity, lighter-styled, lean, compact wine that is easy to drink. The 1984 and 1985 estate bottlings of Sauvignon Blanc and Chardonnay are both extremely well made and reasonably priced at under $10. This winery rarely makes a mistake and their wines always represent good values. Production is now in excess of 45,000 cases.

GREEN AND RED VINEYARD (NAPA)

1980 Zinfandel	Napa	($6.99)	75
1981 Zinfandel	Napa	($6.49)	83
1982 Zinfandel	Napa	($6.99)	83

This tiny winery, located in the remote Chiles Valley in Napa Valley, specializes in Zinfandel that has been generally sound but uninspired.

Prices are certainly realistic, but for specialists in one type of wine, I would like to see higher quality. The Zinfandels are made in a supple, forward, spicy, earthy style that in certain vintages tends to be rather vegetal and out of balance (e.g., 1980).

GRGICH HILLS CELLARS (NAPA)

1981 Cabernet Sauvignon	Napa	($16.00)	85
1982 Cabernet Sauvignon	Napa	($20.00)	87
1983 Chardonnay	Napa	($18.50)	88
1984 Chardonnay	Napa	($18.50)	88
1984 Fumé Blanc	Napa	($10.99)	78
1982 Zinfandel	Alexander Vly.	($10.99)	85
1983 Zinfandel	Alexander Vly.	($10.99)	84

This winery is run with great enthusiasm by one of California's most respected winemakers, Miljenko Grgich, who built his reputation during the mid-'70s by making splendid wines at Château Montelena. His Napa winery produces just over 20,000 cases of wine and has done extremely well with a big, rich, oaky, intense, lush, very concentrated Chardonnay that has been superb in vintages such as 1983 and 1984. The Zinfandel, made from grapes purchased in Alexander Valley, is another winner here—intense, spicy, loaded with berry flavors, and deftly touched by a sojourn in oak barrels. The Cabernet Sauvignons from Grgich, both the 1981 and 1982, have been tannic, fairly intense wines with a heavy overlay of tannin and spicy oak. The 1981 is perhaps the firmer, more structured wine, capable of 7–8 years of aging; the 1982 is lusher, richer, and more supple. Grgich wines are hardly values at their high prices, but they are expressive examples of high-quality winemaking that rarely disappoint.

GROTH VINEYARDS AND WINERY (NAPA)

1982 Cabernet Sauvignon	Napa	($14.00)	87
1983 Cabernet Sauvignon	Napa	($14.00)	85

1984 Cabernet Sauvignon	Napa	($16.00)	90
1982 Chardonnay	Napa	($12.50)	84
1983 Chardonnay	Napa	($12.50)	87
1984 Chardonnay	Napa	($12.50)	87
1984 Sauvignon Blanc	Napa	($9.00)	84

The Groth Winery, founded in 1982, has already raised its production to 30,000 cases, but the smartest decision it has made to date was to hire the brilliant winemaker Nils Venge away from Villa Mount Eden Vineyard. Venge has an impeccable track record for producing some of California's best Cabernets and Chardonnays, and the genius he demonstrated at Villa Mount Eden has hardly stopped now that he is working for Dennis Groth. The first releases have been remarkably impressive and, for their quality, very reasonably priced. Venge is a big believer in dramatic wines made from fully ripe grapes. His Cabernets have gone from one strength to another, starting with an excellent 1982 Cabernet Sauvignon loaded with blackcurrant fruit and married beautifully with oak. The 1983, while less concentrated and a trifle more herbaceous, is still rich and very fruity, with quite a long finish. His 1984 looks to be his best yet for the Groth Winery. It is an opulent, very rich, intense wine with layers of fruit. Nils Venge thinks his 1985 is even better; so it appears we have plenty to look forward to from this young but emerging star in Napa Valley.

GUENOC WINERY (LAKE)

1982 Cabernet Sauvignon	Lake	($8.99)	78
1983 Cabernet Sauvignon	Lake	($8.49)	82
1983 Chardonnay	North Coast	($8.99)	85
1984 Chardonnay	North Coast	($8.99)	83
1982 Petite Sirah	Lake	($6.99)	82
1982 Zinfandel	Lake	($6.49)	85

| 1983 Zinfandel | Lake | ($6.99) | 82 |

Guenoc is another of those California wineries that gets little publicity, but the wines are very solidly made and every once in a while something really special comes out at a remarkably modest price. This was the case with the 1982 Zinfandel and certainly the Chardonnays have been rather toasty and oaky, and in vintages like 1983 also buttery and lemony, with very good concentration of fruit. The winery can also do a decent job with Petite Sirah, though consumers seem hesitant to give this maligned varietal the credit it deserves when well made, as are the Guenoc Petite Sirahs. The Cabernet Sauvignon tends to be light, somewhat herbaceous and, to my taste, less successful than the other varietals. The production at Guenoc has bulged to 75,000 cases, so there is good distribution of these reasonably priced, generally well-made wines.

GUNDLACH-BUNDSCHU WINERY (SONOMA)

1982 Cabernet Sauvignon Batto Ranch	Sonoma	($10.00)	80
1982 Cabernet Sauvignon Rhine Farm	Sonoma	($10.00)	65
1983 Chardonnay	Sonoma	($8.99)	78
1984 Chardonnay	Sonoma	($12.00)	83
1982 Merlot	Sonoma	($7.50)	80
1983 Merlot Rhine Farm	Sonoma	($10.00)	72

One of Sonoma Valley's oldest, this winery was originally founded in 1858 and reactivated by the Bundschus in the early 1970s. Production has grown to over 40,000 cases as the winery produces the entire range of wines from Riesling to Chardonnay, Cabernet Sauvignon, Merlot, Gewürztraminer, and even some Pinot Noir. After a rather spotty record in the late '70s the quality has measurably increased, though the wines lack consistency, with the exception of the Merlot from their Rhine Farm vineyard, which in vintages like 1981, 1980, and 1979 has been particularly impressive. The Chardonnays have been fairly standard, run-of-the-mill-quality wines that are cleanly made, rather medium-bodied, but have one-dimensional, lemony, citrusy flavors without a lot of character and flavor interest. The Cabernets in 1982 were excessively minty and vegetal, which I find an unpardonable defect in this varietal. Even after a long string of successes, the 1983 Rhine Farm Merlot was very vegetal in character. The best Cabernets have come from the Batto Ranch; in 1981 this wine was excellent and in 1982 rather chunky, with good fruit and richness but very little complexity. The Pinot Noir produced here is light and typical of the great majority of California Pinot Noirs—spicy, but with really no complexity or true varietal character.

HACIENDA WINE CELLARS (SONOMA)

1981 Cabernet Sauvignon	Sonoma	($10.49)	80
1982 Cabernet Sauvignon	Sonoma	($9.99)	84
1983 Chardonnay Clair de Lune	Sonoma	($12.00)	86
1984 Chardonnay Clair de Lune	Sonoma	($12.00)	87
1985 Chenin Blanc	California	($5.99)	84
1985 Sauvignon Blanc	Sonoma	($7.99)	82

This moderate-sized winery of 20,000+ cases in Sonoma tends to make above-average, sound, quality wines that rarely hit the peaks but are rarely disappointing either. The Chenin Blanc can be one of California's better examples of this fruity, soft varietal. The 1985 has a lovely flowery bouquet and easy to appreciate flavors. The top Chardonnays, called Clair de Lune, are perhaps the winery's best wines. The 1983, with its crisp acidity and rich, lemony, buttery fruit, is very good. The 1984 is even better, richer, and with its lovely butterscotch nose and good balance has plenty of flavor authority. The Sauvignon Blanc tends to be above average but a trifle dull compared to the many fine Sauvignon Blancs produced in California, and the Cabernet Sauvignons are dark, tannic, refined, and for me just lacking a bit of drama and personality. In essence, this is a good winery that produces sound, even-keeled wines, its Chardonnays and Chenin Blancs being consistently the best.

HAGAFEN WINERY (NAPA)

1984 Cabernet Sauvignon	Napa	($12.00)	85
1983 Cabernet Sauvignon	Napa	($12.00)	75

| 1984 Chardonnay | Napa | ($12.00) | 82 |

This tiny winery produces wines that have been approved by a Rabbi and are suitable for religious observances. The quality has certainly been sound, the Chardonnay being cleanly made, fruity, with a nice toasty element added for complexity. The 1983 Cabernet Sauvignon leans toward the hard, tannic, austere style, with little charm but no flaws. The 1984 is, however, quite appealing for drinking now.

HANZELL WINERY (SONOMA)

| 1981 Cabernet Sauvignon | Sonoma | ($18.00) | 78 |

| 1982 Chardonnay | Sonoma | ($20.00) | 84 |

| 1983 Chardonnay | Sonoma | ($20.00) | 90 |

| 1980 Pinot Noir | Sonoma | ($16.00) | 79 |

| 1981 Pinot Noir | Sonoma | ($16.00) | 84 |

One of the older wineries in Sonoma, the Hanzell Vineyards, founded in 1957, have been dedicated to producing burgundian-style Pinot Noir and Chardonnay, and have certainly succeeded in capturing a cult following for their scant 2,500 cases of wine produced in a good vintage. The prices are high and the wines often rather inconsistent in quality. The debut Cabernet Sauvignon, the 1981, seemed lean, hard, and austere, without sufficient fruit to back up all the tannin. The 1981 Pinot Noir showed a good chewy, robust character, with plenty of tannin and a smoky, earthy, burgundian-like aroma. On the other hand, the 1980 Pinot Noir tasted more like something from Piedmont, Italy, than a complex Pinot Noir. Among the Chardonnays, the 1982 seemed slightly oxidized and overly oaked the one time I tasted it, but the 1983 had virtually everything I look for in a Chardonnay—crisp acidity, rich buttery oak, a dense intensity of tropical fruit and a clean, long, rich finish. It should be drunk over the next several years. Prices at Hanzell are steep and availability virtually impossible unless you live close to the winery and can buy directly from them.

HARBOR WINERY (YOLO)

1982 Cabernet Sauvignon	Napa	($7.99)	86
1983 Chardonnay Reserve	Napa	($7.99)	86
1978 Mission del Sol		($6.99)	90

The tiny Harbor Winery produces less than 2,000 cases of wine, but what they produce has always intrigued me for its rich, intense fruit, flamboyant character, and rather low prices. The 1983 Chardonnay is buttery, oaky, rich, but well balanced. Their Cabernet Sauvignon is always rather full-bodied, very rich, with an expressive bouquet of ripe berry fruit and spicy oak. The heavenly, rich dessert wine, the Mission del Sol, is exceptional, resembling a rich Muscatel de Setubal from Portugal. Prices remain very modest for the quality one gets here. Unfortunately, the quantity of wine insures that there is very little distribution of it outside California.

HAYWOOD WINERY (SONOMA)

1981 Cabernet Sauvignon	Sonoma	($14.00)	81
1982 Cabernet Sauvignon	Sonoma	($14.00)	81
1983 Cabernet Sauvignon	Sonoma	($11.00)	83
1984 Chardonnay	Sonoma	($10.00)	82
1984 Chardonnay Estate	Sonoma	($12.00)	85

The Haywood Winery in Sonoma produces just under 10,000 cases of wine and has been content to devote the bulk of its attention to its Chardonnays and Cabernet Sauvignons, although some Zinfandel and Riesling are made as well as several generic wines called Spaghetti Red and Spaghetti White. The 1984 Chardonnays show good ripe fruit, toasty oak, clean winemaking, and crisp acidity. The Estate Chardonnay has a bit more richness and complexity than the regular wines. My objection to the Cabernets is that, although they are certainly cleanly made and show a dense color and plenty of ripe fruit, they are often excruciatingly tannic, rather closed wines that seem to be slightly out of balance when you measure the immense levels of tannin against the quantity of fruit present. The 1981 is a bit low in acidity and flat as well; the 1982 has a nice berryish nose but is tight and tannic on the palate, and the 1983 even more so, although the underlying depth seems to be present. I am hard pressed to recommend the Cabernets because of my reservations about how they will age, but certainly they will need 4–5 years, and with some luck the fruit might hold up and one might be surprised.

HEITZ CELLARS (NAPA)

1980 Cabernet Sauvignon	Napa	($14.00)	79
1981 Cabernet Sauvignon	Napa	($11.95)	75
1980 Cabernet Sauvignon Bella Oaks	Napa	($27.95)	87
1981 Cabernet Sauvignon Bella Oaks	Napa	($19.95)	84
1980 Cabernet Sauvignon Martha's Vyd.	Napa	($35.00)	87
1981 Cabernet Sauvignon Martha's Vyd.	Napa	($32.00)	86
1980 Chardonnay	Napa	($10.00)	65
1981 Chardonnay	Napa	($10.00)	55
1982 Chardonnay	Napa	($10.00)	60

Heitz Wine Cellars is one of the magical names of the Napa Valley and, in fact, their Cabernets can be among the best wines of Napa. However, that hardly excuses the rest of the stable here, which includes some very poorly made Chardonnays and some inexpensive wines like its Grignolino, a terribly disappointing wine, as well as their Chablis, which lacks character. Undoubtedly, the fame of this winery is the Cabernet Sauvignon from Martha's Vineyard. For whatever reason, the wines have a unique character that can be recognized on smell alone because of their intense minty, chocolatey, eucalyptus-styled aroma. The great vintages of this wine have been the 1968 and 1970, which continue to age magnificently while losing none of their minty character. The 1974 is also a candidate for excellence. Recent vintages, for whatever reason, have not lived up to the above-mentioned ones. The 1978 was disappointing, the 1979 somewhat better, and the 1980 and 1981 good wines but hardly the type of quality to justify the $30+ price asked. Heitz also has begun to purchase grapes from another excellent vineyard, the Bella Oaks Vineyard in Napa

Valley, and this wine can also be excellent, as it was in 1977, 1979, and 1980. The 1981 is good but not special. The regular Cabernets have taken on a very commercial, straightforward style and while not extravagantly priced are hardly good values. As for the Chardonnays, they are consistently thin, acidic, and lacking in varietal character. One wonders how such a great red winemaker can show so little ability with a white varietal that seems to be easy to make elsewhere. The Grignolino is a poor effort for a cash flow wine and is best served chilled, but its high acid character makes it very unattractive. Heitz, of course, remains an institution in Napa Valley, but proceed with caution since the great reputation here is not always justified by the quality or the price of the wine in the bottle.

THE WILLIAM HILL WINERY (NAPA)

1980 Cabernet Sauvignon Gold Label	Napa	($16.00)	90
1981 Cabernet Sauvignon Gold Label	Napa	($15.00)	87
1982 Cabernet Sauvignon Gold Label	Napa	($16.00)	87
1983 Cabernet Sauvignon Gold Label	Napa	($16.00)	84
1981 Chardonnay Gold Label	Napa	($18.00)	87
1982 Chardonnay Gold Label	Napa	($18.00)	82
1983 Chardonnay Gold Label	Napa	($16.00)	86

Bill Hill is a fervent believer in mountain vineyards, with their cooler temperatures and higher natural acidity in the grapes. His winery, which started with an excellent 1978 Cabernet and huge, oaky style of Chardonnay, has continued to evolve in style. In the short ten years the winery has been in existence, it has built an impeccable reputation with Cabernet Sauvignon and good Chardonnay. The production is inching its way up toward 40,000 cases. The winery also makes a less expensive, ready to drink Chardonnay and Cabernet under what they call a Silver Label, versus the Gold Labels that are now on the market. The Chardonnays, after being too oaky and heavy (as in 1980), have moved toward a crisper, more restrained style, but as Bill Hill promised, they have aged well, contrary to what most California Chardonnays do. The 1981 has developed a Meursault-like, buttery, subtle oak character and is drinking beautifully at the moment. The 1982 is a good bit less impressive, but the 1983 looks to be another Chardonnay that can live 5–6 years in the bottle, a long time by California standards. However, the glories of this house are the beautifully made Cabernet Sauvignons that start off life rather lean and austere but seem to develop richness and character as they age. After the very successful 1978 and more supple, fruity, open style of 1979, the 1980, which seemed tight and hard when first released, has developed magnificently into a truly great California Cabernet that may have at least another 10 years of life ahead of it. It can still be found on the market, so run, don't walk, to get a few bottles for your cellar. The 1981 is a more supple, fruity style of Cabernet and the 1982 again lusher but showing good structure and a very seductive texture, with at least a 5–10 year future ahead of it. Hill's Cabernets are well worth seeking out by those who have the patience to wait for them to develop as they exhibit wonderful blackcurrant fruity flavors, an intelligent dosage of oak, and plenty of concentration and tannin. This is definitely one of the premier producers of Cabernet in California.

THE ROBERT HUNTER VINEYARD (SONOMA)

1981 Brut de Noir	Sonoma	($20.00)	80
1982 Brut de Noir	Sonoma	($20.00)	83

Another of the burgeoning number of sparkling wine producers in California that I predict will all have a difficult time in the competitive sparkling wine business. Robert Hunter sparkling wines to date have been attractively packaged and have sold at prices too high for what are rather tart, lean, crisp wines lacking character and intensity.

INGLENOOK VINEYARDS (NAPA)

1980 Cabernet Sauvignon	Napa	($7.50)	84
1981 Cabernet Sauvignon	Napa	($8.00)	78
1982 Cabernet Sauvignon	Napa	($8.00)	72
1983 Cabernet Sauvignon Kabinett Selection	Napa	($8.00)	73
1980 Cabernet Sauvignon Reserve Cask	Napa	($18.00)	88
1981 Cabernet Sauvignon Reserve Cask	Napa	($18.00)	88

1982 Cabernet Sauvignon Reserve Cask	Napa	($18.00)	87
1983 Cabernet Sauvignon Reserve Cask	Napa	($18.00)	86
1982 Charbono	Napa	($9.00)	85
1983 Chardonnay Reserve	Napa	($15.00)	?
1984 Chardonnay Reserve	Napa	($15.00)	85
1982 Merlot	Napa	($8.00)	78
1981 Merlot Limited Cask Reserve	Napa	($12.00)	75
1983 Merlot Reserve Cask	Napa	($15.00)	?
1984 Sauvignon Blanc Reserve	Napa	($9.00)	78

Inglenook is one of the great old names in California and was one of the pioneers in producing world-class, outstanding Cabernet Sauvignons under the legendary John Daniel. Much has been made of the fact that when the winery was sold to Heublein in the mid-'60s production was expanded significantly and the quality suffered immensely. Certainly, anyone who had tasted the old Inglenook Cabernets from the '50s and early '60s realized how great California Cabernets could be. However, since 1980 the winery has been putting its best foot forward in trying to regain some of its lost prestige and stature. The wines have a new label (which actually resembles the old label used back in the '50s) and the quality seems to be on the rise again. Certainly, 1980 was a very successful vintage for the winery's Cabernets and the Reserve Casks from 1981, 1982, and 1983 all look very good, particularly the flamboyant blackcurrant, cedary-scented, supple 1981 and the exotic, multidimensional 1982. The new Kabinett selections from Inglenook are inexpensive, lighter-styled wines that are simple and straightforward, and of course the winery produces a significant amount of jug wine under the Navalle label. The Chardonnays continue to be a little disappointing in the scheme of things, rather light, citrusy and lemony with just a touch of oak, but one would like to see more intensity. The Sauvignon Blanc Reserve has looked quite good, has a lot of fruit, depth, and character, but the 1984 was surprisingly devoid of flavor intensity. At $10 it is expensive. The winery also continues to make a bit of Chenin Blanc, Gewürztraminer,

Riesling, Pinot Noir, Petite Sirah, and Charbono. One of the most interesting wines in the Inglenook lineup that rarely gets the credit it should is Charbono, of which the 1982 is one of the better examples since the mid-'70s. It is a beefy, rich, spicy, peppery wine with a considerable amount of character. Inglenook's production of 150,000 cases of varietals and another 100,000+ cases of generics puts it among the leaders in terms of total production of wine in California. This winery clearly looks to be on the rebound and merits following to see what the new vintages will offer.

IRON HORSE RANCH AND VINEYARDS (SONOMA)

1983 Blanc de Noirs	Sonoma	($20.00)	84
1983 Blanc de Noirs Wedding Cuvée	Sonoma	($20.00)	84
1982 Brut	Sonoma	($20.00)	83
1983 Brut	Sonoma	($20.00)	83
1981 Brut Late Disgorged	Sonoma	($20.00)	85
1981 Cabernet Sauvignon	Sonoma	($16.00)	72
1982 Cabernet Sauvignon	Sonoma	($16.00)	65
1984 Chardonnay	Sonoma	($12.00)	78
1985 Fumé Blanc	Sonoma	($10.00)	84

Iron Horse is doing one of the best jobs in California with its sparkling wines, though the prices remain a bit stiff. One can find French non-vintage champagne that is superior for less money. Nevertheless, these beautifully labeled wines are certainly worth a try and I applaud the idea of a late-disgorged wine, which adds character and body to the product. With regard to the other wines, the Fumé Blanc tends to be very lean, tart, austere, yet interesting. The 1985 seems less successful than the 1984. The Chardonnay is in the same style, rather herbaceous for a Chardonnay, with lean, tart, citrusy flavors. It is not a style I personally prefer but it is cleanly made and pleasant. The Cabernet Sauvignon tends to be lean, austere, and rather thin. The 1981 was acceptable, but the 1982 tasted more like a Beaujolais and was also spoiled by cardboard aromas in its bouquet.

JAEGER-INGLEWOOD VINEYARD (NAPA)

1980 Merlot	Napa	($12.00)	80
1981 Merlot	Napa	($12.00)	86

William Jaeger is one of the major moving forces in Napa Valley, having a major share of both Freemark Abbey and Rutherford Hill wineries. He has begun to release under his own name a small amount of Merlot from his Inglewood Vineyard in Napa Valley. Production is aimed at 4,000 cases and his debut releases, 1980 and 1981, were both interesting. The 1980 was a rather compact wine with good fruit but a weedy, herbaceous bouquet. However, the 1981 showed a sumptuous, complex, exotic bouquet of saddle leather, coffee, and ripe fruit, and wonderful lushness and depth on the palate.

JEKEL VINEYARD (MONTEREY)

1982 Cabernet Sauvignon	Monterey	($14.00)	?
1981 Cabernet Sauvignon Private Reserve	Monterey	($18.00)	?
1984 Chardonnay Reserve	Monterey	($14.99)	86
1983 Chardonnay Reserve	Monterey	($14.50)	86
1984 Johannisberg Riesling	Monterey	($6.50)	85
1985 Johannisberg Riesling	Monterey	($7.50)	87

This winery, which has a fairly large production of 50,000 cases, started in 1978 and quickly built a reputation for its Riesling. Since then they have added a very powerful, oaky, richly buttery Chardonnay and an intense, very rich, but to my taste excessively vegetal Cabernet Sauvignon. I like and applaud the individualistic style that owner Bill Jekel is aiming for with his rich, dramatic, flamboyant wines, but the Cabernet, as much as I adore its texture, power, and balance on the palate, is difficult to give high marks to because of its pungent vegetal aromas. Both the 1981 Reserve and 1982 are impressive on the palate, but bizarre to the smell. One wine that Jekel seems to consistently do an excellent job with is his Johannisberg Riesling. It was this wine that in 1978 won such plaudits from critics that the name Jekel began to be bantered about in wine circles. I am not a great admirer of California Riesling, which tends to lack acidity and to be heavy and dull, but this Riesling has a wonderfully fragrant bouquet and soft, delicious, fruity flavors balanced by nice acidity in the background. The newly released 1985, made in a true Kabinett style, is as good a dry Riesling as you are likely to find in California.

JOHNSON-TURNBULL VINEYARDS (NAPA)

1982 Cabernet Sauvignon	Napa	($12.50)	86
1983 Cabernet Sauvignon	Napa	($12.50)	82
1984 Cabernet Sauvignon	Napa	($12.00)	85

The tiny Johnson-Turnbull Vineyards produce between 2,000–2,500 cases of Cabernet Sauvignon, their only wine. It is what I have called the poor man's Heitz Martha's Vineyard because of its remarkable similarity to that wine. The wine is characterized by the telltale intense eucalyptus, minty aroma, has wonderful rich fruit, and an aging potential of 5–7 years. The 1982 is the best recent wine and the 1983 and 1984 are certainly very good, but not as deep as the 1982.

JORDAN VINEYARD AND WINERY (SONOMA)

1980 Cabernet Sauvignon	Alexander Vly.	($18.00)	85
1981 Cabernet Sauvignon	Alexander Vly.	($18.00)	86
1982 Cabernet Sauvignon	Alexander Vly.	($18.00)	79
1982 Chardonnay	Alexander Vly.	($16.00)	75
1983 Chardonnay	Alexander Vly.	($16.00)	59

The Jordan Winery, which was built to resemble a Bordeaux château, is one of the top tourist sites in Sonoma County. The first vintage of Cabernet Sauvignon was the 1976, which pleased people when it was released because of its supple, very lush, forward charms. The subsequent vintages of Jordan have continued in the same very supple, plummy, easy to drink style, with a noticeable herbaceous note to the wines. The prices are high for what one actually gets, but the wines have been well promoted and are seen in virtually all the retail shops and on most good restaurant lists. They are appealing young, but be forewarned, 5–6 years seems to be the best one can hope for in longevity for these wines, although the 1980 may last until 1990. Longevity has been compromised for the sake of immediate drinkability; I certainly won't complain, but you should be aware of that before you stock up on cases of Jordan Cabernet expecting it to mature like a fine Bordeaux. As for the Chardonnay, it is straightforward, dull, and quite overpriced for what one receives.

KALIN CELLARS (MARIN)

1980 Cabernet Sauvignon	Santa Barbara	($14.95)	67
1982 Cabernet Sauvignon Reserve	Santa Barbara	($17.95)	86
1984 Chardonnay	Potter Valley	($11.95)	87
1983 Chardonnay Cuvée D	Sonoma	($15.00)	90
1983 Chardonnay Cuvée L	Sonoma	($14.95)	87
1984 Chardonnay Cuvée L	Sonoma	($14.95)	91
1982 Pinot Noir Cuvée DD	Sonoma	($14.95)	87
1984 Sauvignon Blanc	Potter Valley	($8.99)	87
1984 Sauvignon Blanc Reserve	Potter Valley	($11.90)	90
1984 Semillon	Potter Valley	($11.00)	90

Kalin consistently turns out some of the most interesting and well-made complex wines in all of California. Perhaps the fact that owner and microbiologist Terry Leighton is one of the world's great specialists in yeast and believes in making wines very naturally, not centrifuging or filtering them, results in highly intense, original, complex wines with great style. If there is a disappointment, it tends to be occasional vintages of Cabernet Sauvignon that are made from grapes purchased in Santa Barbara. The 1980 was extremely vegetal, spicy, and unattractive. However, the 1982 showed great depth and intensity, with the vegetal component tamed down considerably. This winery makes California's best Semillon wine, with an incredible waxy, lush richness that stands out in vintages such as 1985 and 1984. One can't recommend this dry, Graves-like wine enough. The Sauvignon Blanc Potter Valley is another knockout and potentially one of the great Sauvignons made in California, with some toasty oak in the background and rich, deep flavors that are reminiscent of the great white Graves château Laville-Haut-Brion. The Chardonnays have ranged from a very good Potter Valley Chardonnay in 1984 to absolutely superb Chardonnays from Sonoma, the Cuvée L and Cuvée D. These are unfiltered Chardonnays that actually throw some sediment after several years in the bottle, but they have remarkably intense, rich, buttery, appley, lemony fruit married brilliantly with toasty oak and are as close to the style of a great French Chassagne-Montrachet as one is likely to find in California. The Pinot Noir is tannic but shows every bit of the potential expected of an earthy, smoky, Chambertin-styled wine that can age from 5–10 years. A tiny amount of decadently rich sweet wine called Cuvée d'Or is produced, but your best chance of finding a bottle of this is to buy it directly from the winery or one of its outlets in California. The production of Kalin is now up to 5,000 cases, hardly enough to go around once the splendid quality of the wines being made here is known. This to me is one of the great underpublicized wineries in California, and Terry Leighton, one of California's most adventurous and successful winemakers, has shown that he is willing to take a risk to make something special. One wishes more California wineries would follow in his footsteps.

ROBERT KEENAN WINERY (NAPA)

1983 Cabernet Sauvignon	Napa	($14.50)	82
1982 Chardonnay	Napa	($14.00)	75
1984 Chardonnay	Napa	($14.00)	80
1983 Chardonnay	Napa	($15.00)	70
1982 Merlot	Napa	($15.00)	72
1983 Merlot	Napa	($14.50)	80

This winery produces roughly 9,000 cases and has performed to mostly favorable reviews from the West Coast press. However, as much as I would like to agree, I can't find the quality in the bottle that other critics have found. In fact, there is nothing wrong with the wines, which are technically clean and suffer from no off aromas or technical problems. However, the reds have excruciatingly painful levels of tannin that experience has taught me will never mellow and soften enough to carry what are barely adequate levels of fruit in these wines. It is easy to recommend a big, tannic monster in its youth, but then one comes back to these wines in 8–10 years to find the fruit drying out and the tannins every bit as nasty as they were in the beginning. This appears to be the major problem with many of the Keenan releases. The 1982 Merlot has a dense color, but one is hard pressed to find adequate fruit behind the wall of abrasive tannin. The 1983 shows more fruit, but again I may have been generous in my score because there is still entirely too much tannin and none of the fleshy, fat, lush texture that one looks for in Merlot. The Cabernet Sauvignons, on the other hand, tend to be a bit more consistent and seem to have more fruit to go along with the hard, rough, coarse tannins found in these wines. Whether they will age is debatable; I for one would not be willing to pay the fairly steep price asked to gamble that they will. The Chardonnays from Keenan in 1983 and 1984 have proved terribly disappointing. The 1983 was very acidic, unappealing, lean, and rather devoid of flavor interest. The 1984 has more ripeness and flavor but again tries to out-Chablis Chablis and fails in the attempt.

KENDALL-JACKSON VINEYARD (LAKE)

1982 Cabernet Sauvignon	Clear Lake	($17.49)	68
1983 Cabernet Sauvignon Cardinale	California	($9.00)	82
1983 Chardonnay Royale	Monterey	($11.00)	76
1983 Chardonnay Vintner's Reserve	California	($9.50)	86
1984 Chardonnay Vintner's Reserve	California	($9.50)	85
1985 Chardonnay Vintner's Reserve	California	($9.50)	87
1983 Zinfandel	Mendocino	($8.99)	75
1983 Zinfandel Du Pratt	Mendocino	($10.50)	83

Kendall-Jackson has quickly caught the fancy of many wine consumers with its reasonably priced wines. Its best successes to date have been the Rieslings and Chardonnays, of which the latter have been particularly strong in 1983 and 1984, and exceptional in 1985, especially the Vintner's reserve. They come under different labels, but the consistent winner has been the Vintner's Reserve for under $10. This is a wine loaded with tropical fruit, pineapple and toasty vanillin oak, with a subtle buttery component. However, all the Chardonnays have generally been soundly made and are good values. The Cabernets have not reached the same level. The 1982 Clear Lake is very vegetal, with intrusive alcohol and a hotness on the palate. The 1983 Cardinale is a straightforward, fairly simple wine that has a good measure of supple blackcurrant fruit. The Zinfandels have been above average, even good in the case of the Du Pratt Zinfandel from Mendocino County. But again, this is a winery for taking stock of the whites while approaching some of the reds with a measure of caution.

KATHERINE KENNEDY WINERY (SANTA CLARA)

1981 Cabernet Sauvignon	Santa Cruz	($12.00)	85
1982 Cabernet Sauvignon	Santa Cruz	($12.00)	85

This minuscule winery is specializing in Cabernet Sauvignon, producing just under 1,000 cases. The wines have been well marked by oak aging and have shown ripe cassis flavors and good depth with plenty of breadth on the palate. The prices are not unrealistic; the wines are capable of aging for 4–6 years.

KENWOOD VINEYARDS (SONOMA)

1980 Cabernet Sauvignon	Sonoma	($13.00)	?
1982 Cabernet Sauvignon Artist Series	Sonoma	($25.00)	?
1983 Cabernet Sauvignon Artist Series	Sonoma	($30.00)	?
1981 Cabernet Sauvignon Jack London	Sonoma	($15.00)	?
1983 Chardonnay	Sonoma	($10.00)	78
1983 Chardonnay Beltane Ranch	Sonoma	($15.00)	80
1981 Pinot Noir	Sonoma	($9.99)	76
1984 Sauvignon Blanc	Sonoma	($10.00)	84
1985 Sauvignon Blanc	Sonoma	($10.00)	84

Kenwood Winery has a fairly large production of over 100,000 cases and the wines have performed to rather mixed results in my tastings.

The Cabernets have always been very vegetal and herbaceous but extremely concentrated, tannic, and heady. The Jack London Cabernet Sauvignon has been intense and weedy and the Artist Series that Kenwood puts out is often so heavy and vegetal that I find it grotesque in its texture and intensity. Yet my view may well be the minority position since these unusual wines get strong support by much of the California wine press. The whites, on the other hand, have been much more consistent. The Sauvignon Blanc, which I find again entirely too vegetal and herbaceous to be called classic, is nevertheless a crisp, well-made, deeply fruity wine with varietal character oozing from it. Both the 1984 and 1985 look good. Of the two Chardonnays, the one from the Beltane Ranch is usually the best, with its fat, ripe, buttery, somewhat herbaceous flavors married with plenty of toasty oak. Prices here are hardly expensive, but this is a winery that could use a shift in style, particularly with its reds.

KISTLER VINEYARDS (SONOMA)

1982 Cabernet Sauvignon Veeder Hills	Napa	($14.00)	88
1984 Chardonnay Dutton	Sonoma	($14.00)	87
1984 Chardonnay Winery Lake	Sonoma	($14.00)	87
1985 Chardonnay Winery Lake/Dutton	CA	($14.00)	87
1984 Pinot Noir	Sonoma	($12.00)	84

Kistler Vineyards is dedicated to making natural, unmanipulated wines that have character and aging ability. Burgundy seems to be the source for their inspiration. The winery produces a modest 7,000 cases of wine and only started with the release of Chardonnays in the 1979 vintage. Those wines were met with great critical success, but were followed by the 1980 Chardonnays which were seriously flawed and unfortunately caused a loss of confidence in the winery. Since then they have been right on target and recent vintages of 1983, 1984 and 1985 are strong across-the-board. The Chardonnays in 1984 were their best since 1979. They are made in the so-called Kistler style, one that emphasizes toasty oak from barrel fermentation as well as crisp, buttery fruit. They are forward, fleshy and show lush, buttery, lemony, toasty oak-influenced flavors. The 1985 as well as the the 1984 Winery Lake and Dutton show excellent depth, fruit, and character. As for their Pinot Noir, it tends to be a rather powerful, earthy, smoky wine that has the potential to improve for 4–6 years. The Cabernet Sauvignons in both 1982 and 1983 have shown a great deal of tannin, dark ruby colors, youthful bouquets of spice, oak, and tarry, curranty fruit, and a rather medium- to full-bodied weight with plenty of depth. They should last at least 8–10 years. This is a winery that deserves your attention.

F. KORBEL AND BROTHERS (SONOMA)

N.V. Blanc de Blancs Sparkling Wine	($16.00)	80
N.V. Blanc de Noirs Sparkling Wine	($12.00)	75
N.V. Extra Dry Champagne	($9.75)	65
N.V. Natural Champagne	($12.00)	70

Korbel sparkling wines can be found in most retail shops since the production is said to be in excess of 725,000 cases. The quality of the wines tends to be rather mediocre, with a certain dullness. My favorite has been the Blanc de Blancs, but at $16 a bottle it hardly represents a good value. The Blanc de Noirs, which is another rather nondescript, dull wine with little character, can hardly be recommended. Perhaps the two least attractive wines are the Non-Vintage Extra Dry Champagne and the Non-Vintage Natural Champagne, both rather sweet, with Rieslinglike flavors and a certain musty, almost chemical character that is unattractive.

HANS KORNELL CHAMPAGNE CELLAR (NAPA)

N.V. Brut Sparkling Wine		($10.99)	78
N.V. Natural Champagne		($11.99)	80
N.V. Sehr Trocken	California	($14.00)	80

Hans Kornell produces around 100,000 cases of sparkling wine made largely from the Riesling grape. His best sparkling wine tends to be the Sehr Trocken, which has a Riesling character and, while not exactly to my taste, is austere, floral in aroma, and fairly light. The other wines are adequate, but these sparkling wines generally appeal to those who do not like the taste of dry French champagnes or the more serious California sparkling wines.

CHARLES KRUG (NAPA)

1981 Cabernet Sauvignon		($8.99)	82
1974 Cabernet Sauvignon Lot F1		($35.00)	87
1978 Cabernet Sauvignon Vintage Selection	Napa	($12.00)	84
1983 Chardonnay	Napa	($9.99)	78
1983 Johannisberg Riesling	Napa	($8.99)	68

Charles Krug's wines, which are made by one segment of the omni-present Mondavi family in California, get very little publicity and could use a good PR expert to give them a bit more status in the wine world today. The reds tend to be the best wines here; I find the Riesling rather dull and too acidic and the Chardonnay bland and lacking varietal character. However, the Cabernet can be quite good. The 1978 Vintage Selection Cabernet Sauvignon has a rich black cherry nose dominated somewhat excessively by oak, but it has good flavors and should be drunk now since it appears to have reached full maturity. The 1974 Cabernet Sauvignon Lot F1, which has been rein-troduced into the market, is a very good, even excellent example of a wine from a great vintage for California Cabernet. It has a wonderfully rich, expressive bouquet, dramatically deep, intense flavors, and seems to be at its plateau of maturity now. One suspects that the Krug Cabernets can hold their own against some of the best from California, but it's a shame they don't get more attention from retailers and the press. The production of this winery has topped one million cases, of which a large part is in their jug wine production under the label C. K. Mondavi.

LA CREMA (SONOMA)

1984 Chardonnay Reserve	Monterey	($14.00)	88
1984 Chardonnay	Sonoma	($10.00)	84
1985 Chardonnay	Sonoma	($12.00)	87

This winery, which began only in 1979, has had a mixed reception from consumers and the press. Certain wines (e.g., the 1981 Ventana Chardonnay) were quite excellent whereas others lacked character and seemed to be flawed in one way or the other. The winery changed hands several years ago and there seems to be a renewed effort to get it back on track. So far the only wines that have been released under the new ownership have been the 1984 Chardonnay, which was ripe, spicy, quite well made, and sold at a reasonable price, and very impressive, rich, elegant 1984 Reserve and 1985 Chardonnays. Hopefully, the consistent quality that this winery has lacked will be forthcoming.

LA JOTA VINEYARD (NAPA)

1982 Cabernet Sauvignon Howell Mtn.	Napa	($15.00)	86
1983 Cabernet Sauvignon Howell Mtn.	Napa	($15.00)	86

This new winery is producing 5,000 cases of wine each year and its winemaker is none other than the famous Randy Dunn, who helped make such superb wines at Caymus before starting his own winery at a nearby location on Howell Mountain. The winery plans to specialize in Cabernet Sauvignon and Zinfandel. Its first Cabernet, the 1982, showed the Howell Mountain and Randy Dunn style—rich, dark ruby color, tannic yet impressive, with a subtle bouquet of mint and ripe berry fruit. It has plenty of muscle as well as tannin. I doubt that it will be fully mature until at least the late 1980s. The 1983 is just as impressive, but needs 4–5 years of cellaring. This appears to be a winery to watch carefully.

LAKESPRING WINERY (NAPA)

1982 Cabernet Sauvignon	Napa	($11.00)	82
1983 Chardonnay	Napa	($12.00)	82
1983 Merlot	Napa	($10.00)	78
1984 Sauvignon Blanc	Napa	($10.00)	80

Lakespring Winery seems to produce rather sound yet uninspiring wines that to my taste and smell border on being too vegetal for all four of these wines. The 1983 Merlot, which the winery billed as their best Merlot yet, seemed to have extremely lean, tannic flavors and was quite vegetal in its aroma. The Chardonnay tends to be overtly herbaceous and rather extreme in style. Prices are moderate for the wines from this 16,000-case winery in Napa Valley.

LAMBERT BRIDGE (SONOMA)

1981 Cabernet Sauvignon	Sonoma	($12.00)	55
1983 Chardonnay	Sonoma	($12.00)	82
1984 Chardonnay	Sonoma	($12.00)	83
1981 Merlot	Sonoma	($12.00)	60
1982 Merlot	Sonoma	($12.00)	65

Lambert Bridge Winery, a lovely winery tucked in the hills of the Dry Creek area of Sonoma, has never enthused me with the quality of their wines. The Chardonnays have been the best wines released, but taste more like Sauvignon Blancs than Chardonnay. Nevertheless, they have good balance, richness, depth, crisp acidity and are certainly above average as wines, although the herbaceous element is something one associates with Sauvignon, not Chardonnay. The Cabernets and Merlots have been borderline disasters for the simple reason that they are incredibly weedy and vegetal, and often resemble a purée of asparagus while showing none of the rich blackcurrant, cassis fruit that one finds in the top California Cabernets. The winery should either change their source of grapes or give up these wines altogether since they have little appeal and are very defective examples of Merlot and Cabernet Sauvignon.

LANDMARK VINEYARDS (SONOMA)

1983 Chardonnay	Sonoma	($9.00)	85
1984 Chardonnay	Sonoma	($9.00)	84
1984 Petite Blanc	Sonoma	($5.00)	82
1985 Petite Blanc	Sonoma	($5.00)	82

Landmark Vineyards is definitely a winery to seek out when you are looking for white wines that represent excellent values. The inexpensive Petite Blanc, a blend of Chardonnay, Sauvignon Blanc, and Chenin Blanc, has been especially good over the last several vintages, showing a wonderful freshness yet some real body and flavor on the palate. The Chardonnays here seem to be on a hot streak at the moment. The 1984 is wonderfully refreshing, with good varietal character, a subtle buttery, lemon character to the fruit, and soft, medium-bodied finish. The 1983 is even better, with lush, buttery, lemony fruit, fairly big body, and a soft, spicy finish. At the price, one can hardly ask for more. The winery produces 23,000 cases of wine; Chardonnay has been their best effort to date. Some Cabernet Sauvignon and Pinot Noir are made also.

LAUREL GLEN (SONOMA)

1981 Cabernet Sauvignon	Sonoma Mt.	($12.99)	87
1983 Cabernet Sauvignon	Sonoma Mt.	($12.99)	81
1984 Cabernet Sauvignon	Sonoma Mt.	($15.00)	90
1982 Merlot	Sonoma	($8.99)	75

Winemaker/owner Patrick Campbell is producing close to 5,000 cases of wine that were the first to have the appellation "Sonoma Mountain" on them. Before he opened his winery, he sold his grapes to several Sonoma wineries. His debut wine, the 1981 Cabernet Sauvignon, was a rich, beautifully made, well-structured wine with intense fruit, full body, and deep layers of flavor, with 5–7 more years of aging potential. This was followed by the 1982 Merlot, which was rather feeble in color, light in body, and rather herbaceous, with somewhat diluted flavors. However, the 1983 Sonoma Mountain Cabernet Sauvignon was a return to the more impressive style of the 1981. Campbell's 1984 Cabernet Sauvignon, his best produced yet, is a rich, opulent, intense wine with great flavor concentration and plenty of backbone for aging of 5–10 years. So far this winery has been content to produce only Merlot and Cabernet Sauvignon, and aside from the off year of 1982, three of the first four vintages have been considerable successes and merit serious attention from wine enthusiasts.

CHARLES LEFRANC-ALMADEN (SAN JOSE)

1981 Cabernet Sauvignon	San Jose	($7.99)	84
1982 Cabernet Sauvignon	San Benito	($8.99)	83
1983 Cabernet Sauvignon	San Benito	($8.99)	85
1984 Chardonnay	Napa	($15.00)	85

1984 Chardonnay	Tepusquet	($7.49)	78
1984 Pinot Noir	Cienga Vly.	($12.50)	85
1984 Premium Red	California	($6.99/1.5 l)	83
1985 Premium White	California	($6.99/1.5 l)	82
1982 Sauvignon Blanc Late Harvest	San Benito	($12.00)	84

The huge Almaden Winery in San Jose, with a production in excess of eight million cases a year, is more and more separating its premium line of wines called Charles Lefranc away from the bulk wine production of Almaden. Winemaker Klaus Mathes has been given greater independence and flexibility to produce wines of high quality for Charles Lefranc. The first evidence of this was the 1981 Cabernet Sauvignon, the best Cabernet produced yet by Almaden under their premium Charles Lefranc label. A rich, densely colored wine, it should drink and evolve well for another 5 or more years. The 1982 is somewhat less impressive, but still a good wine, the 1983 the best yet from this winery looking for newly found prestige and respect. The Chardonnays that have been released include an impressive, expensive Napa Chardonnay in 1984 that had a complex bouquet of hazelnuts and toasty, buttery fruit. The palate impression was one of balance and restrained elegance. The other 1984 Chardonnay from grapes grown in the Santa Barbara area from the Tepusquet Vineyard was a more tart wine with scents of tropical fruit, particularly pineapples. The Late Harvest Sauvignon Blanc that Charles Lefranc is producing also looks to be a winner, as does their 1984 Pinot Noir. Most serious wine consumers turn their heads the other way when looking at some of the huge wineries that are primarily involved in jug wine production; Almaden, however, is clearly setting new standards with their Charles Lefranc label and they bear watching as well as tasting as the wines are released. The new Premium generic red and white table wines are delicious: the white, supple, lush, very fruity; the red, cherry-scented and obviously Cabernet dominated. Both offer quality and value.

LEEWARD WINERY (VENTURA)

1983 Chardonnay Ventana Vineyard	Monterey	($14.95)	86
1984 Chardonnay Ventana Vineyard	Monterey	($15.00)	88

1983 Chardonnay	Bien Nacido	($13.00)	74
1983 Chardonnay	Central Coast	($12.00)	55
1984 Chardonnay	Central Coast	($11.00)	87
1983 Chardonnay MacGregor Vyd.	Edna Vly.	($15.00)	78
1984 Chardonnay MacGregor Vyd.	Edna Vly.	($15.00)	85

The smallish Leeward Winery (which produces just over 9,000 cases of wine) specializes in vineyard-designated Chardonnays from locations throughout the central coast and Santa Barbara areas. A little bit of Cabernet and Zinfandel is made, but I have never tasted it. The Chardonnays have generally been made in the big, buttery, oaky, tropical fruit style that has dramatic character and rich levels of fruit and intensity. The most consistent two Chardonnays have come from the Ventana Vineyard in Monterey and the MacGregor Vineyard in Edna Valley, although the 1983 MacGregor seemed almost Sauvignon Blanc in character, with a very grassy bouquet and very high acidity. The 1983 Central Coast and Bien Nacido also suffer from the same problem of excessive herbaceousness, and for the former, excessive oxidation as well. However, the 1984s look ripe, rich, and loaded with character in the buttery, oaky style. This is clearly a winery to search out when looking for dramatic, very flavorful, barrel-fermented Chardonnay.

J. LOHR (SANTA CLARA)

N.V. Cabernet Sauvignon	California	($5.49)	69
1983 Cabernet Sauvignon	California	($6.99)	72
1984 Cabernet Sauvignon	California	($6.99)	84
1983 Cabernet Sauvignon	Napa	($6.99)	76
1983 Chardonnay Greenfield Vineyards	Monterey	($8.99)	83
1984 Chardonnay Greenfield Vineyards	Monterey	($8.99)	84
1982 Chardonnay Reserve	Monterey	($8.99)	74

1984 Fumé Blanc Greenfield Vineyards   Monterey   ($7.99)   84

The J. Lohr Winery in San Jose produces just over 300,000 cases of wine from extensive vineyard holdings as well as purchased grapes. Some of the wines from the late 1970s were terrible, but in recent vintages, particularly 1984, quality has jumped to a moderately good level and some of the J. Lohr wines now represent excellent values in the scheme of California wine pricing. Once more people learn of the quality of their 1984 Fumé Blanc and Chardonnay from the Greenfield Vineyards, as well as their 1984 California Cabernet Sauvignon (the best, I believe, they have made), prices will no doubt climb upward. The Fumé Blanc stood out extremely well in several tastings I did for its fresh, lively fruitiness, subtle herbaceous quality, and well-balanced, concentrated feel on the palate. Both the 1983 and 1984 Chardonnays from the Greenfield Vineyard in Monterey have performed admirably, but the 1982 Chardonnay Reserve was acidic and tart, with very little length and fruit. However, the 1983 Greenfield Chardonnay had a lovely nose, was medium-bodied, and crisp with appley, tart flavors. The 1984 is even better, with more toasty oak integrated into a rather medium- to full-bodied palate impression. The winery also makes a decent Petite Sirah and a proprietary blend of Riesling and Pinot Blanc called Jade, which tends to be fruity, soft, but somewhat dull. This winery should definitely be considered at the moment for its fine Chardonnay, Sauvignon Blanc, and 1984 Cabernet Sauvignon. The best Chardonnays and Sauvignon Blancs seem to be coming out of their Greenfield Vineyard in Monterey, where they own 240 acres —a winery that appears to be on the move up.

LONG VINEYARDS (NAPA)

1980 Cabernet Sauvignon	Napa	($30.00)	?
1981 Cabernet Sauvignon	Napa	($25.00)	88
1983 Chardonnay	Napa	($25.00)	90
1984 Chardonnay	Napa	($25.00)	92
1984 Johannisberg Riesling "Botrytis"	Napa	($15.00)	90
1984 Sauvignon Blanc	Sonoma	($10.00)	86

The tiny Long Vineyard produces less than 1,500 cases of wine and has it strictly allocated to a few select wine shops in this country. The

Chardonnay is consistently one of the great Chardonnays of California —not terribly long-lived, but in its first 3 or 4 years of life a wine to be enjoyed for its immense richness, remarkable length and huge, oaky, barrel-fermented, buttery, toasty style. The last two vintages, 1983 and 1984, have shown a bit more restraint than some of the monster wines produced in 1979 and 1980. The Cabernet Sauvignon is another dense, broodingly dark-colored, very rich wine with a textbook bouquet of blackcurrant fruit. However, it has been difficult to project how they will develop in the future because they are so tannic and backward. Certainly, they seem to need all of 7–10 years of aging and do appear to have the requisite depth of fruit to hold up to the high level of tannins. But one can never be quite sure with a wine this tannic. Long also makes a wonderfully rich, subtly herbaceous but oak-influenced Sauvignon Blanc that is one of the better examples in California. The 1984 is particularly successful. Lastly, the Auslese-styled, sweet Riesling made here is one of California's finest—flowing with ripe tropical fruit scents, rich, well balanced, an altogether decadent drinking experience. But these wines may be very hard to find.

LYETH VINEYARD AND WINERY (SONOMA)

1981 Red Table Wine	Alexander Vly.	($15.00)	86
1982 Red Table Wine	Alexander Vly.	($15.00)	87
1983 Red Table Wine	Alexander Vly.	($15.00)	82
1984 Red Table Wine	Alexander Vly.	($15.00)	90
1982 White Table Wine	Alexander Vly.	($9.00)	87
1983 White Table Wine	Alexander Vly.	($9.00)	86
1984 White Table Wine	Alexander Vly.	($9.00)	86

The Lyeth Winery, which was founded only in 1981, is one of the new breed of California wineries that has taken the varietal name off the label and featured a proprietary blend for both its red table wine (composed of Cabernet Sauvignon, Merlot, and Cabernet Franc) and its white wine (Sauvignon Blanc and Semillon). The quality has clearly matched the price for the red and the white wine represents a good value. The style aimed at here is very Bordeaux in orientation, the white wine resembling a very fine Graves, with a percentage of Semillon blended in for its creamy, soft qualities. The red table wines have a good deal of Cabernet Franc and Merlot blended in and have shown remarkable elegance in 1981, more power and tannin in 1982, a more austere quality in 1983, and the wonderful, opulent, rich, layered quality of a fine Pomerol in 1984. Their label is one of the more interesting in California, with engraved gold etching on the face of the bottle. This winery plans to raise their production up in the neighborhood of 30,000 cases and if the quality continues at the current level they should have no problem selling them. I'm impressed.

LYTTON SPRINGS (SONOMA)

1981 Zinfandel	Sonoma	($9.00)	85
1982 Zinfandel	Sonoma	($9.00)	86
1984 Zinfandel	Sonoma	($10.00)	87

Lytton Springs remains faithful, despite sagging sales of Zinfandel, to its belief that high-quality Zinfandel can be made. I can offer no objections since the wines made here, if lacking elegance and a bit of finesse, show the power and richness Zinfandel can achieve in the best vintages. These are dense in color, highly extracted, tannic, bold, peppery, rich wines that are powerful, robust, and mouth-filling. The 1984 is the best of this impressive trio. They would be best consumed within the first 6–7 years of their lives.

MCDOWELL VALLEY VINEYARDS (MENDOCINO)

1983 Cabernet Sauvignon	McDowell Valley	($10.00)	78
1983 Chardonnay	McDowell Valley	($12.00)	67
1984 Chardonnay	McDowell Valley	($12.00)	82
1985 French Colombard	McDowell Valley	($4.99)	84
1984 Fumé Blanc	McDowell Valley	($8.99)	83
1981 Syrah	McDowell Valley	($9.99)	75

McDowell Valley Vineyards, with its distinctive label, was founded in 1978 and production has risen to 70,000 cases a year. Prices are moderate and the quality somewhat standard. The Syrah, which the winery tends to promote, is rather tart, lean, and not particularly interesting. The 1984 Chardonnay was pleasant and fruity with some oak, but the 1983 showed a great deal of oxidation and an overly oaked, flat character. The 1983 Cabernet Sauvignon is straightforward and supple, with some varietal character but little complexity. The winery also tends to make a good French Colombard, of which the 1985 is extremely aromatic, crisp, fruity, and an absolute delight to drink as an apéritif. Overall, this winery seems to do a much better job with its white wines, particularly the French Colombard and Sauvignon Blanc (which they call Fumé Blanc), than its reds.

MANZANITA (NAPA)

1982 Cabernet Sauvignon	Napa	($14.00)	85
1984 Chardonnay	Napa	($14.00)	87

This tiny winery specializes in both Chardonnay and Cabernet and as of 1986 the production was only 1,600 cases. My first impressions of the wine have been quite positive. The 1982 Cabernet Sauvignon is a densely colored, tannic yet well-balanced wine that shows the potential to improve and soften for at least 5–6 years. The 1984 Chardonnay has an attractive marriage of fruit and oak, and buttery, lemony flavors balanced well by acidity. It is too soon to know if the winery will be able to consistently produce wines of this quality, but the debut releases look hopeful.

MARK WEST VINEYARDS (SONOMA)

1985 Chardonnay	Russian River Valley	($12.00)	75
1980 Chardonnay Vintner's Library Selection		($12.00)	55
1984 Gewürztraminer	Russian River Valley	($7.99)	80

Mark West Winery has a reputation for producing some of California's better Gewürztraminer; however, having been weaned on the Gewürztraminers from Alsace, I am not a great fan of what they call Gewürztraminer in California. The wine Mark West produces, while called Gewürztraminer, tends to lack the varietal character one finds in those from Alsace. It is, however, a crisp, fruity, slightly sweet but well-balanced wine that is an enjoyable beverage. The Chardonnays on the other hand have not been terribly impressive. The 1980, re-released by the winery, has an old, moldy, oxidized taste that hardly resembles

Chardonnay. The 1985 is flat, light golden in color, with one-dimensional fruit, and is lacking in freshness and varietal character.

MARKHAM WINERY (NAPA)

1979 Cabernet Sauvignon Yountville Vyd.	Napa	($9.99)	74
1980 Cabernet Sauvignon Markham Vyd.	Napa	($10.99)	75
1983 Chardonnay	Napa	($12.00)	80
1984 Gamay Blanc	Napa	($5.99)	83
1983 Sauvignon Blanc	Napa	($7.99)	68
1984 Sauvignon Blanc	Napa	($7.99)	80

The Markham wines have not done well in comparative peer group tastings I have held. The two Cabernets I found abrasively tannic, and while fairly deep in color, they seem to be gambles in my opinion since they are not showing much charm or fruit at the present. In addition, the 1979 shows the rather vegetal, weedy character that one finds in entirely too many California wines whether they be Cabernet, Merlot, or Pinot Noir. The 1983 Sauvignon Blanc is now oxidized and drying out. The 1984 would be a better bet for drinking over the next 12 months. It again proves the fact that California white wines often fade incredibly fast after bottling. One wine I do like from this winery is the Gamay Blanc, a sort of pale blush wine with surprising character and very appealing dry flavors, with a floral, fruity nose. Prices here are moderately high, especially given the record of quality.

LOUIS M. MARTINI (NAPA)

1980 Barbera	California	($5.79)	72
1982 Burgundy	Calfornia	($4.99)	70
1982 Cabernet Sauvignon	North Coast	($7.50)	74
1981 Cabernet Sauvignon La Loma	Napa	($15.00)	84
1980 Cabernet Sauvignon Monte Rosso	Sonoma	($16.00)	86

1978 Cabernet Sauvignon Sp. Sel.	Napa	($9.00)	86
1984 Chardonnay	North Coast	($7.50)	84
1983 Chardonnay Los Vinedos	Sonoma	($10.00)	84
1983 Chardonnay Vineyard Selection	Napa	($12.00)	82
1983 Pinot Noir	Napa	($6.99)	65
1980 Pinot Noir Las Amigas	Napa	($9.99)	73
1983 Merlot	North Coast	($6.00)	72
1980 Merlot Private Reserve	Napa	($7.50)	84
N.V. Moscato Sparkling Wine	California	($5.99)	87
1983 Zinfandel	North Coast	($5.99)	72

This well-known winery's products can be found in every market in America. The strength of Martini has always been its red wines— some old vintages of Cabernet Sauvignon and Barbera from the '50s and '60s can still be marvelous today. The style produced here is very light by northern California standards, and my notes also show a surprising inconsistency since the mid-'70s. Yet in certain vintages Martini's Barbera can still be one of California's best wine buys. (For example, the 1979 is very, very good, the 1980 quite mediocre.) The other two great bargains here include the Special Selection Cabernet Sauvignon—the 1978 is fully mature, rich, cedary, and supple—and the Chardonnay from the Los Vinedos Vineyard of which the current release, the 1983, is fresh, lively, and filled with fruit. Martini has two single-vineyard Cabernet Sauvignons that also merit attention, although they are not bargains. The La Loma from Napa Valley and the Monte Rosso from Sonoma are Martini's two richest, densest-colored wines, meant to take at least 10 years of aging. My notes have consistently shown a preference for the richer, more complex Monte Rosso over the La Loma. If you visit the winery, be sure to ask for Martini's remarkably vibrant, fruity, flowery, absolutely delicious sparkling Moscato, which can only be purchased there. One wishes he would make much more of this wonderful wine. Over recent vintages, the other wines here (particularly the feeble Pinot Noirs) have been con-

sistently dull, very light, somewhat oxidized, and too often dominated
by the smell of redwood. However, chosen carefully, Martini's wines,
particularly the Special Selections, can offer considerable rapport in
quality/price.

PAUL MASSON VINEYARDS (SANTA CLARA)

1981 Cabernet Sauvignon	California	($5.49)	69
1982 Cabernet Sauvignon	Sonoma	($6.49)	73
1984 Chardonnay	Monterey	($10.00)	77
1984 Emerald Dry	California	($3.25)	74
1984 Sauvignon Blanc Pinnacles	Monterey	($5.99)	80

Paul Masson Winery, located in Monterey, produces a staggering
8,000,000 cases of wine. Owned by the Seagrams Wine Co., the prices
range from inexpensive to around $10 for their top-of-the-line Char-
donnays and sparkling wines. The quality has improved somewhat
with the inauguration of their best lots of wine, which appear under
the Pinnacles Estate Selections. In addition, in 1983 they began to
buy their Cabernet Sauvignon from growers in Sonoma County. The
wines tend to have very light-intensity flavors, unfocused varietal
character, and often rather soft, slightly sweet flavors. The proprietary
wine, Emerald Dry, is a slightly sweet but fresh, very light, casual
wine. The Chardonnays have tasted like some sort of generic white
table wine, totally lacking varietal character, which is somewhat
amazing given the fact that they come from Monterey, where splendid
Chardonnay grapes can be produced. The Sauvignon Blancs have
been up and down in quality, and are often very herbaceous and
green. The Cabernet Sauvignons, under the California appellation,
tend to be rather cooked and pruny, not bad, but not good either. The
1982 Cabernet Sauvignon shows an increase in quality; although it is
very light and watery, it does have simple, fruity flavors. The sparkling
wines are generally sweet, flabby, and terribly uninteresting. One
can't question the commercial success of operations like this, but the
quality level of the wines is hardly inspirational.

MASTANTUONO WINERY (SAN LUIS OBISPO)

1981 Zinfandel Centennial	San Luis Obispo	($20.00)	?
1981 Zinfandel Dusi		($9.49)	72

This winery produces a whole range of California wines, but the only ones I have tasted are the Zinfandels, which are some of the heaviest, densest, richest, most tannic Zinfandels made in California. Moreover, they have very little complexity and are often raisiny and extremely tiring to drink after one or two sips. The $20 1981 Zinfandel Centennial is a particularly heavy-handed, thick wine that one should approach as a port-type wine rather than a dry table wine. Production is claimed to be around 8,000 cases.

MATANZAS CREEK WINERY (SONOMA)

1983 Chardonnay	Sonoma	($12.00)	88
1984 Chardonnay	Sonoma	($15.00)	86
1983 Chardonnay Estate	Sonoma	($12.00)	90
1984 Chardonnay Estate	Sonoma	($18.00)	87
1983 Merlot	Sonoma	($11.99)	81
1984 Merlot	Sonoma	($12.50)	89
1984 Sauvignon Blanc	Sonoma	($11.99)	87

This winery, with a tiny production of only 6,000 cases, has a well-deserved reputation for producing some of California's greatest Chardonnays and certainly one of its very finest Sauvignon Blancs. The Chardonnays come in two types, one made from purchased grapes in Sonoma, the other an estate-bottled Chardonnay. They are brilliant examples of marrying the wonderful, opulent, ripe Chardonnay fruit obtained in California's best vineyards with toasty oak, yet are balanced beautifully by crisp acidity. The Estate always seems to be a little richer and longer. The 1983s are superb, the 1984s slightly less so, but still excellent and well worth a special trip to find. The 1984 Sauvignon Blanc is loaded with wonderful fruit, good acidity, and a lushness that one rarely finds in this wine. The 1983 Sauvignon Blanc, which should now be drunk up, was one of the greatest Sauvignon

Blancs I have ever tasted from California. The red wines here have always lagged behind the quality of the whites. Interestingly, the Cabernet Sauvignon has now been dropped from the winery's offerings. The Merlots have shown steady improvement, the 1983 being angular but with moderately intense, supple fruit. The 1984 looks to be a real winner since winemaker David Ramey seems to have learned his lessons well by working in Pomerol with Christian Moueix. The 1984 Merlot is a wonderfully opulent, ripe, fleshy-textured wine with super depth and remarkable appeal. Now that some of California's finest white wines are produced here, it looks as if their Merlot will enter the top league and put Matanzas Creek on the map for top-quality red wine as well.

MAYACAMAS VINEYARDS (NAPA)

1978 Cabernet Sauvignon	California	($18.00)	87
1980 Cabernet Sauvignon	California	($18.00)	85
1981 Cabernet Sauvignon	California	($18.00)	83
1982 Cabernet Sauvignon	California	($18.00)	88
1983 Chardonnay	California	($16.00)	85
1984 Sauvignon Blanc	California	($10.00)	85

Mayacamas is one of Napa's oldest wineries, having been originally founded in 1889 and resurrected by the Travers family in 1941. The reputation of this house has been built on California's longest-lived Cabernet Sauvignon, a wine that ages as slowly as the great Latour in Pauillac. A vertical tasting attended recently showed such wines as 1968, 1970, and 1974 still evolving, the last vintage not yet close to being ready to drink. Recent vintages have performed less spectacularly than such greats as the 1974, 1973, and 1968, but one always wonders (when tasting this wine) if its true personality and flavor intensity are really showing through since it is such a notoriously slow starter. Of the recent vintages, certainly the 1982 looks like a big winner, but it should not be drunk until the mid-1990s. It has more accessibility than most Mayacamas Cabernets, while the 1981 seems particularly hard, backward, and without the inner core of strength and muscle this wine normally exhibits. The unreleased 1984, tasted from cask, looked to be a pretty stunning wine, with all the muscle and tannin as well as the opulence a great Napa Cabernet should have. The Chardonnays are also remarkably slow developers. The 1975 remains in healthy condition, proof that not every California Chardonnay begins to fall apart after 3 or 4 years. It remains one of the greatest Chardonnays I have ever tasted. Recent vintages have not shown the same character, but then, I always ask myself, am I drinking them too soon? The Sauvignon Blanc is married nicely with toasty, spicy oak, shows good fruit, and seems to be the only Mayacamas wine that one must drink in its first 4 or 5 years. One should also keep an eye out for the late-harvest Zinfandel that this winery occasionally makes. It can be the best example of late-harvest Zinfandel produced in California.

MAZZOCCO VYDS. (SONOMA)

1985 Chardonnay	Sonoma	($12.50)	87
1985 Chardonnay River Lane Vyd.	Alexander Vly.	($16.50)	90

These debut releases mark an auspicious beginning for this winery. Both Chardonnays are excellent examples of the barrel-fermented, complex, toasty school of winemaking. They have crisp acidity, surprisingly low alcohol, authoritative varietal character, and gobs of flavor. The River Lane Vyd. is longer on the palate and has a wonderful bouquet. An impressive newcomer to the California wine scene.

MERRY VINTNERS (SONOMA)

1984 Chardonnay	Sonoma	($12.00)	85

This brand new winery is specializing in Chardonnay and everyone is waiting with great anticipation because the winemaker here is the former star winemaker for Matanzas Creek's wonderful Chardonnays (as well as those of Mount Eden). When Merry Edwards makes wine, people take notice. Her first Chardonnay, the 1984, while good, hardly showed her formidable abilities; I expect one will have to wait for the release of the 1985 to see all her talents displayed in the wine.

MILANO WINERY (MENDOCINO)

1983 Chardonnay	Sonoma-Mendocino	($9.99)	82
1984 Chardonnay	Mendocino	($9.99)	83

1982 Johannisberg Riesling Select Late-Harvest   ($25.00)   90

The small Milano Winery has built its production up to 10,000 cases and while they run the gamut of major California varietals—Cabernet Sauvignon, Zinfandel, Pinot Noir, Gewürztraminer, Sauvignon Blanc —I have been most impressed with their Chardonnay and Trockenbeerenauslese-styled Late-Harvest Riesling. Their Chardonnays tend to be lush, intense, fairly oaky, but rich and soft, and delicious if drunk within the first 2–3 years after the vintage. The 1982 Johannisberg Riesling was fabulous, with great intensity of fruit and a very intense bouquet of honey, caramel, and brown sugar and baked apples. It is extremely sweet, so be forewarned. Their Cabernets are disappointing.

MIRASSOU VINEYARD (SANTA CLARA)

1980 Blanc de Blancs	Monterey	($12.00)	78
1981 Blanc de Noir	Monterey	($12.00)	82
1981 Brut Champagne	Monterey	($12.00)	58
1982 Brut Champagne	Monterey	($12.00)	82
1982 Cabernet Sauvignon Harvest Reserve	Napa	($10.49)	85
1984 Chardonnay Harvest Reserve	Monterey	($10.50)	80
1984 Fumé Blanc Harvest Reserve	Monterey	($7.50)	72
1984 White Burgundy	Monterey	($4.99)	84
1985 White Burgundy	Monterey	($4.99)	84
1981 Zinfandel Harvest Reserve	Monterey	($9.00)	80

The Mirassou Winery is one of the great old historic wineries in California, having been founded in 1854. It remains family-owned in a time when wineries this size (300,000+ cases) are being gobbled up by large corporations. The quality of the wines here ranges from good to occasionally below average. One of the great buys offered by Mirassou has consistently been their white burgundy, a wine made from Pinot Blanc grown in Monterey County. It has been a success in every vintage I have tried, with the 1984 and 1985 fresh, loaded with fruit and broad flavors, and, at under $6 a bottle, unquestionably a "best buy." The top wines are called Harvest Reserve and the Chardonnays have tended to be rather oaky and buttery, with a certain earthy character. In certain vintages they have turned out slightly thin and vegetal. The Fumé Blanc tends to be very vegetal and smoky, but is certainly interesting. Among the red wines, the Cabernets have been persistent disappointments, extremely herbaceous and green and rather unpleasant to drink. After decades of drawing their grapes from Monterey for Cabernet, the Mirassous in 1982 began to put their Harvest Reserves under a Napa appellation and the 1982 Cabernet Sauvignon is their best Cabernet in memory. The winery also dabbles a bit with Zinfandel, which tends to be very high in alcohol, rich, lush, and intense (as the 1981 is). The winery has also made some Pinot Noir, a rather big wine but again painfully green and herbaceous. Sparkling wines are also part of the huge stable of offerings at Mirassou—I have had remarkably thin and again vegetal-tasting wines as well as rather odd, unidentifiable-smelling sparkling wines. However, the 1982 Brut Champagne and 1981 Blanc de Noir seem to be harbingers of better and more interesting sparkling wines. We shall see with the release of their 1983s. Many wine consumers tend to dismiss this winery as not making serious wine, but they can do very well with certain varietals; their decision to go to Napa for their Cabernet Sauvignon can only be looked upon as a positive step in the right direction.

ROBERT MONDAVI WINERY (NAPA)

1982 Cabernet Sauvignon	Napa	($12.00)	82
1978 Cabernet Sauvignon Reserve	Napa	($52.00)	91
1979 Cabernet Sauvignon Reserve	Napa	($35.95)	86
1980 Cabernet Sauvignon Reserve	Napa	($29.95)	87
1981 Cabernet Sauvignon Reserve	Napa	($29.95)	87
1982 Cabernet Sauvignon Reserve	Napa	($29.95)	83
1984 Chardonnay	Napa	($12.00)	82
1984 Chardonnay Reserve	Napa	($22.00)	91

1984 Fumé Blanc	Napa	($10.00)	83
1983 Fumé Blanc Reserve	Napa	($15.00)	86
1984 Moscato d'Oro	Napa	($5.99)	84
1980 Pinot Noir Reserve	Napa	($16.95)	84
1981 Pinot Noir Reserve	Napa	($17.95)	86
1982 Pinot Noir Reserve	Napa	($17.95)	86

It's hard to believe that Robert Mondavi only started his winery in 1966. It seems like he has been around forever since he has become an American institution and certainly one of the greatest influences on the California wine scene. There are those who often find some trivial matter to criticize him for, but looking at what he has accomplished, it is hard to find fault with anything he has done, with the possible exception of the bold pricing policy established here. The quality of his wines at the reserve level is usually outstanding, and many of the regular bottlings, while more commercial in orientation, are still very drinkable, well-made wines with which one is rarely disappointed. The production at his Oakville winery, pictured on the label, is up to 300,000 cases, with over one million cases produced at his plant in Woodbridge. Yet, most people tend to think that the Robert Mondavi Winery is one of those small, quality-conscious, boutique Napa Valley wineries. Needless to say, his marketing staff has promoted the right image. As for his wines, certainly his Fumé Blanc Reserve, made in a rich, opulent, oaky, intensely concentrated style, is one of the most unique and greatest wines of its type in California, and with it he has led the way with regard to the potential of the Sauvignon Blanc grape. The Chardonnays—from the regular, rather pleasant but straightforward bottling to the luxuriously rich, buttery, oaky, exotic, reserve bottlings—have been superb in vintages like 1981, 1983, and 1984 where they are truly world-class Chardonnays. They have even tended to last 5–6 years in the bottle, a lot longer than many California Chardonnays. His regular Cabernets have been increasingly dull after a splendid Regular Cabernet in 1974 which today is still drinking beautifully; perhaps one will have to wait for the wonderful regular bottling of 1984, which has not yet been released, to again experience such quality. However, at the reserve level Mondavi does not miss a step. Recent vintages for his reserve Cabernets have been 1971 (still an astonishing wine in its full bloom of maturity); 1974, a rather controversial, minty, chocolatey wine that may not prove to be as great as he predicted; the 1975, an elegant Bordeaux-style wine that is ready to drink; the 1978, a wine that continues to get richer and more complex as it ages and may prove to be one of his greatest successes and the 1981, rich, velvety and complicated. The 1982 is a very minty, light, simple wine that lacks richness and depth. Mondavi can also turn a trick or two with his Pinot Noirs, which he is constantly experimenting with and seems to be moving closer and closer to an elegant, ripe cherry fruitiness married with new, toasty, vanillin oak in such vintages as the 1981 Reserve, a wine remarkably similar to a fine Volnay. Zinfandel was unfortunately dropped by the winery, although they never seemed to give it the attention it deserved. The other wines to look for from Mondavi include a flowery, fruity, seductive Chenin Blanc that is slightly sweet but one of the very best on the market, and his wonderfully fragrant, slightly sweet Moscato d'Oro. Of course, there are many other Mondavi wines, including the generic wines of white and red which are simple and straightforward, but Mondavi has in 20 years established remarkably high quality standards and all the success he has attained seems, in my opinion, well deserved.

MONTEREY VINEYARDS (MONTEREY)

1982 Classic California Red	California	($4.00)	83
1984 Classic California White	California	($3.99–$4.49)	81
1984 Pinot Blanc	Monterey	($4.99)	82

This winery is known mainly for its soundly made red and white table wines called Classic California White and Red. They have consistently represented good value in the market and have been well made in every vintage. The current vintages are not complex wines but show straightforward, fruity flavors, moderately intense concentrations, and clean winemaking. The winery also makes approximately 50,000 cases of varietal wines that seem less impressive than their generics. The 1984 Pinot Blanc is one of the better varietal wines, with clean, stylish, medium-bodied flavors and an interesting bouquet of fruit and mineral scents.

MONTEVINA (AMADOR)

1981 Cabernet Sauvignon Shenandoah Vly. California		($7.49)	83
1985 Fumé Blanc	Amador	($7.99)	85
1984 Semillon	Amador	($6.50)	82
1981 Zinfandel Estate	Amador	($7.99)	84
1984 Zinfandel Montino	Amador	($5.99)	82
1982 Zinfandel Winemaker's Choice	Amador	($9.99)	84

Montevina was one of the first wineries to bring significant attention to Amador County and in particular the Shenandoah Valley viticultural area. The wines have tended to be very realistically priced and are often good values. The light, fruity, Beaujolais-style Zinfandel is called Montino and the Winemaker's Choice Zinfandel is a huge, rich, powerful wine with tremendous extract. The winery makes a little bit of Sauvignon Blanc and Semillon (which I have been underwhelmed by) and a Cabernet Sauvignon that tends to be a sleeper pick in their selections. The 1976 and 1978 continue to drink well and the 1981 is a lush, rich, supple wine with plenty of berry fruit and chocolate aromas and scents. At under $8 a bottle, this Cabernet represents a particularly good value. Production has reached 35,000 cases, and their bold, intense, high-extract style of winemaking of the mid-70s has lightened up considerably in the '80s.

MONTICELLO CELLARS (NAPA)

1982 Cabernet Sauvignon Corley Reserve	Napa	($15.00)	80
1982 Cabernet Sauvignon Jefferson Cuvée	Napa	($12.00)	76
1983 Cabernet Sauvignon Jefferson Cuvée	Napa	($14.00)	90
1984 Chardonnay Estate	Napa	($14.00)	85
1984 Chardonnay Jefferson Reserve	Napa	($15.00)	88
1985 Chevrier Blanc	Napa	($6.99)	86

1984 Pinot Noir	Napa	($9.99)	87

1985 Sauvignon Blanc	Napa	($6.99)	84

This winery, which has been built to look like the famous Virginia home of Thomas Jefferson, was founded in 1980 and seems to be showing dramatic improvement in the quality of its wines with each passing vintage. The unreleased 1984 Reserve Cabernet Sauvignon looks to be the best wine yet from Monticello Cellars and the 1984 Pinot Noir from Napa, of which only 175 cases were made, a wonderfully complex, rich, berry-fruited wine with a remarkable similarity to a top Volnay with its sweet, broad, round flavors. The 1982 Cabernets, both the Corley Reserve and the Jefferson Cuvée, hardly do justice to the memory of Thomas Jefferson. They are tart, lean, angular wines with good color, rather hard tannins, but little personality or charm. While the same can be said for the 1984 Sauvignon Blanc, the 1984 Chardonnays are both very good, with a toasty, buttery richness, good balance, and lively fruit. The 1985 Sauvignon Blanc is much better than the 1984, and the 1985 Chevrier, with its 80% Semillon, a very interesting wine of character and elegance. The newly released 1983 Cabernet Sauvignon is superb, with at least a decade of life ahead of it, and a barrel sample of the 1984 Cabernet Sauvignon Reserve looked even better. This is surely a winery to watch.

MORGAN WINERY (MONTEREY)

1985 Chardonnay	Monterey	($12.99)	90

1984 Chardonnay	Monterey	($12.99)	88

1985 Sauvignon Blanc St. Vrain	Alex. Vly.	($8.99)	85

This small, excellent winery of 5,000 cases is apparently making only two wines, Chardonnay and Sauvignon Blanc. The first releases were in 1982, the same year the winery was founded. Winemaker Dan Lee has had plenty of top-notch experience at both Jekel Vineyards and Durney Vineyards. The 1984 Chardonnay is a wonderfully deep-flavored, richly scented, toasty, buttery wine with layers of fruit, good acidity for balance, and a wonderfully long, full-bodied finish. The 1985 is very similarly styled but tasted even more complex. The 1985 Sauvignon Blanc St. Vrain is fresh and lively, with clean, fruity aromas and a dry, medium-bodied feel. This would appear to be a winery to keep an eye out for.

J. W. MORRIS WINERY (SONOMA)

1982 Cabernet Sauvignon	Alexander Vly.	($6.49)	82
1983 Cabernet Sauvignon	Alexander Vly.	($6.59)	75
1984 Chardonnay	California	($6.49)	84
1983 Port Black Mountain	Sonoma	($10.00)	88
1984 Sauvignon Blanc	Alexander Vly.	($6.49)	85

J. W. Morris is generally associated with its high reputation for California ports. They have been the best produced in California and are often indistinguishable from a top vintage port when placed in blind tastings. The newest release is the 1983, which competes favorably with the excellent 1983 vintage ports from Portugal: dense, tarry, with chocolatey cassis flavors and tremendous power and strength. However, one should not dismiss the varietal wines made here since they are very reasonably priced and offer exceptional value (such as the 1984 Sauvignon Blanc from Alexander Valley, a wonderfully fruity, spicy wine that has impeccable balance). The 1984 Chardonnay shows plenty of ripe fruit, some toasty oak, and clean, well-defined varietal character. Among the recent Cabernets, the 1983 is too weedy and lacks true varietal character, though it has plenty of depth; however, the 1982 is a much better wine, with a supple, lush fruitiness and straightforward appeal. These wines should be drunk in the first 5 years of their lives.

MOUNT EDEN VINEYARDS (SANTA CLARA)

1982 Cabernet Sauvignon	Santa Cruz Mts.	($18.00)	78
1983 Chardonnay	Santa Cruz Mts.	($20.00)	90
1984 Chardonnay	Santa Cruz Mts.	($20.00)	90
1982 Pinot Noir	Santa Cruz Mts.	($16.00)	81
1983 Pinot Noir	Santa Cruz Mts.	($15.95)	84

Mount Eden Winery has always had a cult following for some of California's most spectacular Chardonnays, which are ripe, buttery, toasty, and very much in the full-bodied, barrel-fermented style of winemaking. The Pinot Noir has, in my opinion, been somewhat overrated, but some of the vintages can be particularly aromatic, spicy, smoky, or at the very least interesting, if not always in total harmony. I have had less experience with the Cabernet Sauvignons, but the 1982 (not a good vintage in this area) is quite herbaceous, soft, and obviously overpriced. This is a winery that has gone through a tremendous change of winemakers and managers since it was founded in 1961. The production of 3,500 cases does not go far, but I would seek out with great enthusiasm any of the Chardonnays produced here, even the secondary Chardonnay that is sold under the MEV label from purchased grapes from the Ventana Vineyard in Monterey County.

MOUNT VEEDER WINERY (NAPA)

1981 Cabernet Sauvignon Mt. Veeder Vyds.	Napa	($14.00)	86

1984 Chardonnay	Napa	($14.00)	85

This tiny winery has always had a good reputation for its deeply scented, densely colored, tannic, rather long-lived Cabernet Sauvignons. The winery changed hands in 1982 when it was sold. They have continued to produce Cabernet in the same tannic, ageworthy style and have added Chardonnay to their line of wines. The 1984 Chardonnay shows a toasty, barrel-fermented character, with nice tropical scents of pineapples and ripe, appley fruit. Its wonderful aroma followed through on the palate. The 1981 Cabernet Sauvignon, which should age for at least 10 or more years, has a rich blackcurrant aroma, an oaky, woody component, and plenty of firm tannins in the finish.

MURPHY-GOODE (SONOMA)

1985 Chardonnay	Alexander Valley	($9.99)	85

1985 Fumé Blanc	Alexander Valley	($7.49)	85

The debut releases from this new winery exhibit flashy varietal fruit, good balance, a sense of style, and are quite captivating, charming wines.

NAPA CREEK WINERY (NAPA)

1981 Cabernet Sauvignon	Napa	($12.00)	84
1984 Merlot	Napa	($12.00)	86

This winery was founded in 1980 by Jack Schulze, who had worked in administration for Beringer. The wines here are all made from purchased grapes in Napa Valley and the reds seem much stronger than the handful of whites I have tried, including the 1981 Chardonnay and 1981 Fumé Blanc, both of which were oxidized and flat. However, the 1984 Merlot is wonderfully fleshy, with a toffee, chocolatey, rich bouquet and lush opulent flavors that will get plenty of attention from those who enjoy rich, intense wines. The 1981 Cabernet Sauvignon still has a good bit of tannin left, but has an attractive, smoky, earthy, blackcurrant aroma and medium-bodied flavors. This winery has only a handful of vintages out and, though they have been fairly reliable for the reds and less so for the whites, it is hard to get a feel for what the overall quality level is likely to be. The 1984 Merlot is a very positive sign.

NEWTON VINEYARDS (NAPA)

1981 Cabernet Sauvignon	Napa	($12.50)	84
1982 Cabernet Sauvignon	Napa	($12.50)	87
1983 Chardonnay	Napa	($16.00)	87
1984 Chardonnay	Napa	($16.00)	87
1982 Merlot	Napa	($12.50)	87
1984 Sauvignon Blanc	Napa	($10.00)	82

The Newton Vineyard, founded in 1978 by one of the former partners of Sterling Vineyards, is clearly trying to stylize its wines in a French fashion with barrel-fermented, rich Chardonnays, oaky Sauvignons, and tightly knit, well-made, potentially very promising Cabernet Sauvignons and Merlots. The Chardonnays have been very good for those who prefer the toasty, oaky style of wine since the wines have plenty of aggressive oak but also plenty of flavor, depth, and concentration. The 1984 is a bit more restrained than the 1983. The Sauvignon Blancs have been similarly styled and are among the more unique Sauvignons produced in California, with an oaky character and a similarity to the richer, oaky style of white Graves wines. The Cabernets have tended to be very closed and tight, so their ratings may sometimes be a bit ungenerous given their obvious potential for 7–10 years of further evolution and improvement in the bottle. Both the 1981 and 1982 show good acidity, plenty of spicy oak, and rich, berrylike flavors tightly integrated with plenty of tannin and acidity. The 1982 is lusher and riper, but both wines need until the end of this decade to reach maturity. The 1982 Merlot is one of the best I have tasted from Napa, yet needs until 1988–1990 to reach full maturity.

NEYERS WINERY (NAPA)

1982 Cabernet Sauvignon	Napa	($11.99)	78
1985 Chardonnay	Napa	($12.00)	85
1984 Chardonnay	Napa	($12.00)	85

This small winery, founded by Bruce Neyers and his wife Barbara, has turned out good to excellent Chardonnays, but the Cabernets have been entirely too weedy to get high marks. The 1983 Chardonnay is a Napa classic, with wonderfully rich, well-knit, stylish flavors and just the right amount of oak. The 1984 is a bit restrained and slightly lighter but still very good. The Cabernets on the other hand seem overly herbaceous and weedy, though well made, fruity, and medium-bodied. The prices seem realistic. Production has inched up toward 4,000 cases but should remain small since Bruce Neyers continues to do most of the marketing work as a full-time employee of the Joseph Phelps Winery.

NIEBAUM-COPPOLA ESTATES (NAPA)

1978 Rubicon	Napa	($30.00)	88
1979 Rubicon	Napa	($30.00)	90
1980 Rubicon	Napa	($30.00)	90

This winery, founded in 1978, is dedicated to producing luxury-priced, proprietary wines from blends of Cabernet Sauvignon, Cabernet Franc, and Merlot from an old established vineyard in Napa Valley. It is owned by the famous movie producer/director Francis Ford Coppola, who has said that he wants his wines to last 100 years. They are certainly impressive wines, rich, full-bodied, intense, with power and character. The 1979 was released first and has a rich bouquet with a tarry, black cherry fruit note. It is very concentrated, full-bodied, and while drinkable now will keep for at least 8–10 more years. The unreleased 1978 is an even bigger wine, still a little rough around the edges, but loaded with black cherry fruit, cedar and tar scents. There is enough tannin and acidity to easily last another decade. The 1980 looks to be the best of the first three vintages of Rubicon; rich yet graceful, powerful, but with finesse, it should be quite long-lived. Prices have been high, but with a production of 3,500 cases and winemaking that seems to spare no expense and make no compromises, these dramatic, unique, distinctive wines will attain quite a following by wine enthusiasts.

OPUS ONE (NAPA)

1979 Opus One	Napa	($55.00)	87
1980 Opus One	Napa	($55.00)	89
1981 Opus One	Napa	($55.00)	87
1982 Opus One	Napa	($55.00)	90

No wine has received more publicity in the last ten years in California than the Opus One, a joint venture between Napa's famous Robert Mondavi and Bordeaux's equally famous and flamboyant Baron Philippe de Rothschild. The first vintages have been made at Robert Mondavi's winery in Napa, although plans have been proposed for construction of a separate facility to house Opus One. The price of the wine has been criticized throughout the country, but the quality of the wine has ranged from excellent to outstanding. The best vintage to exemplify the combination of the rich Napa Valley grapes and the broad winemaking experience of the French has been the 1982, an elegant yet still powerful, rich wine that shows impeccable winemaking and looks to be the best Opus One to date. The 1980 is very Californian in style, having plenty of power and richness but also plenty of depth. The 1979 and 1981 are lighter-styled wines with a little bit less concentration, but still very good (and very pricy as well). In spite of the prices asked for the wines and the hoopla surrounding them, it remains to be seen if these wines can fully live up to all of their advance publicity. However, the quality has been very good to excellent and reports are that both the 1983 and 1984 are even better than the outstanding 1982. Whatever people may think, this operation has generated a tremendous amount of attention for the California wine business.

PARDUCCI WINE CELLARS (MENDOCINO)

1982 Cabernet Sauvignon	Mendocino	($6.99)	84
1980 Cabernet Sauvignon 50th Anniv.	Mendocino	($7.99)	84
1984 Chardonnay	Mendocino	($7.50)	84
1983 Chardonnay Cellarmaster	Mendocino	($11.00)	84
1985 French Colombard	Mendocino	($4.49)	83
1985 Gewürztraminer	Mendocino	($6.99)	78
1978 Petite Sirah Cellarmaster	Mendocino	($7.50)	84
1985 Sauvignon Blanc	Mendocino	($6.49)	85

The Parducci clan have long fought for recognition of Mendocino as one of the better viticultural areas of California. The winery, founded in 1932, has grown by leaps and bounds to produce over 300,000 cases of wine. The style of the wine here rarely disappoints the taster—they are fruity, with their varietal character well displayed, are cleanly made, and always enjoyable. Their Sauvignon Blanc, which often suggests that a slight amount of residual sugar is still present, is wonderfully fruity, round, lush, and altogether captivating. The same can be said for their very aromatic, off dry French Colombard, one of the best of its type made in California for this grape varietal and a lot more appealing than most consumers have realized. The Chardonnays tend to be mostly fruit, are straightforward in style, always well made, clean, with no oxidation and no overly oaky character. The Gewürztraminer has always been rather lean and insufficient to my taste, but the Cabernet Sauvignons are fat, grapy, immensely fruity, delicious wines that all seem to be drunk while young, though a 1970 drunk last year showed that they can age surprisingly well. Cellarmaster selections are meant to be the pick of the bunch from this winery. By no means ignore the Petite Sirah from Parducci, a peppery, densely colored wine in which Parducci seems to extract more fruit than tannin, making it wonderfully appealing but also capable of aging for

7–8 years. I find little to criticize from this winery, which makes remarkably sound yet interesting, fruity wines that have immense crowd appeal and are sold at realistic prices.

PAT PAULSEN VINEYARDS (SONOMA)

1982 Cabernet Sauvignon	Sonoma	($10.99)	72
1983 Chardonnay	Sonoma	($12.00)	80
1984 Muscat Canelli	Sonoma	($8.99)	85
1983 Sauvignon Blanc	Sonoma	($10.95)	82

It is no joke that Pat Paulsen, the well-known comedian, runs this vineyard that he founded in 1980. After selling grapes to Chateau St. Jean for several years he decided to go on his own. His best wine, in my opinion, is the wonderfully fragrant, delicate, perfumed, off dry Muscat Canelli, which I find ideal as an apéritif. Drink it within the first several years of its life. The Chardonnays tend to be a bit weedy and lean and too acidic or overacidified, whichever the case might be. This seems to have been a common component of both the 1983 and 1982. The 1983 Sauvignon Blanc shows wonderful crispness and freshness, good varietal character, but again tends toward the austere, lean style of winemaking. The Cabernet Sauvignon is quite herbaceous and though fruity would appeal only to those who like a strong vegetal character in their wines.

ROBERT PECOTA WINERY (NAPA)

1983 Cabernet Sauvignon	Napa	($10.00)	80
1984 Chardonnay	Napa	($8.99)	84
1984 Chardonnay Barrel-Fermented	Napa	($8.49)	82
1985 Moscato di Andrea	Napa	($8.00)	85
1985 Sauvignon Blanc	Napa	($9.00)	79

This winery is located in the very northern end of Napa Valley in Calistoga and makes one of the fruitiest and loveliest apéritif wines, Moscato di Andrea, which explodes from the glass with a wonderfully perfumed, flowery bouquet. It is soft, with a slightly fruity, sweet taste on the palate balanced nicely with wonderful freshness and acidity. This is clearly the best wine in an otherwise decent group of wines that sell for realistic prices. The two Chardonnays offer different textures and flavors. The barrel-fermented is toasty, oaky, and has barely enough fruit to hold up to the oak. Drink it now. The other 1984 Chardonnay is lively, fruity with a lemony, citrusy character that is appealing. The Cabernet Sauvignon is straightforward, with lots of berry fruit, soft tannins, and a medium-bodied format. It doesn't have much complexity and is made to be drunk over the next several years. The winery used to make a wonderfully aromatic, fruity French Colombard and hopefully they have not discontinued it, although I have not seen it since the excellent 1983 vintage. Sauvignon Blanc is a winner here, and if you should see the 1985, be sure to drink it within the first several years of its life because this is not a type of wine that ages at all.

J. PEDRONCELLI WINERY (SONOMA)

1982 Cabernet Sauvignon	Sonoma	($6.99)	82
1980 Cabernet Sauvignon Reserve	Sonoma	($13.99)	86
1984 Chardonnay	Sonoma	($8.99)	82
1984 Sauvignon Blanc	Sonoma	($5.99)	84
1985 Zinfandel Rosé	Sonoma	($4.99)	83

As often happens, the wines of the J. Pedroncelli Winery seem to be consistently underrated by wine writers and wine consumers alike. This winery has a surprising number of good wines in its stable, from its Zinfandel Rosé, one of the best blush wines on the market, to its Cabernet Sauvignon Reserve, which can compete with some of the best in Napa. The 1980 in particular shows wonderful ripeness and richness, with plenty of tannin and at least another 5–6 years aging potential. The regular 1982 Cabernet Sauvignon is a straightforward wine with a lot of berry fruit but not much complexity. The Sauvignon Blanc made here tends to be crisp, fruity, clean, and slightly herbaceous, the Chardonnay less consistent, but in vintages like 1984, crisp, slightly toasty, with a pleasant, understated varietal flavor. The winery also produces a range of other wines, from a dull, watery Gamay Beaujolais to a Pinot Noir that is too vegetal and often tart and harsh as well. Nevertheless, for Sauvignon Blanc, Cabernet Sauvignon, and Zinfandel Rosé, and occasionally Chardonnay, Pedroncelli offers very good value for your money.

ROBERT PEPI (NAPA)

1984 Chardonnay	Napa	($9.99)	75
1984 Sauvignon Blanc	Napa	($8.99)	82

Located in Oakville, this winery has stressed both Sauvignon Blanc and Semillon in its line up of wines. The Chardonnay has been somewhat of a disappointment in a couple of vintages that were overly herbaceous, but the 1984 is certainly pleasant, if too understated and innocuous. The 1984 Sauvignon Blanc is crisp, fresh, light, well made, with appealing character. I have not tasted the recent Semillons, but several of the older vintages were certainly soundly made if uninspired wines.

PERRET VINEYARDS (NAPA)

1983 Chardonnay Perret Vineyard	Napa	($15.00)	85
1984 Chardonnay Perret Vineyard	Napa	($15.00)	86

This winery, founded in 1983, is producing approximately 2,000 cases of Chardonnay from the owner's own vineyard in the cool Carneros area of Napa. The wines show that a percentage of the wine is fermented in oak since they have a toasty, buttery character backed up by good acidity and plenty of tropical fruit flavors. The prices are hardly timid, so don't come here to look for values in their Chardonnay; but the quality certainly looks to be good for the first three vintages released by this new winery.

JOSEPH PHELPS VINEYARDS (NAPA)

1981 Cabernet Sauvignon	Napa	($12.00)	80
1982 Cabernet Sauvignon	Napa	($12.00)	?
1981 Cabernet Sauvignon Backus	Napa	($25.00)	84
1983 Cabernet Sauvignon Backus	Napa	($25.00)	87
1981 Cabernet Sauvignon Eisele	Napa	($27.00)	87

1982 Cabernet Sauvignon Eisele	Napa	($28.00)	85
1983 Cabernet Sauvignon Eisele	Napa	($28.00)	88
1981 Cabernet Sauvignon Insignia	Napa	($25.00)	87
1982 Cabernet Sauvignon Insignia	Napa	($28.00)	86
1982 Chardonnay	Napa	($11.95)	78
1983 Chardonnay	Napa	($12.99)	75
1984 Chardonnay Sangiacomo	Sonoma	($14.00)	84
1983 Delice du Semillon	Napa	($15.00)	90
1985 Gewürztraminer	Napa	($8.99)	82
1985 Johannisberg Riesling Late-Harvest	Napa	($25.00)	88
1985 Sauvignon Blanc	Napa	($8.99)	83
1985 Scheurebe Late-Harvest	Napa	($20.00)	87
1979 Syrah	Napa	($10.50)	84
1982 Syrah	Napa	($7.50)	75
1980 Zinfandel	Alex. Vly.	($8.99)	87
1982 Zinfandel	Napa	($8.99)	70
1986 Zinfandel Nuovo	Napa	($5.99)	82

The Joseph Phelps Winery is unquestionably one of the great California wine producers. Since their inception, when much of the wine world praised the winery for its great Late-Harvest white wines, there has been a remarkable succession of both great Late-Harvest Rieslings and, starting in 1974, fabulous Cabernets and every once in a while a sensational Zinfandel. The record in the '70s was one of unparalleled brilliance and consistency. The top-of-the-line Cabernets are all vineyard-designated, including one of the first luxury proprietary red wines launched in California, the Insignia. The other top Cabernets include the fabulously rich, tannic, monumental wine from the Calistoga vineyard of Milton Eisele and, since 1977, the Backus Vineyard designated Cabernet from Napa. So in essence there are four Cabernets offered—the regular, the Eisele Vineyard, Backus Vineyard, and the proprietary luxury blend, Insignia. In addition, there are two Zinfandels, the Napa Valley Zinfandel and the Alexander Valley Zinfandel, of which the latter has been the most interesting and even fabulous in years like 1975, 1976, and 1980. The Phelps Winery in the '70s produced a bevy of great Cabernet Sauvignons that stand out in the history of California winemaking. The 1974 Insignia, 1975 Eisele, 1976 Insignia, 1977 Insignia and Eisele, 1978 Eisele, and 1979 Eisele are all very special wines. Regular Cabernets that were sensational included the 1975 vintage. Despite this fabulous record of success, recent vintages, especially the 1982, have shown a slight drop in quality. However, the 1983s and 1984s from Phelps look to be a return to the top rank, particularly the 1984 red wines. The 1980s were good, the 1981s also good, but the 1982 vintage for this winery was somewhat plagued by problems, for whatever reason. The Backus Vineyard Cabernet Sauvignon was never released because of a technical problem with the wine, the Eisele was somewhat of a disappointment for that particular wine, and the regular Cabernet was fruity and soft but lacking complexity. Even the Insignia is not up to its normal quality. As for the Chardonnays here, this has never been a winery that has greatly impressed me with its ability to make top-notch Chardonnays. The best has generally been the barrel-fermented Chardonnay from Sangiacomo Vineyard in Sonoma, whereas the non-barrel-fermented Schellville tends to be rather straightforward and fruity but lacking complexity. However, if there was a little slump in the early '80s, the Late-Harvest Rieslings and Scheurebes made by this winery have been consistently superb, particularly the Late-Harvest or Select Late-Harvest wines which resemble respectively Beerenauslese and Trockenbeerenauslese wines. They are decadently rich, intense and fragrant, and can challenge the greatest of the German late-harvest sweet wines. In 1983, Phelps added a sweet 1983 Delice, produced from 75% Semillon and 25% Sauvignon Blanc. It is a brilliant achievement and has a frightening resemblance to a great Sauternes. The Sauvignon Blanc here has taken on more complexity and richness with the addition of Semillon, and the Gewürztraminer, a varietal that I find does not do very well in California, can be one of the best made in California. Phelps also has experimented with the true Syrah grape, with mixed results. The 1979 showed some of the peppery, Rhône-like character one would expect, but the 1982 tastes like a dilute Beaujolais with little character and a somewhat stinky nose. All in all, this remains a great winery despite an off year in 1982. The 1984 Cabernets across-the-board are the best overall vintage for Joseph Phelps since 1978. This winery, where production has remained around the 60,000-case level, is certainly one to always take note of.

R. H. PHILLIPS VINEYARD (YOLO)

1983 Cabernet Sauvignon	Yolo	($5.99)	84
N.V. Cabernet Sauvignon/Merlot Night Harvest Cuvée		($5.99)	82
1985 Chardonnay	California	($6.99)	85
1984 Chardonnay Reserve	California	($8.99)	78
1985 Chenin Blanc	Yolo	($4.99)	83
1985 Chenin Blanc Estate	Yolo	($4.99)	84
1984 Sauvignon Blanc	Yolo	($5.99)	82
1985 Sauvignon Blanc/Semillon Night Harvest Cuvée	Yolo	($5.99)	85
1984 Semillon	Yolo	($6.99)	72

The youthful R. H. Phillips Vineyard, founded only in 1983, has 250+ acres of vines in Yolo County. It is making a quick reputation for very good quality wines at honest prices. The white wines here have been sparkling examples of what modern technology can render if one wants to produce wines that are wonderfully fresh, fruity, and easy to drink young. The Sauvignon Blancs have been slightly herbaceous but remarkably fresh and crisp, whereas the Night Harvest Cuvée of Sauvignon Blanc with some Semillon added in has been a winner in every vintage where it has been produced. The 1985 is the best yet, with depth, complexity, crispness, freshness, and loads of fruit. The winery's barrel-aged Semillon has had its fruit covered up by too long a sojourn in oak barrels. The Chardonnays here are also good values, with the 1985 Chardonnay fresh, fruity with light-intensity, appley, buttery fruit, wonderful crispness and freshness, and a soft texture. The 1984 Reserve is a bigger, richer, more oaky wine but lacks the freshness of the 1985. There are two Chenin Blancs usually made, one, the estate-bottled, slightly sweet and the other completely dry. Both have the wonderful flowery fragrance that makes Chenin Blanc so popular; the Phillips Winery seems to be very consistent in successfully turning out these wines. Until recently, I did not know this winery was capable of producing good reds, but the 1983 Cabernet Sauvignon at $6 was quite a bargain, with lush, supple flavors that suggested cassis and a medium-bodied format that was easy to drink. The Night Harvest Cuvée of Cabernet and Merlot, a non-vintage, is a wonderfully fruity, soft, straightforward wine that would be an ideal restaurant wine. R. H. Phillips has yet to establish its reputation nationwide, but this should change once the quality and prices of its wines are better known.

PINE RIDGE WINERY (NAPA)

1980 Cabernet Sauvignon Andrus Reserve	Napa	($35.00)	92
1982 Cabernet Sauvignon Rutherford Cuvée	Napa	($12.00)	78
1983 Cabernet Sauvignon Rutherford Cuvée	Napa	($14.00)	75
1982 Cabernet Sauvignon Stag's Leap	Napa	($14.00)	80
1983 Cabernet Sauvignon Stag's Leap	Napa	($14.00)	72
1983 Chardonnay Oak Knoll Cuvée	Napa	($12.95)	85
1983 Chardonnay Stag's Leap	Napa	($13.49)	81
1983 Merlot	Napa	($12.00)	78

Pine Ridge Winery was founded in 1978 and the moving force behind it has been Gary Andrus who, having had significant training in Bordeaux, has sought a style of wines oriented in the direction of France. There have been some interesting wines here, but they have all, with the exception of the fabulous 1980 Andrus Reserve Cabernet, turned out a little tart, with moderately intense flavors but no real drama or much character. I wish the winery would pursue a more distinctive style rather than playing it safe with technically very well-made wines that do not "sing." Perhaps it will be necessary to wait until 1984 to see more drama and complexity in Pine Ridge's Cabernets since from the cask the 1984s looked consistently very good, with the Rutherford Cuvée and Andrus Reserve potentially outstanding. Pine Ridge's production of 20,000 cases a year also includes a little bit of Sauvignon Blanc blended with some Semillon, and a very delicate, floral Chenin Blanc.

PIPER SONOMA (SONOMA)

1981 Blanc de Noir	Sonoma	($15.99)	84
1982 Blanc de Noir	Sonoma	($14.00)	75
1981 Brut	Sonoma	($16.00)	84
1982 Brut	Sonoma	($20.00)	78
1980 Tête de Cuvée	Sonoma	($30.00)	85
1981 Tête de Cuvée	Sonoma	($25.00)	80

This joint venture, which combines the considerable talents of Rodney Strong, winemaker at Sonoma Vineyards, and the Piper Heidsieck champagne firm, started production with their wholly successful 1980s, including an especially good Tête de Cuvée, a rather complex, toasty wine that seemed to suggest that world-class sparkling wine could be made in California. However, recent releases have not demonstrated the consistency or fulfilled the hope engendered by the earlier wines. The 1981 Tête de Cuvée is remarkably overpriced at $25 a bottle, as was the 1980, but unlike the 1980, the 1981 is rather tart, seemingly less complex and less rich than the 1980. The 1982 Brut and 1982 Blanc de Noir are cleanly made, with small, well-defined bubbles, but taste rather neutral and devoid of much flavor interest, particularly the Blanc de Noir. If these wines are examples of what we are to expect from one of the better producers of sparkling wines, the California sparkling wine industry is in for difficult times since there are much better sparkling wines increasingly available from Italy, Spain, and even France for under $10 with more flavor interest and more character than these bland wines.

PRESTON VINEYARDS (SONOMA)

1985 Chenin Blanc	Dry Creek	($5.99)	84
1985 Sauvignon Blanc Cuvée de Fumé	Dry Creek	($6.99)	84
1984 Sauvignon Blanc Estate	Dry Creek	($8.99)	84
1982 Zinfandel	Sonoma	($6.99)	83
1983 Zinfandel	Sonoma	($6.99)	84
1984 Zinfandel	Sonoma	($7.99)	84

The modest-sized Preston Vineyards, with a production of 12,000 cases, seems to be doing its best job with a wonderfully Loire Valley-like Cuvée de Fumé that sells at a remarkably reasonable price of $6–$7, and a light fragrant Chenin Blanc. All the recent vintages have been very good and this wine often has a character much like a Pouilly-Fumé from France. Curiously, the wine often has a little bit of Chenin Blanc and Semillon added to its Sauvignon Blanc character. It requires drinking up within a couple of years of the vintage. The regular Sauvignon Blanc tends to be rather aggressively herbaceous yet crisp, with good fruit and surprising character. The Zinfandel is straightforward in style, supple, with a lot of rich berry fruit, a little spice and some pepper, but medium-bodied and attractive for drinking within its first 4–5 years of life.

QUAIL RIDGE WINERY (NAPA)

1982 Cabernet Sauvignon	Napa	($14.00)	84
1983 Chardonnay	Napa	($14.00)	72
1984 Chardonnay	Napa	($14.00)	82

This winery, founded in 1978, produces less than 8,000 cases of wine, but the pride and joy of the house has been its barrel-fermented, toasty, buttery Chardonnay, of which the 1980 and 1981 were excellent. The 1982 seemed to fall off in quality and the 1983 was surprisingly flat and uninteresting when tasted. The 1984 looks to be back to form, though not quite at the level of the wonderful 1980 and 1981. The 1982 Cabernet Sauvignon was the first released and while it lacked complexity, it did have an elegant, medium-bodied, blackcurrant taste to it and at least 3–4 years' further longevity.

QUPÉ WINERY (SANTA BARBARA)

1982 Chardonnay	Santa Barbara	($10.00)	74
1983 Chardonnay	Santa Barbara	($10.00)	78
1984 Chardonnay	Santa Barbara	($10.00)	84

This winery's first Chardonnays have clearly made a statement, for they have been almost overbearing in their intense, oaky, rich, butterscotch scents and aromas. I like the fact that a winery is trying to make an individualistic Chardonnay and I like the flavor and intensity this winery is aiming for, but the 1982 tasted surprisingly flat and low in acidity, and the 1983, while having better acidity and a more vigorous feel on the palate, seemed hollow once one fought past the wall of oak. However, the 1984 looks like the toasty, buttery, tropical fruit intensity is sufficiently there with enough depth to balance the tremendous amount of oak in the wine. It may be the best Chardonnay this winery has yet made. The winery is also trying its hand with real Syrah from Paso Robles, but I have not tasted it.

A. RAFANELLI WINERY (SONOMA)

1980 Zinfandel	Sonoma	($6.99)	85

I have not seen a recent vintage of Zinfandel from Rafanelli, but based on the 1980 and several of the vintages that owner/proprietor Americo Rafanelli produced in the mid-'70s, this winery takes its winemaking seriously, aiming for individualistic, distinctive, full-bodied, full-blooded Zinfandels of richness and character. Several of the older vintages tasted, the 1978 in particular, seem to be aging as well as most red wines made in California. A winery to watch, but the production of less than 3,000 cases rarely seems to get beyond the Zinfandel fanatics residing in California.

RAVENSWOOD WINERY (SONOMA)

1983 Cabernet Sauvignon	Sonoma	($12.00)	83
1984 Cabernet Sauvignon	Sonoma	($12.00)	83

1983 Merlot	Sonoma	($12.00)	87
1984 Merlot	Sonoma	($12.00)	90
1982 Zinfandel	Napa	($8.00)	84
1982 Zinfandel Dickerson Vyd.	Napa	($8.00)	84
1984 Zinfandel Dickerson Vyd.	Napa	($9.50)	89
1981 Zinfandel Dry Creek Benchland	Sonoma	($7.99)	86
1984 Zinfandel Old Hill Vyd.	Sonoma	($11.00)	90
1984 Zinfandel Vintner's Blend	Sonoma	($5.99)	87
1981 Zinfandel Vogelsen Vyd.	Sonoma	($9.00)	86
1984 Zinfandel 60% Sonoma, 40% Mendocino		($8.50)	86

Ravenswood, with a production of only 5,000 cases, has been causing quite a bit of talk in wine circles. Winemaker Joel Peterson seems to have the magical touch with both Zinfandel and Merlot. His Cabernet Sauvignon can be good, but it never seems to be a match for his handcrafted, intense, wonderfully ripe and opulent Zinfandels and his Merlots, which seem to get more spectacular with each vintage. Perhaps the best wine made yet by Ravenswood is the 1984 Merlot, a wine of unbelievable richness and stunning opulence that should drink beautifully for its first 7–8 years of life. The 1983 Merlot is also an excellent wine, with an almost gamey, exotic, Rhône-like nose and loaded with luscious berry fruit and a soft, unctuous texture. Of the Zinfandels, it is almost impossible to make a mistake with any of this winery's Zins. They are all densely colored, high in extract, with rich, berrylike flavors of raspberries and cassis, and lush, long textures. They come from different vineyards, but always keep an eye out for the Ravenswood Vintner's Blend, an inexpensive Zinfandel made from purchased grapes. The 1984 might be one of the great wine buys from California. It is one of four super Zinfandels Ravenswood produced in 1984. All in all, it seems like one can hardly make a mistake with a Ravenswood wine since they represent the best of what California should be doing more frequently—producing individualistic, dramatic wines with plenty of personality. Prices can only go up because the demand already exceeds the supply, so move quickly and try the very special wines of Ravenswood, and make a mental note to jump on the 1984s with great enthusiasm as they appear on the market.

MARTIN RAY VINEYARD (SANTA CLARA)

1982 Chardonnay	Santa Cruz Mts.	($15.00)	86
1982 Chardonnay Dutton Ranch	Sonoma	($14.00)	89
1983 Chardonnay Dutton Ranch	Sonoma	($15.00)	68
1981 Pinot Noir Winery Lake	Napa	($14.00)	85

Martin Ray Winery, which was founded in 1946 and run by the famous, late Martin Ray, makes wines that are sought after the country over for their rich, intense flavors. Most of the vineyards are now owned by Mount Eden in nearby Santa Cruz and many of the grapes seem to come from areas to the north in Sonoma and Napa. The 1982 Chardonnays were outstanding for their richness and length; however, the 1983 proved to be a big disappointment, which was particularly surprising since there were a number of outstanding 1983 Chardonnays made from grapes grown on the Dutton Ranch in Sonoma. The 1981 Pinot Noir Winery Lake shows toasty, earthy, exotic scents and should prove pleasing after another several years of aging. I have not recently tasted the Merlot or Cabernet Sauvignon that are being made from Napa Valley grapes. Prices seem high, although future Chardonnays, if they are as good as the 1982s, will certainly justify the prices.

RAYMOND VINEYARD AND CELLAR (NAPA)

1981 Cabernet Sauvignon Reserve	Napa	($16.95)	83
1983 Chardonnay	Napa	($12.95)	85
1984 Chardonnay	Napa	($12.95)	82
1984 Chardonnay California Selection	Napa	($14.00)	83
1984 Chardonnay Reserve	Napa	($16.95)	85

1982 Johannisberg Riesling Late-Harvest   Napa   ($10.50)   86

The family-owned Raymond Winery has been a success from its founding in 1970. Production has climbed toward 60,000 cases and the hallmark of this house has always been the oaky, buttery, opulently styled Chardonnay that is never shy but always loaded with fruit as well as plenty of vanillin and spicy, toasty oak. All the recent vintages have generally been solid, including the 1983 and 1984 Reserve, although the 1984 California selection seemed a bit dull. Raymond can also do interesting things with Cabernet Sauvignon, but most of the time the wine tends to be fairly straightforward, ripe, and intense, without a lot of complexity. However, the 1981 Cabernet Sauvignon Reserve is one of Raymond's best Cabernets to date and shows that when he puts his mind to it he can make good Cabernet. Its lushness and richness dictate drinking over the next 3–4 years. The winery also makes a little Zinfandel that I find average in quality, but every once in a while a splendid Late-Harvest Johannisberg Riesling is made. The current version (1982) has a wonderful bouquet of caramel and pineapples and is rich and sweet on the palate. It is a perfect dessert wine. Raymond made a great classic in 1978 when he produced a Trockenbeerenauslese-styled wine of great intensity and depth that is still drinking well today.

RICHARDSON VINEYARDS (SONOMA)

1984 Chardonnay	Sonoma	($13.95)	78
1984 Pinot Noir	Sonoma	($10.99)	84
1983 Zinfandel	Sonoma	($10.00)	75

This tiny winery (a production of just over 2,000 cases) also produces Cabernet Sauvignon, which I have not tasted. The successes to date have been their Pinot Noir, which is plump, rich, spicy, and very good though not always very varietal, and their Zinfandel, which borders on the late-harvest style with intense flavors and a full-bodied palate impression. The 1984 Chardonnay tastes heavy and overly oaky. It is too soon to know exactly what this winery is capable of doing since I have been unable to follow their wines in every vintage because of their tiny production.

RIDGE VINEYARDS (SANTA CLARA)

1981 Cabernet Sauvignon	Napa	($12.00)	78
1982 Cabernet Sauvignon Howell Mt.	Napa	($16.00)	85
1983 Cabernet Sauvignon Howell Mt.	Napa	($16.00)	82
1980 Cabernet Sauvignon Monte Bello	Santa Cruz	($35.00)	86
1981 Cabernet Sauvignon Monte Bello	Santa Cruz	($30.00)	90
1982 Cabernet Sauvignon Monte Bello	Santa Cruz	($30.00)	82
1983 Cabernet Sauvignon Monte Bello	Santa Cruz	($30.00)	88
1981 Cabernet Sauvignon York Creek	Napa	($12.00)	85
1982 Cabernet Sauvignon York Creek	Napa	($14.00)	75
1984 Chardonnay	Santa Cruz	($15.00)	84
1981 Petite Sirah York Creek	Napa	($9.00)	85
1983 Petite Sirah York Creek	Napa	($12.00)	86
1982 Zinfandel Geyserville	Sonoma	($9.99)	86
1983 Zinfandel Geyserville	Sonoma	($10.99)	87
1984 Zinfandel York Creek	Napa	($11.99)	84
1984 Zinfandel Geyserville	Sonoma	($11.99)	90
1984 Zinfandel Lytton Springs	Sonoma	($11.99)	90
1982 Zinfandel York Creek	Napa	($10.99)	86

Ridge Vineyards and its winemaker, Paul Draper, are justifiably very highly respected, not only in the United States but in the world. Paul Draper has consistently produced spectacular, long-lived Cabernet Sauvignons that have 15–20 years' aging potential and usually California's finest Zinfandels from a half-dozen or so vineyard locations. A little Chardonnay is also made here that tends to be oaky and often not terribly interesting, but the 1984 showed very well. The reasons for Ridge's success are numerous, but their belief in either no or minimum handling of the wine once it has been made results in wines that are generally made with wild yeasts from the vineyards, the minimum of fining, and no filtration whatsoever. Consequently, they all have character and plenty of flavor intensity. The jewel of this house is its Cabernet Sauvignon from the Monte Bello Vineyard next to the winery, which sits strategically and beautifully overlooking Silicone Valley and San Jose. The drive up to Ridge is both beautiful and steep. The Ridge Monte Bello Cabernets start off life almost like Château Latour Cabernets do in Bordeaux. Many writers dismiss them as being too tannic and too lean when in truth there are layers and layers of flavor underneath. The great Monte Bellos have been the 1964, still in spectacular condition when I last tasted it in 1985, the 1968, 1970, an incredibly great 1971, 1974, and a monumental 1977 that needs another 10 years to reach its peak. In the 1980s, the vintages have been slightly less successful, although the 1984 tasted from the cask looked to be outstanding and both the 1981 and 1983 are very strong. The Ridge Monte Bello Cabernet is a wine that has rich fruit, an almost gravelly, mineral extract, and develops like no other Cabernet I have experienced in California. I have consistently mistaken a 10- or 12-year-old Ridge Monte Bello for a first growth Bordeaux. The other Cabernets made here range from the fairly chunky, medium- to full-bodied York Creek made from grapes purchased in Napa to a fairly tannic, closed, rather reserved yet very ageworthy Howell Mountain Cabernet also made from purchased grapes in Napa. The winery has always done a great job with Zinfandels, and until the Ravenswood Winery in Sonoma got started, Ridge rarely had any competition for producing the best Zinfandels in California. Their Zinfandels come from a horde of different locations, but the best ones have consistently been produced in Sonoma (Geyserville and Lytton Springs). The 1984s are the best in recent memory. These wonderfully rich Zinfandels are loaded with berry fruit and should age beautifully. Perhaps the next best Zinfandel is that from the York Creek Vineyard in Napa, which often contains a little bit of Petite Sirah. This again is a rich, intense, long-lived Zinfandel that can seemingly last for 8–10 years with no difficulty. Other Zinfandels are from Fiddletown Vineyard in Amador (a robust, rich wine), the Dusi Ranch in Paso Robles, and, every once in a while, the Jimsomare Ranch, which is located lower down the mountain from Ridge. The 1970 Jimsomare Zinfandel remains for me the single greatest bottle of Zinfandel I have ever tasted. Having had it several years ago, I can report with great astonishment that it is still not fully mature. The winery also makes a splendid Petite Sirah that is deep, dark, rich, and loaded with peppery extract and blackcurrant, cassis flavors. The best Petite Sirah always comes from the York Creek Vineyard in Napa Valley. Sometimes Paul Draper adds a dollop of Zinfandel to give it some additional character. In fact, a 1974 Petite Sirah York Creek drunk in 1984 had an astonishing resemblance to a great Côte Rôtie from Guigal. So perhaps this wine has even more potential for aging than any of us have ever given it credit for.

RITCHIE CREEK WINERY (NAPA)

1982 Cabernet Sauvignon	Napa	($12.50)	84

1984 Chardonnay	Napa	($14.00)	88

This micro-winery with a production of just under 800 cases is rarely seen outside its native state of California. The winery specializes in broadly flavored Cabernet and rich, buttery Chardonnay. The 1982 Cabernet Sauvignon is a rich, supple, tannic, densely colored wine with lots of power and flavor but very weedy and herbaceous to smell. It seems to need all of 4–5 years to reach maturity. Older vintages of note are the 1980 and 1978. This is certainly a wine worth buying given the moderate price, but it is very difficult to find.

ROMBAUER VINEYARDS (NAPA)

1982 Cabernet Sauvignon	Napa	($12.00)	77

1984 Chardonnay French Vineyard	Napa	($12.00)	70

1983 Merlot	Napa	($12.00)	75

This new winery was founded in 1980 and has bulked its production up to 3,500 cases, with plans to build to 10,000. The wines so far have left me unimpressed. They are technically correct, but lack concentration, seem lean, and express no character or personality. I just can't see making wines like this in the competitive wine business when there are numerous generic jug wines that have every bit as much flavor and character.

ROSENBLUM CELLARS (ALAMEDA)

1983 Cabernet Sauvignon	Sonoma	($9.99)	81
1983 Cabernet Sauvignon Groth Vyd.	Napa	($11.99)	84
1982 Petite Sirah St. George & Rich Vyds.	Napa	($7.99)	84
1983 Petite Sirah St. George & Rich Vyds.	Napa	($8.99)	86

This is another small winery that seems to get very little distribution outside of California. The production is just under 5,000 cases and while some Chardonnay and other varietals are made, the emphasis seems to be on a fat, rich, big, somewhat too herbaceous Cabernet Sauvignon and a Petite Sirah that is peppery and densely colored, with excellent levels of fruit intensity and harmony. Prices remain reasonable given the quality, although I would like to see some of the weedy, herbaceous components of the Cabernets removed; otherwise, they are rich, intense, interesting wines.

ROUDON-SMITH VINEYARDS (SANTA CRUZ)

1982 Cabernet Sauvignon-Nelson Ranch	Mendocino	($7.99)	83
1984 Pinot Blanc	Santa Maria	($6.99)	84
1982 Zinfandel-Chauvet	Sonoma	($7.99)	84

Roudon-Smith Winery was started in 1972 and production has remained fairly constant over recent years at about 10,000 cases. The owners purchase grapes from many different locations in California and produce rich, powerful, intense Zinfandels, somewhat tannic, austere Cabernets, and though I have not tasted a recent vintage, often excessively oaky, dull Chardonnays. The 1984 Pinot Blanc, which has a bit of Chardonnay blended in, suggested a movement in style from over-oaked white varietals to more emphasis on lush, fresh fruit and only a subtle hint of oak. Prices for Roudon-Smith wines remain modest, so good values can sometimes be found from this winery.

ROUND HILL (NAPA)

1983 Cabernet Sauvignon Reserve	Napa	($8.99)	85
1982 Cabernet Sauvignon	Napa	($8.99)	85

NV Cabernet Sauvignon Lot 5	California	($5.99)	83
1984 Chardonnay	California	($5.99)	82
1985 Chardonnay	California	($4.99)	84
1985 Fumé Blanc	California	($5.49)	84

The Round Hill label operates much like a *négociant* in France since they own no vineyards—the production of over 100,000 cases is totally from purchased wines. The quality seems consistently good and the prices remarkably fair. While the winery makes a little bit of Fumé Blanc, Chenin Blanc, and Riesling, the stars here are their Cabernet Sauvignons, which are usually supple with good blackcurrant fruitiness touched by oak, and a straightforward, tropical fruit-scented, lushly textured Chardonnay. Consumers should give this winery more attention since the wines are rarely disappointing and represent considerable value.

RUTHERFORD HILL WINERY (NAPA)

1981 Cabernet Sauvignon	Napa	($12.50)	83
1982 Cabernet Sauvignon Partner's Sel.	Napa	($8.99)	80
1978 Cabernet Sauvignon Reserve	Napa	($17.00)	84
1983 Chardonnay	Napa	($10.99)	84
1984 Chardonnay Partner's Selection	Napa	($12.00)	84
1981 Chardonnay Reserve	Napa	($18.00)	86
1981 Merlot Partner's Selection	Napa	($8.99)	85
1984 Sauvignon Blanc	Napa	($8.99)	84

Rutherford Hill Winery, located on a hill above the famous Napa restaurant Auberge du Soleil, rarely produces great wines, though it consistently produces good wines that are often fairly priced. The successes have been the Chardonnay, which is always oaky and rich in buttery, lemony fruit, and the Merlot, which has shown surprising richness and a deep, fleshy, lush character, making it drinkable at an early age. Unfortunately, the winery dropped its excellent Zinfandel made from old vines on Atlas Peak, but continues to make a very good Cabernet Sauvignon and a good Sauvignon Blanc. A dull Gewürztraminer is also offered. Production is in the neighborhood of 150,000 cases of wine and growing all the time. The new series of Partner's Selection wines seem to be less expensive and, for the moment, offer excellent value in Chardonnay and Merlot.

ST. ANDREWS WINERY (NAPA)

1983 Chardonnay	Napa	($12.99)	85

This small winery has been content to devote almost all of its 5,000-case production to Chardonnay. It sells many of its grapes to Domaine Chandon for its sparkling wine production but keeps the best for its own richly fruity, subtly oaky, medium-bodied Chardonnay that shows a refined, elegant, balanced style. The plans are to add Sauvignon Blanc and Cabernet Sauvignon to the stable here.

ST. CLEMENT VINEYARDS (NAPA)

1983 Cabernet Sauvignon	Napa	($14.95)	76
1983 Chardonnay	Napa	($14.99)	82
1984 Chardonnay	Napa	($14.50)	82
1985 Sauvignon Blanc	Napa	($9.00)	86

St. Clement, founded in 1975, has continued to produce around 10,000 cases of Chardonnay, Sauvignon Blanc, and Cabernet Sauvignon. The Chardonnays seemed much stronger in the '70s than they do in the '80s where they have taken on a more compact, leaner, austere style that seems to lack flesh and charm. The same can be said for the Cabernet Sauvignon, which in 1983 tasted watery, over-acidic, and rather charmless. However, the Sauvignon Blanc continues to be one of the best made in California, with its figlike, melonlike, subtle, herbaceous flavors and wonderful exuberant freshness and crispness on the palate. Prices for the Chardonnay and Cabernet Sauvignon seem out of line for the quality of recent vintages, but the Sauvignon Blanc is still a decent value at less than $10 a bottle.

ST. FRANCIS VINEYARD (SONOMA)

1985 Chardonnay	Sonoma	($10.99)	86
1984 Chardonnay Barrel Select	Sonoma	($10.99)	84
1984 Chardonnay Poverello	Sonoma	($7.00)	72
1983 Merlot	Sonoma	($10.99)	86
1981 Pinot Noir	Sonoma	($10.99)	72
1985 Pinot Noir Blanc	Sonoma	($5.99)	78

St. Francis Vineyard was founded in 1979 and has increased its production to 24,000 cases with the help of many purchased grapes. The strongest wines have been the Chardonnays, with the 1985 and 1984 very good wines. The 1985 is loaded with fruit. Both admirably show the style of this winery, having crisp acidity, medium-bodied, attractive, ripe appley fruit, and subtle oak. The 1984 Poverello seemed bizarre and very unvarietal when tasted. The winery also produces a bit of Pinot Noir that suffers like many California Pinot Noirs from an aggressive vegetal quality and some bitterness as well. A wine to search out is the 1983 Merlot, an elegant, spicy, richly fruity wine with a great deal of class. Prices are a little steep here for the quality offered.

SAINTSBURY WINERY (NAPA)

1985 Chardonnay	Carneros	($11.99)	87
1984 Chardonnay	Carneros	($10.99)	87
1984 Pinot Noir Carneros	Carneros	($9.99)	87
1984 Pinot Noir Garnet	Carneros	($8.00)	84
1985 Pinot Noir Garnet	Carneros	($8.00)	84

The Saintsbury Winery is proving that very good, even stunning Pinot Noir can be made from grapes grown in the cool region of Carneros. The two young owners, David Graves and Richard Ward, seem to have learned their lessons well and with each vintage the quality improves. The 1984 and 1985 Chardonnays are their best Chardonnays to date, with a wonderfully complex, toasty, buttery, moderately intense bouquet of spices and ripe apple fruit. Both wines show remarkable balance, medium body, long flavors, and seem very French in their orientation. The winery produces two Pinot Noirs. The lighter-styled Garnet Pinot Noir in 1984 and 1985 seems richer and a trifle firmer than the previous editions, with a lush raspberry fruitiness and true Pinot Noir personality. The one to get really excited about, however, is their 1984 Carneros Pinot Noir, one of the most impressive Pinot Noirs to come out of the Carneros region in the last 10 years. It seems to have an aging potential of 5–7 years but can be drunk now for its intense raspberry fruitiness and smoky, rich Pinot Noir character. This winery has maintained sensible prices even as the quality has improved. I recommend paying plenty of attention to Saintsbury. Production has inched up to 15,000 cases.

SAN MARTIN (SANTA CLARA)

1983 Chardonnay	California	($7.49)	80
1983 Soft Chenin Blanc	California	($5.99)	72
1984 Soft Johannisberg Riesling	California	($3.99)	80
1982 Zinfandel	Amador	($6.00)	73

This huge winery, with a production in excess of 400,000 cases, has pioneered the idea of "soft" wines, which are in fact off dry, slightly sweet, very fruity, supple wines that are made to have broad commercial appeal. The best examples of this tend to be the Johannisberg Riesling and Chenin Blanc, which in certain vintages can be exuberantly fruity, flowery, and very easy to drink though hardly complex. The other wines have tended to be very standard in quality, lacking somewhat in varietal character, uninteresting, and a little dull.

SANFORD WINERY (SANTA BARBARA)

1983 Chardonnay	Central Coast	($10.00)	72
1984 Chardonnay	Central Coast	($10.00)	78
1982 Pinot Noir	Santa Maria	($10.99)	72
1983 Pinot Noir	Central Coast	($9.95)	80

| 1984 Sauvignon Blanc | Central Coast | ($8.99) | 82 |

This winery has had a tough go of it in my tastings, as have many wineries from the Santa Barbara area. Not that fine wine can't be made there, because it can, but for whatever reason Sanford wines have a consistent problem and that is one of an overt, aggressive, vegetal character that permeates the wines from their overly vegetal Sauvignon Blanc to the weedy, stemmy qualities of their Pinot Noir and Sauvignon Blanc character of their Chardonnay. The Pinot Noirs show a lot of flavor and bouquet, but they are spoiled by the weediness. The Chardonnays seem bland as well so there is not much I can recommend from this winery at present.

SANTA CRUZ MOUNTAIN VINEYARD (SANTA CRUZ)

1981 Cabernet Sauvignon Bates Ranch	Santa Cruz	($13.95)	87
1982 Duriff	Santa Cruz	($9.00)	85
1983 Duriff	Santa Cruz	($9.00)	82
1983 Merlot	California	($11.95)	84
1981 Pinot Noir	Santa Cruz	($15.00)	86

Owner Ken Burnap is much like the individualistic, rich, full-bodied, interesting wines that he produces—big and extroverted. His Pinot Noirs will not remind anyone of what this grape can do at its heights in Burgundy, but they remain fascinatingly rich, stunning, smoky, extroverted, exotic, occasionally bizarre examples of this varietal. They are never timid wines, but incredibly rich, intense, with smoky, tarry flavors and sometimes seem more like a full-style Barolo than Pinot Noir. However, in vintages like 1981 the wine has remarkable appeal even if it is somewhat unusual. His Cabernets from the Bates Ranch in the Santa Cruz Mountains are from the same ilk, unfiltered, rich, smoky, with remarkably intense flavors. In certain vintages like 1978, 1980, and 1981 they have been stunning wines. Burnap has added Merlot to his stable and his 1983, produced from purchased grapes, is a richly fruity, soft, supple wine with instant appeal. Unlike most of his other wines, it should be drunk soon rather than aged. This winery also produces a Duriff, a grape variety that is indigenous to the Middle East and parts of the Rhône Valley. The 1982 was a wonderfully smoky, robust, chocolatey, rich, rather massive wine with

5–6 years of further aging potential ahead of it. The production of Santa Cruz Mountain Vineyards is not large, averaging only around 3,000 cases, but these are highly individualistic, unique wines with flamboyant personalities. They are all worth a try.

SARAH'S VINEYARD (SANTA CLARA)

1984 Chardonnay Sarah's Vineyard	Santa Clara	($18.49)	87
1984 Chardonnay Ventana Vineyard	Monterey	($18.49)	90
1981 Zinfandel	Dry Creek	($9.99)	85

This small winery in Santa Clara produces less than 3,000 cases of wine, but the quality has been very good, even exceptional. The new releases continue to show this winery's increasingly fine touch with Chardonnay. Both 1984s show wonderfully ripe, luscious fruit, medium- to full-bodied palate impressions, and just enough oak to add complexity to the succulent, rich, tropical fruit and lemony, ripe appley, buttery flavors. The Ventana Vineyard seems to be a bit more intense in fruit than Sarah's Vineyard, but both are excellent Chardonnays. As for the Zinfandels here, they tend to be rather big and rich, with tremendous ripeness and intensity, and probably as much complexity as one can get in wines of this style. The 1981 from Dry Creek borders on being late-harvest but is dry, very rich, and full-bodied, with plenty of impact. The winery also makes a little bit of Cabernet Sauvignon, but I have not seen a recent vintage. Since production here is so tiny, these wines are almost impossible to find outside of California.

V. SATTUI WINERY (NAPA)

1983 Cabernet Sauvignon	Napa	($10.99)	75
1982 Cabernet Sauvignon Preston Vyds.	Napa	($12.99)	86
1983 Cabernet Sauvignon Preston Vyds.	Napa	($12.99)	86

This is a rather curious winery. It tends to make very good, underrated Cabernet Sauvignon. The production of 15,000 cases is, remarkably, sold entirely at the winery, which is located right on the main road going through St. Helena. The winery also produces several other varietals, including Zinfandel, Chardonnay, Sauvignon Blanc, and Riesling, but I have not tasted them. However, the Cabernets can be very good, although the 1983 regular bottling seemed entirely too herbaceous and lacked intensity and concentration of fruit. The 1983 from Preston Vineyards showed wonderful blackcurrant and black cherry fruit dominated somewhat by toasty, spicy oak, but with plenty of depth and good length. The 1982 version seemed a touch lighter but also very good. Prices for the Sattui wines seem reasonable for the quality; this should be a definite stop on your next visit to the Napa Valley.

SAUSAL WINERY (SONOMA)

1984 Chardonnay	Sonoma	($9.99)	80
1982 Zinfandel	Sonoma	($9.00)	85
1985 Zinfandel White	Sonoma	($6.00)	82

The Sausal Winery produces 8,000 cases with the emphasis clearly on Zinfandel and Chardonnay. The quality of the wines is good, prices reasonable, and the Chardonnay made in a lemony, moderately toasty, buttery, barrel-fermented style. The Zinfandel comes in two varieties, the regular Zinfandel and a private reserve. It tends to be made in the big, ripe, full-bodied, heavily extracted style, but has good balance overall and layers of ripe berry fruit.

SCHRAMSBERG WINERY (NAPA)

1982 Blanc de Blancs	($19.00)	70
1982 Cuvée de Pinot	($18.00)	71
1979 Reserve Sparkling Wine	($30.00)	75

Schramsberg of course has a great reputation, but I have never been overwhelmed by the quality of their sparkling wines. Despite all the hype, the reality is that recent releases have been less interesting than many of the releases that pre-date the mid-'70s. This is unfortunate because this historic winery has led the California sparkling wine industry from its founding in 1965, and obviously inspired many a vintner to try his or her hand at making sparkling wine. The 1982 Blanc de Blanc tastes like a green Muscadet that has been carbonated. The nose is odd, there is no middle range of flavor, and it has a sharp finish. The 1982 rosé, the Cuvée de Pinot, has a charming color but little else. There is no flavor, though what is present is clean and crisp with absolutely no follow-through. The 1979 Reserve, priced "modestly" at $30, has some body and flavor but no real focal point of interest. Schramsberg can make better sparkling wines than this, and though one gets a famous name here, a higher level of quality can be found in many *vins mousseux* from France as well as the numerous inexpensive Italian and Spanish sparkling wines. This winery produces approximately 50,000 cases of sparkling wine.

SCHUG CELLARS (NAPA)

1982 Cabernet Sauvignon	Napa	($14.95)	85
1984 Chardonnay A. Hollinger Vyds.	Napa	($10.99)	60
1983 Chardonnay Beckstoffer Vyds.	Napa	($10.99)	75
1984 Chardonnay Beckstoffer Vyds.	Napa	($10.99)	78
1983 Pinot Noir Beckstoffer Vyds.	Napa	($10.49)	78
1982 Pinot Noir Heinemann Vyds.	Napa	($10.49)	74

Walter Schug is the German-born and -trained winemaker who did so much to help establish the Joseph Phelps winery in the 1970s as one of California's great producers of Cabernet Sauvignon and late-harvest Riesling. He began his own winery in 1980 as another winemaker fanatically obsessed with making excellent Pinot Noir in California. Ironically, his first releases of Pinot Noir, the 1981, 1982, and 1983, have largely been disappointing. They are not bad wines, but they show the problems that even a genius winemaker can have with this temperamental grape varietal. The 1982 Heinemann Vineyards is a very mediocre wine that seems lifeless and dull. In the Beckstoffer Vineyards slightly more fruit is present, but it too is flawed by a sharp, angular texture. His Cabernet Sauvignon, a 1982 from Napa, though quite limited in availability, is rich, full-bodied, with plenty of blackcurrant fruitiness and a good measure of tannins. It will take at least 5 more years of aging to reach total harmony. The winery also makes some Chardonnay in its production of 8,000 cases, but recent vintages have been quite mediocre.

SEA RIDGE WINERY (SONOMA)

1984 Chardonnay	Sonoma	($10.00)	82
1982 Pinot Noir	Sonoma	($10.00)	86
1981 Pinot Noir Bohan Vyd.	Sonoma	($15.00)	87

The Sea Ridge Winery, located in the very mountainous western area of Sonoma, is dedicated to burgundian-style Pinot Noirs. The results to date have been impressive. The 1981 Pinot Noir from the Bohan Vineyard is quite good, and the 1982 from Sonoma spicy, smoky, with an excellent bouquet of cedar, violets, and berry fruit. The winery has not enjoyed the same success with their Sauvignon Blanc and Chardonnay, which have been terribly inconsistent, but for Pinot Noir this is a winery to watch with great anticipation and excitement.

SEBASTIANI WINERY (SONOMA)

1981 Cabernet Sauvignon Eagle Label	Sonoma	($25.00)	84
1982 Cabernet Sauvignon Eagle Label	Sonoma	($25.00)	84
1983 Cabernet Sauvignon Eagle Label	Sonoma	($25.00)	85
1980 Cabernet Sauvignon Prop. Res.	Sonoma	($13.95)	85
1984 Chardonnay Proprietor's Reserve	Sonoma	($10.00)	78
1984 Sauvignon Blanc Prop. Res.	Sonoma	($10.00)	81
1980 Zinfandel Proprietor's Reserve	Sonoma	($12.00)	84

One of Sonoma's most famous wineries, with a production in excess of 2,000,000 cases, the Sebastiani Vineyards (founded in 1904) has gone through a tumultuous period from 1980, when the patriarch of the firm, August Sebastiani, died, until 1985, when his son, Sam Sebastiani, was dismissed from the company by his mother. Sam had attempted to give Sebastiani a brand new look, improving the quality and dropping some of the wines that made up the bulk wine production of this winery. At this time, it is too early to know what direction this winery will go, but there are a number of good quality wines under the Sebastiani label in existence. The strength of the house has always been their red wines, with the Zinfandel especially good, as well as a generally sound Cabernet Sauvignon. The introduction of the super-expensive Eagle Label was met with praise from the critics but a price too steep for most consumers. It has tended to be an inky, rich, very tannic, intense wine that requires aging. The winery also produces a range of white wines, with the best of it being a somewhat underrated Muscat with a slight sweetness but wonderfully perfumed aroma, and a blush wine called Eye of the Swan. The Rosa Gewürztraminer, which has a rosé-type color, is another wine that has tended to be consistently good. The Pinot Noirs have erred on the light side, the Gamay is dull and uninteresting, and the Chardonnays and Sauvignon Blancs are well behind the quality one expects from this winery. Sebastiani is going through a period of major changes, and it will be interesting to see if the style of the wines produced here changes as well.

SAM SEBASTIANI (SONOMA)

1983 Cabernet Sauvignon		($15.00)	84
1985 Sauvignon Blanc	Napa/Sonoma	($10.50)	85

Since his exile from his family's winery, Sam Sabastiani seems determined to forge ahead with some quality wines of his own. The Sauvignon is a daring sort of wine—extroverted, flashy, and loaded with fruit. The Cabernet is deep in color, rather austere, but shows good potential if cellared for 2–3 years.

SEQUOIA GROVE WINERY (NAPA)

1982 Cabernet Sauvignon	Napa/Alex. Vly.	($12.00)	83
1983 Cabernet Sauvignon	Napa/Alex. Vly.	($12.00)	80
1983 Chardonnay Estate	Napa	($12.00)	85
1984 Chardonnay	Sonoma	($12.00)	70

This smallish winery (a production of 8,000 cases) is run by the charming Allen family, who specialize in a variety of Cabernet Sauvignons and Chardonnays from both Napa and Sonoma Counties. The Chardonnays have shown a stylish fruitiness in a medium-body format, with the varietal character well displayed but not overstated. The Cabernets have tended to be fruity, soft, medium-bodied, very straightforward in style, and made for drinking within the first 4–5 years after the vintage. Prices are moderate.

SHAFER VINEYARDS (NAPA)

1982 Cabernet Sauvignon	Napa	($12.00)	84?
1983 Cabernet Sauvignon	Napa	($12.00)	65
1982 Cabernet Sauvignon Reserve	Napa	($16.00)	86?
1982 Chardonnay	Napa	($12.50)	87
1983 Chardonnay	Napa	($12.50)	84
1984 Chardonnay	Napa	($12.00)	84
1983 Merlot	Napa	($12.00)	72

The Shafer Winery quickly established its reputation for a rich, full-bodied Cabernet Sauvignon and Zinfandel in 1978, the debut vintage. As production has grown to 12,000 cases, the winery continues to specialize in Cabernet Sauvignon, Chardonnay, and a little Merlot. Unfortunately, the big, rich Zinfandels were dropped from the roster. The 1982 Cabernets were remarkably variable from bottle to bottle, although the best bottles showed wonderful richness and intensity, particularly the Reserve bottling. The 1983 Merlot has never impressed me since it suffers from an intense vegetal aroma and hard, harsh tannins that render it charmless, as does the vegetal and petrol-scented bizarre 1983 Cabernet. Shafer Vineyards produced one of Napa Valley's very finest Chardonnays in 1982 and followed it with good rather than great efforts in 1983 and 1984. Prices remain moderate for wines that are generally quite soundly made, although I wonder about the bottle variation in quality of the 1982 red wines.

CHARLES F. SHAW VINEYARDS (NAPA)

1983 Chardonnay	Napa	($12.50)	86
1984 Chardonnay	Napa	($12.50)	83

1985 Gamay Nouveau   Napa   ($4.99)   82

The Charles Shaw Winery set off to produce Beaujolais-type wines
from the Gamay grape and has succeeded in producing consistently
pleasing, fruity, lively wines in the last several vintages. This is the
type of wine that must be drunk up within a year after its release to
fully appreciate its fresh, fruity character. The winery has since added
Chardonnay to its lineup with the help of the brilliant winemaker Ric
Forman, one of California's best winemaking talents for both Chardonnay and Cabernet. The two Chardonnays to date (1983, 1984) have
not gotten a great deal of publicity but are very good wines, with a
medium-bodied, subtle, toasty, lively feel on the palate and good varietal fruit. The winery also makes a little bit of Fumé Blanc. Production is in excess of 20,000 cases, the bulk of it being the Gamay
Nouveau.

SILVER OAK CELLARS (NAPA)

1982 Cabernet Sauvignon   Alexander Vly.   ($20.00)   90

1981 Cabernet Sauvignon   Alexander Vly.   ($18.00)   87

1982 Cabernet Sauvignon   Napa   ($20.00)   90

1981 Cabernet Sauvignon   Napa   ($18.00)   90

1981 Cabernet Sauvignon
Bonny's Vyd.   Napa   ($35.00)   90

The Silver Oak Winery specializes in one wine (Cabernet Sauvignon),
but from three appellations—Napa, Alexander Valley, and a very
limited amount of single-vineyard Cabernet from Silver Oak's own
vineyard called Bonny's Vineyard (named after winemaker Justin
Meyer's wife). The Cabernets have been consistently among the top
wines made in California. The Napa always tends to be a bit firmer
and more structured. The Alexander Valley tends to be more opulent
and rich with a lush, full, ripe fruitiness. The Bonny's Vineyard is a
great Cabernet of outstanding depth and richness. One has to applaud
what this winery does. The wines are highly extracted, very individualistic, with sensational bouquets, and are not released until the
winery feels they have some bottle age. (The 1982s, for example, were
just released and the great 1984s that I tasted from cask are not
scheduled to be released until 1989.) This is definitely a winery to seek

out despite the relatively high prices because the Cabernets are simply excellent. Most of them have been ready to drink between their sixth and tenth birthdays and show no signs of falling off, including some of the old classics such as the 1977s and 1978s, the first two wines made under the Silver Oak label by Justin Meyer.

SILVERADO VINEYARDS (NAPA)

1982 Cabernet Sauvignon	Napa	($11.00)	82
1983 Cabernet Sauvignon	Napa	($12.00)	69
1982 Chardonnay	Napa	($12.00)	85
1983 Chardonnay	Napa	($12.00)	85
1984 Chardonnay	Napa	($10.00)	75
1985 Sauvignon Blanc	Napa	($9.00)	84

This winery was started in 1981 by the famous Walt Disney family. Production has peaked at 50,000 cases and the wines are consistently good and fairly priced. The top two wines have been the Chardonnays (although the 1984 was thin and citric) and Sauvignon Blancs, followed by a less impressive but still pleasant (except for the lean, angular 1983) Cabernet Sauvignon. The winery is one of the most beautifully situated in the Napa Valley, overlooking the southern part of the valley on a small ridge next to the Silverado Trail. The Chardonnays tend to be made in the very balanced, correct style, with just enough toasty oak and the emphasis clearly on the lemony, ripe appley, fruity scents of Chardonnay rather than the big, butterscotchy, barrel-fermented style. The Sauvignon Blanc tends to be fresh and lively, with the aggressive herbaceous character of this varietal well controlled.

SIMI WINERY (SONOMA)

1981 Cabernet Sauvignon	Sonoma	($12.00)	78
1982 Cabernet Sauvignon	Sonoma	($14.00)	83
1978 Cabernet Sauvignon Reserve	Sonoma	($20.00)	76

1980 Cabernet Sauvignon Reserve	Sonoma	($20.00)	85
1983 Chardonnay	Mendocino/Sonoma	($12.00)	85
1984 Chardonnay	Sonoma	($12.00)	86
1981 Chardonnay Reserve	Sonoma	($20.00)	84
1982 Chardonnay Reserve	Sonoma	($20.00)	90
1985 Rosé of Cabernet	Sonoma	($6.99)	85
1984 Sauvignon Blanc	Sonoma	($9.99)	86

The historic Simi Winery, founded in 1876, has always made good wine, but the decision to bring on board the outstanding winemaker Zelma Long (in 1979) has meant a succession of better wines. Zelma Long's specialty is Chardonnay, and one can hardly go wrong with a Chardonnay produced here. The regular Chardonnay, often a blend of both Sonoma and Mendocino grapes, is wonderfully fruity, gently touched by aging in oak barrels, and consistently successful in every vintage since 1980. The Reserve Chardonnay, released much later, is barrel fermented and made in the very opulent, rich, full-bodied, oaky style, but in vintages like 1982 the balance between fruit and oak is struck, whereas in 1981 the oak seemed to play the dominant role. The Cabernet Sauvignon has not matched the quality of the Chardonnays here, but the 1982 regular bottling and 1980 Reserve, though more tannic and tough, show very good depth and character. The regular bottling of 1981 and 1982 Cabernet Sauvignon are rather straightforward, simple wines. The Sauvignon Blanc has increased in quality; the 1984 is certainly the best example yet from this winery. The Rosé of Cabernet is arguably one of the finest rosé wines made in California, remarkably fresh, lively, and with plenty of flavor and character, particularly for a rosé. Prices for the Simi regular bottlings remain fair, although Reserve prices are expensive at $20–25 a bottle, but in the case of the Chardonnay, well worth it.

SOLETERRA WINERY (NAPA)

1982 Pinot Noir Three Palms Vyd.	Napa	($12.00)	83
1983 Pinot Noir Three Palms Vyd.	Napa	($12.00)	82

This new winery, founded in 1982, is specializing in Pinot Noir, of which the first two vintages have been pleasant, above-average-quality wines, though hardly inspired efforts. The price is realistic, but I would expect more in quality for this wine to be able to compete successfully in the very competitive California wine market.

SONOMA-CUTRER VINEYARDS (SONOMA)

1983 Chardonnay Cutrer Vineyard	Sonoma	($11.00)	89
1984 Chardonnay Cutrer Vineyard	Sonoma	($16.00)	89
1983 Chardonnay Les Pierres	Sonoma	($16.00)	90
1984 Chardonnay Les Pierres	Sonoma	($16.00)	90
1985 Chardonnay Russian River Ranches	Sonoma	($12.00)	87
1984 Chardonnay Russian River Ranches	Sonoma	($12.75)	87

The youthful Sonoma-Cutrer Winery has a glittering display of high technology used to make wine in a very traditional way. I have never seen grapes and wines so carefully handled, nor have I seen a winery with any more technology than this showpiece winery in Windsor, California. The results have been brilliant, with the 1983 and 1984 Chardonnays both sensational vintages for this winery. Bill Bonetti, the winemaker here, has a remarkable track record when it comes to Chardonnay, and he has had full control over things at Sonoma-Cutrer. The three Chardonnays that are offered include a fruity, forward, very delicious Russian River Ranches, a rather opulent, tropical fruit-scented, subtly oaky Cutrer Vineyard, and a classic, austere, mineral-scented but long, rich, intense, ageworthy Les Pierres Vineyard Chardonnay. Prices continue to inch up for the 25,000 cases of Chardonnay that are produced, but the wines also continue to be on allocation as demand has simply outstripped supply. These Chardonnays are some of the best of their kind in California, three distinctively different wines, of which the Les Pierres and Cutrer are among the handful of California Chardonnays that have the potential and the structure to last and improve in the bottle for more than 4 or 5 years. The 1984s tend to be a bit more opulently forward and fruity than the classic 1983s. The winery also plans to produce a sparkling wine after it has spent 5–7 years aging on its lees. This is a Chardonnay producer of the highest quality, and worth every effort to search out and follow.

SONOMA VINEYARDS (SONOMA)

1980 Cabernet Sauvignon Rodney Strong Alexander's Crown	($11.00)	84
1982 Chardonnay Rodney Strong Chalk Hill	($10.00)	55
1982 Chardonnay Rodney Strong River West	($10.00)	68
1983 Sauvignon Blanc Rodney Strong Alexander Valley	($6.99)	60

Sonoma Vineyards produces in excess of a half-million cases of wine from extensive vineyard holdings in Sonoma. The wines have appeared under a number of different labels, including the Sonoma Vineyards, Windsor Vineyards, and more recently the Rodney Strong labels, alluding rather strongly to winemaker Rodney Strong. The Chardonnays, for whatever reason, seem to be released late onto the market, when they are already starting to lose their fruit and have become oxidized. This is precisely the problem with the 1982s. The best wines have been the Cabernet Sauvignon from the excellent Alexander's Crown Vineyard in Sonoma. The 1980 is successful, though not nearly as rich and intense as the great wines made at this vineyard in 1974 and 1976. Another wine to keep a lookout for is the rich, intense, almost late-harvest style Zinfandel made from old vines of the River West Vineyard in Sonoma. I have not seen a vintage of this since 1978.

SOUVERAIN CELLARS (SONOMA)

1982 Cabernet Sauvignon	Sonoma	($7.50)	78
1980 Cabernet Sauvignon Vintage Selection	Sonoma	($12.00)	72
1982 Chardonnay Vintage Selection	Sonoma	($12.00)	70

1982 Zinfandel Sonoma ($4.49) 70

How things change might be an appropriate comment for this historic winery that was founded by the famous J. Leland Stewart. Stewart gave the country many excellent Cabernet Sauvignons in the late '60s and early '70s. The last great wine made at Souverain was the 1974 Vintage Selection Cabernet Sauvignon, a wine that today is still remarkably rich and alive. The current crop of offerings are dull, simple, and generally devoid of varietal character. The exceptions tend to be the Cabernet Sauvignons, which have adequate blackcurrant fruit but little else. The Chardonnays are dull and simple, and the same can be said for the Pinot Noirs, Zinfandels, Fumé Blancs, and Gray Rieslings. The Petite Sirah can provide surprisingly good character, although I have not seen a vintage of it since 1978. The wines are not inexpensive for their mediocre to below-average quality level.

SPOTTSWOODE VINEYARD AND WINERY (NAPA)

1982 Cabernet Sauvignon Napa ($20.00) 90

1983 Cabernet Sauvignon Napa ($20.00) 85

1985 Sauvignon Blanc Napa ($12.00) 86

This winery, which was only opened in 1982, stunned both consumers and critics alike with a great Cabernet from that same vintage. It is a type of Cabernet that one rarely sees from California: rich, tannic, with gorgeous balance and enough extract and balance to age gracefully for over a decade. The 1983, while slightly less impressive, was still a good wine, and barrel samples of the 1984 and 1985 seem to verify that this winery will make another great wine in 1985 and certainly a very good one in 1984. The winery is also producing small quantities of Sauvignon Blanc, of which the 1985 is very, very good. Production is only 1,500 cases, but the quality level is impeccably high, with prices to match.

SPRING MOUNTAIN VINEYARDS (NAPA)

1982 Cabernet Sauvignon Napa ($15.00) 77

1983 Cabernet Sauvignon Napa ($15.00) 72

This winery, known by television viewers as Falcon Crest, started off in 1968 producing very interesting wines, particularly Cabernet Sauvignon and occasionally Chardonnay. For whatever reason, the wines have become increasingly commercial and dull in style, and recent vintages, though expensive, rarely deliver the complexity and flavor intensity one would hope for.

STAG'S LEAP WINE CELLARS (NAPA)

1983 Cabernet Sauvignon	Napa	($15.95)	84
1978 Cabernet Sauvignon Cask 23	Napa	($30.00)	92
1979 Cabernet Sauvignon Cask 23	Napa	($25.00)	82
1983 Cabernet Sauvignon Cask 23	Napa	($30.00)	87
1981 Cabernet Sauvignon Stag's Leap Vyd.	Napa	($14.50)	82
1982 Cabernet Sauvignon Stag's Leap Vyd.	Napa	($14.50)	78
1983 Cabernet Sauvignon Stag's Leap Vyd.	Napa	($14.50)	85
1984 Chardonnay	Napa	($13.50)	85
1983 Merlot	Napa	($14.00)	85
1984 Sauvignon Blanc	Napa	($9.00)	84

Stag's Leap Wine Cellars, although only founded in 1972, has a worldwide reputation for making some of California's finest wines, particularly Cabernet Sauvignon. The wine that owner Warren Winiarski built his reputation on is his sumptuous and luscious Cask 23 Cabernet Sauvignon. It is not a wine that I have found to be long-lived, but, given its sheer intensity of flavors and wonderful fleshy suppleness and great rich bouquet, it can be a knockout in vintages such as 1974, 1978, and 1984, and can completely dominate other wines in tastings, not because of its power, but because of its sheer succulence and complexity. The regular Cabernets here have been somewhat light in style and a bit disappointing given the reputation of the winery. The 1981 is beginning to fall apart, the 1982 is rather watery and loosely knit, and the 1983 is somewhat better but very soft, forward, and not terribly complex. However, the 1983 Stag's Leap Vyd. shows fine depth, and the excellent Cask 23, while more austere and tannic than usual, is nevertheless rich, deep, broadly flavored wine that will age well for 5–8 years. The winery does a nice job with Sauvignon Blanc, which often has a little bit of Semillon blended in, and the Chardonnay tends to be slightly toasty, with good lemony, appley, buttery fruit. The secondary label is Hawk Crest, which can often represent good value, particularly in the Cabernet Sauvignon. The performance record over the last decade is surprisingly inconsistent, but for the Cask 23 and for some of the special lots of Cabernet, this is a winery that can produce world-class, fabulously rich, seductive wines. For the future, the 1984 vintage here looked awfully good and the most consistently successful vintage for this winery's Cabernets since 1978.

STAG'S LEAP WINERY (NAPA)

1979 Petite Sirah	Napa	($9.99) 85

The personable Carl Doumani runs this tiny vineyard with a 10,000-case production, making mostly red varietals from his favorite grape, the Petite Sirah, but also a little bit of Merlot and tiny quantities of Chardonnay. His Petite Sirah tends to be one of the best made in California, with older vintages like the 1974 and 1973 remarkably intense, distinctive wines. The most recent vintage that I have tasted, the 1979, is also another excellent Petite Sirah—still not ready to drink, but impressive for its peppery, dense fruit and richness. The secondary label here is called Pedregal.

STELTZNER VINEYARD (NAPA)

1982 Cabernet Sauvignon	Napa	($14.00) 83
1983 Cabernet Sauvignon	Napa	($14.00) 85
1984 Cabernet Sauvignon	Napa	($15.00) 86

This famous vineyard, which until 1983 sold its grapes to some of the better California wineries, has quickly established a record for making very elegant, medium-bodied wines that recall the style of Bordeaux more than most Napa Cabernets. Both the 1982 and 1983 have moderately intense, complex bouquets of subtle herbs, cherry fruit, and spicy, toasty oak. The 1983 seems a trifle more complex but also more angular, while the 1982 is more supple. The unreleased 1984 shows a more opulent, forward character than either the 1983 or 1982. Production of Steltzner wines is at 5,000 cases and the prices of $14–$15 a bottle a little on the high side for the quality of the wine produced.

STERLING VINEYARDS (NAPA)

1985 Cabernet Blanc	Napa	($5.99)	84
1982 Cabernet Sauvignon	Napa	($12.00)	55
1982 Cabernet Sauvignon Diamond Mt.	Napa	($14.00)	86
1983 Cabernet Sauvignon Diamond Mt.	Napa	($15.00)	72
1984 Chardonnay	Napa	($15.00)	75
1983 Chardonnay Diamond Mt.	Napa	($15.00)	72
1984 Chardonnay Diamond Mt.	Napa	($15.00)	85
1983 Merlot	Napa	($10.00)	80
1984 Sauvignon Blanc	Napa	($10.00)	85
1985 Sauvignon Blanc	Napa	($10.00)	85

Sterling Vineyards, with a production of 75,000 cases, is unfortunately just a shadow of what it was in the early and mid-'70s when winemaker Ric Forman made an absolutely remarkable string of Cabernets, Merlots, and Chardonnays. When the winery was sold to Coca-Cola in 1978, quality began to slip immediately. In 1983 the winery was again sold, this time to Seagrams, and there seems to be a renewed effort to try to get things back on track, although no red wines made under the new management have yet been released. In any event, one could almost cry when looking at the fabulous Reserve Cabernet Sauvignons of 1973, 1974, 1975, and 1976 and then comparing them to the Cabernets that were made in the late '70s and early '80s. The 1974 Reserve Cabernet remains one of the single greatest California Cabernets I have ever tasted, and at 13 years of age it is just now coming into its plateau of maturity. Even the Chardonnays that Ric Forman produced were immensely rich and long-lived by California standards. Today the most consistent wine has been the blush wine called Cabernet Blanc, one of the better of its type made in California. The 1984 and 1985 Sauvignon Blancs also showed quite well in my tastings of this varietal, and their lean yet firm, subtle complexity holds plenty of attraction for Sauvignon Blanc drinkers. The recent Merlots have been rather straightforward, fruity, a little tart, and not ageworthy at all. What a shame when one looks back at the 1974 and 1975 Merlots, which remain in great shape today. The 1982 Cabernet Sauvignon Diamond Ranch shows proof positive that this winery can still turn out top-notch wine. It is rich, ripe, medium- to full-bodied, deep and long, and should hold well for at least 5-6 years. However, the 1983 Diamond Ranch Cabernet is austere and painfully tannic, and the regular 1982 Cabernet Sauvignon unusually thin and intensely vegetal. Hopefully, Sterling will rebound strongly under its new ownership for it owns a significant amount of acreage and can easily draw from its own well-situated vineyard sources, something that many California wineries do not have the ability to do.

STONEGATE WINERY (NAPA)

1981 Cabernet Sauvignon	Napa	($12.00)	78
1980 Cabernet Sauvignon Vail Vista	Alexander Vly.	($12.00)	84
1982 Merlot Spaulding Vyd.	Napa	($12.00)	84
1983 Sauvignon Blanc	Napa	($8.00)	68
1984 Sauvignon Blanc	Napa	($8.00)	75

Stonegate Winery, located in the northern end of Napa near Calistoga, tends to produce a rather dull group of wines ranging from a fairly bland Sauvignon Blanc to straightforward Chardonnays. Merlot has looked to be the best wine in the 1980s, being fairly lush and fleshy, with a nice, supple fruitiness. The Cabernet Sauvignon has performed to mixed reviews, but the 1980 Vail Vista, though made in the very minty style, has plenty of depth and richness and 5–10 years of aging potential.

STONY HILL VINEYARDS (NAPA)

1981 Chardonnay	Napa	($15.00)	90
1982 Chardonnay	Napa	($12.00)	80
1983 Chardonnay	Napa	($12.00)	88
1984 Chardonnay	Napa	($16.00)	92

Stony Hill is one of the great old wineries of California, having been founded in 1952 and now run with great enthusiasm by Eleanor Mc-

Crea. The Chardonnays are certainly among the handful of exceptions from California in that they actually improve in the bottle for 4–5 years, longer in some vintages. The 1981 is now fully open and shows the splendid richness and balance that this wine has when mature. The 1982 is a disappointment, but the 1983, though tightly knit, shows very good underlying richness and ripeness and should be another candidate for extended aging, as will the 1984, a rich, opulent, yet tightly structured Chardonnay of great style and class.

STORYBOOK MOUNTAIN VINEYARDS (NAPA)

1982 Zinfandel	Sonoma	($8.49)	85
1983 Zinfandel	Napa	($8.99)	85
1984 Zinfandel	Sonoma	($8.99)	86
1981 Zinfandel Reserve		($10.99)	84

This winery in the northern end of Napa in Calistoga produces almost 5,000 cases of full-blooded, robust, intensely flavored Zinfandels from vineyards in Napa and Sonoma. The style is one of aggressive richness, peppery, spicy aromas, and layers of berry fruit. Thank goodness there are still wineries that believe in this varietal.

SULLIVAN VINEYARDS WINERY (NAPA)

1982 Cabernet Sauvignon	Napa	($18.00)	88
1983 Cabernet Sauvignon	Napa	($18.00)	?
1984 Cabernet Sauvignon	Napa	($18.00)	90
1983 Chenin Blanc	Napa	($7.99)	60
1983 Merlot	Napa	($15.00)	55

This tiny winery produces very rich, highly extracted Cabernet Sauvignon and Merlot, as well as a little bit of bizarre Chenin Blanc. A tiny bit of Zinfandel is also produced in certain vintages, although I have not tried it. The Chenin Blanc is aged in oak barrels and, from its taste, is fermented in them as well. Consequently, the delicate flowery fruitiness is obscured by a cascade of toasty oak. I like Chardonnay in oak, but to give Chenin Blanc this kind of treatment is rude and unnecessary. The Cabernet Sauvignons here are massive wines and one applauds the Sullivans for producing wines that are bold, dramatic, and very Californian. Both the 1984 and 1982 were a great success, rich, intense with layers of flavor, and each should drink well for at least another 5–7 years. I have experienced significant bottle variation with the 1983, and even at its best it is not up to the 1982, but it is still a chewy, rich wine with a lot of character. The 1983 Merlot seems to have technical problems since its bouquet is rather bizarre and off. Sullivan Vineyards is somewhat of a hit-or-miss proposition with the quality of their wines, but when they hit they are among the most interesting wines made in Napa.

SUTTER HOME WINERY (NAPA)

1982 Zinfandel	Amador	($6.25)	80

1985 Zinfandel White	California	($5.00)	84

Sutter Home makes an enormous amount of wine (600,000 cases) and has achieved a great deal of commercial success with its white Zinfandel. It is pale salmon in color, wonderfully refreshing, fruity, soft, and quite aromatic. In 1985 they added a sparkling white Zinfandel that is slightly sweet but has more character than many of the super-expensive California sparkling wines that are bland and neutral. The Zinfandels here have a good reputation, but I have always been left asking myself why I find them rather straightforward and unimpressive.

JOSEPH SWAN VINEYARDS (SONOMA)

I have not tasted a Joseph Swan wine since some of their Pinot Noirs in the mid-'70s, but the legendary Zinfandels and Pinot Noirs made here continue to elicit rave responses from the few who are lucky enough to try them. The tiny production of 1,200 cases is sold to a mailing list of loyal customers. Prices tend to be very reasonable ($10–$12 a bottle for Zinfandels). The winery also produces Pinot Noir and Chardonnay. Based on the older vintages I have tried, the Pinot Noir is certainly good, though perhaps overrated because of its rarity.

ROBERT TALBOTT VINEYARDS (MONTEREY)

1983 Chardonnay	Monterey	($18.00)	88

The first wine I tasted from Talbott Vineyards was the 1983 Chardonnay, a wonderfully rich, barrel-fermented wine with great extract, good, crisp acidity, and plenty of complexity and character. I have no idea how it will age, but it seems to have a lot of promise. It is not inexpensive, but it is in one of the most distinctive and expensive bottles any California winery puts their Chardonnay. This could well be a winery to watch. The vineyards consist of 47 acres planted in Monterey, with a production expected to average around 3,000 cases a year.

TREFETHEN VINEYARDS WINERY (NAPA)

1982 Cabernet Sauvignon	Napa	($13.00)	82
1984 Chardonnay	Napa	($14.50)	87
1983 Chardonnay	Napa	($14.00)	86
1981 Pinot Noir	Napa	($9.00)	80

With little fanfare the Trefethen Winery has built up a production of 60,000 cases and specializes in a wonderfully rich yet elegant, understated Chardonnay, one of the handful of wines made from this varietal in California that can age 7–8 years. The 1984, 1983, 1981, 1980, and 1978 are all wonderfully successful. The 1982 proved to be somewhat of a disappointment, given the high level of quality usually obtained here. The winery also produces a Cabernet Sauvignon that I find to be a bit oaky and a trifle too vegetal to receive high marks, but it is generally richly fruity and supple. A small amount of Pinot Noir is also made that, while not resembling a French burgundy, does have ripe, plummy fruit and plenty of character. Two of the most successful wines produced by Trefethen are their excellent nonvintage Eschol white and red wines, blends that are expertly put together and offer immediate gratification for less than $6 a bottle.

MICHEL TRIBAUT (MONTEREY)

N. V. Brut	($12.99–$13.99)	84
1983 Brut	($13.99)	85

Two Frenchmen, Michel Tribaut and Bertrand Devavry, are trying to produce sparkling wine in the traditional manner from Pinot Noir and Chardonnay in Monterey. Their debut releases, the N.V. Brut and 1983 Brut, showed much more depth of flavor and personality than most of the dull, bland, tart, high acid, sparkling wines coming out of

California. Furthermore, both were released at very sensible prices. Compared to the other sparkling wines from California, they are fuller-bodied, riper, and have a much more creamy character to them on the palate. Hopefully, the debut releases will augur even better things for the future. An impressive start.

TUDAL WINERY (NAPA)

1981 Cabernet Sauvignon	Napa	($12.00)	84
1982 Cabernet Sauvignon	Napa	($12.00)	65

This winery, which specializes in Cabernet Sauvignon with a tiny bit of Chardonnay made from purchased grapes, produces only 3,000 cases and has shown the potential to make very good Cabernet Sauvignon, as they did in 1980 and 1981. However, the 1982, for whatever reason, turned out extremely vegetal in its aroma, thereby spoiling a wine that had good ripeness as well as plenty of depth. However, I would keep an eye on future Cabernets from Tudal.

TULOCAY VINEYARDS (NAPA)

1982 Cabernet Sauvignon-Egan	Napa	($10.00)	?
1981 Pinot Noir	Napa	($10.99)	80
1982 Pinot Noir Haynes Vyd.	Napa	($13.99)	60

I continue to get reports from friends in California that winemaker/ owner Bill Cadaman has the right touch with Pinot Noir. To date I have found the wines entirely too overtly vegetal and his Cabernets a bit bizarre and green as well. I would like to believe there is hope here, but I have yet to experience it in tasting the wines.

VICHON WINERY (NAPA)

1982 Cabernet Sauvignon	Napa	($12.00)	78
1983 Cabernet Sauvignon	Napa	($12.00)	82
1982 Cabernet Sauvignon Fay Vineyard	Napa	($14.50)	80
1984 Chardonnay	Napa	($15.00)	67

1984 Chevrier Blanc	Napa	($10.99)	72

1985 Chevrier Blanc	Napa	($10.99)	84

From the very beginning (1980), this winery has promoted the ubiquitous concept of "food wines," meaning wines that will not interfere with food. In essence, what the food wines provided were wines that were so neutral and bland in character that they were inoffensive to all those who drank them. That is not what winemaking nor California wines are all about. Since then, after having financial problems, the winery was sold to the Robert Mondavi family. One of the interesting wines made here is a 50-50 blend of Sauvignon Blanc and Semillon called Chevrier Blanc. This wine seems to have a great deal of popular appeal, but the 1984 tasted exceptionally lean, oaky, and lacking in character, quite surprising in view of the high percentage of Semillon, which tends to add flesh and a waxy, creamy character to the wine. The 1985 looks to be more promising. The Cabernets have generally been made in the same stylistic vein: lean, tart, austere wines about which one can be nice and call elegant, but which in fact lack any real focal point of interest. The 1983s have some flavor interest, but it is the 1984s, tasted from cask samples, that look to be a bit riper and more opulent in style, and with more flavor character than heretofore. I find the Vichon wines to be generally standard in quality and overpriced for what one gets.

VILLA MT. EDEN WINERY (NAPA)

1980 Cabernet Sauvignon Reserve	Napa	($22.00)	90

1982 Cabernet Sauvignon Reserve	Napa	($25.00)	85

1982 Chardonnay	Napa	($14.00)	74

1983 Chardonnay	Napa	($10.00)	73

1980 Pinot Noir Tres Ninos	Napa	($5.99)	75

1981 Pinot Noir Tres Ninos	Napa	($3.99)	80

This is one of Napa's oldest wineries, having originally been founded in 1881. Production has remained modest (18,000 cases) and under the great winemaker Nils Venge, this winery in the mid-'70s produced a series of monumental Cabernets that included a 1974, 1978, and

1980 Reserve, all of which have shown the potential to last 15 or more years in the bottle. The 1974 is drinking fabulously now and should live on for at least another decade. Since Venge left to become a winemaker at Groth, the track record here has been a bit more spotty; one hopes that things will get back on the right track. The Chardonnays, which were excellent under Venge, have been a bit inconsistent in recent vintages and the Cabernets somewhat leaner and less complex. Hopefully, the 1982 Reserve will point to better things, though this wine does not have the richness of any of the Nils Venge productions. The winery has also produced an inexpensive Pinot Noir called Tres Ninos from its vineyard in Napa Valley. This vineyard has since been replanted and there will no longer be a Pinot Noir.

WENTE BROTHERS WINERY (ALAMEDA)

1985 Chardonnay	California	($7.99)	84
1985 Sauvignon Blanc Estate	California	($6.49)	82

Wente Brothers specializes in inexpensive wines, of which the best tend to be their whites, particularly the Sauvignon Blanc and occasionally the Semillon from fairly old vineyards planted in the Livermore Valley. Every once in a while the Chardonnay can also be good. The other wines tend to be dull, with little varietal character present.

WILLIAM WHEELER WINERY (SONOMA)

1982 Cabernet Sauvignon	Dry Creek	($10.99)	60
1981 Cabernet Sauvignon Priv. Res.	Norse Vyd.	($14.49)	85
1983 Chardonnay	Sonoma	($9.99)	84
1984 Chardonnay	Sonoma	($10.99)	86
1985 Chardonnay	Sonoma	($10.99)	86
1985 Sauvignon Blanc	Sonoma	($8.99)	85
1982 Zinfandel	Dry Creek	($8.99)	83
1985 Zinfandel White	Sonoma	($5.99)	84

The William Wheeler Winery, started in 1981, is now up to producing 15,000 cases of very successful white wines. The Sauvignon Blancs have consistently been attractively fruity, dry, crisp, well-balanced wines with the herbaceous quality subtle and not overwhelming. The Chardonnays have ranged from outstanding, as was the case with the 1981 made from Monterey grapes, to very good, which has been the case with the last three vintages of Chardonnay made from Sonoma County grapes. The style is one of ripe fruit balanced nicely with toasty oak. Their blush wine, the 1985 White Zinfandel, is among the leaders of this category of wine. The disappointments have come from some of the Cabernets, which have been surprisingly vegetal and awkwardly styled from a textural perspective. The best Cabernet to date has been the 1981 Private Reserve Cabernet from the Norse Vineyard, a wine with a good measure of herbaceousness but also with fine concentration and depth. Whether it will ever attain elegance or harmonious balance remains to be seen. The winery also produces some Zinfandel.

WHITEHALL LANE WINERY (NAPA)

1983 Cabernet Sauvignon		($12.95)	83
1983 Chardonnay Cerro Vista Vyd.	Napa	($14.00)	85
1984 Chardonnay Knight's Valley Vyd.	Napa	($10.00)	83
1982 Merlot Knight's Valley Vyd.	Napa	($12.00)	85
1983 Merlot Knight's Valley Vyd.	Napa	($12.00)	85

With a production of 20,000 cases of wines that appear to be in demand the country over, the young Whitehall Lane Winery seems to be doing everything right with its toasty, oaky, buttery Chardonnay from the Cerro Vista Vineyard and its big, lush, dense Merlot from the Knight's Valley Vineyard in Napa. Both the 1982 and 1983 Merlots have the fleshiness and breadth of flavor one expects from this supposedly easy to drink, easy to like varietal. The 1983 Cabernet is a bit leaner and more austere, no doubt because the vintage produced many wines like that. But it is still well made. The winery also produces a little bit of Sauvignon Blanc and Chenin Blanc. Prices are moderate given what looks to be a consistently very good level of quality; reports are that the 1984s and 1985s are very successful. This new winery is well worth seeking out for its Chardonnay, Merlot, and Cabernet Sauvignon.

WOLTNER (NAPA)

1984 Cabernet Sauvignon Cask 654	Central Coast	($5.99)	85
1984 Chardonnay Cask 639	California	($5.99)	84
1984 Merlot Cask 573	North Coast	($5.99)	85

These are splendid values from the Woltner family, who now reside in California after selling their beloved Bordeaux château, La Mission-Haut-Brion. The two red wines are very good. The Merlot has a raspberry-scented bouquet, lush, spicy flavors, and immediate appeal. The Cabernet is a much bigger wine, rich, deep, with plenty of blackcurrant, herb-flavored fruit, and 3–4 years of cellaring potential. The Chardonnay is fresh with an applelike, lemony, fruity character, medium body, and crisp finish. All three are top-drawer values.

ZACA MESA WINERY (SANTA BARBARA)

1983 Cabernet Sauvignon	California	($10.00)	81
1981 Cabernet Sauvignon American Reserve	Santa Ynez	($12.00)	69
1982 Cabernet Sauvignon Toyon	California	($6.00)	70
1984 Chardonnay American Reserve	Santa Ynez	($12.00)	85
1984 Chardonnay Toyon	California	($6.59)	75
1984 Sauvignon Blanc	Central Coast	($6.99)	84

The Zaca Mesa Winery has historically performed to mixed results. However, most of their recent releases have shown surprisingly well. For example, the 1983 Cabernet Sauvignon showed none of the vegetal character that plagued earlier offerings. It had a straightforward, ripe berry fruitiness and suppleness that was attractive, if somewhat simple. The Chardonnays have been more interesting wines, with plenty of oak, a slight herbaceous quality, but plenty of fruit. The less expensive Toyon Chardonnay has consistently represented a very good value. The winery's Sauvignon Blanc tends to be a bit grassy, but in 1984 this aspect was tamed down and the wine is fruity and ripe. This winery, which has a significant production of 85,000 cases, does seem to have a sensible view with respect to prices for its wines, and if the new releases are any indication, higher quality can be expected.

ZD WINERY (NAPA)

1981 Cabernet Sauvignon	Santa Maria	($10.50)	68
1982 Cabernet Sauvignon	California	($12.00)	84
1984 Chardonnay	California	($15.00)	91
1985 Chardonnay	California	($16.00)	90
1982 Pinot Noir	Napa	($12.50)	83

The ZD Winery has since 1969 made some of the richest, lushest wines across the entire spectrum of its offerings. Its Chardonnays are excellent and tend to be fat and buttery, with tropical fruit scents and layers of ripe decadent fruit. The 1984 and 1985 continue the line of outstanding Chardonnays produced by this small winery with a production of 10,000 cases. Like all the Chardonnays produced by ZD, both should be drunk within 1–2 years of its release date, since the wines tend to be a little low in acidity. The Pinot Noirs are rather robust and richly fruity, with great density; not terribly elegant, always deep, fat, and bordering on being heavy, they are nevertheless unique and distinctive. The Cabernets tend to range widely in quality since the winery buys grapes from all over California, from Santa Maria in the south to Napa in the north. The 1981 Santa Maria is incredibly vegetal and unattractive, but the 1982 has plenty of sweet oak, nice ripeness and richness, and a fat, low-acid style that has plenty of appeal for drinking over the next 3–4 years. When I think of ZD, I think of good quality wines, with the Chardonnays usually stunning, Cabernets somewhat variable, and the Pinot Noirs always interesting, but don't expect them to taste anything like a good red burgundy.

STEPHEN ZELLERBACH VINEYARDS (SONOMA)

1983 Chardonnay	Alexander Valley	($9.95)	82
1980 Merlot	Alexander Valley	($10.00)	85

1982 Merlot   Alexander Valley   ($8.50)   84

This winery, which was recently sold, had a good track record of making very fine Merlot, rather rich, straightforward Cabernets, and a rather lighter-style yet toasty, straightforward Chardonnay. The pricing policy was always fair and the wines generally represented good value. It is too soon to comment on what direction the wines will take now.

7. OREGON: AMERICA'S NEW WINE STAR

In the late seventies an Eyrie Vineyard 1975 Pinot Noir, in a blind tasting against Premier and Grand Cru red burgundies from top producers, and tasted by a French panel, came in second place. It was thought to be a French wine and the results were considered a shock. This tasting made the headlines but, curiously, it did not have the same positive effect on the prestige of Oregon wines that the famed Steven Spurrier Paris tasting of the mid-seventies—in which California Cabernets and Chardonnays were pitted against the wines of Bordeaux and Burgundy—had for the reputation and respect of California wines.

Now at last Oregon is about to be catapulted into stardom not just for its startling Pinot Noirs but also for its Chardonnays. The focal point for your attention should be the 1983 and 1985 vintages, both perfect growing years for the Pinot Noir and Chardonnay grapes.

For the proud and fiercely independent winemakers of Oregon, the wait for respect and recognition has taken too long. As of 1985, there were 46 bonded wineries and 2,000 acres of vineyards. Most of the wineries are quite small. Even the three largest wineries—Tualatin (83 acres and 18,000-case production), Knudsen Erath (93 acres and 24,000-case production), and Sokol Blosser (45 acres and 23,000-

case production)—are by California standards rather small. Virtually all of the top wineries specializing in Pinot Noir and Chardonnay are located in the Tualatin Valley and Yamhill County just west of Portland. A few wineries are also located to the south of Portland in the Salem and Eugene areas.

The climate in this area is significantly different from that of Mendocino, Napa, Sonoma, and other viticultural regions to the south in California. Cooler weather and more daylight hours (on average, two more than California's north coast per day, as in Burgundy) allows the grapes to mature at a slower pace and thus retain their natural acidity. Unlike California, where the addition of acidity to the finished wine is routinely employed to give the wines balance, in Oregon acidification rarely takes place. In California, only a few Chardonnays are put through a malolactic fermentation to lower acidity, because their acidity levels are already low. In Oregon, all of the Chardonnays go through malolactic and as a general rule are barrel fermented rather than tank fermented.

In short, the general style of the wines of Oregon is one with an undeniable European character. The wines develop and improve not only after being poured into the glass, but develop and improve in the bottle. Both the Pinot Noirs and Chardonnays are remarkably similar to their French counterparts and, as my blind tastings proved, often impossible to pick out as being "made in the U.S.A."

The best Pinot Noir producers in Oregon look to be Eyrie, Amity, Peter Adams, Adelsheim, Oak Knoll, Ponzi, and Bethel Heights, followed by Rex Hill, Sokol Blosser, and Elk Cove. For Chardonnay, Tualatin, Shafer, and Eyrie produced stunning wines in 1985 and 1983, and Peter Adams, Adelsheim, Ponzi, Knudsen Erath, Sokol Blosser, and Alpine have all proved that they can do something special with Chardonnay, given a good vintage.

Chardonnay and Pinot Noir are not the only top-quality wines made in Oregon. The Riesling is light, flowery, crisp, and aromatic. Eyrie Vineyards produces exceptionally good, dry Pinot Gris and Muscat that remind one of these same wines from Alsace. Shafer produces one of this country's best blush wines, a dry, vibrant Pinot Noir Blanc, and Oak Knoll a sweet raspberry wine that is the Chateau d'Yquem of American fruit wines. But for Cabernet Sauvignon and Merlot, California is still the unchallenged king.

The availability of Oregon wines is still rather poor. The top wines are available in small quantities, and despite the excellent quality of many of the wines, the trade has regarded Oregon as somewhat of a stepchild of the California wine industry. And not surprisingly the majority of the California wine press, forever cheerleaders for that state's wine industry, has done little to encourage consumer interest in Oregon's wines. This all should change as consumers get a chance to taste these wines of Oregon; the quality and excitement of their wines will be obvious to both the neophyte and the connoisseur. In addition, the prices are lower than those charged for California wines.

The tasting notes are arranged alphabetically by winery. Please note that many of the excellent 1985 Pinot Noirs, though already bottled, will not be released until late 1987 or early 1988.

QUICK VINTAGE GUIDE

1985—After the rainy, disappointing year of 1984, everyone in Oregon is immensely pleased with the 1985 vintage. It is generally a very good to excellent year for all varietals, but particularly Pinot Noir, Chardonnay, and Pinot Gris. This will be a vintage to buy.

1984—A poor year plagued by rain and cool weather. The wines are tart, lean, and lack charm.

1983—The vintage that finally brought Oregon wines their long-deserved publicity. Textbook climatic conditions and sunny, hot weather resulted in fully mature grape, excellent sugar contents, and an array of very impressive Pinot Noirs and Chardonnays that will age gracefully for 4–8 years. Quantities produced by the best growers were small and have largely disappeared from the marketplace.

1982—A good, above-average vintage of soft, medium-weight wines with decent ripeness and charm. The wines should be drunk up since they will not be long-lived.

1981—A good, even very good, vintage that produced very fine Pinot Noir and Chardonnay. The wines from the top producers are now in their prime and should be drunk up.

RATING OREGON'S PRODUCERS

* * * * * (OUTSTANDING PRODUCERS)

Eyrie Vineyards

* * * * (EXCELLENT PRODUCERS)

Peter F. Adams   Ponzi Vineyards
Adelsheim Vineyard   Rex Hill Vineyards
Amity Vineyards

* * * (GOOD PRODUCERS)

Alpine Vineyards

Bethel Heights

Elk Cove Vineyards

Knudsen Erath

Oak Knoll

Shafer Vineyard Cellars

Sokol Blosser

Tualatin Vineyards

Yamhill Valley Vineyards

* * (AVERAGE PRODUCERS)

Chateau Benoit

Forgeron Vineyard

Henry Estate

Hidden Springs

Hinman

Siskiyou

Valley View Vintners

Veritas Vineyard

PETER F. ADAMS (YAMHILL COUNTY)* * * *

If I knew only that this winery's T-shirt says "Real Wine Throws Tartrates," I would no doubt be kindly predisposed toward the Adams wines. Making only Pinot Noir (6½ acres planted) and Chardonnay (4½ acres planted), Adams made his first vintages at the Adelsheim winery. The quality of the 1982s and 1983s that I tasted was excellent, the prices shockingly low. His winemaking style seems to emphasize rich, pure flavors touched noticeably by aging in new oak barrels. Adams's wines are real winners. Fame and higher prices are sure to come, so move quickly. Availability is very limited.

1981 Chardonnay	($11.00)	89
1982 Chardonnay	($11.00)	85
1983 Chardonnay	($11.00)	87

There is nothing about the 1982 and 1983 Chardonnays to suggest that they will not surpass the wonderful 1981s; they are just so young and promising that, unlike California Chardonnays, they simply beg for 2–3 years of cellaring. The 1981 is the breathtaking Chardonnay, with a striking resemblance to a fine Meursault. An intense bouquet of buttery, rich fruit and toasty, vanillin oak is first-class. Quite fat, deep, medium-bodied and packed with flavor, it also has gorgeous balance. The 1982 is lower in acidity and less complex but still quite good. The 1983 is a powerful, oaky, rich, buttery wine with excellent length, acidity, and depth. It needs 1–3 years of cellaring.

1981 Pinot Noir	($11.00)	86
1982 Pinot Noir	($11.00)	86
1983 Pinot Noir	($11.00)	88
1984 Pinot Noir	($11.00)	82

All of these wines are extremely impressive Pinot Noirs. All have what looks to be good potential to develop and improve for 2–5 more years. The 1982 is the most evolved, exhibiting a real burgundian, smoky, oaky, ripe, fruity bouquet, lush, deep flavors, medium body, a spicy fruitiness, and an excitingly long finish. Expect it to drink well for 3–4 more years. The 1983 is still quite young and unevolved, but hints at being very complex. At present it has a vibrant, bright ruby color, a bouquet of ripe, smoky fruit and new oak, medium body, rather astonishing fruit intensity, and plenty of tannins. It should make quite a memorable bottle in 1990. The 1981 is the lightest, but fragrant, very burgundian, and ready to drink. Lastly, the 1984, a terrible year, is a top success for the vintage. It has a smoky, spicy, fruity nose and tannic flavors.

ADELSHEIM VINEYARD (YAMHILL COUNTY)* * * *

This 8,000-case winery is one of the up and coming stars on the domestic wine scene. The first vintage for Adelsheim was in 1978. Much of Adelsheim's winemaking education came from Oregon's most successful and best-known winemaker, David Lett of Eyrie Vineyard. Surprisingly, the winery makes a little Merlot and Cabernet Sauvignon (which I have not tasted), but its real stars are the Côte de Beaune-like Pinot Noir and Chardonnay. A good Pinot Gris in the Alsatian style is made, but it is not yet comparable to that of Eyrie Vineyard. The prices charged for Adelsheim's wines, in keeping with other Oregon wine prices, are extremely reasonable. Despite the small production, the wines have good distribution and are distinguished by their distinctive labels.

1982 Chardonnay	($10.00)	85
1983 Chardonnay	($10.00)	87

1984 Chardonnay   ($9.00)   72

These Chardonnays typify what makes the wines of Oregon so special and ageworthy. Barrel fermented, put through malolactic, and bottled with no acid adjustments, they are, not surprisingly, very similar in smell and texture to French white burgundy. The 1982 and 1983 are initially closed and predominantly oaky when first poured. However, with 10–20 minutes of airing, the buttery, rich layers of fruit swell in the glass. The long, crisp finish is unmistakable. The 1982 is more accessible and developed than the 1983, which is a more powerful, more deeply concentrated wine. It will be fascinating to see how these two wines develop over the next 1–4 years. The 1984, however, is green and tart, with little appeal.

1985 Pinot Gris   ($7.50)   80

This is a rather light wine with high acidity, that has as its principal attributes freshness and one-dimensional charm. Drink immediately.

1982 Pinot Noir   ($11.00)   85

1983 Pinot Noir   ($11.00)   87

When tasted blind against some good Côte de Beaune reds, these wines are impossible to pick out as domestic Pinot Noir. Adelsheim seems to know how to get a lush, intense, velvety, ripe cherry fruitiness in his Pinot Noir and he admirably complements it with some toasty, spicy, vanillin, new oak flavors and scents. The 1982 has oodles of cherries and spice, excellent balance, medium body, and crisp, long finish. It should only get better for 2–3 years. The 1983 has a gorgeously complex bouquet of ripe berry fruit and oak, lush, deep flavors, a haunting similarity to a Drouhin red Beaune Clos des Mouches, and 4–5 years of further evolution.

ALPINE VINEYARDS (NEAR EUGENE)* * *

This small 3,700-case winery makes an assortment of wines: Pinot Noir, Chardonnay, Riesling, Gewürztraminer, and Cabernet Sauvignon. My tasting experience has been with the Chardonnay and Pinot Noir, of which I preferred the former.

1982 Chardonnay   ($9.00)   82

1983 Chardonnay   ($9.00)   85

The 1982 Chardonnay has a lean, rather restrained and austere Chablis-like style. There is a good dosage of oak present and it seems to need 2–3 years of aging. The 1983 is similarly styled, only the fruit is more accessible and certainly more concentrated. Both wines are quite French in character.

1982 Pinot Noir	($10.00)	73

1983 Pinot Noir	($10.00)	78

Both Pinot Noirs have light-intensity flavors, rather light color (even for Pinot Noir), and short finishes. The 1982 is rather thin and frail. The 1983, ready to drink now is a little watery, but cleanly made, has elegant but faint cherry flavors, and a soft texture. Both wines require drinking over the next 1–2 years.

AMITY VINEYARDS (YAMHILL COUNTY)* * *

This Yamhill County winery is run by Myron Redford and is gaining an international reputation for its excellent Pinot Noir. The winery also makes Riesling, Chardonnay, and a proprietary blend called Solstice Blanc. As good as the Pinot Noir is, I cannot say the winery enjoys the same success with its other varietals. The current level of production is 8,500–9,000 cases.

1983 Chardonnay	($12.00)	84

1982 Chardonnay	($10.00)	76

1982 Chardonnay Winemaker's Reserve	($15.00)	87

1984 Gewürztraminer	($7.00)	72

1983 Solstice Blanc	($4.00)	75

Except for the very fine 1983 and 1982 Winemaker's Reserve Chardonnay, which have deep fruit, a rich yet restrained, oaky, spicy bouquet, a long finish, and still rather unevolved flavors, the other wines are rather nondescript and bland, with little varietal character, particularly the Gewürztraminer. The 1982 is deficient in fruit, the Solstice Blanc just boring and innocuous.

1981 Pinot Noir	($12.00)	78

1982 Pinot Noir	($12.00)	80

1983 Pinot Noir	($15.00)	84

1983 Pinot Noir Estate	($15.00)	87

1982 Pinot Noir Winemaker's Reserve	($18.00)	85

1983 Pinot Noir Winemaker's Reserve	($25.00)	89

Both the Amity 1983 Estate and Winemaker's Reserve Pinot Noirs are gorgeous wines, certainly among the finest Pinot Noirs I have ever tasted in this country. Unlike most Oregon Pinot Noirs, which I find to have a vivid cherrylike fruitiness, these two wines are Côte de Nuits-like with big, spicy, cinnamon-scented, smoky, earthy, ripe fruity bouquets. Both these Gevrey-Chambertin look-alikes are tremendously concentrated and deep, but also terribly young. You can buy the 1983 regular bottling, which has smoky, ripe, fragrant aromas, lusher, softer, more accessible flavors, and light tannins. The 1982 Winemaker's Reserve is medium ruby in color, rather young on the palate, but shows awfully good fruit and structure and a big, smoky nose. The 1982 regular is mature, with a soft cherry fruitiness, medium body, and light tannins. I found the 1981 to be a trifle too vegetal and tough and awkward on the palate.

CHATEAU BENOIT (CARLTON)* *

The specialty here is white wines, primarily German-inspired ones such as Müller-Thurgau and Riesling. To date, the red Pinot Noirs have been feeble efforts.

1982 Chardonnay Select Cluster	($8.00, 375 ML)	86

1985 Müller-Thurgau	($7.00)	82

1985 Sauvignon Blanc	($7.00)	83

The Müller-Thurgau is moderately sweet, very perfumed, light, and makes a fine apéritif. The Sauvignon Blanc has a smell of fresh straw, is aromatic, crisp and very pleasant. The sweet dessert wine, the Chardonnay, is rich and unctuous and should continue to drink well for 4–5 years.

1983 Pinot Noir	($8.95)	70

Very light in color, this is a diluted, surprisingly weak wine in what was an excellent vintage for Oregon Pinot Noir.

BETHEL HEIGHTS (SALEM)* * *

There is little we can say yet about this new winery in Salem, Oregon. Bonded in 1984, the Casteel and Webb families have heretofore been amateur winemakers and growers. Their 48-acre vineyard is planted with 21 acres of Pinot Noir, 14 of Chardonnay, and the balance in Gewürztraminer, Riesling, and Chenin Blanc. The 1983 Bonny Doon Pinot Noir made from grapes from the Bethel Heights vineyard was very good. I also tasted the 1983 noncommercial Pinot Noir made by Casteel and Webb; it was explosively rich and fruity with pure, intense, Pinot fruit. This should be a winery to watch.

1984 Pinot Noir ($12.00) 83

For a poor vintage, this wine has turned out surprisingly well. Soft, deep berry fruit offers plenty of appeal. The Pinot character is spicy and very fruity.

ELK COVE VINEYARDS (YAMHILL COUNTY)* * *

This 9,200-case winery has a good reputation already for its Chardonnay and Pinot Noir. The first crush here was in 1977 and the winery now has eight acres of Pinot Noir, seven of Riesling, five of Chardonnay, and four of Gewürztraminer. I have only tasted the Pinot Noir and Chardonnay. Based on what I have seen, the wines are good, with the Pinot Noir the most exciting entry.

1982 Chardonnay Dundee Hills ($12.00) 84

1982 Chardonnay Estate ($9.00) 78

Both of these Chardonnays may ultimately improve in score. Both are young and rather closed. The 1982 Estate seems a little short on fruit and slightly acidic in the finish. The 1982 Dundee Hills has more of a ripe fruit, toasty bouquet, good body, crisp, well-balanced flavors, and a good finish.

1983 Pinot Noir Dundee Hills Reserve ($15.00) 75

1982 Pinot Noir Estate ($15.00) 85

1983 Pinot Noir Estate ($15.00) 86

As Oregon Pinot Noirs go, these are rather expensive, but except for the 1983 Dundee Hills, which I found too vegetal on the nose but ripe and round on the palate, I liked the style of Pinot at this winery. The

1982 Estate is quite easy to confuse with a good Beaune. The bouquet of ripe cherries, damp earth, and spices is elegant and complex. The flavors are beautifully balanced with crisp acidity and soft, light tannins. It is a lovely wine for drinking over the next 1–3 years. The 1983 Estate is slightly riper, richer, and more multidimensional than the 1982. It seems to swell up in the glass after 10–15 minutes of airing. It should provide delicious drinking for 4–5 years.

EYRIE VINEYARDS (YAMHILL COUNTY)* * * * *

As the song goes, "Nobody does it better," and in winemaker and proprietor David Lett's case, no one did it any earlier. Lett planted his first vines in 1966 and opened his winery in 1970. He has been an inspiration to his winemaking peers in Oregon, who speak of him in admiring terms. His 1975 Pinot Noir was the first Oregon wine to get international recognition in the Paris tasting I mentioned in my introductory comments. One has only to taste this man's wines to realize that this is a very serious winemaker who knows exactly what he is doing. I have followed Eyrie's Pinot and Chardonnay since 1981 and I expect them to be very good, but he makes Oregon's and America's finest Pinot Gris, and his dry, aromatic Muscat, made in a style that clearly recalls similarly styled wines of Alsace, is quite an intriguing and delicious wine. Despite his stature as the "father" of the Oregon boutique wineries, one gets the impression that he just wants to remain small. His total case production is still tiny at 5,000. He has more challengers today, but his Pinot Noir remains Oregon's best example of the heights this temperamental grape variety can reach.

1985 Chardonnay	($12.50)	88
1983 Chardonnay	($12.50)	88
1984 Chardonnay	($12.50)	82

Extremely impressive Chardonnays, both the 1985 and 1983 seem to need 15–30 minutes to open and develop complexity. It will be interesting to see how they develop over the next 1–3 years in view of their tightness and structure. The 1985 is more accessible and shows a restrained, buttery, appley fruitiness, good body, a rich, long, crisp finish, and blossoming complexity. I think it will improve for 3–4 years. The 1983 tastes slightly more powerful and even deeper, but is still quite unevolved and needs 1–2 years. The 1984 is much lighter, rather oaky, but, given the difficult vintage, a success. These wines are barrel fermented and put through malolactic fermentations.

| 1982 Pinot Noir | ($12.00) | 85 |

| 1983 Pinot Noir | ($15.00) | 87 |

| 1984 Pinot Noir | ($12.00) | 77 |

| 1981 Pinot Noir Reserve | ($25.00) | 87 |

| 1982 Pinot Noir Reserve | ($25.00) | 86 |

| 1984 Pinot Noir Reserve | ($18.00) | 81 |

Like all of David Lett's wines, his Pinot Noirs also seem to magically
unfold in the glass. At first the nose is closed and the wine tastes
impressive but tight on the palate. Thirty minutes later, aromas of ripe
raspberries, spicy, toasty oak, and other smoky scents emerge and
the real show begins. I cannot say enough about these wines. The
1981 Reserve is a gorgeously deep, rich, spicy wine that still needs
4–5 years of cellaring. The bouquet of raspberries and cinnamon is
quite promising. Deeply colored, rich, yet tannic, it is a brilliantly
made Pinot. The 1983 regular Pinot Noir is quite tightly knit; I am
sure it needs 3–5 years to show its best, but one can even now be
impressed by the rich, ripe, plummy fruit, deep, intense Pinot flavors,
fragrant bouquet, and long finish. For drinking now, the 1982 Pinot
Noir is ideal. Richly aromatic with scents of cherries, oak, and spices,
this velvety soft, lovely wine has light tannins and should be drunk
over the next 1–2 years. The 1982 Reserve offers deeper, richer, more
tannic flavors than the regular bottling. It needs another 1–2 years.
The 1984 Pinot Noir is quite light and not up to recent standards. The
1984 Reserve has good, soft, jammy, Pinot fruit, but light body, and it
finishes short.

| 1985 Muscat Ottonel | ($8.50) | 84 |

| 1985 Pinot Gris | ($8.50) | 85 |

| 1984 Pinot Gris | ($8.50) | 82 |

Eyrie produces both a lovely Pinot Gris and dry Muscat. The 1984
Pinot Gris is good, but the 1985 has richer, more intense, spicy, distinctive flavors and begs for a fillet of Pacific northwest salmon. It is
long and rich on the palate, with surprising length. The 1985 Muscat
is dry, quite aromatic and seductive to the smell with crisp, clean

flavors. It would be ideal as an apéritif wine or as an accompaniment to creole cooking.

FORGERON VINEYARD (ELMIRA)* *

Located in the warmer southernmost part of the Willamette Valley, Forgeron was bonded in 1977 and has 20+ acres under vine producing Riesling, Pinot Noir, Chenin Blanc, and Cabernet Sauvignon. The **1982 Chardonnay ($6.99)**, 72, was dull-tasting and not very varietal. The **1983 Chenin Blanc ($6.99)**, 80, was quite good, crisp, slightly sweet and refreshing. The **1985 White Riesling ($7.49)**, 80, is a one-dimensional, slightly sweet wine that is fresh and simple.

HENRY ESTATE (UMPQUA VALLEY)* *

Located south of Eugene, Oregon, in Umpqua, the Henry Estate's wine did not fare well in the comparative blind peer group tastings. The **1981 Chardonnay ($7.99)**, 72, had a nice touch of oak but too little fruit and tasted like a minor Mâcon-Villages wine. The **Non-vintage Pinot Noir ($4.99)**, 73, has light color, some pleasant fruit in the nose, but is a little watery. The **1982 Pinot Noir ($10.00)**, 65, is light and has a decaying vegetation taste. The **1983 Pinot Noir ($9.95)**, 75, has a correct light ruby color, and clean, rather watery flavors. For Oregon, these are standard to below-average-quality wines.

HINMAN (EUGENE)* *

This winery began in 1979 and has a good reputation for Gewürztraminer and Riesling. Unfortunately, I have only tasted a good **1983 Chardonnay ($10.00)**, 82, made from Washington grapes; it has attractive, buttery, pineapple fruit, medium body, and a crisp, clean finish. The **1983 Pinot Noir ($10.00)**, 78, from Oregon grapes, was medium ruby, soft, clean, and pleasant. It, like the Chardonnay, should be drunk over the next 2 years. The winery's production of all varietals is 14,000 cases.

KNUDSEN ERATH (YAMHILL COUNTY)* * *

One of Oregon's three biggest wineries, and one of its oldest (started in 1969), this winery seems to produce consistently good Chardonnay, Pinot Noir, and Riesling. The current production is just in excess of 24,000 cases. Knudsen Erath's wines showed consistently well in my tastings. Rather than being big and overblown, they are elegant, rich in fruit, but balanced and quite accessible and forward. Whether they will evolve and age as long as the wines of Eyrie, Adelsheim, Adams, and Ponzi is for time to tell.

1982 Chardonnay	($9.00)	68

1983 Chardonnay	($9.00)	86

I am not sure what went wrong in 1982, but the Chardonnay is excessively oaky, very acidic, slightly oxidized, and suspiciously deficient in ripe fruit. On the other hand, the 1983 exhibits an impressive oak/fruit balance, good intensity of flavors wrapped in toasty oak, real elegance, and a crisp, lively finish. The 1983 should last and improve for at least 3–4 years.

N.V. Pinot Noir	($5.99–$6.99)	74

1980 Pinot Noir Vintage Select	($10.00)	83

1982 Pinot Noir Vintage Select	($10.00)	84

1983 Pinot Noir Vintage Select	($13.00)	84

The Non-vintage is clean, fruity, simple, and pleasant. It does taste like Pinot Noir. The 1980 Vintage Select is quite an elegant, very burgundian-like wine with a savory cherry fruitiness, medium body, and soft yet short finish. The 1982 Vintage Select has a sweet, jammy, soft midrange that is very reminiscent of a good Côte de Beaune, a soft, lush finish with light tannins still in evidence, and an attractive, moderately intense bouquet. The 1983 Vintage Select is surprisingly closer in style to the 1982 than what I normally saw from other Yamhill County wineries when comparing their Pinot Noirs of 1982 with 1983. Slightly deeper in color than the 1982, medium-bodied, the bouquet offers pure cherry and toasty oak aromas, but the flavors are relatively closed. Drink the 1982 and age the 1983 for two years.

OAK KNOLL (TUALATIN VALLEY)* * *

This winery, fairly old by Oregon's standards (bonded in 1970), specializes in not only Pinot Noir, Chardonnay, and Riesling, but also fruit wine of which the raspberry and loganberry are reputed to be among the best in this country. Total production varies, but in 1983 was 23,000 cases. Based on my tastings, the Chardonnays have yet to catch up in quality with the Pinot Noirs. I have never tasted it, but the 1980 Vintage Select Pinot Noir made by Oak Knoll has been one of the greatest Pinots made in this country.

| 1982 Chardonnay | ($9.00) | 70 |

| 1983 Chardonnay | ($9.00) | 84 |

What a difference a vintage makes. The 1982 is thin, overly oaked, and just deficient in fruit. It borders on being unattractive in its meagerness of flavor. The 1983 seems to have gotten things right. Light golden, with an attractive balance of fruit and oak, medium body, crisp acidity, and a good finish, the 1983 is a good Chardonnay, and will be even better with 6–12 months of bottle aging.

| 1983 Pinot Noir | ($12.00) | 82 |

| 1982 Pinot Noir Vintage Select | ($14.00) | 85 |

| 1983 Pinot Noir Vintage Select | ($14.00) | 86 |

I found Oak Knoll's Pinot Noirs absolutely indistinguishable from a good French Côte de Beaune. They are extremely elegant, fragrant, and much more accessible and presumably earlier maturing than some of the more profound, statuesque, and ageworthy Pinot Noir wines from the likes of Eyrie, Peter Adams, and Amity. The 1982 Vintage Select is mature and exhibits a lovely ripe cherry fruitiness with just the right touch of oak. Lush and savory, it makes one think of a good Beaune when drinking it. The 1983 regular bottling is light and elegant, with a touch of spicy oak to add complexity, has clean, pure Pinot Noir fruit, and a good finish. It should drink well for 3–4 years. The 1983 Vintage Select is remarkably similar to a fine red Premier Cru Beaune. It has a rich, ruby color, a full-intensity, fine, smoky, oaky, ripe cherry fruit bouquet, lush yet firm flavors, rather intense fruit, medium body, and a good finish. It is a lovely wine with character, finesse, and charm. It should drink well for 1–3 years.

PONZI VINEYARDS (TUALATIN VALLEY)* * * *

I like everything I have tasted from this small winery and everything I have read and heard about it. First, and most important, the wines are made very naturally (no cold stabilization) in an elegant, subtle style. The winery was bonded in 1974 and now produces nearly 4,000 cases of Riesling, Chardonnay, Pinot Noir, and Pinot Gris. Prices charged for the Ponzi wines are extremely modest given the quality.

1982 Chardonnay	($9.00)	78
1983 Chardonnay	($10.00)	85
1982 Chardonnay Reserve	($9.49)	84
1985 Pinot Gris	($8.99)	85

Vividly different levels of fruit intensity and depth are apparent in the two regular bottlings of Chardonnay. The 1982 is similar to a Chablis, lighter, crisp, lean, with good acidity, a pleasant oakiness, and a refreshing quality, although somewhat simple. On the other hand, the 1982 Reserve has an elegant ripeness of fruit, medium body, a refreshing crisp acidity, and real solid flavor authority. The 1983 is initially rather closed and oaky to smell, but as it sits in the glass, ripe, spicy, deep fruit swells noticeably. It needs 12 months or more to totally gain harmony, but already shows impressive structure, balance, and excellent winemaking. The 1985 Pinot Gris is delicious, spicy, fresh, and a peerless match for grilled salmon.

1980 Pinot Noir	($10.00)	79
1982 Pinot Noir	($10.00)	83
1983 Pinot Noir	($12.00)	85

These are lovely Côte de Beaune-styled Pinot Noirs. The 1980 starts off well, offering smoky, ripe berry fruit, and a touch of oak in its complex bouquet, but falls off in the mouth and finishes short. The 1982 regular bottling has a seductive bouquet of ripe berry fruit and smoky oak, some tannin, and noticeable acidity and good length. It should be at its peak in 1–2 years. The 1983 is richer and deeper, with medium ruby color, a rich, smoky, ripe cherry fruit bouquet, good intensity of flavors, moderate tannins, and fine balance. It should be close to maturity by 1987–88.

REX HILL VINEYARDS (YAMHILL COUNTY)* * * *

A sparkling new winery, Rex Hill will produce 5,500 cases of Pinot Noir, Chardonnay, Riesling, and Gewürztraminer. The only wines I have tasted are three 1983 vineyard-designated Pinot Noirs. This appears to be a winery to watch, given the commitment, both physical and financial, to excellence.

1983 Pinot Noir Archibald Vyds.	($16.50)	87

1983 Pinot Noir Dundee Hills	($16.50)	81

1983 Pinot Noir Maresh Vyds.	($16.50)	86

All three of these wines show impressive winemaking. My least favorite is the Dundee Hills, because of the vegetal aspect to its bouquet. Otherwise it exhibited very good fruit, medium body, and good depth. Both the Archibald and Maresh recalled Cortons from the Prince de Mérode, particularly the Archibald. Both have beautiful deep ruby color (the Maresh is a shade darker). The Archibald has an expansive bouquet of ripe cherry fruit, new oak, rather tannic, youthful flavors with a touch of mint, and a good finish. It needs 4–5 years. The Maresh is more concentrated and fuller-bodied, slightly minty, very long on the palate, and pretty intense and aggressive. It needs 4–5 years of cellaring. I would have scored it higher except for the minty eucalyptus nose that I personally do not like.

SHAFER VINEYARD CELLARS (TUALATIN VALLEY)* * *

To date I have been extremely impressed by this winery's Chardonnay and Pinot Noir Blanc. The Pinot Noirs I have tasted have been rather light and pale-colored, though flavorful. The prices are very fair.

1982 Chardonnay	($9.99)	87

1983 Chardonnay	($9.99)	86

Stylistically, the Shafer Chardonnays are as close to the French style of white burgundy as any I have tasted. Rather reserved and closed in at first, they develop beautifully in the glass. The 1982 has a slight edge; it is more open and developed, quite multidimensional, with deep flavors complemented admirably by crisp acidity. The 1983 shows the exact same style, only it is younger, more closed, but has impeccable balance and quite a long finish. It will be interesting to see how these two wines develop.

1983 Pinot Noir	($10.00)	81

This is a lighter-colored Pinot Noir than most 1983s from Oregon. It is also close to full maturity. Light ruby with an intensely fragrant, spicy, slightly minty, smoky, fruity Pinot bouquet, soft on the palate with medium body and light tannins, this wine should provide nice drinking for 1–2 more years.

1985 Pinot Noir Blanc   ($6.49)   82

Shafer's rendition of a blush wine is one of the best. Quite dry, crisp, delicate, and ever so refreshing, this medium-bodied wine makes a lovely apéritif.

SOKOL BLOSSER (YAMHILL COUNTY)* * *

One of the three largest Oregon wineries (the 1983 production was 23,000 cases) Sokol Blosser has probably done the best promotional job of getting their wines into different markets around the country. To date, the Pinot Noirs have stood out as the winery's best, but the Chardonnay can be good, as well as the Riesling and Sauvignon Blanc. Prices are very moderate.

1982 Chardonnay Reserve   ($12.00)   84

This is a moderately intense Chardonnay that exhibits good concentration, a toasty, vanillin oakiness, crisp acidity, and medium body. It has a good finish and should continue to evolve and improve.

1983 Pinot Noir Hyland Vyd.   ($9.95)   84

1983 Pinot Noir Red Hills   ($11.95)   86

Two very different Pinot Noirs: the 1983 Hyland is ready to drink, soft, fruity, and spicy, with a charming berry fruitiness and medium body. It should drink nicely for 2–3 years. The 1983 Red Hills is altogether a more serious, deeper, richer, more concentrated wine. Rich in black cherry fruit, darker in color, more obviously tannic, it is an impressive Pinot Noir that needs 1–2 years of cellaring.

TUALATIN VINEYARDS (TUALATIN VALLEY)* * *

A well-established winery (the first crush was in 1973), the strength of Tualatin's wines appears to be its whites, particularly Riesling and Chardonnay. The Chardonnays, along with those of Eyrie and Shafer, are, in my opinion, the best I have tasted from Oregon. Tualatin has not had the same success with Pinot Noir. This is a large vineyard (by Oregon standards) of 83 acres, consisting of 33 in Riesling, 21 in Chardonnay, 14 in Gewürztraminer, and 11 in Pinot Noir.

1981 Chardonnay   ($10.00)   87

1982 Chardonnay   ($10.00)   80

1983 Chardonnay ($10.00) 88

The 1981 is an excellent Chardonnay with complex, earthy, smoky, buttery aromas and outstanding length and balance. The 1982 is less interesting, rather austere and lean, without the deep depth of fruit the 1981 has. Look out for the 1983, a real winner. Quite rich yet, in the Oregon style, it has a restrained power, a very complex, buttery, oaky, smoky bouquet, crisp, natural acidity, and super length and balance.

1981 Pinot Noir ($9.90) 62

Intensely herbaceous, vegetal aromas, light ruby/orangish color, and thin, tart flavors make for an unpleasant drinking experience.

VALLEY VIEW VINTNERS (JACKSONVILLE, OREGON)* *

This small winery (under 10,000 cases) in the southern part of Oregon emphasizes Cabernet Sauvignon and Merlot, although Chardonnays, Gewürztraminers, and some Pinot Noirs are produced. I have a few tasting notes for Valley View's wines and they are mixed. A 1983 Pinot Noir ($4.49), 75, was simple and pleasant and fairly priced. The 1980 Cabernet Sauvignon ($10.00), 70, was entirely too vegetal and herbaceous; however, the 1981 Merlot ($10.00), 84, has rich, chocolatey, spicy, intense flavors, a chunky texture, and good depth.

VERITAS VINEYARD (YAMHILL COUNTY)* *

A new winemaking operation, Veritas's first wines are from the excellent 1983 vintage. The 1983 Pinot Noir ($9.00), 81, has dark color, a ripe, rather jammy, chunky texture, good fruit, but not as much complexity as one normally finds in Oregon's Pinots. Nevertheless, it has appeal. The 1984 Chardonnay ($9.00), 72, is a little light and lacking in flavor authority, but offers light to moderately intense flavors, some spicy vanillin, buttery scents, and a short finish.

YAMHILL VALLEY VINEYARDS (YAMHILL COUNTY)* * *

Another brand new winery, the first wines were released in the fall of 1985. The only wine I have tasted was extremely impressive, a 1983 Pinot Noir ($14.00), 87. Quite rich and fragrant, with oodles of ripe, plummy, smoky Pinot fruit, it had a long, concentrated feel on the palate and moderately soft tannins. It should reach maturity by 1988.

Other Oregon Wines

Of the other wines I tried, my notes show an impressive rating for the 1983 **Arterberry Pinot Noir** ($10.00), 84, poor marks for a 1981 **Siskiyou Pinot Noir**, which had a cardboard-like aroma and watery flavors, poor marks for an unvarietal-tasting 1983 **Hidden Springs Reserve Riesling**, a 1982 **Hidden Springs Pinot Noir**, as well as a 1981 **Hillcrest Riesling**.

8. OTHER AMERICAN VITICULTURAL REGIONS

One can find vineyards in almost every state, most of them tiny and with purely local supporters. While the great majority of the wines I have tasted from other areas outside Oregon and California have left me unimpressed, there are isolated cases in at least ten other states of high-quality winemaking as well as potential. The following wineries are those at which wine consumers should give a serious look. Except for the several large wineries in Washington state, most of these wineries' products will rarely be found outside their state of origin.

Connecticut

The standout winery in this state is **Crosswoods** in North Stonington. The Chardonnay ($12) is a delicious, ripe, lemony, buttery wine that shows toasty oak and plenty of body. In power and depth, it is more akin to something from California's central coast than New England. The production here is 4,000 cases.

Idaho

One winery again dominates this state's wine production. The **Ste. Chapelle** winery in Caldwell produces in excess of 100,000 cases of wine using grapes from growers throughout the state as well as from Washington. Their red wines have been mediocre at best, but the white wines, particularly their moderately sweet Johannisberg Riesling and slightly sweet Chenin Blanc, each priced at $4–$7, are quite well made. The winery promotes its Chardonnays, but they have been uninspiring and bland.

Maryland

There are a number of good wineries in Maryland, yet few are known outside the state because of tiny productions. The most famous winery is Dr. Hamilton Mowbray's **Montbray Vineyard** in Westminster. The crusty and feisty Mowbray produces the finest Seyval-Villard in America, a wine that is easy to confuse with a white burgundy from the Côte Chalonnaise. His Cabernet Sauvignon is also good (the 1982 is excellent) and the barrel-fermented Chardonnay can make many a French Chablis look thin. Mowbray is a very serious winemaker and his 3,000-case production is quickly sold out to local enthusiasts.

The East Coast's best Cabernet Sauvignon is made by **Byrd Vineyard** in Myersville, Maryland. With hillside vineyards planted in the foothills of the Appalachian Mountains, Byrd's rich, black ruby-colored, tannic Cabernets are closest in spirit to those of Mayacamas in Napa Valley. They have been immensely impressive young, particularly the 1980, 1982, the blockbuster 1983 and the 1984 (all sell for $12–$14). Each needs a decade to show its true potential. Unfortunately, Byrd's other wines tend to be dull, overoaked, and uninteresting.

Other Maryland vineyards to take note of are **Catoctin Vineyards** in Brookeville, which produces above-average Chardonnay and Cabernet, and a newcomer, **Basignani Wine Cellars** in Sparks, which has good Chardonnay, Seyval-Villard, and promising Cabernet Sauvignon.

Massachusetts

One taste of the **Commonwealth Winery's** Chardonnay or Riesling is convincing proof that fine wines can be made in this northern state. A cranberry sparkling wine is also produced by this Plymouth winery.

New Jersey

The **Tewksbury** Winery in Lebanon, New Jersey, is the uncontested leader here. Again, the red wines are run-of-the-mill, but the white wines are a different story altogether. Seyval-Villard, white Riesling, Gewürztraminer, and Chardonnay all merit interest and sell at reasonable prices of $6.50–$8.50 a bottle.

New York

New York has the greatest number of wineries of any state after California and Oregon. My tasting notes show I have tasted wine from over 50 of the 65+ wineries in existence. The two major viticultural areas are the beautiful Finger Lakes region and Long Island. Like most viticultural regions in the Northeast, the red wines are generally insipid and in many cases frankly repugnant. Many of the best wineries do not even make a red wine, but one winery has miraculously excelled with Cabernet Sauvignon and Merlot. The **Hargrave Vineyard** in Cutchogue, Long Island, makes very good, sometimes excellent, Cabernet Sauvignon that is one of the two best red wines produced in the East (the other is Byrd's Cabernet Sauvignon). The winery also does an excellent job with Sauvignon Blanc and Chardonnay.

Elsewhere in New York, Chardonnay, Riesling, and Seyval-Villard are the principal grape varietals that have proved successful. For Chardonnay, the finest producer in the East, and one of the best in the country, is **Wagner Vineyards** in Lodi. Their 1980, 1981, and 1984 Chardonnays had remarkable depth of flavor as well as complexity. Wagner may be at the summit in terms of Chardonnay, but there are a bevy of fine producers of this wine. **Bridgehampton** on Long Island, **Plane's Casa Larga, Finger Lakes Wine Cellars, Glenora,** and **Knapp,** all near the Finger Lakes, **Pindar** on Long Island, **Schloss Doepken, West Park, Wickham Vineyards,** and **Hermann J. Wiemer** are all reliable producers of Chardonnay. Other than Wagner's explosively rich Chardonnay, the style of New York Chardonnays is more austere, leaner, and less opulently fruity than those found in California.

Several other wineries of note are **Clinton,** a producer of very good Seyval, **Benmarl,** a good producer of Seyval, and the idiosyncratic **Bully Hill,** a good producer of white wine hybrids.

Ohio

There is a small but flourishing wine industry in Ohio. I have had little experience with many of this state's wineries, but I do recommend one winery that has pleased me time and time again. The **Markko Vineyard** in Conneaut does a good job with a Chardonnay that has a lemony, fresh apple fruitiness, good, clean varietal character, and plenty of body. The price is a reasonable $9 per bottle.

Pennsylvania

This state's wineries have never, to my judgment, demonstrated the potential for making fine wine. However, there is one notable exception, the small **Allegro Vineyards** in Brogue. There is no one more serious about his winemaking than owner John Crouch. If he can overcome the enormous economic strains of financing a new winery, I predict big things for him and his wines. To date, the successes have been the beautiful Cabernet Sauvignon; the 1980, 1982, and 1983 all revealed rich blackcurrant fruitiness married intelligently with toasty new oak. Crouch's Seyval-Villard is also good and his Chardonnay seems to get better with each vintage, the 1984 being the best yet. Prices here range from $6 for the Seyval to $12–$15 for the reserve Cabernets. Another good winery to keep an eye out for is Naylor's.

Rhode Island

I have often wondered how the 10,000-case **Sakonnet Vineyard** in Little Compton can make good wine so far north. Yet this winery makes very interesting, well-made wine ranging from good Riesling and Chardonnay to a particularly interesting Pinot Noir. The winery's very good blush wine in 1985 was called Eye of the Storm after the savage hurricane "Gloria" that wreaked havoc on the northeastern coastline that year. Prices are extremely reasonable, ranging from $4 for the hybrids to $8 for the vinifera-based wine.

Texas

Texans are unusually chauvinistic about anything grown, produced, or located in that state, but everyone should pay more attention to the handful of wineries in this state that are making very fine wine. For Cabernet Sauvignon, the **Pheasant Ridge Winery** in Lubbock is turning out delicious, lush, intense wines with plenty of character. The bold $15–$20 price is Texas-proportioned. For Chardonnay, the **Llano Winery** in Lubbock made an exquisite 1984 and good 1985 Chardonnay for $12 a bottle. For fruity, fresh, slightly sweet Chenin Blanc, both the aforementioned Llano Winery and **Fall Creek** in Tow are worthy of attention. There are at least another half-dozen wineries sprouting up in Texas, but for the moment, these three wineries can compete in quality with anybody.

Virginia

The state of Virginia and its producers actively promote the state's wines, but I cannot see any reason for their enthusiasm. There has been a great deal of money invested in winery operations, but for a state that is quite hot and extremely humid, though lovely, one has to be cautious about the future for quality wine here. To date, the **Meredyth Winery** in the historic town of Middleburg has done a credible job with the hybrids, but the Chardonnay and Cabernet have left me consistently unimpressed. I have not yet tasted a good Cabernet or Merlot from Virginia, but the winery of **Mont Domaine** in Charlottesville is getting close to producing very good red wines. With respect to Chardonnay, the outlook is hardly any better. The best Chardonnays have come from three wineries: **Ingleside Plantation** in Oak Grove, **Naked Mountain** in Markham, and **Piedmont Vineyards**. These Chardonnays tend to be well marked by oak, but are correct and pleasant. For Riesling, **Rapidan River Vineyards** in Culpepper has, since 1978, produced a series of very flavorful, interesting wines. Lastly, **Piedmont Vineyards** also produces a very good, interesting Semillon.

I hope these Virginia wineries succeed, but in all truthfulness, the quality of most of their wines does not stand up well when compared to what else is available from around the world. The one exception appears to be the wines of Piedmont Vineyards.

Washington

With the emergence of its neighbor, Oregon, as a wine star, Washington must be wondering when it will have its day in the sun. I for one am not nearly as enthusiastic as others seem to be about the prospects for many Washington wines, but in all fairness, most of the serious wineries have just gotten started. Red wines produced in Washington have been patchy at best. Certainly the huge **Ste. Michelle Winery** has been the production leader with its adequate, but often vegetal Cabernet Sauvignon (a deeper reserve bottling is also inconsistent) and Merlot, followed by **Columbia Winery**, Haviland, and the tiny **Woodward Canyon**. It is this last winery that has shown the best potential for serious red wines in Washington.

Despite all the problems with red wine, white wine, particularly the cool climate varietals such as Riesling, has done better in Washington than anywhere outside of Germany. Wineries such as **Hogue**, **Ste. Michelle**, **F. Wilhelm Langguth**, **Hinzerling**, and **Arbor Crest** have produced excellent Rieslings—light, fresh, aromatic, and beautifully balanced. **Ste. Michelle, Bernard Griffin, Arbor Crest,** and **Columbia** have demonstrated equally talented hands at making Sauvignon Blanc and Semillon. Chardonnay is also made in increasing quantities in Washington state, and the best wines I have tasted have come from the following wineries: **Kiona, Arbor Crest, and Woodward Canyon.**

Other Washington wineries that have performed less consistently but can do good things with white wines are **Snoqualmie, Preston,** and **Covey Run.**

Whether Washington's wineries can survive the global competition by consistently making very good Riesling remains to be seen.

THE BEST OF THE REST

Australia
The Middle East
South America

9. AUSTRALIA, THE MIDDLE EAST, SOUTH AMERICA

AUSTRALIA

Another Emerging Star

For the next decade, I see three wine-producing countries emerging into stardom and popularity. Spain, Chile, and Australia all have had enormous potential, but the introduction of more modern technology, the explosion of interest in fine wine and fine wine values, and the increasing prices for the glamour wines of France have all combined to focus more and more attention on these three countries. However, Spain and Chile's strong points are their red wines. In Australia, they can do everything well and they are.

Traditionally, this has been red wine country, but the new wave of Chardonnays from the Aussies have left me remarkably impressed. In addition, some of the late-harvest, decadently sweet dessert wines and tawny and vintage port look-alikes from here are strikingly beautiful wines. High quality, increasingly good availability, and modest prices should propel Australia's wines into international prominence over the next several years.

RECENT VINTAGES

Vintages are especially hard to appraise because in this vast country there are major differences in climatic conditions in Victoria and

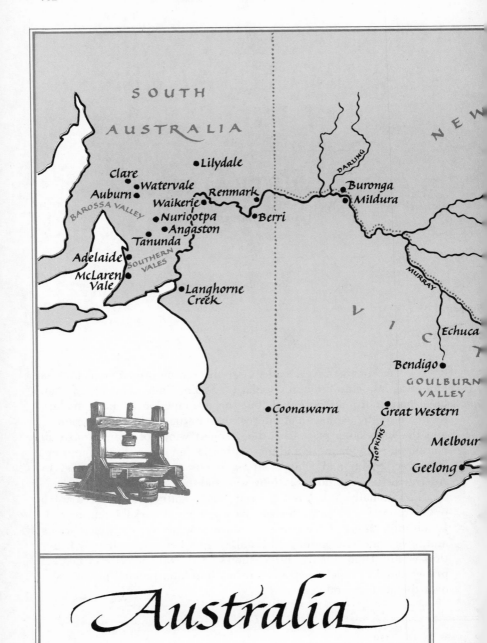

Australia

SOUTH WALES

Mudgee

Muswellbrook

HUNTER

Rothbury

HUNTER
VALLEY

Pokolbin

Cessnock

LACHLAN

Forbes

Cowra

Rooty Hill

ABERCROMBIE

Cobbitty

Sydney

Yenda

Griffith

Young

LACHLAN

MURRUMBIDGEE
IRRIGATION AREA

Wagga Wagga

Canberra

THE RIVERLAND

Barooga

Corowa

N

W   E

herglen

S

enrowan

Milawa

AUSTRALIAN ALPS

R   I   A

ahbilk

YARRA
VALLEY

50   100
MILES

50   100   150
KILOMETERS

Northern
Territory

Queensland

Western
Australia

South
Australia

New
South Wales

Victoria

Melbourne

New South Wales, the two best-known wine regions, and Queensland, Northern Territory, South Australia, and Western Australia. Most Australian authorities claim that 1984, 1985, and 1986 were the best recent vintages, 1983 the worst. Nevertheless, most of Australia's viticultural regions enjoy a hot, sunny, Mediterranean-type climate.

What You Need to Know

Like any wine-producing region, knowing the finest growers/producers here will give you the maximum benefit. The labels of Australian wines are as confusing as those of Germany. Special "bin" selections, wines called Riesling that have Chardonnay or Semillon in them, Cabernets blended with Sirah (called Shiraz), and other anomalies are normal here since virtually anything goes. Knowing the finest producers will narrow the risk and ease the pain of making a terrible choice. Therefore, I have concentrated on the producers of the Cabernet and Shiraz as well as the Chardonnay. But there is so much more here. For example, the sparkling wines made by **Yellowglen** (priced at under $11) put to shame anything coming out of California. The remarkable old fortified Muscats and Tokays of **William Chambers** and **Brown Bros.** ($15–$75 a bottle) are among the most sublime after-dinner drinks I have ever tasted. The Rieslings will not strike any fear in the hearts of German winemakers, but they are superior to anything produced in North America. However, some of the late-harvest Rieslings, Semillons, and Sauvignon Blancs from producers such as Petaluma, Rosemount, and Peter Lehmann are phenomenal and can successfully rival, sometimes surpass, their German and French counterparts, at one-third the price.

Yet it is the Chardonnays and red wines, particularly the Cabernets and Shiraz-based wines, that can compete with the best in the world. When one tastes the likes of a **Penfolds** Bin 95 Grange Hermitage ($35) or a **Rosemount** Chardonnay ($16–$25), there is no doubt that these two wines are among the world's elite. And there are other growers making wines almost as spectacular as these. For Chardonnay, in addition to Rosemount, look for **Leeuwin, Montrose, Tyrrell, Petaluma,** and **Lindeman.** For Cabernet and Shiraz, see the ratings of the producers and growers; there are simply too many fine producers to mention.

A GUIDE TO AUSTRALIA'S BEST PRODUCERS OF CABERNET SAUVIGNON AND SHIRAZ

***** (OUTSTANDING PRODUCERS)

Penfolds (South Australia)

Petaluma (South Australia)

Alkoomie (Western Australia)
Baileys (Victoria)
Balgownie (Victoria)
Brand's Laira (Coonawarra)
Chateau Tahbilk (Victoria)
Huntington Estate (New South
    Wales)

Lake's Folly (New South Wales)
St. Huberts (Victoria)
Seville Estate (Victoria)
Taltarni (Victoria)
Virgin Hills (Victoria)
Wolf Blass (Victoria)

*** (GOOD PRODUCERS)

Brokenwood (New South Wales)
Bowen Estate (South Australia)
Brown Bros. (Victoria)
Fern Hill (McLaren)
Lindeman's (New South Wales)
Mildara (Victoria)
Montrose (Mudgee)
Moss Wood (Western Australia)

Mount Avoca (Victoria)
Redman (Coonawarra)
Saxondale (New South Wales)
Seppeit (Barossa)
Vasse Felix (Western Australia)
Wrights (Western Australia)
Wyndham Estate (South
    Australia)

A GUIDE TO AUSTRALIA'S BEST PRODUCERS OF CHARDONNAY

***** (OUTSTANDING PRODUCERS)

Rosemount Estate (New South
    Wales)

**** (EXCELLENT PRODUCERS)

Arrowfield (New South Wales)
Huntington Estate (Mudgee)
Lake's Folly (New South Wales)
Leeuwin (Western Australia)
Lindeman's (New South Wales)
Miramar (Mudgee)

Montrose (Mudgee)
Moss Wood (Western Australia)
Petaluma (South Australia)
Seppeit (Barossa)
Mark Swann (South Australia)
Tyrrell (New South Wales)

Balgownie (Victoria)   Rothbury Estate (New South
Brown Bros. (Victoria)   Wales)
Hungerford Hill (New South
   Wales)

THE MIDDLE EAST

The top wine of the Middle East is a story in itself. Thirty kilometers (18 miles) from the savage and senseless civil war that has torn apart Beirut is **Château Musar,** a winemaking estate founded in the thirties and one that makes superlative wines from a blend of Cabernet Sauvignon, Syrah, and Cinsault. Owner/winemaker Serge Hochar has had vintages wiped out because no harvesters would risk their lives to pick the grapes, but still he continues. His wine training came from his father and a stint in Bordeaux, but the wines made here remind me of the best and most complex Châteauneuf-du-Papes. They are quite full-bodied, very fragrant, rich and supple enough to drink young, but if the very good 1966 and exquisite 1970 tasted last year are any indication, they will last 10, even 20 years. The vintages now on the market are the 1975, 1977, 1978, and 1979, retailing for less than $8 a bottle, undeniable bargains given the quality here. The 1977 is deeper and has more potential than the 1975. The 1979 is gorgeously fragrant and velvety. Musar is still relatively unknown; as long as the disastrous civil war continues to rage, the future is uncertain here, but this estate does indeed produce outstanding wine.

SOUTH AMERICA

Argentina and Chile dominate winemaking in South America. Argentina seems to have an endless array of incredibly cheap, solid, pleasant wines that, if rarely exciting, are hard to ignore at their ridiculously low prices. On the other hand, Chile has enormous potential but also chronic political instability and nineteenth-century winemaking techniques that have kept them from reaching their full capabilities. Yet Chile is the only major viticultural area in the world that never suffered from the phylloxera plague of the last century, and many of the older vineyards here consist of ungrafted European root stocks that history says produce the greatest wines. Certainly the Cabernet Sauvignons from **Cousino Macul** and Sauvignon Blancs from **Canepa** can stand head to head in the best of company.

I have been quite pleased with red wines from Argentina, especially Cabernet Sauvignon and Sirah from **Aberdeen Angus**. Prices are $2.99–$3.99 per bottle. Another good producer of red wine is **Etchart,** whose Cabernet called Cafayate sells for $4.99. For white wines, things are more tricky, but if you stick to Etchart's Torrontes ($4.99) in only the most recent vintage and the **Resero** Blanc ($2.99) from the winery of the same name, you are unlikely to be disappointed.

For Chile there are a bevy of wineries that are modernizing and taking their winemaking more seriously than ever, but two merit serious consideration. Chile's and South America's finest wine is the world-class Cabernet Sauvignon Antiguas Reserva from **Cousino Macul.** The 1978, 1979, and 1980 ($8.49 per bottle) all show layers of classic blackcurrant fruit, medium to full body, an intense, complex, smoky, cedary bouquet, and enough tannin to continue to evolve gracefully for 5–10 years. A 1947 Antiguas Reserva drunk in 1986 showed that in certain vintages this wine can live as long as a top Bordeaux. Cousino Macul produces two other wines of special significance. Their regular bottling of Cabernet ($5.99) is meant to be drunk upon release. Both the 1981 and 1982 are particularly attractive and supple. The Chardonnay produced here never sees a wood barrel and is bottled quickly to preserve its freshness. It is a soft, creamy, very fruity wine that for $6 a bottle represents a very good buy. The 1985 and 1986 must be consumed within two years of the vintage.

Another top grower is **José Canepa,** a very modern winery that produces an excellent Sauvignon Blanc that I would put up against my favorite California Sauvignons any day. It sells for an unbelievably low $6 per bottle. Both the 1986 and 1985 are delicious, full of freshness and character. This fine winery also makes a Gran Brandis Cabernet Sauvignon for $7 that is not up to Cousino Macul's standards, but is certainly above average.

Other Chilean wineries to look for are that of Spain's **Miguel Torres, Tarapaca, Concha y Toro,** and **Chateau Andrew.** None of their wines should cost more than $6.50 a bottle. Wineries that have left me unimpressed are **Santa Carolina** and **Undurraga.**

Consider buying Chilean wines very seriously—you are likely to be very favorably impressed.

HOW TO BUY, STORE, SERVE, AND DRINK WINE

HOW TO BUY WINE

On the surface, having made your choices in advance, buying wine seems simple enough—you go to your favorite wine merchant and purchase a few bottles. However, there are some subtleties in buying wine that must be appreciated in order to ensure that the wine is in healthy condition and unspoiled.

To begin with, take a look at the bottle of wine you are about to buy. Poor storage generally is revealed by the condition of the bottle in your hand. First of all, if the cork has popped above the rim of the bottle and is pushed above the lead or plastic capsule that covers the top of the bottle, then look for another bottle to buy. Wines that have been exposed to very high temperatures expand in the bottle, thereby putting pressure on the cork and pushing it upward against the capsule. And it is the highest-quality wines, those that have not been overly filtered or pasteurized, that are the most subject to abusive transportation or storage, and they will show the effects in this manner. A wine that has been frozen in transit or storage will likewise push the cork out, and while the freezing of a wine is less damaging than the boiling of it, both are hazardous to its health. Remember: Any cork that is protruding above the rim of the bottle is a bad sign

and the bottle should be returned to the shelf and never, ever purchased.

Another sign that a wine has been poorly stored is the presence of
seepage ("legs") around the rim of the bottle. This is the sometimes
sticky, dried residue of wine that has expanded and seeped around
the cork and dripped onto the rim. This condition is almost always
due to excessively high temperatures in transit or storage. Few merchants take the trouble to wipe this evidence off, and it can often be
spotted, particularly in wines that are shipped during the heat of summer or brought into the United States through the Panama Canal in
containers that are not air-conditioned. In any case, avoid buying any
wine that shows dried seepage legs originating under the capsule and
trickling down the side of the bottle.

Also be on the alert if a young wine (less than four years old) has
more than half an inch of air space between the cork and the liquid
level in the bottle; it may still be a very sound wine, but given modern
bottling operations that generally fill the bottle to within a quarter to
an eighth of an inch of the cork, more than half an inch of air space,
or ullage, is a suspicious sign—why take the risk if there are other
bottles with better fills?

Finally, another sign of a badly treated and abused bottle of wine
can generally only be determined after the wine has been decanted,
though sometimes this culprit can be spotted in the neck of the bottle.
Wines that have been exposed to very high temperatures, particularly
deep, rich, intense red wines, will often form a heavy coat or film of
coloring material on the inside of the glass. One must be careful here
because this is the same type of sediment that vintage port regularly
throws, and often the huge, rich Rhône wines and Piedmontese wines
will do the same thing. But in Bordeaux a coating such as this in a
wine less than three years old generally indicates that the wine has
been subjected to very high temperatures and has undoubtedly been
damaged.

On the other hand, there are two conditions consumers frequently
think are signs of a flawed wine when nothing could be further from
the truth. Many consumers return bottles of wine for the very worst
reason—because of a small deposit or sediment in the bottom of the
bottle. Ironically, this is actually the healthiest sign one could find in
most bottles of red wine. However, keep in mind that white wines
rarely throw a deposit, and it is rare to see a deposit in wines under
two to three years of age. However, the tiny particles of sandlike
sediment that precipitate to the bottom of a bottle simply indicate that
the wine has been naturally made and has *not* been subjected to a

flavor and character eviscerating traumatic filtration. Such wine is truly alive and usually full of all its natural flavors.

Another erroneous reason wine consumers return bottles to retailers is the presence of small crystals called tartrate precipitates. These crystals are found in all types of wines, but appear most commonly in white wines from Germany and Alsace. They often shine and resemble little slivers of cut glass, but in fact they are simply indicative of a wine that somewhere along its journey was exposed to temperatures below 40° F in shipment, and the cold has caused some tartaric crystals to precipitate. These are harmless, tasteless, and a totally natural occurrence in many bottles of wine. They have no effect on the quality and they normally signify that the wine has *not* been subjected to an abusive, sometimes damaging, cold stabilization treatment by the winery for cosmetic purposes only.

Fortunately, most of the better wine merchants, wholesalers, and importers are more cognizant today of the damage that can be done by shipping wine in unrefrigerated containers, especially in the middle of summer. A general rule is that heat is much more damaging to fine wines than cold. Unfortunately, there are still plenty of wine merchants, wholesalers, and importers who treat wine no differently than they treat beer or liquor, and the wine buyer must therefore be armed with a bit of knowledge before he or she buys a bottle of wine.

HOW TO STORE WINE

Wine has to be stored properly if it is to be served in a healthy condition. All wine enthusiasts know that subterranean wine cellars that are vibration free, dark, damp, and kept at a constant 55° F are considered perfect for wine. However, few of us have our own castles and such perfect accommodations for our beloved wines. While such conditions are ideal, most wines will thrive and develop well under other circumstances. I have tasted many old Bordeaux wines from closets and basements that have reached 65–70° F in summer and the wines have been perfect. In cellaring wine keep the following rules in mind and you will not be disappointed by a wine that has gone over the hill prematurely.

First of all, in order to safely cellar wines for ten years or more keep them at 65° F, and *no* higher. If the temperature gets up to 70° F or higher, then be prepared to drink your red wines within ten years. Under no circumstances should you store and cellar white wines more than one to two years at temperatures above 70° F. Wines kept at temperatures above 65° F will age faster, but unless the temperature exceeds 70° F, will not age badly. If you can somehow get the temperature down to 65° F or below, you will never have to worry about the condition of your wines. At 55° F, the ideal temperature according to the textbooks, long-lived wines actually will evolve so slowly that your grandchildren are more likely to enjoy the wines than you. Constancy in temperature is most essential, and changes, if any, should occur slowly. White wines are far more fragile and sensitive to temperature changes and higher temperatures than red wines. Therefore, if you do not have ideal storage conditions, buy only enough white wine to drink over a one to two year period.

Second, be sure that your storage area is odor free, vibration free, and dark. A humidity level above 50% is essential; 80–90% is ideal. The problem with humidity over 80% is that the labels become moldy and deteriorate. A humidity level below 50% will keep the labels in great shape, but will cause the corks to become very dry and the potential lifeline of your wines will be threatened. Low humidity is a great threat to a wine's health as is high temperature.

Third, always bear in mind that wines from vintages that have produced powerful, rich, concentrated, full-bodied wines travel and age significantly better than wines from vintages that produced lighter-weight wines. It is often traumatic for a fragile, lighter-styled wine from either Europe or California to be transported transatlantic or cross-country, whereas the richer, more intense, bigger wines from the better vintages seem much less travel-worn after their journey.

Fourth, in buying and storing wine I always recommend buying a wine as soon as it appears on the market, assuming of course that you have tasted the wine and like it. The reason for this is that there are still too many American wine merchants, importers, wholesalers, and distributors who are indifferent to the way wine is stored. This attitude still persists, though things have improved dramatically over the last decade. The important thing for you as a consumer to remember, after inspecting the bottle to make sure it appears to be healthy, is to stock up on wines as quickly as they come on the market and to approach older vintages with a great deal of caution and hesitation unless you have absolute faith in the merchant from whom you bought the wine. Furthermore, you should be confident your merchant will stand behind the wine in the event it is flawed from poor storage.

HOW TO SERVE WINE

There are really no secrets for proper wine service—all one needs is a good corkscrew, clean, odor free glasses, a sense of order as to how wines should be served, and whether a wine needs to be aired or allowed to breathe. The major mistakes that most Americans, as well as most restaurants, make are 1) fine white wines are served entirely too cold, 2) fine red wines are served entirely too warm, and 3) too little attention is given to the glass into which the wine is poured. (It might contain a soapy residue or stale aromas picked up in a closed china closet.) All of these things can do much more to damage the impact of a fine wine and its subtle aromas than you might imagine.

Most people tend to think that red wines must be opened and allowed to "breathe" well in advance of serving. Some even think a wine must be decanted, a rather elaborate procedure but only essential if sediment is present in the bottle and the wine needs to be poured carefully off. With respect to breathing or airing wine, I am not sure anyone has all the answers. Certainly, no white wine requires any advance opening and pouring. With red wines, 15–30 minutes of being opened and poured into a clean, odor- and soap-free wine decanter is really all that is necessary. There are of course examples that can always be cited of wines that improve for seven to eight hours, but these are quite rare and unusual.

While breathing seems to dominate all the discussion in wine circles, to me a much more critical aspect is the temperature of the wine and the glass in which it is to be served. The temperature of red wines is very important, and in America's generously heated dining rooms, temperatures are often 75–80° F, more than is good for fine red wine. A red wine served at such a temperature will taste flat and flabby, with its bouquet diffuse and unfocused. The alcohol content will also seem higher than it should be. The ideal temperature for most red wines is from 62° F to 67° F; light red wines such as Beaujolais should be chilled to 55° F. For white wines, 55–60° F is perfect, since most will show all their complexity and intensity at this temperature, whereas if they are chilled to below 45° F, no one will know if they are drinking a Riesling or a Chardonnay.

In addition, there is the all-important issue of the glasses in which the wine is served. An all-purpose, tulip-shaped glass of 8 to 12 ounces is ideal for just about any type of wine. But the important thing is that no matter how clean you think the glass might look, be sure to rinse the glass or decanter with unchlorinated well or mineral water just before it is used. A decanter or wine glass left sitting for any time is a wonderful trap for room and kitchen odors that are undetectable until the wine is poured and they yield their off-putting smells. That, and soapy residues left in glasses, has ruined more wines than any defective cork or, I suspect, poor storage from an importer, wholesaler, or retailer. I myself put considerable stress on one friendship simply because I continued to complain at every dinner party about the soapy glasses that interfered with the enjoyment of the wonderful Bordeaux wines being served.

The other critical element in serving wine is to have a sense of the flavor intensity levels of the different dishes one is serving and to match them with similarly intense wines. The general rule is that delicate courses go best with delicate wines and richer, more exotic, intensely flavored foods with more intense and dramatic wines. Food and wine combinations are not nearly as important to this writer as to many others; this field has been overly legislated, to the detriment of the enjoyment of wine. Many of the greatest wine connoisseurs I know will serve a great red wine with a seemingly conflicting fish course, the explanation being that they happen to love red wine and they happen to love fish, so they have them together regardless of what everyone says. The point is, red wine often doesn't work so well with fish, but there are many more possible combinations than most writers have led people to believe. For me, the rule is simple: If you match the intensity of the dish with the intensity level of flavor in the wine, whether the wine be white or red, you will generally have a successful presentation.

As far as the actual order of wines, I always recommend that one proceed from the lighter, more delicate wines to the richer, more intense wines. If such an order is not followed, a delicate wine will often taste pale and watery having followed a fuller-bodied, richer wine. In addition, I always recommend serving wines from youngest to oldest. This tends to be the traditional manner and I think it makes sense; the grapier, younger, more astringent wines show better when followed by more mellow, more complex, more mature wines.

INDEX

ABOUT THE AUTHOR

Robert M. Parker, Jr., is the author and publisher of *The Wine Advocate* and a regular contributor to the magazines *Food and Wine* and *Connoisseur*. He is also the author of the book *Bordeaux: The Definitive Guide for the Wines Produced Since 1961*.

Much of the material in this book is based upon tastings and research done by Robert Parker in conjunction with the publishing of *The Wine Advocate*, an independent consumer's guide to fine wine that is issued six times a year. A one-year subscription to *The Wine Advocate* costs $28.00 for delivery in the continental United States, $35.00 for Canada, and $50.00 for air-mail delivery anywhere in the world. Subscriptions or a sample copy may be obtained by writing to The Wine Advocate, P.O. Box 311, Monkton, MD. 21111.